www.wadsworth.com

www.wadsworth.com is the World Wide Web site for Thomson Wadsworth and is your direct source to dozens of online resources.

At *www.wadsworth.com* you can find out about supplements, demonstration software, and student resources. You can also send email to many of our authors and preview new publications and exciting new technologies.

www.wadsworth.com
Changing the way the world learns®

Theories of Human Learning

What the Old Woman Said

FIFTH EDITION

Guy R. Lefrançois

University of Alberta

THOMSON

WADSWORTH

Australia • Brazil • Canada • Mexico • Singapore • Spain
United Kingdom • United States

Theories of Human Learning: What the Old Woman Said, Fifth Edition
Guy R. Lefrançois

Publisher: Vicki Knight
Psychology Editor: Marianne Taflinger
Assistant Editor: Jennifer Keever
Editorial Assistant: Lucy Faridany
Marketing Manager: Chris Caldeira
Marketing Assistant: Nicole Morinon
Marketing Communications Manager: Laurel Anderson
Project Manager, Editorial Production: Candace Chen
Creative Director: Rob Hugel
Art Director: Vernon Boes
Print Buyer: Karen Hunt

Permissions Editor: Stephanie Lee
Production Service: Forbes Mill Press
Text Designer: Carolyn Deacy
Photo Researcher: Myrna Engler
Copy Editor: Robin Gold
Interior Illustrator: Gloria Langer
Cover Designer: Denise Davidson
Cover Image: Harry Briggs
Cover Printer: Coral Graphic Services, Inc.
Compositor: International Typesetting and Composition
Printer: R.R. Donnelley/Crawfordsville

Printed in the United States of America
1 2 3 4 5 6 7 09 08 07 06 05

For more information about our products, contact us at:
Thomson Learning Academic Resource Center
1-800-423-0563

For permission to use material from this text or product, submit a request online at
http://www.thomsonrights.com.

Any additional questions about permissions can be submitted by e-mail to
thomsonrights@thomson.com.

Library of Congress Control Number: 2005922852

ISBN 0-534-64152-0

Thomson Higher Education
10 Davis Drive
Belmont, CA 94002-3098
USA

Asia (including India)
Thomson Learning
5 Shenton Way
#01-01 UIC Building
Singapore 068808

Australia/New Zealand
Thomson Learning Australia
102 Dodds Street
Southbank, Victoria 3006
Australia

Canada
Thomson Nelson
1120 Birchmount Road
Toronto, Ontario M1K 5G4
Canada

UK/Europe/Middle East/Africa
Thomson Learning
High Holborn House
50–51 Bedford Row
London WC1R 4LR
United Kingdom

This book is dedicated to an old woman, Emerilda Francœur, and to an old man, Hervé Lefrançois, both of whom taught me things I would never otherwise have known.

(Editor's Note: This is the Old Woman's motto, thumbprint, seal, and signature—all of which are apparently necessary to make a document true and binding.)

Brief Contents

Contents

PART TWO

Mostly Behavioristic Theories

PART THREE

The Beginnings of Modern Cognitivism

PART FOUR

Mostly Cognitive Theories

Chapter 7   Three Cognitive Theories: Bruner, Piaget, and Vygotsky 214

Chapter 9   *Learning and Remembering* 292

PART FIVE

Summary

Read This First

. . . not just because it's at the beginning of the book, but because if you don't, you'll wonder what the devil is going on.

Let me get right to the point: The most unusual thing about this book is that it wasn't written by one of us. Truth is, the first edition was written by Kongor.

It all started about three decades ago. I still have the notes I made at the time, right here in this shoebox, size 10. Looking back at the very first entry, I see that I had been sleeping on the riverbank when I thought I felt something tugging on my toe. At first, I thought I was dreaming, but when I woke up, I was looking right into the big, bulbous eyes of a dwarfish, blue-skinned creature with pink tufts of hair on its chest and above its ears.

Turned out it was Kongor, a behavioral scientist from Koros, a planet in the Androneas system. As part of his training, he'd been sent to Earth to report on the dominant life form thereon.[1] He stayed with me for about a year, during which time he prepared a series of reports for his superiors. One of these reports summarized the then-current state of our knowledge about learning. When he was recalled to Koros, he left me the report with his permission, in writing, to do whatever I wanted with it. That report was the first edition of this book, published in 1972 with the title *Psychological Theories and Human Learning: Kongor's Report.*

---

[1] That Kongor was male has never been clearly established, despite my grandmother's strong suspicions following his disappearance with Sylvia during the dance that Saturday. Nor do we have any convincing reason to believe him female. And "it" didn't seem appropriate. Hence the "he." (GRL)

A decade later, users began to complain that some of what Kongor had originally written was misleading, inaccurate, or irrelevant. And although he

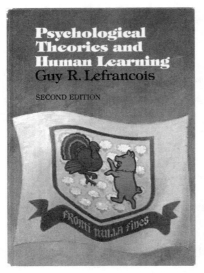

had promised to sonarduct back some of his other reports so I could put together some staggeringly useful texts in biochemistry, biology, sociology, and goat herding, the so-and-so never did. So I was forced to prepare the second edition myself. It was published in 1982.

Then, almost two decades after Kongor's visit, I was down on the west quarter checking out beaver damage and looking for mushrooms and chokecherries when—I'm quoting almost directly from my journals here—I heard a kerplumf! in the beaver pond behind me. I thought, Shoot, there goes another dang beaver. Sure enough, when I turned and looked, I could see the expanding circle of ripples where the beaver had smashed his tail down on the water.

But it wasn't a beaver at all. It was Kro, Kongor's cousin. "Oops. Missed," he spluttered as he dragged himself onto the beaver dam, leaning to one side and pounding the opposite side of his head to spill the slough water out of his ears. It turned out that Kro[2] had been sent here to update Kongor's original report, which he did. That was the third edition: *Psychological Theories and Human Learning: Kro's Report*, published in 1995. My

reward for helping him was about a billion Koronian credits, which is nothing to sneeze at, I'm told. Unfortunately, at this moment I can't even use them to paper the walls of my bush cabin because they're just a number in a computer somewhere. But if I ever get to Koros, you can bet I won't be hunting mushrooms or selling chokecherries for a living.

A few years later, the Old Man showed up, claiming he had updated, corrected, polished, and perfected all previous editions. That was the fourth edition, which the Old Man insisted I should record on tape while he read it to me. I did as he said, suffering the hardships of trudging after him for many long days, until I had on tape an entire book: *Theories of Human Learning: What the Old Man Said.*

---

[2] We had the same problems determining Kro's gender, if any, even after my aunt Lucy, a quite-good chicken sexer, attempted to examine him. Kro once claimed to be all sexes but could not easily prove it. (GRL)

And the Old Man disappeared.

Then, just a short while ago, an old woman showed up in my bush cabin. "Things change. Science doesn't stand still," she muttered without preamble. "So I brought you the next edition." And when I asked her who she was, did she know the Old Man, where had she come from, all she did was laugh darkly and ignore all my questions. "You can call me the Old Woman," she said. "Now pay attention while I read you the next edition."

This is it. Only this preface, the epilogue, some footnotes, and a few little bits (always in italics) were written by me. The rest, organized into 12 chapters, is what the Old Woman said. She read the book from a ragged, handwritten manuscript, insisting that I record her words as she read them and that I make handwritten notes as well. "Just make notes for posterity," she said when I asked why.

I changed nothing of what the Old Woman said; I was only a clerk. When she spoke "off the record," she insisted that the recorder be turned off. If what she said in those circumstances seemed important, I put what I could remember, or what I could decipher from my notes, into footnotes.

The Old Woman wanted it made perfectly clear that although she spoke all these words as she told me this book, they were certainly not all her words and thoughts. She asked that I explain very carefully that this is a revision—an updating and a correcting of what Kongor and then I and then Kro and then the Old Man, put together for the first four editions. She said that many of our words and our examples are still in this fifth edition and that she could have done better had she had time to start from scratch, but that they wouldn't let her. She did not clarify who "they" were.

The few comments I have permitted myself in this fifth edition, always italicized or in footnotes, serve only to tell something of the Old Woman, to describe where she was and what she was doing at this moment or that. Very rarely, I asked questions; sometimes she responded, mostly she didn't. When she did, I included what I remembered of her replies as well—but always only in footnotes or in italics.

What's in the Fifth Edition?

This fifth edition is a survey and interpretation of some of the important theories and findings in the psychology of learning. It presents a historical look at the development of behavioristic and cognitive theories and describes and evaluates the most important of these theories, including current brain-based research as well as approaches such as connectionism (neural net models) and models of memory, motivation, and social learning.

The emphasis throughout is on clarity of presentation, relevance and practical implications of topics, and maintenance of high interest.

The book is written primarily for students of human learning, teachers, counselors, social workers, industrial psychologists, nurses, social psychologists, numismatists, physicians, lawyers, dentists, engineers, housewives, farmers, judges, fishermen, tree planters, glass blowers, vagabonds, poets, philosophers, farmers, retired types, and all others—in that order.

About the Flag on the Back Cover

That's the Koronian flag, which I first saw when Kongor planted it near the beaver dam close to the southwest corner of the northwest quarter of Section 15, Township 48, Range 23, west of the 4th Meridian. It's made of synthetic fibers and boasts both a pig rampant and a turkey glissant on a field of flowers that look suspiciously like dandelions. Kongor's undershorts boasted the same design, said Aunt Lucy. About the Old Woman, we are less certain.

Acknowledgments

The Old Woman wanted me to pass on her appreciation to about 500 different people, all of whom she said deserved emoluments, credits, applause, and many wet kisses. I said there's no room, this isn't an encyclopedia. She said okay but you have to say thank you to the publisher (Vicki Knight), the acquisition editor (Marianne Taflinger), the assistant editor (Jennifer Keever), the editorial assistant (Lucy Faridany), the production project manager (Candace Chen), the production editor and copy editor (Robin Gold), the interior and cover designers (Carolyn Deacy, Harry Briggs and Denise Davidson, respectively), your grandmother (Emerilda Francœur), Lord Thompson, the guy you borrowed the boat from, your office cleaning company—and then I said, whoa, that's enough, are you trying to get all 500 in? And she said no, but please thank the reviewers, they were so amazingly competent and clever: Aneeq Ahmad, Henderson State University; Cindy Arnold, Bethel College; Sandra Harris, Troy State University; Yvonne Lippa, Miami University; Mary McNaughton-Cassill, University of Texas at San Antonio; Debora Scheffel, University of Northern Colorado; Jerome Wagner, Loyola University Chicago; and Mark Winkel, University of Texas, Pan American.

The Old Woman also wanted me to indicate that she is not responsible for any errors and misinterpretations that remain in this text. "If any errors creep in," said she, "it'll be the fault of reviewers, editors, and other publishing types." That, of course, is absolutely untrue. The Old Woman is fully responsible for any weaknesses and flaws in the book.

Guy R. Lefrançois

P.S. Many thanks to Claire, who succeeded in photographing Kro, and to Claire and Liam, who came closer than anyone to getting recognizable photos of the Old Man and the Old Woman (see page 410). Unfortunately, no one came close enough to earn the reward I had promised for a good shot of their faces. (GRL)

Human Learning: Science and Theory

The two primary motives for research in the behavioral sciences are to develop scientific theories and to solve problems that occur in everyday life.
R. Hastie (2001)

It ain't so much the things we don't know that get us into trouble. It's the things we know that just ain't so.
Artemus Ward

When I came to feed the birds that cold March morning, there was smoke coming from the stovepipe and I thought, "Dang, somebody's snuck into the bush cabin!" and I opened the door gingerly, calling out, "Who's there?"

Who was there, sitting in front of the hot stove with the one-eyed cat curled on her lap, was an Old Woman. "Get your tape recorder and your notebook, and pay attention," she said, as if we had known each other for a long time. "There've been some important changes since the last edition." She waved a handful of ragged pages at me.

"What . . . where did you. .wh. . ?" I spluttered a mouthful of unfinished questions. But the Old Woman ignored all my questions. Instead she said again to get the recorder, she was ready to start.

"We can talk later," she said. "We'll talk when what I have to say isn't so important." I thought she might be mocking me.

I fetched the recorder and turned it on. The Old Woman started to talk. This is what she said.

hat the Old Woman Said: This Book

This book, *she explained as she threw a fresh piece of birch into the stove,* summarizes what your psychologists know and believe about human learning. It presents a historical view of the development of psychological theories related to human learning. It describes the major principles and the practical applications of each theory, and it evaluates each theory's main strengths and weaknesses.

Objectives

Tell your readers, the Old Woman said, that this first chapter is a bit of a preamble: It defines important terms and sets the stage for what comes later. Explain to them that after studying this chapter, they should know with stunning clarity:

- *What is meant by the term* learning
- *What psychological theories are*

- *How theories are developed*
- *How theories can be evaluated*
- *What the principal information gathering methods are in psychology*
- *Some of the advantages and weaknesses of these methods*

Psychology and Learning

Let me begin at the beginning, *said the Old Woman.* **Psychology**[1] is the science that studies human behavior and thinking. It looks at how experience affects thought and action; it explores the roles of biology and heredity; it examines consciousness and dreams; it traces how people develop from infants into adults; it investigates social influences. Basically, it tries to explain why people think, act, and feel as they do.

Of course this book doesn't tackle all of psychology but is limited to psychological theories that deal with human learning and behavior—and animal learning too because studies of learning in animals are inextricably linked with the development of theories of human learning. So it's important from the outset to know what learning is.

Knowledge and Consciousness

What do we learn? What do we know? What is knowledge?

These questions define the branch of philosophy known as **epistemology.** Epistemology asks how we know the world. It also asks how we know that what we think is real, actually is.

Some of the ancient Greek philosophers, like Aristotle (384–322 BC), answered these questions by proposing the theory that whatever is out there in the world is copied onto the **mind.** What happens, he explained, is that the act of perceiving something results in a copy that we then somehow *know.* Thus, we can never know reality directly; all we know is indirect, resulting from our knowledge of copies of reality. We know not so much as a result of our senses, he argued, but more as a result of our reason. Thus, the educated person, whose mind is presumably better able to reason, knows reality more clearly than does the less educated person. "The roots of education are bitter," said Aristotle, "but the fruit is sweet."

Plato (428–347 BC), another well-known Greek philosopher who was actually Aristotle's teacher, also believed that we know only ideas (although he and Aristotle disagreed on the nature of ideas). Hence the importance of educating people, of making them into thinkers, into philosophers. "And may we not say," asked Plato, "that the most gifted minds, when they are ill-educated, become the worst?" (Plato, 1993, p. 491).[2]

But, asked other philosophers, how do we even know that there actually is a *reality* out there if all we have are copies in our minds. Maybe, some suggested, reality only exists in our minds—a belief sometimes referred to as *idealism* as

---

[1]Boldfaced terms are defined in the glossary at the end of the text, starting on page 411. Unlike most of the text, glossary items and footnotes are not the Old Woman's words but mine. (GRL)
[2]In this text, references are cited in the style approved by the American Psychological Association (APA)—that is, the name of the author(s) is followed by the year of the relevant publication. The list of references at the end of the book provides complete information about the source.

opposed to *materialism*. Whereas materialism holds that everything that actually exists is physical (or material), idealism suggests that ideas are the only knowable reality.

These issues are at the core of a big issue in psychology: the **mind-body problem.** Simply stated, this problem asks about the relationship between the mind and the body. How can something purely physical, like a cat, produce something purely mental, like the *idea* of a cat? And how can the idea of a cat be translated into an act, like that of looking for a cat?

The French philosopher and mathematician, René Descartes (1596–1650), presented one of the earliest and most influential resolutions for this problem, at the same time penning one of the most widely known and repeated phrases ever produced by any philosopher: *I think; therefore I am.* Descartes arrived at this insight by first pretending that everything he was thinking was not real—was simply like a dream. He writes,

> "But immediately upon this I noticed that while I was trying to think everything false, it must needs be that I, who was thinking this, was something. And observing that this truth 'I am thinking, therefore I exist' was so solid and secure that the most extravagant suppositions of the skeptics could not overthrow it, I judged that I need not scruple to accept it as the first principle." (Anscombe & Geach, 1954, pp. 31–32)

I think; therefore I am. The Latin form of this sentence, the language in which learned philosophers and scientists of Descartes' age wrote, is *Cogito, ergo sum.* As a result, this principle is commonly referred to as Descartes' *Cogito.* One very important conclusion that flows from this principle, said Descartes, is that all ideas must come from God because humans are clearly not perfect enough to generate them on their own (Vrooman, 1970). Hence, the mind and the body must be separate, insisted Descartes. Furthermore, the existence of ideas proves that what we think is out there actually is out there, because God would surely never give us ideas that are false. Thus, ideas are pure and innate because they come from God. In contrast, the body is physical or material; its functioning is like the functioning of a machine.

It follows that there are two basic substances in the world, says Descartes: material and immaterial. The material includes things such as bodies, bats, and beverages, all of which actually exist in space and all of which can be compared to machines in their functioning. The immaterial includes the mind, or, to use what Descartes considered an equivalent term, the soul. The soul is more closely related to God than to a machine. Thus, mind and body are fundamentally different and separate. This *Cartesian* (referring to Descartes) position is labeled **dualism.** Descartes is referred to as an *interactive dualist* because he believed that even though the mind and the body are separate (are *dual*, in other words), they are, in a sense, united in the brain. The brain allows the body to influence the mind and the mind to influence the body: Hence *interactive dualism.*

Descartes thought that communication between body and mind was accomplished by means of a small organ in the brain known as the **pineal gland.** Why the pineal gland? Because as far as Descartes knew, the pineal gland was the only structure in the brain that didn't have a duplicate. Most other brain structures are duplicated in each of the brain's halves (called *hemispheres;* see Chapter 5 for a discussion of the anatomy and functions of the brain). We now know that Descartes was wrong about the functions of the pineal gland.

Descartes' speculations about the mind and the body underlined a very important problem for psychologists: What is consciousness? Put another way, how are physical sensations translated into the subjective world so that we become aware of reality?

One way around this problem is simply to ignore mind or consciousness, which can't be observed directly, and instead look for the laws that govern observable human behavior. In fact, this solution has permeated a great deal of early research and theorizing about learning.

Learning

Ask someone what learning is and the most likely answer will have something to do with the acquisition of information. If I tell you that the bird over there is a pine siskin and next time you see such a bird you correctly identify it as a pine siskin, I might infer that you have learned something. In this case, the nature of the information that you've acquired is obvious. Note, too, that *your behavior has changed as a result of experience.* In this case, the specific experience of my telling you that this bird is a pine siskin affects your response when you next see a bird of this species.

In many cases, what is acquired during learning isn't so obvious. For example, Toch and Schulte (1961) used an apparatus (a stereoscope) to present police recruits with a split-second glimpse of a different image for each eye— one image neutral and the other showing some form of violence. Almost invariably, third-year trainees saw significantly more violent pictures than did novices.

The term *learning* is more complex than is implied by a definition that restricts it solely to the acquisition of information. It certainly isn't clear exactly what information the police trainees might have acquired during their three years of training that would lead them to actually *see* one class of image more often than the other. They had apparently learned something, but the learning didn't involve regurgitating information; yet here, too, behavior had changed.

Psychologists usually look for evidence of learning in the changes that occur in people's behaviors as a result of experience. But not all changes in behavior are examples of learning. If someone hits you hard enough on the head or feeds you strange drugs, your behavior might change in bizarre ways. This is possibly what happened to a student who reportedly thought his closet housed a pair of small dragons and who ran madly down the street shouting for help. Here is a striking change in behavior, but to say that this change is an example of learning is to stretch the term beyond reasonable limits.

Behavior changes that are the temporary results of things like fatigue or drugs don't illustrate learning. Similarly, changes that are mainly biologically determined, like physical growth or sexual maturation, or that result from injury or disease (especially of the brain and other parts of the nervous system), are not examples of learning.

Experience	Learning	Change in Behavior
Contact with, participation in, exposure to external or internal events to which the organism is sensitive.	*All relatively permanent changes in potential for behavior that result from experience but are not caused by fatigue, maturation, drugs, injury, or disease.*	*Actual or potentially observable changes following experience that provide evidence learning has occurred.*

Figure 1.1 Evidence of learning is found in actual or potential changes in behavior as a result of experience. But learning is, itself, an invisible, internal neurological process.

Definition

To summarize, **learning** is generally defined as all relatively permanent changes in potential for behaviors that result from experience but are not caused by fatigue, maturation, drugs, injury, or disease. Strictly speaking, of course, learning is not defined by actual or potential changes in behavior. Rather, learning is what happens to the organism (human or nonhuman) as a result of experience. Changes in behavior are simply evidence that learning has occurred. (See Figure 1.1.)

Performance versus Learning

Note that the definition specifies changes in *potential* for behavior rather than simply changes in behavior. Why? Because the permanent effects of experience are not always apparent. In a classic experiment, Buxton (1940) left rats in large mazes for several nights. These mazes had start boxes at their beginnings and goal boxes at their ends (without food). After these few nights in the maze, there was no evidence that the rats had learned anything at all. Later, however, Buxton gave them a small taste of food in the goal boxes and then placed them in the start boxes. Now more than half of them ran directly to the goal boxes without making a single error! Clearly, they had learned a lot during the first nights in the maze. But their learning was **latent** rather than actual. That is, it was not evident in their **performance** until there had also been a change in their **dispositions**—in this case, in their reasons for going through the maze.

So learning may involve changes in capability—that is, in the *capacity* to do something—but also in disposition—in the *inclination* to perform. And evidence that learning has occurred may depend on the *opportunity* to perform as well; hence the need to define learning as a change in potential for behavior rather than simply as a change in behavior. As you read this book, for example, some astounding changes may occur in your capabilities. That these changes should mostly remain potential, becoming apparent only if you are given the opportunity to perform—on a test, for example—makes them no less real.

heory [3]

Behavior is a complicated thing; there are all sorts of factors involved in determining what you do. The main task of the learning psychologist is to understand behavior and behavior change. And from understanding comes the ability to predict and sometimes to control, both of which are useful and important functions. For example, teachers' predictions about how well students are likely to perform are critical for decisions relating to teaching and evaluating.

To understand something as complicated as behavior, psychologists need to simplify, to discover regularity and predictability, to invent metaphors (comparisons). Man looks for order where there is none, said Francis Bacon (perhaps not yet realizing that woman is as guilty of this as man). And Bacon may have been correct that humans would look for order even if there were none; that they seem to have a need to find order. But we have long assumed that there *is* considerable order in the world. This assumption has guided our research and colored our theories, claim Ballou, Matsumoto, and Wagner (2002). Discovering this assumed regularity and trying to explain it is what theory building is all about. "Theories are systematic statements of principles that explain natural phenomena," explain Sommer and Sommer (2002, p. 3).

Humans like to build theories, says Stagner (1988). Years ago, they devised theories about the lights in the sky, about why babies look like their parents, about the shape of the earth. Often, these theories were expressed as metaphors: the sun is a chariot, racing across the sky; dreams are the adventures of souls walking in parallel worlds while the body sleeps. Modern scientific theories, too, can often be explained and understood as metaphors: The heart is a pump; the brain is a computer; the eye is a camera. In Chapter 6, we look in more detail at metaphors in psychology.

Theories, Principles, Laws, and Beliefs

A scientific **theory** is a collection of related statements whose main function is to summarize and explain observations. In a simplified sense, theory building works something like this: Theorists begin with certain assumptions (unproven

---

[3]At this point, the Old Woman asked me did I need a break, should we continue later, but I said no it was okay and I didn't really think the reader would need a break yet. Well, they won't ask if they do, she said, that's the way students are. Besides, she continued, some of the brighter ones might be asking themselves some philosophical questions right now, so they should maybe take a break. When I asked her what these philosophical questions might be, she said, Free Will and Determinism. She explained that this was another of those really big issues in philosophy and in psychology. Determinism, she explained, is the belief that all behaviors result from identifiable causes—even if we don't know what these causes are—and that they don't result from the exercise of free will. Lots of philosophers think the two are incompatible, she said, meaning determinism and free will. She said that learning theorists pretty well have to assume that behavior is determined. That's one of the essential assumptions of science, she said shaking her head and I couldn't tell if it was because she was sad or confused. So does that mean there's no free will? I asked, and she replied, well, that's the philosophical question. Then she went back to her notes.

beliefs) about human behavior, perhaps based partly on their observations of regularity or predictability in behavior. As a result, they develop tentative explanations for what they observe. This leads them to believe that certain relationships exist—that *if* this, *then* that. These *if-then* statements, or educated predictions, are called **hypotheses.** Now the theorist gathers observations (data) to test the validity of the hypotheses. As Sommer and Sommer (2002) note, in scientific research, it is extremely important that hypotheses be testable. Nontestable hypotheses have little place in scientific theories. Hypotheses that are supported by evidence permit theorists to make generalizations—statements that summarize relationships and become part of the theory. Some of these statements might take the form of principles; some might be expressed as laws; others might simply be beliefs.

behavior

Principles are statements that relate to some predictability in nature or, more important for psychology, in behavior. Principles of learning, for example, describe specific factors that affect learning and remembering. A very general principle of learning, which we discuss in more detail in later chapters, might be worded as follows: *Behaviors that are followed by certain consequences, such as food, sex, or praise, become more probable.* As Pashler and Medin (2002) point out, theorists have long hoped that a few simple principles of this kind might explain vast chunks of human behavior. This principle, for example, seems to be widely evident. It is apparent in the fact that birds come to winter feeders, that dogs who are fed, petted, or praised quickly learn to roll over, that children who are rewarded for studying hard continue to study hard. But, as we see in Chapter 5, not all children study harder when they are praised or given high grades for so doing; not all dogs willingly roll over for a dog bone; and some birds shy away from the best stocked of winter feeders. By definition, principles are probabilistic and uncertain. Although they represent generally agreed-upon conclusions based on pretty solid evidence, they are nevertheless tentative. With new evidence, principles are subject to change.

Such is not the case with respect to laws. **Laws** are statements whose accuracy is beyond reasonable doubt. They are conclusions based on what seem to be undeniable observations and unquestionable logic. Unlike principles, by definition laws are not ordinarily open to exceptions and doubt. The statement $E = mc^2$, for example, is a law. Laws should not be confused with *truth*, however, since any law can be refuted given sufficient contrary evidence. By definition, truth can never be found to be untrue.

Beliefs describe statements that are more private and more personal than are principles or laws. For example, the notion that redheaded people are more prone to anger than are dark-haired people is a belief rather than a principle or a law. Note that, like principles and laws, beliefs attempt to describe general fact. Unfortunately, they are often treated as though they were as universal as principles (or even laws). Beliefs are often formed very early in life, notes Pajares (1992), and they are not always based on objective observation or reliable logic. Furthermore, they tend to be maintained even in the face of strong contradiction. They act as a sort of filter through which people view and understand the world; beliefs guide thought and action.

Bubba Psychology and Folk Beliefs

All societies have developed large bodies of commonly held beliefs about human behavior. These beliefs are part of what Kelley (1992) calls **bubba psychology** (*bubba* means grandmother). Hence, the term indicates an intuitive sort of folk psychology, also sometimes labeled *implicit* or *naive* psychology.[4]

The beliefs of folk psychology are often correct. If they weren't, people would constantly be surprised at what others say and do. Most people know enough about human behavior to be able to predict that, for example, those who are sad might cry, those who are overjoyed might smile and laugh, and those who are outraged might do outrageous things.

Quite often, though, the beliefs of folk psychology are wrong. For example, it might seem obvious that many people don't dream, that some women are more likely than others to give birth to sons, and that most people are altruistic enough to try to help someone being raped, mugged, or beaten. In fact, however, all normal people dream, although not all can remember doing so; it is the man's sperm and not the woman's ovum (egg) that determines the infant's sex; and some studies indicate that many people will not try to help someone being raped, mugged, beaten—or even killed (for example, Darley & Latané, 1968).

Because they are often misleading or flatly incorrect, personal beliefs can be very dangerous in science. Yet, even educated and trained professionals are often victims of false beliefs. For example, Gilovich (1991) found that many nurses believe that childless couples that adopt are more likely to have a child of their own. Some are also convinced that more infants are born during a full moon. Both these beliefs are wrong.

Purposes of Theories

Clearly, however, not all personal beliefs are wrong. One of the things that theories do is provide a basis for judging the accuracy and usefulness of beliefs. The most important function of a theory is to simplify and organize observations, and to provide a basis for making predictions. In the end, the usefulness of a theory in psychology may depend a great deal on how accurately it predicts. Thus, a theory that tries to explain how humans learn through experience should provide a basis for predicting the most likely effects of different experiences. Similarly, such a theory should lead to suggestions for arranging experiences in such a way that behavior will change in desired ways.

In addition to their practical usefulness for predicting and controlling behavior, theories also suggest which facts (observations) are most important as well as which relationships among these facts are most meaningful (Thomas, 2000). Theorists may have dramatically different ideas about what is important,

---

[4]When I pointed out to the Old Woman that in this age of political correctness it isn't wise to single out identifiable groups as examples of anything that might seem in any way negative, she shot back that she wasn't real interested in being politically correct. "If the book isn't sufficiently politically correct," she said, using what I soon learned was a variation of one of her favorite expressions, "well bugger them."

however, so a large number of theories may emerge in the same area of investigation. And although these theories may be quite different, none will necessarily be totally incorrect, although some may be more useful than others. In the final analysis, a theory cannot easily be evaluated in terms of whether it is right or wrong. Instead, it must be judged mainly by its usefulness.

Characteristics of Good Theories

Good theories in psychology are not only useful, explains Thomas (2000), but can also be judged by several qualities:

1. The best theories are those that summarize and organize important facts (observations). Theories are based on observations and should reflect them accurately.

2. A good theory should be clear and understandable.

3. Theories should simplify, should impose order where there might otherwise be complexity and chaos. Put another way, theories should be **parsimonious.** A parsimonious statement is the simplest and shortest statement that adequately covers the fact. The *principle of parsimony*, also termed **Occam's razor,** holds that where there are two competing theories that each explain or summarize a set of observations, the least complex is better. Accordingly, a parsimonious theory is one that describes all important relationships in the simplest but most accurate terms possible. Theories that are unnecessarily detailed and complex are said to lack parsimony.[5]

4. A theory should be useful for predicting as well as for explaining. In fact, one of the most important criteria of a good theory is that it should lead to predictions that are potentially false—that is, that are *falsifiable*. This is because a theory that doesn't lead to falsifiable predictions cannot be proven to be incorrect and therefore cannot be proven correct either.

5. As we saw earlier, predictions and explanations based on a theory should have some usefulness, some application in the real world—for example, in education or in therapy—or in the further development of theory.

6. Theories should be internally consistent rather than contradictory. Poorer theories sometimes lead to contradictory explanations and predictions. Such theories cannot easily be tested and are of limited usefulness.

7. Theories should not be based on a large number of **assumptions** (beliefs accepted as fact but essentially not verifiable). Theories that are based on

---

[5]Should you maybe explain this just a bit more—this business of parsimony and simplicity, I asked the Old Woman, and she laughed that mocking laugh of hers. She said that the human preference for parsimony and simplicity seems highly revealing. Of what? I asked, and she laughed her sardonic laugh again. Of intellectual limitations, she answered. Of limitations evident in a widespread inability to understand chaos and an aversion to detail and complexity. And of a stubborn reluctance to separate reason and emotion. You've lost me, I said, and she retorted that simplicity just *feels* better to people than complexity.

Table 1.1 *Criteria of a good theory, applied to Grandma Francœur's fertilizer theory. This theory holds, in part, that horse manure stimulates potatoes and carrots, that chicken droppings invigorate cabbages, and that dried cow dung excites flowers.*

Criteria of a good theory	Grandmother Francœur's theory
Does it reflect the facts?	Yes, if carrots, potatoes, and other plants behave as expected under specified conditions.
Is it clear and understandable?	It is quite clear and understandable except to the very stupid, who are seldom asked to judge theories.
Does it reflect the use of Occam's razor?	It is perhaps less parsimonious than it might be, long-windedness being a family characteristic.
Is it useful for predicting as well as explaining?	Very. For example, the theory allows the gardener to predict in the spring what will happen in the fall depending on the fertilizers used. And the predictions are clearly falsifiable. Thus, the theory can be tested directly.
Is it practically useful?	Clearly, yes, for those engaged in the growing of vegetable things.
Is it internally consistent?	Unfortunately, no. The old lady has sometimes claimed that chicken droppings are better than horse manure for potatoes.
Is it based on many unverifiable assumptions?	No. The assumptions upon which it is based could be verified—or falsified.
Is it satisfying and thought provoking?	Oh yes!

many assumptions are difficult to evaluate. And if the assumptions on which they are based are invalid, the theories may be misleading. Still, as pointed out in an earlier footnote, scientific theories are generally based on the inescapable assumption of **determinism**—in other words, that behavior results from predictable relationships among causes and effects rather than from what might be termed *free will*.

8. Finally, a good theory should be thought-provoking as well as providing satisfying explanations. Theories that have the greatest impact on a field are often those that give rise as much to opposition as to support. Such theories typically lead to research designed to support, to refute, or to elaborate. They are said to have high **heuristic** value in the sense that they lead to new research and to new discoveries.

These criteria are summarized in Table 1.1 and illustrated with respect to Grandma Francœur's theory of wastes.[6]

---

[6]The grandma in question is my own grandmother. When I was younger, my cousins and I had a less polite word for what the Old Woman called grandma's theory of wastes. We called it grandma's **** theory. (Bleeped by the editorial committee.)

Science and the Development of Psychological Theories

Many of the most stubborn and widespread beliefs about human behavior, often based on what is termed **common sense,** are wrong; common sense doesn't always make sense. For example, Gilovich (1991) points out that there are about 20 times more astrologers than astronomers in North America. Yet, there is no good evidence that the beliefs and predictions of astrology are the least bit valid. Similarly, more people believe in ESP, a collection of phenomena that science has not been able to verify, than believe in evolution, a theory that has received enormous scientific support.

One of psychology's important tasks is to determine which beliefs about human behavior make sense. How can psychology accomplish this? The answer can be given in one word: **science.**

What Is Science?

In one sense, science is a collection of information related to a field of study. The science of physics, for example, is a collection of information relating to the nature and properties of matter. The science of psychology is a collection of information relating to the nature and properties of human thought and behavior.

In another sense, science is a way of dealing with information. The scientific approach to information is evident in (a) an attitude toward the search for knowledge that emphasizes replicability, objectivity, and consistency; and (b) a collection of methods for gathering and analyzing observations, designed to ensure that conclusions are objective and generalizable.

Science is psychology's most powerful tool for separating fact from fiction.

Rules of the Scientific Method

A useful way of looking at the meaning of the term *science* is to think of it as an attitude rather than simply as one of several bodies of knowledge or as a series of recipes for acquiring and systematizing knowledge. As an attitude, science insists on objectivity, precision, and replicability; it accepts as valid only those observations that have been collected in such a way that others can repeat them under similar circumstances.

This view of science leads to a clear set of methods for gathering information. These methods collectively make up what is often referred to as the scientific method. For more than 100 years now, note Haslam and McGarty (2001), the social sciences have used the scientific method to reduce uncertainty and to search for knowledge.

The scientific method can be simplified to five rules:

1. Ask the Question
Do people who are most highly rewarded always work hardest? Is punishment effective in eliminating undesirable behavior? Are adoptive parents more likely

to have children of their own after they adopt? There is no shortage of questions in the study of learning and behavior. As a method, science makes no judgments about whether questions are trivial or important; it simply insists that they be clear.

And it absolutely refuses to jump to conclusions. There are certain procedures to be followed, certain logical steps to be taken first.

In practice, the researcher's first step after identifying a problem is to find out what is already known about it. Usually this involves doing library research, conducting computer searches, or consulting other sources such as experts and professionals in the field.

2. Develop a Hypothesis

Once the scientific researcher has uncovered relevant background information, the next step is to arrive at a tentative conclusion, or hypothesis, which is an educated guess that guides the research. It usually takes the form of a prediction or a statement of relationships. Hypotheses are often based on theories. By definition, they are *unproven* and *falsifiable*. As a result, the outcome of a scientific investigation can lead to the *rejection* of a hypothesis.

3. Collect Relevant Observations

The scientific study of all phenomena always begins with observations, which are the basis of all science. Observations are, after all, what science tries to explain and understand.

Science suggests several different ways of gathering observations. The most powerful of these is the **experiment** (discussed shortly). Experiments sometimes make use of **surveys,** which are ways of making observations concerning the behaviors, the beliefs, the attitudes, and other characteristics of a sample representing some population. Surveys often use **questionnaires** (lists of predetermined questions to which subjects respond), **interviews** (where investigators question participants), or different kinds of tests and measurements (such as intelligence or personality tests, or measures of weight and height).

4. Test the Hypothesis

The reason for gathering observations is to determine the validity of hypotheses. The whole point of the exercise is to answer the questions that inspired the research in the first place.

If conclusions are to be valid, observations must be accurate and meaningful. Science is very concerned that observations might just be chance occurrences— that, in other words, they might not *mean* very much. For this reason, researchers often use one or more of a number of special mathematical procedures to separate chance events from those that are **significant.** Simply put, these *statistical* procedures help us determine the likelihood that what is observed is not simply a chance occurrence. Many scientific conclusions are based on the assumption that observations that would be expected to occur only very rarely by chance must have some identifiable cause.

5. Reach and Share a Conclusion

In scientific research, conclusions usually take the form of accepting or rejecting the hypotheses that have guided the investigation. Sometimes, of course,

the results are unclear or are contrary to what is expected. Often research outcomes suggest another question rather than an answer, or lead to another hypothesis. Thus, conclusions are often tentative rather than final. Sometimes,
too, a series of unexpected observations and conclusions may lead to major
changes in the theories upon which hypotheses are based.

And, if science is to progress, the results of its research must be shared.
One fundamental principle of academic science is that its fruits belong to
everyone.

Experiments

The **experiment,** says Gould (2002), is science's most powerful tool for reliably
determining the validity of hypotheses. An experiment is a situation in which
the investigator systematically manipulates some aspect of the environment
(termed a **variable**) to determine the effect of so doing on some important outcome. What is manipulated is the **independent variable;** the effect of this control or manipulation is reflected in the **dependent variable.**

Consider, as an example, the hypothesis that *rewards for current learning
have a positive effect on subsequent learning.* The first step in conducting an experiment to test this hypothesis is to define the abstract terms involved in
such a way that they can be manipulated, controlled, and measured. Such definitions are labeled **operational definitions.** Operational definitions usually
involve defining something by the means used to measure it. For example,
hunger might be operationally defined in terms of number of hours without
eating, and "subsequent learning," could be operationally defined in terms of
performance on a specific test following a clearly defined learning experience.
Similarly, an operational definition of "rewards for current learning," might
refer to objective, measurable outcomes such as receiving money or prizes,
being granted privileges, or being showered with verbal praise. Furthermore,
the operational definitions would need to specify several other details such as
whether or not the learner had prior expectations of being rewarded, and so
on. Thus, a simple experiment designed to examine this hypothesis (*rewards
for current learning have a positive effect on subsequent learning*) might consist of
an arrangement whereby some learners are paid for their grades and others
not, all are subsequently exposed to a learning experience, and the performance of the rewarded group is compared with that of the unrewarded group.
In this case, the independent variable (that which is controlled by the experimenter) is the money reward; the dependent variable is the learner's subsequent performance.

Identifying dependent and independent variables is a relatively simple matter when an experiment is phrased as an if-then statement. The objective of an
experiment is to determine whether it is true that "if this, then that." The "if"
part of the equation represents what is controlled or manipulated—hence the
independent variable(s); the "then" part represents the consequences or outcomes—
hence the *dependent* variable(s). Virtually any hypothesis can be phrased as an
if-then statement. Thus, the previous example can be rephrased as follows: *If a*

learner is consistently rewarded for performing well, *then* subsequent learning will improve.

Sampling and Comparison Groups

An important step in carrying out most experiments in psychology is to select participants for the experiment (often referred to as *subjects*). Clearly, experimenters are seldom able to conduct their investigations with the entire **population** in which they might be interested (for example, *all* grade five learners; *all* left-handed males; *all* three-year-olds). Instead, experimenters conduct their research with small groups (or sometimes with single individuals)—termed a **sample**—*selected* from a larger population.

In an experiment, it's very important that participants be selected at **random** from the population to which the investigator wants to generalize. Random selection means that everybody has an equal chance of being a participant. Common, *nonrandom*, ways of selecting participants are to have them volunteer or to select them from institutions or classrooms.

The problem with nonrandom selection of subjects is that systematic biases may be introduced. For example, people who volunteer for experiments may be more adventurous than those who don't—and the investigator's conclusions might then be valid only for those who are adventurous. Similarly, students may be systematically different from nonstudents (and institutionalized people from noninstitutionalized people) in interests, motivation, background, and other characteristics. As a result, conclusions based on studies that use nonrandom samples may not be valid for the larger population.

Having selected participants, the investigator then assigns them *randomly* to one of two groups: **experimental** or **control groups** (control groups are sometimes also called *comparison* or *no-treatment* groups). These two groups are as identical as possible, except that experimental group members are given some *experimental treatment* (such as being rewarded for grades) whereas members of the control group are not. Without a control group, it might be impossible for the investigator to know for certain that any changes observed after the experimental treatment are actually caused by the treatment and not by something else.

Evaluating Psychological Research

One important limitation in psychological investigations is that the observations with which psychology deals are not always undeniable fact. In some ways, observations in other sciences such as chemistry or physics are less open to doubt. Thus, it is a fact that apples fall when they become detached from trees. And if a lazy Newton is sleeping below the tree directly under the apple, it *will* hit him on the head. Put another way, gravity is more than simply a belief or even a principle: It is a law. But that rewarding children for being good increases the probability of their behaving well is not so much a law as a principle. And, as we see in Chapter 10, it's not always a very straightforward principle; there are circumstances under which rewarding children may have unexpected results.

The characteristics of children are highly variable and complex; at least in some ways, apples are more predictable.[7]

Psychological investigations are also limited by the amount of control psychologists have over relevant variables. Two rats reared in identical cages and subjected to the same daily routines from birth may reasonably be assumed to have had highly comparable experiences. The same assumption can't be made as confidently about two children who are raised in different homes. Because their parents, friends, siblings, relatives, and so many other important aspects of their worlds are different, their experiences will also have been very different. Control in psychological experimentation needs to take into account these, and many other, important differences among subjects.

Consider the following illustration:

Problem To determine the relationship of sleep deprivation to problem-solving behavior.

Subjects All students in a private school are selected for the study. They are randomly divided into two groups.

Hypothesis Sleep-deprived subjects will perform significantly more poorly on a problem-solving test.

Experimental Treatment One group is allowed to sleep as usual; the other is kept awake all night. In the morning, the test is given to all subjects, and results for the two groups are compared.

Results The sleep-deprived group does significantly better.

Is the conclusion that sleep deprivation is related to problem-solving ability warranted? The answer is yes, *providing that a number of other relevant variables have also been controlled.* For example, if the rested group were on average more or less intelligent, all male or female, or had had previous training in problem solving, these variables could also account for differences in test performance. It would then not be logical to conclude that sleep is the significant factor. But because participants were *assigned* at random to either of the two groups, there is a greater chance that they are similar on each of these important variables.

Random selection and assignment to groups is one way to match groups on important variables—and also to make sure that the sample is a good representation of the population. Another possibility is to try to match the groups directly, making sure that the composition of the groups is highly similar for variables such as intelligence, sex, previous training, and so on. In fact, however, it's usually

---

[7]When I said to the Old Woman that this might not be entirely clear to everyone and that she made it sound as if we shouldn't place too much faith in the results of psychological investigations, she said no, not at all. She explained that it shouldn't be inferred from these comments that physical facts are more "factual" than psychological facts. Indeed, she said, in this chaotic and relativistic world, the word *fact*—be it physical or psychological—is a statistical concept of varying probability. The point, she concluded, is that it's simple to observe an apple falling, but it's far more difficult to evaluate things like the effects of rewards, or children's attachment to their mothers, or how punishment affects dogs and cats and people, and on and on.

impossible to account for all relevant variables in psychological experimentation. Investigators have to be aware that the outcomes of experiments might not always mean what they seem to mean. Science insists that investigators, and consumers of research, think critically. At the very least, says science, when interpreting and evaluating psychological research ask the following questions:

Have I Committed the Nominal Fallacy?

Luria (1968) reports the case of S, whose memory was so remarkable that he could remember completely accurately the most trivial of details—not just for minutes, hours, or days, but also for decades. He seemed never to forget even the most meaningless of sounds, the most nonsensical of words. "Yes, yes," he would say when Luria asked him to remember some jumbled paragraph or a complex table of digits he had been asked to learn years earlier. "Yes, this was a series you gave me once when we were in your apartment . . . you were wearing a gray suit and you look at me like this . . ." (Luria, 1968, p. 12)

Why did S remember so well? Do you suppose it was because he had what is popularly called a *photographic memory?* Or did he remember so well because he was a professional **mnemonist**—a professional memorizer?

Neither of these possibilities is correct. In fact, neither is even an explanation. S did not remember because he was a mnemonist or because he had a photographic memory. These are just labels for someone with a good memory; they don't *explain* why the person is exceptionally good at remembering. All they do is name something; they don't say anything about what underlies actual performance. The assumption that names are explanations is the **nominal fallacy.**

Nominal fallacies are quite common. For example, if you think some children have difficulty learning because they are mentally retarded or learning disabled, you are guilty of a nominal fallacy. To say that children have difficulty learning because they are learning disabled or mentally retarded is not to say anything at all about *why* they have difficulty.

Is the Sample Representative?

The samples on which conclusions are based have to be representative of the groups to which they are generalized. So investigators try to select *unbiased* samples (samples whose characteristics are much the same as those of the general population) using random selection whenever possible. However, research is sometimes limited to groups, such as students, institutional inmates, or residents of a housing complex. In such cases, to ensure that a sample represents a larger population, it's necessary to compare the two on important variables such as age, sex, and educational background. If the sample is *biased* (different from the population), conclusions might apply only to the sample upon which they are based.

Can Subjects Be Believed?

Sometimes research runs into memory problems. How well can participants remember their fourth birthday? Do they remember the age of their first menstrual period? Their first ejaculation? Can they remember what the thief was wearing? The color of her eyes?

Sometimes the problem is one of honesty. Questionnaires that probe into highly personal areas are especially vulnerable to deliberate distortion. And if there is something to be gained or lost by presenting a certain image, that too must be taken into account by the critical consumer of research.

Is There a Possibility of Subject Bias?

In a historic study, Roethlisberger and Dickson (1939) tried to increase the productivity of a group of workers at Hawthorne Electric by changing aspects of their work environment. Over a series of experiments, the researchers did things like increase or decrease number of work periods, shorten or lengthen breaks, increase or decrease illumination, and provide or take away bonuses. Strangely, it didn't matter what the experimenters did, production increased. It seemed that subjects were simply responding to the knowledge they were being studied. Maybe they just wanted to please the investigator.

Although this **Hawthorne effect** is not often apparent or usually very large (see Rice, 1982), it may still be an important factor in some psychological research. Participants in experiments are often anxious to please the investigator; consequently, their responses may occasionally be misleading. To guard against this possibility, subjects are often not told that they are members of experimental groups, or they are compared with others who also think they are part of the experiment but actually aren't.

Is There a Possibility of Experimenter Bias?

Margaret Mead, the well-known anthropologist/sociologist, had a profound belief that cultures shape people. Her studies of isolated inhabitants of New Guinea uncovered three very different tribes (Mead, 1935). Among the cannibalistic Mundugummor, both men and women were ruthless, aggressive, and very masculine by North American standards. In contrast, both sexes among the agricultural Arapesh seemed traditionally feminine (noncompetitive, non-aggressive, warm, and emotional). And in a third tribe, the Tchambuli, where the men spent most of their time adorning themselves and devising new dances while the women gathered food, there appeared to be a reversal of sex roles. This is striking evidence of the power of culture in shaping important characteristics like masculinity and femininity, claimed Mead.

Not so, argues Freeman (1983). After six years of research in Samoa, where Mead had done much of her work on culture, Freeman found little evidence of cultural differences as striking as those described by Mead. Her observations and conclusions, he writes, were highly subjective and largely undocumented. Freeman suggests that Mead was so convinced of the importance of culture that her biases blinded her to contradictory evidence.

In the same way that subjects are sometimes not told whether they are members of the experimental or control group to guard against the possibility of subject bias, so too can experimental observers be kept ignorant of who is an experimental subject and who isn't. This is called a **single-blind procedure.** A **double-blind procedure** is when neither subjects nor experimenters know which subjects received which treatment. For example, tests might be scored and interpreted without the investigator knowing whether or not the testee is part of an experimental group.

Participants in Psychological Investigations

Even psychologists who are mainly interested in human behavior often use animals as experimental subjects. In well-known psychological investigations, for example:

- Infant monkeys have been separated from their mothers at birth and reared in cages with inanimate wire models with bizarre looking masks.
- Blowflies have had a nerve between their brains and their foreguts severed and have been observed to eat until they burst.
- Worms have been trained, ground up, and fed to other worms.
- Rats have been given electric shocks.
- Cats have been caged within sight and smell of (presumably) succulent morsels of fish.

These investigations have provided us with potentially useful information about infant attachment, the mechanisms that control eating, the nature of memory, the relationship between negative consequences and learning, and the role of trial and error in learning. They serve as good examples of one of the advantages of using animals in psychological investigations: specifically, that many of the procedures sometimes used with animals cannot ethically be performed with humans.

Using animals rather than humans in psychological research has several other distinct advantages: For example, an animal's experiences can be very carefully controlled; such is not often the case with human subjects. Also, most animals can reproduce many generations over a relatively short period, and of course, mates can be selected for them in accordance with the requirements of the investigation. This can be especially useful in studies of genetic influences. Humans reproduce more slowly and typically insist on choosing their own mates.

In many cases, results of animal studies can be generalized, at least tentatively, to humans. Still, there is always the possibility that conclusions based on animal research might not apply to people. And ultimately, psychology is most interested in people.[8]

---

[8]Here the Old Woman stopped and asked me to turn off the recorder. She said this wasn't really part of the book, but she wanted to explain that throughout their history, many humans have been at great pains to demonstrate that they are fundamentally different from nonhuman animals and many have devoted much time and effort to trying to discover exactly how it is that they are different. She said that some, like Aristotle, proposed that it is the *soul* that separates the two; others have suggested *language* or *consciousness*. Still others claim that some Maker made humans according to a self-likeness, and this accounts for a critical, basic difference. She pointed out that some psychologists argue that because humans and nonhumans are different, animals make poor subjects in investigations of human behavior; others argue that in some ways they are very similar, and because certain experimental procedures are better performed with animals, it makes sense to use animals in psychological research.

Ethics of Animal Research

In this age of greater sensibility, awareness, compassion, and political sensitivity, some of the procedures used in experiments such as those just mentioned are considered by some to be unacceptable on moral and ethical grounds. As Tannenbaum (2001) explains, many oppose the use of animals in research. Some argue that even though the goal of science is to improve human welfare, this does not automatically justify causing pain and suffering to an animal (and often even sacrificing it). The use of animals rather than humans, some argue, reveals that animals are less *valued* than humans. Many animal rights activists suggest that not only should animals be protected from pain and suffering, but that they are entitled as well to pleasure and even happiness. Some believe that under no circumstances should animals be harmed in the interests of science.

On the other side of this highly controversial and emotional issue are those who insist that the benefits that might ultimately be derived justify animal research under certain circumstances (Brody, 2001). Animal researchers must become more active in public education, suggests Morrison (2001), so that the potential benefits of animal research become more apparent and to demonstrate that research animals are humanely and ethically treated.

The Association for the Study of Animal Behavior (Guidelines for the . . . 2002), as well as the American Psychological Association (APA, 2002, available online at http://www.apa.org/science/anguide.html), presents a number of principles intended to guide the conduct of scientists doing research with animals. Among them are the following:

- Animal care must comply with existing laws and regulations.
- All animal research must be supervised by a psychologist trained in the care of laboratory animals.
- All animal workers should be explicitly trained in animal care.
- Every effort must be made to minimize animal pain and suffering.
- Animals should be subjected to surgery, pain, and discomfort only when this is justified by the potential value of the research.
- If animals need to be killed, this should be done quickly and painlessly.

Humans as Subjects

Human subjects are seldom subjected to pain and suffering as obvious as that among monkeys whose experimental participation requires that they develop experimentally induced ulcers, or rabbits who are exposed to allergenic cosmetics. But there are experimental treatments with humans that are psychologically stressful; some might even have lasting negative consequences. As a result, the American Psychological Association (APA) has developed a set of guidelines governing the conduct of research with human subjects. The most important principle underlying these guidelines is that of *informed consent*. Subjects are to be made aware of the nature and purpose of the research, and are to be given complete freedom *not* to participate. This is especially important where investigators are in a position of power over potential participants—as is the case for students or for residents in homes for the elderly.

In practice, almost all investigations conducted in North American schools, whether with animals or with humans, are subject to approval by ethical review committees. The purpose of these committees is to ensure that appropriate ethical standards are met—standards whose purpose is to protect participants. The APA's guidelines for research with human participants include the following (Sales & Folkman, 2000):

- The investigator is responsible for evaluating the ethical acceptability of the research.

- Investigators need to determine whether subjects are "at risk" or "at minimal risk."

- Before the investigation, all participants should be made fully aware of all aspects of the research that might affect their willingness to participate.

- When an investigation requires that participants be deceived, investigators need to (a) determine whether the potential benefits of the study justify the use of deception; (b) determine whether other nondeceptive approaches might answer the same questions; (c) provide participants with a "sufficient" explanation as soon as possible.

- Participants must be free not to participate.

- Participants must be protected from physical and mental danger or discomfort. Procedures that might result in harm to participants may be used only when failure to use them might have even more harmful consequences, or where the potential benefits are very significant and all participants have given fully informed consent.

- Where there *are* harmful consequences to participants, the investigator is responsible for removing and correcting these.

- Information about participants is confidential unless otherwise agreed in advance.

Ⓛ earning Theory: A Brief Overview

Because learning involves changes in behavior that result from experience, the psychology of learning is based on observations of behavior and behavior change. Not surprisingly, the terms **learning theory** and *behavior theory* are often synonymous in psychological literature.

Learning theories (or behavior theories) result from psychologists' attempts to organize the observations, hypotheses, hunches, laws, principles, and guesses that have been made about human behavior. Not surprisingly, the earliest learning theories were, in many ways, somewhat simpler than more recently developed theories. Theories have become increasingly complex with new findings, and with the recognition that earlier theories don't account for all the facts. Still, the earliest theories continue to have a profound influence on current theories and research.

Recent Origins of Learning Theory

Among the origins of contemporary psychological theory are early attempts by psychologists to explain behavior on the basis of instincts and emotion. Early psychologists—for example, William James and Edward Bradford Titchener—relied heavily on **introspection** (examining one's own feelings and motives and generalizing from these) as a way of discovering things about human learning and behavior. Recall that Descartes, too, used this approach in his efforts to understand human nature. This approach differs dramatically from the more objective methods of science that eventually dominated psychology.

The establishment of a psychological laboratory in Leipzig, Germany, by Wilhelm Wundt in 1879 is considered by many as the beginning of psychology *as a science*. Although Wundt and his followers—both in Europe and in North America—continued to deal with mentalistic concepts such as consciousness, sensation, feeling, imagining, and perceiving, they attempted to use the more objective methods of science to study them.

Classifications of Learning Theories

By the early 1900s, psychologists (especially in the United States) began to reject subjective and difficult topics like mind and thinking, choosing instead to concentrate on the more objective aspects of *behavior*. This orientation eventually became known as **behaviorism.** It led to learning theories concerned mainly with objective events such as stimuli, responses, and rewards. *Stimuli* (conditions that lead to behavior) and *responses* (actual behavior), behavioristic theorists argued, are the only directly observable aspects of behavior; hence, they are the objective variables that can be used to develop a science of behavior. "The essence of behaviorism," explains Mills, "is the equating of theory with application, understanding with prediction, and the workings of the human mind with social technology" (1998, p. 2). Behavioristic theories include those of Pavlov, Watson, and Guthrie (Chapter 2); Thorndike and Hull (Chapter 3); and Skinner (Chapter 4). Other theories that share many beliefs of the behaviorists, but in which there is greater use of biological (Chapter 5) or mentalistic (Chapter 6) concepts serve as a transition to the second major division of theories—**cognitivism.**

Cognitive psychologists are interested in human mental activity, and specifically in three dimensions of human mental activity: information processing, representation, and self-awareness (Mandler, 1985). Gestalt theories, with their interest in perception and awareness, are important early examples of cognitive theories (Chapter 6). Other examples include Bruner, Piaget, and Vygotsky (Chapter 7). More recent information-processing approaches, evident in computer

Table 1.2 *Major Divisions in Learning Theory*

	Variables of interest	Representative theorists
Behaviorism	Stimuli	Thorndike
	Responses	Pavlov
	Reinforcement	Guthrie
	Punishment	Watson
		Skinner
		Hull
A transition: the beginnings of modern cognitivism	Evolutionary psychology	Rescorla-Wagner
	Sociobiology	Wilson
	Stimuli	Hebb
	Responses	Tolman
	Reinforcement	Koffka
	Mediation	Köhler
	Purpose	Wertheimer
	Goals	
	Expectation	
	Representation	
Cognitive theories	Representation	Bruner
	Self-awareness	Piaget
	Information processing	Vygotsky
	Perceiving	Computer models
	Organizing	Information processing
	Decision making	Models of memory and motivation
	Problem solving	
	Attention	
	Memory	
	Culture	
	Language	

models of thinking (Chapter 8) as well as in current investigations of memory (Chapter 9) and motivation (Chapter 10), are also unmistakably cognitive. (See Table 1.2.)

The main importance of the distinction between behavioristic and cognitive approaches is that it permits a simple classification of explanations of human learning; this makes it easier to understand, remember, and apply learning theories. Be warned, however, that behaviorism and cognitivism exist only as convenient labels for extremely complex theories. Even theories that might appear very different often share common ideas. Few are clear examples of only one theoretical approach.

Preview of the Text

The Old Woman said we were about done with Chapter 1, but before going on to the next chapter, she would present little previews of each of the remaining 11 chapters of the book. She explained that these were being offered as hors d'oeuvres. She said that like hors d'oeuvres, they might whet your appetite, satiate you completely if your appetite is extraordinarily tiny, or make you quite ill. She thought that some of you might choose to go directly to the entrée, and she said there would be no dessert and probably no wine either, and she laughed so suddenly the one-eyed cat got up and left, not even looking back at anyone.

Chapter 2. Early Behaviorism: Pavlov, Watson, and Guthrie

They say Watson liked to impress his friends with his dog's intelligence. So at dinner one night, he knelt with the dog and began to bark the way an intelligent dog might. The dog listened politely and then ate. The next night Watson did the same thing again. He knelt and barked and howled while, again, the dog listened attentively and then ate its supper. Watson was trying to teach the dog to bark—not just in an ordinary way but intelligently—for its supper. The procedure, called conditioning, half worked. At the end of two weeks, the dog still wouldn't bark, but it absolutely refused to eat until Watson had knelt and barked. Why?

Chapter 3. The Effects of Behavior: Thorndike and Hull

Some professors complain that their students often go to sleep when they present their magnificent lectures on Hull. They think that the students are bored, but perhaps most of them are simply suffering from symbol shock.

What does this mean: $_SE_R = {_SH_R} \times D \times V \times K$?

Chapter 4. Operant Conditioning: Skinner's Radical Behaviorism

A bright psychologist once decided that he would show a rat how to eat. "Pshaw," his grandmother croaked, "rats already know how to eat." That's not what her grandson meant; he intended to teach this rat how to eat properly, using a tiny

spoon, sitting at th⌐ ... 　　its mouth closed. He also expected the
rat ... 　　⌐ps delicately on a napkin after an espe-

⌐cceeded. Unfortunately, both the rat and
⌐e learning program was completed.

⌐ **Psychology:**
⌐**d the Brain**

⌐er and living with his grandmother, Lefrançois says
⌐zens every winter.[9] But one night when the stew was
⌐, or the rabbit diseased, all who had been at dinner be-
⌐tly afterward. From then on, says he, he does not molest
⌐en write about them.

Chapter 6. A Transition to Modern Cognitivism: Hebb, Tolman, and the Gestaltists

A poverty-stricken graduate student in psychology, driven by hunger (for food and for knowledge), accepted a summer job at an isolated fire-lookout tower. They flew him to the tower by helicopter and left him—completely alone.

The second morning, his radio broke.

The sixth morning, the helicopter came back with a radio repair technician. But the student was gone. He had scribbled a note: *Can't take it. Going home.* Home was only 300 miles of spruce forest and muskeg away. He was never seen again.

Why? Not why was he never seen again, but why did he leave? He wasn't stupid.

Chapter 7. Three Cognitive Theories: Bruner, Piaget, and Vygotsky

If I say to you, "Red hair, blue eye, scar," do you simply see a thatch of reddish hair, a single eyeball with a blue iris, a length of surgical scar?

Or have you already built a face, added a nose and ears, drawn your scar from ear to jowl?

Could you help going beyond the information given?

---

[9]I have no doubt my grandmother told the Old Woman something very much like this story because the important parts of it actually happened—although not exactly as described.

Chapter 8. Neural Networks: The New Connectionism

Can machines think? How do they think? What do they think? Can they deliberately lie?

Chapter 9. Learning and Remembering

In a carefully guarded psychological laboratory of a large North American university, a small, bespectacled, shabbily dressed undergraduate student sits on a straight-backed kitchen chair. Her name is Miranda. In front of Miranda is a dish filled with curled, grayish pieces of food. She doesn't know what the food is, but when well salted and peppered it's quite palatable. She hasn't been fed for 24 hours and is now busily eating.

Just before being given this meal, Miranda was given a simple problem in advanced calculus—which she failed miserably. Now, after eating four dishes of this food, she's expected to be able to solve the problem. Why? And do you really believe this one?

Chapter 10. Motivation

Three radical student leaders are cleverly coerced into volunteering for a psychological investigation. They later discover that they will be required to write an essay strongly advocating a pro-Establishment, nonradical point of view. None of them dares refuse for fear of incurring the wrath of the psychology instructor. For their efforts, one student is paid $50, the second is paid $10, and the third is presented with a single $1 bill. The students are told that their essays are quite good and that the authorities would like to see them published. The money is ostensibly payment for publication rights. The students agree to allow their work to be published. A day later, a skilled interviewer uncovers how each of the subjects really feels about the Establishment. A human grandmother would almost certainly predict that the student who was paid $50 dollars would be most likely to feel better about the Establishment. But the grandmother would be wrong. Why? She isn't stupid.

Chapter 11. Social Learning: Bandura's Social Cognitive Theory

Twelve-year-old Ronald, who has been a rule-abiding child all his short life, is allowed to spend the summer with his cousin, Edward. One day shortly after returning home at the end of the summer, he smashes his thumb with a hammer while helping his dad build a chicken coop. @#!%**&, says Ronald with impressive conviction. His dad had never before heard Ronald say @#!%**&.

What might Ronald's saying @#!%**& suggest about Edward? What might it suggest about Ronald?

Chapter 12. Analysis, Synthesis, and Integration

There are many different ways of learning, distinct outcomes of the learning process, and varied models of the learner. For example:

Instructional and Other Applications of Learning Theories

Learning, as we saw, involves relatively permanent potential or actual changes in behavior as a result of experience. Learning theories are systematic attempts to explain these changes. Good learning theories allow us to explain behavior and to predict and perhaps to control it.

The business of education is to change behavior—and at the same time, to predict and control it. Predicting, controlling, and changing behavior is also the business of parenting, of therapy, of sales, and of many other human endeavors.

In most cases, then, good learning theories will be practically useful for each of these undertakings. Accordingly, each chapter in this text contains one or more sections that deal specifically with the educational implications of learning theories, as well as with some of their applications in other fields.

Summary

1. Psychology is the science that studies human behavior and thinking. Its roots lie in *epistemology*, which deals with the nature of knowledge and of knowing. The *mind-body problem* asks about the relationship between the mind (consciousness) and the physical world (including the body).

2. Learning can be defined as relatively permanent changes in *potential* for behavior that are the result of experience. Hence learning is not always apparent in performance.

3. Theories are collections of related statements intended to summarize and explain important observations. These statements are seldom laws (verifiable fact; beyond reasonable doubt), but more often take the form of principles (statements relating to some general predictability) and beliefs (more personal convictions, sometimes accurate, and sometimes not; the basis of bubba psychology).

4. Learning theories are attempts to systematize and organize what is known about human learning. They are useful for explaining and for predicting and controlling behavior, and they may lead to new information.

5. Good theories reflect the facts, are clear and understandable, are parsimonious, are useful for predicting as well as explaining, are useful in practical ways, are internally consistent, are based on few unverifiable assumptions, and are satisfying and thought provoking in that they lead to further research (have heuristic value).

6. Science refers to collections of related information (chemistry or physics, for example) as well as to an attitude toward the search for knowledge (it insists on objectivity, replicability, consistency) and a collection of methods to ensure objectivity (ask the question; make a hypothesis; collect relevant observations; test the hypothesis; reach and share a conclusion).

7. Experiments are science's most powerful tool for determining the validity of hypotheses. They involve systematically manipulating some aspect of the environment to determine the effect of so doing. They can be thought of as ways of testing if-then statements, where the "if" refers to independent variables that can be manipulated to see what the effect will be on dependent variables (the "then").

8. Psychological research should be subjected to critical questions such as: Does it provide an explanation or does it simply label? Is the sample on which conclusions are based representative? Is there a possibility that the subjects were dishonest or behaved as they did because they knew they were part of an experiment? Might the investigators have been influenced by their own expectations?

9. Findings based on animal studies have to be generalized to humans with caution. In addition, there are important ethical guidelines for research with both animals and people.

10. The traditional divisions in theories of learning are based on the primary concerns of different theorists. Behaviorism describes an approach that deals mainly with the observable aspects of human functioning; cognitivism refers to a preoccupation with topics such as perception, information processing, concept formation, awareness, and understanding.

Early Behaviorism: Pavlov, Watson, and Guthrie

> Mind, n.—A mysterious form of matter secreted by the brain. Its chief activity consists in the endeavor to ascertain its own nature, the futility of the attempt being due to the fact that it has nothing but itself to know itself with.
> **Ambrose Bierce**

The Old Woman was already on the lake when I arrived, although I couldn't tell how she had come. She had said "I'm gonna catch me a goldurn whitefish," and that I should meet her at Pigeon Lake.

"Do you like this car?" she asked when she saw me, waving a full-page magazine ad in front of me. I no longer recall what kind of car it was, but I remember that a long-legged model lounged over its hood.

"How about this one?" she asked, showing me another advertisement, another near-perfect female form, another car.

"I know you like them," she said somewhat aggressively, not giving me time to think an intelligent response. "And I'll tell you why."

I waited for her to tell me why. But instead, she said to turn on the recorder, that the explanation would be in the second chapter. I asked could I maybe fish too while she spoke, but she said, "No, pay attention. Besides, you'll need both hands to take notes. I'll catch enough." Then she began to read her manuscript.

This Chapter

The first chapter of this book, *she read*, defined important terms and concepts in the study of human learning, and described approaches in theory building. This second chapter traces the early beginnings of *behaviorism*, which is an explicit concern with actual behavior in contrast to a concern with more *mental* things like knowing and thinking. The chapter describes one of the simplest forms of learning: classical conditioning.

Objectives

Tell your readers, said the Old Woman, that after they finish this chapter, they may be overcome by an overwhelming urge to stop complete strangers on the street and explain to them:

- *What classical conditioning is*
- *The meanings of US, UR, CS, CR, extinction, spontaneous recovery, generalization, discrimination, transfer*
- *How emotions might be learned*
- *Why models sell cars*

- *Similarities among Pavlov, Watson, and Guthrie*
- *Differences among them*
- *The difference between contiguity and reinforcement*
- *Why it is so hard to teach a cow to sit up*

Explain to them, too, that if they don't know these things when they finish, they should not bother asking their grandmothers. Instead, write to Lefrançois, she said.[1]

---

[1]This is just the Old Woman's strange sense of humor. So don't write unless you're sending gifts. Just ask your grandmother.

Scientific Psychology's Beginnings

As mentioned in Chapter 1, early psychologists relied heavily on introspection as a tool for investigating human behavior. After all, they had no access to the kinds of sophisticated instruments we now use to measure mental activity (for example, the electroencephalograms and magnetoencephalographs discussed in Chapter 5, or the computers, discussed in Chapter 8). Using introspection, the psychologist would systematically analyze and interpret personal thoughts and feelings, trying to arrive at an understanding that could then be generalized to others. Introspection, sometimes called "arm-chair research," was the method Descartes used as he struggled to understand the meaning of reality, of knowledge, and of mind. It was also the method used by William James, widely recognized as the father of American psychology. James tried to understand human experience and consciousness as a *whole*, claiming that it could not meaningfully be chopped up into little bits like stimuli and responses, or understood in terms of sensations or associations. "A river or a stream are the metaphors by which it is most naturally described," he insisted—from whence the common expression "stream of consciousness" (James, 1890/1950, p. 239).

At the time that James was lecturing and writing in America, another powerful movement was well under way in Europe. This movement was strongly influenced by biology and physiology. Instead of relying solely on the highly subjective method of introspection, it attempted to apply a more scientific approach to the study of the mind. Its methods were those of **psychophysics,** the measurement of physical stimuli, and their effects.

Early Psychophysics

Imagine you are standing in a completely darkened room staring in the general direction of an unlit, 100-watt light bulb. As long as the light is off, you won't see it. And even if the light is turned on, if it's kept sufficiently low, you still will see nothing. In fact, you will continue to see nothing until light intensity has reached a sufficient, minimum level.

Absolute Threshold

Early psychologists, such as Wilhelm Wundt and Gustav Theodor Fechner in Europe, and Edward Bradford Titchener, one of Wundt's students, in the United States, were interested in questions such as these: What is the minimum amount of light the human eye can detect? The softest sound that can be heard? The lightest touch that can be felt? What they wanted to do through their psychophysical measurements is determine exactly the **absolute threshold** for each sense—that is, the least amount of stimulation required for sensation. (See Wundt biography).

It turns out that this is not possible because there is no single level of light or sound or pressure that always leads to sensation, whereas all stimulation below this threshold goes undetected. Some people are more sensitive than others (have better hearing or better vision, for example). But for each individual, there is a lower limit below which a stimulus will never be detected and an upper limit

Wilhelm Wundt (1832–1920)

Wundt was one of four children born to a Lutheran minister and his wife who lived in Mannheim, Germany; only he and one brother survived childhood. He was reportedly a profoundly introverted boy whose only friend was somewhat older and mentally handicapped. Wundt's upbringing was extremely strict; he often was locked, terrified, in dark closets when he had misbehaved.

Wundt's early school career was difficult and not very successful, but when he went to university, he became fascinated by the anatomy and mysteries of the brain and, almost overnight, became a scholar. At the age of 24, he obtained a medical degree and subsequently became an instructor in physiology.

He spent 17 years at Heidelberg University on the medical faculty, 1 year in Zurich as a professor of philosophy, and 42 years at Leipzig, where he founded the psychological laboratory that is generally associated with the beginning of psychology as a science. He was apparently a quiet, unassuming man who seldom left his laboratory and his home. He wrote almost constantly, producing more than 500 books and articles. Boring (1950) estimated that Wundt wrote an average of one published word every 2 minutes, day and night, for 68 years. His major textbook on psychology appeared in three volumes in its first edition: 553, 680, and 796 pages of very complex German.

above which it will always be detected. Between the two, there is a point at which it will be detected 50% of the time. This point is called the absolute threshold, although it is more approximate than absolute.

Differential Threshold

Psychophysicists measured not only thresholds but also what they called the **differential threshold** often referred to as the **just noticeable difference (JND).** You can tell the difference between weights of 1 and 2 pounds—as you can easily demonstrate if you lift a sack containing 1 pound of black beans and another containing 2 pounds; the difference between the two is a *noticeable difference*. Fechner (1860/1966) and his brother-in-law, Max Weber, were interested in finding out the least amount of change in stimulation that would be noticeable—that is, the *differential threshold* or *just noticeable difference* (JND).

If you can tell the difference between 1 and 2 pounds, does that mean that the JND for weight is something less than 1 pound? No, says Weber. You can tell the difference between 1 and 2 pounds, and perhaps between 6 and 7 pounds, but you can't so easily tell the difference between 10 and 11 pounds, much less between 99 and 100 pounds. In the same way, you can tell the difference between a

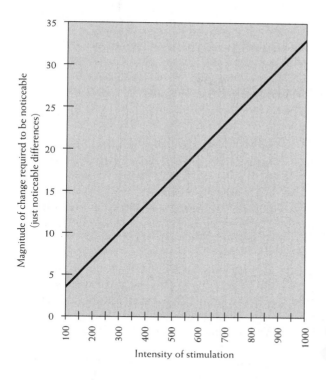

Figure 2.1

A graphic portrayal of Weber's law. As intensity of stimulation increases, proportionally greater increases in stimulation are required if they are to be noticeable.

25-watt bulb and a 60-watt bulb, a difference of 35 watts. But you can't discriminate between 1,000 watts of light and 1,100 watts. Even though the difference is almost three times greater in the second case, it is not a noticeable difference.

JNDs, said Weber, are a *constant proportion* of a stimulus. For lifted weights, for example, the constant is about 1/30. This means that a weight lifter who normally lifts 300 pounds would probably not notice an addition of 5 pounds, but would notice a difference of 10; one who lifts 600 pounds would require an addition of 20 pounds before noticing the difference (Figure 2.1). Fechner labeled this conclusion **Weber's law.**

Unfortunately for psychophysics, Weber's constants are not very constant. Some people are more sensitive to stimulus changes than are others; furthermore, people's sensitivity can vary from day to day, or even from moment to moment, depending on fatigue and other factors. Nevertheless, Weber's law appears to be true as a general principle (Falmagne, 1985).

Ivan P. Pavlov (1849–1936)

Fechner, Weber, Titchener, Wundt, and other early psychologists were as much physiologists as psychologists. Another physiologist who had a profound influence on the development of psychology throughout the world was the Russian, Ivan Pavlov. (See Pavlov biography.)

Ivan Petrovich Pavlov (1849–1936)

Pavlov was born to a poor village priest in Russia and set out to follow his father's footsteps and become a priest. He did rather poorly in elementary school; no one would have dreamt that he would one day win a Nobel Prize.

His early postsecondary education was at the Riazan Ecclesiastic Seminary. But, says Windholz (1997), the young Pavlov was so influenced by Russian translations of Western scientific writings, and particularly with their Darwinian overtones, that he promptly abandoned his religious training. Instead, he went to the University of St. Petersburg where he specialized in animal physiology and in medicine.

After he received his medical degree, Pavlov went to Germany, where he studied physiology and medicine for another 2 years before returning to St. Petersburg to work as an assistant in a physiology laboratory. He was later appointed professor of pharmacology and, at the age of 41, head of a physiology department. His work continued to deal almost exclusively with physiological topics, specifically with digestive processes. It wasn't until the age of 50 that he began to study classical conditioning, these studies lasting another 30 years. His international reputation was so great, says Windholz (1997), that he was one of the few Soviet scientists of his era who could openly criticize the Bolshevik regime and who could defend human rights with impunity. In 1923, when he was 74 years old, the famous scientist and Nobel Prize winner visited the United States. And in New York's Grand Central Station, Pavlov was mugged (Thomas, 1997).

To the end, Pavlov insisted he was a physiologist and not a psychologist. In fact, he viewed psychology with such disdain that he fined any of his laboratory assistants who used psychological rather than physiological terms (Watson, 1971). Yet he wrote papers and provided theoretical explanations for psychological topics such as hypnosis and paranoia and made invaluable contributions to the early development of theories of learning (Windholz, 1996a, 1996b).

The experiment for which Pavlov is most famous was the result of an almost accidental observation. Pavlov had been studying the role of various juices in digestion, one of these being saliva, and he had developed a procedure that allowed him to detect and measure salivation in the dogs he used in his experiments. In fact, in 1904 he was awarded a Nobel Prize in medicine and physiology for his work on digestion—work that, claims Smith (1995), illustrates Pavlov's remarkable experimental and inferential skills.

During this work, Pavlov happened to notice that some of the dogs in his laboratory began to salivate before they were fed. He saw, too, that this occurred only in dogs that had been in the laboratory for some time.

Figure 2.2 What Pavlov first noticed was that the sight of the handler alone was enough to cause many of his experimental dogs to salivate. Through further experiments, he studied the learning processes involved.

Classical Conditioning

In trying to find some scientific explanation for the salivation of his dogs before they were fed, Pavlov devised a series of now-famous experiments in **classical conditioning.** In these experiments, he demonstrated that not only could the sight of food eventually bring about salivation in his dogs, but almost any other distinctive stimulus could have the same effect if paired with food often enough. Ever the physiologist, Pavlov thought he had discovered "psychic secretions."

In his demonstration, Pavlov refers to the food as an **unconditioned stimulus** (US). It is called a stimulus because it is an environmental event that affects the organism, and it is labeled *unconditioned* because it leads to a response (muscular or glandular reaction) without any learning taking place. The salivation in response to the food is called an **unconditioned response (UR)** because it is associated with an unconditioned stimulus. Hence, an unconditioned response is a response that occurs without any learning.[2]

What Pavlov showed repeatedly is that if a US (food, for example) is paired with another stimulus often enough, this other stimulus will eventually lead to the response originally associated only with the US (in this case, salivation). For example, if a buzzer is sounded every time food is presented to the dog, eventually the buzzer—called a **conditioned stimulus (CS)**—will elicit the response of salivation—now a **conditioned response (CR).** Illustrations of this procedure are given in Figures 2.2, 2.3, and 2.4.[3]

---

[2]In fact, said the Old Woman as an aside, Pavlov didn't really use the words "conditioned" and "unconditioned." He used "conditional" and "unconditional," terms that make a lot more sense if you think about it. It's the translators who screwed it up, she harrumphed.
[3]"So," said the Old Woman at this point, "Do you now know why half-dressed human forms sell cars?" But, according to my notes, she continued before I could answer. Chapter 11 provides an answer.

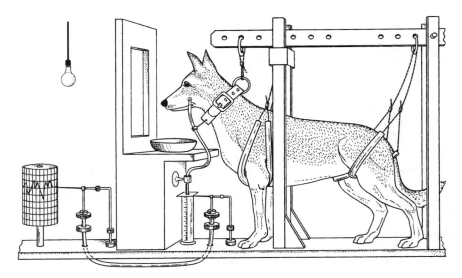

Figure 2.3 In his experiments, Pavlov often placed his dogs in a harness like this one. Food powder can be placed either in the dog's mouth or in the dish. A tube is surgically inserted into the duct of the parotid gland so that the amount of saliva produced can be measured as it drops down the tube, causing movement in a balancing mechanism at the other end of the tube. This movement is in turn recorded on a revolving drum. In the experiment illustrated here, the US (food) is paired with a CS (light shining in the window).

Classical conditioning is also referred to as *learning through stimulus substitution.* That's because the conditioned stimulus, after being paired with the unconditioned stimulus often enough, can then be substituted for it. The CS will evoke a similar, but weaker, response. It is also sometimes referred to as *signal learning* because the conditioned stimulus serves as a signal for the occurrence of the unconditioned stimulus. For example, in the Pavlov demonstration, the buzzer is a signal that food will soon follow.

In classical conditioning, learning always begins with an unlearned response (UR) that can reliably be elicited by a specific stimulus (the US). This unlearned stimulus-response unit is called a **reflex.**

Figure 2.4
Classical conditioning. Food elicits salivation in a dog, but a buzzer does not. After successive pairing of food and buzzer, the buzzer begins to elicit salivation.

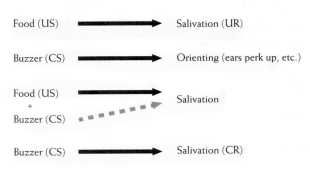

Food (US) ➡ Salivation (UR)

Buzzer (CS) ➡ Orienting (ears perk up, etc.)

Food (US)
+
Buzzer (CS) ➡ Salivation

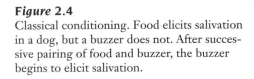

Buzzer (CS) ➡ Salivation (CR)

Human Reflexes

Reflexes are defined as simple, non-intentional, unlearned behaviors. In a sense, they are pre-wired stimulus-response units. The stimulus *food* reliably leads to salivation, whether you intend to salivate or not; your response is reflexive; that is, it is involuntary and largely uncontrollable. Similarly, when somebody strikes your patella, your knee jerks. In the same way, you blink if something potentially threatening approaches your eye.

Humans are born with a number of reflexes, many of which are very important for survival. The **sucking reflex,** which causes the infant to suck when the mouth is appropriately stimulated, is clearly related to infant survival. So is the **Moro reflex,** although its relationship to survival is somewhat less obvious. The Moro reflex is the infant's startle reaction. It involves throwing out the arms and feet symmetrically, and then pulling them back in. Some speculate that this reflexive response could have been important for tree-dwelling primate infants who might, as a result of this reflexive action when suddenly dropped by a careless mother, be lucky enough to catch a branch and save themselves. (See Table 2.1).

Most reflexive responses that can reliably be elicited by a stimulus can be classically conditioned both in humans and in nonhuman animals. Thus, the knee-jerk reflex, the eye-blink reflex, and the pupillary reflex can all be conditioned to various stimuli. In addition, some glandular responses (such as salivation) and other internal reactions can be conditioned. The term **interoceptive conditioning** is used to describe the conditioning of actions involving glands or involuntary muscles. For example, blood vessel constriction or dilation, which is brought about by the external application of cold or hot packs, can be conditioned to a bell or a buzzer. Urination can also be classically conditioned.

Table 2.1 *Some Reflexive Behaviors in the Newborn Human*

Reflex	Stimulus	Response
Sucking	Object in mouth or on lips	Sucks
Rooting (head turning)	Stroking the cheek or the corner of the mouth	Turns head toward side being stroked
Swallowing	Food in mouth	Swallows
Sneezing	Irritation in the nasal passages	Sneezes
Moro reflex	Sudden loud noise; loss of support	Throws arms and legs out symmetrically
Babinski reflex	Tickling the middle of the soles	Spreads and raises toes
Toe grasp	Tickling the soles just below the toes	Curls toes around object
Palmar grasp	Object placed in infant's hand	Grasps object tightly
Swimming reflex	Infant horizontal, supported by abdomen	Coordinated swimming movements
Stepping reflex	Infant vertical, feet lightly touching flat surface	Makes coordinated walking movements

If sufficient air is introduced into a person's bladder, pressure increases inside the bladder and urination occurs. If the introduction of air is paired with a bell or buzzer, after a relatively small number of pairings the bell alone will elicit urination.

Related to this, Keller (1969) describes a procedure in which subjects are asked to dip their right hands in pitchers of ice water. This causes an immediate drop in the temperature of that hand and, interestingly, also causes a more easily measured drop in the temperature of the other hand. If the hand is dipped in the ice water at regular intervals (3 or 4 minutes) and each dip is preceded by a buzzer, after 20 or so pairings the buzzer alone will cause a measurable drop in hand temperature.

Another type of response that can readily be classically conditioned involves **taste aversion**—a powerful disinclination to eat or drink something. Some taste aversions are hereditary; they prevent animals, and people, from eating bitter-tasting substances (which, incidentally, often taste bitter precisely because they're toxic). (Classical conditioning of taste aversions is discussed in more detail in Chapter 5.)

How easily a classically conditioned response is acquired is related to a number of factors. Not the least important is the distinctiveness of the conditioned stimulus. Buzzers and other tones have been particularly good conditioning stimuli in animal experimentation because they can be highly distinctive stimuli.[4]

Explanations for Stimulus-Response Associations

Basically, conditioning theory offers two different explanations for learning: **contiguity** and **reinforcement.** Contiguity, the simultaneous or nearly simultaneous occurrence of events, is the explanation used by Pavlov—and, as we will soon see, also by theorists such as Watson, and Guthrie. These theorists believed that for behavior to change (that is, for learning to occur), it is sufficient that two events be paired—sometimes only once, sometimes more often.

Reinforcement is a more complex concept having to do with the *effects* of a stimulus. One kind of reinforcement, for example, is positive reinforcement, in

---

[4]When she finished this section, the Old Woman said she had another example but I should turn off the tape recorder. When I asked why, she explained that she, personally, didn't care one way or another but that after reading the pre-revision reviews of the old fourth edition of this book she had come to the conclusion that it might be important for various reasons, including political correctness, to shield student readers from exposure to certain topics. She reminded me that one of the reviewers had written, in reference to another passage, "Our purpose is to educate, not titillate." So I turned off the recorder. The Old Woman paused while she baited the wireworm, turning it at right angles to the line and then dropping it down the hole, bending to check its depth. Then she began to describe the details of a study by Letourneau and O'Donohue (1997). Unfortunately, my notes here are almost illegible because in the middle of the telling, the Old Woman caught a whitefish and when I went to help her, my notebook got wet and the ink ran. What I recall is that in this study, 25 women aged 18 to 40 years were shown clips from erotic videos in a conditioning study where the videos were paired with an amber light and the women's sexual arousal was measured using physiological measures like vaginal impulse amplitude and vaginal photoplethysmograph recordings. Different sorts of pairings of the light and the videos were used, and results showed that sexual arousal can be classically conditioned so that these women could then be "turned on" with a stupid amber light. "But there's no need to put that in the book," the Old Woman explained.

which an effect (such as the satisfaction of hunger) leads to learning. Reinforcement is defined in more detail and illustrated in the next chapter.

Variations in Contiguity

Events are contiguous when they occur at the same time and place. Contiguity does not imply **contingency.** Events are said to be contingent when the occurrence of one depends on the occurrence of the other. Thus, event A is contingent on event B when the occurrence of A depends on the occurrence of B. For example, if being given a new car depends on selling X amount of CLEANSOAP, receiving the car is *contingent on* selling the soap. Pavlovian conditioning is based on *contiguity* rather than *contingency.* In contrast, reinforcement-based theories such as B. F. Skinner's operant conditioning use *contingency* as an explanatory principle.

Contiguity in classical conditioning does not always mean that the CS starts and ends at exactly the same time as the US. Actually, this arrangement, termed **simultaneous pairing** (or *simultaneous conditioning*), is not the most effective way of classically conditioning a response.

Far more effective is **delayed pairing** (or *delayed conditioning*), in which the CS is presented before the US and continues during presentation of the US. It is termed *delayed* because of the time lag between the presentation of the CS and beginning of the US. In **trace pairing** (or *trace conditioning*), the CS starts *and ends* before the US so that there is a very brief time lapse between the two (with time lapses longer than half a second or so, trace conditioning is usually not very effective.)[5] In **backward pairing** (or *backward conditioning*), the US has already been presented and removed before presentation of the CS.

In the classical Pavlovian demonstration, simultaneous pairing requires that the buzzer be sounded at the same time as food powder is injected in the dog's mouth; delayed pairing would occur when the buzzer is turned on slightly before the food powder is injected into the dog's mouth, and then the buzzer is turned off at the same time as the food injection ends; trace pairing would require that the buzzer be turned on and then off again *before* food powder is injected in the dog's mouth; and in backward pairing, food powder is injected first, and then, after a brief time lapse, the buzzer sounds. These four options are shown in Figure 2.5, in order from most to least effective.

Backward Conditioning and Biological Predispositions

Backward conditioning—or *backward pairing*, in which the CS follows the US—was long thought to be completely ineffective. In fact, in most circumstances classical conditioning does not ordinarily occur with this arrangement. However, in a small number of highly specific experiments, investigators have succeeded in bringing about backward conditioning. In one experiment representative of these studies, Keith-Lucas and Guttman (1975) classically conditioned an avoidance response in rats by shocking them electrically (US) and afterward placing a plastic hedgehog

---

[5]One exception in which conditioning is effective even after a long lapse between the CS and the US is taste aversion learning, discussed in Chapter 5.

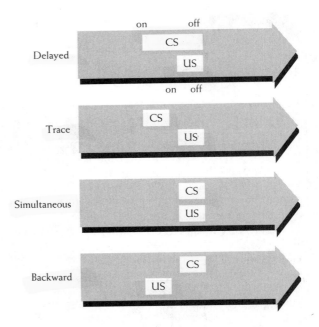

Figure 2.5
Impact of variations in CS-US procedures. The pairing sequences are shown here in the order of effectiveness. Conditioning takes place most quickly in the delayed sequence, when the conditioned stimulus (for instance, the buzzer) is presented shortly before the unconditioned stimulus (food powder) and continues throughout the time the US is presented.

toy in their cages (CS). A significant number of rats responded with apparent fear when shown the plastic toy the following day, providing it had been placed in their cages within 10 seconds of the electric shock. Those that had experienced a 40-second delay showed little fear.

The significance of this study and of related studies is not so much that they establish that conditioning through backward pairing is possible but, rather, that they add to the growing evidence that some types of learning are far easier for certain organisms than are other types. As is shown in Chapter 5, people seem to be *prepared* to learn certain things (language, for example); by the same token, people also seem to be prepared *not* to learn certain other things (for example, avoidance of sweet foods, a type of learning for which humans may be *contraprepared*). Similarly, rats are prepared to learn to fear hedgehogs; they are not prepared to learn language. The discovery and elaboration of these biological constraints on learning constitute an important and growing area of psychological research and theorizing (see Chapter 5).

Phenomena in Classical Conditioning

During more than 20 years of detailed experimentation on classical conditioning, Pavlov and his students discovered a range of phenomena, many of which continue to be investigated.

Acquisition
For example, Pavlov and his students found that **acquisition**—the formation of the stimulus-response association—requires a number of pairings of CS and US.

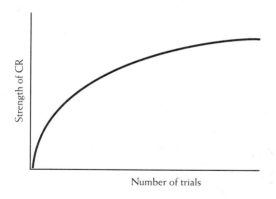

Figure 2.6
A hypothetical learning curve. Note that the strength of the conditioned response increases rapidly at first and then levels off.

After only one or two pairings, the CS alone does not ordinarily lead to a CR. But with increasing numbers of pairings, the CR occurs more frequently *and more strongly*. For example, in the salivation experiment, amount of salivation in response to the CS increases until it reaches a peak, after which it levels off. Psychology researchers and students have plotted thousands of **learning curves** illustrating this. One is shown in Figure 2.6.

Learning curves are affected by the number of US-CS pairings and by the strength of the US. In general, the stronger the US (the bigger the steak; the louder the noise; the stronger the puff of air), the more quickly the CR will reach its peak.

Extinction and Recovery
Another important Pavlovian finding is that classically conditioned associations are remarkably durable. A dog conditioned to salivate to a tone and then left alone to do nothing but dog things for months will immediately salivate again (although perhaps in a more restrained way) when brought back into the laboratory and presented with the same tone. Similarly, Maurice, who had several terrifying experiences with snakes as a young boy, would, if you showed him a snake today, break into a cold sweat even if he hasn't actually seen a snake for many years.

But classically conditioned responses can be eliminated—a procedure that Pavlov called **extinction.** One way to extinguish a conditioned response is to present the conditioned stimulus repeatedly without the unconditioned stimulus. For example, if the buzzer keeps buzzing, but no food is presented, the dog will soon stop salivating. Interestingly, however, if the CS (the buzzer) is presented again later, the dog will again salivate, although at lower intensity—a phenomenon called **spontaneous recovery.** To completely extinguish the response, it would be necessary to present the CS without the US again—and perhaps to repeat the procedure a number of different times. Eventually, there would no longer be evidence of spontaneous recovery. (See Figure 2.7.)

Generalization and Discrimination
Pavlov demonstrated that when a dog is conditioned to salivate to a given tone, it will then usually salivate in response to a wide range of tones. This phenomenon

Figure 2.7
A hypothetical representation of spontaneous recovery following extinction. Note how the strength of the CR is less following each extinction period, and how progressively fewer trials are required for extinction.

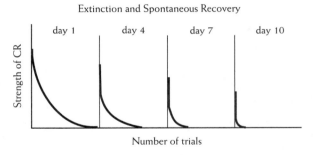

Extinction and Spontaneous Recovery

is referred to as **stimulus generalization.** It involves making the same, or similar, responses when presented with any of a number of related stimuli. An opposite phenomenon, **stimulus discrimination,** involves making different responses to related but distinctly different stimuli. Pavlov illustrates stimulus discrimination by reference to studies showing that dogs conditioned to salivate in response to a tone can also be conditioned *not* to respond to a second tone that varies in pitch only slightly from the original conditioned stimulus.

Higher Order Conditioning

A dog conditioned to respond to a tone will eventually salivate readily in response to that tone—and perhaps in response to other similar tones (stimulus generalization). If the tone is then paired repeatedly with another stimulus—say a light—but the second stimulus (in this case, the light) is never paired with food, the dog may nevertheless learn to salivate simply in response to the light. This is an example of what Pavlov labeled **second-order conditioning** (a form of **higher-order conditioning**). Now if the light is paired with yet another conditioning stimulus, such as a black square, the black square will eventually elicit salivation. This example of higher-order conditioning is sometimes labeled *third-order conditioning*.

As we see later, many behaviorists, including Skinner, used the concept of higher-order conditioning extensively in their theories. Higher-order conditioning expands the applicability of conditioning theories enormously. It provides an explanation for the observation that responses, stimuli, and reinforcers often become linked in complex ways.

Educational Implications of Pavlov's Classical Conditioning

Although we are often not aware of it, classical conditioning, especially of emotional responses, occurs in all schools, pretty well at all times. It is at least partly through unconscious processes of classical conditioning that learners come to like or dislike school, teachers, and specific subjects.

To illustrate, we can assume that in the beginning a given subject such as mathematics is a neutral stimulus. That is, it doesn't lead to a strong positive or negative emotional reaction by most students. It follows from what we know about classical conditioning that nonneutral stimuli that are repeatedly present when the learner is exposed to mathematics can serve as unconditioned stimuli. These unconditioned stimuli might be associated with positive reactions (a smiling, friendly teacher, a comfortable desk, a friendly environment), or they might be associated with negative reactions (a stern, demanding teacher with an unpleasant, grating voice; a cold, uncomfortable desk; an unfriendly environment). After a time, mathematics may become a conditioned stimulus associated with either negative or positive reactions depending on the unconditioned stimuli with which it is repeatedly paired. Thus, it is entirely possible to teach mathematics while teaching students, through classical conditioning, to like or dislike mathematics (see Figure 2.8 on page 52).

Among the most useful educational implications of Pavlov's classical conditioning are the following (Lefrançois, 2000):

- Teachers need to do whatever they can to maximize the frequency, distinctiveness, and potency of pleasant unconditioned stimuli in their classrooms.

- Teachers need to try to minimize the unpleasant aspects of classroom learning to reduce the number and potency of negative unconditioned stimuli in their classrooms

- Teachers need to know what is being paired with what in their classrooms.

Pavlov's Classical Conditioning: An Appraisal

As will become clear in the following chapters, Pavlov's description of classical conditioning has served a crucial role in the early development of psychology. It's absolutely remarkable that the work done by this Russian physiologist, exemplified in the single classical study of a dog learning to salivate in response to a tone, should, more than a century later, still form an essential part of every introductory psychology course in most countries of the world. Moreover, many of the principles of classical conditioning (of generalization and extinction, for example) continue to be applied in clinical psychology, in education, in industry, and elsewhere.

John B. Watson (1878–1958)

Profoundly influenced by Pavlov's model of classical conditioning, a determined young rebel set out to revolutionize American psychology—and succeeded. His name was John Broadus Watson.

Behaviorism

In the early 20th century, psychology was an intuitive and highly subjective discipline. Its early development was based largely on ideas developed by Wundt. Wundt saw psychology as a discipline whose principal methods of inquiry were contemplation and speculation (introspection), and whose most important questions had to do with consciousness. As Watson described it, most of the followers of psychology believed it to be "a study of the science of the phenomena of consciousness" (1914, p. 1). That, argued Watson, has been a mistake. He thought that because of this belief, there had been no significant discoveries in psychology since Wundt established his laboratory. It has now, said Watson, "been proved conclusively that the so-called introspective psychology of Germany was founded upon wrong hypotheses" (1930, p. 5). "The subject matter of human psychology," he insisted, "*is the behavior of the human being*" (p. 2; italics in the original). To make a science of this approach, it is essential that it be completely objective; that it concern itself only with actual *behavior* and not with mentalistic things like thoughts and emotions. The science would be called behaviorism.

In 1913, Watson wrote a brief article, now often referred to as the behavioristic manifesto, entitled "Psychology as the Behaviorist Views It." The opening sentence makes his position—and his antagonism to introspection—very clear: "Psychology as the behaviorist views it is a purely objective experimental branch of natural science. Its theoretical goal is the prediction and control of behavior. Introspection forms no essential part of its methods" (p. 158).

Watson firmly believed that consciousness is an irrelevant concept because human actions can be understood through actual behaviors that can readily be observed and studied. Limiting psychology to actual behaviors, he insists, would do away with much of the contradiction that exists in psychology. "Consciousness," he insists, "is neither a definite nor a usable concept" (Watson, 1930, p. 2).

The term *behaviorism* has come to mean concern with the observable aspects of behavior. This orientation assumes behavior comprises responses that can be observed and related to other observable events, such as conditions that precede and follow behavior. "Behaviorism is the scientific study of human behavior," wrote Watson. "Its real goal is to provide the basis for the prediction and control of human beings: Given the situation, to tell what the human being will do; given the man in action,[6] to be able to say why he is reacting in that way" (1928, p. 2). The ultimate goal of behaviorism is to derive laws to explain the relationships existing among antecedent conditions (stimuli), behavior (responses), and consequent conditions (reward, punishment, or neutral effects).

Put simply, and in what Watson referred to as "technical language," the behaviorist's job is "given the stimulus, to predict the response—given the response, to predict the stimulus" (Watson, 1928, p. 2).

Mills summarizes the basic beliefs and purposes of early behaviorism as follows:

> All (behaviorists) denied any intrinsic life to the mind, none believed that the mind was psychology's primary area of study, and all believed that introspection was a futile and misleading way of gathering psychological data. . . . All shared the faith that behaviorist doctrine could be applied directly to human beings and that experimentation with humans was a direct route to knowledge. Almost all also believed that psychological research would have direct social implications. (1998, p. 3)

---

[6]And, presumably, the woman too, the Old Woman muttered as an aside. Watson lived in a more chauvinistic, less politically correct age.

Behaviorists tried to limit psychology to the study of actual, observable behaviors.

Learning: A Classical Conditioning Explanation

Watson's (1930) explanation for learning is based directly on Pavlov's model of classical conditioning. Humans are born with a number of reflexes, says Watson. These include physical and glandular reactions, such as salivating in response to food or blinking in response to a blast of air, and a handful of emotional responses like fear and rage and love. Each of these reflexes can be brought about by a specific stimulus. For example, feelings of love might result from being stroked; fear, from being dropped suddenly from a height; and anger, from being restrained. Pavlov's model of classical conditioning makes it clear, insists Watson, that any distinctive stimulus that is present at the time a reflexive response is brought about can serve as a CS. If this stimulus is present often enough, it will eventually become associated with the response.

Emotional Learning

It follows, says Watson, that emotional behavior, like all other behavior, is simply another example of classical conditioning. He assumed that individual differences are virtually nonexistent to begin with—that is, all people are born with the same emotional reflexes of fear, love, and rage. These reflexive responses initially occur only in response to certain specific stimuli like loud noises, sudden loss of support, or fondling. Eventually, however, humans react emotionally to a variety of things that previously had no emotional significance at all. Watson proposed to explain this important phenomenon using classical conditioning. All later emotional reactions, he explained, result from the pairing of initially neutral stimuli with stimuli that are associated with emotional responses. To illustrate and validate this belief, he, assisted by his then-student Rayner, performed one of his

John Broadus Watson (1878–1958)*

The founder of American behaviorism, John Watson was born in Greenville, South Carolina, in 1878. He was apparently an aggressive boy and was arrested at least twice (once for fighting; another time for firing a gun within city limits). By his own admission, he was not an especially good student, although on one occasion he was the only person who passed a Greek final exam. He later claimed he was able to do so because he spent the previous afternoon cramming and drinking an entire quart of Coca-Cola™[7] syrup (Murchison, 1936).

Watson took his graduate training at the University of Chicago, working his way through school as a rat caretaker. After he graduated, he lectured at the University of Chicago. Several years later, when he was only 29, he was offered a full professorship at Johns Hopkins. He moved rapidly through the ranks, partly because of the misfortunes of his department head, James Baldwin, who, having been caught in a police raid on a Baltimore bordello, had been forced to resign. Watson stepped easily into Baldwin's position, directing the development of psychology at Johns Hopkins and editing one of the most influential publications in psychology at that time: *Psychological Review*. At the age of 36, Watson became president of the American Psychological Association. By then, he had become one of the most powerful contemporary voices in psychology.

A few years later, Watson undertook the study for which he is most famous: the conditioning of Little Albert (described in the text). His assistant for this experiment was a young graduate student named Rosalie Rayner. Watson, who was then 42, began an affair with Rayner, which came to the attention of his wife.[8] She sued for divorce, and during the messy trial that followed, used love letters from Watson to Rayner (that she had stolen from Rayner's room) to underline Watson's depravity. The divorce settlement, remarkable for the 1920s, left Watson with less than one-third of his university salary (see Buckley, 1994). The ensuing scandal led to Watson's being forced to resign from Johns Hopkins.

Watson then went to New York, married Miss Rayner on New Year's Eve of 1920, had two more children (he had already fathered

---

*Based in part on Benjafield, 1996; Buckley, 1994; Burnham, 1994; Todd and Morris, 1994.

[7]I said to the Old Woman that the symbol ™ was not really necessary, but she explained that she had no wish to subvert the natural order—or to become embroiled in some legal action for lack of social, political, or legal sensitivity and correctness.

[8]It was in reference to this passage, and in reference to the third edition's mention of the widely reported but totally unsubstantiated rumor that Watson involved Rosalie Rayner in a series of investigations of physiological changes during sex, that one of the third edition reviewers exclaimed, "The discussion of Watson's sexual history is completely inappropriate in a textbook. Our purpose is to educate, not titillate" (Reviewer E). When I brought this to the attention of the Old Woman, she snorted that there was no mention of Watson's unsubstantiated sex research in this fifth edition. And she explained that she had left out much of the interesting stuff on Watson's personal life, like, for example, when Burnham interviewed different people who knew Watson and concluded, "he may well have been one of the great lovers in all history" (Burnham, 1994, p. 69). Burnham based his conclusion on the fact that what people seemed to remember most clearly about Watson were his allegedly numerous romantic adventures. "I learned a great deal that I did not want to know, some of it of the most intimate nature," says Burnham (p. 70).

two), and went to work in advertising with the J. Walter Thompson Company at a salary of some $25,000 per year—more than four times his university salary.

During his time as an advertising executive and later, as vice president of J. Walter Thompson Company, Watson wrote popular psychology articles for magazines such as *Harper's*, *McCall's*, *Liberty*, *Collier's*, and *Cosmopolitan*. With Rayner, he also wrote a book on infant and child care, advocating rigid and controlled approaches to dealing with children.

These activities, for which he was well paid, did little to endear him to his former colleagues, who spent some time and effort criticizing the articles and books. (Rayner also wrote popular articles, including one entitled, "I Was the Mother of a Behaviorist's Sons," which appeared in *Parents* magazine in 1930.)

Watson never returned to academic life. But in 1958, just before he died, the American Psychological Association honored him for his outstanding contributions to psychology, presenting him with a gold medal.

---

most famous and controversial investigations: the study of Little Albert (Watson & Rayner, 1920).

Little Albert

The study of Little Albert is more a demonstration than an experiment; it involves a display of emotional conditioning rather than the systematic manipulation of a variable to investigate its effect on another. In fact, note Paul and Blumenthal (1989), the original study is scientifically weak and has often been embellished by later writers.

The subject of this study was "Little Albert," an 11-month-old boy. At the beginning of the demonstration, Little Albert showed no fear of a great variety of objects and people. "Everything coming within twelve inches of him was reached for and manipulated," said Watson (1930, p. 159). And among the things he always reached for was a white rat that he had played with for weeks.

But Watson and Rayner quickly established that Albert, like most infants, would react with fear to a loud noise. "A steel bar about one inch in diameter and three feet long, when struck with a carpenter's hammer, produced the most marked kind of reaction," Watson informs us (1930, p. 159). And so began the study with Little Albert, at the age of 11 months, 3 days, sitting on his mattress, reaching for the white rat, his hand just touching it when—Kaboom!—Watson pounded the bar "just behind his [Albert's] head," and poor Albert "jumped violently and fell forward, burying his face in the mattress." But Albert was a staunch little fellow; he didn't cry. In fact, he reached for the rat again—and again, Watson (or Rayner; the point isn't clear from Watson's notes) banged on the steel bar just as Albert's hand touched the rat. This time, Albert began to whimper and, as Watson put it, "On account of his disturbed condition, no further tests were made for one week" (1930, p. 160).

A week later, the procedure was repeated, the rat and the loud sound being combined a total of five more times. Now Albert's behavior had changed dramatically. When the rat was presented alone, he no longer reached for it. In Watson's words, "The instant the rat was shown the baby began to cry. Almost instantly he turned sharply to the left, fell over, raised himself on all fours and began to crawl away so rapidly that he was caught with difficulty before he reached the edge of the mattress" (1930, p. 161).

Watson considered this demonstration extremely important to his theory. "Surely this is proof of the conditioned origin of a fear response," he argued. "It yields an explanatory principle that will account for the enormous complexity in the emotional behavior of adults" (1930, p. 161).

Transfer

The explanatory principle has two facets: (1) Emotional responses are conditioned to various stimuli as a result of pairings that occur between conditioned stimuli such as distinctive sounds, smells, sights, or tastes, and unconditioned stimuli such as those that produce fear or love or anger; and (2) emotional responses can spread to stimuli to which they have not been conditioned, but that resemble conditioned stimuli.

Both these principles are clearly illustrated in the Little Albert demonstration. First, after only seven separate pairings of the rat with the noise, Albert had become very frightened of the rat. And second, when Little Albert was tested again five days later (at the age of 11 months, 15 days), he was afraid not only of the rat but also of a white rabbit, a seal coat, white cotton wool, a white-bearded Santa Claus mask, and Dr. Watson's hair—all objects with which he had previously played.[9]

This phenomenon, which Watson called **transfer,** or *spread*, is what Pavlov described as stimulus generalization—the making of similar responses for a variety of related stimuli. Stimulus generalization is what occurs when a dog that has been conditioned to salivate to a given tone also salivates in response to a variety of other tones. And this is precisely what happened when little Albert, conditioned to fear a white rat, *generalizes* the fear response to other similar stimuli such as white beards and white cats.

Positive Emotions
The Little Albert study indicates that it is possible to condition negative emotional reactions by repeatedly pairing a stimulus ordinarily associated with some negative emotion with another distinctive stimulus. Similarly, it is also possible to condition positive emotional reactions to neutral stimuli. It is highly probable, for example, that if the white rat had been paired with a dish of ice cream or a wet kiss, Little Albert might very soon have come to love white rats with some passion. Similarly, even after being conditioned to respond with fear to the presence

---

[9]Because this study makes such a good story, says Gilovich (1991), it has been exaggerated and misrepresented by many textbook writers. Some have had Little Albert fearing cats, white gloves, his own mother, or a teddy bear. Others have insisted that Watson later cured Little Albert of his fear. He didn't, as the Old Woman explains in another paragraph or so.

of a white rat, it might still have been possible to condition a positive response to the rat—a procedure termed **counterconditioning**. (Counterconditioning is illustrated later in this chapter, in the section on Edwin Guthrie.) It seems clear from the original article that Watson had intended to do just that (see Harris, 1979; Prytula, Oster, & Davis, 1977). Unfortunately, Albert was Watson's subject only because he happened to be in a hospital at the time. And, as luck would have it, he was released from the hospital the day before Watson was to have begun his counterconditioning procedures. That these procedures would probably have been successful was demonstrated four years later when Mary Cover Jones found a small boy, Peter, who had a profound fear of rabbits. She cured him of his fear through a classical conditioning procedure (Jones, 1974).[10]

The Controversy

Although the study of Little Albert is well known and widely cited as an example of emotional conditioning, it remains controversial for a number of reasons—apart from the fact that it has often been misreported. First, only a single subject was used in the study, and many who have tried to replicate the findings have experienced difficulty (Eysenck, 1982). Second, Watson seems to have been unclear about exactly what he did with Little Albert. Samelson (1980) found that in one published report, Watson complained that whenever Little Albert was upset, he would stick his thumb into his mouth—and then calm down. In fact, as long as he had his thumb in his mouth, he showed no signs of the conditioned fear response, so that when Watson and Rayner were trying to film the experiment, they continually had to pull Little Albert's thumb from his mouth. Samelson raises the interesting possibility that Little Albert could have been crying not because he was afraid of the rat, but because they wouldn't let him suck his thumb! And although Watson doesn't suggest it, it is conceivable that thumb sucking might also have been a classically conditioned response.

Watson's Environmentalism

A recurrent theme in psychological literature is the controversy over the nature and nurture question—the **nature-nurture controversy**: Are humans primarily a product of genetic makeup, or are they molded and shaped mainly by environment? The chief spokesman for the nature position at the turn of the 20th century was Francis Galton (1870), a cousin of Charles Darwin. He believed that genes are largely responsible for the differences that exist among people. Accordingly, he advocated that people should be selected and bred for desirable characteristics, such as intelligence and strength, in much the same way as horses are bred

---

[10]"Advertisers are keenly aware of the power of emotional conditioning," the Old Woman said, showing me the car ad with the picture of the striking model. "Many people have a strong positive conditioned emotional reaction when they look at this ad. And that's exactly what the advertisers want. If you really like the model, you're going to really like the car without even knowing why." "Don't look so confused," she said, "we'll talk more about this in Chapter 11." I don't think I was confused.

for speed, dogs for appearance and hunting instincts, and turkeys for breast size. This practice is termed **eugenics.**

The chief spokesman for the environment (nurture) camp was Watson (1930). He was convinced that there are no individual differences at birth, that what people become is a function of their experiences. "There is no such thing," claimed Watson, "as an inheritance of *capacity, talent, temperament, mental constitution* and *characteristics*" (1930, p. 94; italics in original).

When Watson arrived on the scene, John Locke, the philosopher, had already given scholars his **tabula rasa** doctrine, which presented the metaphor that the mind is a blank slate upon which experience writes its message. Watson accepted the proclamation wholeheartedly. "Give me the child and my world to bring it up in," he wrote, "and I'll make it crawl or walk; I'll make it climb and use its hands in constructing buildings of stone or wood; I'll make it a thief, a gunman, or a dope fiend. The possibility of shaping in any direction is almost endless" (Watson, 1928, p. 35).

Some years later, Watson published another version of this same declaration in what may be his most widely quoted (and longest) sentence: "Give me a dozen healthy infants well-formed," he said "and my own specified world to bring them up in and I'll guarantee to take any one at random and train him to become any type of specialist I might select—doctor, lawyer, artist, merchant-chief and yes, even beggar-man and thief, regardless of his talents, penchants, tendencies, abilities, vocations, and race of his ancestors" (1930, p. 104).[11]

The controversy surrounding the relative roles of experience and heredity in shaping human development is far from resolved. Nevertheless, most psychologists readily admit that both heredity and environment interact in determining most facets of human behavior and personality. As Anastasi (1958) puts it, the important question may not be "how much" environment or heredity contributes but, rather, "how" each exercises its influence.

Higher Learning

All learning, said Watson, is a matter of responses that are selected and sequenced. Even complex sequences of behavior result from a conditioning process whereby the most recent behavior is linked with a stimulus through a sort of chaining of sequences of responses. More complex learning simply requires the conditioning of more stimulus-response sequences, eventually leading to what he called **habits.** Even something as apparently complex as language begins as simple stimulus-response links. Speech, Watson claimed, involves actual movements of the vocal cords and the larynx, as well as of the mouth, tongue, and lips. These movements are conditioned to occur in the presence of appropriate stimuli. As he put it, words are simply substitutes (through conditioning) for objects and situations. And

---

[11]It's interesting, said the Old Woman, that everybody ends this quotation right here. Actually, Watson's very next printed words are highly revealing. "I am going beyond my facts," he writes, "and I admit it, but so have advocates of the contrary and they have been doing it for many thousands of years" (p. 104). He may not have been nearly as adamant in his beliefs as is often portrayed.

thinking is nothing more complicated than *subvocal* speech. Watson believed this subvocal speech is accompanied by minute movements of the larynx, which he attempted to measure and describe. He referred to these movements as *implicit* rather than *explicit* behaviors.

Educational and Other Applications of Watson's Psychology

Watson's unwavering conviction that experiences determine all that people do and know leads logically to the belief that all humans are basically equal—that the differences between the eminent and the unknown, the rich and the poor, the brave and the timid are simply a question of different experiences and opportunities. This inherently egalitarian view of the human condition has proven immensely popular. As Stagner (1988) notes, it fit remarkably well with the *Zeitgeist*—the spirit of the times.[12]

But the theory also lends itself to rigid prescriptions for child rearing and education, as well as for training and control in the military, in industry, and elsewhere. It asserts that people's behavior can be controlled through the judicious and clever arrangements of stimulus and response events. Don't kiss and cuddle your children, Watson urged; shake their hands, and then arrange their environments so that the behaviors you desire will be brought under the control of appropriate stimuli.

Attitudes and Emotions

As we saw in out discussion of the educational implications of Pavlov's theory, simple models of classical conditioning are very useful in explaining emotional learning. That's because many emotions appear to be learned as a result of an often-unconscious process of classical conditioning. Figure 2.8, for example, illustrates how something like a math phobia might be classically conditioned.

Behavior Modification

In the same way as a phobia might be acquired through classical conditioning, it might also be removed using similar principles. The deliberate application of

---

[12]That's not really your Zeitgeist, the Old Woman said, motioning that I should pause the recorder, explaining that what she was about to say wasn't really part of the book. She explained that true egalitarianism is not part of our Zeitgeist at all. She said today's Zeitgeist, at least in the Western industrialized world, is one of political correctness. She explained that although one aspect of political correctness means going out of your way *not* to say or do things that might be offensive, inappropriate, tactless, unfair, or demeaning, this doesn't imply egalitarianism at all. She said that political correctness is an insincere motive for treating people with respect and love and fairness, that it leads to paying lip service to egalitarian principles, but that the fact is that most societies don't behave as though they actually believe that all people are initially equal (and, by extrapolation, equally valuable). She said many other cynical things, and then she said to be quiet, there was a fish looking at her hook—although I had not yet said anything. Then she began to read the book once more and I thought the fish must have moved away. I turned the recorder on again.

Before Conditioning

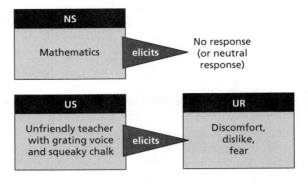

Mathematics elicits no strong emotional response; the unconditional stimulus elicits negative reactions.

Conditioning Process

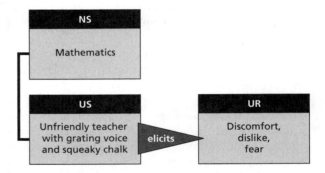

Mathematics is paired repeatedly with the unconditioned stimulus (teacher).

After Conditioning

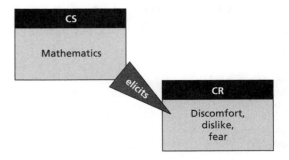

Figure 2.8
Classical conditioning of a math phobia. From Guy R. Lefrançois, *Psychology for Teaching* (10th ed.). Used by permission.

Mathematics has become a conditioned stimulus associated with negative reactions.

theories such as Watson's in efforts to change or control undesirable behavior is labeled **behavior modification.** One well-known example of the use of classical conditioning in behavior modification is provided by Mowrer and Mowrer's (1938) technique for curing nocturnal bedwetting (enuresis). In their procedure, a water-detecting device is placed under the bed sheet. A single drop of moisture is enough to activate the device, causing an alarm to sound and awaken the child, who then goes to the bathroom. Within a relatively short time, the child goes to the bathroom as necessary, even when the alarm is no longer connected. Why?

In classical conditioning terms, the noise of the alarm is an unconditioned stimulus (US) linked with the unconditioned response (UR) of waking up, which causes a tightening of the muscles so that urination doesn't occur immediately. After a few pairings, the US (alarm) quickly becomes associated with the sensation of a full bladder (a CS). Through classical conditioning, the CS (sensation of full bladder) eventually substitutes for the US (the alarm), leading to the conditioned responses of waking up and not urinating in bed. (Other behavior modification techniques are discussed in Chapter 4.)

Watson's Behaviorism: An Appraisal

As we just saw, Watson's theory, which became immensely popular in the United States, had a profound influence on child-rearing and educational practices. It also had an enormous influence on the development of psychological thinking and theorizing in North America. "By the early 1920s," writes Mills, "behaviorism had come to mean the doctrines of John B. Watson" (1998, p. 55). These doctrines were a form of psychology that dismissed mental and other abstract qualities as unworthy of study, while emphasizing the importance of social agents, and especially of the mother, in shaping the child. Watson strongly advocated the application of this doctrine of behaviorism to produce humans with desirable characteristics.

As will become clearer when we consider the development of more recent psychological theories, much of what earlier theorists such as Watson and Pavlov believed has been greatly elaborated and qualified, or simply no longer fits well with the spirit of contemporary times. As O'Donohue and Ferguson (2001) point out, Watson was probably guilty of exaggerating the role of learning in determining behavior, and underemphasizing the role of heredity. In addition, it now seems clear that he tried to explain too much with an overly simple model. In effect, the model views humans as both simpler and more similar than they actually are.

Watson appears to have been more of a spokesman for behaviorism than a rigorous researcher actively looking to discover new facts about human behavior. Not surprisingly, for example, some of Watson's early theorizing about emotional development has not stood the test of objective inquiry. Despite his attempts to deal only with objective variables, fear, rage, and love are emotional reactions that remain difficult to identify in young children. Controlled studies have shown, for example, that babies left completely unclothed in temperature-regulated environments show as much rage as do babies wrapped in cumbersome clothing (Irwin & Weiss, 1934).

It remains true, nevertheless, that many human behaviors are the result of classical conditioning: fear in response to the sound of a gunshot, although the *sound* of shot has never hurt; salivating on seeing food (usually with more restraint than a dog); and countless other automatic responses that result from previous stimulus pairings.

Watson's contribution to the understanding of human behavior is difficult to assess, largely because the behavioristic approach for which he was clearly the strongest spokesman continues to exert a profound influence on contemporary psychological thinking. Among other things, he did much to make the science of psychology more rigorous and more objective, he popularized the notion that environmental experiences are potent forces in shaping behavior patterns, and he elaborated a learning model (classical conditioning) that explains at least some aspects of animal and human behaviors. In addition, he exerted a profound influence on the thinking of other psychologists such as Guthrie, whose theory we look at next.

Edwin Guthrie (1886–1959)

In retrospect, it is perhaps astounding that virtually all learning textbooks still discuss someone who wrote as little as did Edwin Guthrie (a handful of books and articles), who had almost no students and followers (unlike most other well-known psychologists of that time, such as Pavlov, Watson, and Thorndike), and whose theory consisted of only a single law with virtually no original experimental support. That one law of learning must be pretty big.

Like Watson, Guthrie believed that psychology should deal only with what is seen rather than with what has to be inferred. "Only the observable conditions under which learning occurs are of any use for a theory or for an understanding of learning," he insisted (1935, p. 143). But he didn't share Watson's determination to revolutionize American psychology, overthrowing the mentalism of his predecessors and putting in its stead a completely objective, experimental behaviorism. In fact, Guthrie performed only one experiment (Guthrie & Horton, 1946). In this experiment, a cat is placed in a cage from which it must escape if it is to obtain food that is left a short distance outside the box. To escape, the cat has to engage in a series of new behaviors leading to the unlatching of an escape door. Most reasonably intelligent cats soon solve the problem and obtain the food.

Guthrie's Law of One-Shot Learning

Guthrie explains the cat's behavior the same way he explains all learning, using a single, all-encompassing law of learning: *"A combination of stimuli which has accompanied a movement will on its recurrence tend to be followed by that movement"* (italics in original; 1935, p. 26).

Edwin R. Guthrie (1886–1959)

 Edwin Guthrie was born on January 9, 1886, in Lincoln, Nebraska. This was rural ranch country, and it isn't surprising that when he later felt the need to illustrate his theory, many of his examples dealt with horses and dogs.

Guthrie received an arts degree from the University of Nebraska in 1907. Three years later, he received a master's degree with a major in philosophy and a minor in mathematics—and an additional minor, almost as an afterthought, in the fledgling discipline of psychology. Subsequently, he spent three years as a high school teacher.

Guthrie then went to the University of Pennsylvania, where, in 1912, he obtained a Ph.D. in philosophy. Most of the remainder of his 42-year academic career was spent at the University of Washington. The philosopher Edgar Arthur Singer, who believed that many philosophical problems could be reduced to problems of behavior, strongly influenced Guthrie's shift to psychology, which occurred in 1919. A contemporary of Watson's (he was only 8 years younger), Guthrie was also profoundly influenced by Pavlov's classical conditioning, an influence that is strongly reflected in his theory. Mills (1998) reports that, unlike Watson, Guthrie had the advantage of having access to translations of Pavlov's work.

The most important of Guthrie's writings is his book, *The Psychology of Learning*, published in 1935 and revised in 1952. Later, he also coauthored a book on educational psychology (Guthrie & Powers, 1950). He was widely recognized during his academic career, served as dean of graduate studies at the University of Washington, and was honored by the American Psychological Association (of which, like Watson, he was president for a time).

What the Law Means

"This is a short and simple statement," claims Guthrie (1935, p. 26). He was only half right: It's short, but only superficially simple. What the law says, in effect, is that when an organism does something on one occasion, it will tend to do exactly the same thing if the occasion repeats itself. Furthermore, claims Guthrie, the full strength of the "bond" between a stimulus and a response is reached during the first pairing; it will neither be weakened nor strengthened by practice. In behavioristic terms, if a stimulus leads to a specific response now, it will lead to the same response in the future. Thus, learning occurs, and is complete, in a single trial!

But this isn't true, you protest. He must have meant something else.[13]

---

[13]The Old Woman liked to pretend she knew what you, her readers, would be thinking.

One-Shot Learning

Yes, it is true, says Guthrie. People, and animals, learn in one shot. What they learn is not a connection between two stimuli (as happens in Pavlovian classical conditioning, for example), but a connection between a stimulus and a response. If you do X in situation Y, you will do X again the next time you're in situation Y. To learn X, you don't need to repeat it over and over again; nor does it need to be rewarded. If X has been performed once in response to Y, the link between X and Y is as strong as it will ever be.

So if a woman shouts, "Guy!" and you turn your head in her direction, does this mean that every time this woman shouts your name, you will turn your head in her direction?

No, says Guthrie. Note the wording of the law, which is worth repeating at least once: *A combination of stimuli which has accompanied a movement will on its recurrence tend to be followed by that movement.* Guthrie uses the word *tend* because, as he puts it, "the outcome of any one stimulus or stimulus pattern cannot be predicted with certainty because there are other stimulus patterns present" (1935, p. 26). So the answer is yes, you will *tend* to turn again in the woman's direction because that is the last thing you did when you were previously in this situation. But the answer is also no, you might not turn in her direction because the "combination of stimuli" will not be identical the second time. Any number of things might be different: You might be tired; her voice might be more plaintive or more strident; there might be other voices in the background; you might be paying attention to something else; your head might be in the refrigerator.

Practice

Hence the value of practice and repetition. What practice does is clear, says Guthrie: It provides an opportunity for making the same response in a wide variety of different situations. "An act is learned in the single occurrence," he insists. "The need for repetition comes from the need for executing the act in a *variety* of circumstances" (1935, p. 138). The more often an action has been practiced, the wider the range of combination of stimuli to which it has been exposed *and connected.* Hence, the more likely that it will be repeated in a given situation.

One-Shot Classical Conditioning

Does this mean that Pavlov's dog learned to salivate in response to a buzzer in a single trial? Yes, says Guthrie, even though Pavlov reported that in his earlier work he sometimes needed as many as between 50 and 100 pairings of CS and US before the CS reliably elicited salivation. According to Guthrie, the large number of trials was necessary because the conditions under which the learning was taking place were not perfectly controlled. As he puts it, "standing in the loose harness the dog can shift his weight from one leg to another, turn his head, prick up his ears, yawn, stretch, in fact alter his whole pattern of proprioceptive stimulation, and a certain amount of his exteroceptive situation" (1935, p. 98).

(**Proprioceptive stimulation** refers to internal sensations such as those associated with movements of muscles; **exteroceptive stimulation** relates to sensations associated with external stimuli and involving the senses of vision, hearing, taste, and smell.) As a result, the learning required dozens of trials simply to ensure that the response would be associated with most of the various combinations of stimuli possible. That Pavlov was later able to condition salivation in dogs in as few as 10 to 20 trials simply reflects the fact that he was now better able to control stimulus conditions.

Movement Produced Stimuli (MPS)

To understand Guthrie's law of learning—which actually implies his entire theory—it's important to understand that a stimulus is not just one sensation but, rather, is a combination of numerous sensations. In Guthrie's words, learning involves associating a response to a *combination of stimuli*.

Similarly, for Guthrie, a response is not just a single, final act; rather, it is a sequence of actions. To simplify, the sound of a bell leads to a number of alerting responses: turning of the ears, movements of the eyes, perhaps movements of the head and neck, and so on. "Every such motion," says Guthrie, "is a stimulus to many sense organs in muscles, tendons, and joints, as well as the occasion for changing stimuli to eyes, ears, etc." (1935, p. 54). Guthrie labeled these stimuli **movement produced stimuli (MPS).** Movement produced stimuli in turn give rise to other responses, which can also have an effect on muscles, glands, and tendons, thus giving rise to more stimuli.

Contiguity Through MPS

Thus, the sequence between the initial presentation of a stimulus and the occurrence of response is filled with a sequence of responses and the proprioceptive (internal) stimulation that results (MPS). Each of these responses and their corresponding MPS are in contiguity (occur at the same time). And so each becomes associated, or learned. These learned associations are what guide behavior, claims Guthrie. "One movement starts another, that a third, a fourth, and so on" (1935, p. 54). And the entire sequence is learned because each individual MPS is present at the same time as the response occurs. One of the clearest examples of MPS is found in the learning of athletic skills. These skills often consist of long sequences or chains of responses. Each response in the sequence serves as a signal for the next response. Thus, like Watson, Guthrie believed that even very complex sequences of behavior result from the *chaining* of sequences of stimuli that are often internal.

Habits

Learning, Guthrie insists, occurs in one trial. But this does not mean that a complex behavior can be learned in one trial. What it means is that each individual component of the vast number of stimulus-response associations that make up a complex act requires only a single pairing. A number of trials might be required, however, before all have been associated as they need to be. When they are all linked so that a particular combination of stimuli reliably leads to a particular combination of responses, what we have is a habit—a stereotyped, predictable pattern of responding.

But humans are seldom completely predictable. They don't respond exactly the same way every time they're placed in the same situation. There are several possible explanations for this, according to Guthrie. One is that if responses to two stimuli are different, it's because the stimuli are not exactly identical; another is that it may be that through one of a number of procedures, a new habit has replaced an old one. The old one is not forgotten—it is merely replaced.

Forgetting

Guthrie (1935) tells the story of two young boys whose Friday afternoons were "made dreary" by the pastor's weekly visit, during which they were required to unharness, groom, feed, and water that good man's horse. One day they got the bright idea of retraining the horse. One of them stood behind the animal, shouted, "Whoa" and, at the same time, jabbed it sharply with a pitchfork. It isn't clear, says Guthrie, how many times they did this; nor does the story report exactly what happened later when the pastor drove his horse home and shouted, "Whoa!" But apparently the boys were quite happy with the outcome.

The point, explains Guthrie, is not that the horse had forgotten how to stop; that is hardly likely. Rather, the old habit of stopping in response to the command "Whoa!" had been replaced by a different habit.

The best explanation for forgetting, says Guthrie, is not that associations are wiped out with the passage of time, but that time allows new learning to replace the old. It follows from the theory that whatever response was last performed in a stimulus situation will tend to be repeated again when that situation next arises.

Reward and Punishment

For this reason, reward is sometimes important in learning. According to Guthrie, reward doesn't do anything to strengthen the link between stimulus and response. But what it does is change the stimulus situation, thus preventing the animal (or person) from learning something different.

Punishment, too, can change a stimulus situation and serve, in Guthrie's words, to "sidetrack" a habit. The important point is that because learning depends on contiguity (that is, on the simultaneity of stimulus and response events) to be effective, punishment has to occur during the response, or very soon afterward. And because punishment works by interrupting the unwanted habit, anything that grabs attention and brings about a different behavior will work. "Picking up a small child and tossing him or swinging him by the heels," writes Guthrie, "is just as effective in overcoming a balky fit as is a sound spanking" (1935, p. 141).[14]

Practical Applications of Guthrie's Theory: Forming and Breaking Habits

Guthrie was very interested in making his theory highly practical. As a result, his writing is filled with examples of how learning and remembering can be improved, both with animals and with people.

What this "one-shot theory of contiguity learning" means from a practical point of view, says Guthrie, is that to bring behavior under control, it is necessary to arrange for the behavior to occur in the presence of stimulus conditions that are under control. If you want a dog to come when you call it, he explains, you first have to get him to come to you, either by holding up a bone, running away from him, pulling him toward you, or doing whatever else you suspect might entice the dog to approach. If, at the same time, you yell, "Come," an association may soon form between the command and the action.

Note that the dog has not learned a new response; he already knew how to run toward you. Here, as in all learning, what changes are associations between the response of running toward a person and a signal. What makes it easy to teach a dog to come, says Guthrie, is that this is something that dogs do, just as they fetch sticks, lie down, roll over, and so on. "We can not teach cows to retrieve a stick because this is one of the things that cows do not do," claims Guthrie (1935, p. 45).[15]

Consistent with his theory, Guthrie maintains that responses are never forgotten; they are merely replaced by more recently learned responses. "Unlearning becomes merely a case of learning something else," he says (1935, p. 66). Hence, the best way of breaking a habit is to find the cues that initiate the habit and to practice another response to these same cues. For example, if you smoke, a wide range of stimulus conditions will have become associated with the action of smoking: finishing eating; drinking, watching television, meeting a friend who smokes, getting up in the morning. A general *unconditioning* of all these links is a long process, says Guthrie, which requires that the smoker attach other responses to the situations associated with the beginning of the smoking sequence.

Guthrie (1952) describes three specific techniques, or methods, for sidetracking (breaking) habits: the **fatigue technique,** the **threshold technique,** and the **method of incompatible stimuli.** What each of these has in common

---

[14]Speaking of tossing children, the Old Woman said, Guthrie doesn't explain where the child should be tossed. But in the Middle Ages, reports deMause (1974), baby tossing was one sport by which the gentry amused themselves. It involved throwing infants from one gamesman to another. One of the unlucky babies was King Henry IV's infant brother, who was killed when he fell while being tossed from window to window.

[15]It appears that Guthrie had never seen a cow sitting up, smoking cigars, and reading, said the Old Woman, as an aside. She seemed dead serious.

is that it involves what Guthrie terms *inhibitory conditioning*—that is, the conditioning of a response that inhibits the habit that is to be broken.

The Fatigue Technique

Sometimes termed *flooding*, the fatigue technique involves presenting the stimulus repeatedly to elicit continued repetition of the undesired response. Eventually the organism will become so fatigued that it can no longer perform the response; at that point, a different response will be emitted (even if that response is to do nothing). It follows from Guthrie's theory of one-shot learning that this new response, because it is the most recent reaction to that stimulus, will be repeated if the stimulus is presented again. In this way, the original undesirable habit has been broken.

The Threshold Technique

This technique involves presenting the stimulus that forms part of the undesirable S-R (for stimulus-response) unit (habit) but presenting it so faintly that it doesn't elicit the undesirable response. If it doesn't elicit the undesirable behavior, then it probably elicits another response; again, it may simply be the response of not reacting. The stimulus is then presented with increasing intensity over a succession of trials, but the degree of increase is carefully kept so small that the undesirable response will never be elicited. By the time an intensity level is reached that would initially have stimulated the undesirable behavior, a different habit has been formed.

The Method of Incompatible Stimuli

The third technique involves presenting the stimulus when the response can't occur. Because the undesirable reaction is prevented, a different response takes its place and eventually replaces the old habit entirely.

Horse Illustrations

Each of these techniques can be illustrated in the training of horses—a subject about which the Nebraska-raised Guthrie knew something (see Figure 2.9).

A bucking horse, most people will readily admit, has a bad habit—a bad S-R chain, as the behaviorists would say. The stimulus part of this habit is represented by various things, such as saddles and people that are put onto a horse's back, leading it to react in an antisocial manner. The response part is represented by the antisocial activity—the bucking response. Guthrie's theory suggests three different techniques for modifying the horse's behavior.

The common "rodeo" technique of breaking a horse is simply to throw a saddle on its back and to ride the living _____[16] out of it. When it gets sufficiently tired, it will stop responding in an undesirable way, and if the rider is still on its back, the horse may eventually begin to respond by standing, walking, or running. This is Guthrie's fatigue technique.

---

[16]The Old Woman had originally filled this space with some surprisingly colorful expressions. Editorial wisdom being what it is, they have been deleted. Those of you who are old enough, and strangely curious, might try writing and begging for a copy of the original.

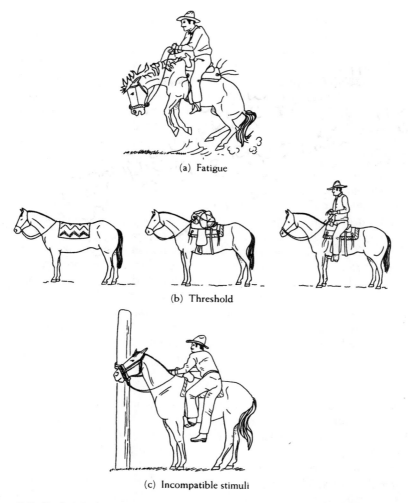

(a) Fatigue

(b) Threshold

(c) Incompatible stimuli

Figure 2.9 Guthrie's three ways of breaking habits. In (a) the horse is "broken" in the traditional sense, being allowed to buck until fatigued. In (b) the horse is "gentled" by having progressively heavier weights placed on its back, beginning with a blanket and culminating with a saddle and rider. In (c) the horse is tied down so it cannot buck when mounted.

The threshold method is also commonly used for breaking horses. It breaks as many horses as the rodeo technique but fewer riders. This method involves "gentling" the horse—beginning by placing a light blanket on its back and increasing the weight (that is, increasing the intensity of the stimulus) over successive trials. Given sufficient time and patience, a horse may be broken in this fashion.

The third technique, that of incompatible stimuli, is probably used less frequently with horses but can also be effective. It involves presenting the stimulus (saddle and rider on the horse's back) when the response can't occur. The incompatible stimulus usually involves tying the horse to a post ("snubbing short") so that it can't buck.

Human Illustrations

Each of Guthrie's three techniques can be applied to people. Of course, it's quite unacceptable to break a child in the same manner that a horse would be broken. But, with due consideration for the *humanity* of children, and without having to hold each of them up by their heels or toss them about, it's possible to remove certain bad habits that might be acquired even in the very best of homes. Consider, for example, the purely fictitious example of a small boy who habitually responds to the sight of his grandfather with intense fear, which he acquired because the old man once punished him with a short whip. In the manner of Jones and her subject, Peter, one can remove the boy's fear by having him eat something pleasant while the grandfather stands quietly in the distance. Over succeeding trials, grandpa can be invited to move a little closer each time but never close enough to bring about the old fear reaction (threshold method). Eventually the fear response will be replaced by a more desirable behavior.

Guthrie's threshold technique is similar to another approach popularized by Wolpe (1958), sometimes called counterconditioning, or *systematic desensitization*. This method has often been successfully employed with patients suffering from severe fears (phobias). Janssen (2002) also reports its use with a sexual offender given to sexual fantasies of rape. Counterconditioning, in combination with other treatments, eventually led to a significant reduction in sexual fantasizing.

When used to treat phobias, counterconditioning typically requires that the patient list all stimuli associated with the phobia. These are ranked hierarchically, beginning with the stimulus associated with the least amount of fear, progressing through other stimuli associated with increasing fear, and culminating with those associated with the most intense fear reaction. Following this first step, the therapist trains the patient in one or more of a variety of relaxation techniques. Therapy, which generally occurs over a number of sessions, then involves having the subject imagine or describe a situation low on the hierarchy of fear-producing stimuli. While this is happening, the patient is continually instructed to relax. The object of the procedure is to have the patient imagine fear-producing stimuli without feeling anxiety. Care is taken to ensure that the stimuli being imagined remain below the threshold for fear—in other words, that they do not lead to the phobic reaction (hence the similarity to Guthrie's threshold method). In the end, if the therapy is successful, the undesirable fear reaction will have been replaced by a response that is essentially incompatible with it—a response of relaxation.

Lefrançois's Uncle Renault

The fatigue method and the method of incompatible stimuli can also be used to correct various behavior and emotional problems, a fact of which Lefrançois's Uncle Renault is still painfully aware.[17] The story is that his sweet tooth would have led him unerringly in the direction of juvenile criminality had it not been for his grandmother's cunning and resourcefulness. You see, Renault, as devious

---

[17]This is another of those stories told to the Old Woman by my grandmother. In the first tellings, it was entirely true. But with the passage of the years, it has become greatly exaggerated.

as any other fledgling criminal, had become so successful at pilfering doughnuts, pies, cakes, and other assorted delights from his grandmother's kitchen that the poor lady was quite at her wit's end. She had eventually realized that beating little Renault with her poplar cane wasn't likely to teach him anything other than to dislike poplar and to fear the old lady herself. And cleverly inserting vinegars, mustards, pickles, and other surprises in her pastries had done nothing but make him more cautious. Now, like a dog, he sniffed everything before he ate it. But eat it he did, almost as fast as the old lady baked.

At one point, the old lady considered the method of incompatible stimuli. "Make a muzzle for him," she told Frank, Renault's grandfather, "and he'll have to leave my baking alone." But the muzzle was never made; they both realized that Renault would learn little from wearing a muzzle, other than not to eat with a muzzle on.

As a last resort, Renault was exposed to the fatigue technique. The story has it that one June day, Renault's grandmother started baking at dawn: pies and cakes; creamy tortes and almond cookies; chocolate wafers and sugar doughnuts; lemon meringues and cherry cupcakes. And Lefrançois's Uncle Renault ate. Sitting on a straight-backed wooden chair, his grandfather encouraging him, he ate—jubilantly at first, then less gladly, and finally, quite reluctantly. In the end, he said he was certain he could eat no more. But even then, he ate a little more, because he had no choice. "Eat. You never have enough. You're going to sit there and eat everything." Renault no longer much likes desserts.

Guthrie's One-Shot Learning: An Appraisal

Guthrie's is a highly appealing and, in some ways, relatively simple theory. In fact, among its principal virtues are its clarity and its simplicity. True to his behavioristic orientation, he insisted that the psychologist should look not at mental states or at vague concepts such as reinforcement but, rather, at objective stimuli and responses. To understand behavior, argued Guthrie, it's essential to look at specific responses and the conditions under which they occur.

Guthrie's is also a highly practical theory. He went to great lengths to point out how stimulus and response events could be arranged to bring about learning through the formation of habits—and how those habits might be changed or replaced once they had been formed.

Although the simplicity of the theory is one of its main attractions, it's also one of its weaknesses. The theory lacks the sort of detail required to make clear what concepts such as habits, movement produced stimuli, and, indeed, responses and stimuli are. In this theory, stimuli are what lead to responses; responses are what result from stimuli. Hence, these two variables, both of which are central to the theory, are defined only in terms of each other, explains Mills (1998).

Early Behavioristic Theories: Evaluation

Pavlov, Watson, and Guthrie were concerned mainly with discovering and explaining regularities that underlie relationships among stimuli and responses. Among the important regularities that these theorists discovered were those now described as Pavlovian or classical conditioning.

But how good are these theories relative to the criteria discussed in Chapter 1? For example, how well do they reflect the facts, keeping in mind that facts are simply the observations on which theories are based? The answer is that they fit the facts reasonably well *as the facts were known then*. As is shown in later chapters, many observations had yet to be made. In addition, the "facts" explained by these theories are those that the theorists in question thought to be most in need of explanation—an observation that is true of virtually all psychological theories. That the theories did relatively little to explain "higher" mental processes, such as language, thought, problem solving, perception, and so on, is really not a valid criticism of the theories *as theories*. These theories were concerned with accounting for "behavior"; hence, the observations to which they paid attention—the "facts" they tried to explain—relate directly to observable behavior.

With respect to the other criteria, the theories fare quite well. They tend to be clear and understandable, they are relatively parsimonious, they are internally consistent, and their insistence on objectivity generally means that they are not based on many unverifiable assumptions. Their contributions to the subsequent development of learning theories can hardly be overestimated. In fact, the terms and concepts used today in investigations of classical conditioning are almost entirely terms and concepts first explored and labeled by Pavlov almost a century ago! And, finally, these three early behavioristic theories have proven to be highly practical in a variety of applied situations. For example, Carrillo, Thompson, Gabrieli, and Disterhoft (1997) describe how classical conditioning of the eyeblink reflex can be used as a diagnostic tool for detecting and measuring brain damage as well as for assessing the effectiveness of related drug therapy. Similarly,

Dadds, Bovbjerg, Redd, and Cutmore (1997) explain how classical conditioning procedures can be used to treat patients suffering from severe phobias or from disorders resulting from traumas.

These early behavioristic positions don't explain all of human learning. However, doing so was not every theorist's goal. Many theorists, such as Pavlov, were concerned mainly with investigating one or two interesting and important phenomena in detail. They believed that other phenomena, many of which might seem more important and more interesting, would eventually be understood— that science needs to progress in increments, beginning with simple concepts and progressing toward the more complex.

The explanations of these early behaviorists provide valuable insights into human and animal functioning. They should not be dismissed because of their failure to explain symbolic functioning or so-called higher mental processes. Instead, they should be reviewed for their contribution to the development of a science that might not yet explain all of human behavior but that explains more behavior, more clearly, with each succeeding theoretical contribution.

Summary

1. William James used introspection to try to understand human behavior; others, such as Wundt and Fechner in Europe and Titchener and Weber in the United States, used objective measurements of physical stimuli and their effects (psychophysics: for example, absolute thresholds and JNDs) to understand behavior.

2. Pavlov, a physiologist, is famous for his elaboration of classical conditioning. In this procedure, a neutral (conditioned) stimulus (CS) is paired with an unconditioned stimulus (US: linked with an unconditioned response or UR) until it can eventually substitute for it in bringing about a conditioned response (CR)—like salivation on the part of Pavlov's dog in response to a tone. Classical conditioning explains learning on the basis of contiguity— the simultaneity of the stimuli that become associated—rather than on the basis of reinforcement.

3. Stimuli need not be perfectly simultaneous in classical conditioning; the pairing can also be delayed (CS before US but overlapping: most effective), trace (CS starts and ends before US), or backward (US occurs before the CS: least effective). Organisms seem predisposed to learn certain behaviors.

4. Acquisition depends on the number of CS-US pairings as well as on the strength of the US. CS-US bonds are remarkably durable but can be extinguished by repeatedly presenting the CS without the US. Spontaneous recovery normally occurs after a period following extinction. Subsequent extinction is faster.

5. Watson originated and preached behaviorism in North American psychology. His position was a carefully objective reaction to an earlier, more mentalistic psychological orientation. He based much of his theory on Pavlov's work.

6. Watson found classical conditioning useful for explaining the learning of emotional responses in people. Reactions of fear, love, hate, and so on, can often be traced to experiences where previously neutral stimuli are associated with emotion-producing

stimuli. Through generalization, these responses can then be associated with other related stimuli.

7. Watson was a strong believer in the power of the environment in determining people's behavior. Probably the most often quoted statement attributed to Watson is his claim that he would be able to make anything he wished out of a dozen healthy infants if he were given a free hand in determining their environments.

8. Guthrie's explanation of learning, referred to as a one-shot learning theory, is based on contiguity. He maintained that whatever response follows a stimulus is likely to follow that stimulus again when the stimulus is repeated. In addition, the strength of the bond between the stimulus and the response is fixed after the first pairing.

9. In Guthrie's system, practice is important because it permits an association to be formed between a behavior and a variety of stimulus complexes. Reinforcement is effective because it changes the situation, preventing the person (organism) from learning another response. Similarly, punishment works because it disrupts the learning sequence, forcing the individual to perform (and therefore learn) some other response.

10. The notion that stimuli and responses occur in temporal contiguity was made plausible by Guthrie through his statement that external stimuli give rise to muscular and glandular movements that produce internal (proprioceptive) stimuli, termed *movement produced stimuli* (MPS). These MPS are stimuli for other responses in the chain of response events that is maintained between the presentation of a stimulus and the occurrence of a response.

11. Sequences of stimuli and responses form habits. These are never forgotten, but may be replaced. Guthrie describes three ways of breaking habits: repeated presentation of a stimulus (fatigue technique), presenting the stimulus so faintly that a response is not elicited (threshold technique), and presenting the stimulus when the response cannot occur (method of incompatible stimuli).

12. It is fairer to evaluate these theories by their enormous contributions to the development of psychological theory, rather than by their shortcomings.

The Effects of Behavior: Thorndike and Hull

> A *new scientific truth does not triumph by convincing its opponents, but rather because its opponents die, and a new generation grows up that is familiar with it.*
> **Max Planck**

The Old Woman motioned for me to turn off the recorder and said to shush and listen, the one-eyed cat was coming, and we could hear the dry grasses and the leaves rustling as he made his way through the willows below the bush cabin. Then for a long time there was silence as though the cat had paused. Earlier we had watched as he crossed the beaver dam holding up one paw, limping uncertainly on three legs, his right ear tattered, a splash of blood across his blind-side cheek, dark black on his orange fur, a streak of mud across his back as though the fight had just now ended and he had not yet had time to do his toilet.

He was a long time coming through the willows, and the Old Woman called him once using a strange name, sadly not recorded, but the cat made no response and the Old Woman pulled her hat down low over her face against the morning sun and her eyes were lost in its shadow. She arranged her notes across her knees as though she were about to continue into the third chapter, but for a long time she said nothing.

And then the cat eased himself from the willows and ambled across the clearing more strut than walk, using all four legs but stepping lightly on his right forepaw so that we knew we had not dreamt his pain. His face was now fresh-cleaned, glistening where he had rubbed the smirch with wetted paw, his orange fur laid wet against his back, the mud all gone.

He curled himself carefully against the Old Woman's leg, and the Old Woman asked did I think the cat thought he'd fought a good fight? Did I think he'd deliberately stopped to clean his fur before presenting himself to us? Did I think it was his macho pride that made him strut so and pretend that, no, nothing hurt because he was a Real Cat?

But before I could answer, she said to turn on the recorder and she began to read once more:

This Chapter

On earth, *said the Old Woman bending to her notes,* this is sometimes called **anthropomorphism**—giving nonhuman animals or objects characteristics, such as motives and values, which belong solely to humans.

But who is to say that cats don't think? Who is to say what characteristics of emotion and intelligence are solely human? These might seem to be simple questions, but they have no simple answers.

At about the time that scientific psychology was being born, Charles Darwin's highly influential *The Origin of Species* (1859/1962) seemed to suggest that humans are just another species of animal—evolved with certain distinctly different characteristics to be sure, but nevertheless basically animal. Did this mean that nonhuman animals, too, might possess capacities that had previously been considered beyond the abilities of "dumb" animals? Might they be intelligent in a human sense?

These questions interested Edward Thorndike, whose theory is discussed in the first part of this chapter. The second part of the chapter looks at the theory developed by Clark Hull. Both these theories are behavioristic in that they are mainly concerned with observable behaviors and with discovering the laws that govern relationships among behaviors (responses) and the conditions that lead to and follow behavior.

Objectives

Explain to your readers, said the Old Woman, that after they finish this chapter, they should be able to describe in words so simple and clear their grandmothers would be astounded:

- *The principal features of Thorndike's connectionism*

- *Thorndike's laws of effect and readiness, and the main subsidiary laws*

- *Changes in Thorndike's thinking after 1930*

- *The nature of Hull's system*

- *Relationships among input, intervening, and output variables*

- *What fractional antedating goal responses are*

- *What is meant by a habit-family hierarchy*

The Old Woman bent to scratch the injured cat, but the creature rose, walked across to the woodpile, and lay down in the shade of the splitting stump. The Old Woman continued to read from her notes.

Ⓔdward L. Thorndike (1874–1949): Connectionism

So, do "dumb" animals possess humanlike capacities of thought and reason? Maybe. Certainly, Darwin's writings contained numerous anecdotes illustrating what seemed to be animal intelligence—for example, describing how monkeys who cut themselves with a sharp object never make the same mistake twice; or how monkeys who have been fed sugar lumps wrapped in paper and who are then given a wrapped sugar lump that also contains a wasp, reason that they must from then on hold the wrapping to their ear to hear whether there might be a wasp inside.

People are anxious to find intelligence in animals, claims Edward Thorndike (1898). If a dog gets lost and then happens to find its way home over a long distance, newspapers all run stories about how intelligent dogs are. But there are no stories about the hundreds of other dogs who go out for an evening stroll in the neighborhood, stupidly make a wrong turn, and never find their way home again.

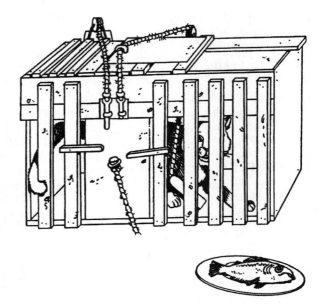

Figure 3.1
Thorndike's puzzle box. To get out of the box, the cat has to pull a string to release one of the door locks, step on the lever to release the second, and then flick one of the door latches. From "Animal Intelligence: An Experimental Study of the Associative Processes in Animals," by E. L. Thorndike, 1898, *Psychological Review Monograph Supplement*, 2(8).

Similarly, if a cat stretches upward on the refrigerator, seeming to reach toward the handle with its paw, people immediately assume that the cat has somehow figured out the connection between the handle and the door. Hogwash, says Thorndike. Anecdotes make a poor source of evidence for scientific theories. If psychology is to determine whether animals can actually reason out complex relationships in their solutions of day-to-day problems, researchers should carry out controlled experiments to this end.

Puzzle Boxes and Animal Intelligence

And so Thorndike devised a number of what he called puzzle boxes. The most typical, shown in Figure 3.1, is designed so that a cat locked into the box can escape only if it does three things: pull a string to release one lock, step on a lever to release a second, and flip a latch upright to finally open the door. To make sure the cat is interested in getting out of the cage, some tidbit of food—like a dead fish—is placed not far away, but beyond reach. Most cats have a number of ready-made solutions for this problem—like trying to squeeze between the bars, scratching and clawing at the door or at the floor, or meowing indignantly for help. Of course, the puzzle box is designed so that none of these works.

Basically, the cat can solve this problem in two ways. One is to try a dozen different actions, or 100 or 200, until all three required actions have been performed and—voilà!—the door is open. The other is to sit back, look the situation over, think about possible courses of action, and suddenly—bang!—figure

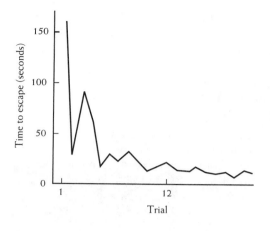

Figure 3.2

The behavior of one cat in Thorndike's puzzle box. The cat took almost 3 minutes to escape the first time, but almost always less than 1 minute after the first successful escape. From "Animal Intelligence: An Experimental Study of the Associative Processes in Animals," by E. L. Thorndike, 1898, *Psychological Review Monograph Supplement*, 2(8).

out what needs to be done. The psychologist Wolfgang Köhler (whose theories are considered in Chapter 6) carried out a similar experiment with chimpanzees and decided that this second solution is essentially what chimpanzees do. In a typical Köhler (1927) experiment, a caged chimpanzee cannot reach a bunch of bananas hanging outside the cage until, in a sudden flash of insight, it occurs to the animal to use a stick or to pile boxes one on top of the other to reach them.

But Thorndike's cats didn't do that at all; instead, they used the first approach, the trial-and-error approach. As Figure 3.2 shows, it didn't take them very long to get out of the cage; only about three minutes the first time. But after that, it seldom took them more than a minute.

The conclusion, says Thorndike, is that there is no easily demonstrated, high-level reasoning among cats—nor, indeed, among monkeys. As additional evidence that this is so, notes Thorndike, there appears to be no real imitation—based on understanding and ideas—among animals. That one dog should follow another through a field is not evidence that the dog that follows figures out mentally that, for one reason or another, it is wise to follow a fellow dog. Rather, this is simply evidence of a natural behavior, or of a behavior learned through associations that have previously had satisfying consequences. Thorndike demonstrated repeatedly that a naive cat, dog, or monkey can be allowed to witness a trained cat, dog, or monkey performing some behavior to escape from a puzzle box, but will not learn that behavior as a result (Thorndike, 1911).

It seems clear, concluded Thorndike, that cats don't learn by developing some special insight into a situation. Instead, they learn through **trial and error.** Simply put, in a given situation the organism makes a number of responses, one or more of which leads to a solution or, in Thorndike's words, to "a satisfying state of affairs." Subsequently, a connection is formed between the response and the situation. This connection is learned, or "stamped in" as Thorndike puts it.

And people, he insists, learn in the same way: "These simple, semi-mechanical phenomena . . . which animal learning discloses, are the fundamentals of human learning also" (Thorndike, 1913b, p. 16).[1]

Contiguity or Reinforcement

How does this learning, or "stamping in," occur?

As we saw earlier, in learning theories that are based on the formation of connections or associations (conditioning theories), one of two different explanations for learning is typically advanced: contiguity or reinforcement. A contiguity explanation says that an association is formed between stimuli, or between stimuli and responses, because they are presented in contiguity (simultaneously, or in close temporal proximity). The second alternative, reinforcement, maintains that learning occurs because of the consequences of the behavior—more specifically, because the behavior leads to pleasant consequences or the elimination of something unpleasant (or both).

Ivan P. Pavlov, John B. Watson, and Edwin Guthrie used contiguity to explain learning. Pavlovian (classical) conditioning is based on the notion that the simultaneous presentation of two stimuli leads to the development of some sort of equivalence between them. For example, the buzzer becomes at least partly equivalent to food when it elicits a response similar to that elicited by the food. Guthrie maintained that a link is formed between a stimulus and a response because they are simultaneous (in contiguity). To maintain this position given the apparent time lag between the presentation of most stimuli and their responses, he borrowed the concept of movement produced stimuli (MPS) from what was known of the physiology of muscles—where MPS are series of internal (muscular, glandular, neural) stimuli and responses that occur between an overt stimulus and a response.

Clearly, says Thorndike, contiguity is only part of the story. Surely, the cat would not learn to escape from the puzzle box were it not for the consequences of so doing.

Thorndike's Pre-1930s Theory: Emphasis on Practice

Traditionally, psychologists have made two types of statements with respect to both people and animals, notes Thorndike: those that have to do with consciousness and those that have to do with behavior. But, he cautions, statements about consciousness are uncertain and difficult, especially in animals and young children.

---

[1]Speaking of people, said the Old Woman, motioning toward the recorder so that I would know that this was an aside, Thorndike seemed to consider humans fundamentally different from animals, although he remained unclear about what the differences were. He didn't believe that language and reason alone distinguished humans from other animals, the Old Woman explained, reading a passage from Thorndike's 1911 book: "I said a while ago that man was no more an animal with language than an elephant was a cow with a proboscis. We may safely add the statement that man is not an animal plus reason" (p. 127). But he did accept that humans can learn by associating ideas and believed that this does not seem to happen among other animals.

Edward Lee Thorndike (1874–1949)

Like Pavlov, Thorndike was the son of a minister—a fact whose significance probably relates to the somewhat greater probability that the children of ministers and pastors would receive a college education. In fact, three Thorndike brothers, including Edward, later taught at Columbia University. Edward's upbringing is reported to have been strict and to have emphasized hard work and good manners, and he grew up to be extremely industrious and self-controlled (Joncich, 1968).

Thorndike began his academic career studying English at Wesleyan and then went to Harvard, where he switched to psychology. While at Harvard, he raised chickens in the basement of William James's house, using them in studies of animal intelligence. Later Thorndike transferred to Columbia, where in 1898 he obtained a Ph.D. in psychology. His thesis on animal intelligence, published that same year, is still a classic (he was then 24). He tried to establish, through experimentation, that animals (specifically cats) learn through a gradual process of trial and error that eventually leads to the "stamping in" of the correct response. Much of his later career in psychology involved generalizing this observation to human learning and demonstrating how humans, too, learn through trial and error as a function of reward or punishment. Interestingly, Thorndike claimed never to have been very interested in animals or in animal research. "The motive for my first investigations of animal intelligence was chiefly to satisfy requirements for courses and degrees. Any other topic would probably have served me as well. I certainly had no special interest in animals . . ." he wrote (Thorndike, 1936/49, pp. 3–4).

Thorndike wrote extensively, publishing more than 78 books and more than 400 articles. His writing deals with a wide range of topics in education and psychology (it's said that all of his course outlines eventually became books). He almost single-handedly defined and established educational psychology when, in 1913 and 1914, he published his three volume book entitled *Educational Psychology* (Thorndike, 1913–1914); he changed the study of child development into an objective science; he established the use of tests and statistical methods in psychology and education; he was instrumental in the psychological testing movement in psychology; and he conducted literally hundreds of experiments on learning and transfer using human subjects. During his lifetime, he was widely honored, not only in North America but also in Europe.

And in adults, they are based mainly on introspection, which is a scientifically suspect approach. At least in part, argues Thorndike, psychology can be "as independent of introspection as physics is" (1911, p. 2). Hence, Thorndike emphasizes experimentation rather than introspection, and behavior rather than thought (although he did not consider himself a behaviorist but, rather, a *connectionist*).

For Thorndike, learning consists of the formation of bonds between stimuli and responses—bonds that take the form of neural connections (hence the label **connectionism**). Learning, Thorndike explains, involves the stamping in of stimulus-response (S-R) connections; forgetting involves stamping out connections.

Thorndike's theory summarizes the effects of classical conditioning's three important variables (recency, frequency, and contiguity) in a single law: the **law of exercise.**

Law of Exercise

The law of exercise states that bonds between stimuli and responses are strengthened through being exercised "frequently," "recently," and "vigorously" (Thorndike, 1913a). As we will see, this law played a very minor role in Thorndike's final system, but it had a tremendous influence on educational theory and practice in the early decades of the 20th century. Although Thorndike did not invent the notion that practice and repetition improve learning (these ideas had long been the basis of classical education), his early belief in the effectiveness of "exercising" S-R connections did a great deal to encourage the repetitive "drill" approaches to learning that became increasingly popular in the 1930s and 1940s. Ironically, however, following later revisions of his theory, Thorndike would certainly not have recommended mere repetition and practice as an instructional process.

Law of Effect

Thorndike believed that whether a connection is stamped in or not depends far more on its consequences (its *effects*) than on how often it is exercised. Hence, Thorndike's most important law is the **law of effect** (Thorndike, 1913a).

Simply stated, the law of effect maintains that *responses just before a satisfying state of affairs are more likely to be repeated.* The converse also applies, although it is less important in explaining learning: *Responses just before an annoying state of affairs are more likely not to be repeated.* Thus, what Thorndike calls *satisfiers* and *annoyers* are critical to learning.

Whoa! Staunch behaviorists might object at this point: Terms like *satisfying* and *annoying* are not very objective, not very behavioristic. These sound a lot like the sorts of mentalistic terms favored by psychologists given to introspection and contemplation and not at all like the kinds of terms that would appeal to experimentally inclined, more objective psychologists such as Thorndike— or Watson.

But, responds Thorndike to his would-be critics, satisfiers and annoyers can be defined completely objectively. A satisfying state of affairs is simply one that the animal (or person) either does nothing to avoid or actively attempts to maintain. An annoying state of affairs is one that the animal (person) does nothing to preserve or attempts to end (Thorndike, 1913b). Note that the definition has nothing to do with the organism's feelings, but only with behavior.

The law of effect is basically a model of what is often termed **instrumental learning.** An organism performs a response that leads to a satisfying state of affairs (a response that is *instrumental* in bringing about this satisfying state), and a connection is formed between the response and the stimulus preceding it.

One important aspect of this model of instrumental learning is the assumption that the connection is formed between the stimulus and the response rather than between the reward and the response.[2] This is fundamentally different from the positions described by Pavlov and Watson, which maintain that an association forms between two stimuli because of repeated pairings no matter what their consequences. Recall that Pavlov and Watson are contiguity theorists; Thorndike's position is based on the effects of reinforcement. As is made clear later in this chapter, Hull, too, accepted Thorndike's view and made it one of the central features of his system (Bitterman, 1967).

Law of Readiness

A third major law formed an important part of Thorndike's pre-1930 system: the **law of readiness.** This law has to do mainly with the learner's motivation (forces that lead to behavior). It recognizes that certain behaviors are more likely to be learned (stamped in) than others. When a conduction unit is ready to conduct, says Thorndike, to do so is satisfying and not to do so is annoying. Similarly, when a conduction unit is not ready to conduct, being forced to do so is annoying.

Although Thorndike's use of vague expressions like "conduction unit" and "ready to conduct" detract from the objectivity of his system, the law of readiness has been made more concrete, and more useful, in educational practice. Readiness, Thorndike explains, is closely related to the learner's maturation and to previous learning, and it has much to do with whether an activity is satisfying or annoying. Specifically, a pleasant state of affairs results when a learner is ready to learn and is allowed to do so; conversely, being forced to learn when not ready—or prevented from learning when ready—leads to an annoying state of affairs. As Rita Watson (1996) notes, for a theory of readiness to be useful in education, it has to take into consideration what we know about children's development, as well as what we know about instruction.

---

[2]At this point, the Old Woman got up from the stump and motioned that I should turn off the recorder, and I thought maybe she just wanted to stretch. But no, it seemed a spider had dropped upon her arm from an overhanging branch, and now she bent so that it might walk down the length of her arm and across the back of her hand onto a smooth boulder by the fire pit. While she did this, she explained that this business of Thorndike's describing how connections form between responses and stimuli might seem like a small point, but that it's a fundamentally important one. She said I should repeat it when I transcribe her words into this fifth edition. She said I shouldn't simply assume that you are bright enough to understand everything the first time you're told, that all important things should be repeated at least once or maybe twice, or even three times. I defended you, praised your intelligence, said you would be bored rather than enlightened if I were to repeat the Old Woman's words more than once. She took her hat off and looked at me for a time, but I could not read her expression. Then she put the hat back on, sat down, nodded that I should turn the recorder on once more, and continued reading this report. For a moment, I was distracted from her words, watching the spider as it ambled up the smooth side of the white stone and began to cross what must have seemed like a vast desert expanse. Did it wonder why its world had changed? Did it understand where it was? Did the heat of the sun-warmed stone reassure it?

The cat reached out with its paw and smashed the spider hard against the rock.

Subsidiary Laws

As a result of his many experiments with both human and nonhuman animals, Thorndike arrived at several additional laws of learning. Five of these are an especially important part of Thorndike's explanation for learning.

1. Multiple Responses

The **law of multiple responses** states that in any given situation, the organism will respond in a variety of ways if its first response does not lead immediately to a more satisfying state of affairs. In other words, an individual will attempt to solve problems through trial and error—an observation well illustrated in the most famous of Thorndike's hundreds of experiments, the cat-in-the-puzzle-box study described earlier.

2. Set or Attitude

The second law recognizes that learning is partly a function of **attitude,** or **set** (defined as a predisposition to react in a given way). The **law of set** applies to satisfiers and annoyers and to the nature of the responses that will be emitted by a person. There are culturally determined ways of dealing with a wide variety of problems. For example, many cultures find it generally acceptable to react to aggression with aggression. Individuals in these cultures are *set* to respond aggressively. Presumably, doing so has the potential of leading to a satisfying state of affairs for the aggressor—and perhaps an annoying state of affairs for those aggressed upon.

3. Prepotency of Elements

Thorndike suggests, in his **law of prepotency of elements,** that it is possible for a learner to react only to the significant (prepotent) elements in a problem situation and be undistracted by irrelevant aspects of the situation. For example, recognizing that a figure is a square rather than a rectangle requires only that the subject respond to the relationship among the sides of the figure and not to its color, placement, and so on. For this problem, stimuli associated with shape are *prepotent;* others are irrelevant.

4. Response by Analogy

The fourth principle (**law of response by analogy**) recognizes that a person placed in a novel situation may react with responses that might be employed for other situations that are in some ways similar or that, in Thorndike's words, share *identical elements.* When Cindy uses a subtraction rule she learned at school to determine that if she buys 40 cents worth of black jellybeans, she'll still have 60 cents left from her dollar, she is responding by analogy. The reason she does so, explains Thorndike, is that she recognizes important similarities between her current situation and a problem-solving situation in school. This allows her to *transfer* what she has learned. This principle, Thorndike's theory of transfer, is sometimes referred to as the **theory of identical elements.**

Thorndike's theory of identical elements was his explanation for how people respond in novel situations—that is, how they transfer or generalize responses. When faced with a new situation, " [People's] habits do not retire to some convenient distance," he explains (1913a, p. 28). Instead, people recognize aspects of the novel situation as being similar to some more familiar situation, and they respond accordingly. And if the first response doesn't lead to a satisfying state of affairs, a second is emitted; then perhaps a third, a fourth, and so on.

Cox (1997) notes that Thorndike's theory of identical elements still plays an important role in current explanations of transfer of training. For example, many computer-related models of human behavior, such as those discussed in Chapter 8, reflect the understanding that the number of elements two different situations have in common can be used as a basis for deciding whether to make similar responses in each situation.

5. Associative Shifting

The last of the five subsidiary principles describes what might also be called *stimulus substitution*. **Associative shifting** recognizes that it is possible to shift a response from one stimulus to another. Thorndike illustrated this process by training a cat to stand. Initially, the cat stands because the experimenter holds up a piece of fish. Gradually the amount of fish is decreased until the cat stands even when no fish is presented.

A clear experimental illustration of associative shifting is provided in a study by Terrace (1963). He trained pigeons to discriminate between red and green by rewarding them with four seconds of access to a food hopper when they pecked a key back-lit with a red light and denying access to food when they pecked the key when filters were used to make it appear green. Once the pigeons had learned to discriminate readily between red and green, Terrace superimposed a vertical line over the red key and a horizontal line over the green one. The pigeons, having learned the link between red and a satisfying state of affairs, continued to peck the red key and not the green. Terrace then slowly faded out the color over a series of trials until the keys had nothing but a vertical or a horizontal stripe on them. He found that these pigeons had, without error, transferred their responses so that they now pecked vertically striped keys but not those with a horizontal stripe.

In a variation of this procedure, Terrace superimposed stripes on the keys over a number of training trials but did not gradually fade the colors. Pigeons trained this way later made numerous errors when presented with keys containing only stripes.

Associative shifting may explain the effectiveness of countless advertising campaigns that pair a stimulus associated with positive emotions (or with greed or lust) with what might otherwise be a relatively neutral stimulus—for example, liquor brands with deliriously happy juveniles; macho hombres with cigarettes dangling from their lips; ecstatic couples with fists full of lottery tickets.

Thorndike's Post-1930 Theory: Emphasis on Reinforcement

Although many of Thorndike's beliefs about human learning remained unchanged throughout his long career, he is nevertheless one of several theorists who remained active long enough, and open to change long enough, that the

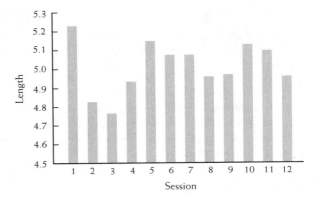

Figure 3.3
Median lengths of 3,000 separate lines drawn by a single subject with eyes closed, over 12 sessions, when instructed to draw a line 4 inches long. Data from *Human Learning*, by E. L. Thorndike, p. 9 (Table 1). Cambridge, MA: MIT Press, 1931.

system underwent some major modifications. Beginning around 1930, Thorndike admitted he had been wrong about some things.

Repeal of Law of Exercise

For one thing, I was wrong about the law of exercise, he confessed. Why? Because he had determined, through experimentation with humans (rather than simply with cats or chickens), that mere repetition does not cause learning. In one relevant experiment, for example, subjects were each given a large pad of paper and a pencil, and were asked to draw, with one quick movement, a line intended to be about 4 inches long—with their eyes closed (Thorndike, 1931). They were to do this over a number of sessions on successive days, until they had drawn a total of 3,000 lines—always with their eyes closed.

Results for one subject are shown in Figure 3.3. The results illustrate two general truths, claims Thorndike: "(1) that of multiple response or variable reaction and (2) that of the failure of repetition of the situation to cause learning" (1931, p. 10). In other words, exercise—or repetition—does not affect learning. "The repetition of a situation may change a man as little as the repetition of a message over a wire changes the wire," writes Thorndike. "In and of itself, it may teach him as little as the message teaches the switchboard . . . the more frequent connections are not selected by their greater frequency" (1931, p. 14).

Half a Law of Effect

What does lead to learning is not repetition, Thorndike insists, but the *effects* of the action. Specifically, as he had always maintained, actions that lead to satisfying states of affairs tend to be stamped in and maintained. But recall that he had also thought that responses leading to annoying states of affairs tend to be stamped out. I was wrong, Thorndike admitted again, now claiming that annoying outcomes do relatively little to the strength of a connection.

To investigate the law of effect, Thorndike (1931) devised several experiments. In one of these, nine non-Spanish-speaking subjects were asked to select one from among five possible meanings for 200 different Spanish words whose meanings they could not easily have guessed correctly. After each correct selection, the experimenter said, "Right"; for each incorrect selection, the experimenter

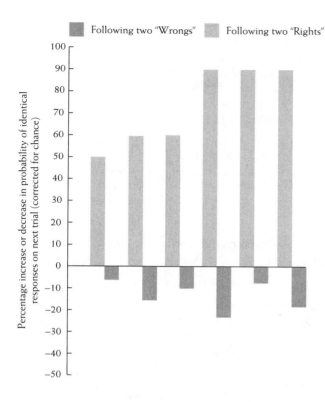

Figure 3.4
The influence of two consecutive "Rights" or "Wrongs" on the next choice of possible word meanings for an unknown word for nine subjects in six experiments. Data from *Human Learning*, by E. L. Thorndike, p. 44. Cambridge, MA: MIT Press, 1931.

said, "Wrong." The procedure was then repeated a second time, then a third, and a fourth. The object was to see whether there would be an increased tendency to select meanings that were initially followed by the response, "Right." And, not surprisingly, there was. Subjects were between 50% and 90% more likely to select a meaning that has twice been followed by the response, "Right." Was there a corresponding reduction in the probability of selecting a response followed by a "Wrong"? The answer is no. In fact, subjects were only between 7 and 23 percent less likely to select an incorrect response already selected twice (see Figure 3.4). "Other things being equal," says Thorndike, "an announcement of 'Right' strengthens the connection which it follows and belongs to much more than the announcement of 'Wrong' weakens the one which it follows and belongs to" (1931, p. 45).

Learning by Ideas

Thorndike revised his theory in several other important ways after 1930. His changes were typically prompted by a need to take into account observations about human learning that didn't readily fit the original theory. Because these observations tended to reveal that thoughts, or ideas, are important in human learning, his theory hinted at cognitive concerns. For example, Thorndike (1931) now spoke of "ideational learning"—a "higher" form of learning that involves analysis, abstraction, and meaningfulness. As an illustration of these notions, he refers to the apparently simple task of taming a monkey. To accomplish this task, he says, you cannot simply reach over, grab the monkey, and feed it. Chances are, it simply won't get the idea. If, on the other hand, you let it approach on its own and then feed it, the behaviors associated with tame behavior will eventually be stamped in. On the other hand, humans in the same situation may well form associations among *ideas* relating to being grabbed by a keeper and subsequently being fed. In Thorndike's words,

> Learning by ideas is, as the name implies, characterized by the frequent presence of ideas as situations or as responses or as both. Whereas the bulk of the learning which dogs and cats and chicks and rats display consists of connections leading from external or perceptual situations straight to bodily acts or to impulsive tendencies closely attached to such acts, the insight learning of man operates with the aid of ideas which are free from narrow confinements. (1931, p. 138)

Although terms such as *ideas*, *analysis*, and *insight* are not defined very clearly in the system, they are reflected in two additional concepts that Thorndike investigated and incorporated into the system. The first is the **principle of belongingness,** evident in the finding that if two or more elements are seen as belonging together, they are more easily learned. One of Thorndike's (1931) studies illustrating this principle asked subjects to pay attention while the experimenter read out 1,304 pairs of words and numbers. Among these were four words that each recurred 24 times, each time being preceded by exactly the same number. Afterward, subjects were asked to write which numbers came after specific words (including the four frequently repeated words) as well as which words came after specific numbers (including the four numbers each repeated 24 times).

Their performance was no better than would be expected solely by chance. Why? Because, explains Thorndike, they thought each word belonged to the number that followed it, rather than to the number that preceded it.

The second post-1930 Thorndikean concept relevant here is labeled **spread of effect.** It relates to Thorndike's discovery that when a response is followed by a satisfying state of affairs, other related responses also seem to be affected. As an illustration, Thorndike (1931) had subjects choose any number between 1 and 10 to go with each word in a series, among which were a number of frequently repeated words. Whenever the subject chose the number the experimenter had previously selected for each often-repeated word, he was told he was right. Not surprisingly, "right" numbers increased in frequency. More surprising, numbers immediately preceding and following these "right" numbers also increased, although not as dramatically.

An Appraisal of Thorndike's Connectionism

Thorndike's laws and principles present a relatively clear picture of his view of learning. According to this view, learning consists of the formation of physiological bonds or connections between stimuli and responses. The bonds are stamped in because of the satisfying nature of their consequences, influenced as well by the individual's sense of what goes with what—what belongs.

Basically, according to Thorndike, humans arrive at appropriate responses largely through trial and error. They may also respond in given ways because of a predetermined set, or attitude, perhaps determined by culture or by more immediate aspects of the situation. For example, a hungry person will respond to food in a different way than will someone who is not hungry. Some responses will be based on behavior learned in other, somewhat similar situations (response by analogy), whereas others may have resulted from a conditioning procedure (associative shifting). In many cases, the person will engage in behavior only in response to the most important aspects of a situation (the most prepotent elements).

Critics point out that much of Thorndike's theorizing was based on informal observation. Nevertheless, Thorndike was largely responsible for the introduction of controlled investigations of both animals and people as a means of verifying predictions made from theory.

Critics also point out that Thorndike often appealed to vague, internal states as a basis for explaining learning. Satisfying and annoying states of affairs are ill-defined and difficult concepts. As we see in the next chapter, later theorists devoted considerable efforts to finding more objective ways of describing the effects of behavior.

Despite the difficulties associated with Thorndike's use of concepts like "satisfyers" and "annoyers," one of his most important contributions to the development of learning theory is the emphasis he placed on the consequences of behavior as determiners of what is learned and what is not. The significance of the law of effect in the development of learning theory is apparent in its long-lasting influence. The notion that the effects of reinforcement are central in learning has largely dominated psychology since Thorndike (Bitterman, 1969).

Thorndike also made significant contributions in the practical application of psychological principles, particularly in teaching. A large number of his writings are devoted specifically to pedagogical problems in specific areas such as arithmetic (Thorndike, 1922), Latin (Thorndike, 1923), and the psychology of interest (Thorndike, 1935).

Thorndike serves as an example of a theorist strongly committed to a clear and definite point of view, yet willing to examine other views, to make dramatic changes in his own thinking, and also to admit that there was still much that his theory could not explain. "The connectionist theory of life and learning," he writes, "is doubtless neither adequate nor accurate. Its explanations of purposive behavior, abstraction, general notions, and reasoning are only a first and provisional attack on these problems. It has many gaps and defects" (1931, p. 131).

Since Thorndike, many others have tried to fill the gaps and fix the defects.

Clark L. Hull (1884–1952): A Hypothetico-Deductive System

Among these was Clark L. Hull, probably the most ambitious of the behavior theorists. Hull's dream was to use the rules of logic and of experimentation to discover and to deduce (to infer logically) the laws that govern human behavior: hence the label **hypothetico-deductive system.** The result is a system of such complexity and scope that only a brief glimpse of it can be given here.

In its entirety, the system is based on 17 laws (called postulates) from which he derived more than a hundred theorems and many corollaries (Hull, 1943, 1951, 1952).

Overview of Hull's System

Science has two essential aspects, Hull tells us (1952). One is concerned with the actual observations (facts) of the discipline; the other tries to make sense of the observations by organizing them into a coherent, logical system or theory. The theory then serves as an explanation for the observations and as a basis for understanding and for making predictions.

That, in one paragraph, is what Clark L. Hull intended to do in psychology. This energetic, mathematically oriented, and very scientific young man proposed to develop a logical, scientific, and mathematical system that would fully explain human learning and behavior.

Hull called the 17 laws that make up the system postulates rather than laws because, science being a young discipline, "a certain amount of uncertainty surrounds these basic laws" (1952, p. 1). These 17 postulates, together with the 133 specific theorems and numerous corollaries he derived from them, describe relationships among the many variables thought to be involved in human behavior.

Although the 17 postulates that are the foundation of Hull's system can't easily be tested, the theorems and their corollaries can be. Each is precise and mathematical; each gives rise to specific predictions that can be tested experimentally. Results can then be interpreted as providing support for—or refuting—not only the theorems or their corollaries but also the postulates on which the theorems are based.

Hull's system is elaborated in two major books. He had also planned a third book describing the application of the system to behavior in social interactions. Unfortunately, he died at about the time he was finishing the second book; the third was never begun.

Main Components of Hull's System

Hull's explicitly behavioristic system is marked by all the behaviorist's concerns for objectivity, precision, and rigor. Thus, although he began by inventing postulates—which might sound like a pretty mentalistic undertaking—his main concern was to derive specific, testable hypotheses from them. Then he attempted to verify them in laboratory situations. As is clear from an examination of the system, this was a monumental task.

True to the behavioristic approach, Hull looked at human behavior through stimuli and responses. Like Pavlov, Watson, Guthrie, and Thorndike, Hull was convinced that environmentally conditioned responses underlie behavior (Weidman, 1994). However, he dealt with stimuli and responses in considerably more detail than did most of his contemporaries. For Hull, stimuli consist of

Clark Leonard Hull (1884–1952)

Hull was born in Akron, New York, on May 24, 1884. His family was poor, and he apparently missed a lot of school because he had to work on the family farm. His health was bad throughout much of his childhood, he had extremely poor eyesight, and he was laid low by poliomyelitis for a lengthy period during his early college years (a disease that left him crippled in one leg). Still, at the age of 17, he spent a whole year teaching in a one-room school in Michigan before continuing his education at Alma Academy, also in Michigan. He had considerable talent for mathematics (as well as philosophy), and his initial aspiration was to become a mining engineer. But after reading James's *Principles of Psychology*, Hull switched to psychology and went on to the University of Wisconsin, where he obtained a Ph.D. in 1918.

Hull's early interests included systematic investigations of human and animal aptitudes, of thinking machines (robots), of hypnosis (to which he devoted a full 10 years of study and research), and of the effect of tobacco on intellectual functioning. In 1929, he went to Yale, where he became a research professor and generated (with a number of ardent disciples) the monumental system that, in extremely simplified form, makes up the rest of this chapter. Following his first major descriptions of this system in *Principles of Behavior* (1943), he rapidly became the most frequently cited psychologist in the United States. A final revision of this book was published just after his death in 1952.

all the conditions that affect the organism but that might or might not lead to behavior. He referred to these conditions as **input variables;** responses are described as **output variables.** Several of his postulates are devoted to explaining the nature of input and output variables as well as the relationships that exist between the two. A third set of behavior variables, which forms a central part of Hull's system, is referred to as **intervening variables.**

Important aspects of input and output variables can be observed and measured; in contrast, intervening variables are purely hypothetical. They are inferred from input and output. They are the scientist's best, most educated guesses about what might be happening between the presentation of a stimulus and the occurrence of a response.

Hull's interest in intervening variables is a significant departure from the preoccupations of the early behaviorists such as Watson and Guthrie, who actively shunned speculation, trying to keep the study of behavior as objective as possible. For this reason, Hull described himself as a **neobehaviorist,** rather than simply as a behaviorist, and saw himself as an S-O-R theorist rather than an S-R theorist. The "O" stands for organism, and indicates that instead of just dealing with stimuli and responses (as Watson did, for example), he also took into account events that occur within the organism.

Hull was greatly impressed by Pavlov's work on reflexive behavior and classical conditioning. This Pavlovian influence is reflected in part by the fact that the cornerstone of Hull's system is his belief that all behavior consists of S-R connections. Hull thought that conditioning provides a good explanation for the *mechanics* of learning. But his system goes beyond these mechanics and attempts to explain the *motivation* that seems to be clearly involved in behavior. Here the influence of Thorndike, and especially of his law of effect, is most apparent. The influence of reward on learning is the essence of Hull's motivational system and became the main explanatory notion in the final theory.

Graphic Summary of Hull's System

It might seem backward to begin this discussion with a summary. In this case, however, the summary, presented in Figure 3.5, serves as a useful outline of the pages that follow.

Note that the system is jammed with symbols and mathematical terms and values—all of which seem highly complex. In fact, the symbols simplify the theory, although they might impose some strain on memory. Although the theory is very complex in scope and detail, its most basic ideas are quite straightforward.

First, to simplify the model in Figure 3.5, think of it not as a general description of human behavior but as representing only one specific behavior for one person at one given time. Understanding how the system can describe one behavior makes it much easier to comprehend.

Next, keep in mind that Hull, the precise and logical mathematician, truly believed that human behavior could be predicted if psychologists had the right information and the right equations. Hence, his main goal, like Watson's, was to develop a system that would allow him to do just that—to predict a person's behavior given knowledge about the stimulus and about the person's history relating to this stimulus.

Input Variables: Predictors

In Hull's system, summarized in Figure 3.5, input variables are predictors. They represent the information the psychologist needs to correctly predict how a person will respond (the output variables represent the response, or what is predicted). In different terms, the stimulus variables are independent variables, and the response variables are dependent variables.

In brief, input variables represent a stimulus. But a stimulus is not just a simple sensation (like the sound of a bell), but is a complex product of a large number of preceding events. As Figure 3.5 indicates, complete knowledge of input requires knowing the following: how many times in the past the S-R bond in question has been reinforced (N); something about the physical intensity of the stimulus (S); the drive conditions of the organism (C_D); the reward attached to

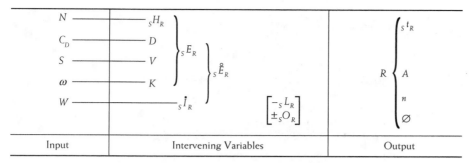

Input variables

N = number of prior reinforcements
C_D = drive condition
S = stimulus intensity
ω = amount of reward (weight)
W = work involved in responding

Intervening variables

${}_sH_R$ = habit strength
D = drive
V = stimulus-intensity dynamism
K = incentive motivation
${}_sE_R$ = reaction potential
${}_s\overset{.}{I}_R$ = aggregate inhibitory potential
${}_s\overset{o}{E}_R$ = net reaction potential
${}_sL_R$ = reaction threshold
${}_sO_R$ = oscillation of reaction potential

Output variables

R = the occurrence of a response, measured in terms of ${}_st_R$, A, and n
${}_st_R$ = response latency
A = response amplitude
n = number of nonreinforced trials to extinction
$\varnothing$ = no response (not used as a symbol by Hull)

Figure 3.5 The Hullian system. Adapted from *Theories of Learning* (3rd ed.), by E. R. Hilgard and G. H. Bower. New York: Appleton-Century-Crofts, 1966.

responding (ω); and the amount of work required in responding (W). All these variables, in combination, would allow prediction of the output variables—at least theoretically. Hence, one of the major difficulties in applying this system to predict behavior is that the psychologist needs a tremendous amount of knowledge about the subject's experiences.

Intervening Variables

Although input and output variables are the only directly observable and measurable events described in Hull's system, intervening variables are probably more important for understanding what his theory is really about. These variables have important links with the external variables; they intervene between stimulus events and response events to determine whether a response will occur for a stimulus. They are the "O" in Hull's description of his theory as an S-O-R system rather than simply an S-R system (recall that the "O" stands for *organism*).

Intervening variables determine responses, or the lack thereof. But note that the power of intervening variables in determining responses is completely determined and controlled by input variables. In a sense, the intervening variables are a mathematical description of S-R relationships. That is, each stimulus (input) variable has a specific intervening variable related to it by some mathematical function. Thus, characteristics of input variables (such as number of prior reinforcements) are reflected in the value of intervening variables that, in turn, determine whether a specific response will occur.

Keep in mind that Hull's objective was to develop a mathematical system that would make it possible to calculate human behavior given sufficient knowledge about prior conditions—a sort of human behavior calculator. Viewed in this way, the intervening variables are much easier to understand. Each of Hull's nine intervening variables is described in turn in the following sections.

1. $_SH_R$

The most important intervening variable, **habit strength ($_SH_R$)**, is defined as the strength of the bond between a specific stimulus and response. Habit strength, explained Hull, is determined largely by the number of previous pairings of a stimulus with a response, *provided that reinforcement occurred on every trial*. Here, Thorndike's influence on Hull is most evident. Unlike contiguity theorists, both Thorndike and Hull maintained that the strength of a habit (of an S-R bond) is a function of reinforcement rather than of simple repetition. Hull introduced specific numerical functions to illustrate the precise relationship between number of reinforced S-R pairings and habit strength. These are now of historical interest, but of little practical value.

2. D

Habit strength is crucially important in determining behavior, but it is not the most important intervening variable—**drive (D)** is. Basically, drive is a motivational concept closely tied with reinforcement. Within Hull's system, drive is the cause of behavior. Accordingly, the system is referred to as a *drive-reduction* theory. Responses become connected with stimuli (that is, become learned), says Hull, when they lead to a reduction in drive.

Drive can be primary or secondary (as can reinforcement because it involves reducing drive). Primary drives are those associated with physiological needs such as the need for food or water; secondary drives are conditioned to primary drives through contiguity—for example, the need for high grades or money. Drive, as an intervening variable, corresponds to the input variable *drive condition*, which is defined by number of hours of deprivation. Hull identified two components of drive: the *drive proper* increases as a direct function of the length of deprivation, and the *inanition component* is recognition that drive decreases if deprivation (starvation) lasts too long.

Drive has three central functions in Hull's theory: (1) It provides for reinforcement, without which learning would not occur; (2) it activates habit strength—meaning that without drive, behavior will not take place even if there is a strong previously established habit ($_SH_R$)—and (3) drive stimuli become attached to specific behaviors through learning. Otherwise, people might engage in completely inappropriate behavior. They might drink when hungry, eat when cold, or cover up when thirsty. Essentially, this distinctiveness of drive stimuli determines whether a response will be reinforcing.

As we note later, research has established that even in animals, learning can occur in the absence of drive (when drive is defined in terms of deprivation). This observation does not necessarily invalidate Hull's system, although it does point to some of its inadequacies.

3. V

As Pavlov had demonstrated, the physical intensity of a stimulus increases the probability that a response will occur. This effect is manifested in the intervening variable **stimulus-intensity dynamism (V)**. Stimulus-intensity dynamism interacts with habit strength and drive to determine the probability of a response.

4. K

The symbol K in Hull's system stands for **incentive motivation**.[3] Incentive motivation, which is determined by amount of reward (ω as an input variable), was added to Hull's system as a function of some important experiments reported by Crespi (1942). These experiments made it apparent that drive (D) alone could not account for motivation. In Crespi's experiment, three groups of rats received different amounts of reward (food pellets) for running to a goal box. The fact that the rats that received the greatest reward ran faster than those that received less supports Hull's original notion that drive is reduced more by greater reward, hence leading to a stronger habit. But Crespi also found that when these three groups of rats were subsequently given an identical amount of reward, those that had previously had the least amount now ran fastest, whereas those who had received the greatest amount reduced their speed the most. As a result, Hull now had to modify his system to account for the fact that previous reinforcements are also effective in determining behavior. Their effects, described by Hull as involving *incentive motivation*, interact with other intervening variables (including drive) to determine the probability that a response will occur.

5. $_SE_R$

The four intervening variables described thus far ($_SH_R$, D, V, and K) make up the first and most important term in the equation Hull used to determine the

---

[3] The Old Woman paused here. She said that some of you—actually, she said the brighter ones among you—might be interested in knowing why Hull chose the letter K for incentive motivation. She said I might want to tell you that he did so to honor his prize pupil, Kenneth Spence. Spence worked closely with Hull in developing his theory—so closely that the system is often referred to not as Hull's theory, but as the Hull-Spence system. She said those less bright wouldn't be interested in this little historical footnote. I defended you, said there weren't likely any of you noticeably less bright. The Old Woman yawned and said nothing for a long time. I thought she might be going to sleep. Then she continued.

Decreased drive after too many hours of deprivation (or satiation)

probability that a stimulus would lead to a response, or what he called **reaction potential ($_SE_R$)**: $_SE_R = {_SH_R} \times D \times V \times K$. Reaction potential, sometimes called *excitatory potential*, is essentially a measure of the potential that a stimulus has for eliciting a specific response. As the formula indicates, this potential will depend on how many times the stimulus has been paired with the response and with reinforcement, how intense it is, how great the reward, and how strong the drive (in other words, $_SE_R = {_SH_R} \times D \times V \times K$).

Note that because reaction potential is a multiplicative function of these variables, if the value for any of them is zero, reaction potential will also be zero. In practical terms, what this means is that in the absence of drive, it makes no difference how intense the stimulation, how great the reward, or how strong the habit, the response (R) will not occur. Similarly, in the absence of the appropriate stimulus at sufficient intensity, a reaction will not occur; in the absence of reward, there will be no response; and in the absence of a previously learned habit, there will be no response. Consider the case of a person sitting at a table on which is set a variety of appetizing dishes. If that person has just eaten, not a single dish may be touched, despite the fact that the stimulus, the reward, and the habit are all very strong. In this case, drive would be too low. By way of further illustration, consider the other possibilities: no food (K = 0); the person is blind and cannot smell (V = 0); or the person has not learned to eat ($_SH_R = 0$). In none of these cases will the eating response occur.

Note, too, that the probability of responding ($_SE_R$) is a multiplicative function of drive, habit strength, and so on. What this means is that identical changes in one of these variables will have different absolute effects, depending on the values of the other variables. Doubling drive, for example, will make a greater difference if habit strength ($_SH_R$) is already large than if it is small. Put another way, increasing the motivation of a professional golfer should have more effect than increasing that of a rank amateur.

The significance of the magnitude of reaction potential in this system is that a minimum amount of potential is required before behavior will take place. Increasing reaction potential will be reflected in shorter response latency ($_St_R$),

Symbol Shock

more response amplitude (A), and longer extinction time (n)—all of which are characteristics of the output end of Hull's equation.[4]

6. ${}_s\overset{\circ}{E}_R$

Hull used two similar symbols to denote reaction potential. The first, as we just saw, indicates the organism's tendency to respond and is a function of factors such as number of prior reinforcements or intensity of the stimulus. This second symbol refers to **net reaction potential.** Put simply, it is the result of subtracting the individual's tendency not to respond (called *inhibitory potential*) from the tendency to respond—or *reaction potential*.

7. ${}_s\overset{\circ}{I}_R$

The tendency that the organism has not to respond is labeled **aggregate inhibitory potential (${}_s\overset{\circ}{I}_R$)** (reactive inhibition plus conditioned inhibition). It results partly

---

[4]At this point in the first four editions, there appeared in bold print, page center, the expression: ~~BULLSHIT~~. An accompanying footnote explained: "The indelicate expression (delicately crossed out) is not a description of content but simply an antidote to the symbol shock that might by now have overcome the careful reader." When she got to this point the Old Woman said, "I've taken it out, you know, your indelicate expression, the one you got away with for more than two decades now. You should pay more attention to your reviewers." Then she quoted from the reviewer of the second edition who said, in 1982, "This is probably not as exciting now as it was in 1972," and from a third edition reviewer who said, "This strikes me as out of place in a textbook." And she began to quote from another reviewer who said he was deeply offended, but I said, Hey, wait, the expression wasn't meant to excite students or to offend them so much as to startle them out of their symbol shock—a sort of shock therapy. And she said, well, it's gone, and besides, that wasn't a very intelligent cure for symbol shock, and then she started to read the fifth edition out loud once more without explaining what a good cure for symbol shock might be.

from the amount of work involved in responding (W) and partly from any habits of not responding that the organism might have learned, usually as a function of repeated performance of the responses. According to Hull, responses requiring a high expenditure of physical energy are less likely to be engaged in than are those that require less work. Also, with continued repetition of a response, inhibitory potential accumulates. Its effect is to lower the net reaction potential until eventually the response no longer occurs. That is, if inhibitory potential is equal to or greater than reaction potential, then it follows mathematically that net reaction potential will be zero or negative—in which case, no behavior will occur. Inhibitory potential resulting from repetition and fatigue dissipates quickly, notes Hull, so that the response might reoccur again very soon.

8. $_sL_R$

The **reaction threshold ($_sL_R$)** is the magnitude that net reaction potential must exceed before a response will occur. (If $_s\mathring{E}_R > {_sL_R}$, a response, R, occurs; if $_s\mathring{E}_R < {_sL_R}$, no response (∅) occurs).

9. $_sO_R$

Even given relatively complete information about input variables, predictions are not always accurate. Guthrie's answer for this problem was simply that the stimulus situation has changed. Hull's answer was that reaction potential is not exactly fixed, that it varies around a central value. He labeled this variation **behavioral oscillation ($_sO_R$).**

Output Variables: The Predicted

The response variables of interest to Hull include the time lapse between the presentation of the stimulus and the appearance of the response (**response latency, $_st_R$**), the physical amplitude of the response (**response amplitude, A**), and the number of nonreinforced responses that would occur before extinction (n). Hull believed that response latency would decrease with increasing reaction potential. That is, the response would occur more rapidly. At the same time, both resistance to extinction and amplitude of response would increase with higher reaction potential.

Two additional symbols standing simply for the occurrence of a response (R) or its nonoccurrence (∅) have been included in Figure 3.5. The following formula is essentially a summary of the contents of that figure:

$$\text{If } {_sE_R}\ [= ({_sH_R} \times D \times V \times K) - {_s\mathring{I}_R}] > {_sL_R}, \text{ then R}$$

This expression reads as follows: If net reaction potential—which is the product of habit strength, drive, stimulus-intensity dynamism, and incentive motivation, minus aggregate inhibitory potential—is greater than the threshold, a response will occur.

Note how this is very much the kind of mathematical formula that a logic machine charged with predicting human behavior might produce. In fact, Hull was very interested in robotics and actually designed a type of computer to sort and score some of his tests.

Not surprisingly, Hull's main problem turned out to be the near impossibility of arriving at precise mathematical functions for each of the variables in the equation. Nevertheless, the system led to the development of several additional concepts, two of the most important of which are *fractional antedating goal reactions* and *habit-family hierarchies.* These concepts represent significant departures from theories that had preceded Hull.

Fractional Antedating Goal Reactions

Recall that Hull's major explanation for learning is reinforcement. Specifically, he maintains that reinforcement consists of drive reduction, where a drive is a powerful urge or tendency. Hunger and thirst are clear examples of drive. The ordinary way of reducing a drive is to attain a goal, or, in Hull's words, to make a *goal reaction.* Goal reactions, as described by Hull, are often responses of consuming (eating or drinking; termed *consummatory responses*). A **fractional antedating goal response (r_G)** (called "little *r g*") is a conditioned response made by an organism before the actual goal reaction. One of Hull's examples is that of a rat that has learned that there is food at the end of a maze. Through conditioning, the rat's goal reaction (eating) has become linked with the food box as well as with various other stimuli also present, such as other sights and smells. Hull suggested that because many of these smells and sights are also present in other parts of the maze, the rat's antedating goal responses might eventually occur when it is first put into the maze. Although overt behaviors might be associated with these antedating goal reactions, such as the rat's licking its chops, they are conditioned internal responses.

These antedating (Hull sometimes called them "anticipatory") responses are important because they serve as stimuli that maintain behavior toward a goal. It's as though there are strings of associated stimuli (little s g's) and responses (little r g's) (labeled r_G-s_G) that precede goal reactions. In this sense, they serve the same purpose as Guthrie's movement produced stimuli (MPS). But unlike MPS, r_G-s_G are linked with reinforcement and therefore become rewarding.

Foresight and Expectancy

Perhaps most significant, Hull's notions of antedating goal response foreshadowed some fundamental cognitive notions. In effect, what Hull attempted to do with r_G-s_G's was explain in precise, measurable behavioral terms behaviors that most people might explain using more vague mentalistic terms such as "knowing" or "anticipating." It was a clever and distinctive contribution to the development of learning theory.

Even though he was determinedly behavioristic, Hull could hardly avoid the use of nonbehavioristic ideas. In a section of his 1952 book entitled "Terminal Notes: Foresight, Foreknowledge, Expectancy and Purpose," he admits that "since time out of mind, the ordinary man has used the words *expect, expectation, expectancy,* and *expectative* in a practically intelligent and intelligible manner" (p. 151). Hull goes on to explain that although the fractional antedating goal response is a conditioned mechanism, because it occurs before a response, it "constitutes on the part of the organism a molar foresight or foreknowledge of the not-here and the not-now. It is probably roughly equivalent to what Tolman has called 'cognition'" (p. 151).

What Hull was trying to do was to show that it is possible to predict behaviors without resorting to subjective definitions and interpretations. Thus, in a sense, his fractional antedating goal responses are objective, behavioristic ways of accounting for intention and expectancy and even purpose. Although the term *purpose* "has a bad metaphysical history," he wrote, "it represents an undoubted aspect of mammalian behavior" (Hull, 1952, p. 151).

Habit-Family Hierarchies

In the course of learning—or acquiring habits (S-R bonds)—an individual will learn a number of different responses for the same stimulus. And in many cases, each response will lead to the same goal. These alternative responses constitute a **habit-family hierarchy** (Figure 3.6). They are referred to as a *family* because they are related to the same goal and therefore share common fractional antedating goal reactions; they are a *hierarchy* because one alternative will usually be preferred over another—presumably because it has been rewarded more often in the past, and as a result, the reaction potential ($_sE_R$) associated with it is higher. Thus, in the hypothetical habit-family hierarchy shown in Figure 3.6, all responses are related to escaping the danger associated with the stimulus "bear." The most probable response for this individual, *running*, has presumably been most reinforced in the past.[5]

Appraisal of Hull's Formal Behaviorism

At first glance, Hull's behavioristic system might seem unduly abstract and difficult. In fact, however, its most important ideas can be explained clearly and simply. Basically, the theory says that behavior is lawful and predictable.

Hull believed, much as did Thorndike and Guthrie, that an organism placed in the same situation on different occasions will generally respond in the same way each time. If the response is different but the situation is identical, it simply means that the organism has changed. The main purpose of

---

[5]Here, the Old Woman stopped reading from her notes. "Listen," she said to me, "I didn't want to explain this any farther because we'd be getting ahead of ourselves. But for sure some of your brighter students will be asking themselves what the devil happens if this is the first time you come across a bear and therefore you've never been reinforced one way or another in that situation, either for running or singing or praying or what-have-you." I said yes, that's a good point. Then the Old Woman said, "Well, tell them, if they haven't already figured it out, that reinforcement doesn't always have to be direct. Tell them . . ." The Old Woman interrupted herself. "On second thought," she said, "they can wait until Chapter 11 to find out about vicarious reinforcement." And then she continued reading.

Input   possible responses

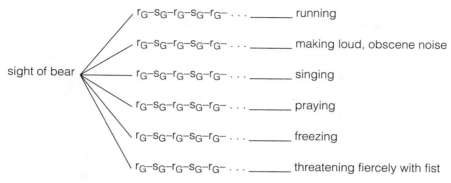

Figure 3.6 A hypothetical habit-family hierarchy. The stimulus input "bear" can lead to a number of different responses, each of which has in common that it is linked with the goal of not being molested by this animal. The preferred response—that which is highest in the hierarchy—is the one that, because of the individual's learning history, has become associated with a higher probability of being reinforced (that is, of leading to the desired goal).

the theory is to discover the relationships that exist between stimuli (input variables) and responses (output) to predict output given knowledge about input. This aspect of the system is clear and simple; what is more complex are the mathematical formulas Hull invented to describe links between input and output variables.

One of the important criteria we have been employing to evaluate psychological theories concerns the extent to which the theory reflects the facts. In one sense, the "facts" of psychological theories are the observations on which the theories are based. To the extent that Hull's system reflects valid observations about input and output, it does reflect the facts well. But at another level, the system deals with hypothetical properties—properties that cannot be observed. That is, much of Hull's system consists of what are termed **logical constructs.** These are entities that are inferred—they follow logically from what is observed but cannot themselves be observed. Thus, *reaction potential, aggregate inhibitory potential, behavioral oscillation, incentive motivation,* and the raft of other related "intervening" variables cannot be shown to be facts. This does not mean that they are invalid or that inferred entities have no place in psychological theorizing—quite the contrary. Logical constructs, like other theoretical "truths," should be judged by their usefulness.

So, are Hull's intervening variables useful? Clearly, within the system itself, they are immensely useful, providing a compelling logic. That they contribute to explanations of human behavior, that they lead to more accurate predictions than would otherwise be the case, that they are clear and understandable, and that they are based on few unverifiable assumptions is not nearly so apparent.

Ironically, then, despite the impressive logic and mathematics that are fundamental to the Hull system, the theory does not fare particularly well with respect to some of our criteria. But Hull's system contributed in many tangible ways to the advancement of psychological theory. First, introducing concepts such as fractional antedating goal reactions foreshadowed more cognitive concerns. The concept smacks of intention or purpose, and as we shall see, intention is an important variable in some cognitive theories of learning and motivation.

Second, Hull has profoundly influenced how psychological investigations are conducted. This influence has resulted largely from his insistence on precision, rigor, and quantification, as well as his emphasis on logical consistency. These qualities are well illustrated in a variety of experiments in which Hull systematically compared abilities of hypnotized and awake patients in an attempt to refute current misconceptions. Page (1992) notes that many of Hull's typically thorough and highly controlled investigations in this area have led to experimental methods and to conclusions that are still valid. It is perhaps Hull's insistence on systematic experimentation and the application of logic that most sets his system apart from that of other learning theorists.

Third, Hull, along with Thorndike and B. F. Skinner, is often credited with popularizing and systematizing the notion that reinforcement is one of the most important forces in shaping behavior. In this sense, note Purdy, Harriman, and Molitorisz (1993), these theories involve a Darwinian sort of natural selection: Responses that are accompanied by favorable consequences tend to become more frequent; other responses eventually disappear. It's a principle of natural selection whereby the "fittest" behaviors—those that survive—are those that are reinforced.

In summary, Hull significantly influenced the development of psychology. In fact, for many years, he was seen as the leading proponent of systematic theories of behavior. As Mills (1998) notes, Hull was very ambitious and very interested in his own personal success as the main spokesman and developer of a complete theory of behavior. At the same time, he was apprehensive, and perhaps a little upset, at the apparent popularity and success of the Gestalt psychologists (which we discuss in Chapter 6). "These gestalt people are so terrifyingly articulate," he wrote in a letter to his student and collaborator, Spence. "Practically every one of them writes several books. The result is that whereas they constitute a rather small portion of the psychological population of this country, they have written ten times as much in the field of theory as Americans have" (reported by Mills, 1998, p. 112).

Webster and Coleman (1992) note that for about a dozen years following the publication of *Principles of Behavior*, Hull was one of the most influential of all American psychologists. Yet Hull provided very little research to validate his theories and support his corollaries. By the late 1950s, his influence had diminished dramatically, perhaps because no one had yet succeeded in plugging in values in the basic Hullian formulas and predicting, with anything approaching machinelike accuracy, what the organism would do in various situations. Perhaps it shouldn't be surprising that subsequent theories of learning have typically been much smaller in scope and ambition.

Educational Implications of Thorndike and Hull

As we noted, Thorndike almost single-handedly defined and established educational psychology. Also, he popularized the use of tests and statistical methods in education, as well as in psychology. Moreover, he changed child psychology into an objective discipline. Both Thorndike and Hull conducted countless experiments on learning. It is hardly surprising that both their theories should have important educational implications.

Perhaps more than anything else, their recognition of the importance of the consequences of behavior—of behavior's *effects*—profoundly affected practices in schools. Thorndike's theory, for example, stresses that rewards and punishments need to follow correct trials, and that they also have to be tailored to the situation. Among other things, the child's *readiness* needs to be considered.

Thorndike's subsidiary laws also stress the importance of taking students' attitudes into consideration, the importance of drawing attention to the most important aspects of a situation, and the importance of teaching for transfer (for generalization). Thorndike suggested that teachers can facilitate transfer by pointing out how different situations are similar.

Although Hull's theory is not so clearly directed at improving educational practice, he is largely credited with popularizing the notion that reinforcement is centrally involved in learning. As we see in the next chapter, Skinner expanded this notion into an enormously influential system.

Summary

1. Thorndike's theory of trial-and-error connectionism is based partly on his attempts to determine whether animals think—whether they are intelligent in human terms.

2. Contiguity and reinforcement are the two main behavioristic explanations for the formation of relationships between stimuli (S-S), between responses (R-R), or between stimuli and responses (S-R). The contiguity explanation maintains that the co-occurrence of the events in question is sufficient; the reinforcement position takes into consideration the consequences of behavior. Watson and Guthrie were contiguity theorists; reinforcement is central in Thorndike's and Hull's theories.

3. Thorndike described learning as involving the formation of bonds (connections) between neural events corresponding to stimuli and responses. Learning involves stamping in bonds; forgetting involves stamping out bonds.

4. The *law of effect* is Thorndike's major contribution. It specifies that the *effect* of a response is instrumental in determining whether it will be stamped in or out. After 1930, he stressed that *satisfiers* (defined objectively as that which the organism does nothing to avoid, instead often doing things to maintain or renew the situation) are much more effective in stamping in responses than *annoyers* are in stamping them out. Before 1930, he also believed

that repetition (the law of exercise) was important, but he rejected this notion after 1930.

5. Readiness was an important part of Thorndike's pre-1930 system (when an organism is ready to learn, to do so is satisfying); belongingness (things that are seen as belonging together are learned more readily) became more important after 1930.

6. Thorndike's system includes a number of subsidiary laws. Most important is the law of multiple responses (learning occurs through trial and error). Other laws state that culture and attitude affect behavior (set, or attitude), that people are selective in responding (prepotency of elements), that behavior is generalizable (response by analogy), and that stimulus substitution or transfer (associative shifting) occurs.

7. Among Thorndike's most important contributions are his emphasis on the importance of the consequences of behavior (reward and punishment), popularization of the use of animals in psychological research, and a determined attempt to apply psychological principles to real problems, particularly in the area of education.

8. Hull's analysis of behavior is a highly formalized attempt to account for behavior through the precise relationships thought to exist between input, intervening, and output variables. This hypothetico-deductive system is based on 17 laws (called postulates) from which more than a hundred theorems and many corollaries are derived.

9. A summary of the major Hullian variables and the relationships that exist between them is given by the equation $_sE_R = {_sH_R} \times D \times V \times K$. It reads: Reaction potential is the product of habit strength, drive, stimulus intensity dynamism, and incentive motivation. If reaction potential (the tendency to respond) minus inhibitory potential (a tendency not to respond based on work involved and previous habits of not responding) is greater than a threshold value, a response occurs. However, even within this system, behavior is not completely predictable because the value of reaction potential varies (oscillates) around a fixed point.

10. Two Hullian concepts of special significance in the development of learning theories are fractional antedating goal responses and habit-family hierarchies. Fractional antedating goal responses are sequences of internal responses that precede reaching a goal and thus become conditioned. In Hull's system, they are seen as strings of internal stimuli and responses, labeled s_G-r_G sequences). Habit families are hierarchical arrangements of habits that are related because they have common goals.

11. The concept of fractional antedating goal responses illustrates Hull's belief that it is possible to predict and explain behaviors using precise, quantifiable notions, without resorting to mentalistic and unquantifiable terms. In a sense, these are behavioristic definitions of cognitive concepts such as expectancy or purpose.

12. Despite the impressive mathematics and logic of Hull's system, it has not resulted in useful predictions of behavior. Nevertheless, its contribution to the further development of learning theories is vast. In addition, Hull's work profoundly influenced how psychological investigations are conducted (emphasis on objectivity and experimentation), and he is credited with popularizing the notion that reinforcement is important in learning.

Operant Conditioning: Skinner's Radical Behaviorism

> It is dangerous and foolish to deny the existence of a science of behavior in order to avoid its implications.
> **B. F. Skinner (1973)**

That evening we walked through the woods, the Old Woman and I, following the trail that goes north from the fork below the cabin on the other side of the main beaver pond. She walked ahead of me because the trail is too narrow for us to walk side by side. She likes to walk in front, mostly because she's not very tall and she likes to see where she's going rather than just looking at my back.

When we came to the tree with the osprey nest, the Old Woman stopped. She said the osprey was an amazing bird, even though there was no osprey to be seen. She explained how it's related to both the hawk and the vulture and how it lives only on fish and that it plunges into the water feet first to catch them alive and how with its 5- or 6-foot wingspan it can lift itself from the water soaking wet, grasping a squirming fish with its reversible outer toe and the ingenious tiny sharp spines under its feet. Amazing bird, she said again, pointing out how it can even close its nostrils when dragged under water by a heavy fish, which is something extremely rare among birds except for ducks and coots and other aquatic fowl, and how it always builds its nest over water or close to it like here with Coal Lake just down the valley below us, and how every fall the osprey migrates all the way to South America and how one of the first planes that could fly horizontally like any conventional plane but that could also land and takeoff vertically by tilting its propellers was called the V-22 Osprey.

We sat on a fallen tree on the edge of the valley looking out over Coal Lake with the sun setting at our backs, our shadows long across the slope of the hill and everything seemed as perfect as it ever does and the Old Woman spoke of osprey and fish for a while longer, explaining that there is much to be learned from the behaviors and the adaptations of animals, that early psychologists believed it would be a lot easier to discover the laws of human behavior by studying animal behavior than by studying the behavior of humans.

This Chapter

Skinner was one of those, explained the Old Woman, motioning that I should now turn on the machine, that she wanted to record the next chapter, explaining that this chapter deals with what is undoubtedly the most influential and the best known of all the behaviorist positions, that of Burrhus F. Skinner. She predicted that some of you, when you finish this chapter, will have been converted to **radical behaviorism,** saying it almost as though it might be some form of religion.[1]

---

[1]"Don't look so confused," said the Old Woman, turning from her notes. "I don't mean radical like Skinner was a wild revolutionary, bent on vandalizing and looting other people's theories and maybe burning them." She said Skinner used the description *radical* in a 1945 article where he was insisting that to be a science, psychology must deal only with public events. In this sense, *radical*

Objectives

The Old Woman said to tell you that you would know this has happened when the dreams—perhaps even the nightmares—that awaken you in the night are no longer about the lotteries you fantasize winning or the dramas of which you are the perpetual hero. They will deal instead with the following:

■ *Respondents and operants*

■ *The basics of operant learning*

■ *Effects of different schedules of reinforcement*

■ *The nature and uses of punishment*

■ *Possible origins of superstition*

■ *What is meant by terms like* fading, generalization, discrimination, aversive control, *and* rat

Is Skinner's Radical Behaviorism Antitheoretical?

That Skinner even has a theory may seem strange and inaccurate to some, given that he is widely considered to have been deliberately antitheoretical. In 1950, he wrote an article entitled, "Are theories of learning necessary?" (Skinner, 1950). His answer, in one word, was "no." In a later article, he declared that theories, though they could be amusing to their creators, were of little practical value (Skinner, 1961).

Hordes of Skinner's critics—and supporters as well—concluded that Skinner was against all theories, that he had, as Westby (1966) put it, developed the "Grand Anti-Theory." Skinner disagreed. "Fortunately I had defined my terms," he said of his original article (Skinner, 1969, p. vii). The type of theory he objected to is expressed very clearly in that article: "Any explanation of an observed fact which appeals to events taking place somewhere else."

As an example of the kind of theorizing to which he most strongly objected, Skinner (1969) described an educational film he had recently seen. To illustrate a reflex, this film showed electrical impulses (which looked like flashes of lightning) running up neural pathways, finally appearing on a television screen in the brain. A little man in the brain would then burst into action, pulling a lever that sent return flashes of lightning scurrying down the neural pathways to muscles, which then responded to complete the reflex.

---

means *root*. What Skinner was saying was that public events, rather than mental states, are the root of psychology. But, said the Old Woman, this does not mean denying the private event. Thus, a toothache may be private, but it is also an actual physiological stimulus. The label *radical behaviorism* is commonly used to distinguish between Skinner's behaviorism and that of other theorists who were not nearly as insistent as Skinner on *not* making inferences about mental states. Most specifically, the Old Woman explained, it draws an unmistakable distinction between Skinner's theory and Tolman's *purposive* behaviorism—which is discussed in Chapter 6.

This is a very old explanation for human behavior that dates back to the ancient Greeks, who attributed behavior to a little **homunculus**—a little man inside the big man (or woman, presumably). In Skinner's view, psychological theorizing often takes the form of inventing "little men" in the brain: for example, Freud's notions of the subconscious or cognitive psychology's descriptions of mental maps or other unobserved "fictions" (Skinner's term). These are misleading and wasteful, Skinner claims; they suggest mysterious intellectual activities and do little to advance science. Behavior, he claims, should be studied and explained in the most direct way possible (Smith & Vetter, 1996). "Behavior is one of those subject matters," says Skinner, "which do not call for hypothetico-deductive methods. Both behavior itself and most of the variables of which it is a function are usually conspicuous" (1969, p. xi).

Accordingly, it wasn't *theories* to which Skinner objected. Rather, he objected to speculation about unobservable events and processes. In fact, his acceptance of the central function of theories could scarcely be more explicit: "A theory is essential to the scientific understanding of behavior as a subject matter" (Skinner, 1969, p. viii). His point is simply that theory should be limited to organizing relationships and events that can be observed. The emphasis of radical behaviorism, as Smith (2002) points out, is on the practical usefulness of the science of human behavior rather than on testing formal theories.

Skinner's Radical Behaviorism: An Overview

One way to look at theories, suggests Larsen (1999), is to view them as stories that, among other things, reflect the life-experiences of their authors. She points out that Skinner's behavioral approach tells a story of behavior *in context*. That is, the theory looks at the actual behavior of organisms in the context of the definable and observable conditions that precede the behavior and the consequences that follow.

Skinner did not object to theories. What he objected to were theories that appealed to unobservable states of affairs or events to explain behavior. For example, he thought Hull's use of *intervening variables* wasteful and fruitless. Accordingly, there are two overridingly important characteristics of his radical behaviorism: (1) explanations of behavior rely exclusively on directly observable phenomena; and (2) psychology is considered an objective *science* whose methods involve the analysis of behavior without appeal to subjective mental events or speculative physiological events (Vargas, 2001).

Basic Assumptions

Skinner's theory is based on two fundamental assumptions. First, he believed that human behavior follows certain laws. Second, although psychology has typically looked for the causes of behavior *within* the person, Skinner started (and ended) with the absolute conviction that its causes are *outside* the person, and that these can be observed and studied. Accordingly, Skinner's theory is the result of a search for the laws that govern behavior. As such, it takes a clearly objective, descriptive form and not an inferential, speculative one. Interestingly, it is precisely for this reason that his work remains free from sound, invalidating

Table 4.1 *Skinner's System*

Independent variables	Dependent variables
Type of reinforcement	Acquisition rate
Schedules of reinforcement	Rate of responding
	Extinction rate

criticism. The main critics are those who interpret Skinner's system as implying that principles of **operant conditioning** can eventually be used to explain and control *all* human behavior and that the principles can then be misapplied. Other critics include those who feel that the Skinnerian view of behavior as lawful and therefore explainable through laws makes humans less than they are. We look at these criticisms again toward the end of this chapter.[2]

The Experimental Analysis of Behavior

The causes of behavior, Skinner insisted, are outside the organism. The whole point of a science of human behavior, then, is to discover and describe the laws that govern interactions between the organism and the environment. To do so, the psychologist must specify three things: "(1) the occasion upon which a response occurs, (2) the response itself, and (3) the reinforcing consequences" (Skinner, 1969, p. 7).

Skinner describes his system as involving the **experimental analysis of behavior.** As an experimental analysis, it deals with two kinds of variables: independent variables (factors that can be directly manipulated experimentally, such as reinforcement) and dependent variables (the characteristics of actual behaviors, such as rate of responding). Dependent variables are not manipulated by the experimenter but are affected by the independent variables. The goal is to describe the laws that govern relationships between dependent and independent variables. Achieving this goal would make it possible to increase and refine control over dependent variables—in other words, to control behavior. The essential elements of the system, viewed as dependent and independent variables, are summarized in Table 4.1.

---

[2]The Old Woman reached over and shut off the recorder, grumbling that the sun had set, it was dark, and she could hardly see the pages anymore and besides there were too dang many mosquitoes out here; we should go back to the cabin and finish the chapter indoors. After a while, we got there and she called the cat to sit on her lap, which the animal refused, while I rummaged through the box looking for matches to light the lamp so she could continue reading. She said the biography would come next, explaining there was one for every major theorist in the book. She said biographies might not seem that important to some of you, but sometimes they are, that they're not just there to be interesting or inspiring. She explained that many psychologists think that people's personal lives often profoundly influence their professional lives. For example, Demorest and Siegel (1996; Siegel, 1996) made a detailed study of Skinner's life and of his autobiographical writings. Among other things, they suggest that Skinner's radical behaviorism is a sort of defense reaction that allowed him to cope with repeated failures—specifically, his apparent failure as a novelist following college. I found the matches and lit the lamp. The Old Woman began to read Skinner's biography. The cat got up and went outside.

Burrhus Frederic Skinner (1904–1990)

B. F. Skinner—he was called Fred; Burrhus was his mother's maiden name—is one of the giants of 20th-century psychology. Only Freud is more readily recognized as an important psychological figure of the 20th century (O'Donohue & Ferguson, 2001).

Skinner was born in Susquehanna, Pennsylvania, on March 20, 1904, to a staunchly Presbyterian (and Republican) family. His father was a successful, though largely self-taught, lawyer. His mother was an attractive woman who, Skinner claimed, always stood for 20 minutes after every meal to maintain her figure and her posture. Skinner also confessed that he thought she was frigid.[3]

Skinner attended the same one-room school that both his parents had attended. As a child, he read a great deal, which may have been apparent in his desire to become a novelist. He also displayed remarkable mechanical skills, building wagons, roller skates, scooters, gliders, rafts, and even musical instruments—skills that he put to good use in devising and constructing the devices he later used in his experiments.

Like many of psychology's pioneers, when Skinner went to college, he did not intend to become a psychologist, majoring instead in English (Hamilton College in New York). At the end of his undergraduate career, he met Robert Frost, who read some of the things Skinner had written. Frost's suggestion that he might have some talent convinced Skinner he should be a novelist, and so he asked his father to support him for a year while he wrote his first novel. His father reluctantly agreed, and Skinner spent what he was later to describe as "my dark year at Scranton" discovering that he had nothing to say. Subsequently, he undertook graduate studies at Harvard University.

Skinner found psychology fascinating. From the very beginning, he was an avowed behaviorist who already dreamed of "making over the entire field to suit myself" (Skinner, 1979, p. 38). In 1931, he obtained his Ph.D. in psychology and spent the next five years doing research before beginning a career as lecturer, researcher, and writer (at the University of Minnesota, Indiana University, and Harvard University, in that order). Chief among his early works was *The Behavior of Organisms* (1938), which laid the groundwork for operant conditioning principles. A novel, *Walden Two* (1948), did much to popularize his conception of an ideal society based on scientific principles of human behavior and engineered in such a way that positive rather than aversive techniques of control would predominate. By the late 1950s, Skinner had become recognized as the leading proponent of the behavioristic position, a position that he continued to develop and defend throughout his life.

In addition to about 200 clearly written scholarly books and articles, Skinner wrote three autobiographical books totaling more than a thousand pages (Skinner, 1976, 1979, 1983).

---

[3]"Do we really care if Skinner thought his mother frigid?" asks Blind Reviewer E, implying that this passage should be deleted. "Leave it in just the same," said the Old Woman, explaining that maybe that conviction, or at least suspicion, is reflected in Skinner's operant conditioning.

Table 4.2 *Classical and Operant Conditioning*

Classical (Pavlov)	Operant (Skinner)
Deals with respondents that are elicited as responses to stimuli and appear involuntary	Deals with operants that are emitted as instrumental acts and appear voluntary
Type S (stimuli)	Type R (reinforcement)

Respondent and Operant Learning

In his attempts to explain behavior, Skinner had available the classical conditioning explanation that had already been proposed by Ivan Pavlov and elaborated on by people like John B. Watson and Edwin Guthrie. Although Skinner (1996) expressed considerable admiration for Pavlov, he disagreed with the basic Pavlovian notion that a study of the conditioning of reflexes could explain a large number of important human behaviors. Skinner believed that classical conditioning explained only a very limited variety of human and animal behavior. Specifically, classical conditioning explains the acquisition of behaviors *only* where the initial response can be elicited by a known stimulus. The learning that then occurs results from pairing this stimulus with another over a number of trials.

Though Skinner accepted this model as accurate for explaining some behavior, he insisted that many human responses don't result from obvious stimuli. He further maintained that the stimuli, whether observable or not, are often not important for an accurate and useful explanation of learning.

Responses elicited by a stimulus are labeled **respondents;** responses simply emitted by an organism are labeled **operants.** In respondent behavior, the organism reacts *to* the environment, whereas in operant behavior it acts *on* the environment. In a sense, respondents correspond to involuntary behavior, whereas operants are more voluntary. Skinner would probably not have said this, however, because the terms imply what he would have considered unnecessary speculation. We don't need to ask or wonder whether the organism wants or doesn't want to do something, Skinner insists; we need only note what it does, the circumstances under which it acts, and the consequences of its actions. These three things, taken together, are the *contingencies* of behavior. And the experimental analysis of behavior requires nothing more—or less—than the analysis of these contingencies.

Skinner suggested that classical conditioning only works on respondent behavior. Skinner called this type of learning *Type S* (for stimulus) conditioning. He advanced a different model to explain learning based on operant behavior: the model of operant or instrumental conditioning, also referred to as *Type R* (for response) conditioning. The distinctions between these two forms of learning are detailed in Table 4.2.

Prevalence of Operant Behavior

Skinner (1938) believed that most of the important behaviors in which people engage are operant. Walking to school, writing a letter or a textbook, answering a question, smiling at a stranger, scratching a cat's ears, fishing, shoveling snow, skiing, and reading are all examples of operant behavior. Even thinking is an operant—a covert (internal) form of verbal behavior. Although there might be some known and observable stimuli that reliably lead to some of these behaviors, the point is that these stimuli are not central in any learning that takes place. What is central are the consequences of the responses.

Charles Darwin's Influence

Skinner's most important ideas owe much to Charles Darwin as well as to Edward Thorndike. In many ways, explained Skinner, learning seems to involve the selection of responses in much the same way as evolution involves the selection of characteristics. Darwin believed that in nature, all sorts of different traits appear; forces of nature act to select those that contribute to survival—precisely because they *do* contribute to survival. Similarly, in behavior all sorts of responses appear. Some have consequences that seem to benefit the organism; others don't. The effect of these consequences is that some responses are selected and others are eliminated.

Thorndike made the observation that consequences lead to the "stamping in" or "stamping out" of responses the cornerstone of his theory of trial-and-error learning. Skinner based his theory of operant learning on much the same idea. Briefly, operant learning is the survival (and death) of responses. "Both in natural selection and in operant conditioning," Skinner wrote, "consequences take over a role previously assigned to an antecedent creative mind" (1973, p. 264).

Pavlov's Harness and Skinner's Box

When Pavlov placed a dog in a harness and injected food powder or an acid solution into its mouth, the dog salivated. That is a clear and unambiguous example of a respondent—of a stimulus reliably eliciting a predictable response.

In his investigations, Skinner used a dramatically different, highly innovative piece of equipment now known as a **Skinner box** (he called it an *experimental chamber*). The most typical of these experimental chambers is a cage-like structure that can be equipped with a lever, a light, a food tray, a food-releasing mechanism, and perhaps an electric grid through the floor (see Figure 4.1).

When a naive rat is placed in this box, it doesn't respond as predictably and automatically as does the dog in the Pavlov harness. In fact, Gallo, Duchatelle, Elkhessaimi, Le Pape, and Desportes (1995) identified 14 distinct behaviors that a rat might display in a Skinner box. For example, the rat might cower for a while, then it might sniff around the cage, occasionally rearing up on its hind legs to smell the bars, spending a little more time near the food tray as it senses the faint odors of some other rat's long-eaten reward. Eventually the rat might happen to depress the lever, causing a food pellet to drop into the tray. The rat will eat this pellet; in time, it will depress the lever again. After a while, the rat will run straight to the lever whenever it is put into the cage. Its behavior has changed as a result of that behavior's consequences: The rat has been operantly conditioned.

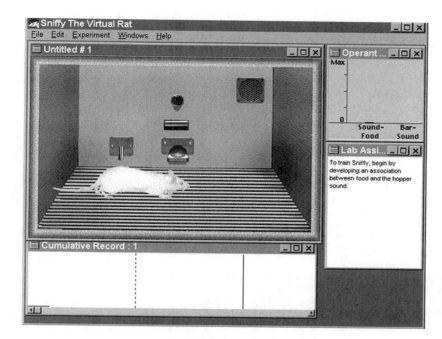

Figure 4.1
Sniffy the Virtual Rat explores his cage, frequently referred to as a Skinner box. Skinner, however, called it an "experimental space."

Operant Learning

Stated very simply, the operant conditioning explanation says that when a reinforcer follows a response—regardless of the conditions that might have led to its emission—the result will be an increase in the probability that this response will occur again under similar circumstances. Further, the explanation states that the circumstances surrounding reinforcement may serve as a **discriminative stimulus** (abbreviated S^D) that can come to have control over the response.

Any behavior that is acquired because of reinforcement can be interpreted as an illustration of operant conditioning. Figure 4.2 shows one example.[4]

Not S-R Learning

Note that unlike Thorndike's connectionism, Skinner's theory of reinforcement does not involve the formation of associations between stimuli and responses. In fact, Skinner took pains to point out that he was not an S-R theorist. By definition, an operant is *never* elicited. Thus, although the rat in the Skinner box might eventually learn to press the lever only when a light is turned on, this particular discriminative stimulus does not *elicit* bar pressing, claims Skinner. It

---

[4]You can put in your own example, the Old Woman said. So I did. When we were on Pigeon Lake that day, and the Old Woman wouldn't let me fish so I could take notes, I saw how she stopped using the Wetaskiwin Lure after she pricked herself a few times. And I saw, too, how her hand movements became progressively more agitated as she began to catch more fish. "Isn't your hand getting tired?" I asked, offering to fish for a while. "Why should it be tired?" she asked. "All I'm doing is holding a line with a tiny little lure at the end." She wasn't even aware that the fish had shaped her behavior.

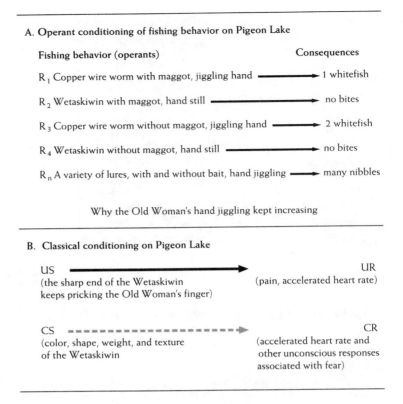

Figure 4.2
Two types of conditioning.

simply allows the rat to discriminate reinforcing situations from those that aren't reinforcing.

Ⓡeinforcement

Skinner's explanation of learning through operant conditioning is based squarely on the notion that the consequences of behavior determine the probability that the behavior will occur again. This is very similar to Thorndike's belief that responses that lead to "satisfying states of affairs" are more likely to be learned. But, determined as he was to be objective, Skinner had no place in his theory for subjective terms like *satisfying* and *annoying*. Thus, Skinner defines a **reinforcer** as *an event that follows a response and that changes the probability of a response's occurring again*. **Reinforcement** is simply the effect of a reinforcer.

This is a clear example of what is meant by an *operational* definition: Reinforcers are defined by observable and measurable behaviors (or operations). Skinner's emphasis on this type of definition, notes Wyatt (2001), has had a profound and long-lasting influence on psychological theory. One important advantage of defining terms operationally is that doing so makes it unnecessary to wonder about subjective states. Defining reinforcement operationally, for example, eliminates the need to speculate about what is pleasant or unpleasant. Whether an event is reinforcing or not depends solely on its effects; its intrinsic nature is irrelevant. Thus, the same event might be reinforcing on one occasion, but not on another.

To illustrate, consider Henry, a freckle-faced, lovable little school child of 10. Henry takes a spelling test for which he has studied very hard, using a number of mnemonic devices. For example, to remember how to spell *separate*, he talked himself into remembering that there is "a rat" in the word. He receives a score of 95% on his spelling test. This event serves as a reinforcer; it increases the probability that Henry will again use mnemonics.

Now consider Agnes, a bright little girl who always gets 100% in spelling without using mnemonic tricks. But this time she does use one; in fact, she uses the same mnemonic device as Henry. Unlike Henry, though, she becomes confused on the test and thinks there is "e rat" in *separate*. She also receives a grade of 95%. This event is not a reinforcer for Agnes, however, and will probably have the opposite effect on her behavior.

Positive and Negative Reinforcement

Skinner distinguishes between two types of reinforcement: positive and negative. **Positive reinforcement** involves what Thorndike had labeled a "satisfying" consequence of a behavior. In behavioristic psychology, a consequence is more properly referred to as a **contingency.** Defined in objective Skinnerian terms, positive reinforcement occurs when the consequences of the behavior, when *added to* a situation after a response, increase the probability of the response's occurring again in similar circumstances. In common speech, this type of reinforcement is similar to *reward*. It involves a positive contingency.

Negative reinforcement involves a response that results in the elimination or prevention of what Thorndike would have labeled an "annoying" outcome. It occurs when the probability of a response's occurring increases as a function of something being *taken away from* a situation. In everyday speech, negative reinforcement is similar to *relief*. It involves the removal of a *negative* contingency.

Note that the effect of both positive and negative reinforcement is to *increase* the probability of a response's occurring. Note, too, that the effect of the event— not the nature of the stimulus itself—determines whether it is reinforcing.

Punishment

Like reinforcement, **punishment** is also defined by its effects. In this case, however, the effect is not a strengthening of the behavior (as it is for *both* negative and positive reinforcement) but, rather, a suppression of it.

In the same way as there are two types of reinforcers—positive (reward) and negative (relief)—there are two types of punishment, each the converse of a type of reinforcer. One is the kind of punishment that occurs when a positive contingency is removed (what might be termed a *penalty*—sometimes referred to as *positive* punishment); the other, where a negative contingency follows a behavior, is what is more commonly thought of as punishment (sometimes referred to as *negative* punishment).

Punishment versus Negative Reinforcement

Because both often involve aversive consequences (negative contingencies), punishment and negative reinforcement are often confused, but they are really quite different. Negative reinforcement is a procedure that *increases* the probability of a behavior; punishment does not. Consequently, negative reinforcement typically involves the *termination* of an event that might be considered aversive (the termination of a negative contingency); punishment involves introducing a negative contingency or terminating a positive (*appetitive*) one.

Any lingering confusion can easily be clarified by referring to Table 4.3, which shows the four possibilities that result when either positive or negative contingencies (appetitive or aversive events) follow behavior or terminate following behavior. In everyday speech, these four possibilities represent reward (positive reinforcement), relief (negative reinforcement), castigation (one kind of punishment, sometimes called presentation punishment), or penalty (another kind of punishment, sometimes referred to as removal punishment). Each of these four possibilities is illustrated with a rat and then with a person in the following section.

Illustrations of Reinforcement and Punishment

The rat illustrations relate to the behavior of Arnold, a rat in a Skinner box; the people illustrations refer to the behavior of Bill, a toddler in his house.

Positive Reinforcement (Reward)

If the consequences of Arnold's depressing a lever in a Skinner box is that the food mechanism releases a pellet of food into the tray (positive contingency), the effect may be an increase in the probability that bar-pressing behavior will occur again. In this case, the food is a **positive reinforcer;** its effect is positive reinforcement. It leads to an increase in the preceding behavior.

If toddler Bill offers to kiss his mother one morning, and she praises him for this touching filial gesture, there may be an increase in the probability of this kind of behavior in the future. Mama's praise is a positive reinforcer.

Negative Reinforcement (Relief)

If the current is on continuously in the grid but is turned off every time the rat presses the lever (removal of negative contingency), there will again be an increase in the probability of bar-pressing behavior. In this case, termination of the electric current is a **negative reinforcer;** its effect is negative reinforcement. It, too, leads to an increase in the behavior that precedes it.

Table 4.3 Reinforcement and Punishment

	Positive contingency (Appetitive)	**Negative contingency (Aversive)**
Added to a situation after a response	Positive reinforcement (reward) [Sam is given a dollar for behaving well] **behavior strengthened**	Presentation punishment (castigation) [Sam has his ears pulled for misbehaving] **behavior weakened**
Taken away from a situation after a response	Removal punishment (Type II: penalty) [Sam has his dollar taken away for misbehaving] **behavior weakened**	Negative reinforcement (relief) [Sam's ears are released when he behaves well again] **behavior strengthened**

If toddler Bill is later isolated in his room while having a temper tantrum or crying fit (because his mother insists that no, he can't sit on the cat like on a horse), allowing him to come out when he stops crying illustrates negative reinforcement. This event may increase the probability that he will stop crying when again in this situation.

Presentation Punishment (Castigation)
If the rat, which must stand on the electric grid when it depresses the bar, is given a mild shock every time it does so, it will probably attempt to avoid the bar in the future (negative contingency). The shock in this case is one type of punishment (termed *negative* or *Type I punishment*, commonly referred to as *castigation*). It may lead to what is termed *avoidance learning* (where the rat tries to avoid the situation associated with this negative contingency) or *escape learning* (where the rat, when placed in a situation previously associated with negative contingencies, tries to escape). It does *not* lead to an increase in the rat's bar-pressing behavior.

Note, however, that although the electric shock in this case serves as punishment for bar pressing, it is also an example of negative reinforcement *with respect to avoidance learning*. That is, if the removal of the shock leads to an *increase* in avoidance behavior, it serves as negative reinforcement for that behavior. If, at the same time, it leads to a *decrease* in bar pressing, it serves as punishment for *that* behavior.

If toddler Bill kicks his sister in the posterior, and she turns around and whacks him on the side of the head, he may be less likely to kick her again in similar circumstances or places. The sister's whack is a castigation kind of punishment with respect to Bill's kicking.

Removal Punishment (Penalty)
Once the rat has been trained, if the experimenter *removes* the food pellet (removal of a positive contingency) unless the rat gets to it within a specified time after pressing the lever, the rat may soon stop dawdling and licking its chops on

the way to the food tray. In this illustration, removal of the food pellet is an example of punishment involving a penalty (sometimes called removal, penalty, or Type II punishment). The responses being punished are those that delay the rat.[5]

If toddler Bill has his jellybeans taken away at lunchtime because he licked them, rubbed them on the wall, ground them into the floor, and then hurled them at his sister, this is an example of a penalty punishment. It might decrease the probability of some of his jellybean behaviors.

Primary and Secondary Reinforcers

In addition to distinguishing between positive and negative reinforcement, Skinner identifies reinforcers that are primary or secondary. **Primary reinforcers** include events that are reinforcing without any learning having taken place. Examples of primary reinforcers are stimuli such as food, water, and sex, each of which satisfies basic, unlearned needs (primary needs).

Secondary reinforcers include events that are not reinforcing to begin with but become reinforcing as a result of being paired with other reinforcers. The light in the Skinner box is sometimes used as a secondary reinforcer. Suppose that over a succession of trials, the light is turned on every time the animal is fed (given a primary reinforcer). Eventually, the animal will respond simply when the light goes on. At this point, the light has acquired secondary reinforcing properties.

The expression **generalized reinforcer** is sometimes used to describe a learned reinforcer that appears to reinforce any of a wide variety of behaviors. For humans, generalized reinforcers include things such as money, prestige, power, fame, strength, intelligence, and a host of other culturally prized contingencies. These are extremely powerful in determining human behavior.

Reinforcement Schedules

To develop a science of behavior, Skinner insisted, the psychologist needs to observe what the organism does, under what circumstances, and to what effect. These are the basic units in the *experimental analysis of behavior*. In the studies that proved most useful for developing his views of operant conditioning, rats depressed levers or pigeons pecked at disks. These are easily observed behaviors that Skinner could quantify by how rapidly they were acquired (acquisition rate), how many responses were emitted over a given period (rate of responding), and how long it would take for the responses to stop if reinforcement were

---

[5]This, the Old Woman admitted, is a hypothetical illustration. She said she could find no evidence in the literature that anyone had actually conducted this experiment. And she claimed she had no time to do it herself.

discontinued (extinction rate). Recall that these represent *dependent* variables; they are not under the investigator's direct control.

Probably the most easily manipulated and most effective *independent* variable in operant conditioning is the way rewards are administered. In a carefully controlled laboratory situation, experimenters can determine precisely what reinforcements will be used and how and when they will be used. In other words, experimenters are in complete control of **schedules of reinforcement.**

Continuous or Intermittent Reinforcement

Basically, the experimenter has two choices: **continuous reinforcement,** in which case every desired response is reinforced, or **intermittent** (or partial) **reinforcement,** where reinforcement occurs only some of the time (see Figure 4.3). If reinforcement is continuous, there are no further choices to make; every correct response is rewarded in the same way. (It is entirely possible, however, to use a combination of continuous and intermittent reinforcement schedules. This type of arrangement is sometimes referred to as a *combined schedule.*)

Interval or Ratio Schedules

If experimenters use an intermittent schedule of reinforcement, they can make one of two further choices. The intermittent schedule can be based on a proportion of responses (termed a **ratio schedule**) or on the passage of time (called an

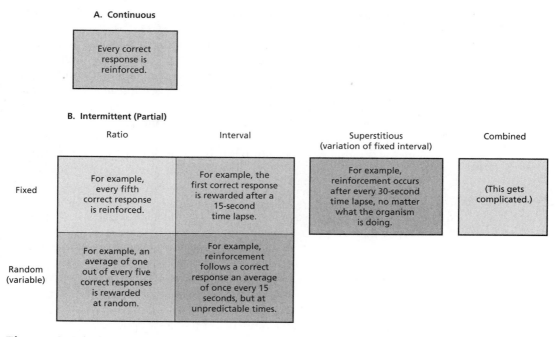

Figure 4.3 Schedules of reinforcement. Each pattern of reinforcement tends to generate a predictable pattern of responding.

interval schedule). For example, a ratio schedule might reinforce one out of five desired responses; an interval schedule might provide reinforcement once every five minutes.

Fixed or Random Schedules

An experimenter using either of these intermittent schedules (ratio or interval) would further have to decide whether the reinforcement would be administered in a fixed or in a random (variable) way. A **fixed schedule** is one in which the exact time or the precise response that will be followed by a reinforcing event is predetermined and unchanging. For example, in the case of a fixed-ratio schedule, reinforcement might occur after every fifth correct response. In fixed-interval reinforcement, the reinforcement will be available as soon as the chosen time interval has elapsed, immediately following the next correct response.

Random schedules provide reinforcing events at unpredictable times. A random ratio schedule of reinforcement based on a proportion of one reinforcement to five responses might involve reinforcing the first 4 trials, not reinforcing the next 16, reinforcing numbers 21 and 22, not reinforcing the next 8 trials, and so on. After 100 trials, 20 reinforcers would have been administered.

Superstitious Schedules

As we noted earlier, the consequences of behavior can involve positive or negative contingencies. Note that, by definition, contingencies are *consequences*. Clearly, however, not all of the positive and negative events that follow behavior are actual consequences of that behavior. Put another way, in many cases, outcomes are *noncontingent;* their occurrence or their failure to occur has nothing to do with the organism's behavior.

A **superstitious schedule** of reinforcement is a special kind of noncontingent fixed-interval schedule in which reinforcement occurs at fixed time intervals *without the requirement that there be a correct response.* It follows from the law of operant conditioning that any behavior just before reinforcement is strengthened. Whether the reinforcement is a consequence of the behavior is not always important. It seems that for both humans and other animals, temporal contiguity alone is enough to establish a relationship between reinforcement and behavior.

Numerous examples of superstitious behavior in animals are cited in the literature. In fact, it appears that in most conditioning sequences there are behaviors that accidentally precede reinforcement and temporarily become part of the animal's repertoire. For example, a rat that has just learned to depress a lever may do so with its head always to the right or with its left leg always dangling. Both actions are examples of superstitious behavior.

Skinner (1951) left six pigeons on a superstitious schedule overnight; they received reinforcement at fixed intervals no matter what they were doing. By morning, one bird regularly turned clockwise just before each reinforcement, another always pointed its head toward one corner, and several had developed unnatural swaying motions.

Skinner suggests that people often develop superstitious behaviors unconsciously. If you were holding your head just so when you were lucky enough to find a coin, there may be a greater tendency for you to hold your head just so in other similar circumstances, no matter how inelegant the posture might be. During a final exam, for example, you might find students scratching their heads; others frown; some move their lips, hands, legs, or feet; some chew their hair, and others engage in a variety of behaviors not directly related to clear thinking.

Effects of Different Reinforcement Schedules

Responses like pressing a bar or pecking at a key are easily observed and measured. Skinner, displaying his boyhood mechanical skills, devised a simple and ingenious way of recording such responses by having a pen trace a line on a continually moving drum of paper. Every response (bar press or key peck) causes the pen to jump up one step, thus providing a **cumulative recording** of the number of responses on the y- (or upright) axis. The rate of responding, which is the number of responses emitted during a fixed period of time, is indicated by the slope of the line; the faster the animal responds, the steeper will be the line on this recording. A line that stays parallel to the x-axis indicates that no response occurred during the period marked.

Figure 4.4, for example, shows a cumulative recording produced by Skinner (1938) of the bar-pressing responses of an initially untrained rat. In the training session, all lever-pressing responses were reinforced. Note how the first three reinforcements (responses, and hence reinforcements, are indicated by the first three upward steps in the recording) seemed to have little effect; the rat took almost 2 hours to press the lever three times. But immediately after the fourth reinforcement, the rate of responding zoomed upward so that almost 100 responses were emitted within the next 30 minutes. When conditioning bar pressing in rats, it isn't uncommon to reach close to a maximum rate of responding in 30 minutes or less.

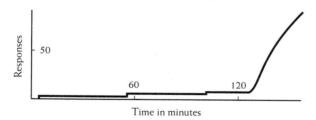

Figure 4.4 A cumulative recording showing the responses of an untrained (naïve) rat on a continuous schedule of reinforcement. Passage of time is shown on the x-axis; total number of responses on the y-axis. Note how, after four reinforcements, this rat's rate of responding, represented by the slope of the graph, increased dramatically. From *The Behavior of Organisms: An Experimental Analysis*, p. 67, by B. F. Skinner. Copyright © 1938 by Appleton-Century-Crofts. Reprinted by permission of Prentice-Hall, Inc.

Effects of Schedules on Acquisition

When training rats to press levers or pigeons to peck disks, Skinner typically deprived the animal of food for 24 or more hours (sometimes reducing its weight to 80% of normal) to increase the effectiveness of the reinforcer. Initial training usually begins with "magazine training" during which the animal is trained to eat from the food tray and, consequently, is exposed to the noise made by the food mechanism as it releases food pellets. After magazine training, all correct responses—and sometimes even responses that merely approximate the desired behavior—are reinforced.

Initial learning is usually more rapid if every correct response is reinforced (a continuous schedule). In contrast, changes in responding appear to be haphazard and slow if any of the intermittent schedules of reinforcement are used.

Effects on Extinction

One measure of this kind of learning is rate of responding—that is, number of responses in a given period; another is the rate of extinction after the withdrawal of reinforcement—that is, the amount of time that passes before the organism stops responding.

Interestingly, although a continuous schedule of reinforcement results in a faster rate of learning than does an intermittent schedule, it also leads to more rapid extinction after withdrawal. Further, the fixed schedules of reinforcement, although they have shorter acquisition times associated with them than variable schedules, also lead to more rapid extinction than the variable schedules do. Hence, the best training combination for an animal is usually a continuous schedule initially, followed by a variable-ratio schedule. (The ratio may also be varied over training sessions, with a decreasing ratio of reinforced to nonreinforced trials usually leading to even longer extinction periods.)

Figure 4.5 shows four typical extinction curves. In each case, reinforcement has been discontinued at the beginning of the 1-hour period (indicated on the x-axis). Note how rate of responding (indicated by the steepness of the curve)

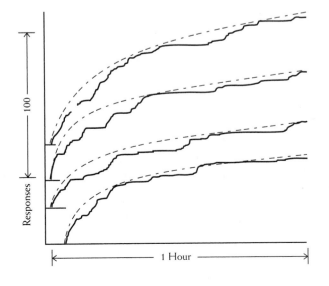

Figure 4.5
A cumulative recording showing four typical extinction curves. Note how rate of responding is high immediately after reinforcement stops (indicated by the steepness of the curve), and then occurs in sporadic outbursts until, less than an hour later, few responses still occur (curve is almost flat). From *The Behavior of Organisms: An Experimental Analysis*, p. 75, by B. F. Skinner. Copyright © 1938 by Appleton-Century-Crofts. Reprinted by permission of Prentice-Hall, Inc.

remains unchanged for the first few minutes after reinforcement stops, but then rapidly flattens out showing that few or no responses are occurring.

Spontaneous Recovery

Recall that a classically conditioned response (like salivation in response to a tone) can be extinguished by presenting the CS (tone) repeatedly without the US (food). Remember, too, that if the CS is presented again after the passage of some time, the CR (salivation) might occur again—a phenomenon Pavlov labeled **spontaneous recovery.**

Spontaneous recovery also occurs in operant learning, as is illustrated in Figure 4.6. "If the rat is replaced in the apparatus at a later time," wrote Skinner, referring to a time *after* a behavior has been extinguished, "a small extinction curve will be obtained" (1938, p. 78). In the case shown in Figure 4.6, for example, the steep slope of the graph during the first half hour followed by its leveling shows initial extinction of bar pressing in a rat over a 1-hour period without reinforcement. The next 1-hour period shows recovery of the same rat's bar-pressing response when placed back in the cage *48 hours later.*

Extinction and Forgetting

In Skinner's system, the terms *extinction* and *forgetting* describe different events. As we saw, **extinction** occurs when an animal or person who has been reinforced for engaging in a behavior ceases to be reinforced; the outcome is a relatively rapid cessation of the responses in question. Forgetting, in contrast, is a much slower process that also results in the cessation of a response, but not as a function of withdrawal of reinforcement. According to Skinner, forgetting occurs simply with the passage of time when there is no repetition of the behavior during this time.[6]

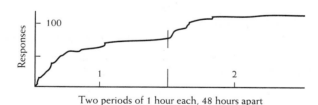

Two periods of 1 hour each, 48 hours apart

Figure 4.6 A cumulative recording showing initial extinction over a 1-hour period (left half of the graph), and spontaneous recovery of the rat's bar-pressing responses over a second 1-hour period when placed back into the Skinner box 48 hours later. Note how much more rapidly extinction occurs during the second period (flatter slope). From *The Behavior of Organisms: An Experimental Analysis,* p. 69, by B. F. Skinner. Copyright © 1938 by Appleton-Century-Crofts. Reprinted by permission of Prentice-Hall, Inc.

---

[6]There is a more detailed discussion of remembering and forgetting in Chapter 9.

These concepts can be illustrated by reference to a pigeon that has been conditioned to peck at a colored disk. If food is used as the reinforcer for this response and this reinforcement is suddenly withdrawn completely, the pigeon will in all likelihood continue to peck at the disk sporadically for some time. In a relatively short time, however, it will cease pecking entirely, at which point extinction will have occurred.

As noted earlier, a behavior that has been extinguished through withdrawal of reinforcement often reappears (that is, spontaneously recovers) without any further conditioning when the animal is again placed in the same situation. The extinction period following spontaneous recovery is almost invariably much shorter than the first. Assume that the pigeon that has been conditioned to peck at a disk is taken out of the cage and not allowed to return to it for a very long time. If it does not peck at the disk when it is reintroduced into the cage, one can say that forgetting has occurred. Skinner reported the case of at least one pigeon that had still not forgotten the disk-pecking response after six years. He also reported one instance of a pigeon that emitted 10,000 pecks before extinction.

Effects on Rate of Responding

A third measure of learning is rate of responding, which is a dependent variable that is remarkably sensitive to schedules of reinforcement. In general, an animal behaves as would be expected if it is valid to assume that the animal develops

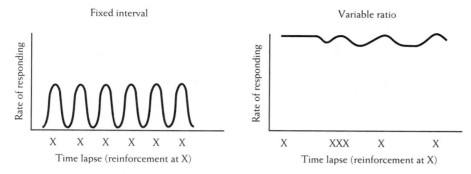

Figure 4.7 Highly idealized representation of the effects of two schedules of reinforcement on rate of responding.

expectations and has some sense of time. For example, under variable schedules of reinforcement, when the animal is less likely to develop an expectation of receiving a reward at a given time, the rate of responding will be uniformly high and relatively unvarying. If the variable schedule is a ratio schedule rather than an interval one, the rate of responding will be uniformly higher. Under a fixed-interval schedule of reinforcement, the rate of responding drops dramatically immediately after reinforcement and often ceases altogether. Just before the next reinforcement, however, the animal again responds at a high rate (see Figure 4.7).

Skinner, of course, would not normally use mentalistic concepts such as *expectation* or *goal* or *purpose* to explain why people or animals do things. When he does use such terms, which he does freely when discussing the implications of his science of behavior, he defines them in terms of the organism's reinforcement history. "What gives an action its purpose?" he asks. "The answers to such questions," he then responds, "are eventually to be found in past instances in which similar behavior has been effective" (1969, p. 105).

Schedules of Reinforcement in Everyday Life

Among the most powerful reinforcing events for humans are money, praise, satisfaction, food, and sex. Two of these stimuli, money and food, appear to be on fixed-interval schedules. For a large number of people, money arrives regularly in the form of a paycheck, and food is taken routinely in the form of meals. For both of these rather important reinforcers, however, often there are no immediate, simple operants that predictably result in their presentation. The operants involved in acquiring money have become so complex and so remote from the actual source of reinforcement that it has become difficult to see the relationship between the two. The confusion is further compounded by the fact that the reinforcers themselves are inextricably bound together. That is, money allows one to buy food and—in some cases—praise, satisfaction, sex, and other reinforcers as well.

The relationship between behavior and reinforcement is not always simple or obvious. But this doesn't invalidate the conclusion that reinforcers and their scheduling affect many human behaviors. Indeed, in many cases, the person whose behavior is affected remains completely unaware of the relationship between behavior and its consequences. There are countless examples of how behavior is controlled and modified by reinforcements.

Illustration 1
Iris has panned for gold in the same stream for 22 years, gleaning at least a few flecks every outing, as well as finding the occasional heart-stopping nugget (continuous reinforcement). Now, after devastating spring floods, she suddenly stops finding any gold whatsoever (withdrawal of reinforcement). After four fruitless trips to the stream, she stops going altogether (rapid extinction following continuous reinforcement).

Illustration 2
Esmeralda has also spent 22 years panning for gold. Sometimes she finds a little something, sometimes not. On occasion, she finds barely a fleck during an entire season, but she has found as many as five kick-in-the-rump nuggets on a single day (intermittent reinforcement). Now she, too, stops finding gold (withdrawal of reinforcement). Still, even many years later, she continues to pan the same stream (slow extinction following intermittent reinforcement).

Illustration 3
Zachary is given his first rattle, not knowing that a cruel but clever psychologist has yanked out its innards. Zachary holds the rattle up, looks at it, shakes it, bites it, strikes his knee with it, drops it, and forgets it. (The unreinforced response of shaking the rattle is not strengthened.)

Illustration 4
Zachary is now given a rattle that has been carefully kept from all psychologists. He looks at it, shakes it, looks at it again, and then proceeds to shake it vigorously for some time (the sound of the rattle serves as a reinforcer and strengthens the operant that precedes it).

Shaping

Why is it so easy to train a rat to press a bar, or a pigeon to peck a disk? Simply because these are among the things that rats and pigeons do. They are operants that almost invariably appear within just a short period in the experimental chambers that Skinner and his followers have provided for these animals. But, as we saw in Chapter 2, Guthrie assures us, "We can not teach cows to retrieve a stick because this is one of the things that cows do not do," (1935, p. 45). Elsewhere, he argues, "It would be a waste of time to try to teach a cow to sit up" (Guthrie & Powers, 1950, p. 128). The same is thought to be true of horses. Yet at the National

Shaping

Finals Rodeo a short time back, there was a guy with a horse that not only fetched things the man would throw—much like a dog might—but that also sat down when he was invited to do so.[7] This horse's behavior had been *shaped* using operant conditioning techniques.

Shaping is the technique used to train animals to perform acts that are not ordinarily in their repertoire. It isn't required for behaviors like pressing a bar in a Skinner box, because bar pressing is one of the behaviors the rat emits in the course of exploring the environment. But if the experimenter wanted to train a rat to go to corner A of the cage, pick up a marble in that corner, carry it to corner B, drop it there, return to the center of the cage, lie down, roll over, get up, return to corner B, pick up the marble again, and carry it to corner C, the rat would probably die of old age before it just happened to emit the operant.

Nevertheless it is possible, through shaping, to teach a rat to engage in behaviors that are very impressive, if not as complex as the behavior just described. An experimenter using the technique of shaping reinforces every behavior that takes the animal closer to the final response, instead of waiting for the final desired response to be emitted. For this reason, shaping is sometimes referred to as the *method of successive approximations*, or as a method involving the **differential reinforcement of successive approximations** (Skinner, 1951).

Most animal trainers employ techniques that amount to shaping procedures. That's how parrots are trained to walk on tightropes, parachute, play tunes, and ride bicycles; porpoises to jump incredible heights with military precision in predetermined order; bears to play guitars, dance, roll somersaults, and clap hands; chickens to play ball; and horses to sit down and bark.

---

[7]I'm sorry I missed the rodeo that night. The Old Woman went with my grandfather, ostensibly to do research. "Looking for examples for the book," she said. Apparently she found one.

One important requirement for the successful use of shaping procedures is that the environment be controlled. For example, the Skinner box is constructed so that the rat can't perform very many responses other than those the experimenter wants to reinforce. Similarly, a professional animal trainer would not attempt to condition a dog when the dog is chasing a rabbit but would first confine the dog and get its attention. In other words, the environment is arranged to facilitate the appearance of the desired response.

Chaining

An important phenomenon in operant learning is **chaining,** the linking of sequences of responses. Even a behavior as apparently simple as pressing a bar in a Skinner box involves sequences of different responses. "Most of the reflexes of the intact organism are parts of chains," said Skinner (1938, p. 52),[8] going on to describe how chains integrate all behavior. For example, he explained, a rat in a Skinner box makes all sorts of responses. Some of those made in the vicinity of the food tray become learned as a result of being associated with discriminative stimuli (S^D), such as the sound of the food mechanism, that have become secondary reinforcers. Initially, the discriminative stimuli that become secondary reinforcers are those directly associated with reinforcement (like the sound of the food mechanism). Over time, though, those discriminative stimuli that are further removed (like the smell of the lever) can also become secondary reinforcers. Thus a chain of responses can be woven together by a sequence of discriminative stimuli, each of which is a secondary reinforcer associated with—in this case—food as a primary reinforcer.

"Such movements become fully conditioned," Skinner wrote, "and are made with considerable frequency by a hungry rat" (1938, p. 53). Each movement, in sequence, changes the situation and hence the discriminative stimuli, giving rise to the next response. Vastly simplified, the chain involved in bar pressing might be something like this: the sight of the inside of the cage serves as an S^D associated with the response of turning toward the bar; the sight of the bar is an S^D for approaching the bar; proximity to the bar is an S^D for pressing it; the sounds and muscular sensations associated with pressing it are discriminative stimuli for turning toward the food tray; the sight of the food pellet is a stimulus for responses associated with eating.

Skinner argued that most human behaviors, even if they appear simple, consist of chains. For example, combing your hair, should you have any, may require a range of sequential acts: walking to the bathroom, opening a drawer, retrieving

---

[8]You might point out to your readers, said the Old Woman, that Pavlov, the then-current giant in psychology, profoundly influenced Skinner. That's why Skinner used the term *reflex* throughout his first major work, although he was not speaking about simple reflexes of the type investigated by Pavlov. In his later writing, Skinner largely abandoned the term in favor of *operant*, or simply *response* or *behavior.*

a comb, looking at yourself in a mirror, and going through your usual combing motions. If reinforcement (such as your mother saying, "Good girl, Sally,") is contingent upon you combing your hair, the entire chain of related behaviors is in effect reinforced.

Chains in Shaping

When a behavior is shaped, chains are established. What the professional animal trainer tries to do is link a series of discriminative stimuli and responses long enough to astound you and perhaps even your grandmother (although she's seen a lot more than you have). This way, in the final performance the trainer doesn't have to hold a steak above the dog's head, yell "Somersault," and move his or her hand quickly backward when the dog leaps for the steak, forcing the animal to describe a crude semicircle in the air. (Your grandmother wouldn't be impressed.)

Holding the steak over the dog's head and "forcing" the somersault is the first step in the chain, because all chaining works backward from a primary reinforcer. During training sessions, a clever trainer arranges for the conditioning of chains by *differentially reinforcing* certain responses leading to the final and complete sequence of responses. In the end, the dog will bound onto the stage, race through an obstacle course, rescue a drowning baby, spell its name with wooden letters, and finally do a most amazing somersault. And neither you nor your grandmother will ever see the steak.

Shaping in Human Learning

Human learning often involves shaping. For example, when learning complex motor tasks involving muscular coordination (such as golfing or fly fishing, for example), a large number of inappropriate or ineffective responses need to be modified or abandoned. At the same time, more appropriate (and consequently reinforced) responses become more firmly established and linked in chains.

People's verbal behavior is also highly susceptible to the effects of reinforcement (Skinner, 1957). Greenspoon (1955) illustrates this through what he calls *verbal conditioning*, a process in which participants are asked simply to say words. The participants, who have no idea what words are required, begin to speak. Each time they make some predetermined utterance, such as plural nouns, the experimenter reinforces them by saying "Mmhm." During a single training session, the incidence of plural nouns generally increases significantly.

Although this type of experimental procedure may at first glance appear to be somewhat remote from the realities of everyday life, on closer examination it becomes evident that people engage in many behaviors that are examples of the effects of verbal conditioning. For example, a high-pressure door-to-door salesperson often gets customers to commit themselves by employing a verbal conditioning technique. First, the salesperson suggests that the customers are intelligent, and then he or she reinforces all declarations of intelligence made spontaneously by the customers. Eventually, they will have realized that being so intelligent, they are sufficiently concerned for their children to purchase an encyclopedia.[9]

Fading, Generalization, and Discrimination

Shaping is one technique employed in training animals to perform complex behaviors. Another is **fading,** a process that involves both generalization and discrimination. Recall that **generalization** involves making similar responses in different situations; **discrimination** involves making different responses in similar but discriminably different situations.

Illustration 1: Teaching Pigeons to Read

Fading is best explained through illustration. For example, Reese (1966) describes a fading procedure whereby a pigeon is taught to "read" the words *peck* and *turn*. If the pigeon pecks when it sees *peck* and turns when it sees *turn*, says Reese, it will have satisfied the typical conditions for our saying it can read.

This type of training presents some special problems. Although it is relatively simple to train a pigeon either to peck or to turn when shown the appropriate word, the bird will then immediately generalize the learned response to the other word. If the pigeon is taught to peck in response to the word *peck*, it will also peck in response to the word *turn*. But if the two stimuli are made highly different so that the pigeon can easily discriminate between the two, it can be taught to respond appropriately to each stimulus through shaping. For example, the word *turn* might be printed in large black letters and the word *peck* in small red letters (pigeons have excellent color vision). After the pigeon has learned to peck and to turn as instructed, the differences between the stimuli are slowly *faded out* over a number of sessions: The large black letters become smaller, and the small red letters become both darker and larger, until finally each word is black and the letters are of uniform size. Through *fading*, the pigeon has learned to *discriminate* between two stimuli; in one sense, it has learned to read.

Illustration 2: Deceiving Amorous Quail

"Copulatory behavior," Domjan, Huber-McDonald, and Holloway inform us, "rarely occurs in responses to an arbitrary inanimate object" (1992, p. 350). But such behavior can be conditioned through fading. These investigators arranged

---

[9]"Maybe the author could find a different example," writes one reviewer. "There are a lot of parents, and maybe some encyclopedia salesmen, who won't like this." That's what I, too, told the Old Woman. But she refused, declaring that the truth is the truth, no matter how ugly it might be or how politically incorrect. She said that as far as she was concerned, there was no room for political correctness *for the sake of being politically correct* in a textbook. "Besides, if they don't like it," she grumbled, "bugger them." In the dim glow of the kerosene lantern, she seemed almost angry but her eyes laughed. After a while, the cat meowed. "Let him in," the Old Woman said. "He has no political motives."

for male Japanese quail to copulate with live female quail while being exposed to a terry-cloth-covered dummy, prepared by a taxidermist, that had a head and neck made of real female skin and feathers. Over 15 to 20 conditioning trials, the "birdness" of the dummy was gradually faded out as it was progressively covered with terry cloth. In the end, many of the male quail tried to copulate with the cloth-covered lump.

Relevance to Human Learning

Generalization and discrimination are very important in human learning. Generalization involves engaging in previously learned behaviors in response to new situations that resemble those in which the behaviors were first learned. One example is that of the pigeon turning in response to the word *peck* before it has learned to discriminate between *turn* and *peck*. Another is the perhaps even more impressive finding that pigeons can learn with relative ease to discriminate between spherical and nonspherical stimuli and will, after fewer than 150 trials of training, generalize the "concept" spherical to hundreds of other stimulus objects (Delius, 1992).

Generalization

Examples of generalization in human behavior are numerous. Any five-minute segment of behavior in the life of a normal person is likely to be filled with instances of old behaviors being generalized to new situations. New cars are driven in ways similar to those used in driving old ones; someone who hits a stranger accidentally may apologize although she's never hit this particular stranger before; when faced with the problem of adding 27 kangaroos and 28 zebras, a farmer reasons that the sum is the same as that of 27 pigs and 28 horses; people assume that objects fall from mountaintops as they do from treetops; strangers shake hands when introduced; and on and on. All these behaviors are examples of responses to new situations that are based on previous learning. Generalization is important precisely because not all, or even most, situations to which a person must react in a lifetime can be covered in schools or in other learning situations. Teaching for generalization (teaching for *transfer*) is one of the main functions of schools.

Discrimination

As we saw, discrimination is complementary to generalization in that it involves a subject making distinctions between similar situations to respond appropriately to each. The pigeon's learning to respond differently to the two highly similar situations involved in the presentation of the words *peck* and *turn* is an example of discrimination.

Discrimination learning is probably as important for human behavior as is generalization. This is especially apparent in learning socially appropriate behavior. Children must learn to discriminate at relatively early ages between similar situations where different responses are appropriate. Children learn, for

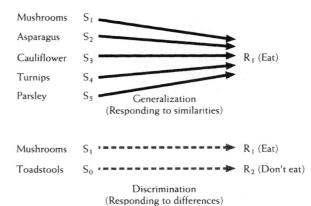

Figure 4.8
Discrimination and
generalization.

example, that it is permissible to kiss one's parents, but not strangers; that sisters should not be punched, but perhaps neighborhood bullies can be under certain *discriminable* circumstances; that it is bad to make noises in quiet churches but permissible to make the same noises in quiet houses; and so on. Thus, socially appropriate behavior is very much a function of having learned to discriminate between similar situations calling for different types of behavior.

The processes of discrimination and generalization are illustrated in Figure 4.8. In the first case, the appropriate response is to eat any of the five vegetables; in other words, a generalization of the eating response is appropriate. In the second case, it is necessary to discriminate between two stimuli. Generalization here is inappropriate.

Applications of Operant Conditioning

Although it was initially developed largely through the study of rat and pigeon behavior in highly controlled environments, Skinner's explanation of operant conditioning is as much a science of humans as of other organisms. Skinner saw no important discontinuity between how humans and nonhumans respond to the contingencies of their behaviors. And he considered criticisms that accused the system of neglecting higher mental processes like thinking to be unfair and inaccurate. "A science of behavior does not, as is so often asserted, ignore awareness," he declared. "On the contrary, it goes far beyond mentalistic psychologies in analyzing self-descriptive behavior" (Skinner, 1969, p. 245). In an article appropriately entitled, "Why I am not a cognitive psychologist," Skinner (1986) makes it clear that he by no means denies the existence and importance of cognitive phenomena such as thinking, problem solving, and imagining. These are interesting topics, says Skinner; but it is a mistake to try to explain them by reference to inferred "cognitive" processes.

Skinner's behavioristic system did not neglect language and thought. As Lana (2002) explains, acquiring and emitting verbal behaviors is subject to the same rules of operant conditioning as any other behavior. For Skinner, concepts such as awareness and purpose depend on verbal rules that result from analyzing the relationship between behavior and its contingencies: "An advanced verbal community generates a high level of such awareness" (1969, p. 245). Initially, argues, Skinner (1989), words were used not to describe awareness, purpose, and feelings but, rather, to describe the specific behaviors or situations in which these occurred. Thus, for example, a word like "love" might be used to describe the action of holding a baby. In time, however, the word would come to be associated with the bodily states—the physiological changes—that accompany the action. Hence, the word eventually describes an emotion and can then be generalized to other situations and behaviors that bring about the same physiological reactions—like kissing someone, or even petting a cat.

That humans are responsive to behavioral contingencies (to the consequences of behavior) seems clear. For example, 25 separate studies reviewed by Kollins and associates (1997) indicate that people are sensitive to variable interval schedules of reinforcement in much the same way as are experimental animals. People's responsiveness to the consequences of their behavior is the basis for behavioral therapies—therapies that systematically manipulate things like rewards and punishments in an effort to change behavior and emotions (Vargas, 2001).

That people are responsive to the effects of reinforcement doesn't mean that they are always aware of the relationships between their behavior and its consequences. In fact, it is possible to control people through the clever manipulation of rewards and punishments without the awareness of those being controlled—and societies do just that, claimed Skinner.

Instructional Applications of Positive Contingencies

As Skinner (1971) notes repeatedly, societies make extensive use of *aversive* contingencies when positive contingencies would be far more humane and probably more effective as well. He writes, for example, that the methods of control of the world's major social institutions are based largely on aversive contingencies. These methods are sorely evident in schools, where reprimands, detention, low grades, and threats of punishment are often a more prominent fact of a student's daily life than are praise, the granting of favors, the promise of high marks, or the possibility of other important reinforcement.

A classroom is a little like a giant Skinner box. Teachers play the role of experimenters: They schedule and administer rewards and punishments. Students play the role of Skinnerian rats (or pigeons, if that seems less offensive): Their responses are shaped by various teacher-controlled contingencies (and by many other contingencies, such as peer approval or ridicule, that are not under the teacher's control). As experimenters, teachers can profit from knowing that reinforcement is effective in bringing about changes in behavior, schedules of

Teacher reinforcement

reinforcement can be varied to good advantage, punishment is not very effective for learning, some reinforcers are more powerful than others, and that there should be as short a delay as possible between behavior and its consequences. For example, if teacher comments on student work, or grades, are used as reinforcement, they should be given to students as soon as possible.

Teachers can also profit from greater knowledge about sources of reinforcement. We tend to think of reinforcers as easily identifiable stimuli. For example, Bijou and Sturges (1959) describe five categories of reinforcers: consumables (such as candy), manipulatables (like toys), visual and auditory stimuli (for example, a bell signal that means "good work"), social stimuli (like praise), and **tokens** (such as disks that can be exchanged for other reinforcers). These stimuli are reinforcing because, as defined by Skinner, they increase the probability of a response occurring. Unfortunately, there are a number of problems with Skinner's definition. One is that it is rather circular: What is a reinforcer? A stimulus that increases the probability of a response occurring. How do we know it is a reinforcer? Because it increased the probability of a response. Why did it increase the probability of a response? Because it's a reinforcer. What is a reinforcer? And on, and on.

A second problem with the Skinnerian definition is that it doesn't take into consideration the fact that reinforcement is relative—that is, it can vary from one organism to another, and even from one situation to another for the same organism. As Kimble (1993) observes, food is reinforcing at the beginning of a meal, but by mid-meal, it might well have become neutral, and at the end of the meal, it might be punishing.

The Premack Principle

Premack (1965) presents a somewhat different approach to identifying rein-forcing events. His approach takes into account the observation that reinforce-ment is relative; it also takes into consideration the fact that reinforcers can be activities, or *responses*, rather than only stimuli. Premack's approach to identify-ing reinforcement, described as the **Premack principle,** states that behavior that occurs frequently and naturally can be used to reinforce less frequent be-havior. Being allowed to run in an exercise wheel, for example, can be reinforc-ing for some rats; others find it more reinforcing to be allowed to chew wood. Similarly, some children find it highly rewarding to watch television; others prefer playing with friends; still others might prefer reading quietly. Note that each of these is a *response*. Moreover, each is a response in which the organism will engage freely if given the opportunity to do so—in much the same way as the organism will also drink and eat. To find out what the best class of reinforcers might be for a given organism, suggests Premack, it is often sufficient to observe what the organism does freely. For example, a "with-it" teacher may notice that when students have free time in class, Tara reads, Amy and Sara talk to each other, William asks to clean the whiteboard, and Trevor draws cartoon characters. Ap-plication of the Premack principle suggests that allowing Tara to read might be reinforcing for her but not necessarily for other students; allowing Trevor to draw cartoons might be highly reinforcing for him.

Behavior analysis, based on conditioning principles, is applied extensively in schools (see, for example, Alberto & Troutman, 2003; Harlan & Rowland, 2002). It is also widely used by therapists in a variety of settings. The deliberate and sys-tematic application of operant conditioning principles in an attempt to change behavior is labeled **behavior modification.** Behavior modification is described and illustrated later in this chapter.

Applications of Aversive Consequences

Skinner describes two types of aversive (or negative) control: punishment and negative reinforcement. Recall that these are fundamentally different from each other: Whereas negative reinforcement increases the probability that a response will occur again, punishment usually has the opposite effect.[10]

The Case Against Punishment

Few topics in child rearing and education have received more attention than punishment. Much of this attention results from the prevalence of punishment rather than from its effectiveness—since Thorndike's (1931) work, there is wide

---

[10]By the way, said the Old Woman as an aside, you might have noticed that the environment con-stantly provides people with a huge number of aversive stimuli that appear to be extremely effective in shaping behavior. Stoves that are hot, insects that bite, mushrooms that poison—all of these quickly lead to important learning. If they didn't, the human species probably would not have sur-vived this many generations. So, although you need to recognize the importance of emphasizing positive rather than aversive control, aversive control should not be dismissed too glibly.

agreement that punishment is much less effective in eliminating undesirable responses than reinforcement is in bringing about desirable ones.

From a learning theory point of view, a number of practical and theoretical objections to the use of punishment can be raised. First, the likelihood that punishment will lead to appropriate behavior is often remote. Essentially, punishment draws attention to undesirable behavior but does little to indicate what the desirable behavior should be.

Second, instead of eliminating behavior, punishment usually only suppresses it; what is affected is the rate of responding. The advantage that nonreinforcement has over punishment is that, theoretically, it leads to the extinction of the unreinforced behavior.

Third, punishment can lead to emotional states that will probably not be associated with love, happiness, or any other pleasant feeling. Through contiguity, these negative emotional states may become associated with the punisher rather than with the undesirable behavior.

A fourth, more general objection to punishment is that it often does not work. Sears, Maccoby, and Lewin (1957) cite evidence to show that mothers who punish children for toilet accidents are more likely to have children who wet their beds, and those who punish aggression are more likely to have children who are aggressive.

Less Objectionable Forms of Punishment

Psychology's most passionate objections to the use of punishment apply mainly to physical punishment, such as spanking (or, perhaps worse, *strapping*). The same objections are not nearly as relevant for several other forms of punishment, some of which are quite common in schools and homes. These include *time-out procedures*, *response cost*, and *reprimands*.

A **time out** is a procedure in which children are removed from a situation where they might expect reinforcement and placed in another situation where they are less likely to be reinforced. Children who are removed from a classroom in response to misbehavior are being punished not by the administration of an unpleasant stimulus (unless, of course, they are sent to the principal's office or given detention) but, rather, by being removed from what is assumed to be a reinforcing environment. Similarly, when children who have received tangible reinforcers for good behavior later have some of these reinforcers taken away for misbehaviors, they are being exposed to **response-cost** punishment.

Other common punishments include the use of **reprimands,** most of which are verbal, but a number of which might be nonverbal (a negative shake of the head or a frown, for example). A series of studies in classroom situations found that the most effective verbal reprimands are those described as "soft" (O'Leary & Becker, 1968; O'Leary, Kaufman, Kass, & Drabman, 1974). Soft reprimands are those given in such a way that only the child involved can hear them. In classes in which teachers employed loud reprimands, there was a significantly higher incidence of disruptive behavior. In this connection, it is also worth noting that praise—a highly effective reinforcer in the classroom—is far more effective if it is "loud." In brief, in most cases, reprimands should be soft, and reinforcement should be more public.

It is potentially revealing, as well, to look at what students consider effective punishment. In one survey of more than 1,600 eighth graders, students ranked "a letter to parents" as the most effective punishment for bad behavior (Casteel, 1997). This type of punishment is "soft" in the sense that it doesn't expose students to humiliation in the classroom. At the same time, however, it exposes the student to the reaction of parents. In a second study of 371 students from four secondary schools, punishment directed at poor behavior was interpreted as being more effective than punishment directed at poor work (Wan & Salili, 1996). Because behavior is under the student's control, punishment of misbehavior is seen as being justified. In many instances, however, poor work may not be under the individual's control; hence, punishment for poor work is interpreted as unfair and may be highly ineffective.

The Case for Punishment

Corporal punishment, or the threat thereof, remains a highly common childrearing practice. Davis (1996) arranged for investigators to observe adults and their children in various public settings, listening for situations in which the adult (presumably the parent or guardian in most cases) threatened the child with physical punishment. Such threats were highly common, and many of the adults actually hit their children following the threat.

That physical punishment continues to be common in industrialized societies serves as a poor justification for it. Still, a number of arguments can be made for the use of punishment. First, although reinforcement, imitation, and reasoning might all be effective in bringing about and maintaining desirable behavior, in many instances they do not appear to be sufficient. As Ausubel (1977) notes, it is not always possible for a child to determine what is undesirable by generalizing in reverse from what has been identified as desirable.

Nor, of course, is gentle persuasion always going to convince the child immediately that certain behaviors are undesirable. If Johnny persists in throwing the cat in the bathtub even after being told that the poor thing cannot swim, punishment might be in order. And although psychologists have long noted that punishment does not appear to be very effective in eliminating undesirable behaviors, there is considerable evidence that it might be very effective in at least suppressing these behaviors (see, for example, Rush, Crockett, & Hagopian, 2001; Atkins, Osborne, Benn, Hess, & Halperin, 2001). Actually, the argument that punishment does not lead to the extinction of the behavior in question is irrelevant. If Johnny now stops throwing the unfortunate cat in the bathtub, his grandmother will surely not believe that he has forgotten how to do so—but she might justifiably hope that he would refrain from doing so in the future.

Despite ethical or moral objections that many feel toward the use of punishment, there are situations in which its use seems the least cruel and the most effective of alternatives. For example, Lerman, Iwata, Shore, and DeLeon (1997) describe an investigation of the use of punishment with five profoundly mentally retarded adults who habitually engaged in episodes of severe self-injurious behavior (SIB), such as pulling their hair out or chewing their flesh. Reinforcement for not engaging in SIBs, or even simple reprimands (a form of punishment), are seldom effective for such individuals. But in this investigation, subjects who were exposed to continuous schedules of punishment (time-out or restraint procedures)—that is, who were punished at the onset of each SIB episode—showed significant reductions in these behaviors. Interestingly, however, when the administration of punishment was changed from continuous to fixed interval, incidence of SIBs rose again to pretreatment levels.

Like reinforcement, punishment appears to be most effective when it immediately follows behavior. However, this observation is far more valid for other animals than it is for humans, presumably because of the human ability to symbolize. This allows for associations between behavior and its consequences even when the consequences occur a long time after the behavior.

In addition, punishment appears to be most effective when administered by a warm and loving parent (or other adult). And there is no evidence that the affection that exists between parent and child is damaged or reduced because of the judicious use of punishment (Walters & Grusec, 1977).

Negative Reinforcement

Recall that both positive and negative reinforcement, by definition, lead to an increase in the probability of a response occurring—one by being added to a situation (reward), and the other, by being removed (relief). Each of these, however, is likely to have very different effects. You might train a rat to jump onto a stool by feeding it every time it does so (positive reinforcement). Or you might train it to jump onto the same stool by giving it an electric shock when it does not do so. In the end, it may jump onto the stool with equal haste no matter how it has been trained, but it's likely that the positively reinforced rat will display considerably more enthusiasm for jumping than will its aversively trained colleague. There is a fundamental difference between learning an approach response (as is generally the case with positive reinforcement) and *escape* or *avoidance* learning (which often results from negative reinforcement).

Much like the rat that has learned to jump onto a stool to escape an electric shock, students who are attentive and studious because of aversive contingencies (negative reinforcement or punishment) cannot be expected to like school as much as those who are attentive and studious because of positive reinforcement.

Perhaps the same is true of those who go to church to avoid hellfire and damnation.[11]

---

[11]The Old Woman went to the cupboard, motioning that I should turn off the recorder saying she was hungry and did I want a sandwich, which I didn't. She laid out a slab of ham from what was left from supper, buttered two of those thick slices of the bread I get from my grandmother, mustarded them, and eased the ham carefully onto one of the slices. The cat rubbed hard against the Old Woman's legs. Yes cat, the Old Woman said and it seemed clear she was speaking to the cat and not to me but what she was explaining to the cat was that this was an old example, the one about the rats and the church, left over from an earlier edition. She said she had paraphrased it because she doesn't know much about hellfire and damnation. She said, too, that she found the use of such remarkably nonbehavioristic images as that of rats jumping on stools "enthusiastically" at least amusing, if not entirely meaningful or appropriate. Then for a long time she stood silent, looking at her sandwich. Afterwards she went to the door and laid the sandwich carefully in the cat's dish. The cat sniffed it gingerly, licked tentatively at a corner of ham sticking out from between the bread, then went back and curled up on the upper bunk. After a while, the Old Woman continued.

Other Applications: Behavior Management

One goal of the fashion and taste industry is to mold and change people's tastes and, ultimately, their behavior. Similarly, one goal of the business of teaching is to bring about learning (which, by definition, involves a change in behavior), and one goal of psychotherapy is to change people's emotional and behavioral responses.

All these can involve what is termed **behavior management,** which is the deliberate and systematic application of learning principles in an attempt to modify behavior. The application of Pavlovian principles is often labeled **behavior therapy;** the systematic use of operant learning principles is more often termed *behavior modification.*

A large variety of specific, conditioning-based behavior management techniques have been developed. Four of the most common are described briefly here.

Positive Reinforcement and Punishment

As we just saw, both positive reinforcement and punishment can be highly effective for modifying behavior, and both are well known and widespread in everyday life. Parents praise children to toilet-train them, employers give bonuses for hard work, and teachers smile at diligent students. Each of these is an example of reinforcement. Parents may also withhold praise or scold when children fail to reach the bathroom in time, employers may withhold pay for tardiness, and teachers might express disapproval toward lazy students: Each of these is an example of punishment.

The systematic use of rewards, and occasionally of punishment as well (often in the form of response-cost or time-out procedures, described earlier), is a common aspect of many behavior modification programs. For example, these might be used to control misbehavior in a classroom, to encourage verbal interaction for children who are shy, or to bring about better study habits. Sometimes the exact relationship between specific behaviors and rewards (or punishments) is spelled out in a written document (labeled a *contingency contract*).

Research indicates that specific, well-planned behavior management strategies are typically more effective than are more informal, less-organized approaches (Jack, Shores, Denny, & Gunter, 1996). The most effective of these programs are often those based on positive rather than aversive contingencies (Carpenter & McKee-Higgins, 1996). When these programs are based on positive reinforcement, they often use tokens as reinforcers. Typically, these can later be exchanged for more meaningful reinforcement. Money is an especially effective token, note Dickinson and Poling (1996), following a review of eight studies that used various schedules of monetary rewards.

Not surprisingly, behavior management consultants who are trained in the development and application of behavior management programs can be very effective in assisting teachers and parents with behavior problems. For example, Cicero and Pfadt (2002) describe a program that used a combination of reinforcement and punishment to toilet train three children with autism. In less than two weeks of training, "urination accidents" had been eliminated for all three children.

Counterconditioning

As we saw in Chapter 2, Guthrie describes how some undesirable habits that have been conditioned to certain stimuli can sometimes be replaced with different, incompatible responses to the same stimuli through a process called counterconditioning.

Counterconditioning has been extensively studied with animals. For example, Bouton and Peck (1992) conditioned a stimulus to the presentation of food (conditioning) and then conditioned the same stimulus to the presentation of shock (counterconditioning). Under these conditions, the animal first learns an appropriate food-related response to the stimulus (eating), but then quickly learns a shock-related response (like jerking its head). Interestingly, however, counterconditioning does not destroy the original association. Bouton and Peck report that after a 28-day lapse, the original response had recovered spontaneously.

Counterconditioning is sometimes used in **psychotherapy** and is well illustrated by *systematic desensitization* (Wolpe, 1958), a method used primarily in the treatment of anxieties and phobias (fears). Highly simplified, systematic desensitization involves three steps. First, the patient describes all the situations that bring about the unwanted behavior, listing these in hierarchical order from least to most likely to produce the behavior. Next, the therapist teaches the patient a response that is incompatible with the unwanted response—almost invariably a relaxation response because relaxing is incompatible with fear or anxiety. The final step is to present the mildest stimulus while the patient is relaxing and to continue presenting progressively more potent stimuli until the patient begins to feel uncomfortable. At that point, the therapist stops, and relaxation is again practiced. The object of the procedure is eventually to present the strongest stimulus without eliciting the unwanted reaction. (This procedure is a sophisticated version of Guthrie's threshold technique, described in Chapter 2.)

Counterconditioning procedures have also successfully been used in the medical field. For example, Smeijsters and van den Berk (1995) treated a patient who suffered from a form of epilepsy that is readily elicited by music (labeled musicogenic epilepsy)—in her case, by almost any kind of music. Over time, these investigators were able to condition imagery and specific keywords to musical stimuli so that, in the end, the woman could listen to certain kinds of music without experiencing seizures. A second example of counterconditioning in medical practice involved pairing pleasant activities with simulated medical routines with young children to countercondition responses incompatible with fear, pain, and anxiety before the actual medical procedures themselves (invasive procedures such as bone marrow aspiration, lumbar puncture, or venipuncture) (Slifer, Babbitt, & Cataldo, 1995).

Extinction

Just as Skinner's rats could be made to stop pressing a lever by disconnecting the food mechanism, so can humans often be made to stop engaging in some unwanted form of behavior by removing their source of reinforcement. This technique can be used whenever a behavior is maintained by positive reinforcement that is under the control of the experimenter or therapist. For example, certain attention-seeking behaviors in young children can be extinguished simply by not paying attention to them. Walker and Shea (1991) describe a situation in which a student, John, continually disrupted his class by making weird noises that made everybody laugh. Each time the teacher drew attention to the behavior by reprimanding John, the class would laugh again (and John would laugh hardest). In the end, the class was instructed to ignore John; all students who did would be rewarded with free time. John continued to make noises for a few days, but no one paid any attention. A week later, the behavior appeared to have been extinguished.

Extinction Using Noncontingent Reinforcement

As a second example of extinction, Hanley, Piazza, and Fisher (1997) successfully treated attention-reinforced destructive behavior in two boys (ages 11 and 16) by deliberately and systematically paying attention to them when they were *not* being destructive. This, the use of noncontingent reinforcement, is a widely used extinction procedure. Essentially, an extinction procedure based on noncontingent reinforcement does not remove the reinforcement that has been maintaining the undesired behavior, but simply rearranges its presentation so that it is no longer contingent upon the undesired behavior. Instead, the reinforcer is presented at other times.

Ⓢkinner's Position: An Appraisal

"Behavioral science," writes Mills, "reached its highest and most complete development in Skinner's writings" (1998, p. 123). More than half a century after the theory was first proposed, it continues to be the most comprehensive and the most researched analysis of human behavior currently available (Vargas, 2001). Not surprisingly, Skinner is widely regarded as one of the "master builders" of psychology; he stands out in the history of psychological thinking as one of its great spokesmen and popularizers.

Although Watson defined behaviorism and many other theorists have contributed significantly to its development, Skinner's name is most often associated with behavioristic psychology.

Contributions

When 186 psychologists were asked to rate psychology's top authors and to list the books that undergraduate psychology majors should read, Skinner's *Beyond Freedom and Dignity* (1971) was among the five books most often listed. These same psychologists also rated Skinner as one of psychology's top five authors (Norcross & Tomcho, 1994).

Probably Skinner's greatest contribution to the understanding of human behavior is his description of the effects of reinforcement on responding. In addition, he extrapolated these findings to individuals and to social groups, and even to entire cultures (see, for example, Skinner, 1948, 1953, 1971). As O'Donohue and Ferguson (2001) note, many of today's problems—overpopulation, pollution, conflict, and war—are problems of human behavior. Skinner's dream was that a science of human behavior that seeks to predict and control behavior would help solve some of these problems.

Through his numerous books and presentations, and because of his remarkable leadership skills, Skinner has had a tremendous influence on many theorists, many of whom have incorporated large portions of his system into their own positions. His theory has also been applied directly in many areas. For example, among the tangible applications of Skinner's work is programmed instruction—a teaching technique premised specifically on principles of operant conditioning. A second very important application of Skinnerian principles, as we saw, is behavior modification.

Evaluation as a Theory

With respect to the criteria for good theories described in Chapter 1, Skinner's system fares relatively well. It is a well-defined, highly researched system that reflects the facts, especially as they relate to the relationships between reinforcing events and the characteristics of responding. It is a clear and understandable system that explains some aspects of behavior remarkably well and allows predictions that can be verified. It isn't based on many unverified assumptions, and it has led to a tremendous amount of research and advancement in the understanding of behavior.

Some Philosophical Objections

Some critics insist that Skinner's operant conditioning does not explain symbolic processes and says little about other topics of interest to contemporary cognitive theorists (decision making, problem solving, perception, and so on). Others are dissatisfied with his attempts to explain language through reinforcement theory. Still others, as we will see in the next chapter, think he neglected the role of biology in learning.

On the other side of the argument are those psychologists who argue that Skinner's system does deal with cognitive topics, and that many have simply confused radical behaviorism's rejection of the usefulness of invoking mental events as explanations with a rejection of the existence of these mental events. Skinner's work has been widely misunderstood, claim Malone and Cruchon (2001). For example, summaries of the theory have tended to overlook his contribution to the understanding of verbal behavior. Similarly, psychology tends to ignore Skinner's explanation for "mentalistic" concepts such as self awareness—which he believed arose from those environmental contingencies that reinforce humans for discriminating (being aware of) their own behavior (O'Donohue & Ferguson, 2001).

If most important human behaviors are operant, the importance of Skinner's explanations can hardly be overestimated. There is controversy, however, about the extent to which behavior is controlled by reinforcement contingencies. Many—most notably humanistic psychologists—consider Skinner's view an assault on human freedom and dignity. If we are controlled by the environment (that is, by the reinforcements and punishments of the environment), the argument goes, then we cannot be free. Thus, on the surface, a Skinnerian position seems incompatible with a concern for human worth and individuality.

"When I question the supposed freedom of autonomous man," Skinner retorted, "I am not debating the issue of free will. I am simply describing the slow demise of a prescientific explanatory device" (1973, p. 261). "Autonomous man," Skinner explains elsewhere, "is a device used to explain what we cannot explain in any other way. He has been constructed of our ignorance, and as our understanding increases, the very stuff of which he is composed vanishes" (1971, p. 200). In brief, as Rockwell (1994) notes, Skinner wasn't trying to provide proof that free will does not exist; rather, he was arguing against what he considered unscientific and futile explanations for human behavior.

That, in a nutshell, is radical behaviorism.

Humans are controlled by their environments, Skinner insists, but humans have built these environments, which they continue to control to some extent. A science of human behavior, the development of which was always Skinner's goal, brings the possibility of applying science for the benefit of all humanity.

In his controversial and sometimes violently attacked novel, *Walden Two*, Skinner (1948) describes how his science of behavior might be applied in a community of about 1,000 people. These people lead what Skinner terms "the good life": they work only a few hours a day; enjoy the highest standards of education, health, and recreation; and are intelligent and happy. "Some readers may take the book as written tongue in cheek," he wrote, "but it was actually a quite serious proposal" (Skinner, 1969, p. 29).

One defense against Skinner's critics, proposed by Amsel (1992), is that most don't attack the system as described by Skinner, but attack, instead, a caricature of the system—an exaggeration of its most obvious features. Skinner's ultimate defense against his critics is that many were objecting not to the theory but to their interpretation of its implications. In short, they don't like what humanity seems to be. But as Skinner noted, "No theory changes what it is a theory about; man remains what he has always been" (1971, p. 215).

Summary

1. Although sometimes interpreted as antitheoretical, Skinner objects not to theories (he considers them essential) but to the kinds of theories that appeal to speculative, mentalistic inventions to explain observed events. Skinner's *radical behaviorism* (*radical* meaning *root*, so-called because he was looking for the *root* causes of behavior) describes human behavior as lawful and insists that psychology should look at external rather than internal factors to explain it.

2. Skinner's experimental analysis of behavior looks for laws that govern interactions between organism and environment. It examines the relationship between independent variables (reinforcement types and schedules) and dependent variables (rate of acquisition, rate of responding, and extinction rate). Influenced by both Pavlov and Thorndike, Skinner identifies two major types of learning: that involving stimulus-elicited responses, explainable using a Pavlovian model (respondents; Type S or classical conditioning); and that involving emitted instrumental acts, explainable because of their consequences (operants; Type R or operant conditioning).

3. Operant learning occurs when there is a change in the probability of a response as a function of events that immediately follow it (response contingencies). Events that increase the probability of a response are termed *reinforcers*. Aspects of the situation accompanying reinforcement become discriminative stimuli (S^D) that serve as secondary reinforcers.

4. Reinforcers can be positive (effective through their presentation; reward) or negative (effective through their removal; relief). Removal punishment involves removing a pleasant consequence (penalty); presentation punishment involves presenting an aversive consequence (castigation) following behavior.

5. Primary reinforcers satisfy basic needs (such as food satisfying hunger); secondary reinforcers become reinforcing through association with a primary reinforcer (for example, a light in a Skinner box, associated with food, becomes reinforcing in its own right). Generalized reinforcers are stimuli that have been paired with a variety of other reinforcers and have become reinforcing for a variety of behaviors.

6. Reinforcement schedules can be continuous (every correct response is reinforced) or intermittent (or partial). Intermittent schedules can be based on proportion of responses (ratio) or on time lapse (interval). Both ratio and interval schedules can be either fixed (unvarying) or random (variable). Superstitious schedules are fixed-interval schedules where reinforcement occurs at fixed times no matter what the organism is doing.

7. Continuous schedules lead to rapid acquisition and rapid extinction. Intermittent schedules lead to longer extinction times but are less efficient for early training. Rate of responding typically corresponds to the expectations of reward an animal or person is likely to develop during training.

8. Extinction (a rapid process, sometimes followed by spontaneous recovery) is the elimination of a behavior through the withdrawal of reinforcement. Forgetting (a slower process) is the elimination of behavior through the passage of time.

9. Shaping, a technique used to bring about novel behavior in animals, involves reinforcing responses that move in the desired direction until the final response has been conditioned. Chaining is the linking of sequences of responses by virtue of discriminative stimuli that are all linked to the same primary reinforcer. Verbal conditioning involves reinforcing certain verbal behaviors, often through nonverbal signs of approval.

10. Fading brings about discrimination learning by exaggerating differences in early training and then phasing them out. Generalization involves transferring one response to other stimuli; discrimination involves making different responses for highly similar stimuli.

11. Social control through the use of positive reinforcement is common and effective. Control through more aversive means (such as negative reinforcement and punishment) is also effective and prevalent. Objections to punishment are based on the observations that (a) it does not tell

the offender what to do but merely what not to do, (b) it often results in suppressing behavior but not eliminating it, (c) it may have some undesirable emotional side effects, and (d) it often does not work, sometimes having effects opposite to those intended. Some forms of punishment (such as reprimands, time-out, and response-cost methods) are not subject to the same criticisms.

12. Some techniques for modifying behavior include positive reinforcement, extinction, and counterconditioning. Another important practical application of Skinnerian principles is programmed instruction.

13. Skinner's system explains and predicts certain behaviors remarkably well, is internally consistent and clear, and reflects some facts well. It has passionate critics, however, many of whom object to its search for explanations outside the person and its apparent denial of freedom and autonomy.

Evolutionary Psychology: Learning, Biology, and the Brain

The Brain—is wider than the Sky—
For—put them side by side—
The one the other will contain
With ease—and You—beside
Emily Dickinson

The Old Woman bent to unfasten each of the straps that bound a canvas knapsack of the kind soldiers might once have taken with them to distant wars, olive green as though army intelligence were uncertain whether the war would be fought in summer or in fall and so had blended the hues of each to hide their soldiers. From it she drew a shape wrapped in wax paper, which she set carefully on her knees. For a long moment she simply stared at it, and then she slowly peeled back the paper, layer after layer, to reveal in the end a glass jar such as might once have contained mayonnaise.

The Old Woman held the jar toward the sun, her gnarled fingers covering the side closest to me so that I could not immediately tell what might be in the jar. A stranger might have thought the look on her face one of wonderment, of amazement, though I could not easily fathom her feelings.

Reaching with her other hand, the Old Woman slowly unscrewed the lid that was dotted with tiny holes where someone might have repeatedly driven a nail through the metal. And then, an orange-colored butterfly, a monarch, emerged hesitantly from the jar, perched delicately on its rim for an instant, and fluttered away. The Old Woman screwed the lid back on, wrapped the jar once more in the wax paper, and put the bundle back into her knapsack.

She said that most adult butterflies live only about 10 days, which is a great sadness for poets, but that the monarch butterfly, which had just now left the jar, survives for months.

She said she expected this monarch would now migrate some enormous distance, probably all the way to Mexico. She said the monarch is very much like the heliconius butterfly. Both are genetically programmed to live a long time by butterfly standards, and both share a remarkable adaptation. She said I would have noticed that the monarch, like the heliconius, is a brightly colored butterfly. She said I would also have noticed that butterflies, especially those that are brightly colored, flit about unpredictably when they fly, the effect being that although their color makes them highly visible to birds and cats, their erratic flight makes it difficult for would-be predators to catch them. She said if I saw one, I would notice immediately that the heliconius, like the monarch, doesn't flit about unpredictably like most other butterflies, but instead flies a slow, deliberate pattern. Yet these butterflies fly among butterfly-eating birds at will, without danger.

Why? Simply because they are so poisonous to birds as to be highly distasteful to them. You see, said the Old Woman, the heliconius is immune to a poisonous vine—the passion vine—that even leaf-eating caterpillars avoid. And the heliconius not only gorges itself on the passion vine but synthesizes its poisons, thus becoming toxic itself. And the monarch does much the same thing when, as a larva, it chomps away at the milkweed plant that contains a compound that is poisonous to vertebrates. The monarch eventually

accumulates enough of this compound to be-
come highly distasteful to the birds that would
otherwise eat it. And so birds avoid these bril-
liant, slow-flying butterflies.

Do they avoid these butterflies because of a
built-in, genetically based aversion? No. In
fact, naive birds attack (and generally con-
sume) just about anything that looks like a
butterfly or a moth. But once they have eaten
one poisonous heliconius or monarch, they
don't eat a second.

They learn this taste aversion in a single
trial. Not only does it prevent them from
getting sick or even dying, but it also saves
the lives of countless slow-flying heliconius
and monarch butterflies.[1]

The Old Woman motioned that I should now
record her words. She leaned back on the grass
by the willow using the knapsack as a pillow.
I couldn't decide where to sit or whether I, too,
should lie down. I stood. It looked like it might
rain.

Ⓣ his Chapter

The Old Woman said that the importance of taste-aversion learning would become apparent in this chapter. She said that the first four chapters of this text
have described two basic types of conditioning: classical and operant conditioning. Theorists associated with each of these—for example, Ivan Pavlov, John B.
Watson, Edwin Guthrie, Edward L. Thorndike, Clark L. Hull, and B. F. Skinner
—typically assumed (a) that these explanations are broad descriptions of learning,
generally applicable in all similar situations, and (b) that the basic explanatory
principles of contiguity and reinforcement also apply in all situations.

Objectives

Tell your readers, said the Old Woman, that
Chapter 5 explains that these views are not
always entirely correct. Make them under-
stand that after they finish this chapter they
will, with startling ease and elegance, be able
to write long dissertations explaining the
following:

■ *The meaning of evolutionary psychology*

■ *The Rescorla-Wagner view of Pavlovian*
conditioning

■ *The significance of phenomena such as*
blocking, instinctive drift, and auto-
shaping

■ *The meaning of biological constraints and*
preparedness

■ *The structures and functions of the human*
brain

■ *Why some long-lived butterflies are flying*
cyanide factories

---

[1]The account of the heliconius is based on Murawski (1993).

Taste Aversion Learning

In psychological terms, the Old Woman explained, what the bird that eats a poisonous butterfly acquires is a taste aversion: a marked dislike for a particular food. As the story of the butterfly shows, taste aversions are sometimes very important in biological terms. If poisons have distinctive tastes, and if they don't immediately kill the organism that eats them but simply make the organism sick, then developing a strong aversion to those tastes might prevent a later poisoning. What is important biologically is that the taste aversion be powerful and that it develop immediately—preferably after a single exposure to the poison.

Conditioning Explanations for Taste Aversions

The conditioning theories described in the early part of this book are of two general kinds: those that deal with behaviors resulting directly from stimulation (respondents) and those dealing with behaviors that are simply emitted by the organism (operants). Behavioristic theories offer two different sets of explanations for respondent and operant learning: classical conditioning and the law of effect, respectively (Herrnstein, 1977).

In their simplest and most basic form, the laws of classical conditioning state that when a neutral stimulus is accompanied or slightly preceded by an effective stimulus (for example, a stimulus that elicits a reflex) often enough, the neutral stimulus will eventually acquire some of the properties previously associated only with the effective stimulus. Thus, a dog eventually comes to salivate (CR) in response to a tone (previously neutral stimulus—CS) after the tone has been paired a number of times with food (effective stimulus—US).

The law of effect, also in its simplest form, maintains that a behavior that is followed by a reinforcing state of affairs will tend to be repeated; one that is not followed by reinforcement will tend not to be repeated. Furthermore, aspects of the situations in which behaviors have been reinforced (or not reinforced) come to exercise a degree of control over the occurrence or nonoccurrence of the behavior. Thus, a dog that is reinforced for rolling over whenever its master says "Roll over" may eventually discriminate between the commands "Roll over" and "Fetch my slippers." At this point, these verbal commands will have acquired stimulus control over the behaviors in question.

Problems with Classical Conditioning Explanations of Taste Aversions
At first glance, classical conditioning might appear to be a good explanation for taste aversion learning. Neutral stimuli (CS), such as the sight and taste of a butterfly, are paired with a powerful unconditioned stimulus (US), such as the poisons in the butterfly, and become associated with the same illness related responses (CR). (See Figure 5.1.)

But several characteristics of acquired taste aversions make a Pavlovian classical conditioning explanation less than perfect. First, a Pavlovian view of

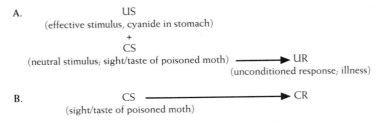

A.   US
          (effective stimulus, cyanide in stomach)
                              +
                             CS
     (neutral stimulus; sight/taste of poisoned moth) ⟶ UR
                                            (unconditioned response; illness)

B.   CS ⟶ CR
             (sight/taste of poisoned moth)

Figure 5.1 A classical conditioning explanation of taste aversion learning. That taste aversions are often learned after a single experience, and that there are sometimes long delays between the UR (illness) and the US/UR pairing (eating of the moth), present problems for this explanation.

classical conditioning, such as that described by Watson, maintains that conditioning results from the *repeated* pairing of stimulus and response events; yet taste aversion learning often occurs in a *single* trial.

Second, learning in Pavlovian classical conditioning is thought to depend on contiguity—that is, on the near simultaneity of events. In taste aversion learning, though, the unconditioned response (the violent illness) sometimes occurs many minutes, or even hours, after the CS.

Third, classical conditioning principles maintain that any neutral stimulus can be associated with any US if paired with it often enough, but in taste aversion learning, organisms often display a marked selectivity in their learning. As a result, certain associations are never learned, but others are learned extremely readily.

These three characteristics of taste aversion learning are well illustrated in controlled experiments with various animals.

- one experience effects for everyone

One-Trial Acquisition of Taste Aversions

Birds don't need to eat bushels of heliconius butterflies before learning to avoid them; a single experience is sufficient. Similarly, rats exposed to a single dose of lithium chloride or radiation so that they become ill after eating will subsequently avoid the food they ate before getting sick. For example, a profound aversion to alcohol can be conditioned in rats following a single dose of lithium chloride (Thiele, Kiefer, & Badia-Elder, 1996). This effect has been found as long as 32 days after a single pairing of food and radiation (Garcia & Koelling, 1966). Under some conditions, taste aversions even increase in intensity following a single pairing of CS and US (Batsell & George, 1996).

Delayed Conditioning of Taste Aversions

Recall that in Pavlovian conditioning, the normal sequence is to present the conditioning stimulus (bell or tone, for example) just before, or overlapping with, the unconditioned stimulus (food powder, for example). *Trace pairing* in classical conditioning refers to a situation in which the unconditioned stimulus (US) is presented after the conditioned stimulus. As noted in Chapter 2, trace conditioning is ordinarily very difficult unless the time lapse between CS and US is extremely short (usually only half a second). Yet taste aversion in rats is learned following a single trial, and it can be extremely powerful even when there is a delay of as much as 24 hours between the conditioning stimulus (the taste of food, in this case) and the effects of the unconditioned stimulus (illness) (Logue, 1988).

In humans, too, taste aversions are powerful and quickly learned. And they are learned by children and by adults. Bernstein and Webster (1980) gave adult patients who were receiving chemotherapeutic drugs (which cause nausea) one of two distinctly flavored ice creams. Subsequent testing revealed that these adults had developed strong aversions to flavors they had tasted before chemotherapy. This happened even though these adults knew that the cause of their illness was the drug and not the ice cream.[2] In fact, in some studies of humans, taste aversions are learned even with CS-US delays of more than 6 hours (Logue, 1988).

Like other forms of classical conditioning, taste aversion learning can also involve stimulus generalization. Thus, aversions are often generalized to other foods that taste or smell similar (Chotro & Alonso, 2003). In the same way, taste aversions can be extinguished after trying an offending food sufficiently often, providing it isn't followed by illness.

[handwritten margin note: - taste aversion to similiar foods]

Latent Inhibition in Taste Aversion Learning

That taste aversions often occur a long time after exposure to an illness-inducing food is referred to as **latent inhibition.** The phenomenon of latent inhibition is marked by an important kind of selectivity. For example, if you eat something new that later makes you violently ill, chances are the taste aversion you develop will not be associated with the utensils with which you ate, the television program you were watching at the time, or any of the other familiar things you ate and drank. Instead, it will be associated only with the *new* taste. And this happens even when the illness occurs hours later.

"But," you say, "we can figure it out. We *know* that the new food is what made us ill." But no: Taste aversions aren't conscious, cognitive decisions; they're unavoidable physical reactions (Baeyens, Vansteenwegen, Hermans, & Eelen, 2001). When you try to poison a rat, for example, and you succeed in getting him to take a small bite of your poison, if that bite later makes the rat ill, it may well develop a powerful aversion to anything that smells and tastes like your poison— but not to any of the other foods it may have eaten at about the same time. That, in fact, is why it's very hard to poison rats. The rat, like most other nonhuman animals, is likely to taste strange foods, but not to eat very much of them if there are other familiar foods around. If the strange new food doesn't make the rat ill,

---

[2]The Old Woman interrupted her reading. She said she wanted to say something here about the human propensity to think that behavior is mostly a function of conscious awareness. She said that taste aversions are just one of many types of behavior that depend not on conscious awareness but on principles of conditioning as well as on evolutionary factors. She explained that other behaviors, like phobias, also illustrate the occasional impotence of reason and conscious awareness—such as how people continue to be afraid of things like spiders or snakes or birds even when they know them to be absolutely harmless. Then she turned to her pages once more. It started to rain a little. She continued reading as if the sudden dampness didn't bother her. I felt cold.

it may well eat a lot more next time. But if the food does make the rat ill, the taste aversion will be associated with the new, rather than with the familiar (Grakalic & Riley, 2002). It's as though the connection between the offending food and its ill effects remain possible (hence, *latent*), until the occurrence—or non-occurrence—of the unconditioned response (illness). If there is no unconditioned response, no aversion learning occurs.

Selectivity in Taste Aversion Learning

If a rat is injected with a solution of lithium chloride while it is drinking saccharin-flavored water, it will later avoid foods that taste of saccharin (although it doesn't become ill until about an hour after the injection). This observation appears reasonable given what is known about contiguity and classical conditioning. But if a rat is made ill and exposed to flashing lights or a distinct noise while drinking saccharin-flavored water, it will develop no aversion to the lights or the sound, but only to the taste (Garcia & Koelling, 1966).

The same point is made even more dramatically in studies of cross-species aversion learning. Wilcoxon, Dragoin, and Kral (1971) produced aversions in rats and in quail by feeding them blue-colored, flavored water and later injecting them with an illness-inducing drug. Both the rats and the quail developed marked aversions, but the nature of these aversions was significantly different. The rats developed an aversion to any liquid with the flavor in question regardless of its color; the quail developed an aversion to all blue-colored liquids regardless of their flavor.

One explanation for these findings is simply that quail have excellent color vision and probably rely to a considerable extent on visual cues to sort what is edible from what is not. In contrast, rats—like most other mammals—depend mostly on olfactory (smell) rather than visual cues. It therefore makes biological sense that rats should make use of smell cues in learning about foods that should be avoided, and it makes biological sense for quail to use visual cues in the same kind of learning (Garcia, Ervin, & Koelling, 1965; Rozin & Kalat, 1971).

The Phenomenon of Blocking

It appears, then, that not just any stimulus can be classically conditioned—as is evident in the fact that quail acquire a powerful aversion associated with color, but rats do not. Thus, there appears to be more involved in taste aversion learning than the simple co-occurrence (contiguity) of events. Another phenomenon that presents problems for a simple contiguity explanation of classical conditioning is a phenomenon known as **blocking.**

In the first well-known demonstration of blocking, Kamin (1969) paired two stimuli (a noise and a light) with an electric shock administered to the feet of a group of rats (we'll call them the A group). The procedure was to turn both the light and the noise on for 3 minutes, then follow them immediately with the electric shock. Classical conditioning theory would predict that after enough pairings with the electrical shock, either the light or the noise would

	Pretraining	Conditioning	Testing	Response
A Group (control)	None	Noise + Light → Shock	Light	Freezing (high fear)
B Group (blocking)	Noise → Shock	Noise + Light → Shock	Light	Bar Pressing (no fear)

Figure 5.2 A representation of Kamin's study of blocking in classical conditioning. For A-group rats, exposed to both noise and light followed by a shock, exposure to the light alone leads to a marked suppression of ongoing bar-pressing behavior. But B-group rats, who had previously learned that noise means shock, failed to learn that light might also mean shock.

bring about reactions similar to those associated with the electric shock. The prediction is correct: A-group rats responded with fear to either the noise alone, or the light alone—an unconditioned response to electric shock.

Now Kamin threw a twist into the proceedings. First, he conditioned a second group of rats using only the noise (we'll call them the B group). As before, he followed 3 minutes of the noise with an electric foot shock. Then, after B-group rats had been conditioned to the noise alone, he conditioned them in exactly the same way as he had the A group—pairing both the noise and the light again for 3-minute periods, then following each pairing with an electric shock. (The procedure is shown in Figure 5.2.)

Now B-group rats were exposed to the light alone. Recall that when the A-group rats were exposed to the light alone they stopped bar pressing. Classical conditioning theory would predict exactly the same outcome for B-group rats, because the light had been paired with the noise equally often for both groups. Amazingly, however, B-group rats continued to press the bar at about the same rate, seemingly unaffected by the light.

Explanations of Blocking

Kamin's pioneering experiments in blocking suggested the need for different explanations of what happens—and why—in certain examples of classical conditioning. Among the most widely accepted of the resulting explanations is the one known as the **Rescorla-Wagner model.**

The Rescorla-Wagner Model
The Rescorla-Wagner model is a mathematical model developed specifically to explain conditioning phenomena such as blocking. What the model says, in effect, is that classical conditioning is the formation of an association between a CS and a US. Furthermore, the likelihood that the CS will lead to the CR, and the magnitude and persistence of the CR, are a function of the strength of the

association between CS and US—their *associative strength*. The model assumes that there is a fixed amount of *associative strength* available for any US-CS pairing, and that the various individual stimuli that make up the CS compete for this associative strength. If the CS, as a compound stimulus, is made up of two or more stimuli, the strength of the association that forms between any one of these component CSs and the US subtracts from the association strength remaining for other component stimuli. Thus, in Kamin's blocking study, the B-group rats first learn an association between noise (CS) and shock (US). That they later fail to learn an association between light and shock, says the model, is explained by the fact that all of the associative strength between the US (shock) and the CS has been used up by the noise-shock pairing.

The Rescorla-Wagner model has proven to be a popular explanation for blocking and related phenomena. Furthermore, it has stimulated an enormous amount of research on classical conditioning. Much of this research has looked at blocking in human learning (for example, Mitchell & Lovibond, 2002). In a typical human blocking study, for instance, participants might be told that a meal consisting of two different foods (X and Y) will be followed by an allergic reaction. If they later learn that X causes the allergic reaction, they will subsequently have trouble learning that Y also causes an allergic reaction in much the same way as the rat that has learned that noise means shock now fails to learn that light might also mean shock. Thus, as Pearce and Bouton (2001) note, theories of blocking have important implications for understanding how humans judge causality.

A Biological Explanation: Learning What Goes with What

There are other more intuitive and more biologically based explanations of phenomena such as blocking. Why, for example, might a rat conditioned to associate a noise with shock subsequently be unable to learn that a light might also mean shock?

Well, said Kamin (1968), the most likely explanation is this: Whenever something important happens to an animal, it immediately searches its memory to see what events could have been used to predict the occurrence. When a red-tailed hawk swoops down on a chicken but narrowly misses, scaring the living begorrah out of the chicken, the chicken searches its memory banks for immediately preceding events. And maybe it remembers a swift shadow darkening its path, or the whistling of wing feathers braking. And forever after, the chicken flees from shadows and whistling noises.

So when the rat receives a mild foot shock, it stops and scans its memory to see what was different and unexpected immediately before this event. Because the A-group rat notes that light and noise always precede the shock, it freezes when it later sees the light—or hears the noise.

But the B-group rat has had different experiences. First, it learned that a noise always precedes a foot shock, and so when it again hears this noise, it cowers and stops pressing the bar. Later it is exposed to both the light and the noise, followed by the shock. But it learns nothing new because the shock is already predicted by the noise; the light provides no new information about the occurrence of the CS. There is no discrepancy between what the subjects expect (the shock) and what occurs (the shock). So, when the B-group rat is later exposed only to the light, it keeps right on pressing the bar. In a sense, having learned that noise means a shock is coming *blocks* the rat from learning that light might mean the same thing.

What this explanation says, in effect, is that classical conditioning means learning what goes with what. Contiguity is not as important as the information a stimulus provides about the probability of other events. Thus, what is learned is a connection or an expectation. Pavlov's dog learns that a buzzer or the sight of a handler means it can expect to be fed; a rat learns that a light or a sound means a shock is about to occur. In Rescorla and Holland's words, "Pavlovian conditioning should be viewed as the learning about relations among events" (1976, p. 184).

Higher-Order Conditioning

In classical conditioning, the organism typically learns about an association between a normally significant event (such as the presentation of food; the US), and one that has less or different importance (such as a tone; the CS). As Pavlov pointed out, though, the relations learned in classical conditioning are not limited to those that might exist between the CS and US but include what is termed **higher-order conditioning.** In higher-order conditioning, another stimulus becomes a significant event in place of the US. For example, Rescorla (1980) describes how a Pavlovian dog learns a connection between a metronome and food. Later the metronome is paired with a second stimulus, a black square. And although the black square is itself never paired with food, in time it too elicits salivation.

As Pavlov (and Watson) interpreted it, higher-order conditioning expands the applicability of classical conditioning tremendously, explaining how associations build on each other to construct a repertoire of responses. For Rescorla, higher-order conditioning is even more important as a way of understanding how associations are formed. In general, says Rescorla, "conditioning [is] the learning that results from exposure to relations among events in the environment. Such learning is a primary means by which the organism represents the structure of its world" (1988, p. 152).

Conditioning as Biological Adaptation

It is clear, according to Rescorla, that contiguity is not sufficient to explain classical conditioning. If it were, Kamin's B-group rats would have learned the same thing about the light as did the A-group rats. In fact, contiguity isn't even necessary for classical conditioning—as is clear in taste aversion studies where the aversive stimulus may be presented after the conditioning stimulus (for example, in the form of an injection or radiation).

One useful way of looking at classical conditioning is to say that organisms "adjust their Pavlovian associations only when they are 'surprised,'" claims Rescorla (1988, p. 153). That is because organisms experience surprise only when expectations are not met (in other words, when there is new information). The B-group rat that has learned an association between noise and shock does not modify that association when noise and light are paired with shock. Thanks to the noise signal, the shock is not a surprise; it doesn't violate expectations. Hence, there is no new information in the light, and no new associations result. Thus, says Rescorla, it is nonsense "that a signal simply acquires the ability to evoke the response to the US" (1988, p. 157), as is suggested by simple interpretations of Pavlovian conditioning.

Learning is essentially an adaptive process. That is, the changes in behavior that define learning are what allow organisms to survive and thrive. At a very basic level, animals need to learn and remember where food sources might be (as does the rat that learns to depress a lever for food); they need to recognize potential enemies (as did the chicken following its near-death experience); they need to avoid potentially harmful substances (as does the bird that has eaten a single heliconius butterfly); and they need to stay away from potentially painful or even injurious situations (such as electric shocks).

Darwinian Natural Selection and Psychology

That biological and evolutionary pressures toward survival should be evident in the principles that govern human and animal learning is hardly surprising. As Robertson, Garcia, and Garcia (1988) note, Darwin was, himself, a learning theorist. He was well acquainted with associationistic explanations of learning, and he invoked these principles in his own theory of natural selection.

Barrett, Dunbar, and Lycett (2002) summarize Darwin's **theory of natural selection** in three clear premises and the consequences that logically follow:

- All individuals of a species vary both behaviorally and physiologically.
- Some of this variation is genetic (heritable), so that offspring will tend to resemble their parents more than the offspring resemble other unrelated individuals.
- Among individuals of any given species, there is typically competition for important resources (such as food, mates, shelter).

The logical consequences of these three premises are clear: Behavioral and physiological variations that allow more success in the competition for resources give certain individuals an edge in the struggle to survive and to procreate. As a result, they produce more offspring who inherit the same, advantageous variations. Similarly, individuals whose behavioral and physiological variations place them at a disadvantage produce fewer offspring. This evolutionary process of natural selection leads to the survival of certain variations—those with the highest degree of **fitness**—and the elimination of those that have less desirable consequences.

As we saw earlier, this theory profoundly influenced conditioning theorists. Theorists such as Skinner and Thorndike noted that all sorts of responses appear when an organism behaves. These different responses are like variations of a characteristic in biological terms. In the same way as the *fitness* of an inherited variation is evident in the likelihood of its becoming more frequent in succeeding generations, the *fitness* of a response, evident in its consequences, is reflected in the probability that it will be retained or eliminated. In brief, conditioning may be described as the survival (and death) of responses. Behaviors whose consequences are most adaptive are most likely to survive.

Evolutionary Psychology

Thorndike's and Skinner's theories can be interpreted as being influenced by, and reflecting, Darwinian ideas. A profound Darwinian influence is also found in works of many other psychologists, who are sometimes labeled *evolutionary psychologists.* Among the first of these was George John Romanes (1848–1894). His classical work on animal intelligence (1883) was based on careful observation of the behaviors of dozens of different animals and insects, always with a view to uncovering the causes and the purposes of their actions. His overall objective was, quite simply, to describe the course of mental evolution, much as Darwin had described the evolution of species (Galef, 1988).

Evolutionary psychologists, notes Wright (1994), continue to fight the doctrine that has dominated psychology for most of the 20th century. Briefly, this doctrine asserts that biology doesn't really matter, that what is most important is the malleability of the mind and the potency of the environment in molding and shaping the mind. This doctrine holds that there really is no such thing as a genetically determined, human nature common to all humans. It is, says Wright, the doctrine of the passive mind, of the *tabula rasa,* the blank slate on which experience writes its messages.

But there is a human nature, Wright insists. Evidence that it exists is found in the overwhelming similarities that one finds between all the world's cultures. Thus, all people have a tendency to be concerned about social status and social relations; all feel love and fear and guilt; all gossip about similar things; almost everywhere, males and females assume complementary roles; all have a sense of justice, of envy, of greed, of retribution, of justice, of love. These feelings are taken for granted and understood everywhere. They are part of human nature.

What is also part of human nature—and this is fundamentally important for biologically oriented learning theory—is a built-in malleability. Malleability is what allows the individual to adapt and survive. But, unlike the malleability described by Watson or Skinner, this malleability has limits—it is subject to biological constraints.

The defining characteristic of **evolutionary psychology,** then, is its attention to biology and genetics as sources of explanation for human learning and behavior. Support for the notions of evolutionary psychologists is sometimes based on situations in which reinforcement and contiguity are inadequate as explanations for learning and behavior. Among these situations are phenomena such as **autoshaping** and **instinctive drift.**

Autoshaping

If a pigeon receives reinforcement at intervals regardless of what it is doing at the time, the result might be what Skinner has described as superstitious behavior. That is, the pigeon may learn some "accidental" behavior such as twisting or swaying.

If a response key or disk is illuminated for a few seconds just before the appearance of food, however, the pigeon will quickly learn to peck at the key or disk (Brown & Jenkins, 1968). That this behavior occurs and is learned despite the fact that the pigeon's pecking bears no causal relationship to the appearance of food has led to the use of the term *autoshaping* to describe the learning involved. As is shown in Figure 5.3, this type of learning is easily explained using a Pavlovian model of classical conditioning. The pecking response is initially an unconditioned response elicited by the food, an unconditioned stimulus. Following the pairing of light and food, however, the pecking response very quickly becomes associated with the light. Subsequently, experimenters can "shape" the pecking response by making food contingent on its occurrence. In this case, key pecking could be viewed as an operant rather than simply a conditioned response.

Autoshaping can also be demonstrated with rats (for example, Reilly & Grutzmacher, 2002). If you place a rat in a cage in which there are two tubes—one, an empty feeder tube, and the second, a spout from which the rat is periodically fed, the rat will lick the empty tube as well as the one through which the food is presented. Eventually, licking the empty tube will become a strong, autoshaped behavior, even though it has nothing to do with the rat's obtaining food. In an experiment, Tomie and associates (2002) brought about binge drinking sessions in rats by placing a saccharin/ethanol solution in the tube, in a study where obtaining food was independent of licking the tube.

Autoshaped responses are remarkably persistent, and remarkably resistant to extinction. This is dramatically illustrated in an experiment by Killeen (2003), in which pigeons were taught to peck at a light in the manner described. Then conditions were changed so that the pigeons' pecking would prevent reinforcement from occurring. Despite this, even very hungry pigeons continued to peck at the light for *thousands* of trials. Nor is autoshaping of key pecking restricted to pigeons. In other studies, blue jays, robins, and starlings have each demonstrated a propensity for learning to peck lighted keys even when there is no tangible reward contingent on so doing (see Kamil & Mauldin, 1988).

Autoshaping poses a problem for a traditional conditioning explanation of learning. First, it provides an example of behaviors that appear to be learned even though they are not associated with reinforcement. Even more telling, these behaviors often persist even when they are clearly associated with withdrawal of reinforcement.

The most important point that studies of autoshaping make, however, is not that reinforcement exercises little control over operant responses. Rather, the point is that pecking among pigeons is not a very good operant behavior for experimental purposes. A good experimental operant is one of several equally probable responses emitted by the organism for no particular reason; the response

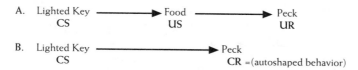

Figure 5.3 Autoshaping. In A, a lighted key is paired with food. The pigeon's response to food is to peck. In B, the pigeon pecks the lighted key even though doing so has nothing to do with obtaining food.

can then be brought under the control of its consequences. Pecking, in contrast, is a highly probable food-related response in pigeons. That a pigeon should continue to peck at a lighted disk even when doing so means it will not be reinforced says more about the pigeon's evolutionary history than about the inadequacies of operant conditioning.

Instinctive Drift

In the early 1950s, two of Skinner's students, encouraged by the remarkable success that experimenters had enjoyed in shaping the behavior of animals, decided to commercialize this process. These students—a husband and wife team, the Brelands—proposed to train a number of animals to perform stunts sufficiently amusing that audiences might pay to see them. Through the "differential reinforcement of successive approximations" (that is, through *shaping*), they taught a raccoon to pick up a coin and deposit it in a tin box; a chicken to pull a rubber loop, thereby releasing a capsule that slid down a chute to where it could be pecked out of the cage; and a pig to pick up large wooden "nickels" and deposit them in a piggy bank. Operant conditioning procedures worked exquisitely; all the animals learned their required behaviors. The Brelands successfully trained more than 6,000 animals (Breland & Breland, 1966).

But not all of these 6,000 animals continued to behave as they had been trained to behave. As Breland and Breland (1951, 1961) put it, many of them eventually began to "misbehave." For example, the pig took longer and longer to bring its wooden nickel to the bank and deposit it, although it clearly knew that reinforcement was contingent on (depended on) doing so.[3] Instead, it spent increasingly longer periods flipping the coins to the ground and then rooting around in the dirt with them, and otherwise behaving as might any other uneducated pig on the trail of the elusive truffle. The Brelands tried to remedy the situation by increasing the pig's food deprivation. But that only made matters

---

[3]The Old Woman said this wasn't very scientifically or accurately worded, that we probably shouldn't say that the pig "clearly knew" anything of the sort. She explained that after all, this was a behavioristic pig, not a humanistic or a cognitive one. She said that all we can say for certain, as behaviorists, is that the pig's shaped responses had been reinforced often enough that the experimenters could justifiably expect it would continue to deposit wooden nickels in piggy banks. She said flatly that what the pig actually thought of the entire process is a matter for speculation, not science.

A. Desired outcome in "banker pig" training procedure:

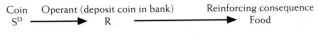

B. Observed outcome in "banker pig" training

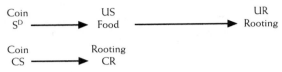

Figure 5.4 Instinctive drift. The desired outcome of the training procedure, shown in A, is explained by the principles of operant conditioning: Depositing the coin in the bank is an operant whose probability should increase as a result of the reinforcing contingency, food. What actually happens, shown in B, is best explained by a model of classical conditioning: The food serves as an unconditioned stimulus that elicits the unconditioned response, rooting. Repeatedly pairing the coin with the food leads to an association between the two so that the coin eventually serves as a conditioned stimulus for rooting.

worse, so that in the end the pig was taking so long to deposit the wooden nickels that it was in imminent danger of starvation.

The raccoon fared no better. It too began to take longer and longer in bringing the coins to the metal box. It often refused to let go of the coins, instead dipping them in the box, bringing them out again, and rubbing them between its paws. And the chicken, not to be left out, became so engrossed in pecking at the capsule that it seemed to quite forget everything else it had learned.

Researchers have now uncovered a large number of situations in which animals initially learn a behavior quickly and well but eventually begin to resort to other behaviors, the nature of which is highly revealing. It is surely no accident that the pig rooted, the raccoon "washed" its coin, or the chicken pecked. These are, after all, what pigs, raccoons, and chickens do with food. "It seems obvious," claimed Breland and Breland, "that these animals are trapped by strongly instinctive behaviors, and clearly we have here a demonstration of the prepotency of such behavior patterns over those which have been conditioned" (1961, p. 683).

In general terms, instinctive drift results when there is competition between a biologically based behavior and a learned response. It appears that with repeated exposure to a situation characterized by this kind of competition, organisms tend to revert to the behavior that has a biological, evolutionary basis. This, the Brelands are careful to point out, does not invalidate general learning principles. In fact, as is shown in Figure 5.4, instinctive drift presents a good example of classical conditioning. But it is an example that emphasizes the importance of biology. Not all behaviors can be conditioned and maintained through the careful arrangement of response consequences.

Biological Constraints

The main characteristic of evolutionary psychology is its attention to biological influences on learning and behavior. Autoshaping, instinctive drift, and the learning of taste aversions are striking examples of biological influences. They illustrate what evolutionary psychologists refer to as **biological constraints** (Hinde & Stevenson-Hinde, 1973; Seligman, 1975; Seligman & Hager, 1972).

A biological constraint is an inborn predisposition that makes certain kinds of learning highly probable and easy and other kinds improbable and very difficult. As Breland and Breland (1966) note, it's very easy to condition a cat or a dog to sit still or stand motionless. For these animals, which evolved as predators, standing still is an extremely useful, survival-related behavior. But, in Breland and Breland's words, "it is almost impossible for a chicken to do nothing" (1966, p. 103). When Breland and Breland tried to teach chickens to stand still, they found these birds absolutely insisted on scurrying around and scratching instead. And, of course, chickens don't have to be trained to scratch. Scratching is how chickens make their living in the wilds; it has clear survival-related benefits for chickens.

The most obvious general principle of a biological constraint is that it will favor behaviors that have survival value and discourage those detrimental to survival. As Kenrick and his associates illustrate, it is possible to predict what will be easy or difficult to learn by reasoning from important social and survival goals (Kenrick, Maner, Butner, Li, & Becker, 2002). For example, that rats (or humans) should learn an aversion to a poisonous taste clearly has survival value. But that they should learn an aversion to a sound or a light when they have been physically poisoned has no such value.

In Seligman and Hager's (1972) terms, organisms are prepared for certain kinds of learning and contraprepared for others—meaning that they are prepared *not* to learn certain things. A rat faced with danger is prepared to flee, fight, freeze, or perhaps become frantic; teaching it to do any of these through the use of aversive stimulation (an electric shock, for example) is a simple matter. But teaching it to engage in a behavior that is opposed to any of these is very difficult. Thus, teaching a rat to depress a lever to escape an electric shock is very difficult (Bolles, 1970). Similarly, a pigeon can easily be taught to peck at a key to obtain food, but not to escape an electric shock. In contrast, the pigeon easily learns to flap its wings to avoid a shock, but not to obtain food.

Biological constraints are clearly involved in the reversion of pigs to rooting and chickens to pecking in the instinctive drift experiments. Similarly, biological constraints affect autoshaped behaviors. For example, pigeons show a marked preference for pecking at keys that are on the floor rather than on a wall—probably because they feed primarily on the ground (Burns & Malone, 1992). Also, biological influences on learning are dramatically evident in single trial taste aversion learning.

It is perhaps less obvious that human learning is strongly influenced by biological factors. People are "prepared" to acquire strong taste aversions very easily. Some also argue that humans are biologically prepared to acquire language, perhaps in much the same way as goslings are programmed to acquire a "following" response if given appropriate stimulation at the right time in their development (Chomsky, 1972). Others insist that many human social behaviors are a direct function of inherited predispositions—that these predispositions and biological constraints shape the nature of human culture (Kenrick et al., 2002; Carporeal, 2001).

Sociobiology: A Precursor of Evolutionary Psychology

The single most important assumption of the discipline labeled **sociobiology** is that humans are biologically predisposed to engage in certain social behaviors rather than others. One of sociobiology's principal spokesmen, Edward O. Wilson (1929–), defines it as "the systematic study of the biological basis of all social behavior" (1975, p. 4). Put another way, sociobiology is the study of the biological determination of social behavior (Kurcz, 1995). But, as Alcock (2001) emphasizes, it is not mainly concerned with *human* social behavior but, rather, with social behavior among all species. Simply defined, social behavior is any form of behavior that requires the interaction of two or more individuals. Thus, mating, aggression, and altruism (helping behavior) are all examples of important social behavior; each requires interaction between at least two individuals.

Sociobiology is based directly on evolutionary theory and draws illustrations liberally from **ethology** (the study of animal behavior in natural habitats). Sociobiologists believe that certain powerful social tendencies have survived evolutionary processes, and are therefore biologically based. Underlying these tendencies is the single most important law of evolution—namely, that processes of natural selection favor the survival of the fittest. Hence, the "fittest" social behaviors (those that have contributed to survival) should be evident as powerful biological predispositions in human behavior.

Inclusive Fitness and Altruism

Note that fitness as defined by sociobiology refers not to the likelihood that a specific individual of a species will survive but, rather, to the likelihood that genetic material itself will survive. Trivers (1974, 2002), Wilson (1976), and other sociobiologists emphasize that the quest for survival is far more meaningful at the group level than at the level of the individual. Hence, the concept **inclusive fitness,** which refers to the fitness of genetically related groups relative to their likelihood of procreation—hence, of survival. What is important, says Wilson, is "the maximum average survival and fertility of the group as a whole" (1975, p. 107).

The concept of inclusive fitness is fundamentally different from the Darwinian notion of the survival of the fittest individual. Inclusive fitness emphasizes that the life of a single individual of a group is important in an evolutionary sense only to the extent that it increases the probability that the genetic material characteristic of the group will survive and reproduce. Thus, a honeybee will sting intruders to protect its hive even though doing so means that the bee itself will die (Sakagami & Akahira, 1960). Similarly, some species of termites explode themselves when danger threatens. The explosion serves as a warning to other termites, which can now save themselves (Wilson, 1975). As Holcomb (1993) points out, these instances of selflessness (or **altruism**) had long puzzled those who interpreted the law of survival of the fittest in the Darwinian sense—that is, as meaning that every single individual does its utmost to survive, come hell or high water. The notion of inclusive fitness presents sociobiology with an explanation for altruism.

Altruism among humans, sociobiologists argue, is a biologically based characteristic ordained by years of successful evolution (see, for example, Hamilton, 1970, 1971, 1972). In its purest form, an altruistic act is one that presents some sacrifice to the doer but results in a net genetic advantage to the species. A blackbird that noisily signals the approach of a hawk may well be detected and eaten, but in the grand scheme of things, that is a small price to pay for the eventual survival of many other blackbirds.

Carrying the argument to its extreme, sociobiology predicts that the extent to which an individual will be willing to undergo personal sacrifice will be a function of the net genetic advantage that results for the species and be directly related to the degree of genetic relatedness between the doer of the good deed and those who benefit most directly. Thus, you might hesitate to save a stranger if the probability of losing your life in the process were high; the net genetic advantage in such a situation would be virtually zero. For the same reason, you should scarcely hesitate to sacrifice your life to save many others, because the net genetic advantage then is high. It also follows that a father will undergo considerably more risk and sacrifice to save his son than to save a stranger because he has a great deal more in common genetically with his son.

Indirect evidence of this is provided by studies of adoption among certain gull species (Bukacinski, Bukacinski, & Lubjuhn, 2000). Among these gulls, it isn't uncommon for as many as one-third of the chicks to leave their nests. Perhaps two-thirds of these orphan chicks are then "adopted" and cared for by other brooding parents; the other third are driven away and typically perish.

According to sociobiological theory, parent gulls should be most likely to adopt chicks to which they are genetically related, and to ignore or drive away those to which they are unrelated. This prediction is, in fact, borne out: Chicks were most likely to be adopted by other related gulls.

Some Reactions to Sociobiology

In February 1978, reports Alcock (2001), E. O. Wilson gave a talk at the annual meeting of the American Association for the Advancement of Science. While he sat on stage waiting to give this talk, a young woman came over and poured a pitcher of cold water on his head. A small group of accomplices then joined her to wave placards and chant, "Wilson, you're all wet."

Sociobiology has often given rise to this kind of highly emotional—and negative—reaction (see, for example, Gould, 2002a, 2002b). Some of this reaction is based on theological arguments that reject the basic notions of evolution (see Cole, 2002); some is based on a misunderstanding of what sociobiology is, on a fear that it belittles human characteristics by reducing them to mechanistic—or animalistic—events over which humans exercise little control (for example, Van Leeuwen, 2002).

In essence, sociobiology suggests that a range of human social behaviors—including aggression and sociopathy, sexual mores, gregariousness, scarification rites, and so on—may have biological bases. Advocates of sociobiology argue that this approach provides a scientific basis for understanding social behavior and for guiding social policy. They insist that the contributions of biology to human behavior have long been underestimated.

As noted, these views have met with a great deal of resistance. Sociologists in particular have reacted very negatively to the notion that much of human social behavior is genetically ordained (see, for example, Gould, 2002a, 2002b). A number have objected to what they think is excessive generalization from a handful of evidence, a great deal of which relates more directly to nonhuman animals than to humans.

While sociobiology was being assailed by a number of critics, the field of *evolutionary psychology* appears to have been steadily progressing (Carporeal, 2001; Siegert & Ward, 2002). Actually, what was once referred to as *sociobiology* is now often termed *evolutionary psychology* (Scher & Rauscher, 2003). Thus, in the last few years, the phrase *evolutionary psychology* appears about seven times more frequently than does *sociobiology* in the PsycINFO database—a database that summarizes psychological research. Evolutionary psychology is a phrase with a much lighter burden of negative connotations than that carried by *sociobiology*.

Evolutionary Psychology: An Appraisal

Early behaviorists were optimistic that their theories would be widely applicable. They had little doubt that if they could take a response as arbitrary as bar pressing in a rat and bring it under the precise control of specific environmental conditions, it would also be possible to take virtually any operant of which an organism is capable and bring it under precise stimulus control. Similarly, in the same way as it was clearly possible to condition salivation in dogs, eye blinking in adults, and sucking in infants, it should be possible to condition virtually any other reflexive behavior to any distinctive stimulus.

Not so. As we saw, there are situations where classical conditioning does not require repeated pairings of CS and US (for example, in the case of one-shot taste aversion learning). Also, classical conditioning does not occur in some situations even after many pairings (as in the blocking studies).

We saw, too, that certain behaviors are easily learned when reinforced (for example, a pigeon learning to peck to obtain food; a pig rooting; a dog fetching—biological preparedness) and others are learned with extreme difficulty (a pigeon flapping its wings for food; a chicken standing still; a cow barking—contrapreparedness). Also, even after certain behaviors have apparently been well learned through operant conditioning, organisms sometimes revert to other more instinctual behaviors that interfere with the learned behavior (instinctive drift).

In brief, there are numerous examples of behaviors that are very difficult or impossible to condition—and of others that are so remarkably easy that they almost appear to be learned automatically. These behaviors, claim evolutionary psychologists, emphasize that learning theorists need to consider biological factors. Although they don't invalidate conditioning explanations, they lead to two important qualifications:

- Classical conditioning is not just a low-level, mechanical process whereby one stimulus (the US) passes its control to another (the CS) as a result of repeated pairings. Rather, as Rescorla (1988), Bolles (1979), and others note, through this process organisms learn what goes with what—they learn what to expect.

- Evolutionary factors are essential in explaining and understanding behavior (Domjan & Galef, 1983). Recognition of the importance of biological factors in learning is reflected specifically in evolutionary psychology's search for the biological basis of social behaviors such as altruism, mate selection, and sexual jealousy (Holcomb, 1993).

In summary, evolutionary psychology recognizes the importance of genetically determined characteristics—of, if you will, human or animal nature. It admits that one of the most important characteristics of human nature is its malleability, but cautions that this malleability has limits. The first step to understanding the contributions of genetics to our learning and development, says Wright, is to understand "We're all puppets, and our best hope for even partial liberation is to try to decipher the logic of the puppeteer" (1994, p. 37).

Some Practical Applications: Biofeedback and Neurofeedback

In addition to their usefulness in developing theories of human learning and behavior, conditioning theories have numerous practical applications. As we saw, these include using many of the concepts and principles of operant conditioning in instructional settings. These deal with the application of positive and negative reinforcement, punishment, generalization, discrimination, and extinction. Other practical applications of conditioning theories include the use of shaping procedures in animal training; chemical aversion therapy for alcoholism, in which patients are given drugs that interact with alcohol so they become ill if they drink; and other techniques of behavior management, described in Chapter 4.

Another application of conditioning principles is **biofeedback,** a procedure by which individuals are given information about their biological functioning. A more specific form of biofeedback that involves feedback about neurological functioning is labeled **neurofeedback.**

Conditioning of Autonomic Responses

Early investigations of classical and operant conditioning led quickly to the conviction that the types of behavior being explained by each were fundamentally different. Most theorists assumed that autonomic (involuntary) behaviors such as salivation or eye blinking could not be brought under stimulus control through operant conditioning, although they responded very well to classical conditioning procedures. Also, it seemed that operants became more or less probable solely as a function of reinforcement contingencies and not as a function of contiguity.

These assumptions were incorrect. Salivation can be conditioned using operant procedures, and so can heart rate, blood pressure, kidney functioning, and a host of other involuntary autonomic functions. Miller (1969) was among the first to demonstrate some of these phenomena when he conditioned increases or decreases of heart rate in rats in response to a combination of a light and a tone. In this experiment, rats were administered curare (a skeletal muscle paralyzer) to ensure that what was being learned by the rats was actual control of autonomic functioning, rather than some combination of muscular movements that affects heart rate.

In a related study, Miller and Carmona (1967) conditioned dogs to salivate or not to salivate simply by rewarding a group of thirsty dogs with water when they salivated spontaneously and rewarding another group of thirsty dogs with water when they refrained from salivating. What these studies show is that operant conditioning procedures can be used to provide animals with some control over behaviors that are autonomic (involuntary).

How Biofeedback Works

One of the important applications of this finding has taken the form of biofeedback, which refers to information an organism receives about its own functioning. Although people are ordinarily unaware of most aspects of their physiological functions (heart and respiration rates, blood pressure, electrical activity in the brain), monitoring devices can simply and accurately provide information about these functions. The use of these devices to control autonomic functioning defines *biofeedback*. When the information is limited to information about neural activity in the brain, the label *neurofeedback* is often used.

In some early biofeedback experiments, for instance, subjects were connected to a device that records brain waves (popularly called an *alpha recorder*) and that emits a distinctive stimulus—usually a tone—whenever the subject produces the right type or frequency of waves (for example, Knowlis & Kamiya, 1970). Subjects were simply instructed to try to activate the tone as often as possible. Experimental results suggested that many participants could quickly learn to control aspects of brain wave functioning. Using an operant conditioning explanation, investigators argued that the tone (or light or other distinctive stimulus) serves as a reinforcer, and the behaviors involved in controlling the autonomic response are operants.

Using more sensitive and sophisticated instruments to monitor brain activity, many researchers have since confirmed that at least some aspects of brain activity can be controlled. Thus, Inoue and Sadamoto (2002) showed that people can learn to exercise control over heart rate even when they are exercising (during this study, 35 women rode exercise bikes). Similarly, Vernon and associates (2003) succeeded in training young adults to increase a type of brain activity often associated with improved memory function. These researchers subsequently found some measurable improvements in certain types of memory.

Among the many practical applications of biofeedback are attempts to alleviate migraine headaches, to reduce blood pressure and heart rate, to control asthma, and to control urinary incontinence. Also, several researchers have been using neurofeedback to treat attention deficit disorders or learning disabilities. In a typical neurofeedback training session for attention deficit disorder, for example, children are connected to brain wave recorders capable of sensing brain wave patterns that indicate attention (and, conversely, those that do not). The children are subsequently rewarded for attention-related brain wave activity (specifically, beta activity) or for suppressing other activity (for example, theta waves), often while engaged in computer-based activities. Over successive training sessions, the activities require progressively longer periods of attentiveness. Many researchers report relatively high levels of success using such procedures (for example, Egner & Gruzelier, 2001; Pope & Bogart, 1996). Replications of these studies have not always yielded positive results, however (Blanchard, 2002). Often, apparent improvements are not maintained for any significant period—perhaps because training sessions are often brief, and there are many opportunities for the extinction of learned responses. Also, equally positive results have sometimes been obtained using simple relaxation training (for example, Blanchard, Andrasik, Ahles, Teders, & O'Keefe, 1980). Given that biofeedback and neurofeedback therapies tend to be very expensive (because of the cost of instruments as well as the cost of the training required), there is clearly need for more research to determine which approaches are most effective, and for what purposes.

The Beginning of a Transition

The rain had gotten a lot heavier, although the Old Woman seemed not to have noticed. Still, as though responding to some nearly forgotten urge, when she rose, she shook herself like a wet dog might. She said we should go back to the cabin, that the cat would be waiting at the door, that he might be hungry. She said we should stop here in any case because we were in the middle of a transition that would take us to another chapter. She said she thought she should say more about the transition, that she was afraid students might miss its importance. She explained that it's more a conceptual than a chronological transition.

She said one way to simplify the transition would be to say that Pavlovian and Thorndikean and even Skinnerian conditioning deal with the somewhat mechanistic (I mean machinelike, she explained) rules and laws governing relationships among objective, observable events. But in this chapter, she said, suddenly we're confronted with phenomena that suggest different explanations— things like one-shot learning and blocking and biological constraints and taste aversions.

(A part is missing here—perhaps a paragraph, perhaps as much as a page. As usual, the Old Woman insisted on leading the way. It was raining very hard. I held the tape recorder inside my coat clamping it to my chest with my left arm, trying to keep it dry, at the same time holding the microphone out toward the Old Woman's back as she plunged through the underbrush. Even in the rain, she didn't like to follow any of the trails that I have so painstakingly cut and maintained through the years, preferring instead to trust her instincts, forging

through swamps and thickets that even wild animals avoid. Between where I got tangled up in the branches of a diamond willow near the east slough and where I again caught up to the Old Woman by the chokecherry bushes on the Big Hill, there is nothing on the tape but the sound of the wind and rain and the swishing and cracking of branches.)

To understand the transition, the Old Woman was saying as I caught up to her huffing her way up the hill, you have to realize that learning is essentially adaptive. That's the whole point of this chapter on evolutionary psychology, she said, explaining that changes in behavior—in other words, learning—are what allow organisms to survive and thrive, and we should not be surprised that animals and people learn to avoid potentially harmful foods in a single trial or that they are prepared to learn certain things and not others. She said psychologists could do a lot worse than look to biology and evolution for guidance and insight about the principles of human and animal learning.

She said, too, that conditioning should be viewed as learning about how events are related, about what goes with what. She said that in a Skinner box, it is as though learning occurs because of the temporal relation between bar pressing and the reinforcing stimulus—and it is as though the rat develops expectations that one will lead to the other.[4]

The Old Woman stopped and turned so abruptly that I almost ran into her. Despite the rain, her words are very clear on this part of the tape. She said that expectations *is too big a word, too mentalistic a word, for where we are in this book. She said we should leave it for the next chapter, which is more clearly a transition between chiefly behavioristic theories and those that are more cognitive.*

I reached to turn off the recorder. I was very wet and very cold. I wanted to go inside and warm up. But the Old Woman stopped me. She said I shouldn't turn off the recorder yet, that there were some very important things about the brain that you should know before we move into the next chapter. She leaned against an old poplar and began to speak about the brain, her voice unexpectedly soft, almost reverential. When I listen to the tape now, I have to strain to make out all her words.

---

[4]But, said the Old woman, the behaviorist would not speculate that the rat "figures out" this relationship. To do so would presuppose that it knows something about the mechanical functioning of levers and food dispensing mechanisms—or something about the minds of psychological investigators. In the behaviorists' view, the rat's "figuring" is limited to a tendency to make associations among things that co-occur, or that always follow one another.

Learning and the Brain

The brain is the most complex structure in the entire universe, with more possible interconnections among its most basic units, **neurons,** than there are particles in the known universe. Estimates are that there are more than 100 billion neurons in the human brain, and perhaps 10 times that number of supporting cells, called *glial* cells (*The Scientific American Book of the Brain*, 1999). In the next chapter, we look at how these neurons function—how they establish connections and communicate with one another.

We have long known that this lump of tissue that we call the brain is at the very center of our ability to learn, to think, to feel—that it, somehow, determines and defines our very essence. We know that experience and learning must result in some relatively permanent changes in the brain, and that thinking and feeling must involve brain activity. Learning, in fact, depends on the formation of connections among neurons in the brain. But until recently, much about how the brain works has remained a mystery, although psychologists have long known, or at least suspected, that different parts of the brain might have different functions.

Studying Brain Functions

On September, 13, 1848, Phineas Gage, foreman of a construction crew building a new rail line in Vermont, had a smooth, cylindrical iron rod, 3 feet, 7 inches long (slightly more than a meter) and weighing a full 13 pounds (about 6 kilograms) shoot out of a blasting hole and penetrate upward through the left side of his face and out the top of his head! The blow threw Phineas to the ground, but he quickly picked himself up and, with the help of his men, made his way to a cart that carried him to the house where he was staying, a little less than three-quarters of a mile away (about one kilometer).

Phineas's physical recovery was rapid and apparently complete. But he was never quite the same person again. He had previously been a kind, gentle man, quiet and hardworking, but now he became moody, fitful, impulsive, selfish, and stubborn. His coworkers no longer recognized him as the man he had been.

Brain Injuries
Brain injuries such as that of Phineas Gage provide one of the earliest clues that different parts of the brain might have different functions. Thus, from Phineas' accident, we might conclude that the part of his brain that was injured had little do to with physiological functions such as breathing (otherwise he would not have survived). By the same token, that part of the brain might have something to do with personality characteristics.

Brain Ablations
The problem with using brain injuries to study brain functions is that the main causes of such injuries—accidents, illness, and tumors—usually have effects that are not often very specific. Typically, large parts of the brain are affected at one

time. In addition, researchers certainly can't control who will suffer from one of these conditions, which can make for poor research.

One way around these problems is to deliberately cut out (*excise* or *ablate*) small, very specific, portions of the brain to see what the effect might be on the organism. Karl Lashley (1924) did this to a number of rats that had been trained to run quickly and correctly through a maze. Lashley was convinced that memories must leave a trace in a tiny part of the brain, and that if you were to succeed in cutting out just the right part, the animal would no longer remember the correct path through the maze. As we see in Chapter 9, Lashley never did find this memory trace (called an *engram*). It seemed that no matter what part, or how much, of the brain he cut out, the rats could still find their way through the maze, although they often moved more slowly. The conclusion, later corroborated by more recent studies, is that most memories are scattered in various parts of the brain.

Electrical Brain Stimulation

Another way of mapping brain functions is to stimulate specific areas of the brain, either with chemicals or electrically, and see what the effects of doing so might be. In a very early study, for example, Olds (1956) implanted electrodes in the brains of rats and accidentally discovered that stimulation of a part of the hypothalamus—a part of the brain located deep inside the brain, near the top of the brain stem (see Figure 5.5)—seemed highly rewarding for rats. When the electrodes were connected in such a way that rats could stimulate their own brains by depressing a lever, they would do so repeatedly. Many rats would even pass up food to stimulate their own brains. Olds reports that one rat stimulated himself more than 2000 times per hour for 24 consecutive hours (1956).

During the same set of experiments, Olds also discovered that if the electrode were implanted somewhat lower in the hypothalamus, the effect of brain stimulation was not rewarding to the rat, but punishing. Now, rats would go to great lengths to avoid having their brains stimulated. But if the electrode is moved slightly in the direction of the **"pleasure center,"** the lure of brain stimulation appears to become almost irresistible: One rat stimulated himself nearly 7000 times in a single hour (Olds & Milner, 1954). Mother rats would even leave their newborn pups to stimulate their own brains (Sonderegger, 1970).

Subsequent research has corroborated that there is a reinforcement center in the brains of a large number of animals, including primates such as humans, located in the brain's **limbic system.** This system, which is concerned generally with emotion, memory, and motivation, includes the hypothalamus, the thalamus, and several other structures. Specifically, a group of nerve fibers termed the **medial forebrain bundle** is linked with reinforcement, and another group of fibers, the **periventricular tract,** is associated with punishment.

Chemical Brain Stimulation

Implanting electrodes in an animal, or human, brain is a difficult and exacting process. A simpler way of stimulating brains is using chemicals such as mood-altering drugs. Evidence indicates, for example, that the neurotransmitter, **dopamine,** is involved in the activity of some of the neurons associated with

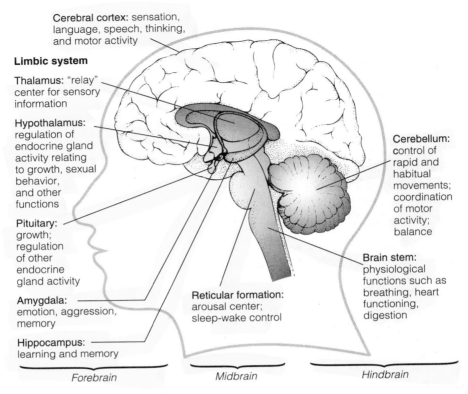

Figure 5.5 A *sagittal* (bisected front to back) view of the human brain showing some of the major structures that make up the forebrain, the midbrain, and the hindbrain, together with their principal functions.

pleasure and motivation (see Chapter 6). Normally, neurotransmitters such as dopamine are released upon neural stimulation, and then quickly recaptured (Wise, 1996). But certain drugs, such as amphetamines and cocaine, prevent the immediate recapture of the dopamine molecules and are, therefore, associated with higher levels of dopamine (Lubin, Cannon, Black, Brown, & Johns, 2003). These drugs are termed **agonists.** An agonist is a chemical that boosts the activity of some naturally occurring chemical. The intensely pleasurable effect of cocaine is probably related to the fact that cocaine prevents or delays the recapture of dopamine molecules so that *dopaminergic* neurons (that is, those that use dopamine for neural transmission) remain active for longer periods. Because dopamine is one of the transmitters associated with neural activity in one of the brain's "pleasure" centers, the ultimate effect of cocaine is to stimulate activity in these centers (Herman & Stimmel, 1997). However, the prolonged use of cocaine leads to the brain's adapting to the drug so that the brain synthesizes less dopamine naturally. As a result, the chronic cocaine user often experiences the opposite of pleasure—depression, sadness, negative moods—in between taking the drug.

Interestingly, electrical stimulation of the brain also leads to the release of dopamine, as do natural reinforcers, such as food, water, and sex, and addictive substances such as nicotine and alcohol (Balfour, Yu, & Coolen, 2004; Kiianmaa et al., 2003).

Brain Imaging Techniques

Researchers now have access to a number of powerful imaging techniques for looking at the brain. Some of these imaging techniques, such as the **electroencephalogram (EEG),** are sensitive to actual electrical discharges in the brain; others detect changes in blood flow associated with neural activity. **Positron emission tomography (PET)** records changes in blood flow by detecting the distribution of radioactive particles injected in the bloodstream. **Functional magnetic resonance imaging (fMRI)** detects extremely subtle changes in magnetic fields that accompany changes in blood oxygen level. And **magnetoencephalography (MEG)** allows researchers to detect at the scalp incredibly subtle changes in magnetic fields that occur with neural activity.

As we see in Chapter 9, these imaging techniques, together with information derived from brain stimulation studies and from examination of patients with brain injuries, have led to a rapidly increasing amount of information about the different structures of the brain and their functions. Much research on memory now uses EEG and MEG recordings to provide measures of what are termed *event-related potentials (ERPs)* and *event-related fields (ERFs)*. These are changes in electrical potential and magnetic fields, respectively, that accompany neural activity in the brain and that are directly related to external stimulation. As a result, ERPs and ERFs can provide researchers with important information about what happens in the brains when, for example, you look at a picture, hear a word, or are asked to solve a problem in algebra (see Chapter 9). To understand this information, it's useful to have some knowledge about the brain's anatomy.

Hindbrain

The human brain can be divided into three basic parts: the hindbrain, the midbrain, and the forebrain. These are thought to have evolved in that order—that is, with the hindbrain being the oldest and the most primitive structure and the forebrain being the most recent and the most advanced. Not surprisingly, the structures of the hindbrain are present and well developed in nonhuman animals, whereas the structures of the forebrain are most developed in humans and other primates.

The hindbrain, physically the lowest part of the brain in an upright human being, includes the lower part of the **brain stem** and what is termed the **cerebellum.** Structures in the brain stem are responsible for basic physiological functions such as respiration and heart rate. The cerebellum (the word means "little brain") is centrally involved in locomotion and balance. Damage to this part of the brain can dramatically impair motor skills such as walking, playing the piano, or catching a baseball. There is tentative evidence, as well, that the cerebellum may sometimes be linked to reading problems and that therapy involving exercises in balance and locomotion might, in some cases, improve performance in reading tasks (Pope & Whiteley, 2003).

Midbrain

The midbrain includes the upper part of the brainstem, sometimes called the **reticular formation,** a structure that, as we see in Chapter 10, is largely responsible for regulating waking and sleeping and for controlling general arousal. We also find the nerve fibers associated with movement in the midbrain. Recall that these nerve fibers are *dopaminergic*, which means that their neural transmission is based on the presence of dopamine. This is why Parkinson's disease, which involves a failure to produce sufficient dopamine, is marked by tremors and other physical motor problems.

Forebrain

The forebrain is the most recent, the largest, and the most complex brain structure; it is also the most important for understanding topics of interest to students of human learning. Its most important structures include the hypothalamus, the thalamus, and other structures of the limbic system, as well as the cerebrum and cerebral cortex.

The Hypothalamus
The **hypothalamus** is a bean-sized structure deep within the brain, near the top of the brain stem. Its major functions relate to regulating physiological functions such as those of the autonomic nervous system and of various glands in the body. Some nerve fibers relating to reward and punishment are also located in the hypothalamus.

The Thalamus
The **thalamus,** another tiny structure at the top of the brain stem, is located just above the hypothalamus and acts as a sort of relay station for sensory information. All incoming neural signals that relate to the senses, except those that have to do with smell, are routed through the thalamus.

The Limbic System
The limbic system is often considered to include parts of the hypothalamus and the thalamus as well as a network of other structures that are found between the cerebral cortex and lower brain structures. Generally speaking, the structures of the limbic system are involved in emotions. Some are also implicated in memories and in conditioning. Among the important structures of the limbic system is the **amygdala,** which processes emotional information for long-term storage (Boujabit, Bontempi, Destrade, & Gisquet-Verrier, 2003). The amygdala is also associated with aggression as well as with classical conditioning (Aguado, 2003). The **hippocampus** plays an important role in long-term memory for facts.

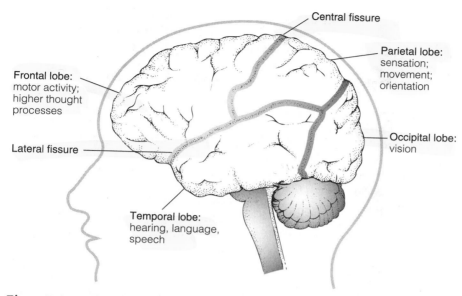

Figure 5.6 The four lobes of the cerebral cortex. The functions of these lobes are highly integrated, so that they cannot easily be separated. Still, each lobe is closely associated with the main functions listed.

The Cerebrum

The **cerebrum,** which divides naturally into two parallel halves (the *cerebral hemispheres*), is the largest and most complex brain structure. Its outer covering, the **cerebral cortex,** which is only about one-eighth of an inch thick, is responsible for our most advanced forms of mental activity: learning, thinking, and remembering. These activities underlie our very sense of consciousness. Interestingly, the cerebral cortex is evolution's most recent legacy and one of the few parts of the brain that continues to develop and grow through childhood and into early adulthood.

The cerebral cortex is highly convoluted, which increases its surface area enormously. It also has a number of fissures running through it. These fissures result in four natural divisions, termed *lobes*, of the cerebral cortex in each of the two cerebral hemispheres (Figure 5.6). Thus, there is both a left and a right one of each lobe.

Toward the front of the cerebral cortex are the **frontal lobes,** structures involved in motor activity as well as in higher thought processes. To either side are the **temporal lobes,** which are involved in hearing, language, and speech. Interestingly, as we see later in this chapter, in most individuals, the left temporal lobe is more involved in language functions than is the right temporal lobe.

Just behind the frontal lobes and above the temporal lobes are the **parietal lobes.** These lobes are strongly implicated in physical sensation, movement, recognition, and orientation. At the very back of the brain are the **occipital lobes,** which are involved in vision.

It's important to note that the division of tasks and responsibilities among the various parts of the brain is far from simple and clear. Although the temporal lobes are involved in language and speech, other parts of the brain are also centrally implicated. Similarly, as we see in Chapter 9, various kinds of memories may be found in many different parts of the brain.

The Hemispheres

As we noted earlier, the brain consists of two highly similar halves separated down the middle, front to back, forming the two cerebral hemispheres. As a result, there are two of each of the four principal lobes of the cerebral cortex. And, although the functions of corresponding lobes are similar in many ways, various studies have shown that the hemispheres do not exactly duplicate each other's functions—a fact referred to as **lateralization.** In general, for example, the right hemisphere controls sensations and movements of the *left* side of the body; the left hemisphere controls functions of the right side of the body. This is referred to as the **principle of opposite control** (Leask & Crow, 1997).

Hemisphere asymmetry is also evident in the fact that about 90% of all people are right-handed and only about 10% are left-handed (Halpern & Coren, 1990). And, in most people, the left hemisphere is somewhat more involved in language production functions than is the right hemisphere. This is true in about 95% of right-handed people and in about 70% of those who are left-handed (Bradshaw, 1989). At the same time, some evidence indicates that the right hemisphere might be more concerned with emotions and with spatial and temporal things—hence, more with music and art.

Findings such as these have led some to speculate that there are "right-brained" and "left-brained" individuals. Those who are left-brained would be expected to perform better on tasks that require logic, math, science, and verbal skills. In contrast, the right-brained would be expected to be more artistic, more musical, and more emotionally intelligent. Some educators argue that schools emphasize the left brain by concentrating on logic, math, science, and language and tend to ignore the right brain (for example, Sonnier, 1991). These educators advocate what is sometimes termed **holistic education**—education that is deliberately designed to teach both sides of the brain. Holistic education, explains Miller (1990), emphasizes the often-neglected artistic and musical interests and talents of children and is more person-centered, more ecologically oriented, perhaps more spiritual.

Unfortunately, it has proven difficult to investigate the separate functions of the cerebral hemispheres. Much of what passes for information, suggests Bruer (1997), is speculation rather than fact. And the information we do have indicates that there is a tremendous amount of overlap between the functions of the cerebral hemispheres. For example, although certain regions of the left temporal lobe are importantly involved in speech and language, when damage occurs to that lobe, speech and language functions are often taken over by other parts of the brain (Bradshaw, 1989). This is especially true if the damage occurs early in life; if it occurs later, there may be less recovery of lost functions. Nor is it clear that the right hemisphere is always more involved in artistic, musical, or spatial functions. For example, an extensive review of studies that have looked at the relationship between the right hemisphere and spatial tasks found that the overall results were highly complex. In general, males seemed to have some slight right-hemisphere preference for spatial tasks, but females did not (Vogel, Bowers, & Vogel, 2003).

As Brown and Kosslyn (1993) suggest, it is misleading and simplistic to insist that the left hemisphere is logical, scientific, and mathematical whereas the right hemisphere is artistic, musical, and emotional. The dichotomy, they explain, is highly relative. That is, one hemisphere is *somewhat* better than the other at certain things, but there is considerable overlap in their functions.

Still, this may not lessen the importance of holistic education's fear that our curricula may neglect important areas of human interest and ability, and its insistence that we should pay more attention to those areas.

The Brain and Experience

Riesen and his associates (1951) raised four baby chimpanzees in a darkened room where they had only about 90 minutes a day of access to diffuse light. After seven months, when these chimpanzees were exposed to a more normal world, none of them had normal vision. The chimpanzees required months before they learned to recognize familiar objects such as their feeding bottles, or learned how to guide their own movements without bumping into things. None ever achieved normal vision.

Many other studies with cats, chimpanzees, and other animals raised in darkness or made to wear goggles that distort the world in different ways illustrate dramatically that most do not learn to see normally when the lights are turned on or the goggles removed. Later examinations of the brains of these animals indicate that they have not developed the same number and kinds of neural connections as animals raised normally (Crawford, Harwerth, Smith, & von Noorden, 1993).

In an early study, Krech, Rosenzweig, and Bennett (1966) raised some rats in a deprived environment: low lighting in tin-lined cages, no toys with which to play, and no interaction with other rats or with humans. Other rats were raised in what, from a rat's point of view, might be considered a highly enriched environment: large, well lit cages, wheels to run on, toys to play with, things to gnaw and look at, other rats with which to socialize, and friendly human experimenters. The eventual differences between these initially identical groups of rats, explain Krech and associates, were remarkable. The enriched group was apparently much brighter, evident in the ease with which they learned to run through mazes, and their brains were measurably different (heavier, more apparent interconnections among neurons, and more of some specific proteins). More recent studies, using more advanced and precise methods for examining the brains of experimental animals, corroborate these early findings (for example, Tropea et al., 2001). Simply enriching an animal's environment (and, presumably, that of a person) results in brains that have more capillaries (tiny blood vessels) per nerve cell, and therefore more oxygen-enriched brains. Enriched environments also seem to lead to the formation of more *synapses*—that is, more connections—between brain cells (Bransford, Brown, & Cocking, 2000).

The general conclusion from these, and numerous other related studies, is that the brain's development depends highly on experience—especially on early experience. The implications of this conclusion for child rearing and education are tremendous.

A Brain-Based Approach to Learning

There are many different ways of looking at human learning. One collection of important approaches, described in the first part of this text, concentrates on behavior and on the events that underlie changes in behavior. Other approaches, some of which are described later in this text, are more *brain-based:* They look at how the brain is involved in learning.

For our purposes, the role of the brain in human learning can be summarized—keeping in mind that this summary is a significant oversimplification—as follows:

1. All information enters the brain by means of our senses. The senses are ultimately our only sources of information about the world. All that brains can know, explains Freeman (2003), results from the hypotheses they make based on the information they receive through the sensory systems.

2. All this sensory information (except for that having to do with smell) is sorted and relayed to appropriate parts of the cerebral cortex via the thalamus. Thus, visual information is sent to what is termed the *visual cortex* in the occipital lobe and auditory information goes to the *auditory cortex* in the temporal lobe. (Sensations having to do with smell have direct links to the *olfactory bulb,* a structure at the base of the frontal lobe.)

3. Important information having to do with non-emotional facts and events is routed through the hippocampus for long-term storage; important emotional information is routed through the thalamus for processing into long-term memory.

4. Actual processing, involving examining information for meanings and associations, occurs in the cerebral cortex.

As Sprenger (2002) explains, this is basically how learning occurs.

Unfortunately, as we see later, the complete picture—which has not yet been entirely drawn, is somewhat more complex than this.

Summary

1. Powerful taste aversions can be learned in a single trial in a process involving delayed conditioning, a phenomenon that has obvious importance as a biological survival mechanism.

2. Taste aversion learning is not well explained by a Pavlovian view of classical conditioning because (a) it may occur in a single trial, (b) it often involves an effect that occurs long after the conditioning stimulus, and (c) it occurs more readily for certain stimuli than others. That taste aversions can be learned using trace pairing with long delays (the effect of

the unconditioned stimulus occurs long after the conditioning stimulus, termed *latent inhibition*) and that animals are highly selective in taste aversion learning suggests that biological and evolutionary pressures might be involved.

3. In blocking, establishing a simple conditioned reaction is prevented by previous learning. Kamin explains blocking relative to the animal's expectations. The occurrence of the unexpected before a significant event leads to the development of an association between the event and the unexpected.

4. Rescorla and Wagner suggest that what is learned in classical conditioning is an association between a variety of component stimuli and a conditioned response. Because a limited amount of associative strength is available, when all of it has been used up for one component of the compound stimulus, none will be left to permit the formation of new associations involving other components of the same compound stimulus: Hence, further learning is blocked.

5. One way of looking at conditioning is to say that it involves learning what goes with what. Higher-order conditioning refers to the process by which various neutral stimuli assume some of the functions of an unconditioned stimulus as a result of being paired with it.

6. Darwin's theory of natural selection is premised on the observation that all species vary behaviorally and physiologically, that at least some of this variation is genetic, and that competition for important resources will lead to an increase in the frequency of those traits that favor success in the competition for resources.

7. Evolutionary psychologists suggest that another useful way of looking at conditioning is to say that it is an adaptive process strongly influenced by biological and evolutionary pressures. Thus, many organisms appear to be predisposed to perform certain behaviors and will often learn these behaviors even in situations where they interfere with reinforcement (autoshaping, such as key pecking in pigeons).

8. Animals that are taught complex behaviors will sometimes revert to a more instinctual behavior even if doing so means that they will no longer be reinforced (instinctive drift).

9. Biological constraints are genetic predispositions that make certain kinds of learning difficult (what Seligman describes as contrapreparedness) and others highly probable and easy (preparedness). Biological predispositions are evident in instinctive drift, autoshaping, and taste aversion learning.

10. Sociobiology is the systematic study of the biological basis of social behavior and assumes that there are genetic explanations for much animal and human social behavior (altruism, for example). These explanations are based heavily on evolutionary theory and on the concept of inclusive fitness, which refers to the fitness of genetically related groups—not individuals—for their likelihood of procreation and survival.

11. Conditioning theory describes two kinds of behavior (respondent and operant) and two sets of laws for explaining them (classical and operant conditioning). Exceptions to these laws are found in taste aversion learning, autoshaping, blocking, and instinctive drift. The exceptions underline the importance of considering biological factors and serve as the basis for evolutionary psychology.

12. Biofeedback defines information that organisms receive about their biological functioning. Neurofeedback refers specifically to information about neural—and especially brain—functioning. Biofeedback research attempts to increase people's control over physiological functioning by providing them with information about it. Biofeedback and neurofeedback

techniques are sometimes used in therapy, particularly for relieving stress, headaches, and a variety of other complaints.

13. Evolutionary psychology, which looks at biological contributions to human and animal behavior, suggests a somewhat less mechanistic approach to explaining learning, and it serves, conceptually, as the beginning of a transition to more cognitive theories.

14. The brain, with its approximately 100 billion neurons, is centrally implicated in everything that we think and do. It is the basis of our consciousness. Information about the brain and its functioning derives from studies of brain injury and disease, surgical procedures and physical examination of the brain, electrical and chemical stimulation of the brain, and imaging techniques such as EEGs and various scanning procedures such as fMRIs, and PET scans.

15. Among other things, studies of brain functioning have identified "pleasure" and "punishment" centers in parts of the hypothalamus and have shown how some neurotransmitters, such as dopamine, may explain the rewarding and addictive effects of electrical stimulation of the brain and of certain drugs such as cocaine.

16. The most recent brain structures in an evolutionary sense, those that make up the forebrain and especially the cerebrum,

are most highly developed in humans and are centrally involved in higher mental functioning. Hindbrain structures, more involved in physiological functioning and in movement, are older and often highly developed in nonhuman animals.

17. The cerebral cortex, the thin, convoluted outer covering of the cerebrum, seems to divide naturally into four lobes on each hemisphere, each of which is primarily associated with one or more functions, although there is considerable overlap and integration of functions (frontal lobes: higher mental processes; parietal lobes: sensation, movement, recognition, and orientation; occipital lobes: vision; and temporal lobes: hearing, speech, and language).

18. Some evidence suggests that the two halves of the cerebral cortex are asymmetrical in their involvement with various functions. Specifically, the left hemisphere is said to be more logical, mathematical, and verbal; the right hemisphere is thought to be more emotional, artistic, spatial, and musical. In fact, cerebral functions overlap considerably.

19. The development of the brain seems to be highly dependent on experience, especially on early experience.

20. Brain-based approaches to learning look at how the brain responds to stimulation and processes information.

A Transition to Modern Cognitivism: Hebb, Tolman, and the Gestaltists

> Logically, a scientific theory should never be believed. It is best regarded as a sophisticated statement of ignorance, a way of formulating possible ideas so that they can be tested, rather than an attempted statement of final truth.
> **Donald Hebb**

The cat was waiting as we neared the cabin, drenched and shivering, rubbing hard against the closed door. Even in the rain, I could smell the beans the Old Woman had put to bake in the oven of the old wood-burning stove, and I was suddenly ravenous. The Old Woman quickly filled the cat's dish with beans and a big chunk of salt port, but she would not let me eat just then. "Not yet," she said, "I want to get into Chapter 6 before dinner," and she rolled her sheets of manuscript out onto the table where I had wanted to eat. But instead of beginning to read from her notes, she turned them aside. She said that before she started the next chapter, she wanted to say something about ideas and theories. She explained that new ideas seldom appear completely out of the blue. She said that if we look carefully at the history of human ideas, we see that long before the appearance of an apparently new idea, there are almost invariably hints that it is coming. Sometimes we find that the idea has appeared fully formed decades or even centuries earlier. Such precocious ideas, and their perpetrators, are often ridiculed loudly and doomed to a premature death—an idea before its time, the philosophers say. But they are wrong, explained the Old Woman, because ideas are never truly before their time; it is people who are behind their own time and therefore cannot recognize the ideas' importance.

The Old Woman was silent for a long time, as though thinking important thoughts. "Are you hungry?" I asked her hopefully, but she seemed not to hear my question. Then, without warning, she motioned that I should turn on the recorder, and she began to read once more from her notes.

🅣his Chapter

Chapter 6 looks at ideas that in many important ways were ideas "before their time"—hints of ideas yet to come. As well, many of these ideas were reflections of ideas already spoken and written. Thus, Donald Hebb's behaviorism reflects the ideas of conditioning theory, but in it are many hints of the connectionism and neural networks that underlie computer models of human thought processes developed decades later (see Chapter 8). Also, Hebb's theory foreshadows current attempts to understand learning and behavior by looking at what happens in the brain. Similarly, the ideas of Edward Chace Tolman and the gestaltists express a growing concern with contemporary cognitive topics, such as perception, problem solving, and decision making.

Objectives

The Old Woman said that when you have read this chapter eight times, you will—she promised—be able (and willing) to mumble your way through astoundingly long discourses on the following:

- *Hebbian cell assemblies and phase sequences*

- *Arousal theory*

- *Tolman's purposive behaviorism*
- *The basic laws of Gestalt psychology*

She said you would also know something, but not a whole heck of a lot, about saber-toothed tigers. And then she began to read from her notes once more.

Hebb's Theory: Higher Mental Processes

The relevance of saber-toothed tigers, *she read*, has to do with the speculation that when a man comes face-to-face with his first saber-toothed tiger, he will turn immediately and run as though the very devil were after him. But when the same man comes to a stream with the intention of crossing it and finds that the stone he had laid there for that purpose is gone, he will stop; perhaps he will sit on the bank with his chin in his hands. Later he may decide to get another stone to replace the first.

In addition to the obvious lack of similarity between a person running from a saber-toothed tiger and one sitting on a riverbank, there is an important distinction between these two behaviors. The first behavior can be interpreted in terms of the now familiar S-R model: The tiger serves as the stimulus; running is the immediate response.

The second behavior presents a different situation, although in a sense, the missing stone is the stimulus and the act of leaving to get a replacement is a response. The problem with this stimulus-response interpretation is that there might be a delay of minutes or even hours between the presentation of the stimulus and the response. Because of this delay, the S-R model is less than adequate.[1]

An important question is this: What occurs during the lapse of time between a stimulus and a response?

---

[1] Here the Old Woman interrupted herself. We could have used the beans as an example, she said to me. She explained that even though I seemed very hungry, my hunger stimulus didn't automatically lead to my eating. She said I was able to delay my response for a variety of reasons, including the fact that I could imagine the consequences both of waiting and of not waiting. She said that the ability to delay our responding, and the ability to imagine the consequences of so doing, is fundamentally important to understanding human behavior. The cat had now finished licking his empty dish, and sat looking at me. My stomach growled.

Higher Mental Processes: Between Stimulus and Response

It's likely, says Hebb, that something related to the stimulus and response must be occurring at least part of the time because the eventual behavior (response) reflects the situation (stimulus). One phrase that labels what goes on between the stimulus and response is **higher mental processes.** In laypersons' terms, higher mental processes are thinking or thought processes. A label, however, is not an explanation or even a description.

Hebb describes higher mental processes as "processes which, themselves independent of immediate sensory input, collaborate with that input to determine which of the various possible responses will be made, and when" (1958, p. 101). In other words, higher mental processes are activities that mediate responses; they are mediating processes. What this means is that they are processes that link stimuli and responses, sometimes over long periods.

From the actor's point of view, these processes are experienced as "thinking." Although Hebb wanted to explain higher mental processes, he is clearly a behaviorist. "The evidence which psychology can be sure of consists of what man or animal *does*," he claims. "The evidence does not include sensations, thoughts, and feelings" (1966, p. 4). But, he hastens to point out, psychology "is essentially concerned with such processes; they are known by inference, not directly" (p. 4). Or, again, "Everything you know about another person's thoughts or feelings is inferred from behavior. Knowledge of behavior is factual. Knowledge of mental processes is theoretical, or inferential" (p. 4).

Here is a profoundly important departure from early behaviorism. With its insistence that the science of behavior be based solely on observations of objective events like stimuli and responses, early behaviorism seemed to deny the existence of mental processes. But behaviorism never really denied that these processes occur, Hebb informs us. What John B. Watson and others emphatically rejected was the *scientific* value of concepts such as consciousness, imagination, and thinking (as well as the scientific value of an approach such as introspection).[2] Hebb is now suggesting that inferences about such processes might be useful if they are based on actual observations, and if the psychologist keeps clearly in mind the distinction between fact (observation) and inference (theory). "Theory is always open to argument," claims Hebb, "but useful argument is possible only when there is some agreement concerning the facts" (1966, p. 4).

Recall that Clark L. Hull, too, had suggested that human behavior can be understood through hypothetical (that is, inferred) variables that mediate between stimulus and response. But one big difference between Hebb's and Hull's

---

[2]The Old Woman shook her head, almost sadly it seemed, when she read this line. You know, she said to me, I find it astounding how your psychologists have treated consciousness. She said she thought we would recognize that consciousness is absolutely central to the experience of being human, but that despite this, it has occupied such an uncertain and controversial role in the development of human psychology. In the beginning, she explained, consciousness was the very center of the science; later it was sometimes ignored or even denied. Psychologists are still not at all certain what they should make of it.

mediational constructs is that Hull's inferences are unrelated to the structure or functioning of the nervous system: They are largely hypothetical. In contrast, Hebb's variables are physiological: They are based on neurological fact and speculation.

The Physiology of Learning

Hebb points out that psychology deals with the behavior of biological organisms; accordingly, it has to be concerned with humans as products of evolution, as well as with the functioning of glands, muscles, and other organs. This view is shared by evolutionary psychology, as shown in Chapter 5. Perhaps most centrally, argues Hebb, psychology needs to take into account the functioning of the nervous system—and especially the brain.

Although other behaviorists, such as B. F. Skinner, accepted the existence and the importance of human physiological systems, and especially of the central nervous system, they deliberately avoided speculation about what these systems do. Such speculations, claimed Skinner (1938), are fictions; they deal with a *conceptual* rather than a *central* nervous system.

Hebb, in contrast, deliberately chose to speculate about what he labeled "the conceptual nervous system." What he proposed was that the mental processes that intervene between stimulus and response can be understood and described as neurological events. This belief forms a cornerstone of his theory, which he described as *pseudobehavioristic* because it is concerned primarily with explaining thought processes and perception—topics not often considered within behavioristic positions (Hebb, 1960).

To understand Hebb's system, it's useful to look at some of the main features of the human nervous system.

Functioning of the Central Nervous System

The human **nervous system** consists of billions of cells called neurons. As we saw in Chapter 5, most of these are located in the brain (perhaps as many as 100 billion) and in the spinal cord, which together make up the central nervous system (CNS).[3] The rest are found throughout the body in the form of complex neural pathways and branches.

A **neuron** is a specialized cell whose function is to transmit impulses in the form of electrical and chemical changes. Neurons form the link between receptors (for example, sense organs) and effectors (muscle systems, glands) and thereby ensure that the responses made by an organism will be related to the stimulation it receives. Bundles of neurons form **nerves** that make up the nervous system.

---

[3]Estimates of the number of neurons vary widely—from as few as 1 to as many as 100 billion neurons. The most recent estimates tend to be very high—100 billion or more. Why don't they just count them, asked the Old Woman?

Donald Olding Hebb (1904–1985)

Hebb was born in the small Canadian town of Chester, Nova Scotia, on July 22, 1904. He spent his childhood in this region, eventually going to Dalhousie University in Nova Scotia. Interestingly, like Skinner, Hebb's early ambition was to become a novelist (Hebb, 1980).

Hebb was reportedly not an outstanding student as an undergraduate; his grade point average was just barely enough for him to be granted a B.A. in 1925. From Dalhousie he went to McGill University, where he was admitted as a part-time graduate student, partly because the chair of the department was a friend of his mother's. He later went to the University of Chicago to study with Karl Lashley. Lashley, who studied memory storage in the brain, profoundly influenced Hebb's theory (Dewsbury, 2002). Hebb obtained an M.A. in Chicago and later went to Harvard University, where at the age of 32, he was granted a Ph.D.

After receiving his Ph.D., Hebb held appointments at Harvard, at the Montreal Neurological Institute, and at Queen's University in Kingston, Ontario. Other positions included a stint as editor of the *Bulletin of the Canadian Psychological Association*, a research position with the Yerkes Primate Laboratory, the presidencies of both the Canadian Psychological Association and the American Psychological Association (he was its first foreign president) and a professorship in psychology at McGill University in Montreal.

Hebb's many honors include the Warren medal (presented by the Society of Experimental Psychologists), which was also won by Hull; a distinguished scientific contribution award, also won by Jean Piaget; and a large number of honorary degrees. Hebb's publications include many important papers and two major books: *The Organization of Behavior*, published in 1949, and *A Textbook of Psychology*, the third edition of which was published in 1972.

Like all cells, neurons consist of a **cell body** and several arms that extend from this cell body. One of these is the **axon;** the others are **dendrites.** (See Figure 6.1.) The axon is a conductor of neural impulses. In most cases, transmission occurs in only one direction: from the cell body outward along the axon. Axons may be microscopically short, but some extend all the way from the brain through the spinal cord, a distance of about a meter (about 40 inches) in an adult. Near their ends, axons branch out and terminate in a number of little bulbs called *terminal boutons* (sometimes called *synaptic knobs*). These are not connected directly to other neurons, but simply end close to them. The gap between the **terminal bouton** and an adjacent neuron is a **synaptic cleft.**

Dendrites are hairlike extensions on a neuron's cell body. Whereas neurons have only one axon, they may have a few or many dendrites. The function of dendrites is to receive impulses and transmit them to the cell body.

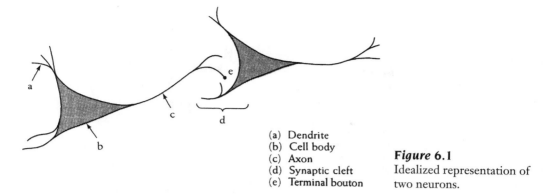

(a) Dendrite
(b) Cell body
(c) Axon
(d) Synaptic cleft
(e) Terminal bouton

Figure 6.1

Idealized representation of two neurons.

Neural Transmission

Transmission of impulses within and between neurons involves both electrical and chemical activity. Think of each neuron as a little battery, capable of generating an electrical impulse. Electricity is the flow of negatively charged particles (called *electrons*) toward a positively charged pole. Electrical impulses in the neuron operate in exactly the same way. A series of chemical changes brought about by stimulation change the *electrical potential* of the cell, causing a flow of charged particles (termed *ions*). This flow is an electrical impulse, called an **action potential,** in contrast to the cell's initial *resting potential.* Within approximately 2 milliseconds of the initial stimulation, the neuron again regains its resting potential. But for a brief period, termed a **refractory period,** it is essentially discharged and so no longer has the potential to generate an electrical impulse.

The chemicals involved in changing the electrical potential of cells, thus leading to neural transmission, are called **neurotransmitters.** As many as 100 different neurotransmitters have now been identified (Sprenger, 2002). The best known of these include dopamine, norepinephrine, acetylcholine, and serotonin.

Dopamine, as we saw in Chapter 5, is involved in the functioning of neurons associated with pleasure and reinforcement. Hence, dopamine is an important neurotransmitter for motivation.

Norepinephrine, sometimes called *noradrenaline,* is a neurotransmitter linked with arousal (see Chapter 10), as well as with memory and learning. At times of crisis, parts of the brain, including the hypothalamus and the amygdala, are suddenly flooded with norepinephrine. This signal of alarm tells the brain that it must now prepare the body to respond to the crisis, perhaps by fleeing, perhaps by turning and fighting.

Acetylcholine is a neurotransmitter involved in activating the muscles, leading to movement. It is also involved in learning and memory. *Serotonin* is involved in neural transmission in much of the brain, especially in areas having to do with emotion. Too low levels of serotonin have been linked with depression, aggression, and even violence.

Figure 6.2
Cell assembly. Cell assemblies consist of activity in a large number of related neurons. They correspond to relatively simple input.

From the learning theorist's point of view, what is most important in all of this is that the effect of stimulation is to activate neural cells, which can then activate one another in sequence as impulses cross the gaps between neurons (the link or bridge between neurons is termed a **synapse**). This ultimately results in the transmission of impulses that cause glands to secrete or muscles to contract. The basic question is this: What changes occur in neurons or in neural transmission when the organism learns?

Hebb's Neurophysiological Assumptions

Although Hebb didn't know the answer to this question, he made a number of important assumptions that suggested an answer highly compatible with what we now know to be correct. The most basic of these assumptions is this: Repeated transmission of impulses between two cells (that is, between two neurons) leads to permanent facilitation of transmission between these cells. Permanent facilitation means, in effect, learning. What Hebb was saying is that if a neurological event—specifically the firing of a sequence of neurons—occurs repeatedly, it will become progressively easier for the first neurons in the sequence to activate subsequent neurons.

A second assumption central to Hebb's theory is that neural cells may be reactivated repeatedly because of their own activity. Stimulation of cell A might cause cell B to fire. This in turn might fire cell C, and cell C might then reactivate the first cell in the sequence, cell A, which again activates B, then C, then A again . . . and again . . . and again (see Figure 6.2). The resulting circular pattern of firing is called a **cell assembly.**

A third important assumption is that if a number of related cell assemblies are simultaneously active, they, too, will become linked in what Hebb labels a **phase sequence** (see Figure 6.3). These hypothetical structures (hypothetical because they are imagined)—the cell assembly and the phase sequence—play important roles in Hebb's proposal for a theory of learning. Each cell assembly corresponds to what Hebb refers to as "relatively simple sensory input"—for example, a color or a sensation. Hence, the recognition of even very simple objects will involve the activation of a large number of such cell assemblies or phase sequences.

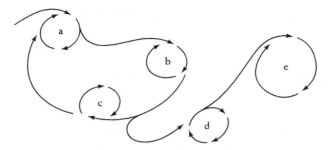

Figure 6.3 Schematic representation of a phase sequence: a, b, c, d, and e can be thought of as cell assemblies. A phase sequence is equivalent to a concept and may consist of activity in a large number of related neurons (see Figure 6.2).

Neurological Changes Underlying Learning

It's important to keep in mind that cell assemblies and phase sequences are hypothetical constructs—Hebb's inventions designed to organize what is known and to lead to new insights. Reassuringly, however, recent evidence of neurological functioning suggests that brain cells tend to fire in groups (assemblies) and to reactivate each other, much as Hebb had speculated they might (see, for example, Amit, 1995; Rosler, Heil, & Roder, 1997). Actually, Hebb's notion of cell assemblies plays an increasingly important role in current psychological research and theory, not only in relation to computer-based neural networks (discussed in Chapter 8) but also in a variety of studies that look at topics such as language learning, amnesia, and memory (for example, Debigare, 1984; Milner, 1989; Mishkin, 1995).

The Aplysia: Habituation and Sensitization

We know that the transmission of neural impulses underlies sensation and behavior, and that it underlies higher mental processes (that is, thinking). But what, exactly, happens when an organism learns something? In other words, what neurological changes occur because of learning?

Studying changes in human neurons is very difficult and complex—especially given that there are more than 100 billion neurons in the human nervous system. But a number of invertebrates have only a few neurons. And some of these have very large neurons whose functioning can be studied. Perhaps most important among these invertebrates is the Aplysia snail, a slug-like snail that can be almost as big as a child's foot. The Aplysia has been extensively studied (for example, Kandel, Schwartz, & Jessell, 2000) and is an especially valuable organism for neurological research: Its nervous system is relatively simple and well mapped, and the electrical and chemical details of neural transmission in the Aplysia are very similar to those of neural transmission in vertebrates. Furthermore, this snail responds predictably by retracting its gills when its siphon (spout) is touched. It quickly habituates to repeated light touches, however, and, after a while, it stops responding. **Habituation** is clear evidence that something has been learned.

Habituation is a highly common phenomenon among most organisms. You quickly stop paying attention to repeated mild stimulation—the sensation of your clothing, the monotonous humming of the air-conditioning unit, the incessant chirping of the sparrows. In the same way, a city dog has *habituated* to traffic noises, and pays them little attention. In contrast, a rural dog may pay considerable attention to the much less frequent traffic noises it hears.

There are instances in which repeated stimulation leads not to habituation, but to its opposite: **sensitization.** This is most likely to occur for highly intense stimulation. Thus, if instead of touching the Aplysia's siphon gently, you administer it one or two electric shocks just about anywhere on its body, then a subsequent very gentle touch of the Aplysia's siphon may cause instant and very decided retraction.

Examination of the Aplysia's neurons before and after habituation and sensitization does not indicate that new synapses are formed (or lost) but, rather, that the axons of the sensory neurons become more or less responsive to stimulation (Kandel, 1985). Specifically, with increasing habituation, the amount of transmitter chemicals released by the stimulated neuron measurably declines. But in the event of sensitization, a second neuron, termed an *interneuron*, becomes active. The net effect is that subsequent stimulation will now lead to measurable increases in the amount of specific transmitter chemicals released. Thus, at least in the Aplysia, a chemical change in the cell itself accounts for changes in behavior (that is, accounts for learning).

The Neurology of Reactivity and Plasticity

In Hebb's theory, as in most other accounts of learning, two properties of the human organism play a central role: reactivity and plasticity. *Reactivity* refers to the capacity of the organism to react to external stimuli; *plasticity* is the property of the organism that allows it to change as a function of repeated stimulation. A simple demonstration can be used to illustrate these two properties. The procedure involves placing a subject 2 or 3 feet in front of the experimenter. The experimenter then, without warning, kicks the subject squarely and soundly where he sits. The subject's immediate behavior is an example of reactivity; subsequent refusal to repeat the experiment is an example of plasticity.[4]

Plasticity—essentially, the capacity to change as a function of experience—is what accounts for learning. Plasticity is evident in the Aplysia snail's habituation, as well as in its sensitization, to stimulation. It is also apparent in the neurological changes that occur following habituation and sensitization. Neurologically,

---

[4]The Old Woman said she didn't like this example. She explained that she was leaving it in because someone had thought of it and we must have decided it illustrated the point. She said she found it demeaning to think of being kicked, or even of kicking someone else, where they sit. The cat watched the Old Woman intently while she spoke. The kerosene lamp's flame danced in its pupil.

sensitization leads to **long-term potentiation (LTP)**—that is, to a lasting increase in the responsiveness of neurons. In contrast, habituation leads to **long-term depression (LTD)**—a lasting decline in the responsiveness of relevant neurons. Current research, involving the electrical stimulation of neurons, illustrates that the facilitation (potentiation) and inhibition (depression) of neural activity involve lasting changes in the release of chemical transmitter substances (Rosenzweig, Leiman, & Breedlove, 1999).

The biochemistry of neurological events involved in learning is now increasingly well understood. As Dayan and Abbott put it, "Activity-dependent synaptic plasticity is widely believed to be the basic phenomenon underlying learning and memory" (2001, p. 281). It's interesting, and impressive, that Hebbian theory attempted to account for behavior in terms of neurological events at a time when all he could do was speculate about these events. Yet, what has now come to be known as the **Hebb rule** is basic to current neurological research. Simply stated, this rule says that if input from neuron A contributes often enough to firing of neuron B, then the synapse from A to B will change and become stronger. Thus, for Hebb, plasticity and reactivity were actual properties of the CNS; they are what account for behavior, rather than being properties of behavior.

Mediating Processes: Hypotheses and Assumptions

Hebb's primary concern was to explain higher mental processes, or thought. His explanation offers a basic hypothesis and makes four principal assumptions related to his view of the physiology of the nervous system.

Basic Hypothesis

The hypothesis, already described, is that mediation (or thinking) consists of "activity in a group of neurons, arranged as a set of closed pathways that will be referred to as a cell assembly, or of a series of such activities, which will be referred to as a phase sequence" (Hebb, 1958, p. 103).

How are cell assemblies formed?

Assumption 1

A cell assembly (or mediating process) is established as the result of the repeated firing of cells. It is the outcome of the repetition of a particular kind of sensory event. That's because the repeated presentation of a specific stimulus will tend to reactivate the same assemblies each time, leading to changes that facilitate transmission of impulses across the synaptic spaces between the neurons involved. Hence, repetition has a facilitating effect on further neural activity. Behavioral evidence of this effect is provided by the fact that it is considerably easier to multiply two numbers if they have been multiplied many times previously. Or, more simply, it is easier to recognize a simple object if it has been presented frequently, than if it has only been seen once. This property of neural transmission partly defines what plasticity of the nervous system means. And, as we saw, there is now neurological evidence of changes in neurons that account for increases and decreases in synaptic strength (Dayan & Abbott, 2001).

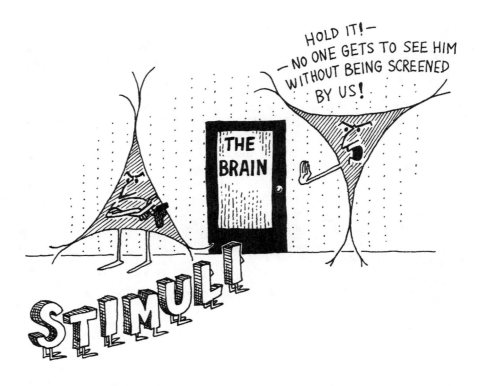

Assumption 2

If two cell assemblies are repeatedly active at the same time, an association between the two will tend to form. In other words, if cell assembly A is always (or
often) active when B is active, the two will tend to become associated neurologically. That is, the firing of cell assembly A may lead to firing in B and vice versa.
The result will be the formation of phase sequences, arrangements of neurons
that tend to fire in sequence, and that can reactivate each other.

This assumption explains conditioning through contiguity. If cell assembly
A corresponds to one specific sensory event and B does also, and if A and B
represent the components of thought (mediation), then establishing a relationship between A and B means that presentation of the event associated with A
may remind a person of the event associated with B. Intuitively, this makes
sense. If you always see George with a cigar in his mouth, then it's likely that
anything that reminds you of George will also bring the cigar to mind. The
smell of wood smoke evokes thoughts of fire; lilacs go with spring; fish mean
water or restaurants; the letter *q* in a word means *u* is next; and motherhood is a
good thing.

This assumption explains learning by contiguity and explains the perception
of objects when incomplete sensory data are available. For example, the lines in
Figure 6.4 are almost always perceived as a triangle, although they really are not.
(This phenomenon, referred to as **closure** in **Gestalt** psychology, is discussed
later in this chapter.) For the sake of simplicity, the cell assemblies associated with

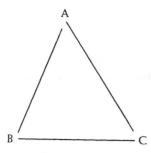

Figure 6.4
Perception with incomplete data. It looks like a triangle, and most people will perceive it as such. But it's really just three lines that don't quite meet.

triangularity can be said to include units representing each of the corners A, B, and C of the triangle, as well as each of the sides. Because these features of triangles have been present in contiguity many times, associations have been formed among the cell assemblies that represent them. It is now sufficient to present only limited sensory input (that is, the three sides of a triangle, but no corners) to evoke activity in the entire sequence of assemblies corresponding to "triangle."

Assumption 3

An assembly that is active at the same time as an efferent pathway (a neural pathway leading outward from the CNS) will tend to form an association with it. This assumption, like assumption 2, allows Hebb to explain the formation of associations between events that are in temporal contiguity. Activity in an efferent pathway may result in some sort of motor activity. Hence, the associations explained by this assumption involve behavioral events and mediation—in other words, thought and behavior. Again, there is ample evidence that such associations are very much a part of human learning. Particular sights, sounds, or smells, for example, become associated with a specific motor activity, so that engaging in the activity recalls the sensory impression. The reverse is also true; activity in assemblies that have often been active during some motor response would tend to elicit the same response. This interpretation is a simple, neurologically based explanation for Pavlovian conditioning. The assemblies relating to the sounding of a buzzer are always present at the time of salivation and are eventually sufficient to elicit salivation.

Assumption 4

Each assembly corresponds to relatively simple sensory input. This property of the cell assembly makes it necessary to involve large groups of such assemblies in explaining the perception of even relatively simple physical objects.

Learning and Thinking in Hebb's Theory

These four assumptions permit Hebb to describe learning and thinking. For Hebb, the term *mediation* is equivalent to the word *thinking*. Mediation consists of activity in assemblies of neurons, and the nature of the mediation (or of the thought) is determined by the specific assemblies involved. Hebb believed that the activated area of the cortex, rather than the nature of the neural activity itself, determines the subjective experience of the organism. For example, it is possible to stimulate the optic nerve electrically or by using pressure. In either case, the effect is the same: The subject sees light (Hebb, 1966, p. 267). In contrast, the activation of specific receptors will always affect the same area of the cortex (and presumably the same cell assemblies). Hence, it is possible to "feel" the same reaction for the same stimulation on different occasions. If this were not true, of course, human awareness as it is now known would not exist.[5]

In Hebb's theory, the repetition of the same sensory event leads to the same pattern of neural firing and, eventually, to the formation of associated assemblies of cells. Conduction among these cells becomes easier with repetition. Put very simply, learning is the "permanent facilitation" of conduction among neural units. What Hebb labels a *phase sequence* is a neurological unit where the transmission of impulses has become so easy that the activation of one part of the sequence is sufficient to activate the entire organization.

Hebb's neurologically based explanation for learning accounts for the formation of stimulus and response associations in connections that are formed between their corresponding neurological counterparts (active cell assemblies or phase sequences). Assumptions 2 and 3 deal with this type of learning. Higher processes involved in learning (insightful problem solving, for example) are assumed to involve the combination of phase sequences (sometimes through chance) in higher order organizational units—*supraordinate phase sequences.*

Hebb's notion of cell assemblies and phase sequences provides an explanation for conditioning and, as we saw, it provides the beginning of an explanation for higher mental processes. It also suggests explanations for two other interesting phenomena: set and attention.

Set and Attention

When a starter at a race tells the contestants that she will fire her pistol a few seconds after saying "On your mark," she is attempting to establish *set* (a predisposition to respond in a certain way). If she succeeds, the contestants will sprint forward when the pistol sounds.

---

[5]The Old Woman interrupted herself and motioned that I should turn the recorder off. "Do you think," she asked, "this means that scientists will one day be able to tell exactly what you're thinking simply by hooking you up to a machine that will detect precisely which neurons are active in your brain?" She got up and put more wood on the fire. Then she said that no, she didn't think scientists would ever be able to tell exactly what you were thinking just by knowing which of your brain cells are active. She said Goldblum (2001) put her finger on it when she said this would never happen because the neurons that are active in your brain when you're thinking that, say, "2 + 2 = 4" are different from the ones active in her brain when she's thinking the same thing. In the end, she says, science might be able to figure out what she's thinking when they detect exactly the same pattern of activity in her brain on different occasions. But if they then detect exactly the same pattern of activity in someone else's brain, all they will be able to do is guess the general area to which the thought relates. Because the same pattern of neural activity might be used to encode entirely different thoughts in different people, they won't know what that other person is thinking. Do you know what I mean? she asked. I wanted to say I wasn't sure but she said to never mind, to turn on the recorder again, that she had more to say.

A superficial behavioristic interpretation of this situation might be that the sound of the pistol is the stimulus that elicits the response of running. But consider what might have happened if the starter had said, "I'm going to fire this pistol to test whether it's working. Just relax." If she then fires the pistol and no one runs, it becomes obvious that the pistol alone is not the stimulus that leads to the running response. Clearly, the initial instructions are also important. In other words, the *set* given to the contestants and the stimulus together influence the behavior.

Consider, further, what would happen if a celebrity strolled along the track just before the sounding of the gun. Would the contestants' perspiration change? Would their blood pressure and heart rate go up? Would their temperature jump? Probably not. But if these same contestants had already finished the race and were lounging around recuperating when the celebrity walked by, the phase sequences activated might be quite different. This illustrates the effect of *attention* on behavior. **Set** refers to selectivity among responses; **attention** refers to selectivity among input.

According to Hebb, both set and attention are functions of the preactivation of specific cell assemblies. When racers are told to get ready to run, they are *set* to respond by running when they hear a bang. When they are paying *attention* to the impending sound, they are less likely to attend to other distracting stimuli.

Educational Applications of Hebb's Theory

Set and attention are especially important for teachers. Attention is essential if learning is to occur and set is involved in choosing appropriate responses. In addition, both attention and set are closely related to **arousal,** a concept that is central to Hebb's theory of motivation. (That theory is summarized and discussed in Chapter 10.) According to this theory, arousal (defined in terms of the alertness of an individual and reflected in physiological measures such as heart and respiration rate and brain wave activity) is an essential condition of learning. Humans behave as though they need to maintain an optimal level of arousal, explains Hebb (1966). Too high a level results in anxiety—perhaps even in panic. Too low a level of arousal results in boredom, lethargy—perhaps even sleep.

Arousal level is, in large part, a function of the amount and variety of stimulation to which the organism is exposed. As we see in Chapter 10, teachers control much of the most significant stimulus input for students in the classroom. The intensity, meaningfulness, novelty, and complexity of what teachers say and do all affect students' attentiveness and arousal level. The aim, suggests Hebb, is to maintain student's arousal level at an optimal level—a level where they are attentive and interested rather than bored or anxious.

In addition to its important implications for student motivation, Hebb's theory, as we saw, provides an explanation for why repetition is important in learning. According to this theory, repetition of stimulation leads to repeated activation of the same sets of neurons and to the eventual formation of cell assemblies and phase sequences. The establishment of these neurological patterns defines learning.

Hebb's Theory: An Appraisal

Hebb's theorizing represents a significant departure from the more traditional S-R theories we have considered earlier. Most notably, it is concerned mainly with internal neurological events, few of which are nearly as objective as the stimuli and responses that interested Watson and Skinner. And Hebb's goal was less to explain the formation of relationships between stimuli and responses than to account for higher mental processes. In this sense, Hebb's ideas serve as a transition between behavioristic and more cognitive theories.

As we noted, much of Hebb's theorizing is based on speculation about the nature of neurological events that mediate between stimuli and responses. Largely because of this, he claimed that his descriptions and assumptions were not really a theory but instead a proposal for one. Nevertheless, his ideas represent a coherent and systematic attempt to explain important observations and can be evaluated as a theory.

Hebb made at least three important contributions to the development of learning theory: First, he brought a consideration of physiological mechanisms back into the study of learning and behavior (much as had Pavlov many decades earlier). Some of the implications of his ideas are now apparent in neural network models, which are described in Chapter 8 (Beltran, 2000.)

Second, as we will see in Chapter 10, Hebb's work on arousal theory gives him an important position as a motivational theorist. This work set the stage for a considerable amount of research on the relationship between motivation and performance.

Third, his work on **sensory deprivation,** also discussed in Chapter 10, has had an important influence on research in learning. Among other things, it called attention to a completely new class of motivational systems relating to things like curiosity, novelty, and exploration.

Hebb's theory, explain Brown and Milner (2004), has significantly influenced research in neuroscience and on brain-based learning, as well as the study of emotions, memory, perception, and human development. In particular, Hebb's suggestions regarding the neurological underpinnings of perception and thinking, and his introduction of the *Hebb Rule* (the notion that repeated simultaneous activation of neurons leads to permanent changes associated with facilitation of subsequent firing of the same neurons) have greatly influenced behavioral neuroscience (Kolb, 2003).

Viewed in light of the criteria we have been employing, Hebb's theory can be described as reflecting some facts rather well. Thus, it is highly compatible with what is known about neurological functioning—despite the fact that instrumentation to detect and measure brain activity was not sufficiently developed in Hebb's time to permit him to verify his neurological speculation. Now there is increasing evidence that neurological functioning in the brain is organized in ways similar to Hebb's description of cell assemblies and phase sequences (Pulvermuller, 1996). It is also clear, as Hebb speculated, that a large range of neural changes are linked with experience, and they appear to underlie learning and remembering. As Kolb and Whishaw (1998) note, these include changes in brain size and weight, in neuron size, in number of dendrite branches, in number and complexity of synaptic connections between neurons, and even in numbers of neural cells. Furthermore, current knowledge about neurological transmission supports Hebb's neurological assumptions. For example, the work of Kandel and others on habituation and sensitization in the Aplysia snail provides evidence of changes in neurological structure and chemical functioning that supports Hebb's notions that repeated co-activation of related neurons facilitates neural transmission among them.

In support of Hebb's theorizing, it's interesting to note that a recent summary of findings from neuroscience reflects some of the key assumptions of Hebb's theory. "Learning," write Bransford, Brown, and Cocking, "changes the physical structure of the brain. These structural changes alter the functional organization of the brain; in other words, learning organizes and reorganizes the brain" (2000, p. 115). That, in a nutshell, is what Hebb said almost half a century earlier.

It bears repeating that the concepts represented by inventions such as cell assemblies have an important explanatory function. Like all theories, Hebb's hypotheses should not be judged by their "truthfulness" but by the extent that

predictions based on these hypotheses agree with actual observations and the
extent to which they provide clear and useful explanations of observations. Indeed, no psychological theory need be blessed with "truthfulness." Science
would not recognize it in any case. Science insists on objectivity, replicability,
consistency, and usefulness—and usefulness is sometimes better judged by history than by science.[6]

From Behaviorism to Cognitivism

Isms seem to have been a little like religions among many psychologists. Even
when dealing with what are meant to be scientific systems of ideas, faith and emotion often seem to have as much to do with people's responses as does science—or
good sense. That's the way it has been with behaviorism and cognitivism.

Amsel describes it well, *read the Old Woman.* He uses a parliamentary metaphor
to describe historical confrontations between behaviorism and cognitivism. "I
like to point out," says Amsel, "that the S-R psychologists, who at one time
formed the government, are now in the loyal opposition, the cognitivists being
the new government" (1989, p. 1). But the change in government from the first
behaviorists (who shunned all mentalistic concepts) to current cognitive psychologists (who have largely abandoned the stimuli and responses of the first behaviorists) didn't happen overnight. It happened slowly. And it happened partly as
a result of the influence of Hebb, Tolman, and others like them.[7]

Uttal (2000), talking about what he describes as "the war between mentalism and behaviorism," describes the two principle points of view in the
early development of psychology. On the one hand, he says, there is the belief
that the subject matter of psychology is mental activity itself, and that it can
be studied directly. The opposing point of view is represented by a collection
of *behaviorisms* that maintain that it isn't the mind but observable behaviors
that should be the target of a science of psychology. The main difference between these two points of view, says Uttal, has to do with whether or not external behaviors can be used to make valid inferences about underlying mental
states.

---

[6]The Old Woman closed her notebook. For a long while she said nothing, just sat there on the straight-
backed chair staring at the window, although it seemed her eyes were focused not on the pane but
on the darkness far beyond. The cat sat on his haunches on the table looking out into the darkness,
his eyes wide and unflinching, his ears turned like a horse's toward what had drawn his attention, no
doubt even in that black night sensing things of which I could not be aware.

And then, as if she had not paused, the Old Woman began to speak once more, although she
didn't immediately reach for her notes. I reached to turn on the recorder, but it had never been off.

[7]Nor, to extend the metaphor, said the Old Woman, has psychology's parliamentary system been
strictly a two-party system. In the government, there have always been other -isms (such as human-
ism), -ologys (such as sociobiology), and -yses (such as psychoanalysis)—some with very loud voices;
others very quiet. And sometimes, I think, there have been revolutions that have perhaps had little
noticeable effect on the established system of government—grassroots revolts by peasants with machine guns and new theories. As if bored, the cat curled up on the table and closed his good eye. I
could not see the other one.

For his part, Hebb was a **neobehaviorist**—a *behaviorist* in that he retained a commitment to the need to preserve the objective, scientific nature of psychological investigation, but *neo* in that he sensed the need to include inferences about profoundly important mental processes such as thinking and imagining. For his part, Tolman—another neobehaviorist—deliberately gave behaviorism a different twist; he gave it a purpose.

Mechanistic Behaviorism

The behaviorism associated with theorists such as John B. Watson, Edwin Guthrie, Ivan Pavlov, and even B. F. Skinner and Edward Thorndike is sometimes referred to as a **mechanistic behaviorism.** These theories emphasize and try to understand the predictable aspects of human behavior—in other words, its *machinelike* qualities. Such theories share several characteristics: First, and perhaps most obviously, they arose largely as a reaction to the more mentalistic approaches that had previously dominated psychology. In contrast to these mentalistic approaches, behaviorism tries to be perfectly objective. Accordingly, its most devoted theorists concentrated almost entirely on aspects of behavior that could be observed and measured. The science of behavior thus became a question of discovering reliable relationships between stimuli and responses. And when theorists such as Hebb and Hull began to break away from this orientation by including intervening (mediating) variables in their systems, they were always careful to link them as directly as possible to observable events.

A second characteristic of behavioristic theories such as those of Watson, Guthrie, and Skinner is that they make few assumptions about the objectives or purposes of behavior except insofar as these can be related directly to specific needs or drives, often defined by measurable conditions of deprivation. Typically, a behavioristic interpretation of a behavior does not ask any questions about the intentions or the wishes of the actor. It simply looks for relationships between response consequences and behavior, or it searches for an understanding of how contiguity of stimuli, responses, and response consequences are important in determining behavior.

Some behavioristic theories, such as those described by Watson and Guthrie, are labeled **reductionist** or *molecular* because they try to explain behavior by analyzing it at a molecular level—that is, through its smallest elements or components. Watson and Guthrie, for example, based their theories on the physiology of the reflex and believed that the most useful approach to understanding and explaining behavior was to look at the most basic (molecular) response. For these theorists, behavior consists of chains of reflexes and reactions.

In contrast to the reductionist or molecular approach, behaviorists such as Hull, Hebb, and Skinner (as well as Tolman) looked at the organism's behaviors from a more *molar* (as opposed to *molecular*) perspective. They assumed that behavior could be understood "as a whole" without being reduced to its individual components.

Edward Chace Tolman (1886–1959)

Tolman was born into a Quaker family in Newton, Massachusetts, on April 14, 1886 (also the year of Guthrie's birth). He attended the Massachusetts Institute of Technology, from which he received a B.S. in electrochemistry in 1911. From there, he went to Harvard, where he obtained his M.A. in 1912 and his Ph.D. in 1915, both in psychology. He became a behaviorist while he was a graduate student at Harvard—although a behaviorist whose theories were very different from those of other behaviorists.

Tolman began his university teaching career at Northwestern University. He was let go three years later, however, apparently because of incompetence as a teacher, but perhaps more likely because of his Quaker-based pacifist convictions in a time of war. From Northwestern, he went to the University of California at Berkeley, where he spent most of the remainder of his academic career. For a few years, though, Tolman was compelled to leave Berkeley as well—this time after refusing to take a controversial loyalty oath spawned by the McCarthy purges. As a result, in 1950 he accepted teaching positions at the University of Chicago and at Harvard. As a member of the American Civil Liberties Union, Tolman was instrumental in bringing about guarantees of certain academic freedoms. As a result of his involvement in this effort, he was able to return to Berkeley in 1953.

Tolman, like Skinner, Hebb, and Guthrie, served as president of the American Psychological Association. Still, he was often accused of not being as serious and single-minded as he might have been regarding the development of his theories. His writings are filled with whimsy and anecdotes, and he wrote somewhat disparagingly about his own theorizing and research. "The system may not stand up to any final rules of scientific procedure," he says. "But I do not much care . . . In the end, the only sure criterion is to have fun. And I have had fun" (Tolman, 1959, p. 140). And perhaps his tongue was at least partly in his cheek when he dedicated one of his most important books to Mus norvegicus albinus—the white Norway mouse, although he probably meant the white Norway rat (Sahakian, 1981; Woodworth & Sheehan, 1964).

Tolman's Purposive Behaviorism

Not all psychologists enthusiastically embraced mechanistic behaviorism's emphasis on the predictable, machinelike qualities of human functioning. There were actually some strong negative reactions to behaviorism, evident in **cognitivism**. Cognitivism is an approach in psychology that is concerned more with decision making, thinking, problem solving, imagining, and related topics, than solely, or primarily, with observable behavior.

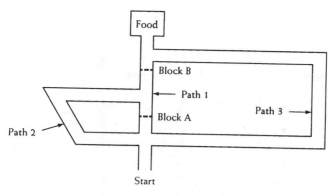

Figure 6.5 In the Tolman and Honzik (1930) blocked-path study, rats that had learned this maze almost invariably selected path 3 when path 1 was blocked at B. It seemed they somehow knew that the barrier at B also blocked the much shorter path 2.

One of the early roots of cognitivism is German Gestalt psychology, which is discussed in the later pages of this chapter. Another is Tolman's theory, which challenged behaviorism's eviction of purpose and consciousness from psychology. All behavior has a purpose, insisted Tolman (1967); all actions, whether they be that of rat or woman or man, are directed toward some goal by **cognitions** (true to his behaviorist roots, he labeled cognitions *intervening variables*). Behavior is never simply the result of mindless S-R connections. But ever a behaviorist, Tolman insisted, "Mental processes are to be identified in terms of the behaviors to which they lead" (1932, p. 2). In other words, his intervening variables, like those described by Hull, are tied to observable behaviors.

Do Rats Have Purpose?

What evidence is there that a rat, for example, directs its behavior as if it had certain purposes? Why should the psychologist believe that cognitions, rather than simply a series of mindless S-R connections, are what drive the rat's behavior?

The Blocked-Path Study

The evidence, claimed Tolman, is convincing. Take, for example, the blocked path study (Tolman & Honzik, 1930). In this study, a rat is released into a maze with several different routes to the goal and is allowed to run freely until it has learned the maze. The next step is to place barriers in some of the paths and then observe the rat's reaction. Figure 6.5 shows an approximate representation of the original Tolman and Honzik maze. The paths vary in length from the shortest, most direct route (path 1) to the longest (path 3).

As expected, once they have learned the maze, hungry rats almost invariably select path 1 when given a choice. Also as might be expected, when path 1 is blocked at point A (see Figure 6.5), rats usually select path 2 (about 93% of the time).

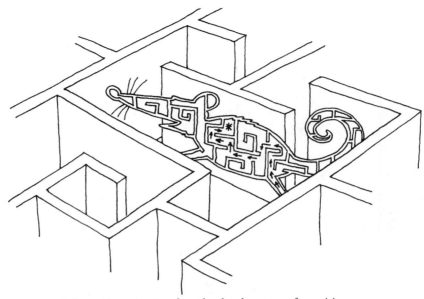

Tolman: Learning involves the development of cognitive maps.

The situation becomes more interesting when path 1 is blocked at point B. S-R theory might still predict that the rat would select path 2 because the entrance to it is not blocked and it is second in overall preference. How can a rat be expected to figure out that the block on path 1 at B also serves as a barrier for path 2 and that there is now only one path to the goal?

Nevertheless, the rat does figure it out. Now the rat consistently selects path 3 rather than path 2 (14 out of the 15 rats involved in the original experiment selected path 3). Should psychology assume that these rats "know" the same thing you and I do—that they have, in fact, developed some sort of cognitive grasp of the maze?

Yes, said Tolman, psychology should assume just that. Experiments such as these illustrate that learning involves the development of **cognitive maps.** A cognitive map is an internal representation of relationships between goals and behaviors as well as knowledge of the environment where the goals are to be found. What happens is that the organism develops a series of expectations with respect to behavior. These expectations are part of what Tolman labels *sign-significate* relationships. A sign is simply a stimulus; a significate is the expectation of reward that results from learning.

An Expectations Study

Even nonhuman animals behave as though they have expectations. Tinklepaugh (1928), one of Tolman's students, placed a banana under a cup in full view of a monkey. Then, when the monkey wasn't watching, he substituted a piece of lettuce for the banana. The monkey was allowed to turn the cup over, which it did very eagerly. The monkey then became extremely agitated, searching here and

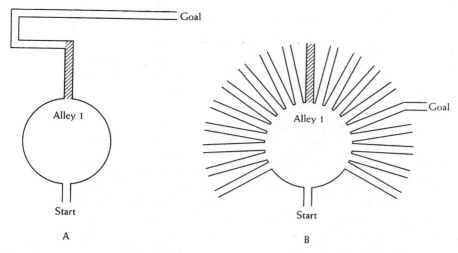

Figure 6.6 Place or direction learning in rats. In the Tolman, Ritchie, and Kalish (1946) study, rats learned a simple maze with an indirect path to the goal. In the second part of the experiment, the position of the goal and of the starting area remained the same, but the original path was blocked and 18 new paths were available.

there and snarling at Tinklepaugh. The monkey's behavior seems to indicate clearly that it had expected to find the banana under the cup. Its agitation and continued search would be difficult to explain using simple conditioning theory.

A Place Learning Study

In a classic experiment, Tolman, Ritchie, and Kalish (1946) trained rats to run across an open, circular area and into an alley that, after three right-angle turns (left, right, and right), eventually led to a goal box with a food tray (see maze A in Figure 6.6). In the next part of the experiment, the alley leading to the goal box was blocked, and 18 new alleys were made available to the rats (maze B). Which alley are the rats most likely to choose?

Behavioristic theory would predict that the rat would most likely choose one of the alleys closest to the original. Because these alleys are closest to the previously rewarded alley, hence most similar to it, the rat would be expected to quickly generalize the learned response to a neighboring alley.

Not so. In fact, far more rats choose alleys that go in the general direction of the original goal box. It appears that what these rats learned was not a series of connected responses, duly reinforced and stamped in, but a place. In Tolman's terms, they developed a cognitive map of the area, together with related expectancies. These expectancies, tied to the cognitive map, directed the rats' behavior.

A second experiment, reported by Macfarlane (1930), makes much the same point in a dramatic way. It also involved rats that were taught to find a goal box in a maze, but these animals had to swim through the maze rather than run. A plausible behavioristic interpretation of this phenomenon would maintain that the specific responses involved in swimming are chained together, reinforced, and eventually learned as a complete sequence. This same interpretation would also predict that if the maze were drained making the learned S-R chains involved in swimming completely useless, the rats would have to learn the maze all over again. In fact, however, when the maze was drained, the rats ran to the goal box without hesitation and with no more errors than they had been making while swimming.

A Latent Learning Experiment

These studies strongly suggest that there is more to learning mazes than the simple acquisition of stimulus-response or response-reward connections—a point that is dramatically underlined by the latent-learning experiment described briefly in Chapter 1. In this study, Buxton (1940) allowed rats to spend several nights in large mazes without feeding them in the maze. Some behavioristic grandfathers would surely predict that these rats would learn very little from their exposure to the mazes. They might be more than a little amazed to find that at least half the rats learned the correct path to the goal box without reinforcement. Buxton determined this by feeding the rat briefly in the goal box and then placing it immediately in the start box; half the rats ran to the goal box without a single error. It appears that rats are capable of developing cognitive maps even in the absence of a food reward. This learning, because it is delayed, is sometimes called latent. Latent learning, as we saw in Chapter 1, illustrates an important distinction between *performance* and *learning*: What is learned is not always immediately apparent in behavior.

Educational Implications and Summary Principles of Tolman's System

Four major themes summarize Tolman's theory of purposive behaviorism. Each has clear implications for educational practice:

Behavior Is Purposive

First, and most important, Tolman believed that all behavior is purposive. By this, he meant that all behavior is guided by expectancies, which are themselves related to goals. In its simplest sense, the purpose that guides the organism's behavior is the expectation of a reinforcing outcome.

It follows from this principle that if teachers are to influence and guide students' behavior, they need to find ways to influence and guide their goals and expectations. The best ways of doing this are implicit in the next summarizing theme:

Behavior Is Cognitive

The expectations that underlie and guide behavior are cognitions. They consist of the organism's awareness of possible (or probable) connections between certain actions and certain outcomes. These cognitions develop after experiences with stimuli and rewards. In effect, what is learned, says Tolman, is not a specific behavior in response to a stimulus or reward but a cognition—an item of knowledge concerning physical space and the possibilities of reward therein. More specifically, what is learned is a sign-significate relationship: knowledge of a link between stimuli and expectancies of acquiring a goal.

Note that a cognition is an abstraction—a theoretical invention. Tolman, a behaviorist, believed that cognitions should only be inferred from behavior, not through introspection.

One of the means by which teachers can influence students' expectations and goals is by arranging for the most desirable, growth-enhancing of their behaviors to be followed by positive outcomes. What students learn, Tolman explains, is an expectation that certain behaviors will lead to certain outcomes. As we saw in Chapter 4, teachers have considerable control over the outcomes of school-based behaviors.

Reinforcement Establishes and Confirms Expectancies

A third underlying theme in this system relates to the role of reinforcement in learning. Tolman's system deals with connections between stimuli and expectancies. Because expectancies develop in situations in which reinforcement is possible, the role of reinforcement is primarily one of confirming expectancies. The more often an expectancy is confirmed, the more likely it is that the stimuli (signs) associated with it will become linked with the relevant significate (expectancy).

This theme reemphasizes the notion that to the extent that teachers, and parents, control and influence the learner's environment and the outcomes of the learner's behavior, they can exercise an enormous influence on learning and behavior.

A Theory of Purposive Behaviorism Is Molar, Not Reductionist

A final important principle of Tolman's system is his emphasis on the molar rather than the molecular aspects of behavior. Unlike Watson and Guthrie, Tolman didn't reduce behavior to its smallest units but dealt instead with large units of behavior that are unified in the sense that they are governed by a single purpose. Purpose (a search for rewarding goals), rather than the reward itself, directs behavior. Put another way, the connections that explain behavior in Tolman's system involve links between stimuli and expectancies rather than between reinforcement and responses or between stimuli and responses. And the expectancies themselves develop as a function of exposure to situations in which reinforcement is possible.

From an educational perspective, this final theme leads to a less mechanistic, less rigid, view of the learner than might be implied by the behavioristic theories discussed in earlier chapters. Tolman's learner is not so much moved blindly this way and that by the rewards and punishments that the world provides; rather, this learner is a more thoughtful being, a learner more likely to develop expectancies and to weigh the possible outcomes of various behaviors.

Tolman's Purposive Behaviorism: An Appraisal

One of Tolman's important and often overlooked contributions to the development of psychology relates to his use of mazes in studies of rat behavior. He and his students designed dozens of ingenious mazes and conducted countless clever experiments with them. As Olton (1992) points out, the study of behavior in mazes continues to be a useful and important way of studying the cognitive mechanisms used to represent space and to direct movement. In addition, maze learning provides an important way of studying memory.

Tolman's principal contribution to the development of psychological theory lies not so much in the advances in knowledge and prediction made possible by his work as in the transition from behavioristic to more cognitive interpretations. Specifically, Tolman's theory departs from behavioristic theories such as those of Skinner, Watson, and Guthrie, which rejected speculation about events that might intervene between stimuli and responses, by emphasizing the importance of cognitive variables such as expectancies. But, notes O'Neil (1991), it is never entirely clear whether Tolman was actually making claims about what he considered to be "real" internal states or processes, or whether he was just speaking "as if." Hence, relative to the criteria described in Chapter 1, Tolman's position might be faulted for a certain inconsistency or lack of clarity.

It would be far from accurate, however, to convey the impression that psychology went directly from the mentalistic concepts of the early introspectionists to the interpretations of behaviorists, such as Watson and Guthrie, and then finally to a more enlightened cognitivism. Actually, cognitivism is approximately as old as behaviorism because Gestalt psychology, one of the earliest forms of cognitive theory, developed at about the same time as early behaviorism. It is nevertheless true, as we noted at the outset, that North American psychology went from a period when Watsonian and Thorndikean behaviorism were supreme, both in theory and in practice, to a later period when interest turned increasingly to cognitive topics (although behaviorism continued to flourish). Thus, it is relatively common in psychological literature to speak of the period during which behaviorism dominated in American psychology (from the 1920s to around the middle of the century) followed by a "cognitive revolution," which began around the middle of the twentieth century (see, for example, Mandler, 1996).

In some important ways, Tolman's thinking reflects something of both schools. This should not be surprising given that—although one of his first courses in psychology used Watson's brand-new and thoroughly behavioristic book—Tolman had traveled to Germany and met with leading gestaltists, including Köhler and his associates, before finishing his graduate work at Harvard (Tolman, 1952). Some 10 years later (around 1923), he returned to Germany to study with the Gestalt psychologists.

Gestalt Psychology: Basic Beliefs

At the time World War I broke out, a young German psychologist by the name of Wolfgang Köhler found himself marooned on the island of Tenerife off the coast of Africa, unable to return to his home because of the war. On Tenerife, there was a research station for studying apes, and Köhler studied them during the four years that he spent on the island. He reported his studies in a book entitled *The Mentality of Apes* (1925).

There are bright apes and stupid apes, Köhler concluded. Stupid apes seem to learn by association and repetition, practicing the same behaviors repeatedly. In their attempts to solve problems, said Köhler, they make "bad errors"—that is, errors based on old and inappropriate solutions. In contrast, bright apes learn very much like people do, repeatedly displaying an astounding capacity for higher mental process. Often, when they fail to solve a problem, they nevertheless make "good errors"—that is, they attempt solutions that, upon reflection, should have worked but didn't for one reason or another.

Köhler designed a variety of studies to observe the problem-solving behavior of apes in cages. These often required that the ape invent or discover a solution for the problem of obtaining a bunch of bananas. In some studies, for example, the ape had to use a long stick to reach the bananas. In some cases, it was necessary to join several sticks together so they would be long enough. In one study, the ape had to use a short stick, which didn't quite reach the bananas, to drag another longer stick within reach. In the "box" problems, the ape had to move a box underneath the bananas or pile boxes one on top of the other to reach the reward.

Insight *versus* Trial and Error in Ape Learning

Thorndike was wrong, claimed Köhler: Intelligent apes don't learn simply by trial and error. They don't just go about their cages lunging repeatedly at unreachable bunches of bananas, climbing the bars, and doing other well-practiced ape things. Instead, at least some apes appear to solve these complex problems very suddenly, as if they had just now grasped the solution. For example, when Sultan, perhaps the most famous of Köhler's apes, found he couldn't reach the bananas with his short stick, he stopped and, in Köhler's words, "gazed about him." Then, as if galvanized into action by his vision of the correct solution, "[he] suddenly carried out the correct reactions in one consecutive whole" (Köhler, 1927, p. 150). The Gestalt term for the process involved in this kind of solution is **insight.**

Insight is the cornerstone of Gestalt psychology. Essentially, it means *the perception of relationships among elements of a problem situation.* This means solving a problem by perceiving relationships between all the important elements of the situation. In Köhler's (1925) words, insightful thinking is a type of *relational thinking.* It requires a mental reorganization of problem elements and recognition of the correctness of the new organization.

But, cautions Köhler, just because the term *insight* or *relational thinking* is used to describe what might be considered an extraordinary accomplishment in an ape, we should not misinterpret it to mean "some special and supranatural faculty producing admirable and otherwise inexplicable results. As I used and intended the term, nothing of that sort should be implied in it" (1929, p. 371). As Köhler uses it, the term applies to understanding common facts and solving general, everyday problems.

Kurt Koffka (1886–1941)
Wolfgang Köhler (1887–1967)
Max Wertheimer (1880–1943)

The ideas and theories of Koffka, Köhler, and Wertheimer are almost inseparable, as are their lives. All were graduates of the University of Berlin (they became known as the "Berlin group"), all had training in philosophy and psychology, and all eventually emigrated to the United States courtesy of Hitler's persecution of the Jews (Koffka and Wertheimer were Jewish). They worked together, sharing their convictions and united in their attacks against both introspectionism and behaviorism, and they were friends: Köhler's 1929 book, *Gestalt Psychology*, is dedicated to Max Wertheimer, and Koffka's 1935 book, *Principles of Gestalt Psychology*, bears the inscription, "To Wolfgang Köhler and Max Wertheimer in gratitude for their friendship and inspiration."

Wertheimer, half a dozen years older than Köhler and Koffka, was born in Prague on April 15, 1880. His initial studies were in the field of law in Prague. Later he went to Berlin, where he studied philosophy and psychology and obtained his Ph.D. in 1904. His many interests included writing poetry and composing symphonies.

Acknowledged as the intellectual leader of Gestalt psychology, Wertheimer did far less to popularize the movement than did Köhler and Koffka. Wertheimer wrote little but designed a number of important experiments, elaborating Gestalt principles in his lectures and recruiting Koffka and Köhler to work with him. The idea for one of his most important experiments reportedly occurred to him during a vacation at the very beginning of his career. Riding on a train, he began to puzzle over the fact that lights that flash sequentially give the illusion of movement. Wertheimer's subsequent investigations of this "phi phenomenon" involved both Köhler and Koffka as his assistants and led eventually to the elaboration of Gestalt psychology. In 1933, Wertheimer immigrated to the United States, where he remained until his death in 1943.

Köhler was born in Reval, Estonia, on January 21, 1887. He obtained his Ph.D. from the University of Berlin in 1909 and subsequently, along with Koffka, worked with Wertheimer in Frankfurt. During World War I, he spent four years on Tenerife, serving as director of the anthropoid station there and studying the behavior of apes (and of chickens, too). The results of his investigations were published in an important book in 1917, translated as *The Mentality of Apes* (1925).

From Tenerife, Köhler returned to Berlin, where he remained until 1935. He published extensively during this time, becoming one of the most important spokesmen for the Gestalt movement. Conflict with the Nazi regime forced him to leave Germany permanently in 1935. He went to the United States, where he had already spent considerable time lecturing and where he stayed until his death in 1967. Köhler continued to write important books in the United States, engaging in fierce battles with behaviorists such as Hull and even publicly debating against Watson. He was awarded the distinguished scientific contribution award by the American Psychological Association and (like Skinner, Guthrie, Tolman, and Hebb) served as president of that association.

Koffka was born in Berlin on March 18, 1886, went to the university there, and obtained his Ph.D. in psychology in 1909. He had earlier studied science and philosophy in Edinburgh. From Berlin, he went to Frankfurt, where he and Köhler worked with Wertheimer. There he began the extensive writings that later became influential in popularizing Gestalt psychology. He was the most prolific writer of the Berlin group, publishing a large number of important and sometimes difficult books.

Like Köhler and Wertheimer, Koffka spent some time lecturing in the United States before moving there permanently in 1927. There he lectured at Smith College and continued to write until his death in 1941 (Boring, 1950; Sahakian, 1981; Woodworth & Sheehan, 1964).

Among the most important of Köhler's convictions is the belief that trial and error play a minor role in problem-solving behavior, even among apes and chickens, and especially among humans. "I am not sure that even after years of trial and error," Köhler writes, "a child would learn to organize [a sensory field]" (1929, p. 177). And organizing what is perceived, he claims, is far more important than the specific properties of what is perceived. Why? Because it is only through an understanding of their organization—through an understanding of their structure—that people know things.

Take, for example, something as simple as a melody. You know that a melody is made up of individual notes. But you cannot understand the melody—you would know nothing of it—were you to hear the notes in completely random arrangement. Similarly, the meaning of a geometric figure derives not from each of its elements (number of sides, dimensions of its parts, angles of corners), but from their relationships to each other.

Gestalt Means "Whole"

That the whole is greater than the sum of its parts is the saying most closely associated with Gestalt psychology. Thus the melody, not its individual notes and rests, is the whole, the organization, the gestalt—as is the trapezoid, the triangle, and the square. Their meaning comes not from summing their parts willy-nilly, but from the ability of humans (and apes) to perceive their organization. To perceive organization or structure is to achieve insight. *Gestalt* is German for *whole*; hence the name for this approach to psychology.

Not surprisingly, one way of summarizing Gestalt psychology is to describe its laws of perception. These laws were developed and elaborated largely by the three men considered to be the founders of the Gestalt movement: Wertheimer (1959), Koffka (1922, 1925, 1935), and Köhler (1927, 1969). Of these three, Wertheimer was the acknowledged leader, but Koffka and Köhler were most responsible for popularizing the movement through their writings.

Gestalt Theory: The Laws of Perception

The first and most basic argument advanced by gestaltists against procedures that emphasize the analysis of behavior is that behavior cannot be understood through its parts—that it cannot be reduced to isolated sensations (as the German psychology of introspection tended to do) or to isolated stimuli and responses (as American behaviorism did). This is not to deny that the whole is composed of parts, or that the parts can be discovered through analysis.

The whole thrust of the argument, notes Murray (1995), is that the whole (the *Gestalt*) is different from the parts, as is evident in countless daily events. As noted earlier, the overall perception when listening to music is not of isolated notes but, rather, of bars or passages. If this were not so, the order of notes and the intervals of time during which they are held, as well as the lapses between them, would not be important. Similarly, physical objects derive their identity from the way their parts are combined rather than only from the parts that compose them. An object as simple as an apple is no longer simply an apple after it has been put through a blender; nor is a house still a house when all of its timbers, nails, and other parts have been taken apart and sorted.

Prägnanz: Good Form
The first concern of the gestaltists was to discover the laws governing the perception of wholes. These laws, first described by Koffka (1935), are summarized briefly here. The laws are primarily perceptual and are most easily described and illustrated as such. Note, however, that Gestalt psychologists see no discontinuity between perception and thinking. They consider these laws applicable to both.

A single overriding principle governs perception and thinking: **prägnanz** (meaning "good form"). As Köhler noted, insightful solutions often seem to involve an "abrupt reorganization of given materials, a revolution, that suddenly appears ready-made on the mental scene" (1969, p. 163). Why is it the right revolution, and how does the person (or the animal) recognize that it is right? At least part of the answer, argues Köhler, is that the brain appears to be directed by a tendency for whatever is perceived to take the best form possible.

The exact nature of that form for all perceptual (and cognitive) experience is governed by four additional principles:

Principle of Closure
Closure is the act of completing a pattern or Gestalt. It is clearly illustrated in the observation that when you look at an incomplete figure (such as in Figure 6.7), you tend to perceive a completed design. The same phenomenon is readily

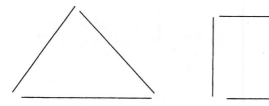

Figure 6.7
Closure: A tendency to perceive incomplete objects (or thoughts) as being complete. The figures tend to be perceived as a triangle and a square, rather than as individual lines that don't meet.

apparent in perception of a melody with missing notes or of incomplete words, such as p–ych–l–gy.

Although the term *closure* was originally employed only with perceptual problems, psychologists now use it in a variety of situations, retaining much of its original meaning but also adding some broader significance. For example, the phrase *achieving closure* is often used to refer to solving a problem, understanding a concept, or simply completing a task.

Principle of Continuity

Perceptual phenomena tend to be perceived as continuous. For example, a line that starts as a curved line (see Figure 6.8) tends to be perceived as having **continuity**—that is, as continuing in a curving fashion.

Principle of Similarity

The principle of **similarity** holds that objects that are similar tend to be perceived as related. For example, a person who hears two melodies at the same time recognizes each as a separate melody rather than hearing both as one. In Figure 6.9, there appear to be 4 rows of identical letters rather than 10 columns of different letters.

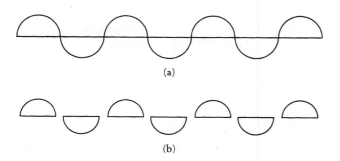

(a)

(b)

Figure 6.8
Continuity: A tendency to perceive things as being continuous. The lines in (a) tend to be perceived as a straight line running through a curved one, rather than as a set of semicircles as in (b).

```
a a a a a a a a a a
g g g g g g g g g g
c c c c c c c c c c
x x x x x x x x x x
```

Figure 6.9
Similarity: A tendency to perceive similar input as belonging together. The figure is seen as 4 rows of identical letters rather than as 10 columns of different letters.

Principle of Proximity

Objects or perceptual elements tend to be grouped by their **proximity.** Figure 6.10(a), for example, shows four sets of curved lines, whereas Figure 6.10(b) is perceived as three faces.

Gestalt Views of Learning and Memory

These four principles, along with several others, were developed by Wertheimer and later applied by Koffka to thinking as well as to perception. Because the gestaltists were not concerned with such molecular aspects of learning and behavior as stimuli and responses, their explanations of learning and memory are considerably more global and nonspecific than those of the behaviorists.

In general, the gestaltist view is that learning results in the formation of memory traces. The exact nature of these traces is left unspecified, but a number of their characteristics are detailed. The most important characteristic is that learned material, like any perceptual information, tends to achieve the best structure possible (prägnanz) relative to the laws of perceptual organization just discussed. Hence, what is remembered is not always what was learned or perceived, but it is often a better gestalt than the original. Wulf (1938) described three organizational tendencies of memory:

Leveling

Leveling is a tendency toward symmetry or toward a toning down of the peculiarities of a perceptual pattern. Figure 6.11 presents a hypothetical illustration of leveling. Koffka assumed that the process of leveling is also applicable to cognitive material. For example, when recalling the feeling of traveling in a train, a person may remember a generalized impression of forward motion and of countryside sweeping by without also remembering the sensation of swaying from side to side.

Sharpening

Sharpening is the act of emphasizing the distinctiveness of a pattern. One characteristic of human memory is that the qualities that most clearly give an object

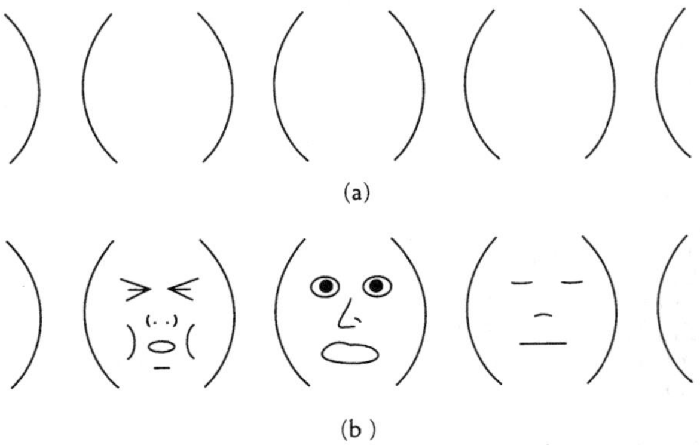

Figure 6.10
Proximity: A tendency to perceive things that are close together as belonging together. Part a is seen as four sets of curved lines; b is seen as three faces.

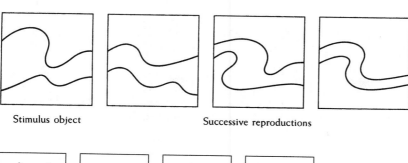

Figure 6.11
Leveling: A tendency toward symmetry, toward reducing abnormalities and peculiarities.

Stimulus object

Successive reproductions

Figure 6.12
Sharpening: A tendency to emphasize the distinctiveness of a pattern.

identity tend to be exaggerated in reproducing that object. For example, Figure 6.12 shows how successive recollections of a face with distinctive eyebrows tend to exaggerate the eyebrows.

Normalizing

Normalizing occurs when the reproduced object is modified to conform with previous memories. This modification usually tends toward making the remembered object more like what it appears to be. A hypothetical illustration of normalizing is presented in Figure 6.13 in which successive reproductions of the same stimulus object over a period of time become progressively more like something familiar (and hence, something "normal").

Beyond Perception: The Behavioral Field

The world as it might be seen and described by physics is one thing, Koffka points out; the world as the individual perceives it is quite another matter. And this, the world of "direct experience," is far more important for understanding the individual's behavior.[8]

---

[8]There is an interesting philosophical issue here, said the Old Woman, let me read to you from this book by Lehar (2003), and she motioned that I should turn off the recorder, but said nothing when I continued to take notes. Then she read different lines from here and there, which seemed to say, according to my hurried notes, that we cannot personally know the reality with which physics deals—but that neither can physics know our personal realities. Consciousness is a "deeply mysterious" thing according to Lehar. He explains that if you think about it, you will eventually realize that the reality you know—your consciousness—is all inside your head. It can't really be anywhere else. What you're observing when you think you're looking at reality is, in fact, *your personal consciousness of reality.* Consciousness, says Lehar, is, in fact, directly observable; the external reality of physics is not. The world is all inside your head, did you know that, asked the Old Woman? Then she turned back to her notes.

Figure 6.13
Normalizing: A tendency to perceive (and remember) the expected.

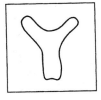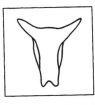

Stimulus object   Successive reproductions

The Lake of Constance

To illustrate, Koffka (1935, p. 28) tells the story of a man on horseback who struggles through a fierce blizzard across an open plain, finally arriving at an inn. "Gawd, which way did you come?" asks the innkeeper. The man, half frozen, points out the direction. "Do you know," asks the innkeeper in amazement, "that you have ridden across the Lake of Constance?" And the man, stunned, drops dead at the innkeeper's feet.

There is only one behavior here—that of riding across a frozen lake through a winter blizzard. The physical environment is fixed and clear. But, Koffka points out, the psychologist knows that the man's behavior would have been very different had he known about the lake. If, after the fact, the thought frightened him so much that it killed him, then he surely would not have crossed the lake if he had been aware of it beforehand.

The Behavioral Field

From the man's point of view, his behavior took place in a quite different environment—in what Koffka calls the **behavioral field** (or the *psychological field*). The behavioral field is the actor's personal view of what is real. In this man's behavioral field, there was a windswept plain. As he later discovered, though, in the real physical world there was a frozen lake.

Both the behavioral field and the physical environment always affect a person's behavior, claims Koffka. And although the physical environment clearly affects the behavioral field, the two are not the same. Koffka describes as another example the behavior of two apes in separate cages, each of which can reach a bunch of bananas only by stacking boxes one on top of the other. One, the bright ape, eventually does so, climbs up, and retrieves the bananas. The other, the stupid one, ends up sitting on one of the boxes, staring sadly at the unreachable bananas. Both these apes are in exactly the same physical field. But in the behavioral field of the bright ape, there are stacking boxes that reach way up; in the behavioral field of the other, there is only a box to sit on and some unreachable bananas.

Appearance versus Reality

The Gestalt laws of perception point out that what people see is not necessarily what is really out there. Your reality, as Lehar (2003) puts it, is all within your head. When you look at the book you are now reading, you are looking at your personal, entirely internal *consciousness* of this book. There may well be an objective, physical reality beyond the confines of your skull, but you can only "know" it *within* your consciousness. And your knowledge of it may not be accurate. Thus, when you saw a complete triangle in Figure 6.7, you did not perceive the physical field accurately. But that there is a triangle in Figure 6.7 becomes an actual part of your psychological reality. Thus does Gestalt psychology emphasize the difference between physical reality and what seems to be real.

The gestaltists believed that to understand behavior, it's necessary to know something of the individual's perception of reality (that is, of the person's behavioral, or psychological, field) (Smith, 1988). This is because people respond to appearance (what they think is real) rather than to reality. The task of psychology, claimed Koffka, is "the study of behaviour in its causal connection with the psychophysical field" (1935, p. 67). In many ways, this is a far more complex task than the behaviorists had set themselves—namely, that of understanding responses to real stimuli in the actual physical environment. At the same time, because the psychological field includes people's individual perceptions of other people (as well as of things, animals, and all else that might be relevant), this approach lends itself more easily to understanding social behavior.

Gestalt Psychology and Contemporary Cognitivism

Gestalt psychology is considered the beginning of contemporary cognitive psychology for two main reasons: first, because of its concern with perception, awareness, problem solving, and insight; and second, because it rejected behaviorism for being overly mechanistic, incomplete, and unsuitable for explaining higher mental processes. Köhler, in particular, felt that approaches such as Hull's were impractical because they were too insistent on objectivity, too determined to reject the usefulness of trying to understand individual perceptions and private awareness.

In several important ways, however, Gestalt psychology and contemporary cognitivism represent different interests and different approaches. Contemporary cognitive psychology deals with subjects such as problem solving, decision making, information processing, and understanding (the theories of Jerome Seymour Bruner and Jean Piaget, discussed in the next chapter, are examples). Cognitive theorists conduct research on a wide range of topics, primarily using human subjects. Topics include understanding prose, memory for words, paraphrasing, language learning, and reading. In contrast, Gestalt psychology made extensive use of animal (as well as human) experimentation and dealt mainly with problems of human perception.

Educational Implications of Gestalt Psychology

Gestalt psychology presents a dramatic contrast to some of the more behavioristic approaches that we have considered in earlier chapters in at least two ways: First, it rejects the trial and error explanations favored by psychologists such as Thorndike. People learn through *insight*, not through trial and error, explain the gestaltists.

Second, Gestalt psychology rejects the "reductionist" approach of early behaviorism. Psychologists who want to understand learning and behavior, insist the gestaltists, should not try to *reduce* it to simple elements like stimuli and responses. Instead, they should look at the more *molar* aspects of behavior—that is, they should look at the whole rather than its parts.

These—the belief that learning occurs through insight, and the belief that psychology should concentrate on the molar rather than the molecular aspects of learning—are two of the important themes that summarize Gestalt psychology. Because Gestalt psychology doesn't present learning principles that are as simple and clear as, say, those of Skinnerian behaviorism, it is not as easily applied to the nitty gritty of classroom practice. But these two underlying themes do have very clear and very powerful implications for teachers.

The rejection of trial and error as a useful way of learning means, very clearly, that teachers and parents should not present learners with problems that require them to attempt a wide variety of different solutions until they finally "get it right." Instead, learning situations should be structured in such a way that learners can eventually achieve *insight*. But how is this to be done?

First, suggests Wertheimer (1959), the problems selected for presentation to a learner should not be problems that can be solved by memorizing a series of steps. People who learn in this way, he explains, are prone to the learning difficulty referred to as *response set*. Response set is a strong tendency to respond, or to perceive, in a predetermined way, even when there are more appropriate responses. Second, Wertheimer argues that problems should be presented in meaningful, real-life situations so that learners can see their importance and their relationship to real, day-to-day problems. And third, learners need to be encouraged to *understand* the problem rather than to attempt to copy a set of prescribed procedures. Accordingly, the guidance that teachers provide students should be geared toward helping them discover solutions for themselves—that is, achieve insight on their own—rather than directed toward imparting all information and procedures from teacher to student.

In the jargon of current educational psychology, the Gestalt perspective supports what is termed **constructivism** rather than *direct teaching* (Lefrançois, 2000). Constructivist approaches are methods that are highly learner-centered and that reflect the belief that meaningful information is *constructed* by learners rather than given to them. In contrast, *direct teaching* implies more teacher-directed approaches. The methods of constructivism encourage discovery learning, cooperative approaches in the classroom, and active learner participation in the teaching/learning process. As we see in the next chapter, these methods are most compatible with cognitive theories such as those of Bruner and Piaget.

Gestalt Psychology: An Appraisal

Gestalt psychology was an important reaction against the introspectionism that had preceded it, as well as against the behaviorism that came to dominate much of American psychology in the first half of the 20th century. Köhler, for example, felt that a behaviorism such as Hull's theory was wrong in rejecting the scientific value of concepts such as consciousness or thinking. "I find myself therefore with a profound aversion and guard against the behaviorist, or any other one-sided and impractical purism in science," wrote Köhler (1929, p. 34). He argued that the behaviorists' insistence on dealing only with objective reality forced them to reject the validity and importance of what he called "direct experience": "There cannot be the slightest doubt for me that, as a child, I had 'direct experience.' . . . There were experiences which belonged to me personally and privately" (p. 20).

In some ways, Gestalt theories don't fare especially well with respect to the criteria listed in Chapter 1. "The theoretical ideas of the Gestaltists were notoriously vague," write Holyoak and Spellman (1993, p. 268). As a result, they are not especially useful for predicting or explaining behavior. "In the view of most contemporary observers," says Gardner, the theoretical program of Gestalt psychology was not well founded . . . there are too many exceptions or indeterminate cases" (1987, p. 114).

One example of vagueness in Gestalt theory, as Latimer and Stevens (1997) point out, relates to their use of the words "whole" and "part," both of which are fundamental to the theory. At times the word "parts" seems to mean specific units of perceptual analysis like notes for music, or angles and lines for geometric shape; at other times, it seems to refer to physiological or neural activity in the brain. In this connection, the Gestalt theorists often spoke of what they called *phenomenal* units, which seem to be subjective units of perception, but the precise nature of phenomenal units remains unclear.

Relative to some of the other criteria, however, Gestalt theory fares very well. For example, Gestalt psychology continues to have useful applications in counseling and therapy (Lobb, 2001). Gestalt-like notions of the behavioral field and of the self play an important role in humanistic theories of counseling such as that of Carl Rogers (he uses the expressions *phenomenological* and *phenomenal field* instead). Rogerian therapy is premised on the notion that to understand a person's behavior, it is essential to look at it from that person's personal view; change in behavior results when the person's views of reality change.

Perhaps even more important, Gestalt theory has proven highly thought provoking and has contributed significantly to the development of later cognitive theories (see Lehar, 2003; Uttal, 2002). In a real sense, notes Epstein (1988), Gestalt psychology has served as a basis for contemporary cognitive theory. Among other things, it provided psychology with the beginnings of a new metaphor.

Ⓜetaphors in Psychology

A metaphor is a comparison. Metaphors abound in literature and especially in poetry, where their purpose is to evoke images (sometimes impossible ones) that are more startling, clearer, and more moving than the reality they represent. For example, in Pablo Neruda's poem "Little America," the woman the poet loves is not just a woman. She is a country, with "boughs and lands, fruits and water, the springtime that I love . . . the waters of the sea or the rivers and the red thickness of the bush where thirst and hunger lie in wait" (1972, p. 110).[9] And in Neruda's "Letter on the Road," love is not simply a feeling; it is seeds and earth and water and fire, so that "perhaps a day will come when a man and a woman, like us, will touch this love and it will still have the strength to burn the hands that touch it" (Neruda, 1972, p. 148).[10]

In psychology, as in poetry, metaphors abound. But their purpose in psychology is less to move or startle than to inform and clarify. In the psychology of cognition, claims Bruner, "it is apparent that there have been nothing but metaphors" (1990a, p. 230). Perhaps the most common of all current metaphors for human cognition is the computer, from which psychology draws notions of humans as information-processing units. Psychologists create cognitive models that speak of processing, storing, retrieving, input, output, and on and on.

But the metaphor was not always entirely welcome in psychology or in science. For years, physical scientists were convinced that the result of their many investigations would be a complete, accurate, and absolutely literal description of the physical world and how it functions. In 1910, there seemed to be little reason to suspect that science might someday discover something about the world that could only be described in terms of black holes, quarks, antimatter, parallel universes, and other metaphorical concepts. Indeed, even in the 21st century, many scientists still do not suspect that there might be something not quite literal about their knowledge.

Metaphors in Behaviorism

And so it was in psychology. During the first half of the 20th century, a period dominated largely by behaviorism, psychologists searched valiantly for reliable facts, laws, and principles that might provide a literal description of human learning and behavior. The emphasis, especially for behaviorists like Skinner and Watson, was on keeping theorizing as close to the data as possible. And even neobehaviorists like Hull and Hebb, who allowed themselves to invent new metaphors in the form of hypothetical somethings that mediate between stimuli and response, nevertheless tried to define things operationally (that is, in terms of actual actions or operations). This was the legacy of "logical positivism"—a philosophy of science premised on the fundamental assumption that things are real and exact and that they can therefore be described and measured literally and accurately.

---

[9]The original is as follows: "ramas y tierras, frutas y agua, / la primavera que amo, / la luna del desierto, el pecho / de la paloma salvaje, / la suavidad de las piedras gastadas / por las aguas del mar o de los rios / y la espesura roja / del matorral en donde / la sed y el hambre acechan."
[10]The original: "Tal vez llegará un día / en que un hombre / y una mujer, iguales / a nosotros, / tocarán este amor y aún tendrá fuerza / para quemar las manos que lo toquen."

But as Smith (1990) points out, the behaviorists also found themselves using metaphors to explain and clarify. Hull, for example, used machine models of human functioning, describing his theory as the "robot approach." "So far as the thinking processes go," wrote Hull in one of his unpublished diaries, "a machine could be built which would do every essential thing that the body does" (quoted in Hays, 1962, p. 820).

Tolman, too, began to glimpse new metaphors in the imagination of the white Norway rat, for it seemed to Tolman that even the rat learns more than just S-R connections. Rather, it develops representations of the world—cognitive maps of what is out there—and notions that somehow connect what is out there with behavioral choices. Tolman called these notions "expectancies," and his view of human learning explored the metaphor of cognitive maps and hypotheses. Thus, Tolman's expectancies are representations of the world. But they are not the literal representations that a logical positivist might seek; they are metaphors.

Even Skinner used metaphors, claims Smith, although he was probably the most determinedly positivistic of the behaviorists and consequently held the "aim of eliminating metaphorical discourse from science" (1990, p. 255). His principal metaphor is a Darwinian, evolutionary one. In the same way as species survive or die out as a function of natural pressures interacting with "fitness," so too are responses selected by their consequences. Behaviors survive or are eliminated as a function of how they are reinforced, ignored, or punished.

Metaphors in Cognitivism

As noted earlier, cognitive psychology is a psychology of metaphors. To explain human functioning, cognitive psychology uses metaphors of mental structures, describing things that don't actually exist to represent things that can't be described literally. All theoretical cognitive concepts—for example, *operations, short-term and long-term memory, neural networks*—are metaphors. And most descriptions of how humans function (that is, of how cognitive structures are developed and used) rely on metaphors, especially computer metaphors. We look at these in succeeding chapters.

Ⓢummary

1. Hebb's model is based largely on knowledge and speculation about neurological and physiological processes. Its aim is to explain higher mental processes—processes that mediate between stimuli and responses.

2. The human nervous system is made up of cells called neurons, which consist of a cell body, receiving extensions called dendrites, and an elongated part called an axon. Transmission among neurons is from axon ends across the synaptic cleft,

which is the separation between the axon end and the dendrites of an adjacent cell.

3. For Hebb, higher mental processes (thinking) involve activity in neural assemblies. He reasons that this activity must take the form of neurons arranged in such a way that they can keep reactivating one another in patterns he calls cell assemblies; arrangements of related cell assemblies are called phase sequences.

4. Research with the Aplysia snail illustrates that habituation (long-term depression or LTD) and sensitization (long-term potentiation or LTP) involve chemical changes at the level of the neuron. This research provides support for Hebb's assumptions about neural transmission.

5. Important assumptions underlying Hebb's theory are the following: that cell assemblies result from the repeated presentation of similar stimulus patterns and therefore the repeated activation of the same neurons; that, if two assemblies are often active at the same time, they will tend to form associations with each other (thus explaining conditioning); that motor activity will become associated with the assemblies that are often active with it; and that each cell assembly corresponds to relatively simple sensory data.

6. *Set* refers to selectivity among responses; *attention* refers to selectivity among input. Set and attention are central processes in learning and perception.

7. The mechanistic behaviorism of theorists such as Guthrie and Watson (and even Skinner and Thorndike) seeks to be impeccably objective, analyzes behavior at a molecular level, and makes no assumptions about any intentions the actor might have. Tolman challenged this approach, claiming that all behavior is purposeful and that explanations for it need to consider the organism's expectations.

8. Tolman believed that all behavior is purposive; behavior involves cognitive elements, evident in expectancies, that can also be described as cognitions or cognitive maps; behavior should be analyzed at the molar rather than the molecular level; and expectancies develop as a function of exposure to situations in which reinforcement is possible (sign-significate relationships).

9. Gestalt psychology is a forerunner of contemporary cognitive psychology. Cognitive approaches to learning are characterized by a preoccupation with topics such as understanding, information processing, decision making, and problem solving.

10. The main beliefs of the gestaltists can be summarized in two statements: (a) The whole is greater than the sum of its parts, and (b) people solve problems through insight. The first gives voice to the belief that the analysis of a subject (or object) into its parts is not likely to lead to knowledge of that subject. The second is a rejection of the role of trial and error in solving problems.

11. The founders and popularizers of the Gestalt school were Wertheimer, Köhler, and Koffka. As a system, Gestalt psychology is closely linked with studies of perception and the formulation of laws of perceptual organization such as prägnanz, closure, continuity, similarity, and proximity. These laws are assumed to apply to thinking as well as perception.

12. Gestalt studies of memory have led to the observation that structural changes in information over time involve the processes of leveling (making symmetrical), sharpening (heightening distinctiveness), and normalizing (rendering more like the object should appear).

13. Gestalt theorists make an important distinction between external reality (the

physical field) and the individual's perceptions (the behavioral or psychological field). Both need to be considered to understand behavior. Our realities are within our skulls—presumably.

14. Psychology, especially cognitive psychology, makes extensive use of metaphors, although early behaviorists sought to be more literal than metaphorical (reflecting a logical positivism). Various machine metaphors have long been popular and are evident in Hull's "robotic approach" and, more recently, in the human-as-computing-machine metaphor.

Three Cognitive Theories: Bruner, Piaget, and Vygotsky

> *The dwarf sees farther than the giant, when he has the giant's shoulders to stand on.*
> **Samuel Taylor Coleridge**

Curled up like a dog in the grass beneath the wild raspberry canes, the Old Woman seemed to be sleeping. She had said I should meet her here below the rock face, that she would say the seventh chapter this afternoon. Anxious to continue, I wanted to awaken her but didn't dare. Thick yellow bees swarmed over the raspberry bushes and ants crawled through the juicy berries the Old Woman had gathered in a bowl. She held the bowl safe in the crook of her arm while she slept, and a smile played at the corners of her mouth.

Suddenly a bird plummeted from the skies in a swoosh of braking wing and tail feathers, curled its outstretched talons almost gently it seemed around the Old Woman's wrist and she was instantly awake, sitting, as though she had never slept, smiling at the peregrine, stroking its dark velvet cheeks, smoothing the blue-black feathers on its back, promising me, although I had not yet heard her acknowledge my presence, that tonight we would dine on rock doves and wild raspberries, and then she shook the bird into the sky

with a screeching cry. Hunt! the Old Woman yelled, and the bird climbed, its short wings churning, climbing, climbing, and the Old Woman explained that the bird was a rare peregrine falcon, the fastest of all the falcons, that it might fly even more than a third the speed of sound. She said that peregrine means "wanderer" or "pilgrim," and still the bird climbed until it was only a speck and then for a long minute it soared until, drawn by the vision of rock doves flying jagged patterns between barn and field on Peterson's farm beyond the road, it folded its wings and streaked like death at the one smooth gray dove it had marked from the flock and stunned it with a single pass, turning wildly to grasp it in its talons and return it to the Old Woman who said that we needed two and loosed the falcon once more till it returned shortly with a sandy-brown dove. And I had not seen or known that the Old Woman had trained a hunting peregrine falcon.

While she plucked the birds, the Old Woman motioned that I should turn on the recorder.

This Chapter

What is a falcon to a pigeon? *the Old Woman mused. Then she was silent for a long time.* And what is a person to a pigeon? *she continued.* What does a pigeon think of people when it swoops above their houses or flies above their fields and forests? Of what does it dream, hunched in a city tree or huddled on the edge of a roof as people scurry about beneath its perch? In the pigeon's thoughts, is a person just another big, earthbound thing, indistinguishable from horses, cows, goats, and trucks? Does the pigeon have a concept of "peopleness"? Is the pigeon capable of any thoughts of this kind?

Objectives

Tell your readers, said the Old Woman, that that's one of the questions this chapter answers as it looks at the topics of cognitive psychology, at what Bruner (1985) describes as the human taste for knowledge, the human hunger for information. More than that, claims Bruner, humans are forever going beyond the information given.

Explain to them, said the Old Woman, that even if they don't go beyond the information given in this chapter, they'll be astounded to discover that once they have finished digesting its contents, they'll be able to (while standing or sitting) answer remarkably complex questions relating to what Bruner meant by the following:

- *Concept formation*
- *Categories and coding systems*
- *Strategies*
- *Going beyond the information given*

They will also know what Piaget meant by

- *Adaptation, assimilation, and accommodation*
- *Play, imitation, and intelligence*
- *Sensorimotor, preoperational, concrete, and formal developmental stages*

And they will have insights into the meanings and educational implications of Vygotsky's notions of

- *The zone of proximal development*
- *Scaffolding*

Even better, said the Old Woman, they will also have stunning new insights into what pigeons know about people.

Cognitive Psychology

It's no easy matter for people to ask pigeons what they know and what they think. But Herrnstein, Loveland, and Cable (1976) gathered some pigeons and, in a fashion, asked them what they thought of people. Even more astounding, the pigeons answered.

What Herrnstein and his associates did was present pigeons with series of slides, some of which contained one or more people doing a variety of things, dressed in different ways (or even nude), and sometimes partly obscured by other objects such as trees. The researchers arranged for pigeons to be reinforced only when they pecked in the presence of a slide containing a person.

Sure enough, the pigeons learned to do this. They seemed to have what Herrnstein and his associates call "natural concepts" that include complex and indeterminate notions such as what a person is. And they were able to identify slides representing this concept even when the "peopleness" of people was disguised in different activities, different contexts, and different clothing.

Pigeons, of course, aren't the only nonhuman animals that can be demonstrated to form concepts. For example, recall Tinklepaugh's (1928) research in which monkeys were shown either a leaf of lettuce or a banana, which was subsequently hidden. If the monkey later remembered where the lettuce or the banana was hidden and subsequently found it, the monkey was allowed to eat it and seemed quite pleased to do so, no matter whether lettuce or a banana was used. But when Tinklepaugh showed the monkey a banana and the monkey later found a lettuce leaf hidden where the banana should have been (because Tinklepaugh had surreptitiously switched the two), the monkey seemed very upset. It not only ignored the lettuce (which it presumably would have eaten had it been expecting to find it), but it continued to search everywhere for the missing banana—clear evidence, claimed Tinklepaugh, that the monkey had learned not only where the object was hidden but also had a clear and stable concept of what should have been hidden in that location.

Studies such as these, note Medin and Ross (1992), present serious challenges to behavioristic explanations. If the simpler behaviors of animals can't be adequately explained using behavioristic positions, then the presumably more complex behaviors of humans might be even less well explained. And if even animals have concepts and apparent thought processes, then psychology should perhaps concern itself with these as well as with more easily observed and described behaviors. Enter cognitivism, an approach to theories of learning concerned primarily with intellectual events such as problem solving, information processing, thinking, and imagining. As we saw in the previous chapter, Tolman's behaviorism, with its description of expectancies, goals, and purpose, foreshadowed contemporary cognitive concerns. And Gestalt psychology's concern with perception, awareness, problem solving, and insight, as well as its rejection of behaviorism as overly mechanistic and incomplete, also reflects cognitive emphases.

Ⓐ Comparison of Cognitivism and Behaviorism

Cognitive psychology is distinguished from behaviorism in a number of important ways.

First, cognitive psychology's principal interests are with higher mental functions. The most important of these higher mental functions have to do with perception (how physical energies are translated into meaningful experiences), concept formation, memory, language, thinking, problem solving, and decision making. As we saw in Chapter 6, these topics are reflected in the sorts of metaphors that characterize cognitive psychology—for example, information-processing or computer metaphors in contrast with Clark L. Hull's "mechanical robot" metaphor.

Second, the shift to cognitivism also saw a shift from an emphasis on animal research to a renewed emphasis on human research. Topics like language learning, reading, strategies in concept attainment, and the growth of logic cannot easily be investigated with rats and pigeons.

Table 7.1 *Principal Differences Between Behaviorism and Cognitivism*

	Behaviorism	**Cognitivism**
Principal concepts	Stimuli, responses, reinforcement	Higher mental processes (thinking, imagining, problem solving)
Main metaphors	Machinelike qualities of human functioning	Information-processing and computer-based metaphors
Most common research subjects	Animals; some human research subjects	Humans; some nonhuman animal research
Main goals	To discover predictable relationships between stimuli, responses, and response consequences	To make useful inferences about mental processes that intervene to influence and determine behavior
Scope of theories	Often intended to explain all significant aspects of behavior	Generally more limited in scope; intended to explain more specific behaviors and processes
Representative theorists	Watson, Pavlov, Guthrie, Skinner, Hull	Gestalt psychologists, Bruner, Piaget, Vygotsky, connectionist theorists (see Chapter 8)

Third, the principal aim of behavioristic theories has typically been to determine the relationships that exist between behavior and its antecedents as well as its consequences. In contrast, the principal goal of cognitive theories is to make plausible and useful inferences about the mental processes that intervene between input and output, and about what we think of as *meaning*.

Fourth, cognitive theories tend to be less ambitious in scope than were behavioristic theories such as B. F. Skinner's or Hull's. There have been few attempts to build systematic and inclusive cognitive theories that would explain all of human learning and behavior. The emphasis in the last several decades has been on intensive research in specific areas, rather than on the construction of general systems (see Table 7.1).

The Main Metaphor of Cognitive Psychology

The dominant metaphor in cognitive psychology, note Massaro and Cowan (1993), is one of **information processing (IP)**—essentially a computer-based metaphor. Information processing refers to how information (input) is modified or changed. The emphasis is on the perceptual and conceptual processes that allow the perceiver to perceive; determine how the actor acts; and underlie thinking, remembering, solving problems, and so on.

The single most important common characteristic of the topics of cognitive psychology is that they presuppose mental representation and, of course, information processing. Accordingly, theory building in the development of cognitive psychology has taken the form of metaphors relating to the nature of mental representation and to the processes involved in constructing and using these representations.

Among important theoretical contributions to the development of contemporary cognitive psychology are those made by Jerome Bruner, Jean Piaget, and Lev Vygotsky; these are discussed in the remainder of this chapter. Subsequent chapters deal with specific areas where current research is primarily cognitive: artificial intelligence, memory, and motivation.

Bruner's Learning Theory: Going Beyond the Information Given

In a classic article, Bruner (1964) compares the development of a child to the evolution of the human race.

Evolution of the Brain

In the beginning, says Bruner, humans were far from the fastest, the fiercest, or the strongest of the predators on this planet. There is little doubt that the fabled saber-toothed tiger or some other awesome beast would have been highly successful in controlling human population had it not been for one simple fact: The human proved, in the end, to be more intelligent than all who preyed on human flesh. So intelligent was this creature that it eventually took the course of evolution into its own hands. It used its brains.

"Brains are wonderful things," Johanson and Shreeve tell us. "There is no better solution to one's environment—no claw so sharp, no wing so light that it can begin to bestow the same adaptive benefits as a heavy ball of gray matter" (1989, p. 262).

Advantages of Brains
At the dawn of civilization, human brains allowed access to food sources that would be overlooked by humankind's finned, feathered, or clawed competitors, many of whom had better noses, keener eyesight, swifter movement, and stronger beaks and jaws. Brains are what permitted people to make the connection between sharp sticks and digging into the ground for roots and tubers, or between heavy rocks and stunned prey (or predators). Eventually brains led to stone and wooden tools, agricultural and hunting implements, the wheel, the rocket, the computer . . . and whatever may come next. And perhaps even more important, brains led to the development of language and of **culture**—and consequently to the possibility of sharing information and of transmitting it among individuals and across generations. Thus, although the raw matter of our nervous systems may be a product of evolution, of genetic transmission, the products of our brains are transmitted in other ways, most of which depend on language or other symbol systems.

Jerome Seymour Bruner (1915–)

Jerome Bruner was the youngest of four children in a Jewish family living in an affluent New York suburb. At the age of 2, he underwent the first of a pair of surgical procedures to correct his early blindness (caused by cataracts), a process about which he retained no memories. He describes his parents as "remote grownups"; the center of his family—the "we" of his childhood—comprised himself, his siblings, and two cousins.

When Bruner was 12, his father died. His mother moved every year after that (to Florida, to California, to "the country"), and the effect on young Jerome was, in his words, "too sudden a transformation" (Bruner, 1983, p. 5). He describes shifting schools constantly but never quite shifting his allegiances before moving again, as though caught up in an endless adolescence. "My formal secondary schooling was appalling," he writes (1983, p. 17), lamenting that he never stayed in one school long enough to develop any good relationships with teachers, although his marks were acceptable.

Bruner describes himself as shy and ill at ease as an adolescent, and he thought himself ugly. At the age of 16, he and some friends acquired a motorized racing hull that they smoothed and polished, and with whose engine they tinkered and played until they had become experts. In 1932, they won the Round Manhattan race ("heady stuff" says Bruner). When, in 1972—at the age of 57—Bruner was named Watts Professor of Experimental Psychology at Oxford University—he and his wife, with a few friends helping as crew, sailed across the Atlantic in his sailboat.

At 17, Bruner entered Duke University in Durham, North Carolina. He obtained a B.A. from Duke in 1937, and 4 years later, he received his Ph.D. from Harvard. He has since been a professor at Harvard as well as at Princeton, Cambridge, Oxford, and at the New York University School of Law. He was one of the founders, as well as a director, of the Center for Cognitive Research at Harvard.

Bruner's research has been highly eclectic and highly influential, in education as well as in psychology. He is widely recognized as one of the leaders of the "cognitive revolution" of the 1950s and 1960s (Bakhurst & Shanker, 2001). He has been a prolific writer, with more than 10 books and many dozens of articles to his name. Even in his 80s, Bruner continued to write about topics such as the development of the self (Bruner, 1997c), the development and meaning of meaning (Bruner, 1996a), and the history and the future of the cognitive revolution (Bruner, 1997d). In 1983, he concluded an autobiographical essay with the note, "I suppose my life has been a good one . . . psychology has certainly helped it to be so, psychology as a way of inquiry rather than as a basis of wisdom" (1983, p. 293).

Maladaptive Brains

The same evolutionary forces that molded other organs also shaped brains, notes Cowley (1989). These evolutionary forces tend to favor behaviors that maximize chances of surviving and reproducing. But they are forces whose effects take shape very slowly over vast stretches of time. On the other hand, the environments in which humans live now change with startling rapidity. As a result, some behaviors that were once highly adaptive persist, even though they are now counter adaptive—witness humanity's peculiar and frightening penchant to destroy its environment and to shorten its lives through resting too much and eating too much of the wrong things. Most of human evolutionary history was spent in Pleistocene environments, Cowley (1989) points out. There, snakes and other wild creatures posed far greater threats than water and air pollution, and ingesting too much fat, salt, or sugar was laughably unlikely. Also, a well-rested and well-fed animal can more easily survive a cold spell or escape from a predator. It's as though the Pleistocene dragons of Sagan's (1977) Eden still whisper in humans' ears when they stand before their refrigerators: "Eat while you can. There may be none tomorrow—if there is a tomorrow."

Evolution of Mental Representation

Still, if you are human, you know there will be food tomorrow, and you know the saber-toothed tiger is not likely to invade your bedroom this night. You can anticipate with startling clarity; you can plan for times that have not yet come but whose coming can be measured to the very second. Not only can you anticipate the future; you can also remember the past. And more than all this, you are conscious of your awareness; you can reflect on your own reflections.

Put simply, you have a mind that is made possible by your nervous system and your brain. The mind, says Alexander (1989), presents the most striking—and the most difficult to understand—gap between humans and all other animals.

Inventions and Mental Evolution

The evolution of the mind, Bruner notes, is evident through three waves of remarkable inventions, each of which served three different functions. First, humans succeeded in developing devices that could amplify their motor capacities: simple machines (levers, pulleys, inclined planes, perhaps even the legendary wheel) and combinations of machines to make weapons (knives, arrows, spears, and hatchets). By amplifying their motor capacities, humans became stronger and faster, better able to build shelters, and far less vulnerable both to predators and to natural catastrophes.

Centuries later—quite recently in human history—a second group of inventions appeared and again dramatically altered the pattern of human evolution. These inventions amplified sensory rather than motor capacities. They include the telescope, radio, television, and all the other instruments that expand humans' ability to see, hear, feel, and sense things they could not otherwise sense.

The final group of human inventions includes those that amplify what Bruner terms *ratiocinative* (intellectual) capacities. These are human symbol systems and theories; they include computer languages and systems. Almost all human mental work, claims Bruner (1997b), is now done with the aid of the technology that cultures provide their members. These technologies enrich human competencies enormously.

Evolution of Representation in Children

Bruner suggests that the representational systems children use as they develop closely parallel the history of human inventions. Thus, at the earliest ages, children represent objects through their own immediate sensations of them. In Bruner's words, things get "represented in the muscles." This representation, termed **enactive representation**, corresponds to the period in human evolution when the emphasis was on the amplification of motor capacities.

Early in development, children progress from a strictly motoric (or enactive) representation to what Bruner calls **iconic representation**. An icon is an image; accordingly, iconic representation involves the use of mental images that stand for certain objects or events. This type of representation corresponds to the period during which human inventions were directed at amplifying sensory capacities.

The most advanced form of representation available to the child is **symbolic representation**, which parallels the development of inventions that amplify intellectual capacities. The fundamental difference between a symbol and an icon is that the icon bears a literal resemblance to its referent, whereas the symbol does not. A symbol is completely arbitrary: The number *2* does not look like a collection of two objects any more than the word *turkey* looks like that bird. Yet humans have absolutely no difficulty in understanding what is meant by either of these or, indeed, by most of the thousands of other symbols in this text.

Although enactive, iconic, and symbolic representation develop sequentially, they don't replace one another. Adults continue to represent both enactively and iconically as well as symbolically. Thus, people "know" how to ride a bicycle, stroke a cue ball, or execute a golf shot not primarily in symbols or in images but in the body—which is why it's so difficult to explain in words how these things are done. In contrast, we recognize faces not in activity or even in symbols but in images.[1]

Representation and Cognitive Theory

In summary, adults have at least three distinct modes for representing not only the effects of sensory experiences but also thoughts. The importance of representation—and especially of symbolic representation—can hardly be overestimated.

A symbolic representational system, most importantly language, is absolutely essential to systematic reasoning, says Newell (1990). In addition, such a system is essential for sharing knowledge among people. Ultimately, representation is fundamental in determining human culture and in shaping the experience of living a human life. Representational systems, claims Bruner, are "a very special

---

[1]And here again, said the Old Woman as an aside, you can't describe *any* face, not even your own, so that some stranger could easily recognize it in a crowd of other faces. Unless, of course, there's something especially odd about your face. And then she added, rather unkindly, perhaps your face is not that good an example.

kind of communal tool kit whose tools, once used, make the user a reflection of the community" (1990b, p. 11). The mind, he argues very firmly, can reach its full potential only through participation in a culture (Bruner, 1996b).

Bruner's Theory of Representation: Categorization

How people build up and use representations is one of Bruner's principal concerns. The metaphor he invents as a basis for his theory of representation is one of **categorization.** All human cognitive activity involves categories, Bruner informs us. Hence, to understand Bruner's theory, it is important to know what a **category** is, how it is formed, and of what value it is.

What Is a Category?

If a man sees a head with long blond hair and an attractive face smiling at him over a sea of foam in a pink bathtub, does he simply see a head with long blond hair and a smiling face over a sea of foam in a pink bathtub?[2]

In a literal sense, yes, that is all he sees. But in another sense, he also sees much more. He sees that this must be a woman who probably has two arms, two legs, toenails, and other things. Yet he can't perceive these things, so what he does, in Bruner's words, is "go beyond the information given" (1957a). First, he decides that this is a woman; second, he makes inferences about this woman based on what is known about all women. According to Bruner, inferences are made possible through using categories—in this case, the category woman. The category woman is a **concept** in the sense that it is a representation of related things; it is also a **percept** in the sense that it is a physical thing apprehended through the senses. Percepts and concepts are roughly equivalent in Bruner's system.

Categories can be compared to the cell assemblies and phase sequences of Hebb's theory. Because categories are essentially classifications of objects relative to properties that are redundant for that type of object, categories are based on associations developed largely through frequency or redundancy. For example, if the first people to arrive from Mars all have warts, eventually warts will become an essential feature of the category Martian. In Hebbian terms, the cell assemblies activated by warts will become associated with others activated by Martians.

Catgegorization, as Markman and Gentner (2001) point out, is closely tied to similarity. That is, objects tend to be placed in the same categories based on the similarities among them—that is, because of the characteristics that are common to them. Thus, cars are categorized as cars because of shared form and function.

---

[2]Maybe you should point out to your readers, saiᴗ the Old Woman, plopping another wild raspberry into her mouth, that the observations that follow would have been just as appropriate had it been a woman looking at a head with curly black hair and a beard smiling at her over a sea of suds in a blue bathtub. I wondered if we would have enough raspberries left for dinner.

Categories as Rules

"To categorize," writes Bruner, "is to render discriminably different things equivalent, to group the objects and events and people around us into classes, and to respond to them in terms of their class membership rather than in terms of their uniqueness" (Bruner, Goodnow, & Austin, 1956, p. 1). Hence, one way of looking at the term *category* is to define it as though it were a rule (or a collection of rules) for classifying things as being equal. This is a logical definition because concepts and percepts, which are achieved through categorizing, are collections of things that are in some way equivalent. For example, the concept (or category) *book* can be thought of as an implicit rule that allows an individual to recognize an object as a book. In fact, this category is a collection of rules that specify that to be a book, an object must have pages, have a cover, contain writing, and have a title (among other things).

Attributes

Categories, as rules, say something about the characteristics that objects must possess before they can be classified in a given way. Characteristics of objects are **attributes.** Bruner defines attributes as "some discriminable feature of an object or event which is susceptible of distinguishable variation from event to event" (1966, p. 26). Attributes are therefore properties of objects that are not possessed by all objects. They are further distinguished by whether they play a role in the act of categorizing. Attributes that define an object are called **criterial attributes;** those that do not are irrelevant. Having female sexual organs is probably a criterial attribute for the category woman; a particular color of hair is irrelevant.

Rules for Categorizing

As rules, categories specify the nature of the similarities (and differences) required for membership in a category. Specifically, categories as rules spell out four things about the objects being reacted to.

First, as we just saw, a category is defined by criterial attributes. Thus, the rule states, for membership in category *y*, it is essential that the object possess attribute *x*. For example, the rule for *car* might specify that the object must have a motor, a place to sit, and certain control devices.

Second, a category specifies the attributes that are criterial and indicates the manner in which they are to be combined. If, for example, all the parts of a car were disassembled and placed in plastic garbage bags, it is unlikely that anyone would treat the result as though it were a car. As the Gestalt psychologists insisted, the whole is greater than the sum of its parts; the rule for the category *car* says that the parts must be assembled in a certain way.

Third, a category assigns weight to various properties. A car might continue to be classified as a car even if it had no bumpers and no windows, and perhaps even if it had no wheels. But if it had no motor and no body, it might be categorized as something else because these properties are more criterial (more essential) for membership in the category.

Fourth, a category sets acceptance limits on attributes. Attributes often vary from event to event; color, for example, can vary tremendously. A rule specifying that a car has four wheels might set the limits of variation at zero. Thus, anything with three wheels or less, or five wheels or more, would not be a car.

Summary of Categorization

People interact with the environment through categories, or classification systems, that allow them to treat different events or objects as though they were equivalent. Incoming information is therefore organized into preexisting categories or causes the formation of new ones. In either case, the end product of the processing will be a decision about the identity of the stimulus input, as well as a number of implicit inferences about the object or event associated with the input. Bruner suggests that all interaction with the world must involve classifying input in relation to categories that already exist. Completely novel experiences are "doomed to be a gem serene, locked in the silence of private experience," writes Bruner (1957b, p. 125). In short, people probably cannot perceive completely new stimulus input; if they can, they cannot communicate it.

Decision Making

All information is processed through an act of categorization, and all decisions also involve classifying. Actually, in Bruner's system, decision making is simply another aspect of information processing that involves categorization.

First, to identify an object is to make a decision about whether it belongs in a given category. Second, once an object is placed in a category and therefore identified, there is inherent in the category a decision about how the object should be reacted to. For example, the almost unconscious recognition that a traffic light is red is the result of interpreting the input in question as though it were an example of events belonging to the category *red light*. Implicit in this act of categorizing is the decision not to walk across the street.

A second aspect of decision making involves the selection of strategies for attaining concepts. These are discussed later in this chapter.

Coding Systems

Categories allow the classification—and hence, the recognition—of sensory input. But going beyond the immediate sense data involves more than simply making inferences based on the category into which the input has been classified. More importantly, it involves making inferences based on related categories. For example, the inference that a new object (let's call it a "korug") is edible might be made not simply because the korug is pearlike and pears are edible, but also because the korug is orangelike and oranges are edible. In fact, the korug is identified and predictions are made about it based on a variety of related categories. These related categories are referred to as a **coding system** (see Figure 7.1).

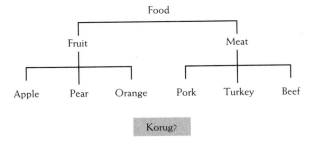

Figure 7.1
Schematic representation of a coding system.
Coding systems are hypothetical groupings of
related categories.

Coding systems can be thought of as hierarchical arrangements of related
categories, such that the topmost category in the system is more generic (or
general) than are all the categories below it. In other words, as one moves up
from the specific instances that define related categories, each subsequent concept (or category) is more abstract—freer of specifics, in Bruner's terms. To remember a specific, it is usually sufficient to recall the coding system of which it
is a member. The details of the specific instance can then be re-created. And
the transfer value of coding systems—that is, the extent to which they help the
individual make generalizations—results because a generic code is really a way
of relating objects and making inferences about them. Thus, a significant amount
of transfer is involved in the decision that an appropriate behavior toward a korug
might be to eat it.

Concept Attainment

Bruner's experimental work in the formation of concepts is a significant contribution to this important area of cognitive psychology. Among other things, his
is the first systematic attempt to examine the belief that people form concepts
by generating and testing hypotheses about the attributes of the concepts in
question. And that he applied a controlled, experimental approach to this difficult cognitive problem did a great deal to make cognitivism more acceptable to
psychologists reared in an experimental—and usually behavioristic—tradition.[3]

For Bruner, **concept attainment** involves discovering the attributes that
may be useful in distinguishing between members and nonmembers of a class.
Concept formation, a slightly different process, involves learning that specific
different classes exist. For example, when Jack learns that there are edible as

---

[3]If I had more time, said the Old Woman as she got up to stretch, I would have found some way to
emphasize more clearly how Bruner's work on concept learning had a tremendous influence on
psychology in the 1950s. She explained that you have to realize that Bruner's early work was done
at a time when American psychology was largely behavioristic. She said that before this work, mentalistic notions such as *concepts* had never seemed particularly amenable to objective experimental
investigation and verification and were very unpopular with the behaviorists. But Bruner demonstrated that solid empirical investigations are possible even in the area of human thinking. Then the
Old Woman sat down, her back resting against the stump. She started to read again.

well as inedible mushrooms, he may be said to have *formed* the concept of edible versus inedible mushrooms. But that Jack has formed this concept does not mean that he can now go out into the forest and bring back only edible mushrooms. When he has learned precisely what the differences between edible and inedible mushrooms are, he will have *attained* the concept. Bruner suggests that the process of forming concepts is predominant in humans until around the age of 15, after which there is a prevalence of concept attainment.

Types of Concepts

Bruner distinguishes among three kinds of concepts based on the attributes that define them—that is, based on the attributes that are *criterial* for them. *Conjunctive* concepts are defined by the joint presence of two or more attribute values. For example, a pen is an object that can be held in the hand and that can be used to write. Both of these conditions must be met if the object is to be a pen; therefore, the concept *pen* is conjunctive.

A *disjunctive* concept, in contrast, is defined either by the joint presence of two or more attributes or by the presence of any one of the relevant attributes. For example, a human with a mental disorder may have delusions of grandeur, an intense fear of persecution, and a mania for stealing, or he or she may simply have the delusions, or the phobia, or the mania. This is a disjunctive concept.

The third variety of concept is referred to as *relational*. It is defined by a specified relationship between attribute values. A rectangle, for example, has four sides, but two sides must also be equal in length and longer than the other two, which must also be equal in length. *Rectangle* is thus a relational concept.

Strategies for Concept Attainment

People form concepts, says Bruner, to simplify the environment and to know how to react to it. Furthermore, to reduce cognitive strain, as well as to ensure that concepts are attained quickly and accurately, they adopt certain **cognitive**

	Number of figures	Number of borders	Shape	Color
Values	1	1	■	red
	2	2	▲	blue
	3	3	●	yellow

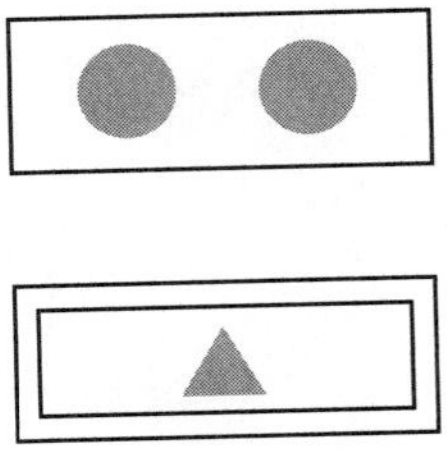

Figure 7.2 An experiment on concept attainment strategies. The chart lists the four attributes and three values that, in all possible combinations, made up the 81-card deck used in the experiment. Two sample cards are also shown.

strategies. These strategies take the form of regularities, or patterns, in the sequence of decisions that are made in determining whether objects belong to given classes.

To investigate these strategies, Bruner and his associates (1956) developed a series of cards, each of which could be used as an example of either a conjunctive, disjunctive, or relational concept. The 81 cards developed for this purpose included all the possible variations of four attributes, each with three values (see Figure 7.2). For the experiments, disjunctive or conjunctive concepts were explained and illustrated, depending on the specific study. A card with two borders and three red circles, for example, could be an example of several conjunctive concepts—such as *red circle*, in which case all other cards also having at least one figure that is both red *and* a circle would be examples of the same concept. If the concept *red circles* were disjunctive, any card with *either* red figures or circles of any color would illustrate the concept. Recall that conjunction means attribute *x and* attribute *y*; disjunction means either attribute *x or* attribute *y*.

The typical procedure in these experiments was to have participants try to discover (that is, try to *attain*) the concept the experimenter had in mind. To make the problem simpler, the experimenter told the subject how many values were included in the concept (usually two) and whether the concept was conjunctive or disjunctive.

Following various studies using these cards, Bruner discovered that subjects used several systematic strategies. One group of strategies for the attainment of conjunctive concepts is discussed here as an illustration. These are called *selection strategies* because the subject was first shown one card that was an example of the concept, and then allowed to select the card to be tested next from the entire deck of 81 cards. After each test, the experimenter told the subject that the card selected was or was not an example of the concept. The object of the "game" was twofold: to arrive at the correct concept and to do it in the least number of trials possible.

Bruner identified four selection strategies for the attainment of conjunctive concepts: *simultaneous scanning*, *successive scanning*, *conservative focusing*, and *focus gambling*.

Simultaneous Scanning

Simultaneous scanning involves generating all possible hypotheses based on the first example (positive instance) of the concept and then using each successive selection to eliminate all untenable hypotheses. For example, if the experimenter presents the subject with a card with two borders and three red circles on it, it would give rise to 15 tenable hypotheses. That is, there are 15 different combinations of two attributes represented by this card (for example, two borders and three figures; three circles; three red figures; red circles; two borders and red figures; two borders and circles; and so on). Unfortunately, the human mind cannot ordinarily consider so many hypotheses simultaneously. As a result, while this strategy is theoretically possible, it is virtually nonexistent in practice.

Successive Scanning

Successive scanning is a strategy that imposes much less cognitive strain because it is simply a trial-and-error approach. It involves making a hypothesis ("Um . . . may be the concept is red circles") and choosing a card to test the hypothesis directly. If the original guess is not confirmed ("Dang, I was wrong!"), a second hypothesis is made ("Maybe it's red squares"). The concept can sometimes be discovered very quickly with this procedure—purely by chance—but sometimes it will never be attained.

Conservative Focusing

For a number of reasons, *conservative focusing* is the best strategy. That's because it imposes relatively little strain on memory or on the capacity to make inferences. Furthermore, it almost guarantees that the concept will be attained.

A subject using conservative focusing begins by accepting the first positive instance as the *complete* hypothesis. For example, suppose the concept is red circles (RO), and the first card has two borders and three red circles (2B3RO). The subject hypothesizes that the concept is 2B3RO and then selects a card that varies from the original in only one value: for example, two borders and two red circles. The experimenter confirms that this card is still an example of the concept. It follows that the changed attribute, number of figures, is irrelevant. The remaining hypothesis is 2BRO. The next selection changes one more value—the color: The card chosen has two borders and three green circles. Because the instance is now negative, color clearly was relevant. The subject now knows that red is part of the concept. If the next choice eliminates number of borders or confirms shape (which it will if only one value is changed), the subject will have attained the concept (see Figure 7.3).

Focus Gambling

In a slight variation of conservative focusing, the participant *gambles* by changing more than one value at a time—hence, *focus gambling*. If the gambler changes two values and the card is still a positive example of the concept, the two values are automatically eliminated, thus leading more quickly to the solution. But if the card chosen is not an example of the concept, the gambler learns nothing, because either or both of the changed values could be criterial.

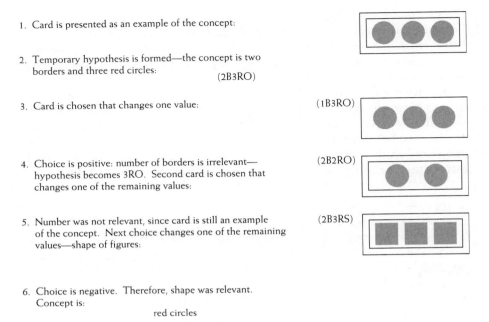

1. Card is presented as an example of the concept:

2. Temporary hypothesis is formed—the concept is two
    borders and three red circles: (2B3RO)

3. Card is chosen that changes one value: (1B3RO)

4. Choice is positive: number of borders is irrelevant—   (2B2RO)
    hypothesis becomes 3RO. Second card is chosen that
    changes one of the remaining values:

5. Number was not relevant, since card is still an example   (2B3RS)
    of the concept. Next choice changes one of the remaining
    values—shape of figures:

6. Choice is negative. Therefore, shape was relevant.
    Concept is:
                                 red circles

Figure 7.3 Decision sequence in attaining the concept *red circles* using a conservative
focusing strategy.

Concept Attainment Strategies in Real Life

The results of Bruner's work on concept attainment are difficult to generalize
to real life situations. That's because people aren't often given systematic examples from which to select experiences. Nor is there usually an authority immediately available to say, "Yes, this is an example of true love" or "No, that is not
an example of true love."

A second difficulty is that Bruner employed adult subjects in his experiments,
but simpler versions of the problems presented to children have not always led
to the identification of the same strategies (Olson, 1963).

A third problem is that even adult subjects in Bruner's experiments often used
no identifiable strategies. Many subjects would guess on one occasion; later, they
might appear to be trying to develop a strategy; then perhaps they would guess
again. Difficult approaches (such as successive scanning) were never employed by
any subject and therefore remain ideal rather than actual strategies.

Despite these problems, some of this work may be related to various aspects
of human behavior. For example, the acquisition of reasoning processes in children may involve learning strategies similar to those investigated by Bruner.
Teaching in schools often involves presenting related examples and information
about class memberships. Although teachers and curriculum materials are seldom
as systematic and rigorous as experimental procedures, they can occasionally be
patterned after these procedures.

More Recent Research on Concepts

Bruner's description of categories and of the processes involved in categorizing continues to play an important role in cognitive research. "A category," write Mervis and Rosch, "exists whenever two or more distinguishable objects or events are treated equivalently" (1981, p. 89)—a definition essentially identical to that first advanced by Bruner a quarter of a century earlier. "Once categories are established," note Markman and Gentner (2001), "people can use them to infer features of a new situation"—a statement highly reminiscent of Bruner's claim that categorizing allows people to "go beyond the information given."

What does more recent research tell us about categorization and concepts?

Developmental Trends in Concept Learning

One simple way of defining concepts is using nouns and verbs. Nouns, like dog, ditch, door, and Dagwood, represent categories of related characteristics that are actually perceived when we interact with one of these. That is, each of these nouns defines a category of perceptual experience. Verbs, on the other hand, express relations between nouns, generally indicating things like states, causes, movements, and other changes.

Linguists tell us that virtually all languages in the world make the noun-verb distinction, and that nouns are in many ways simpler than are verbs. As a result, it's far easier to translate nouns from one language to another than it is to translate verbs. As Medin, Lynch, and Solomon (2000) note, there is far more interlanguage variability for verbs than for nouns.

As might be expected, children tend to learn nouns, and therefore the concepts associated with nouns, before they learn verbs. But, strangely, they don't begin by learning the most specific concept and progressing from there to the most general. Instead, they typically start by learning concepts of intermediate generality and then learn those that are more specific. Later they develop more all-encompassing (sometimes termed *supraordinate*) categories (coding systems, in Bruner's terms). For example, a child doesn't begin by learning the concept *German shepherd*—a highly specific category—but instead learns the concept *dog*. Eventually, concepts such as *poodle, German shepherd*, and others at a similar level of specificity will be learned. Later, the child will be ready to understand the related, but even more generic, concept *mammal*.

Category Boundaries

Items or events that are included in the same category are not all equivalent, even though they may be reacted to as though they were. For example, although a large range of stimulus input will be interpreted as being blue (that is, as belonging to the category corresponding to blueness), some of that input will be interpreted as being more blue and some as less blue. Similarly, some colors will be more green, others more black, some lighter, and some darker; yet under appropriate circumstances, all will be reacted to as though they were blue.

In the same way, those individuals who fit into the categories for thin or fat are not all equally thin or fat. So category boundaries are not always well defined, and the definitions that exist may be somewhat arbitrary and individualistic. Not only might two different people not agree perfectly with respect to the attributes that are criterial for membership in their fat and thin categories, but also, when pressed, they would be forced to recognize that their own personal categories for these qualities have somewhat fuzzy boundaries.

The Neurobiology of Categories

Learning, and hence, the formation of categories, involves changes in the brain. That is, what is learned has to be represented, in some way, in one or more areas of the brain. As we saw in Chapter 5, our exquisitely sensitive imaging and measuring devices have allowed us to detect at least some of the areas of the brain that are involved when, for example, we perceive a dot of light or hear a single note. These measuring devices suggest that perceptual representation of sensory categories occurs in that part of the cerebral cortex labeled the *parietal lobe*. They also suggest that the more abstract aspects of categories are represented in the *frontal lobes* (Keri, 2003). After all, that part of the brain deals with higher thought processes. And abstraction is among the highest—that is, the most *abstract*—of thought processes.

Abstraction

At a superficial level, it might seem that perceiving physical objects requires no more than some knowledge of their physical properties and the availability of an appropriate category in which to place them—that is, perception simply involves matching sensations with appropriate categories. Thus, to recognize someone as belonging to the category *thin* or *fat*, it should suffice to do no more than sense thinness or fatness (probably through vision, or maybe by touch as well). In fact, however, fatness and thinness cannot be sensed directly; they are *abstractions*. Thus, even at the most elementary level of perceptual recognition, abstraction is often involved.

Two Models of Abstraction

Actually, abstraction is involved in virtually all models of categorization (Markman & Gentner, 2001). The main question these models try to answer is this: How do people abstract the central characteristics of a class of objects or events as a result of exposure to examples of that class?

One answer is that people develop a generalized notion of the most typical or representative features of a concept. This abstraction is in effect a **prototype model,** or *generalized model* (Rosch, 1977). Thus, after seeing thousands of different trees, Jane has developed a highly abstract notion of "treeness." If she could represent this abstract notion accurately, she might find that it doesn't resemble any specific tree or kind of tree, but instead it embodies all that is essential in trees. Whenever she sees some new treelike thing, she simply compares it to her prototypical tree.

Another possibility is that while learning about trees, Jane has stored in memory a number of good examples of trees. The **exemplar models** approach argues that concepts are represented by memories of specific examples that have actually been experienced, rather than an abstraction of some ideal prototype (Medin & Florian, 1992). According to this model, a person determines whether a new treelike thing is a tree by comparing it to other examples that define the concept.

One important difference between these two models is that the prototype model assumes a higher level of abstraction. A prototypical category for "birdness," for example, is an abstraction of the characteristics of many examples of birds. In contrast, an exemplar category for bird is defined by examples of real birds.

Rosch (1973) argues that the prototype model is better than the exemplar model because for many concepts it is difficult to find good examples that resemble each other closely. For example, an automobile is a good example of a vehicle, and so is a passenger truck or a van. But a bus is less so, a train even less, and a child's wagon even less than that. In classifying each of these as vehicles, argues Rosch, it is likely that the person relies on an abstract, or prototypical, notion of what vehicles are.

Considerable research has been conducted to evaluate these two approaches. In addition, various other models with a host of new labels have been proposed (see, for example, Anderson, 1995; Markman & Gentner, 2001). Thus far, the research seems to indicate that both highly abstract prototypes and more specific examples are involved in concept learning (Holyoak & Spellman, 1993). As we see in the next chapter, computer-based neural network models present yet another metaphor for understanding how humans learn concepts.

Bruner's Position: An Appraisal

Evaluating a cognitive position such as Bruner's presents an interesting difficulty. Whereas some behavioristic positions attempt to describe a state of affairs in a relatively exact and literal manner and can therefore sometimes be judged by how accurate the description appears to be, cognitive theories such as Bruner's are more abstract. Accordingly, the theory cannot be judged in the same manner as can behavioristic positions. What is being judged is not a description, but a metaphor: It is not an account of things or events that are assumed to actually exist but an abstraction that merely represents (that is, symbolizes).

Still, Bruner's metaphor does not do great violence to what people intuitively suspect about human functioning. More than that, it appears to be relatively clear and understandable, as well as internally consistent. Both of these attributes are important criteria of a scientific theory.

Perhaps the most important question that needs to be asked of any psychological theory concerns its usefulness in predicting and explaining. And although cognitive theories such as Bruner's are not very useful for explaining specific behaviors of the kind most easily explained by behavioristic positions, they can be useful in explaining higher mental processes such as decision making and the use of cognitive strategies.

One of the major contributions of Bruner's writing and theorizing has to do with his role in the so-called cognitive revolution—the revolution by which the cognitive party replaced the behavioristic party in what Amsel (1989) describes as psychology's parliamentary system.[4] "We were not out to 'reform' behaviorism," says Bruner, "but to replace it" (1990b, p. 3).

What was this revolution? "It was," claims Bruner, "an all-out effort to establish meaning as the central concept of psychology—not stimuli and responses, not overtly observable behavior, not biological drives and their transformation, but meaning" (1990a, p. 2). But the revolution was only partly successful, Bruner laments, because the emphasis changed from "constructing meaning" to "processing information." And the dominant metaphor became that of the computer, which unfortunately led to the requirement that new models and theories be "computable." In a more recent article, he argues that there has not been just one cognitive revolution, but that cognitive revolutions are ongoing. And he suggests that the most fruitful direction for the next cognitive revolution is that it should focus on discovering how people construct meaning—that is, how they make sense of the jumble of physical sensations that the senses provide (Bruner, 1997d). There is perhaps a third revolution in the offing, claims Shotter (2001). This next revolution may deal more specifically with the uniqueness of the person, and with the meaning of the self in the context of culture.

The proper study of man, says Bruner in his book of that title, is man (and presumably, women and children too). "There is no one explanation of man," he explains, adding that no explanation of the human condition can make sense "without being interpreted in the light of the symbolic world that constitutes human culture" (1990b, p. 138).

Bruner's more recent work, some of which is described in Chapter 12, deals increasingly with humans in the context of culture. This work places increasing emphasis on the importance of language, on the significance of the stories we tell ourselves about our lives (our personal narratives), and on the analysis of language and of grammar as a way of discovering things about the self (Bruner, 2002; Quigley, 2001).

---

[4]Perhaps he was wrong, the Old Woman chuckled. Maybe it wasn't a parliamentary system after all, but a dictatorship—a benevolent dictatorship. Otherwise, why the need for a revolution? She chuckled again, and then looked at me strangely as though seeing something she hadn't seen before. Maybe I shouldn't laugh about such important matters, she said, turning once more to her notes.

Educational Implications of Bruner's Theory

Bruner's theory fares especially well with respect to its heuristic value (the extent to which it continues to engender research and debate, leading to new discoveries); it also fares very well with respect to its practical implications. Bruner (1966, 1983, 1990c, 1996b) has been especially concerned with pointing out some of the instructional implications of his work. His emphasis on the formation of coding systems, together with his belief that abstract coding systems facilitate transfer, improve retention, and increase problem-solving ability and motivation, has led him to advocate a discovery oriented approach in schools. This emphasis on **discovery learning** is premised partly on his belief that the formation of generic coding systems requires the discovery of relationships. Accordingly, Bruner advocates the use of techniques by which children are encouraged to discover facts and relationships for themselves.

For this purpose, Bruner stresses that some form of spiral curriculum is probably the best. A spiral curriculum is one that redevelops the same topics at succeeding age or grade levels as well as at different levels of difficulty. For example, in early grades learners are exposed to the simplest concepts in a particular area; at succeeding grade levels they are re-exposed to the same area but at progressively more advanced conceptual levels.

Renewed interest in discovery approaches to education is evident in the constructivist approach to teaching advocated by Orlofsky (2001), Gabler and Schroeder (2003a), and others. The whole point of **constructivism,** say Gabler and Schroeder, is to shift students from "the familiar role of listener to that of active learner" (p. xvii). Constructivism is in close agreement with Bruner's argument that learners need to build knowledge for themselves—that, in his words, they need to "make meaning." Numerous books and programs describing specific approaches to constructive education have recently been published (for example, Branscombe, Castle, Dorsey, Surbeck, & Taylor, 2003; Gabler & Schroeder, 2003b).

What is labeled the **conceptual change movement** in education is also in harmony with Bruner's theory (Farnham-Diggory, 1990). The conceptual change movement is a discovery-oriented educational movement in which the emphasis is on encouraging the learner's personal involvement in the learning process. It's an approach that stresses mental reorganization rather than simply increasing the number of facts and procedures learned. A curriculum directed toward conceptual change presents problems and puzzles, challenges old ideas, and leads to the continual construction and reorganization of knowledge.

Not all educators or theorists are as enthusiastic as Bruner about the use of discovery methods in schools (see, for example, Ausubel, 1977; Ausubel & Robinson, 1969). A relatively mild controversy pitting discovery teaching against more didactic approaches (sometimes called **reception learning**) has been going on in educational circles for several decades. Research that has attempted to examine the relative merits of these two approaches doesn't clearly favor one over the other (see Lefrançois, 2000). This need not be of any great concern, though. Teachers do not need to use only one of these methods; they can use both.

Jean Piaget: A Developmental-Cognitive Position

Another cognitive theorist whose research and theories have enormously influenced psychology and education is Jean Piaget. Piaget's system is unmistakably cognitive: Its overriding concern is mental representation. It is also a developmental theory: It looks at the processes by which children achieve a progressively more advanced understanding of their environment and of themselves. In brief, Piagetian theory is an account of human cognitive development. His work covers an enormous range of topics: for example, language (1926); reality (1929); morality (1932); causality (1930); time (1946); intelligence (1950); play, dreams, and imitation (1951); and consciousness (1976)—to name but a few. The theory is scattered in more than 50 books and several hundred articles, many of which were coauthored by Piaget's long-time assistant, Bärbel Inhelder (1913–1997).

The Méthode Clinique

Much of the data on which Piaget based his theories was derived from a special technique he developed for studying children: the **méthode clinique.** This is a semi-structured interview technique in which subjects' answers to questions often determine what the next question will be. It is quite unlike the more conventional approach, in which predetermined questions are asked in a predetermined order.

The méthode clinique is borrowed from clinical psychology, and especially from psychoanalysis. Santiago-Delefosse and Delefosse (2002) speculate that Piaget's psychoanalyst, Sabina Spielrein (1885–1942)[5] may have strongly influenced the development of this research method. As well, the psychoanalyst Pierre Janet (1859–1947), also a contemporary of Piaget's, used this method extensively in his practice. As Piaget describes the method, it requires that the

---

[5] The Old Woman stopped and motioned that I should turn off the recorder. Your students, she said, might want to know how Sabina Spielrein came to be Piaget's psychoanalyst. You could tell them she was born in Russia but her parents, who were Jewish, sent her to Switzerland when she was 19 so that Carl Jung could treat her for some nervous malady she had. Jung had just begun to use Freud's new methods of psychoanalysis. Psychoanalysis fascinated Sabina, so she stayed in Switzerland to study medicine and become a psychoanalyst, and eventually ended up working at the Jean-Jacques Rousseau Institute in Geneva, where Piaget worked. Later, at the age of 38, she returned to Russia with her two little girls. The Old Woman paused for a long time, and I thought she had finished. Then she said that no, even very studious students probably wouldn't be interested in this aside. It's too sad, she said, because, in 1942, Sabina Spielrein, along with her two daughters and a host of other Jewish people, was executed by German soldiers.

interviewer listen while letting the child talk. And it requires, as well, that the interviewer go where the child's explanations and questions lead (Piaget, 1926).

One of the advantages of the méthode clinique lies in the considerable flexibility it permits. Piaget argues that when investigators don't know what all the answers might be, they are hardly in a position to decide beforehand how the questions should be phrased or even what questions should be asked. The "father/experimenter" role of the méthode clinique has sometimes led to surprising observations.

The Hawthorne Effect Studies

Interestingly, the first systematic introduction of Piagetian theory into American psychology, claims Hsueh (2001, 2002), involved the use of the méthode clinique in the now-famous Hawthorne experiments at the Western Electric Company in Chicago (Roethlisberger & Dickson, 1939). In the earliest of these experiments, researchers tried to discover what sorts of variations in work conditions might lead to higher production. Surprisingly, higher production resulted from almost all changes: longer work days, shorter work days, brighter lighting, dimmer lighting, more rest breaks, fewer rest breaks, and so on. The most common current interpretation of these findings is that when subjects are aware that they are members of an experimental group, they often behave the way they think the experimenters would like them to behave. As a result, the outcomes of the experiments can be biased and the conclusions invalid—a phenomenon labeled the **Hawthorne effect**.[6] The possibility of a Hawthorne effect is one of the reasons why, in many scientific experiments, subjects are not told they are part of an experiment.

What happened in the Hawthorne studies, says Hsueh (2002), is that one of the main investigators, Elton Mayo (1880–1949), introduced Piaget's méthode clinique. In a letter to his wife, reports Hsueh (2002), Mayo wrote that the interviewers would be using "the Piaget Method" in an effort to better understand the thinking and the preoccupations of the workers. Mayo's (1930) writings make it clear that even in the 1920s, far before Piaget's work had become popular in the United States, he was very familiar with Piaget's writings and his theory. In 1930, for example, Mayo published an enthusiastic review of one of Piaget's books, along with summaries of four others.

Theoretical Orientation

Consistent with his early training in biology, Piaget borrowed two of the zoologist's big questions: (a) Which properties of organisms allow them to survive, and (b) how can species be classified? These he rephrased and directed at the development of children: What characteristics of children enable them to adapt

---

[6]You might want to tell your brighter readers that the significance and the pervasiveness of the Hawthorne effect have been highly exaggerated, said the Old woman. Rice (1982) reanalyzed the studies and found that in many of the experiments, productivity did *not* increase. Furthermore, the experimental procedures were often poorly controlled and poorly supervised.

Jean Piaget (1896–1980)

Jean Piaget was born in Neuchatel, Switzerland, in 1896, the first child of Arthur Piaget, a professor of medieval literature. Although Jean didn't begin his formal work until some time later, there are indications that he was a precocious child. At the age of 11, he published his first "scholarly" paper: a one-page note on a partly albino spar-row he had found. This early writing was an intimation of the wealth of published material he was to produce later.

Piaget's first interests were primarily in biology, a field in which he obtained his Ph.D. at the age of 22. By the time he was 30, he had already published more than two-dozen papers, most of them dealing with mollusks and related topics.

After receiving his doctorate, Piaget spent a year wandering through Europe, uncertain about what to do next. During this year, he worked in a psychoanalytic clinic (Eugen Bleuler's), in a psychological laboratory (that of Wreschner and Lipps), and eventually in Alfred Binet's laboratory, then under the direction of Théodore Simon, where the famous Stanford-Binet intelligence test originated.

One of Piaget's duties while in the Binet laboratory was to administer an early intelli-gence test, Burt's Reasoning Tests, to young children to standardize the items.

This period probably marks the begin-ning of his lifelong interest in the thought processes of children. It was at about this time, too, that Piaget's first child was born. He and his wife, Valentine Châtenay, had three children, each of whose development he studied in detail. These studies are incor-porated in the origins of his theory. The bulk of Piaget's work is found in *Archives de Psy-chologie* (of which he was coeditor), much of it still not translated.

In 1980, Piaget was still publishing and doing research at an amazing pace. In fact, a book he finished shortly before his death in-troduces important changes and advances in his thinking (Piaget, 1980). And even 20 years after his death, previously unpublished essays and new translations of his work con-tinue to appear (for example, Piaget, 2001). In Piaget's own words, "At the end of one's career, it is better to be prepared to change one's perspective than to be condemned to repeat oneself indefinitely" (quoted in Inhelder, 1982, p. 411).

One indication of his stature in psychology and education is the website www.piaget.org, the official site of the Jean Piaget Society—a group of academics and educators devoted to studying and applying Piaget. The society's official journal is entitled *Cognitive Development* (Nucci & Turiel, 2001).

---

to their environment? And what is the simplest, most accurate, and most useful way of classifying child development? Hence, Piaget's theoretical orientation is clearly biological and evolutionary, as well as cognitive. That is, he studies the development of mind (a cognitive pursuit) in the context of biological adapta-tion. As von Glasersfeld (1997) puts it, the most basic of all of Piaget's ideas is this: *Human development is a process of adaptation. And the highest form of adaptation is cognition (or knowing).*

Assimilation and Accommodation: The Processes of Adaptation

The newborn infant, Piaget notes, is in many ways a stunningly helpless organism, unaware that the world is real, ignorant of causes and effects, with no storehouse of ideas with which to reason or any capacity for intentional behaviors. All the newborn has are a few simple reflexes—and an amazing capacity to adapt.

In the language of the computer metaphor, newborns are remarkable little sensing machines that seem naturally predisposed to acquire and process a tremendous amount of information. They continually seek out and respond to stimulation, notes Flavell (1985). As a result, the infant's simple reflexes—the sucking, the reaching, and the grasping—become more complex, more coordinated, and more purposeful. The process by which this occurs is **adaptation**. And to answer the first of the questions of biology as simply as possible, **assimilation** and **accommodation** are the processes that make adaptation possible.

Assimilation involves responding to situations using activities or knowledge that have already been learned or that are present at birth. To use Piaget's example, an infant is born with the ability to suck—with a sucking **schema**, in Piaget's terms (pluralized as *schemata* or as *schemas*, sometimes used interchangeably with *scheme*). Schemas are important concepts in Piaget's system. Essentially, a schema is a behavior, together with the neurological structures related to that behavior. In Piaget's theory, any distinct activity can be labeled a schema. Thus, there are looking schemas, talking schemas, schemas evident in the child's ability to add 2 and 2, and so on. Objects or situations are said to be assimilated to a schema when they can be responded to using previous knowledge. Assimilation is involved when responding to the object or to the situation requires a change in the schema. Thus, the sucking schema allows the infant to assimilate a nipple to the behavior of sucking. Similarly, a child who has learned the rules of addition can assimilate a problem such as 1 + 1; that is, he or she can respond appropriately because of previous learning.

Often, however, the child's understanding of the world is inadequate. The newborn's sucking schema works for ordinary nipples, but it isn't very effective for fingers or pacifiers. Similarly, preschoolers' understanding of number allows them to keep track of toes and fingers, but it doesn't impress kindergarten teachers. If there is to be any developmental progress, changes are required in information and behavior. These changes define accommodation.

In summary, *assimilation* involves reacting based on previous learning and understanding; *accommodation* involves a change in understanding. And the interplay of assimilation and accommodation leads to adaptation.

Equilibration

All activity, claims Piaget, involves both assimilation and accommodation. The child cannot react to an entirely new situation without using some old learning and some old behaviors (hence, assimilating). At the same time, even reacting to the same situation for the thousandth time nevertheless implies some change, however subtle (hence, some accommodation). Flavell (1985) notes that these activities are simply the two sides of the same cognitive coin.

It is important, explains Piaget, that there be a balance between assimilation and accommodation—an equilibrium. Hence, he uses the term **equilibration** to signify the processes or tendencies that lead to this balance. If there is too much assimilation, there is no new learning; if there is too much accommodation (that is, change), behavior becomes chaotic.

Piaget called assimilation and accommodation *functional invariants* because they are functions, or ways of behaving, that don't change throughout development. These functional invariants are clearly illustrated in two important activities of early childhood: play, which involves mainly assimilation, and imitation, which is mostly accommodation.

Play

When children play, Piaget explains, they continually assimilate objects to predetermined activities, ignoring attributes that don't really fit the activity. For example, when children sit astride a chair and say, "Giddyup," they're not paying particular attention to those attributes of the chair that don't resemble a horse.

This type of play behavior involves little change and thus little accommodation —which is not to deny its importance during development. Indeed, Piaget does quite the opposite, emphasizing repeatedly that although young children engage in activities (such as playing "horse") simply for the sake of the activity, the effect is to stabilize the schema (the activity), to make it more readily available, and consequently, to set the stage for further learning.

Stages of Play

During their development, children progress through a series of stages in the playing of games and, remarkably, a quite different set of stages regarding their understanding of the rules by which they play (Piaget, 1932; see Table 7.2).

Table 7.2 *Piaget's Description of Rules as They Are Understood and Practiced by Children*

Stage	Approximate age	Degree of understanding	Adherence to rules
Stage 1	Before 3	No understanding of rules	Do not play according to rules
Stage 2	3 to 5	Believe rules come from God (or some other high authority) and cannot be changed	Break and change rules constantly
Stage 3	5 to 11 or 12	Understand that rules are social and that they can be changed	Do not change rules; adhere to them rigidly
Stage 4	After 11 or 12	Complete understanding	Change rules by mutual consent

At the earliest stage, before age 3, children have no idea that rules exist and play according to none. By age 5, however, they have developed the belief that rules are eternal and unchangeable, but they change them constantly as they play. During the next half-dozen or so years, they come to realize that rules are made by people and can be changed. Ironically, however, they are now completely rigid in their adherence to rules: They never change them! Finally, by about age 11 or 12, they arrive at a complete understanding of rules. Both in behavior and thought, they accept rules as completely modifiable.[7]

Imitation

Play involves a preponderance of assimilation because, during play, objects and situations are continually assimilated to ongoing activities. Thus, when the child is playing horse—in Piaget's terms, when the "horse riding" schema is active—a chair becomes a horse as easily as does a stuffed teddy bear or the family dog. These objects are assimilated to the "horse riding" schema; the child need not change (that is, need not *accommodate*) to the different characteristics of the chair, the dog, or the teddy bear.

In contrast, imitation is primarily accommodation. When they are imitating, children constantly modify their behavior in accordance with the demands imposed on them by their desire to be something they aren't or to be like someone else. Piaget argues that through the imitation of activity, children's repertoires of behaviors expand and gradually begin to be internalized. **Internalization** is, in Piaget's terminology, equivalent to the formation of mental concepts. Internalization is the process by which activities and events in the real world become represented mentally. Thus, first comes the activity, then comes a mental representation of it. Internalization is the basis of cognitive learning.

Many of the infant's imitative behaviors occur only in the presence of the model being imitated. For example, even very young infants can imitate simple behaviors such as blinking, winking, and opening the mouth (Meltzoff & Moore, 1989), but the imitation does not continue when the model is no longer present. That, says Piaget, is because the infant fails to realize that objects continue to exist independently even when the child isn't actually looking at them, touching them, or otherwise sensing them. The world of the infant, claims Piaget, is a world of the here and now; it does not include an understanding of the permanence of objects (termed the **object concept**).

---

[7]Just as an aside, the Old Woman said, wanting to make sure I didn't include in the text comments that weren't part of her notes, what do you think of this contradiction between the thinking and behavior of children? But it was a rhetorical question, not intended for me to answer. She said this striking inconsistency between behavior and thought might seem excusable given that these are children, and human children come with relatively little prewiring; as a result, they have an awful lot to learn and they make mistakes. But how do you explain, she asked, the astounding number of examples of similar behavior-belief contradictions among human adults? She explained that this phenomenon fuels an enormous gambling industry; that, for example, despite reasonably intelligent humans knowing that the probability of correctly selecting 6 out of 49 numbers is about 1 in 13 million, they continue to give away their money. She was silent for a long moment; then she said that maybe buying a lottery ticket wasn't too high a price to pay for a dream.

At about age 1, an important change occurs when young Ralph puts on his father's jacket, takes his toy shovel, sits on his imaginary car, and pretends he is going to work *after his father has left for work*. Piaget explains that **deferred imitation**—the ability to imitate things and people not immediately present— is evidence that the infant has internalized a representation of that which is being imitated. It is evidence, as well, that the infant has begun to realize that things continue to exist on their own even when out of sensory range—evidence, in other words, of the *object concept*.

Intelligence

Piaget was very familiar with Gestalt theory. In his book *The Psychology of Intelligence* (Piaget, 1950—original written in 1947), he devotes most of a chapter to examining the Gestalt notion that perceptual activity underlies intelligence. In the end, although he greatly admired Gestalt theory and shared its emphasis on perception, he concludes that intelligence is a more active process than portrayed by the Gestalt theorists. Also, his concept of intelligence differs markedly from the traditional measurement approach. Instead of describing intelligence as a relatively fixed quality or quantity, Piaget describes it as *mobile*—that is, as something that moves (that changes). Intelligence, he argues, exists *in action*. As Beilin and Fireman (2000) put it, mental and physical action are the basis of Piaget's theory. In this theory, intelligence is the property of activity that is reflected in maximally adaptive behavior, and it can therefore be understood as the entire process of adapting.

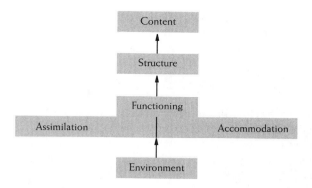

Figure 7.4

Piaget's *intelligence-in-action*. Intelligence is defined by the interactions of an individual with the environment. This interaction involves a balance of assimilation (incorporating aspects of the environment to previous learning) and accommodation (changing behavior in the face of environmental demands). The result of this interaction (of this *functioning*) is the development of cognitive structures (schemas and operations), which in turn are reflected in behavior (content).

To review briefly, adaptation is the process of interacting with the environment by assimilating aspects of it to cognitive structure and by modifying (or accommodating) aspects of cognitive structure to it. Both activities occur in response to environmental demands. Also, both are guided by cognitive structure and result in changes in cognitive structure. However, this entire process can be inferred only from actual behavior (called *content* by Piaget). The substance of Piaget's view of intelligence is summarized in Figure 7.4.

Cognitive Structure

Although this view of intelligence may be useful for understanding some of the processes involved in intelligent behavior, it is not immediately useful for measuring it. But one aspect of the model has implications for developing tests of intelligence: the part defined by the term **structure**.

Piaget's description of structure is essentially a description of the characteristics of children at different ages. It is his answer for the second of the questions he borrowed from biology: What is the simplest, most accurate, and most useful way of classifying or ordering child development? Hence, Piaget's description of changes in structure is a description of the stages of human cognitive development. This is the aspect of his system that has received the most attention.

A Stage Theory

Piaget believed that development progresses through a series of stages, each characterized by the development of new abilities or, more precisely, each consisting of a more advanced level of adaptation. He describes four major stages, and several substages, through which children progress in their development:

- Sensorimotor (birth to 2 years)
- Preoperational (2 to 7 years)
   Preconceptual (2 to 4 years)
   Intuitive (4 to 7 years)
- Concrete operations (7 to 11 or 12 years)
- Formal operations (11 or 12 to 14 or 15 years)

Each stage can be described by the major identifying characteristics of children at that stage and by the learning that occurs before transition to the next stage.

Sensorimotor Development: Birth to 2 Years

The most striking characteristics of child behavior in the first 2 years of life relate to the absence of language and of internal representation. As we saw, the child's world, because it cannot be represented mentally, is a world of the *here and now*. In a very literal sense, it is a world where objects exist only when the child actually senses them and does things with them—hence, the label **sensorimotor intelligence.** At this stage, when objects are not being sensed, they cease to exist; infants have not yet acquired the **object concept** (a realization of the permanence of objects).

The Object Concept
Piaget investigated the development of the object concept by presenting young children with an attractive object and then removing it after they had become interested in it. In the earliest stages of development they show no signs of missing the object—proof, claims Piaget, that out of sight is literally out of mind. In later stages, however, children will look for objects they have seen being hidden; at around age 1, they will search for objects they remember from some previous time.

The development of the object concept may be even more closely tied to language and culture than Piaget had thought. Tomasello (1996) reports, for example, that the child's learning of words for the act of disappearing is closely related to the understanding of object permanence.

Exercising Reflexes
During the sensorimotor stage (first two years), children perfect and elaborate the small repertoire of reflexive schemata with which they are born. At birth, infants are capable of simple reflexive acts like sucking, reaching, grasping, looking, and so on. Much of the first month of life is spent exercising these reflexes (and sleeping). This first month represents the first of six substages of the sensorimotor period described by Piaget, each of which is identified by the nature of its reflexive activity. For example, the second substage (1 to 4 months) sees the appearance of acquired adaptations called primary circular reactions. These activities are centered on the child's body (hence, the term primary) and are circular in that the behavior elicits its own repetition. Thumb sucking is a primary circular reaction in the sense that the activity of sucking produces sensations that lead the child to repeat the activity. Later sensorimotor substages witness the coordination of separate activities, the evolution of language, and so on.

Achievements by Age 2
Piaget's labels for the stages typically reflect the characteristics that are most common throughout the stage rather than the characteristics and abilities a child acquires that lead to transition into the next stage. Thus, the sensorimotor

stage is so labeled because for most of their first two years, children react to the world in a *sensorimotor* fashion. That is, they understand it largely through their sensations of it (hence, *sensori*) and their actions toward it (hence, *motor*). However, each stage is a preparation for the next. Thus, the achievements of each are very important in explaining the transition to the succeeding stage.

Among the most striking and important achievements of the sensorimotor period is the development of the ability to symbolize and to communicate. Language accelerates thinking and makes possible the transition to a more cognitive interpretation of the world. A second achievement, already noted, is the development of the object concept—the discovery that the world continues to exist even when it is not being seen, felt, heard, smelled, or tasted.

The culmination of sensorimotor learning is marked by a third accomplishment: the child's increasing ability to coordinate separate activities. Adults take the ability to coordinate complex activities very much for granted, but it is no small or unimportant achievement for the child. In the absence of cooperation between such simple activities as looking and reaching, the child could never obtain the object looked at and desired. Even for so uncomplicated a behavior as picking up a pen, vision must direct the arm, and the hand, the arm, the shoulder, the torso and perhaps even the head must also be pressed into service.

A final sensorimotor achievement is recognizing cause-and-effect relationships. At birth, infants don't know that if they reach toward an object, they can grasp it and bring it closer to themselves; they must learn this. Moreover, this kind of learning is precisely what allows them to develop intentionality, for until children know what the effects of their activities will be, they cannot clearly intend these effects.

Preoperational Thinking: 2 to 7 Years

The next stage in the cognitive evolution of the child—**preoperational thinking** —brings a marked improvement over the first in the child's increased understanding of the world. But relative to an adult's understanding, the preoperational child's thinking still exhibits serious shortcomings.

The preoperational stage is ordinarily divided into two substages: the preconceptual and the intuitive.

Preconceptual Thinking: 2 to 4 Years

The stage of **preconceptual thinking** is characterized by the child's inability to understand all the properties of classes. Piaget, whose early work typically was based on observations of his own children, illustrates this by reference to his son's reaction to a snail they saw as they were walking one morning. "Papa," said the boy, "regardez l'escargot." Which they did. But later, when they came across a second snail, the boy said again, "Papa, regardez l'escargot. C'est encore l'escargot!"[8]

---

[8]The first conversation means, "Pops, look at the snail." The second one, in response to a different snail, means, "Pops, look at the snail. It's the snail again."

The preconceptual child has acquired the ability to represent objects internally (that is, mentally) and to identify them based on their membership in classes, but now reacts to all similar objects as though they were identical. For a while, all men are "Daddy," all women are "Mommy," animals are all "doggie," and the world is simple. If Samuel sees a teddy bear like his at a friend's place, he knows that it's his teddy bear, and the tricycle at the store is clearly his. Children understand something about classes because they can identify objects. Their understanding is incomplete, though, because they cannot yet distinguish between apparently identical members of the same class (hence, the term *preconceptual*). This mode of thinking occasionally has its advantages for parents: Santa Claus continues to be the one and only individual of his type, even though he may be seen in 10 places on one day.

Another feature of the child's thinking during this stage is that it is **transductive** rather than *inductive* or *deductive*. Deductive reasoning proceeds from the general to the specific. For example, if you accept the generalization that all birds have wings, when you are told that the western water ouzel is a bird, you can *deduce* that it has wings. Inductive reasoning goes from specifics to a generalization. For example, after you have observed a hundred species of birds and have noted that they all have wings, you might *induce* that all birds have wings.

Both inductive and deductive reasoning are valid methods of thinking logically. In contrast, transductive reasoning is a faulty type of logic that involves making inferences from one specific to another. For example, the child who reasons, "My dog has hair, and that thing there has hair; therefore that thing is a dog," is engaging in transductive reasoning. Transductive reasoning can lead to correct conclusions, but is not guaranteed to do so. Thus, the hairy thing might well be a dog, in which case transductive reasoning results in an accurate inference. But if the furry thing is a skunk, the same reasoning process has a less happy outcome.

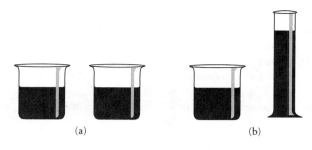

Figure 7.5
Material for a simple conservation of liquid experiment. One of the containers from (a) has been poured into a taller, thinner container in (b). The nonconserving child will assume there is more liquid in this new container because it's "taller"—or less because it's "thinner."

Intuitive Thinking: 4 to 7 Years

By the time children reach the age of 4, they have achieved a more complete understanding of concepts and have largely stopped reasoning transductively. Their thinking has become somewhat more logical, although it is governed more by perception than by logic. Actually, the role played by perception in the stage of **intuitive thinking** is probably the most striking characteristic of this period. The role of perception is evident in the child's lack of conservation, in egocentric thought, and in problems with classification problems.

A typical **conservation** problem goes like this: Children are shown two identical beakers filled to the same level with water (as in part (a) of Figure 7.5). The experimenter then pours the contents of one of the beakers into a tall thin tube (as in part (b) of Figure 7.5). Subjects who had previously said the amounts in each beaker were equal are now asked whether there is as much, more, or less water in the new container. At the intuitive stage, they will almost invariably say that there is more because the water level is much higher in the tube. They are misled by appearance (perception) as well as by a lack of some specific logical abilities.

The thinking of intuitive-stage children shows not only lack of conservation, but also a marked **egocentrism**—an inability to easily accept the point of view of others. To illustrate this, an experimenter holds in each hand one end of a wire on which a boy doll and a girl doll are strung side by side. The child is shown the dolls, which are then hidden behind a screen, but the hands remain in plain view. The child is asked which doll will come out first if they are moved out on the left. The child's answer is noted, the dolls are returned to their original position, and the question is repeated. Again, the dolls come out on the left; thus, the same doll comes out first. The procedure is repeated a number of times.

Reasonably intelligent children generally answer correctly at first. After a while, however, they change their minds and predict that the other doll will come out first. If asked why they think so, they are unlikely to admit that they distrust psychological investigators, because they probably haven't learned to distrust them yet. Instead, they may say something like, "It's not fair. It's her turn to come out next." This solution of a simple logical problem by reference to how things should be from the child's own point of view illustrates the role of egocentrism in intuitive thinking.

Although children at this stage can identify objects based on class membership, they don't yet completely understand how classes can be nested within larger classes. A 4-year-old who is shown a handful of seven candies, two of which are chocolates and five of which are jelly beans, immediately recognizes that they are all candies and, if asked, will probably say so. If, however, the experimenter says "Tell me, are there more jelly beans than candies, or fewer, or the same number?," the child may well say that there are more jelly beans than candies! When a class is broken down into subclasses and children are asked to reason about the subclass (jelly beans) and the larger class (candy), they find it very difficult to do so. For them, the original division destroyed the parent class. (See Figure 7.6 for a summary of the characteristics of preoperational thinking.)

Operations

The preconceptual and intuitive stages are substages of the lengthy preoperational period. The stage is labeled *preoperational* because before the age of 7, the child does not reason with *operations*. As the labels for the next two stages indicate, after the age of 7 (or thereabouts), the average child achieves operational thinking. The term **operation** is therefore central in Piaget's system.

An operation can be defined as an internalized activity (in other words, a thought) that is subject to certain rules of logic. Three of these rules, *reversibility*, *identity*, and *compensation* are described shortly.

Concrete Operations: 7 to 11 or 12 Years

At about age 7 or so, children make an important transition from preoperations to **concrete operations**—that is, from a prelogical, egocentric, perception-dominated kind of thinking to a more rule-regulated thinking. Perhaps nowhere is this more evident than in the acquisition of the concept of conservation.

The Conservations

Conservation, as we saw, is the realization that certain quantitative attributes of objects don't change unless something is added or taken away. In the previously described water-into-a-different-container demonstration (Figure 7.5), children have acquired conservation when they realize that pouring water from one container to another does not change its amount.

There are many types of conservation, each relating to a specific quantitative attribute of an object and each acquired in highly similar order by most children. For example, *conservation of substance* is typically achieved by the age of 7 or 8, whereas *conservation of area* is not learned until 9 or 10, and *conservation of volume* doesn't appear until about 11 or 12 (see Figure 7.7).

The importance of conservation in Piaget's theory is that it illustrates the use of one or more of the rules of logic that now govern thinking—rules such as **reversibility, identity,** and **compensation.** What has happened is that while interacting with things and events—that is, during what Piaget (1972) refers to as "constructing knowledge" (which is the same as what Bruner, 1996a, or Kuhn, 1972, call "meaning making")—the child discovers that logic governs actions and relationships.

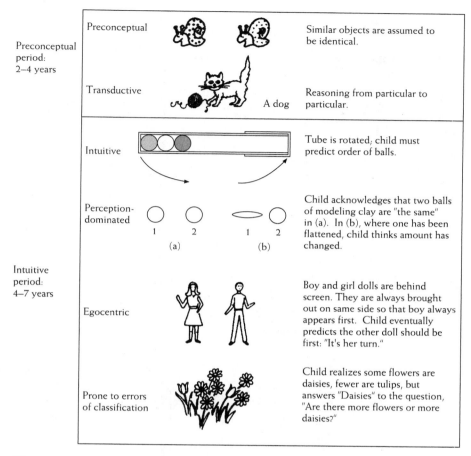

Preconceptual period: 2–4 years	Preconceptual	Similar objects are assumed to be identical.
	Transductive	Reasoning from particular to particular.
Intuitive period: 4–7 years	Intuitive	Tube is rotated; child must predict order of balls.
	Perception-dominated	Child acknowledges that two balls of modeling clay are "the same" in (a). In (b), where one has been flattened, child thinks amount has changed.
	Egocentric	Boy and girl dolls are behind screen. They are always brought out on same side so that boy always appears first. Child eventually predicts the other doll should be first: "It's her turn."
	Prone to errors of classification	Child realizes some flowers are daisies, fewer are tulips, but answers "Daisies" to the question, "Are there more flowers or more daisies?"

Figure 7.6 Characteristics of preoperational thought with illustrations.

A thought (internal action) is *reversible* when the child realizes the action could be reversed and certain logical consequences follow from doing so. For example, with respect to the problem of conservation of liquids described earlier, a child might reason, "If the water were poured out of the tall tube and back into its original container, it would still have as much water as before, so it mustn't have changed." That, in a nutshell, is reversibility.

Alternatively, the child might reason that nothing has been added to or taken away from either container and that there must then still be the same amount in each. This is an example of the rule of *identity*, which states that for every operation (action) there is another operation that leaves it unchanged. Adding or taking away nothing produces no change.

A third way of reasoning might be this: "The tube is taller, but it is also thinner, so it balances out." Piaget and Inhelder (1941) refer to this reasoning as *compensation* (or combinativity), a property defined by the logical consequences of combining more than one operation or, in this case, more than one dimension.

1. **Conservation of number (age 6 or 7)**
Two rows of counters are placed in one-to-one correspondence between the experimenter (E) and the subject (S):

One of the rows is then elongated or contracted:

S is asked which row has more counters or whether they still have the same number.

2. **Conservation of length (age 6 or 7)**
E places two sticks before the subject. The ends are aligned.

S is asked if they are the same length. One stick is then moved to the right:

The question is repeated.

3. **Conservation of substance or mass (age 7 or 8)**
Two modeling clay balls are presented to S. She is asked if they have the same amount of modeling clay in them. If S says no, she is asked to make them equal. (It is not at all uncommon for a young child simply to squeeze a ball in order to make it have less modeling clay.) One ball is then deformed.

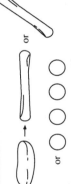

S is asked whether they contain the same amount.

4. **Conservation of area (age 9 or 10)**
S is given a large piece of cardboard, identical to one that E has. Both represent playgrounds. Small wooden blocks represent buildings. S is asked to put a building on his playground every time E does so. After nine buildings have been scattered throughout both playgrounds, E moves his together in a corner.

S is asked whether there is as much space (area) in his playground as in E's.

5. **Conservation of liquid quantity (age 6 or 7)**
S is presented with two identical containers filled to the same level with water.

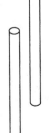

One of the containers is then poured into a tall, thin tube, and the other is poured into a flat dish.

S is asked whether the amount of water in each remains equal.

6. **Conservation of volume (age 11 or 12)**
S is presented with a calibrated container filled with water

and two identical balls of modeling clay. One is squished and placed into the container; the other is lengthened.

S is asked to predict the level to which the water in the container will rise if the longer piece of clay replaces the squished piece.

Figure 7.7 Experimental procedures for conservation of six physical attributes, with approximate ages of attainment.

You might want to clarify these notions further by carrying out some conservation tasks with real children, as shown in Figure 7.7. Note that the ages indicated in parentheses in Figure 7.7 are only approximations.[9]

Can Conservation Be Taught?

Given that the acquisition of concepts of conservation represents a significant achievement in the cognitive development of young children, many investigators have tried to teach these concepts to children earlier than they would acquire them naturally. Success in doing so might translate into significant acceleration of cognitive growth. And, intuitively, it would seem to be a relatively simple task to teach, say, a 5-year-old, that the amount of clay in a ball doesn't really change unless some clay is added or taken way. Actually, however, contrary to what any intelligent grandfather would predict, most attempts to teach young children concepts of conservation have been unsuccessful (for example, Kuhn, 1972; Smedslund, 1961). And those who have been successful in accelerating the appearance of concepts of conservation in some children (never all), have typically succeeded only after extensive, systematic, and theoretically based training (for example, Lefrançois, 1968; Siegler & Liebert, 1972). None of these psychologists has clearly shown that such acceleration studies have a generally beneficial effect on other aspects of child functioning.

Classification

With the appearance of the logical properties of thinking that define operations, children also acquire new skills in dealing with classes, numbers, and series.

---

[9]The Old Woman suggested, as an aside, that it might be amusing for you to perform these conservation demonstrations in front of a grandfather, after having explained the procedure to him and after he has predicted what the child's response will be. She said it's best to use a 4- or 5-year-old to ensure that the grandfather will be wrong.

Piaget assumed that these abilities are highly dependent on interacting with and manipulating real objects. For example, by combining objects, separating them, or arranging them into groups, children learn about class membership and develop the ability to reason about nested classes. The candy problem cited earlier (whether there are more jelly beans or more candies) would present so slight a problem for concrete-operations children that they might well laugh in scorn if the question were put to them.

Seriating

In addition, because of experiences with real objects, children acquire the ability to order them in series and to set up correspondences between more than one series. Piaget investigated the understanding of seriation by presenting children with various objects that can easily be ranked—for example, dolls of different heights. Before concrete operations, children rank objects by comparing two of them at once, but they seldom make the necessary inference that if A is greater than B and B is greater than C, then A must also be greater than C. Preoperational children are not embarrassed about putting C before B if they have just been comparing A and C. The concrete-operations child seldom makes an error of this kind (see Figure 7.8).

Number

The ability to deal with numbers is a logical result of classifying and seriating because a complete understanding of number requires some comprehension of its cardinal properties (the fact that numbers represent classes of different magnitude: one thing, two things, three things, and so on) as well as knowledge of their ordinal meaning (their ordered sequence: first, second, third, and so on).

Formal Operations: After 11 or 12 Years

Formal operations present some important advances over concrete operations. First, concrete-operations children apply their logic directly to real objects or to objects that are easily imagined (hence, the label *concrete*). In other words, children don't yet deal with what is merely hypothetical unless it can be tied directly to concrete reality. Adolescents, in contrast, are potentially capable of dealing with the hypothetical or ideal (the *nonconcrete*).

Combinatorial Analysis

Second, concrete-operations children respond very differently from those in the formal-operations stage when faced with problems that require systematic analysis of a large number of possibilities. In one representative problem, for example, Inhelder and Piaget (1958) presented children with five test tubes containing different chemicals and showed them that a combination of these chemicals would result in a yellow liquid. The children's task was to discover which combination(s) produced the desired result. The experiment is illustrated in Figure 7.9.

Figure 7.8 A test of a child's understanding of seriation. The elements of the series are presented in random order and the child is asked to arrange them in sequence by height. The top row was arranged by a 3½-year-old, and the bottom, by an 8-year-old.

Typical 10-year-olds begin by combining a couple of tubes, then two more, then another two—sometimes maybe trying three at once—until they either stumble accidentally on one of the two correct solutions or give up. Their strategy is to test each combination as a real hypothesis—a reflection of the concrete nature of their thinking.

A bright 14-year-old, in contrast, approaches the problem quite differently, systematically combining all test tubes by twos, threes, or even fours, resulting in all possible combinations illustrated in Figure 7.9. What the 14-year-old has done is imagine all possibilities and then exhaust them—demonstrating the hypothetical and combinatorial nature of formal-operations thinking.

Hypothetical Nature of Thought

As we just saw, the last stage in the evolution of thought is marked by the appearance in behavior of **propositional thinking**—thinking that is not restricted to the consideration of the concrete or the potentially real but instead deals in the realm of the hypothetical. (A proposition is any statement that can be true or false.) Children can now reason from the real to the merely possible, or from the possible to the actual. They can compare hypothetical states of affairs with actual states or vice versa. As a result, they can become profoundly upset at the seeming irresponsibility of a generation of adults that has brought itself to the edge of untold disasters. (See Table 7.3 for a summary of Piaget's stages.)

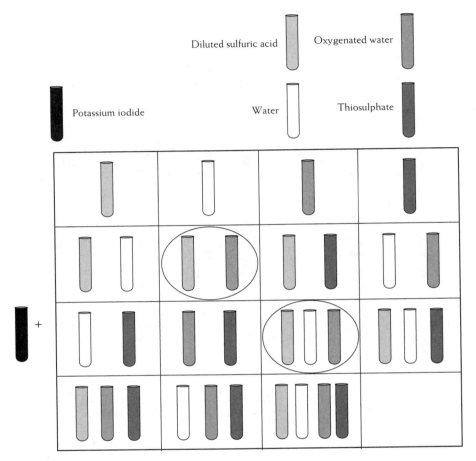

Figure 7.9 All possible combinations of the four test tubes to which the fifth can be added. The experiment requires the subject to discover the combination(s) that yields a yellow liquid when potassium iodide is added. The correct solutions are circled.

Piaget's Theory as a Theory of Learning

Piaget's position is primarily a theory of human development. Largely because of its emphasis on the genesis (or development) of knowledge (what Piaget termed **genetic epistemology**), however, it is also a theory of learning. As a theory of learning, it can be simplified and reduced to the following set of statements:

- The acquisition of knowledge is a gradual developmental process made possible through the interaction of the child with the environment.
- The sophistication of children's representation of the world is a function of their stage of development. That stage is defined by the thought structures they then possess.
- Maturation, active experience, equilibration, and social interaction are the forces that shape learning (Piaget, 1961).

Table 7.3 *Piaget's Stages of Cognitive Development*

Stage	Approximate age	Major characteristics
Sensorimotor	0–2 years	Motoric intelligence
		World of the here and now
		No language, no thought in early stages
		No notion of objective reality
Preoperational	2–7 years	
Preconceptual	2–4 years	Egocentric thought
		Reason dominated by perception
Intuitive	4–7 years	Intuitive rather than logical solutions
		Inability to conserve
Concrete operations	7–11 or 12 years	Ability to conserve
		Logic of classes and relations
		Understanding of numbers
		Thinking bound to concrete
		Development of reversibility in thought
Formal operations	11 or 12–14 or 15 years	Complete generality of thought
		Propositional thinking
		Ability to deal with the hypothetical
		Development of strong idealism

Educational Implications of Piaget's Theory

Piaget (1961) describes four great forces that shape the child's development. As we saw, one of these is the tendency toward *equilibration*—toward finding an optimal balance between assimilation and accommodation. Another is *maturation*, a biologically based process related to the gradual unfolding of potential. A third is *active experience*, which enables the child to know and to *internalize* things. And the fourth is *social interaction*—interaction with other people—that permits the child to elaborate ideas about the world and about others. As is shown in Table 7.4, each of these has important educational implications.

The impact of Piaget's theory on school curricula, on instructional procedures, and on measurement practices is profound and significant. Theories such as Piaget's and Bruner's emphasize that learning is far more than simply moving items of information from *out there* into the child. These theories lead to what is now termed constructivism—an approach to teaching and learning that gives the child a central, *active* role in the *construction* of knowledge. Constructivist methods, explain Gabler and Schroeder, are those that encourage "students to be critical thinkers and independent learners, with the teacher acting as a mentor and a facilitator" (2003a, p. xvii).

Table 7.4 *Four Forces That Shape Human Development*

Force	Explanation	Educational Implication
Equilibration	A tendency to maintain a balance between assimilation (responding using previous learning) and accommodation (changing behavior in response to the environment	Children need to be provided with tasks at an optimal level of difficulty—not so difficult that they are too challenging, but not so easy that they require no accommodation
Maturation	Genetic forces that, although they don't determine behavior, are related to its unfolding	Teachers need to know something about how children think and learn—about their level of maturation and understanding, to optimize their educational experiences
Active experience	Interaction with real objects and events allows individuals to discover things and to invent (construct) mental representations of the world	This supports a constructivist curriculum, one where the learner is actively involved in the process of discovering and learning
Social interaction	Interaction with people leads to the elaboration of ideas about things, people, and self	Schools need to provide ample opportunity for learner-learner and teacher-learner interaction in academic (classroom) and non-academic (playground, library, etc.) areas.

Piaget's work suggests a number of very specific instructional approaches and principles (see Lefrançois, 2000). For example, it follows directly from the theory that in early stages, interaction with real objects is crucial to the growth of knowledge and to the development of the understandings and abilities that underlie thinking. Hence providing opportunities for both mental and physical activity is a basic educational implication of Piaget's theory.

Piaget's theory (as does Vygotsky's) also suggests that schools should take pains to provide students with tasks and challenges of optimal difficulty. Material presented to learners should not be so difficult that it can't be understood (assimilated) nor so easy that it leads to no new learning (no accommodation). Hence, it's very important for teachers to know something about child development, and about how children learn and think. Teachers need to understand both the limitations and the potential of child thought.

In describing the forces that shape the child's development, Piaget gave a very important role to social interaction. Through social interaction, children become aware of the feelings and thoughts of others, they develop moral and games rules, and they develop and practice their own logical thought processes. Instructional methods that reflect Piaget's theory need to provide many opportunities for teacher-learner and for learner-learner interaction. As DeVries puts it, "The obvious general educational implication of Piaget's social theory is to value a socially interactive classroom and foster social exchanges of a cooperative type in order to promote operational development" (1997, p. 14).

Piaget's Position: An Appraisal

Piaget's critics, of which there are a significant number, have advanced a few standard complaints. One of the earliest centered on the small number of subjects in his research: The méthode clinique does not lend itself easily to large samples. This criticism is not particularly relevant, except where more careful studies with larger groups have contradicted Piaget's findings.

Related Research

Thousands of studies have investigated and sometimes elaborated on Piaget's work. An overwhelming majority of these studies supports Piaget's general description of the sequence of intellectual development, especially at the earliest stages (see, for example, Gelman 1978; Opper, 1977). This sequence appears to hold for children from various countries (Dasen, 1972, 1977; Glick, 1975). In contrast, research provides less sweeping support for Piaget's description of the ages at which major intellectual changes occur.

Piaget Underestimated Young Children

Critics point out that Piaget seems to have drastically underestimated the ages at which young children are capable of certain important behaviors. Indications are that verbal difficulties might often have been implicated in Piaget's failure to find certain abilities and understanding during the earlier developmental periods. When the tasks are made simpler and less dependent on advanced language development, children sometimes respond quite differently.

In the "mountains" problem, for example, children are shown three mountains of unequal height set on top of a table and are allowed to walk around the mountains to become familiar with them. In the testing part of the study, subjects are seated on one side of the table, and a doll is placed at some other vantage point around the table. Children are then asked to describe what the display looks like from the doll's point of view. Their initial inability to do so is taken as an example of *egocentrism* (inability to adopt another's point of view). But when Liben (1975) asked preoperational children to describe what a white card would look like from the experimenter's point of view (as well as from their own) when different colored glasses were being worn by the child or the experimenter (pink glasses on the experimenter, for example, and no glasses on the child), the children were often able to answer correctly.

Baillargeon (1987, 1993) also reports studies that seem to indicate young infants have some notion of the permanence of objects much before Piaget thought they did. For example, when 3- and 4-month-old infants saw an object apparently passing through a space that should have been occupied by another solid object, they seemed surprised. Bowers (1989) notes, however, that a 3-month-old infant's fleeting memory of objects does not really contradict Piaget's observation that it will still be some months before that child will deliberately search for a hidden object.

Gelman, Meck, and Merkin (1986) and Aubrey (1993) also point out that preschoolers typically have well-developed understandings of number that Piaget thought more characteristic of older, concrete-operations children.

Formal Operations Are Not Highly General

In his earlier writings, Piaget left little doubt that he considered formal operations to be generally characteristic of older adolescents, as well as of most adults (Inhelder & Piaget, 1958). However, several studies provide convincing evidence that this is probably not the case (see, for example, Modgil & Modgil, 1982). Many of these studies have failed to find much evidence of formal operations among adults, let alone adolescents. When Dulit (1972) tested gifted older adolescents for formal operations, he found that approximately half still functioned at the level of concrete operations; approximately one quarter of average older adolescents and adults operated at a level of formal operations. Similarly, cross-cultural studies have generally been hard-pressed to find much evidence of thinking beyond concrete operations in many cultures (see Gelman, 1978). Ironically, it seems that although Piaget underestimated the abilities of young children, he may have overestimated those of older children and adolescents.

Given these findings, Piaget (1972) modified his earlier position by conceding that the formal-operations stage is probably not nearly so general as he had first thought. Available evidence suggests that formal operations are best viewed as cognitive processes that are potential rather than probable. In short, formal operations are probably impossible in middle childhood or earlier; they are possible but far from completely general in adolescence or adulthood.

The System Is Too Complex

Another criticism has to do with the difficulty of understanding the system and with the use of complex and sometimes nebulous terminology. Morgado (2003), for example, points out that Piaget's use of important terms like *representation* is sometimes ambiguous. In addition, in trying to describe logical thinking, Piaget used a difficult logic whose contribution was not always readily apparent. Lourenco and Machado (1996) suggest that many of these criticisms are based on misinterpretations of Piaget's theory, sometimes resulting from difficulties in translating from the original French to some other language.

How Damaging Are These Criticisms?

These criticisms, although more numerous and detailed than indicated here, are probably not very damaging to the basic theory. At most, the various well-substantiated contradictions of Piagetian theory suggest that the ages of attainment are approximate—a point that Piaget always maintained. They further suggest that children may develop more rapidly in certain areas than Piaget suspected (particularly at the sensorimotor level), and that the final stage in Piaget's description is not generally descriptive—a fact that is not unduly disturbing for Piagetian theorists providing that the preceding stage, concrete operations, remains descriptive of those who have not achieved formal operations.

What the criticisms point out most clearly is the child's cognitive development is far more complex than Piaget had thought—perhaps more complicated than psychologists still think.

An examination of Piaget's system with respect to the criteria described in Chapter 1 reveals, among other things, that the theory is remarkably consistent, coherent, and comprehensive. However, some research indicates that Piaget's system may not reflect all the facts accurately. On occasion, it underestimates children's abilities, but at other times, it may be guilty of overestimating abilities.

Is the theory clear and understandable? Yes and no. At one level—that of describing stages—it can be presented simply and clearly. But there is another level—a level of abstract logical systems—that is less clear, and perhaps not very useful in any case (Russell, 1999).

Does the theory explain and predict well? Again, yes and no. It explains some behaviors that were largely undiscovered previously (conservation, for example), and in a general way, it predicts the type of cognitive functioning that might be expected of children at various stages of development. The predictions are not always entirely appropriate, however, especially when tied too closely to Piaget's approximate ages.

Finally, how useful and influential is the theory? Very. Piaget's impact in psychology and education has been enormous, even if it has also been controversial.

The theory has generated thousands of studies and countless applications in schools. Piaget is largely responsible for converting a generation of teachers, parents, and childcare workers into fascinated observers of children and their development. And although some theorists now argue that the influence of the theory is waning, many continue to praise his contributions and to extend his work (for example, The Jean Piaget Society, 2002).

Lev Vygotsky: A Cultural/Cognitive Theory

Not all psychologists have always praised Piaget's work or sought to extend it. In fact, one of Piaget's contemporaries, the Soviet psychologist Lev Vygotsky, apparently spent a considerable amount of effort attacking and criticizing Piaget's work and trying to get Piaget to engage in debate and dialog with him (Van der Veer, 1996). Piaget, as was his custom, never responded, although it's not clear whether this was because he chose not to respond, or whether it was because he might not have been very familiar with Vygotsky's work. After all, much of Vygotsky's writing was not translated into English until many years after his untimely death (at the age of 38, in 1934). In fact, for several decades after he died, his work was banned in the Soviet Union (see biographical insert).

Main Ideas in Vygotsky's Theory

The central emphasis in Piaget's theory, says Bruner (1997a), has to do with understanding the logical systems involved in the child's construction of meaning. Vygotsky's theory is also concerned with the making of meaning; as a result, his

Lev Semenovich Vygotsky (1896–1934)

Vygotsky was born in the town of Orscha in what is now Belarus, to middle-class Jewish parents. He was raised in Gomel, some 400 miles west of Moscow. His Jewish ancestry placed significant limitations on his educational and career possibilities. As a result, a private tutor educated him during his earliest years before he entered a Jewish high school. That he was later admitted to the University of Moscow was a matter of sheer luck, there then being in place a lottery system by which only a very small number of Jewish youth were admitted to the University each year.

Because his parents insisted, Vygotsky enrolled in the medical school at Moscow University. He quickly decided he didn't want to become a doctor, so he switched to law and simultaneously studied history and philosophy at a second university (Shaniavsky University). After graduating from these two universities in 1917, he went back to Gomel and began teaching in a state school. Some time later, he contracted tuberculosis, apparently while caring for members of his family who had became ill with the disease. Fortunately, he survived this first bout.

Strikingly, although he was to become an outstandingly influential psychologist during his lifetime—and remain so for decades after his death—Vygotsky did not become interested in psychology until 1924, when he was already 28 years old. A mere 10 years later, on the morning of June 11, 1934, he died of tuberculosis. Nevertheless, in the intervening 10 years, he had pioneered research and ideas in developmental psychology and education that still seem fresh and current. Despite the fact that his most famous work, *Thought and Language*, wasn't published until after his death, during this short career, he became one of the most important intellectual forces in the Soviet Union of his time. Sadly, however, his work was suppressed two years after his death and didn't become well known in the West until at least two decades later. Soviet authorities had determined that the child science he had pioneered, known as **pedology**, was a decadent "bourgeois pseudoscience," partly because it used Western tests for assessing and diagnosing learning difficulties.

Toulmin (1978) has described Vygotsky as the "Mozart" of psychology, its child genius. By the age of 28, says Toulmin, Vygotsky had assimilated all of psychology's major theories and findings and had begun to map out new ideas that are still highly influential. What might his career and his contribution have been had he lived as long as Piaget?

theory is often referred to as an example of *constructivism*. But, in contrast to Piaget, Vygotsky emphasizes how culture and social interaction are involved in the development of human consciousness. Thus, whereas Piaget's theory gives a primary role to forces that are *within* the child (the tendency toward equilibration, for example), Vygotsky's system emphasizes forces that are *outside* the child—in other words, the forces of culture.

Three overriding themes unify Vygotsky's far-reaching—and often incomplete and confusing—theory: These deal with the importance of culture, the role of language, and the relationship between educator and educated.

The Role of Culture

The single most important theme in Vygotsky's theory can be summarized in one sentence: *Social interaction is fundamentally involved in the development of cognition.* By *social interaction*, Vygotsky meant the child's interaction with what we label culture. We are very different from other animals, Vygotsky explains. Why? Because we use tools and symbols, and as a result, we create this thing called culture. Cultures are very powerful, dynamic, changing things that exert a tremendous influence on each of us. Culture, for example, specifies what the successful outcome of development is. Cultures determine what it is we have to learn, what sorts of competencies are required for successful adaptation to our worlds. Cultures, as Vygotsky explained, necessarily shape human mental functioning. "Every function in the child's cultural development appears twice," he writes. "First, on the social level, and later, on the individual level; first, between people (interpsychological) and then inside the child (intrapsychological). This applies equally to voluntary attention, to logical memory, and to the formation of concepts" (Vygotsky, 1978, p. 57).

The importance of culture in Vygotsky's theory is highlighted in the distinction he makes between *elementary mental functions* and *higher mental functions.* Elementary functions are our natural, unlearned tendencies and behaviors, evident in the newborn's ability to suckle and gurgle and cry. During development, and primarily because of social interaction—that is, of interaction with culture— *elementary mental functions* are transformed into *higher mental functions.* Higher mental functions include all activities that we think of as *thinking*, such as problem solving and imagining.

The Role of Language

Higher mental functioning, or thought, is made possible largely through language, insists Vygotsky. Without language, the child's intelligence remains a purely practical, purely natural capacity similar to that of animals such as apes. Thus, cognitive development is mainly a function of the largely verbal interaction that occurs between the child and adults. Through these interactions, says Vygotsky, the child develops language and, as a result, logical thinking.

In many important ways, Vygotsky anticipated important aspects of Piaget's genetic epistemology (his description of stages in the development of knowledge). For example, Vygotsky describes how, as a result of social interaction, the child progresses through three stages in the development of speech (Vygotsky, 1962). The first stage, that of **social speech** (also termed *external speech*), mainly controls the behavior of others ("Give me milk!") or expresses simple concepts. **Egocentric speech,** which appears between ages 3 and 7, is a sort of bridge between the highly public, *external*, speech of the first stage, and the more private, *inner*, speech of the third stage. During this stage, children often speak to themselves, as though in an effort to guide their own behavior rather than simply that of others.

The final stage, **inner speech,** is the stage of self-talk—the stage of what William James called the "stream of consciousness" (1890/1950). Our self-talk

Table 7.5 Vygotsky's Stages of Language Development

Stage	Approximate age	Function
Social	To age 3	Control the behavior of others; express simple thoughts and emotions
Egocentric	Ages 3 to 7	Control child's own behavior, but often spoken out loud
Inner	Age 7 onward	Silent, self-talk; makes it possible to direct thinking and behavior; involved in all higher mental functioning

(our *inner speech*) is what tells us that we are alive and conscious. It allows us to observe and direct our thinking and, by the same token, our behavior. Inner speech is what makes all higher mental functioning possible (see Table 7.5).

The Zone of Proximal Growth

Much of the current popularity of Vygotsky's theoretical framework relates to his description of the relationship between learner and teacher—or between parent and child. In Vygotsky's theoretical framework, this relationship involves teaching and learning for both parties (the Russian term for this *teaching/learning* relationship is *obuchenie*) (Scrimsher & Tudge, 2003). That is, the teacher learns from and about the child even as the child learns because of the teacher's actions. This relationship is best summarized by Vygotsky's notion of the **zone of proximal growth.**

The simplest way of explaining the concept of *zone of proximal growth* is to say that it is a sort of potential for developing. To clarify: Take Billy-Bob and Billy-Joe, two 7-year-olds who can both, under normal circumstances, answer roughly the same questions as can average 7-year-olds, and who can accomplish the same tasks in about the same amount of time. The measured intelligence of both these children is about average. But suppose that, when prompted and helped by a competent adult or older child, Billy-Bob can successfully accomplish tasks and answer questions more normally characteristic of 9-year-olds, but Billy-Joe cannot. It would now be accurate to say that Billy-Bob's *zone of proximal growth* is greater than that of Billy-Joe. That is, it spans a greater range of mental functions.

To summarize, Davydov explains the zone of proximal growth as follows: "What the child is initially able to do only together with adults and peers, and then can do independently lies exactly in the zone of proximal psychological development" (1995, p. 18).

Vygotsky's Theory: Educational Implications

The task of the teacher and the parent, explained Vygotsky, is to arrange for children to engage in activities that lie within this zone—activities that, by definition, are not so easy that the child can accomplish them right off the bat, nor so difficult that even with help, they cannot be accomplished.

Scaffolding

If you were to build an especially tall outhouse, it might be very useful to have a scaffold upon which to stand. Initially, the scaffold would be a sturdy affair, solid and low to the ground. And as the structure rose, your scaffold would also rise, making use of its original base to remain strong and in the right location. But the scaffolding might no longer need to be so extensive and so strong. In fact, you might now be able to climb on the wall plates and rafters of your own construction, and eventually right onto the roof, with little need of the scaffolding that was so essential in the beginning.

Scaffolding for teaching/learning works in much the same way, claims Vygotsky. In the early stages of learning, scaffolding (that is, guidance and support) are often essential. A preschooler can hardly be expected to quickly discover the sounds that each letter of the alphabet represents. But in later stages, the bright and successful learner will quickly be able to pronounce brand new words. Older learners who have learned how to learn need far less support, instead building on previous learning and well-rehearsed strategies.

By telling, demonstrating, showing, correcting, pointing, urging, providing models, explaining procedures, asking questions, identifying objects, and so on, teachers and parents build scaffolds for children. As Fernandez, Wegerif, Mercer, and Rojas-Drummond (2002) point out, scaffolding allows children to perform tasks that would be beyond their abilities if they were working alone. Research supports Vygotsky's notion that scaffolding can increase the complexity of children's thinking and affect both learning and development positively (for example, Gregory, Kim, & Whiren, 2003).

Scaffolding, note Hogan and Pressley (1997), is a metaphor that leads to a model of learning through gradual increments. In addition, it emphasizes the importance of interaction between educator and educated. Moreover, it underlines the importance of understanding the principles of child development and learning because the scaffolds that the educator builds need to lie within the zone of proximal development. That is, they must present the learner with challenges that lie within the range of what the child can accomplish with the help of a competent adult or older child.

Vygotsky's Theory: An Appraisal

Like many other cognitive theories, Vygotsky's cultural/cognitive theory can easily be criticized on the grounds that it does not provide precise measurements or lead to many verifiable assumptions—that it is not a highly scientific theory. Interestingly, these are some of the same criticisms that Vygotsky, himself, directed at the Marxist psychology of his day in one of his early works (Vygotsky, 1927/1987). In particular, he was aghast at the notion that "scientific" theories were often supported mainly by references to quotations from Marx and Engels or Lenin. Vygotsky argued strongly that psychology needed to use objective methods of investigation and that it should abandon the more intuitive, introspective approaches that were still widely popular. In addition, he rejected the reductionist approaches of the more behavioristic approaches, preferring to analyze behavior in more holistic terms (Lantolf, 2003).

Vygotsky's theory fares relatively well relative to the major criteria of good theories: it is relatively clear and understandable, it attempts to simplify complex observations relating to human learning and development, it is consistent, and it has very important practical implications, especially in child rearing and education (for example, Kozulin, Gindis, Ageyev, & Miller 2003). Also, it continues to stimulate and guide a considerable amount of research in the social sciences (for example, Lindblom & Ziemke, 2003). But, caution Lambert and Clyde (2003), the application of Vygotsky's theoretical framework to research and education may have been marked by an excess of enthusiasm that might have blinded researchers and practitioners to the possibility that there are better ways of understanding children and of teaching. In addition, Lambert and Clyde suggest, the desire to make his theory fit current practices has sometimes led to taking his writing out of context and to making it conform to current beliefs. But that, to the extent that it's true, is the fault of those who interpret and apply the theory, rather than of the theory or of the theorist.

Summary

1. Cognitive theories are concerned mainly with explaining higher mental processes (perception, information processing, decision making, and knowing), and they are based more on human than on animal research—in contrast with behavioristic theories. Cognitive theories typically presuppose some form of mental representation.

2. Bruner compares the development of the child to the evolution of the human race. Thus, the child progresses from enactive (motoric) representation (corresponding to inventions that amplify motor capacities), to iconic (in the form of images) representation (corresponding to inventions that amplify the senses), and finally to symbolic representation (corresponding to inventions that amplify intellectual capacities).

3. In Bruner's system, categorizing describes both perceptual and conceptual activity. A category can be thought of as a rule for classifying things as being equal. As a rule, it specifies the attributes (qualities) that objects must possess before they can be incorporated into a given category.

4. Information processing (and decision making) involves categorization. An object is identified when it is placed in a category—a process that implies the possibility of "going beyond the information given" (of making predictions about events or objects based on their category membership).

5. Coding systems are hierarchical arrangements of related categories. Higher level categories are more generic in that they subsume more examples and are freer of specifics (that is, are less defined by small details).

6. To form a concept is to arrive at a notion that some things belong together and others do not; to attain a concept is to discover what attributes are criterial (essential) for membership in a given category.

Concepts can be *conjunctive* (defined by the joint presence of two or more attribute values), *disjunctive* (defined by the joint presence of relevant attributes or by the presence of any of them singly or in other combinations), or *relational* (defined by a specified relationship between or among attribute values).

7. Bruner describes several strategies for attaining concepts: *simultaneous scanning* (generating all hypotheses—impractical and impossible for most subjects); *successive scanning* (trial and error—uneconomical); *conservative focusing* (accepting the first instance as the complete hypothesis and varying one attribute value at a time—economical and effective); and *focus gambling* (riskier than conservative focusing—sometimes a faster payoff, sometimes a slower one).

8. Bruner's work has led to considerable current research on categorization. Among the findings from this research are the following: Categories vary in generality, but the most specific category (Holstein cow) is not learned before a more general category (cow); items and events included in the same category, as well as the values that are employed in determining category membership, are not necessarily equivalent; and abstraction is always involved in categorization.

9. The *prototype model of abstraction* says that people abstract highly general notions of concepts from exposure to various examples of the concept; the *exemplar model* (which is less abstract) says people remember specific, representative examples of concepts.

10. Bruner is a strong advocate of discovery-oriented teaching methods.

11. Piaget's theory can be viewed as an attempt to answer two biology-related questions: What are the characteristics of children that enable them to adapt to their environments? And what is the simplest, most accurate, and most useful way of classifying or ordering child development?

12. To assimilate is to respond using previous learning; to accommodate is to change behavior in response to environmental demands. Play involves a preponderance of assimilation; imitation, a predominance of accommodation; and intelligent adaptation, equilibrium between the two.

13. A here-and-now understanding of the world, lack of the object concept, and absence of language characterize the beginning of the sensorimotor stage. Through interaction with the world, the infant begins to build a representation of reality that includes the development of language, the ability to coordinate activities, the appearance of intentionality, and the recognition of cause-and-effect relationships.

14. Errors of logic, transductive (from particular to particular) reasoning, intuitive problem solving, egocentrism, reliance on perception, and absence of conservation characterize preoperational thinking (ages 2 to 7). The stage nevertheless encompasses remarkable advances in language, mathematical understanding, and reasoning.

15. The appearance of the ability to conserve (reflecting logical rules of reversibility, compensation, and identity) marks the transition from preoperational to operational thought. In addition, children can now deal more adequately with classes, series, and number. Their thinking, however, is tied to what is concrete.

16. Formal operations (beginning at age 11 or 12) are defined by the appearance of propositional thinking. The child's thought processes are freed from the immediate and real and are potentially as logical as they will ever be.

17. Among the instructional implications of Piaget's theory are suggestions relating to providing for concrete activity, optimizing the difficulty of tasks, trying to understand

how children think, and providing opportunities for social interaction.

18. Research suggests that sensorimotor children may be more advanced than Piaget suspected, that the sequence he described for cognitive development is generally accurate, and that formal operations may not be generally characteristic of adolescence or adulthood. It is nevertheless a highly influential theory that has stimulated a tremendous amount of research and writing.

19. Lev Vygotsky's cultural/cognitive theory stresses the importance of culture and of its principal invention, language. Culture, and especially language, removes us from a lower-animal-like realm of reflex and reaction and makes higher mental processes (thinking) possible. Children progress through three stages in their learning of language: social (external) speech (before age 3) used mainly to control the behavior of others; egocentric speech (ages 3 to 7) which is often spoken out loud but is often geared toward directing one's own behavior; and inner speech (after age 7) which is "stream of consciousness" self-talk.

20. Vygotsky's *zone of proximal growth* is the child's potential for development, defined by what the child cannot accomplish alone initially, but is capable of with the help of competent others and can subsequently accomplish alone. *Scaffolding* describes an interactive teaching or learning technique where educators or parents provide learners with various forms of support as they learn.

Neural Networks: The New Connectionism

Scientific theories are mountains of sand built grain by grain, and people in the mountain-building business are justifiably wary of anybody who comes their way driving a bulldozer.
W. F. Allman

My brain! That's my second favorite organ.
Woody Allen

The Old Woman said to meet her at night on the ridge behind the bush cabin where the trail forks, that she would be there to tell me the story of the next chapter. "If you're not there," said she, "the thread of the story will be broken." She said that the breaking of the story might not seem a big thing but that it would be far bigger than itself. "All happenings are connected to other happenings," she said very solemnly. And then, very suddenly, she thrust a small black box into my hands.

"Tell me what is in this box?" she said. I turned the box this way and that, searching in vain for a way to open it. "I don't know what's in the box," I said. "I can't open it."

"Is that the only way you can find out what's inside?" asked the Old Woman. But before I could answer, she snatched the box from my hand and whirled quickly around so that I could see only her back. A moment later,

when she turned to face me once more, she held what looked like a fried chicken leg in her hand, which the cat pounced on at once, and I knew that somehow, the Old Woman had opened the box. "How did you . . . ?" I began to ask, but the Old Woman had disappeared into the trees.

I found her that night huddled by a fire not where the trail forks on the ridge's flank but farther back on the edge of the crest where no trees screen the stars, and again she didn't greet me but motioned that I should sit, and nodded her head that I should turn on the recorder. As I did so, a wolf howled. Every time I listen to the tape now, the howl somehow seems more desolate, more mournful.

I squatted on the other side of the fire watching the fire shadows dancing on the Old Woman's face as she spoke this eighth chapter, the recorder laying her words invisibly on its tapes.

This Chapter

She said that much of this chapter deals with how things are connected in vast, complex networks. To understand these networks, she explained, it's important to clarify a mysterious term often used in psychology: **black box.**

Black box is an expression psychologists have sometimes used to describe the contents of the mind. Interestingly, however, psychologists haven't yet decided what a mind actually is—although the term is used constantly, as in, "I've a good mind to . . ." or "I've changed my mind," or "They're always mindful of it," or "She's out of her ever-loving mind," or "Mind the kids now," or "Mind the dog," or "Out of sight is out of mind," or . . . well, never mind.

The expression *black box* implies that the contents of the mind are unknown and perhaps unknowable. So *black box* is often linked with behaviorists such as Watson and Skinner, who thought it was a waste of time to speculate about what happens between the presentation of a stimulus and the appearance of a response.

But, as we saw, some behaviorists thought maybe the black box should be opened—which they couldn't quite do. What they did instead was try to guess as intelligently as possible what sorts of things might be going on up there (or down there) in the mind—or in the brain, because most psychologists believe that if the mind is ever discovered, it'll be found in the brain somewhere.

Neobehaviorists, such as Clark L. Hull, Edward Chace Tolman, and Donald Hebb, invented their own versions of what they thought might be in the black box, being very careful all the while to tie their inventions to things they could actually see and maybe measure. At the same time, cognitivists also tried to crack the black box's lid. Some of them—Jerome Bruner and Jean Piaget, for example—became so engrossed in the structures and processes they glimpsed inside that, in the end, they ripped the lid right off and filled the box with so much jargon and stuff that the lid probably wouldn't go back on at all anymore. And now, far more recently in the history of the black box, a new army of brain/mind explorers, driven by powerful and sometimes intricate computer metaphors, has begun to map regions of the box no one dreamed of. Many of these explorers are no longer content simply to invent metaphors for the mind and the brain. Instead, they try to actually simulate what it is that the brain/mind does. Their theories are, in Harnish's words, "connectionist computational theories of mind" (2002, p. 15).

Objectives

Tell your readers, said the Old Woman, that the paths on which these mind/brain explorers have set out is the subject of this chapter. Try to convince them that once they've finished learning the chapter, they will probably want to rent television time so they might explain to everybody the significance of the following:

- *Artificial intelligence and computer simulation*

- *Symbolic representation systems*

- *Parallel distributed processing and connectionism*

- *Why robots play chess*

Let them know that they will also know more about that lump of tissue inside their skulls that they call a brain. But they will not yet know where the paths of this newer connectionism lead because human history, perversely tied to linear notions of time, provides no glimpse into the future.

The Old Woman fell silent for a moment. The wolf cried again, more moan than howl. Then the Old Woman began reading from her notes.

Computer Simulation and Artificial Intelligence

The field of computer applications in psychology, like the technology of computers themselves, is extremely dynamic. So rapidly does it change that almost everything written as recently as even a decade ago is so far out of date that it isn't even very good history anymore.

Much of the older research, firmly based on a computer metaphor, tried to understand the ways in which brains are like computers and tried to devise computer systems that could accomplish the same things as humans. The field came to be known as **artificial intelligence (AI).** Those who now work in the field are a varied collection of psychologists, neuroanatomists, physiologists, linguists, computer specialists, and others. They are united in their efforts to develop programs, procedures, devices, or mechanisms to simulate or duplicate some of the intelligent functions of human mental activity.

Artificial intelligence is sometimes distinguished from **computer simulation.** Artificial intelligence is concerned with devising systems—primarily computer hardware and computer programs—that can accomplish the same things as humans can (learning language or solving problems, for example). The emphasis in the artificial intelligence enterprise is on the accomplishments of the system. In contrast, computer simulation attempts to mimic the functioning of the human (including errors and biases). Hence, in computer simulation, the emphasis is on the processes rather than on the outcome. The artificial intelligence enterprise might well involve computer simulations of human intellectual activities.

Artificial intelligence, according to Raphael (1976), is a branch of computer science that tries to make computers smarter. Many people think computers are stupid, says Raphael; they think that computers are nothing more than "big fast arithmetic machines" and "obedient intellectual slaves" that can do only what they have been programmed to do. These are myths, claims Raphael. And the first myth—namely, that computers are nothing more than computational machines—is easily dispelled. The functioning of many computers involves countless operations that are not computational, including storing in memory, searching memory, making sequences of decisions, activating and turning off equipment, sensing and responding to external conditions, recognizing patterns, and perhaps even (as is shown later in this chapter) learning to read.

The second myth, that of the computer as slave, is more complex. It's true that computers do what they're programmed to do, and in that sense they are slaves to their programs (or, perhaps more precisely, to their programmers). But this doesn't mean that all computers need always be programmed in such a way that their activities will always be completely predictable. There are computers programmed to play chess or checkers that can beat their programmers. Similarly, there are computers that don't operate in sequential fashion. Their processing is distributed over a large number of connections simultaneously, leading to what is termed **parallel distributed processing (PDP)**—a type of processing that makes it possible for computers essentially to program (or train)

themselves and to respond in unpredictable and sometimes surprising ways. But this story comes later.

Making Computers Smarter

There are at least two good reasons why people might want to make a smarter computer. One is that such a computer might do some marvelous things for people, freeing them to move on to other even more marvelous things. That, in effect, is the goal of the artificial intelligence enterprise, which is aimed at developing computer systems and programs that accomplish intelligent things for humans. One example of this effort can be found in computerized robots—machines that can carry out simple functions like assembling machine parts, or more complex functions such as interacting with people as a psychotherapist might (Brooks, 2002).

The other reason for trying to make a smarter computer, perhaps more important for psychology, is that doing so might clarify many questions about human cognitive processes. As Thomas and Karmiloff-Smith (2003) point out, applying computer models to areas such as individual differences or cognitive development forces researchers to spell out and simplify their thinking about these areas. Not only is the programmer required to clarify and simplify, but whenever the program fails to simulate as expected, perhaps psychology learns something about what it is like to be human (or what it is like to be a machine).

Those involved in the computer simulation enterprise are concerned mainly with the second of these benefits. Their quest is to discover what the study of computers can do for the study of humans. They use computers in two distinct ways: first, to mimic the functioning of the mind; and second, to generate metaphors of human functioning. The hope is that the machines and programs that result will reveal information not previously known. Furthermore, attempts to simulate human processes in machines may serve as a fundamentally important test of what psychologists think they know about these processes—and might have important practical applications in teaching human learners.

Can Machines Think? The Turing Test

What sorts of human activities can computers mimic? For example, can they think?[1] Humans have long struggled with this old but fundamentally important question. Sternberg and Ben-Zeev (2001), for example, suggest that neither the computer simulation of human thought processes nor the development of problem-solving computers provide examples of machines (or programs) that can actually think. Computers *cannot* think, they argue, although they can sometimes be programmed to respond *as if* they were thinking.

Another argument goes like this: If it is true that people can think, and if it is true that a machine can be developed to do everything that a person can do when the person is thinking, then it follows that the machine can think.

Now consider this situation, described by Turing (1950) and since dubbed the **Turing test:** Two people—a man (A) and a woman (B)—are placed alone in a room. An interrogator (C) in another room must discover whether A is a man (X) or a woman (Y). At the end of the game, C must say "A is X, and B is Y" or "A is Y, and B is X." To discover who A and B are, C is allowed to ask them questions. A and B type out their responses. The object of the game for A is to impede the interrogator. He may, for example, answer questions as though he were a woman, or he may tell the truth. B, in contrast, attempts to help the interrogator. Obviously, if she attempts to do so by telling the truth ("I'm B, I'm the woman! Believe me!"), A can do exactly the same thing ("Don't believe him; I'm the woman!").

Turing says it will soon be possible to construct a machine that will stump the interrogator at least 70% of the time, which may be even better than what real people can do. In fact, 50 years after the original Turing paper, Hamburger and Richards (2002) note that it is now widely accepted that a "Turing machine" can be built to carry out pretty well any human function reducible to an algorithm (an algorithm is a step-by-step problem-solving procedure). By implication, then, the answer to the original question of whether machines can think appears to be yes.

---

[1] At this point on the tape, there is a long period when all you can hear is the muted crackling of the fire and, once, the hooting of a great horned owl. I remember that the Old Woman's voice had trailed off as though she were lost in thought, and then she asked that I turn the recorder off for a minute. Then she repeated the question again, "Can machines think?" as though if she asked it of herself, the answer might be clearer. She said that the great French philosopher Blaise Pascal had tried to answer precisely this same question. She said that more than 3 centuries ago, Pascal, whose IQ was estimated by someone clearly less intelligent to be above 200, had invented a primitive, computerlike calculating machine that he called an arithmetic machine. And in one of his Pensées, he had written, "The arithmetic machine does things that are closer to actual thinking than anything that animals do." But, explained the Old Woman, Pascal then concluded this thought by saying, "But, unlike animals, the machine does nothing to indicate that it has willfulness" (Pascal, 1820, p. 184, Vol. 2). When I began to ask her to explain what she meant, the Old Woman said that I should put more wood on the fire and turn the recorder on, and she started to read once more.

"But," the skeptic protests, "the machine wouldn't be thinking. It would just stupidly be churning out responses programmed into it."

Reductio ad Absurdum

Consider a second "Turing test" that doesn't even involve a machine (described by Searle, 1980). Instead, it involves a human student, Bob. Bob finds himself alone in a room, sitting at a table in front of which is a slot. Through this slot, some Chinese psychologists pass a slip of paper on which is written a string of Chinese characters—which are all Greek to Bob. But he has at his disposal a heavy book, and in this book he finds a string of Chinese characters identical to those on the paper, together with instructions to copy out a second string of characters. He does this and passes the paper back through the wall.

The Chinese psychologists examine the characters he has written, nod in approbation, and pass him a second piece of paper with a different string of characters on it. Again he responds as his book instructs. After several repetitions, the Chinese psychologists conclude that the machine—or the room—into which they have been passing these pieces of paper understands Chinese. What they've been doing is asking questions about a story, and Bob has been answering correctly. But he knows, of course, that he understands no Chinese. The Turing test thus is meaningless; it has been reduced to the absurd (*reductio ad absurdum*).

It's a strange thing, notes Searle (1980), that so many psychologists behave as though they believed in the validity of the Turing test. They assume that if a machine simulates intelligent behavior, then the machine must itself be intelligent; that if a machine produces correct responses for complex problems, it must understand these problems; and presumably that if a slot in a wall returns insightful responses in Chinese script, then something or someone beyond the wall knows not only Chinese but also stories. It's a mistake, notes Searle, that people don't make in other areas where computers are used to simulate complex systems: The meteorologist who tracks the movements and implications of weather systems by simulating them on a computer knows that the computer can't generate hurricanes or hailstorms.

Similarly, a computer that accurately imitates humanlike processes, or that selects responses identical to those a human might select, does not become human because of this. As Mellor (1989) points out, simple machine models are poor metaphors for the richness of human thought. Things like the deliberate manipulation of ideas or the conscious analysis of emotions—as well as the unconscious, "automatic" sorts of things that people learn and do—are not easily contained within a feedback-machine metaphor. That is because, says Mellor, "most mental processes are not computations" (1989, p. 47). In particular, things like pains and other sensations are mental processes that represent nothing, and thus they cannot be represented and computed.

Turing's original proposal established that a machine might be as effective as a human in a somewhat trivial task. At best, this suggests what psychologists probably knew all along: Something that imitates something else exactly need not exactly imitate.

So, is there more than one way to solve a problem? To remember a poem? To recognize a word? Will studies of artificial intelligence and computer simulations discover a computer way of thinking quite distinct from the human way? And will humans never know whether a machine can think—until, perhaps, it's too late?

Is it even clear what thinking is? Does the fact that human behavior appears purposive, whereas the behavior of a computing machine does not, prove that humans can think and that the machine can't? Would psychology be more convinced that a machine can think if it could change its "mind"? If it could deliberately lie?

Does the Computer Need to Think?

In the final analysis, that the computer may not be able to think—that it is not a mind, and the mind is not a computer—may not be very important. As Gunderson put it, "In the end the steam drill outlasted John Henry as a digger of railway tunnels, but that didn't prove the machine had muscles; it proved that muscles were not needed for digging railway tunnels" (1964, p. 71).

Similarly, computers don't need to "think," or to feel joy or anger, to do what they do so well. And that they might not be able to think and feel does not imply that computer models are either useless or flatly wrong. But, as DeLancey (2002) notes, their lack of "passion" does underscore that they are *not* human—and perhaps not very *humanlike* either.

The Computer and the Brain

In their characteristically human way, people have assumed all along that a truly smart computer would be quite a lot like a human. It is surely no accident that most of the computers and computerized robots of popular space fiction are given personalities. These computers are superbly "intelligent" in their memory and computational abilities, and they all have a degree of willfulness and of personal idiosyncrasy. Their creators have tried to make them human.[2]

People and Machines: Computer Metaphors

Mechanical metaphors, says Shanks (2002), have been rich sources of inspiration for scientists and philosophers. But these metaphors have not been without controversy. There are those who argue that viewing humans as machines robs them of the most important aspects of their humanity. After all, machines have

---

[2]I find this an astonishingly presumptuous intention, the Old Woman said, explaining that it is clear to all clear thinkers that human-type life forms cannot simply be invented and built, no matter how sophisticated the computing technology available. She said that real robots are simply machines; they do not have personalities because personalities are not properties of machines. She said that this fact explains why the human-invented robots of fiction will always be fictions. She seemed angry but ignored me when I tried to ask her if these things disturbed her. The cat appeared suddenly from the shadows and laid a mouse at the Old Woman's feet. He batted it once with his paw, but it seemed dead. Later he began to eat it and the Old Woman said to turn the recorder back on. The noise of the crunching of the mouse's tiny bones is clear on the tape.

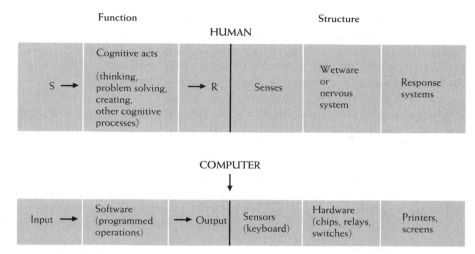

Figure 8.1 Analogies between computer and human structures and functions. The basic computer metaphor compares input to stimuli, output to responses, and the cognitive functioning of the nervous system to the computer's software-driven operations.

no emotion and no volition. Metaphors and models based on machines, explains DeLancey (2002) cannot explain or account for affect (emotion).

It's important to keep in mind that metaphors are, as the term implies, just comparisons. Also, as Penner (2000–2001) points out, models are simply conceptual or physical representations of something else. We need not believe that computers are in any way human for computer metaphors and analogies to be useful. We need only accept that, at least in some ways, computers and humans are sufficiently similar that some features of one can be used as a sort of pattern for some aspects of the other.

Computer metaphors are extremely common in what are sometimes called the cognitive sciences. Similarities that have historically been most important for these computer metaphors have to do with structure and with function. Structurally, computers consist of complex arrangements of electronic components: chips, disks, drives, switches, and so on (called **hardware**). The human brain consists of complex arrangements of neural material: neurons, various other cells, amino acids, chemical transmitter substances, and so on (termed **wetware**). The basic computer metaphor, shown in Figure 8.1, compares hardware to wetware. Similarly, it equates input and output with stimuli and responses.

Although the computer's hardware permits it to function (even as wetware permits humans to function), the computer's instructions or programs (termed **software**) determine whether and how it will function. With respect to functioning, the basic computer metaphor compares the computer's programmed operations with human cognitive processes. Hence, these human cognitive processes are labeled *information processing*. After all, information processing is what computers do.

The potential of the comparison between human and computer functioning lies in the possibility that a truly smart computer—one that responds like an intelligent human being—might function as does a human. Put another way, the memory and programs of a smart computer might in some important respects resemble the memories and cognitive processes of the human.

Keep in mind, however, that even a computer that does very humanlike things might nevertheless use very different processes to do them. A machine can milk a cow every bit as rapidly as Lefrançois's grandmother can, but this certainly doesn't prove that the machine has hands (or that the grandmother has suction tubes!). And it might be important, too, that although the machine doesn't sing as it milks, the grandmother sure as the devil does.

Important Differences Between Brains and Computers

Despite their similarities, brains and ordinary computers are different in some important ways. For one thing, brains are very slow; computers are lightning fast. Transmission of impulses in the brain is maybe 100,000 times slower than transmission in a computer. As Churchland and Sejnowski (1992) note, the brain is a product of evolution, not engineering design, and nature is not always the most intelligent designer.

Yet a single human brain can, in an instant, greet by name a man who has just shaved off his beard, dyed his hair, and changed his clothes; understand five languages spoken in dozens of different accents; recognize a drinking container no matter what style of mug, glass, flask, vessel, goblet, tumbler, cup, jug, beaker, carafe, pot, or flagon it is; write a novel; and on and on.

"What makes a bunch of neurons so smart?" asks Allman (1989, p. 6). He answers his own question by saying that it is a collective phenomenon; it has to do with organization. Or, as Waldrop (1992) argues, what intelligent living things have in common is organization and complexity. Thus, from a physical point of view, the human nervous system is incredibly more complex than even the largest and most sophisticated of modern computers. As a result, claims Allman, from a psychological point of view the brain's "tangled web displays cognitive powers far exceeding any of the silicon machines we have built to mimic it" (1989, p. 3). For example, the human ability to store information in memory is virtually unlimited; no computer even comes close. Also, the human ability to perceive and to recognize complex, changing patterns cannot be matched by computers. Even in the twenty-first century, the most sophisticated modern robots remain laughably incompetent compared with humans with respect to locomoting, recognizing people and objects, discriminating shapes and smells, and on and on.[3]

---

[3]Are you worried that really smart robots might one day take over the world? asked the Old Woman. You shouldn't be, she answered her own question. Brooks (2002) says that even when, or if, robots ever become truly intelligent, you won't have to worry that they will decide that you're stupid and useless, and take over the world. Why? Because, writes Brooks, "there won't be any us (people) for them (pure robots) to take over" (p. ix). You want to know why? asked the Old Woman. And again she answered her own question. It's because by then, according to Brooks, all humans will have robot parts imbedded in them—parts to make their joints and muscles faster and stronger, their hearing more acute, their vision clearer and, yes, even their brains incredibly more powerful. "Robot-humans," said the Old Woman, "will always be a couple of jumps ahead of the pure robots."

In contrast, the computer's ability to retrieve flawlessly from memory and to perform arithmetical computations rapidly and accurately far exceeds that of humans. Computers do complex calculations in elaborate arrays (like spreadsheets) in fractions of seconds. Using the brain to do the same sort of thing, claims Allman (1989), is like using a wrench to pound in a nail: It'll work, but that isn't what it's made for.

So people aren't good at what computers do, says Allman, and computers aren't good at what people do so well. As a result, it would be a mistake to try to compare the brain to a digital computer. That, Allman says, would be a little like trying to understand how airplanes work by studying helium balloons, or like trying to understand how a television works by looking at the wiring diagram in the instruction manual.

Parallel Distributed Processing

The problem, says Rumelhart (1992), is that cognitive scientists have been basing their metaphor on the wrong kind of computer—specifically, the serial processing **digital computer.** They've been asking how the brain is like a computer and, in some ways, forcing their interpretation of the brain's workings to their understanding of the functioning of the computer. Instead, they should ask what kind of computer the brain might be.

One possible answer is that the brain is a computer that doesn't do things one after another with lightning rapidity, arriving at its solutions in less time than it takes to say "Bob's your uncle." The truth is that if the brain actually worked that way, it would take you a staggering amount of time to blurt out "Bob's your uncle." Instead, explain O'Brien and Opie (2002), the brain is more like an **analog computer** that does a whole bunch of things at the same time. A computer that does many things at once is also called a *parallel distributed processing (PDP) computer.*

When the first computer models and simulations of human thought processes were invented, all computers were digital. Now PDP computers are available. However, these are complex and difficult things. Most of the time, what psychologists and others who use computers to simulate human thought processes do is emulate PDP systems on conventional, serial-processing machines such as the ubiquitous PC. In such cases, the PDP system is not actually a different parallel distributed processing machine. Instead, it is simply a set of instructions that makes the machine function like a PDP rather than a serial system.

Ⓢymbolic and Connectionist Models

Just how useful are computers for studying human information processing? Is it possible to design and program them so they perceive the environment as humans do? Can they be made to learn and use language as do humans? Can they be taught to read?

And if a computer can be made to do some (or all) of these things, will its processes be anything like human cognitive processes? Will it then be a "thinking machine?" Will it reveal things about human cognitive processing that are not now known?

In effect, there are two different approaches to the computer-based study of human cognitive processes, each tagged with a sometimes-bewildering array of labels. On the one hand is the **symbolic model** (also associated with the labels *production system* or *declarative knowledge*); on the other is the more recent **connectionist model** (also termed *PDP model* and associated with the labels *procedural*, *automatic*, and *implicit*).

Symbolic Models

Given that all computers were initially digital, serial-processing machines (such as the common personal computer), early models of human thought processes reflect the characteristics of these machines. These models view intellectual functioning largely as a sequence of acts (rather than as a number of acts carried out simultaneously). The tremendous power of the serial computer is that it can carry out a staggering number of operations (calculations) in a very short time—not simultaneously, but successively. In the vernacular of computerese, its strength is one of *brute force*.

The basic assumption of symbolic models is that all meaning, and therefore all thought processes, can be represented by symbols such as language. According to this model, all processing of information—and hence, all thinking—can be interpreted through identifiable rules. Simply put, the external world is represented mentally by symbols; thinking involves manipulating these symbols according to certain logical rules. Therefore, for a computer programmer to simulate thinking, it's necessary to program into the system symbols that correspond to items of information, as well as rules for dealing with these symbols.

Logic Theorist and the General Problem Solver

An early example of a symbolic model is the proposal by Newell, Shaw, and Simon (1958; Newell, 1973; Newell & Simon, 1972) for a theory of human problem solving. The proposal took the form of a complex program designed to discover proofs for theorems in symbolic logic. The program, called Logic Theorist, or LT, was based on *Principia Mathematica* (Whitehead & Russell, 1925) and consisted of storing the axioms of *Principia Mathematica* in the computer, together with all the processes necessary for discovering proofs. The first 52 theorems of the text were then presented to LT; it succeeded in proving 38 of the theorems, almost half of them in less than 1 minute. It even proved a theorem not previously proven.

Although it was reasonably adept at solving mathematical theorems, the Logic Theorist program could not be used to solve other kinds of problems. So Newell and his colleagues developed a more general problem-solving program, aptly titled General Problem Solver or GPS (Newell & Simon, 1972). Simplified, the program uses any of a number of available operations to reduce the difference between the present state of affairs (the problem) and the desired state of affairs (a solution for the problem). That is, the program is designed to allow comparisons between the desired end state and the current state, and to make a succession of changes (using the logical and mathematical operations available to it) until a solution is reached.

GPS has been used to solve a variety of logical and mathematical problems, and the problem-solving steps used by the computer have been compared with those used by human problem solvers. These comparisons, report Newell and Simon (1972) suggest that the behavior of GPS is like that of a human in several ways. Much like humans, GPS solved some problems, though not all; it did better if the information was presented systematically; it performed better with instructions that provided direction; it used processes suggestive of "insight" rather than blind trial and error; it used concepts in solving problems, to the extent that axioms can be considered to be concepts; and it organized itself to do these things, using past discoveries to guide future endeavors. However, GPS didn't actually reveal anything new or very important about human problem solving. It did only what it had been programmed to do, and so it tended to reflect only what was then known or suspected about cognitive processing. But one thing it did reveal, notes Wagman (2002), is that human subjects are far more flexible than GPS. Moreover, humans have a degree of self-awareness and a range of knowledge about the world that cannot easily be programmed into a computer in such a way that it can be brought to bear on a new problem.

SOAR

Newell (1989, 1990) has summarized the processes and components of major symbol-based information-processing models within a theory labeled **SOAR.** In effect, SOAR describes what is sometimes referred to as the architecture of the human cognitive machine (still very much a machine metaphor). Simon defines **cognitive architecture** as a "description of the cognitive system at an abstract, usually symbolic, level" (1990, p. 13). SOAR describes the human cognitive system using 10 components. These include aspects similar to the information and processes given the original GPS, but they also include things that one might not expect to find in a machine model (for example, "intended rationality").

SOAR, claims Newell, "operates as a controller of the human organism, hence is a complete system with perception, cognition, and motor components" (1989, p. 412). Like other symbol-system production models, it is based on the fundamental assumption that all knowledge can be represented by a symbol system, "which means that computation is used to create representations, extract their implications for action, and implement the chosen action" (Newell, 1989, p. 412).

A detailed review of SOAR by Cooper and Shallice (1995) concludes that it is a highly impressive body of research. Newell is widely regarded as one of the principal founders of the field of artificial intelligence (Steier & Mitchell, 1996).

Chess

There is a tendency to think of computers as mechanical wizards endowed with a type of brute cognitive force that humans do not even remotely approach. In the main, this estimate of the computer, though not entirely incorrect, is misleading.

Take a straightforward game like chess, for example. The rules of the game are marvelously explicit; each piece can move only in prescribed ways and only on a conventional, easily defined area. The object of the game—to capture the opponent's king—is simple and clear. At any given point, there are a limited number of possible moves, a finite number of possible countermoves, and so on.

Surely such a powerful brute as the computer can be programmed to consider and keep in memory all possible moves, countermoves, responses to countermoves, and so on, together with the eventual implications of each of these moves. In other words, a well-programmed computer could at least play to a draw, but more likely beat, any chess master in the world.

Not quite so easily. The total number of moves possible in a chess game approximates 10^{120}—a figure that may not look like much sitting here on this page, but that is absolutely staggering. "There haven't been that many microseconds since the big bang," writes Waldrop (1992, p. 151). Hence, no conceivable computer could represent all possible alternatives.

The computer, like people, must rely on *heuristics* rather than *algorithms* for situations such as this. An algorithm is a problem-solving procedure in which all alternatives are systematically considered. An algorithmic solution for chess problems relies on the computer's brute force. In contrast, a heuristic approach to problem solving makes use of various strategies that eliminate and select from among alternatives without having to consider every one separately. A computer programmed to play chess might, for example, make use of heuristics (strategies) designed to protect the king, attack the opposition's queen, control the center of the board, and so on.

When artificial intelligence investigators first began to program computers to play chess, none of their computers was large enough or fast enough to make very good use of brute force; hence, programmers were compelled to build their programs around the kinds of strategies human chess players might use. Chess masters could lick these early chess-playing computers with one hand.

But now computers are much faster and infinitely larger, and some of them can look ahead and see the implications of millions of different moves within seconds or minutes. Modern chess programs, as Campbell, Hoane, and Hsu (2002) explain, have largely given up trying to imitate human chess-playing strategies. They have reverted instead to using sheer brute force, coupled with a few key strategies. Their strength is not that they "think" better chess than average human players, but instead that they can mechanically compute millions of moves and countermoves within a few seconds. In fact, the IBM chess computer, "Deep Blue," is described as a "massively parallel processing" machine whose chips can each consider and evaluate between 2 and 2.5 million moves per second. In total, Deep Blue can attain speeds of more than 300 million positions per second.

So how good are the best chess-playing computers now? Quite good. Chess masters no longer laugh when they watch good computers play each other or when they themselves are challenged. They have to play with both hands, and they now risk losing each time they play. In fact, Deep Blue, which had previously lost to world champion Garry Kasparov, won the rematch in May of 1997 (although the match was close—3$\frac{1}{2}$ to 2$\frac{1}{2}$ in a 6-game match, with 1 point awarded for a win and $\frac{1}{2}$ point for a draw).[4]

Connectionist Models

Chess masters and computers don't play chess the same way. Human chess players do not—in fact, cannot—rely on brute force. Their computational capabilities don't allow them to foresee the consequences of very many moves and countermoves at one time. But what they can do that the machine doesn't do is recognize patterns on the chessboard, based on their previous experiences with similar though probably not identical patterns. And they can select the best move on that basis, in a sense synthesizing the effects of previous experience without necessarily following explicit rules. It's as though the human chess player learns from experience, developing implicit, nonverbalized rules. Moreover, the logic that characterizes the chess player's behavior is not a formal logic that always leads to one correct solution. Instead, it is termed **fuzzy logic**—logic that is relativistic, considers a variety of factors, and has a not entirely predictable probability of being correct (Russo & Jain, 2001).

If all this is true, it suggests that the symbolic model is inadequate or incomplete. Recall that this model is based squarely on the assumption that all information can be represented in symbols (like language), that learning is explicit, and that information processing (thinking) involves the application of identifiable rules.

Two Kinds of Learning

But not all learning is explicit, representable in symbols, conscious, and subject to definite rules. If Martha throws darts at a dartboard long enough, she might eventually reach a point where she will hit the triple- or double-20 spaces almost at will. But she will remain essentially unaware of precisely what it is that she has learned. Her learning will be what is called **implicit learning.** In this case, the learning may be implicit in a complex web of connections between her eye and hand, involving millions of relays among neurons and muscles.

Habitual, well-practiced motor skills are just one example of implicit or unconscious learning. It appears that people also learn all sorts of cognitive things unconsciously. For example, Reber (1989) reports a series of "artificial-grammar" studies in which subjects are shown strings of meaningless letters (for example, PVKPZ) that have actually been generated following precise

---

[4]Deep Blue's victory may not be entirely trivial, said the Old Woman, not just another chess match won and lost. She explained that it might herald the next major blow to humanity's collective ego. She explained that there have already been at least three such blows in relatively recent human history. The first was Copernicus's discovery that humans are not the center of it all. The second was Darwin's suggestion that the human animal is evolved from other animal forms. The third, closely associated with Freudian theory, was the realization that humans are not in complete rational control of everything. And now a computer has beaten a human chess champion. Will the next major blow be the reluctant realization that whatever qualities make *Homo sapiens* human can be duplicated, perhaps even improved, in a machine?

pseudogrammatical rules. In some studies, subjects are aware that rules govern the arrangements of the symbols; in others, they remain unaware of this fact. Later they are asked whether various new strings follow the same rules (that is, whether or not they are "grammatical"). And although human subjects seldom perform very well on complex tasks of this sort, they respond correctly far more often than would be expected by chance—and, by the same token, far more often than they would if they had not been exposed to examples of the so-called grammar. Strikingly, however, they are seldom able to verbalize the rules by which they arrive at their judgments. That they have learned something is clear from their behavior, but what they have learned is implicit rather than explicit.

Much the same thing happens when children learn language. Within an astoundingly short period, they learn to say all sorts of things in ways that are largely correct grammatically. Yet, they cannot make explicit their knowledge of the rules that allow them to generate correct language, or to recognize bad or good grammar.

Cognitive scientists have typically assumed that the mind uses rules and symbols to think, notes St. Julien (1997). And the principal appeal of the computer as a model of cognitive processes rests with the metaphor of information zipping through the brain in the form of electric impulses much as it does in the serial digital computer. But, argues St. Julien, what we know of the physiology of the brain no longer supports this type of metaphor, no matter how useful and instructive and even inspirational it might have been. We now know that cognition occurs in the brain not as a series of processes but more as patterns of activation (much as Hebb had suspected). And we know too that these patterns of activation require that many things be happening both simultaneously and very rapidly.[5]

Cognitive scientists had also assumed that the logic governing human cognitive activities would be a precise and predictable sort of logic—a machinelike logic. And the outcome could, at least theoretically, be duplicated by any machine given access to the appropriate symbols and programmed to apply the underlying logic. As Hamburger and Richards put it, "For every possible algorithm, no matter how complex, there is a TM [Turing Machine] that carries it out" (2002, p. 305). In other words, a machine can be built to do anything that can be represented by an algorithm. The key word, however, is *algorithm*. Recall that an algorithm is a clear, logical, systematic step-by-step procedure for solving a problem. Though a machine can perhaps be built to solve any problem for which an algorithm can be found, many problems don't easily lend themselves to algorithms. As we saw, some problems are more likely to require *heuristics*—more general problem-solving, alternative-eliminating strategies. The logic of heuristics is a fuzzier logic than the logic of algorithms. Activities such as playing chess, learning grammar, recognizing a dog, or mistaking a

---

[5]You might point out to some of your keener readers, said the Old Woman, that as neuroscientists have discovered more about the brain and how it functions, cognitive scientists have had to adapt their models. As a result, there has been what Kobes (1991) describes as a very close co-evolution between the neurosciences and information-processing psychology.

flying shoveller[6] for a mallard illustrate a more typically human, prone-to-mistakes, fuzzy-logic kind of thinking. If computer scientists are to investigate and model this kind of thinking, they clearly need something other than the algorithm-driven, symbol-manipulating, calculating machine that is the serial digital computer.

Neural Networks

What they need—and have—is the PDP computer (or, more often, computer program). This computer gives rise to the PDP (or connectionist) model of cognitive architecture, whose development was pioneered by McClelland and Rumelhart (1986).

All parallel distributed processing models, Kellogg (2003) explains, consist of a set of processing units whose structure (*architecture*) is designed to mimic that of the brain's neurons. Thus, these separate units can be considered to represent words, letters, sounds, elements of visual perception, variables related to financial markets, global weather data, and so on. They are connected to each other in complex and changing ways, as are actual neurons in the brain. The pattern of connections determines what the system knows and how it will respond. Learning within such a system involves changing the strength of connections among units—again in a manner highly reminiscent of Hebb's description of the formation of cell assemblies.

Neural Network Models

The PDP computer serves as a model of how the brain might work—a model labeled connectionism (or connectionist). Recall that the term *connectionism* was first used in Chapter 3 in relation to theories like that of Edward Thorndike. Thorndike was concerned with connections between stimuli and responses. He made inferences about these connections by looking at actual behavior. The new connectionists are concerned with connections among neural units. They make inferences about these connections by looking at the functioning of computers programmed as artificial neural networks.

What the connectionist model supposes is that the brain's collection of neurons is like the processing units in a PDP computer. In effect, they form a **neural network.** No central organizer or processor governs their activities. Instead, thousands (or millions) of these units are simultaneously active, activating each other in turn, establishing new connections, and ultimately learning through experience, achieving understanding, and making decisions.

It's important to keep in mind that in cognitive research, neural networks are not physical arrangements of actual networks of neurons. Rather, what cognitive

---

[6]Tell them that's a kind of duck, said the Old Woman—which it is.

research deals with are artificial neural networks represented by the functioning of PDP computers. As Hu and Hwang put it, "A neural network is a general mathematical computing paradigm that models the operations of biological neural systems" (2002, p. 2). In effect, this approach to understanding human thinking and learning uses the physical hardware and computer software of PDP systems to model the functioning of actual neural networks in humans.

Learning may occur in a neural network in three ways: New connections might develop, old connections might be lost, or the probability that one unit will activate another might change. Connectionists have worked extensively on this last possibility.

An Illustration: NETtalk

It is extremely complex to program into a serial-processing computer all the rules it would need to read a letter, or a poem, as a bright 6-year-old might. How a word is pronounced depends on what words come before or after it, what sorts of punctuation marks follow the sentence in which it is found, when it is being said, by whom, intended meanings and emphases of the reader, and on and on. So many exceptions and qualifications have to be built into such rules that even linguists can't agree on them (Li & MacWhinney, 2002). Actually, it may well be that the 6-year-old doesn't learn to read by first learning all the appropriate rules and exceptions and then applying them as required (a symbol production model) but, rather, that the "rules" are unconsciously made up in the process of learning how to match spoken words to printed symbols (a connectionist model). This is essentially the reasoning that led Sejnowski and Rosenberg (1987) to develop a connectionist program that might learn to read. The result, NETtalk, is at once a machine and a model. It is a machine made up of processing units, and it is what is called a *neural net model*. Hence, its units serve as an analogy for actual neurons in the brain; in the model, they are also referred to as "neurons."

As a machine, NETtalk consists of a "window" that can scan seven letters at a time. Each of the seven slots in this window is connected to 29 neurons (input units), corresponding to the 26 letters of the alphabet plus punctuation marks and space mark. Hence, there are 203 input units. At the output end of the machine are another 26 neurons (output units), each of which is linked with one of the 26 phonemes (simple sounds) that make up the English language. When one of the output neurons selects a phoneme, it is played through a loudspeaker, thus giving NETtalk its "voice." (See Figure 8.2.)

The guts—or, better said, the brains—of NETtalk consist of 80 "hidden units" that intervene between the 203 input units and the 26 output units. Each of the 203 input neurons is connected to every one of the 80 hidden units, as is each of the 26 output neurons. Thus, there are 18,320 connections in this neural network. And each of these 18,320 connections is weighted, meaning that some of the connections are strong (the important ones) and some are weak (those that are irrelevant). The highest of weightings (that is, the strongest of connections) might mean that activation of one unit would always lead to activation of the next; conversely, the lowest of weightings would mean that the activation of a unit would never lead to activation of the second.

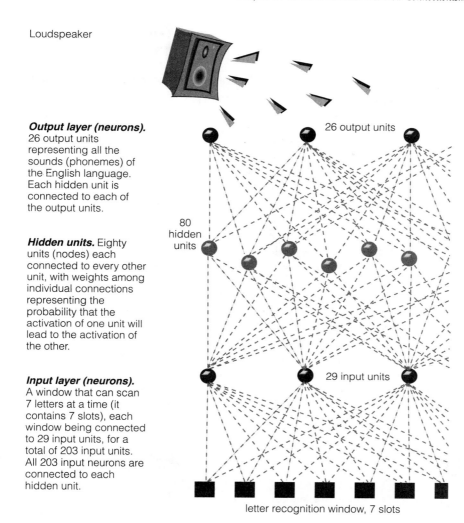

Loudspeaker

Output layer (neurons).
26 output units
representing all the
sounds (phonemes) of
the English language.
Each hidden unit is
connected to each of
the output units.

26 output units

80
hidden
units

Hidden units. Eighty
units (nodes) each
connected to every other
unit, with weights among
individual connections
representing the
probability that the
activation of one unit will
lead to the activation of
the other.

Input layer (neurons).
A window that can scan
7 letters at a time (it
contains 7 slots), each
window being connected
to 29 input units, for a
total of 203 input units.
All 203 input neurons are
connected to each
hidden unit.

29 input units

letter recognition window, 7 slots

Figure 8.2 A schematic representation of NETtalk, a neural network model. The machine is a computer programmed to learn how to translate written English text into accurately spoken words by adjusting the weights among its interconnected units. Only a few of the units and 18,320 possible connections are shown.

The essence of the task for NETtalk is stated simply: Learn to read text. Unfortunately, in English there is no direct, one-to-one link between a letter and a sound, or even between combinations of letters and a sound. The *a* in *can* is quite different from the *a* in *cane*. Although there is a simple rule to cover this situation, how about the *a* in *ah*? Or in *far*? Or the *a*'s in *facade*? Or in *aaaargh*? So the solution for the NETtalk task (learn to read) is not so simple. It requires that the weightings among the hidden units be arranged in such a way that patterns activated by letters lead the machine to select correct phonemes. Sejnowski and Rosenberg (1987) didn't know, of course, what these weightings would be, and so they proposed to let the machine learn them itself by using what is called the **back-propagation** rule. Essentially, a model that uses a back-propagation rule uses information about the correctness or appropriateness of its responses to change itself so that the response might be more correct or more appropriate. In learning to read, for example, a child already knows something about combinations of sounds that are correct (and meaningful); the computer does not.

The solution, Sejnowski and Rosenberg reasoned, might lie in letting the computer know what spoken text should sound like. So they presented NETtalk with 1,000 words of text read by a first grader. And they gave it the back propagation rule, in effect telling the computer to compare its output with the first grader's reading and work back through its hidden units, readjusting weights to reduce the difference between what it says and what the kid said.

And the computer did so. Because the initial weights had been set at random, its first pass through the text produced pure garbage. But over and over again the text was fed through NETtalk's input neurons, and over and over again the computer spluttered and babbled strings of phonemes—initially garbled and meaningless, but eventually clearer and more systematic. It was teaching itself to read.

After a day of practice, NETtalk could read not only most of the 1,000-word text it had been studying so hard but other texts it had never seen. It had learned rules and exceptions, it had learned to generalize, and it had made some of the same sorts of errors that children make when they first learn to read—for example, pronouncing *have* as if it rhymed with *cave* and *rave*. And in much the same way as the human brain, by the end NETtalk used only a small portion of its potential connections.[7]

Connectionist Models: An Appraisal

The point of all this is that neural networks respond very much like humans do. Their fuzzy logic takes the imprecision of the real world into account. In fact, claim Jang, Sun, and Mizutani (1997), the role model for the logic that drives these neural networks is the human mind. As a result, they claim, the notion of truly intelligent machine systems is rapidly becoming a reality.

Like humans, neural networks can make inferences without being given specific rules for so doing. As Allman (1989) notes, if you see the word *bat* along with the words *ball*, *diamond*, and *base*, you know something very different about *bat* than if you see the same word along with *witch*, *Halloween*, and *cave*. The inferences of humans, says Bruner (1957a), are based on experiences that allow

---

[7]I'm sure some of your students would be interested in more information here, said the Old Woman, straying from her notes for a moment. Some, she explained, might want to know that other researchers have developed programs similar to NETtalk, but using feed-forward rather than back-propagation rules. That is, the neural net is so structured that the computer has access to rules designed to eliminate or minimize certain errors. Others have developed similar programs to enable computers to teach themselves how to count. The result can sometimes be quite impressive (see, for example, Ahmad, Casey, & Bale, 2002; Chang, 2002).

them to categorize and relate things. And the neural network computer, given the right series of experiences, might well do exactly the same thing. In a sense, its structure and functioning allow it to reach something that looks like insight. But the conventional computer is quite different; no matter how often it might be presented with bats of various kinds, it would never discover on its own that bat in one context is different from bat in another—unless it were actually given a rule specifying all the possibilities.

So neural network models—and the parallel distributed processing computers that make them possible—may in the end be far better models of some human cognitive processes than symbol-based models. Among other things, these models suggest that people don't always think all that rationally. They don't systematically consider all the pros and cons, bringing the cold rules of logic to bear, calculating (as might a conventional computer) what the correct response is. These models allow for a fuzzier kind of logic, and they emphasize that many aspects of a situation (or of many situations) might be involved in a response or a conclusion. In addition, neural network models have the advantage of more accurately reflecting the actual physiological structure of the human nervous system, with its maze of neurons and interconnections—although the most complex of neural network machines is ridiculously simple compared with the fully functioning human brain.

Neural network models also present a functional analogy for the notion that experience alters the brain's wiring, as Hebb had theorized so long ago. A neural network that adjusts its own connections is highly compatible, for example, with Hebb's notion that neurons that repeatedly activate each other become increasingly more likely to do so.

Connectionist, or neural network, approaches now dominate the study of human cognitive processes. Connectionist models are rapidly leading to new insights in understanding the course of human development, individual differences, and atypical development (Thomas & Karmiloff-Smith, 2003). It is worth noting, as well, that their applications stretch well beyond the cognitive sciences and psychology. Neural networks have been applied to a wide variety of fields, including prediction of the weather and the performance of financial markets, medical diagnosis, and engineering.

Some Cautions and Criticisms

As we have seen, there is a sort of biological realism to connectionist models. Because of their close resemblance to the structure and functioning of the human nervous system, it's easy to mistake connectionist models for the real thing—that is, for real, functioning nervous systems. But they aren't; they're just metaphors. As metaphors, they describe and they suggest, but it would be a mistake to confuse a description or suggestion with an explanation.

Connectionist models are not perfect analogies for human thought processes. There are three standard criticisms of computer simulation models of human thought processes, explains Benjafield (1996). The first is that computers don't simulate human emotions at all well. As DeLancey puts it, the failure to imbue machines with "passions" makes "a strict version of the computational theory of mind untenable" (2002, p. 187).

A second standard criticism is that computer simulations don't reveal the insight of which human problem solvers are capable. In the Gestalt view, such simulations are woefully inadequate models of human cognitive processes.

The third common criticism is that computer programs tell us very little, if anything at all, about how the human nervous system works. For example, as Li (2002) points out, the successful functioning of connectionist models depends on certain properties of their units that are not properties of the human nervous system. Thus, by changing their weightings, these units can inhibit activity in some units while facilitating it in others; neurons in the human brain do not do this.

There are a number of other reasons why connectionist models are not always very informative or useful, and why they should not be taken too literally. A connectionist model with 360 units that successfully duplicates some human cognitive functioning does not reveal that the cognitive function requires 360 neural units in the human brain. The same cognitive activity could conceivably be predicted with a model consisting of only 250 units, or perhaps 400. Massaro and Cowan (1993) point out that neural networks with enough hidden units are capable of generating results that are not only unpredictable but have never been observed in the laboratory. In fact, in a neural net using a back-propagation model, it may be possible to match any input to the desired output if one is given sufficient layers of hidden units and enough time. Thus, it might be possible for a neural network to teach itself to "read" a passage of Spanish as if it were really English. If the input does not matter, then the model again teaches psychologists little about the processes involved in learning. Such models, Massaro and Cowan warn, may not be highly informative.

Another problem for self-taught neural network models has been that of interference. For example, McCloskey and Cohen (1989) have shown that when neural network models train themselves to recognize pairs of words in what is termed paired-associate learning, and are then given a second set of pairs, the initial learning impedes subsequent learning far more than is the case with human subjects. As Estes puts it, "Connectionist models are built to learn, but there are reasons to question whether they can be made to learn like human beings" (1991, p. 23). At the same time, that they learn at all is rather human. And there may be much to be learned by studying some of the ways in which they learn.

E*ducational* Implications

Successful simulation of human learning and thinking has clear educational implications. Ilyas and Kumar (1996), for example, describe how a computer-based tutoring system that can mimic student intellectual activity might also be capable of reasoning about the student's understanding and knowledge. Thus, it might be used to monitor students' progress and to act like a teacher by guiding students, asking questions, uncovering misconceptions and errors, and so on.

Computer simulations that mimic phenomena other than human thought processes also have increasingly important instructional applications. For example, programs that mimic the in-flight responses of specific aircraft are used to train pilots, and others that model the functioning of the circulatory system are used in medical schools. A simulation of a physics or chemistry laboratory can be used to teach students the likely outcomes of combining, chilling, heating, pressurizing, or even eating various substances without the risk of losing an actual laboratory, a school, or a student in the process.

Interactive, computer-based simulations of various environments, labeled **virtual reality (VR)**, also have instructional applications. In education, virtual reality describes a type of computer-learner interaction whereby the learner experiences certain events and environments and makes choices within that environment. Many virtual reality systems, most of which are still in an experimental and developmental stage, involve more than one sensory system. For example, the computer's display systems may include something like helmets and goggles so that the visual presentation occupies the subject's entire visual field and changes as the learner moves. Similarly, learners might wear headphones that provide authentic "surround" sound, as well as "gloves" that give them the sensation of being able to manipulate objects in the virtual world.

One example of a virtual reality program applied directly for educational purposes is that of a Mayan world, called Palenque (Wilson & Tally, 1990). A student interacting in this virtual reality setting can climb a pyramid, explore Mayan tombs, walk through an ancient museum, and so on.

There are, of course, many other applications of computers in education, not all of which involve simulations. For example, what are termed *intelligent tutor systems* are computer-based instructional programs where the computer is used as a source of information, much as a human tutor might be. But unlike a simple information-loaded database, an intelligent tutor system takes into account the student's strengths and weakness. That is, it is programmed to analyze the student's responses and to direct its teaching accordingly—much as might an intelligent human teacher.

Another important use of computers in schools is to teach students programming skills. A well-known program for doing this is **Logo,** a programming language developed by Papert (1980, 1993). The program makes use of a "turtle"—a creature on the computer monitor that can be made to move in different ways. For example, the child types FORWARD 40 to make the turtle move forward 40 small steps. Now, if the child types RIGHT 90, the turtle makes a ninety-degree turn. Very quickly, the child learns to write REPEAT 4 FORWARD 40 RIGHT 90, and the turtle goes forward 40 steps, turns right, advances another 40 steps, turns again, repeating this procedure 4 times and drawing a perfect square—which the child can label SQUARE. The child has easily, almost effortlessly, created a program.

At one level, Logo is a simple tool that allows the child to explore plane geometry. But at another level, it is sophisticated enough to allow children to investigate the world of differential equations. Such programs also teach children the systematic and clear thinking that computer programming requires. They arm children with what is labeled **computer literacy.**

A book edited by Moore, Redfield, and Johnson (2001) describes dozens of other applications of artificial intelligence to education—sometimes abbreviated AI-ED. (Recall that *artificial intelligence* is a general term for models, procedures, devices, or machines intended to accomplish some of the *intelligent* functions of humans.) Several of these applications have been mentioned: intelligent tutoring systems, simulations such as those of a laboratory for teaching chemical reactions, virtual reality programs for teaching history, and programs designed to teach programming and computer literacy skills, such as Logo. In addition, computer programs have been devised for teaching students cooperative learning skills, for fostering proficiency in problem-finding and problem solving, for developing task analysis and study skill, for improving memory, for improving verbal interaction skills, for imitating models—and on and on.

Field in Progress

Much of this book is historical: It deals with theories the meat and gristle of whose principles and assumptions have been well chewed. That, of course, is not necessarily because they are less current than younger fields. It is simply because they are of a greater age and have therefore been around to be gnawed at much longer.

In contrast, the subject of this chapter is of a younger age; it has yet to be digested by generations of scholars and thinkers. And so the chapter cannot really be concluded, nor can the models and theories presented in it be evaluated. History, as is her habit, will judge.

Summary

1. The branch of computer science that tries to develop models, procedures, or devices intended to accomplish some of the intelligent functions of human mental activity is labeled *artificial intelligence. Computer simulation* attempts to mimic actual cognitive functioning.

2. Two myths characterize human reactions to computers: that they are merely computational machines and that they are nothing more than slaves to their programmers. New PDP computers can "learn," however, and they sometimes surprise their programmers.

3. The Turing test says that if A can do x, y, and z, and B can do x, y, and z exactly,

then B must possess whatever attributes A has that allow it to do x, y, and z. The test reduces easily to the absurd and does not answer the question of whether machines can think. They probably don't need to.

4. The basic computer-as-cognitive-processor metaphor sees parallels between computer hardware (physical components) and the human nervous system and especially the brain (wetware), as well as between human cognitive functioning and computer programs (software).

5. Brains are much slower than computers and far inferior at doing computations, but they are much better at recognition tasks and at reasoning where insight and

fuzzy logic are required. They are also enormously more complex in organization and size. Parallel distributed processing (PDP) computers appear to work more like brains, doing many things simultaneously.

6. The *symbolic model* is based on the serial-processing digital computer, and it assumes that knowledge can be represented symbolically and manipulated with rules. An illustration of the symbolic model is Newell, Shaw, and Simon's Logic Theorist (LT), which is capable of finding proofs for theorems in symbolic logic, and their GPS, a more *general problem solver*. The functioning of these programs simulates some aspects of human problem-solving behavior.

7. Newell's SOAR, a model of cognitive architecture, also illustrates a symbolic model, as do most of the chess programs. Chess programs are partly heuristic (that is, they make use of strategies and other systematic shortcuts), but they beat human chess masters mainly through their use of algorithms (systematic problem-solving using brute computing force to consider an enormous number of alternatives with astonishing speed).

8. Not all human learning is explicit and describable in symbols and rules. Much is implicit or unconscious, including motor skill learning and the learning of abstract relationships through experience. Implicit learning is better modeled on PDP machines than on serial-processing machines (or with programs that make digital, serial processing machines function as though they were analog, PDP machines).

9. Neural network (or connectionist) models, premised on PDP machines, consist of interconnected units rather than central processors. Patterns and strengths of connections represent knowledge. Sejnowski and Rosenberg's NETtalk is a neural network model developed so that the machine could "teach" itself to read using a back-propagation rule (knowledge of what the output should be) to modify connections so as to eventually match input (written words) to output (spoken words).

10. Connectionist models lead to machines whose functioning resembles that of humans in some respects. They allow for thinking that isn't completely logical and that sometimes leads to unforeseen results. They also reflect some aspects of human neurological structure well. But they are descriptions rather than explanations, don't always generate plausible results, and don't always function as a human would (for example, they suffer from greater interference effects, do not simulate emotion well, and can't easily be programmed to reflect insight).

11. Artificial intelligence applications in education include the use of intelligent tutoring systems (tutoring systems that take the student's responses into account), simulations of systems and situations to teach things like how to drive a car or conduct experiments in chemistry, virtual reality programs to teach aspects of history or medicine, and a variety of programs designed to teach programming and computer literacy skills, problem solving, memory improvement, verbal interaction skills, and so on.

Learning and Remembering

The world will little note nor long remember what we say here . . .
Abraham Lincoln

The Old Woman said today we would climb the rock face, that my fear of heights was not an issue, that she would show me where to put each foot, each hand, that she would guide me as might a mother her child. She refused my protests, insisted that the ninth chapter would only be told from the top of the cliff, from above the land.

We left at dawn before the sun had warmed the air. The cat lay curled on the sunny side of the largest of the birch trees watching as we inched our way up the smooth face. Within minutes my hands were slick with sweat, my muscles strained with fear. The Old Woman said I should pay attention, do exactly what she did, put my hands and my feet in the holds her hands and feet would show me, trust in the rope that joined us like an umbilical cord. She explained that trust is a thought, a conclusion.

She said that I need only believe it and it would be mine.

But I could not stifle my dread and when I had not yet reached as high as the youngest of the birch, I could climb no more and the Old Woman lowered me to the ground, dropping the rope, useless, like a dead snake at my feet. When I turned to sit weakly against the birch, the cat had left, and when I looked up again at the Old Woman climbing, I saw that the cat waited for her at the very top, although it was not possible that he would have arrived so soon.

The Old Woman climbed swiftly like some hairless simian, scarcely resting, until at last she stood with the cat, and she motioned to my astonishment that I should now record her words, and then she began to shout very loudly, as though enjoying that she needed to do so, the words of the ninth chapter.

This Chapter

Here is what she shouted from that great height while I listened through the early morning, too far away to ask questions.

"My body knows how to climb," she shouted, explaining that much of her knowledge of climbing resides in memories that she cannot easily put into words. "That's why I can't *tell* you how to climb, or how to ride a bicycle." She explained that the memories for actions such as these are *implicit*; they can't easily be made *explicit*. She said that in contrast, she could easily explain how to find the square root of a four-digit number.

This chapter, she said, deals with human memory. It looks at the differences between memories that are implicit and those that are explicit. It explores the astonishing power of human memory, and it recognizes as well, its imperfections and limitations. As Johnson declared, "When put on the witness stand, we can swear before God that we will tell the truth, the whole truth, and nothing but the truth. But the best we can really do is read out what is left of our memories, recollections that have been inevitably altered by time" (1992, p. 233).

Objectives

Let your readers know, said the Old Woman, that they will understand what this means after they have read and studied this chapter— that is, if they remember it. And if their memory serves them well, they will then be able to weave fascinating tales dealing with the following:

- ■ *Sensory, short-term, and long-term memory*

- ■ *Two kinds of long-term memory*
- ■ *Event-related activity in the brain*
- ■ *Theories of forgetting*

They will also have learned a new trick for impressing old people.

Metaphors in the Study of Memory

As I have noted on a number of occasions, *the Old Woman shouted from her lofty perch*, cognitive psychology is a psychology of metaphors. It seeks to understand the grand complexities of human cognitive functioning not so much by uncovering its precise mechanics and exposing its structures and functions but by inventing the most compelling and the most useful of metaphors to describe it. In the end, however, the value of the metaphor will be judged largely by how well it reflects the facts. Thus, the search for the metaphor is premised on the results of scientific investigation. If psychology cannot trust its facts, how can it trust its metaphors?

It bears repeating that the metaphors of cognitive topics such as memory are not the moving figures of speech of literature. They are nothing more than models—often simple models. What they say is not "Attention is a damsel with flowers up her nose," or "Memory is an ancient elephant," or "Motivation is an angel with green hair." Rather, the metaphors of cognitive psychology are prosaic metaphors. They say only that humans behave "as though" or "as if," and they describe what it is that humans behave "as if." These, explain Oswick, Keenoy, and Grant (2002) are the comfortable metaphors of similarity. They elaborate and explain by emphasizing likenesses.

Over the years, an enormous number of different metaphors have been used to describe memory—perhaps testimony to how difficult a concept it is, and how uncertain psychologists have been of their models. The index to Draaisma's *Metaphors of Memory* (2000), for example, lists some 43 different metaphors of memory. Memory, different thinkers have assured us, is like an abbey with many rooms. Or maybe it's more like a book with many pages of information, table of contents, and index. Or perhaps it's like a library, or like a mirror, a loom, a palace, a camera, a purse, a treasure chest, a vault, a wine cellar . . . and on and on (p. 240). Recently, of course, the computer metaphor has become increasingly popular. After all, computers have storage systems and recall systems, and these are two of the essential features of memory. But, as we see in this chapter, the computer metaphor, and indeed all of our common metaphors, do little justice to something as rich and as complex as is human memory.

Basic Concepts and Definitions in Memory

Attention, memory, and learning are inextricably linked. Learning is a change in behavior that results from experience, memory is the effect of experience, and both are facilitated by attention. Put another way, there will be no evidence of learning without something having happened in memory; by the same token, something happening in memory implies learning. Studying memory is, in effect, another way of studying learning.

Still, there is far from unanimous agreement among psychologists concerning what memory is and how it should be studied. The metaphors and models of memory have changed often in the history of psychology, and continue to change—as have the ways in which memory is studied.

Early Studies of Exceptional Memories

Leonard Euler, reports Draaisma (2000), was both a child prodigy and a mathematical genius. He had apparently memorized the entire *Iliad* and could recite it flawlessly until the day he died. They say that one night when he couldn't sleep, he worked out the first six powers for numbers 0 through 99, generating a mental table of 600 numbers that he could read off at will weeks later. He seemed to remember everything that he heard or read, so that even though he was completely blind for the last 15 years of his life, this hardly affected his work. He had a huge slate-covered table installed in the middle of his workroom, and he walked around this table writing down formulas and ideas that his students, including his sons and grandsons, organized, wrote, and read to him. The result was that during the 15 years of his blindness, he published an astonishing 355 scientific papers, mostly in mathematics and applied science.

But not all people with remarkable memories are so well adjusted and so productive. Some extraordinary memories may be quite trivial and useless. For instance, there is the so-called idiot savant—the mentally limited person who possesses a remarkable but highly specific talent, like the guy who could watch a freight train pass by and memorize all the serial numbers on the boxcars. There is, also, the well-documented case of a man known to us only as S, described by Luria (1968). S was in most ways an ordinary man who had not been very successful as a musician or as a journalist, but who had an astounding memory. On one occasion, Luria presented S with the array of 50 numbers shown in Figure 9.1. After examining the table for 3 minutes, S reproduced the numbers flawlessly in 40 seconds. When asked to do so, he recited each of the four-digit numbers in the 12 rows as well as the two-digit number in the last row—again without error, and all within 50 seconds. And one of the absolutely remarkable things about his memory was not so much that he could memorize these tables so quickly but that he could remember them, without error, at any time in the future. In fact, he recalled perfectly lists of words he had learned as

6	6	8	0
5	4	3	2
1	6	8	4
7	9	3	5
4	2	3	7
3	8	9	1
1	0	0	2
3	4	5	1
2	7	6	8
1	9	2	6
2	9	6	7
5	5	2	0
X	0	1	X

Figure 9.1
Luria's subject, S, memorized this table completely within 3 minutes and could then read off from memory any arrangement of the numbers, including the 12 four-digit numbers in the rows, all four-digit diagonals in the array, or the four vertical columns. Also, he was able to convert the entire array to a single 50-digit number and read it off, a feat that required 1½ minutes. From *The Mind of a Mnemonist: A Little Book About a Vast Memory*, by A. R. Luria, p. 17. Copyright © 1968 by Basic Books. Reprinted by permission of the author.

much as 16 years earlier, without having been asked to remember them once in the interim. The only difference was that when asked to remember after several months (or years) had gone by, he needed a few minutes to "revive" the memory. He would usually sit with his eyes closed, Luria tells us, and he might comment, "Yes, yes . . . This was a series you gave me once when we were in your apartment . . . You were sitting at the table and I in the rocking chair . . . You were wearing a gray suit and you looked at me like this . . . Now, then, I can see you saying . . ." (1968, p. 12).

Most memories are not so phenomenal, as is well illustrated by "memory curves" that represent the results of some of the first experiments on retention (many of which were carried out by the pioneer memory researcher, Ebbinghaus (1885/1964)). Figure 9.2 shows an idealized summary of these curves. The most striking thing the curves indicate is that people tend to forget most of what they learn almost immediately after learning it. In Ebbinghaus's original investigations, subjects were typically asked to learn a list of nonsense syllables—meaningless combinations of letters such as kiv, gur, or lev. Even though these subjects could successfully recall all of the syllables immediately after learning, within about 20 minutes, they had usually forgotten more than 40% of them; within an hour, more than half had been forgotten. At the same time, however, the 20% or 30% of the nonsense syllables that were remembered for half a day were still largely available for recall a month later. Hence, although the bulk of what humans learn (at least with respect to meaningless items) tends to be forgotten very quickly, some information is retained over long periods. These characteristics of human memory are reflected in most current theories of learning and forgetting.

Defining Memory

In everyday speech, the term **memory** refers to the availability of information and implies being able to retrieve previously acquired skills or information. It clearly presupposes learning; that is, memory involves change. The computer metaphor leads naturally to the notion that to remember is to be able to retrieve

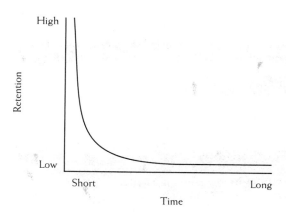

Figure 9.2
An idealized memory curve, based on Ebbinghaus (1885/1964).

from storage. Not surprisingly, says Hintzman (1990), one assumption of an intuitive understanding of memory is that if a memory is to influence behavior, it has to be retrievable.

But this is not so. There are numerous examples of what is sometimes termed *implicit memory* (or *unconscious* memory), as Freud argued so convincingly. For example, past learning that cannot be remembered consciously can nevertheless affect later behavior—as happens when someone relearns a long-unused and apparently forgotten language. Similarly, some amnesiacs know all sorts of things, but they cannot remember having learned them.

Goldblum (2001) distinguishes between two different types of memory. There is, on the one hand, all your general knowledge—the things you know relatively *permanently*, like your name, your telephone number, the names of the planets, a poem you learned in school, where you went on your last vacation. On the other hand, there are a wide variety of things you know that are far more temporary—like what you had for breakfast today, where you plan to eat, what you're going to do after you finish reading this chapter. Connectionist models, which are based on the notion that repeated experiences lead to changes in the probability that neurons will activate each other, can be used to explain permanent memory, notes Goldblum. But these models say little about temporary memories. As we see shortly, current models of memory take into consideration different kinds of memory as well as different ways of storing memories and different storage locations.

Remembering and Knowing

Remembering, says Tulving (1989), is not the same thing as knowing. He explains that trees with their growth rings, just like musical recordings and card files, have memory; in a sense, they know things. But they remember nothing.

To clarify these concepts, Tulving (2002) suggests that psychologists need to pay attention to the two distinct aspects of memory: storage and retrieval. What trees and card files have is storage of certain effects; what humans have is storage and retrieval. Being able to retrieve presupposes storage, because things that have not been learned can't be recalled. However, not all that has been stored can be retrieved. And there is now evidence that different parts of the brain are involved in storage and retrieval (D'Esposito & Postle, 2002).

Current memory metaphors speak of three different kinds of storage: sensory, short-term, and long-term. They also speak of at least two different kinds of retrieval from storage: episodic and semantic. These terms are explained and illustrated later in this chapter.

Forgetting

If the coin of learning has two sides, memory is one side; **forgetting** is the other. Like memory, forgetting relates to both storage and retrieval. Thus, forgetting, which implies a loss of memory, might involve either an inability to retrieve or an actual change in, or loss of, the physiological effects of experience. Or perhaps it can involve both.

Early Memory Research

It can be said that a person remembers if behavior or responses reflect previous learning, whether or not that person remembers the learning consciously. If Ralph stays away from snakes because he had a frightening experience with one when he was three, it's accurate to say that this early snake experience changed his behavior—that is, that he learned *and remembers* something about snakes because of that experience. That he no longer consciously recalls anything about the experience does not contradict that fact. However, most early studies of memory dealt only with conscious retrieval. Most often, they simply looked at people's ability or inability to reproduce items of information that were presented to them.

Studies of this kind can sometimes lead to unclear results if participants have learned related things previously. One way of getting around this problem is to use material that is entirely new for all learners. For example, Ebbinghaus (1885/1964) solved the problem by inventing more than 600 nonsense syllables. For a number of years, he sat faithfully at his desk at periodic intervals, memorizing lists of nonsense syllables and testing his retention of these. The plotted results of these experiments, with Ebbinghaus as the sole subject, provided the first memory curves. As noted earlier (and illustrated in Figure 9.2), these curves show that the bulk of what is forgotten is lost very rapidly. At the same time, what is retained for a longer period (say, 10 days) is less likely to be forgotten even after a much longer passage of time (for example, 40 days).

Subsequent early research on memory continued to make extensive use of nonsense syllables in a variety of experimental situations. Sometimes these syllables were paired with other syllables—or meaningful words were paired with other words—and subjects were required to learn what went with what. This is called *paired-associate learning*. At other times, subjects were asked to learn sequences of stimuli (this is called *serial learning*).

In numerous studies, subjects learned two different sets of material and were then asked to recall one or the other in an attempt to determine whether recall would be interfered with. It often was. When earlier learning interferes

Table 9.1 Testing Retroactive Interference

	Experimental group (A)	**Control group (B)**
Time sequence	1. Learn X	1. Learn X
	2. Learn Y	2. Do unrelated things
	3. Recall X	3. Recall X

Note: Lower scores of group A relative to group B indicate the extent to which learning Y has interfered with the recall of X.

Table 9.2 Testing Proactive Interference

	Experimental group (A)	**Control group (B)**
Time sequence	1. Learn X	1. Do unrelated things
	2. Learn Y	2. Learn Y
	3. Recall Y	3. Recall Y

Note: Lower scores of group A compared with group B indicate the extent to which X has interfered with Y.

with the recollection of subsequently learned material, **proactive interference** is said to have occurred (proactive meaning moving ahead in time). When subsequent learning reduces recall of material that had been learned earlier, **retroactive interference** is said to have taken place (see Tables 9.1 and 9.2). If you half-learn a language such as French and later on try to learn a related language such as Spanish, you might well find yourself recalling French words when searching for newly learned Spanish words. This is an illustration of *proactive* interference. Later, when you have mastered Spanish, you might find it very difficult to remember some of the French words you previously knew. This is an example of *retroactive* interference.

Three-Component Model of Memory

One important contribution of early studies of memory, in addition to their many isolated findings, takes the form of several closely related models of human remembering. The best known of these, sometimes termed the *modal model* (Baddeley, 1997), is that proposed by Atkinson and Shiffrin (1968). It makes an important distinction between **short-term memory** and **long-term memory,** as well as between a third component relating to sensation called **sensory memory** (also called the *sensory register*). The modal model is summarized in Figure 9.3.

Keep in mind that this model, like most psychological models, is a metaphor. As such, it probably says as much about the ways psychologists choose to investigate and talk about memory as it does about memory itself. In brief, there is

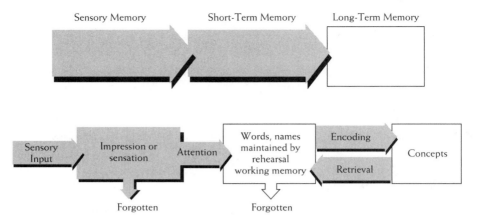

Figure 9.3 The three components of memory in Atkinson and Shiffrin's model. Sensory information first enters sensory memory. From there, it may go into short-term memory (also called working memory), where it is available as a name, a word, an image, for example, as long as it is rehearsed (attended to). Some of the material in short-term memory may then be encoded for long-term storage, where it might take the form of concepts (ideas) and where it might be available for retrieval into short-term memory when needed. It is important to note that these three components of memory do not refer to three different locations in the brain or other parts of the nervous system but, rather, refer to how we study memory.

not a particular "box" or other structure in human brains that corresponds to short-term memory and another that corresponds to long-term memory. These are not physical structures but abstractions.[1]

Sensory Memory

Sensory memory is a term for the immediate, unconscious effects of stimuli. It is illustrated in the *cocktail party experiments*, so called because they investigate situations similar to those of crowded social situations where there are many simultaneous conversations. The cocktail party phenomenon is the ability of individuals to carry on their own conversations while they apparently remain oblivious to other simultaneous conversations. But if someone else in the room

---

[1]Do you see what I mean about metaphors? the Old Woman shouted from the top of the rock face, throwing her arms out wide almost as if she were about to break into a sermon—or about to leap into space and plunge, or glide, down to where I stood. But she had neither of those acts in mind. Do you see, she asked rhetorically, how this model of memory is one more example of how selective humans have been in their attempts to explain what's inside the "black box," and how they have been guided by the metaphor of the day. In the case of memory, for example, for a long time their explanations were shaped by a metaphor that saw the human mind as some sort of filing cabinet that slipped items of information into logically ordered files—many of which were later lost. Another metaphor viewed the human mind as a kind of motion picture camera that makes a continuous record of everything it experiences. And a current metaphor pictures human memory as an information-processing system whose storage is determined by the nature of the processing it does.

... the guilty one is Lefrançois...

The cocktail party phenomenon

mentions a topic of interest once, their attention might switch immediately. This phenomenon indicates that even those sensory impressions to which the individual is not paying attention appear to have at least a momentary effect.

Cherry (1953) was among the first to investigate this cocktail party problem. In one study, he used headphones to feed different messages to each of a subject's ears. Under these conditions, subjects seemed to be able to listen to either ear simply by intending to do so.

In a variation of this study, Broadbent (1952) had subjects repeat everything they heard in one ear, as they heard it—a process called "shadowing." Using this approach, Broadbent discovered that subjects don't remember what goes on in their other ear. When the language was changed from English to German in the unattended ear, the subject remained completely unaware of it. Moray (1959) found that even if the same word were repeated as many as 35 times, the subject was not able to remember having heard it. But if the subject's name was said a single time, that was often enough to cause a shift in attention. Wood and Cowan (1995a, 1995b) replicated this finding later. They also found that subjects who hear their names called in the irrelevant channel appear to monitor that channel for a short time afterward. Also, Moray found that if the investigator interrupted the tape, subjects could recall what had just been said in the unattended ear (although with longer time lapses, the probability of recalling correctly declined dramatically). Apparently, sensory events have some momentary effect even when they're not being attended to. These effects define what is meant by sensory memory.

Sensory memory is also evident in studies such as Sperling's (1963), in which he used a tachistoscope (an instrument that flashes stimuli for fractions of a second) to project on a screen three rows of four letters each. Immediately after the presentation, subjects heard one of three distinct tones signaling which of the three rows they were to try to recall. Under these conditions, most subjects could almost always remember all four letters in the indicated row (accuracy of recall was well over 90%). But if subjects were asked to recall all 12 letters, they remembered only an average of 4.5. And the longer the delay was between the presentation of the letters and the request to recall, the less successful were the subjects.

What this experiment illustrates most clearly is that a limited number of stimuli remain accessible for a very brief period following presentation, even if they are not attended to. This type of sensory memory is very much like an echo—so much so, in fact, that Neisser (1976) called it *echoic* (for auditory stimuli) or *iconic* (for visual stimuli) memory.

Short-Term (or Working) Memory

Another way of looking at sensory memory is to say that it precedes attention—that, in other words, it's something that occurs without the individual being aware of it occurring. When the individual attends to (becomes aware of) a stimulus, it passes into short-term memory (STM).

Sensory memory refers to a phenomenon that lasts milliseconds; short-term memory is a phenomenon that lasts seconds—not hours or even minutes. Specifically, short-term memory refers to the awareness and recall of items that will no longer be available as soon as the individual stops rehearsing them. Short-term memory is what Goldblum (2001) calls *temporary memory*. STM is what makes it possible for secretary Olga to find a number in a telephone directory and dial it without having to look at the second digit after dialing the first, at the third after dialing the second, and so on. That she forgets the number as soon as she has finished dialing—and that she has to look it up again if she has to redial—are also characteristics of STM. Long-term memory (LTM) is what would be involved if Olga decided she might need to use the number again and attempted to "memorize" it; it would also be involved if the symmetry and poetry of the number so moved her that she found herself remembering it the next day.

A Classical Study of STM

Among the most common early techniques for studying short-term memory was one developed by Peterson and Peterson (1959) in which subjects are presented with a single nonsense syllable and then asked to recall it. Immediate recall is typically close to 100% (errors are usually caused by misperception of the original syllable). But greater delay between the presentation of the word and its recall results in lower recall, the extent of which depends on the subject's intervening activities. Subjects who are not required to do anything and who know they will be asked to recall the syllable usually rehearse it to make sure they can remember it. But if subjects are asked to engage in some unrelated activity beginning immediately after presentation of the nonsense syllable (such as counting backward in time to a metronome), retention is interfered with. For example, in

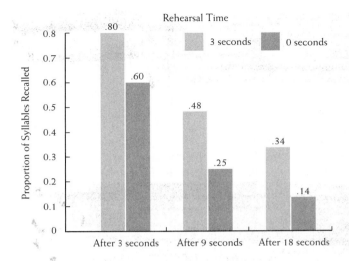

Rehearsal Time

Figure 9.4
Proportion of nonsense syllables recalled correctly in the Peterson and Peterson study as a function of rehearsal and time lapse. Subjects in the zero-time-for-rehearsal group were asked to start counting backward from a three-digit number immediately after they heard the nonsense syllable. Those in the other group experienced a 3-second delay before they were given the digit from which they were to count backward. From "Short-term Retention of Individual Verbal Items," by L. R. Peterson and M. J. Peterson, 1959. In *Journal of Experimental Psychology*, *58*, p. 197.

the Peterson and Peterson (1959) study, subjects recalled the syllables correctly 80% of the time when given 3 seconds to rehearse them, but only 60% of the time when given no opportunity to rehearse them. Eighteen seconds after the stimulus had been presented, subjects still remembered correctly 33% of the time if they had been given an opportunity to rehearse for 3 seconds; but they were correct only 14% of the time when given no opportunity to rehearse (see Figure 9.4).

Limited Capacity

Short-term memory refers to the ongoing availability of a small number of items—an availability that begins to deteriorate within seconds and is usually completely gone within 20 seconds in the absence of rehearsal. Short-term memory is what makes it possible for readers to "keep in mind" the words that they are currently reading (or writing) long enough to make sense of the whole. Put another way, short-term memory is what is conscious at any given time. As Baddeley (2002) explains, it is a sort of "scratch pad" for thinking. For this reason, short-term memory is often called *working memory*.

Following his investigations of short-term memory, Miller (1956) concluded that the average adult's short-term memory capacity is seven, plus or minus two items. According to Miller, it is as though there are about seven slots in STM—plus or minus two. When these are filled, there is no room for more until one or more of the slots are again emptied, which, given the nature of STM, happens within seconds.

Chunking

The limited capacity of short-term memory is not a great problem for most people, says Miller (1956), because the items that fill each of these slots don't have to be unitary (a digit or a letter, for example). Instead, they might be composed of several other items—a **chunking** of items, so to speak. Thus, the short-term memory slots might be filled with seven letters, or with seven words. The seven words represent chunks of information that are far more economical (and probably more meaningful) than seven unrelated letters. Miller explains *chunking* by making an analogy to a change purse that can only hold seven pieces of money (here is the "change purse" memory metaphor). If there are seven pennies in the purse, it will be full; however, it could have held seven quarters or seven dollars (or seven $1,000 bills).

Baddeley's Model of Working Memory

Just how does working memory work? (Recall that *working memory* is simply another label for *short-term memory*.) Baddeley and Hitch (1974) propose an intriguing, though somewhat complicated model. First, they explain, there must be some sort of controlling process or system overseeing the entire process. They label this system the **central executive system.** Second, what we know about the workings of short-term memory suggests that there must also be at least two other systems, referred to as *slave systems* because of their relationship to the central executive system. The two slave systems are the **phonological loop** and the **visual-spatial sketch pad** (see Figure 9.5).

The most important functions of the central executive system are (1) to regulate the flow of information from sensory storage (that is, to bring information into conscious attention), (2) to process information for longer-term storage, and (3) to retrieve information from long-term storage (Baddeley, 1997).

The main functions of the slave systems are to maintain information so that it remains available to working memory. Thus, the phonological loop maintains verbal information, such as words or numbers, and is important in learning such things as new words. Similarly, the visual-spatial sketch pad is concerned with the processing of material that is primarily visual or spatial (Gathercole & Baddeley, 1993).

What this model suggests is that there are two different and independent types of processing available in working memory. Experimental evidence that this might be so comes from studies using a dual task paradigm devised by Baddeley and his associates. For example, subjects might be asked to learn a list of words that are being presented visually (an executive control system task) while retaining a sequence of six or fewer numbers (a slave system task). One might expect that there would be tremendous interference between these tasks. But there is typically only minor interference—strong evidence, suggests Baddeley (1997), that the executive control system and the slave system represent different processes.

Additional evidence that the slave systems represent distinct processes comes from studies that look at brain activity while subjects are engaged in memory tasks. These studies indicate that distinctly different regions of the brain are involved in the different aspects of working memory (for example, Henson, 2001).

Referring back to the modal model of memory depicted in Figure 9.3, Baddeley's model represents what might be involved in sensory as well as in working memory. What the Baddeley model says, in effect, is that the slave systems maintain (as a sort of loop, if you will) the effects of sensory stimulation so the central executive might have access to them. Note, too, that in this model, one

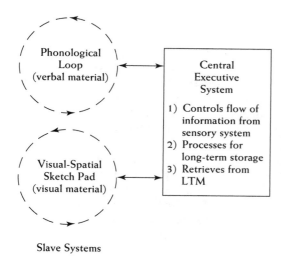

Figure 9.5
A representation of Baddeley and Hitch's model of working memory. The central executive system controls the flow of information from sensory storage, processes it where appropriate, and retrieves from long-term storage. The slave systems maintain sensory material so it is momentarily available to the central executive system.

important function of the central processor is to transfer material into long-term storage as well as to retrieve from storage. These topics are discussed in the upcoming section on long-term memory.

Levels of Processing

There are several different theories to explain why short-term memory is limited to only a few items, and why forgetting occurs. **Decay theory** holds that memory traces vanish quickly with the passage of time (in the absence of continued rehearsal). **Displacement theory**—essentially the Miller (1956) analogy—suggests that there are a limited number of slots to be filled in short-term memory and that incoming information displaces old information. **Interference theory,** which is highly similar to displacement theory, advances the notion that previous learning (rather than subsequent information) might somehow interfere with short-term memory.

Craik and Lockhart (1972) suggest that loss from short-term memory is simply a matter of **levels of processing.** The main difference between short- and long-term memory, they claim, involves how input is processed. For example, a simple stimulus such as a word might be processed relative to its physical appearance—a relatively low level of processing referred to as orthographic. Alternatively, a word might be processed by its sound (phonological processing—a somewhat deeper level of processing). Or it might be processed for its meaning (semantic processing—the deepest level of processing). Craik (1977) devised experiments in which subjects were given word analysis tasks that required them to process words at different levels, but they didn't know they would be required to remember the words later. For example, subjects might be asked whether or not a word was in capital letters (shallowest processing: orthographic); whether it rhymed with another word (intermediate processing: phonological); or whether it meant the same thing as another word (deepest level of processing: semantic).

Not surprisingly, the proportion of words later recognized by participants increased with depth of processing.

In the sensory register, notes Craik, no processing occurs. At the STM level, a "shallow" level of processing occurs, consisting mainly of the recognition of stimuli through perceptual analysis. With deeper processing (involving activities such as analysis, organization, and recognition of meaning), material is transferred to long-term memory and hence is not lost immediately. Forgetting in short-term memory thus is presumed to result from inadequate processing (Cermak & Craik, 1979).

Nairne's (2002) review of studies that have looked at forgetting in STM suggests that Craik's levels-of-processing explanation may be valid and useful. Neither decay nor lack of rehearsal is a very good explanation for most of the forgetting that occurs in STM, says Nairne. Rather, forgetting is most often tied to faulty retrieval cues, or the absence of cues. What happens when an item of information is rehearsed or processed is that the learner establishes certain cues that can then be used for subsequent recall. When these cues permit recall that last more than a handful of seconds, the material is said to have been encoded for storage into long-term memory. It is probably largely because of this that, as Groeger (1997) notes, most researchers have not been very concerned with forgetting in short-term memory. After all, the function of short-term memory is simply to retain information for only as long as it's useful and then to discard it. If people didn't function this way, it's likely that their long-term memories would be cluttered with all sorts of useless information, and retrieving from LTM might be far more difficult than it is now.

Loss of material from short-term memory stores becomes a significant problem in those cases when disease, injury, or aging shorten STM to the point that ongoing functioning suffers. That, essentially, is what happens when people forget what they were going to say after they've started to say it. Or what they were going to write next . . .

Long-Term Memory

Before the 1950s, most research on memory dealt not with the transitory and unstable recollections of STM but with the more stable and, by definition, longer lasting remembrances of long-term memory. Psychologists did not begin to recognize the usefulness of distinguishing between LTM and STM until the mid-1950s.

Two other changes in memory research have been (a) a shift from the use of nonsense syllables and paired associates to the use of meaningful material, and (b) a change in emphasis from measuring memory span and the effects of interference to examining models for long-term storage and retrieval.

All that a person can remember that has not just now occurred makes up long-term memory. Thus, all that is retained of educational experiences, a complete working knowledge of language, and all stable information about the world are in long-term memory. Among the characteristics of long-term memory, four are especially important:

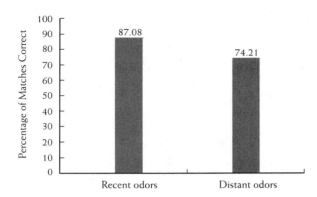

Figure 9.6
Accuracy of memory for recent and distant odors. In this study, 30 17- to 22-year-old students correctly matched odors with names at least two out of three times. Based on "Very Long-Term Memory for Odors: Retention of Odor-Name Associations," by W. P. Goldman and J. G. Seamon, 1992. *American Journal of Psychology, 105*, pp. 549–563 (Table 1, p. 553). © 1992 by the Board of Trustees of the University of Illinois. Reprinted by permission of University of Illinois Press.

1. Long-Term Memory Is Highly Stable

Much of what you remember today and tomorrow, you will also remember next week, and perhaps even next year. The faces and other perceptual patterns you recognize today, you will also recognize tomorrow. And the general information you have retained to date from your schooling will also in all likelihood be retained next month (Jenkins, Burton, & Ellis, 2002; Magnussen, Greenlee, Aslaksen, & Kildebo, 2003). In fact, some recollections, such as those having to do with smells, are astonishingly resistant to the passage of time. Olfaction, notes Annett (1996), has only recently been systematically and extensively investigated. Before the mid-1970s, current cognitive models of memory dealt mainly with visual and verbal information. Since then, however, the amount of research on olfactory memory has increased dramatically. This research reveals that memory for odors is unique, that it is independent from memory for verbal or visual information, and that it is resistant to interference. In an intriguing study, for example, Goldman and Seamon (1992) bottled 14 odors, half of them associated with childhood (for example, crayon shavings, Play-Doh, finger paints, bubble soap) and the other half partially or entirely associated with adulthood (chocolate, popcorn, soap shavings, cigarette tobacco). Adults correctly identified about 90% of recent odors and more than three-quarters of sometimes very distant odors (see Figure 9.6). "Significant memory for odor-name associations remains even over very long recall intervals," Goldman and Seamon conclude, "much longer than any tested to date" (1992, p. 562).

2. Long-Term Memory Is Generative

"Memory," note Schacter, Norman, and Koutstaal, "is not a literal reproduction of the past but instead depends on constructive processes that are sometimes prone to errors, distortions, and illusions" (1998, p. 290). Preconceived notions and beliefs about what goes with what, sometimes termed *schemata* or *scripts*, profoundly influence memories. These schemata may lead people to remember things that have never happened—in other words, to *generate* rather than *reproduce*. For example, Johnson, Bransford, and Solomon showed subjects this passage (1973, p. 203):

> John was trying to fix the birdhouse. He was pounding the nail when his father came out to watch him and to help him do the work.

Later, subjects were shown the previous two sentences along with several others, one of which was the following:

> John was using the hammer to fix the birdhouse when his father came out to watch and to help him do the work.

Most subjects were more convinced that they had seen this sentence rather than either of the sentences they had actually seen. Why? Because, say Johnson and associates, although the word hammer was not mentioned in either of the first two sentences, subjects recalled the idea of the sentences clearly, and, based on their knowledge that hammers are what is used to pound nails, they *generated* the word into their recollections.

That memory tends to be highly generative (or constructive) has especially important implications in judicial systems that tend to rely heavily on human testimony. Investigations by Loftus, Feldman, and Dashiell (1995) show, for example, that under a variety of circumstances, witnesses can be expected to remember incorrectly or to remember events that have not occurred.

3. Understanding Influences Long-Term Memory

What people remember is often a meaning—a central idea. We don't recall the detail so much as the *gist*, explain Koriat, Goldsmith, and Pansky (2000). For example, when Len hears a story and then repeats it, typically what he remembers of it is its general "drift"—its setting and punch line. When he repeats the story, he doesn't remember each of the sentences, pauses, and gestures of the original storyteller. Instead he generates his own, based on his understanding of the story.

The relationship between understanding and long-term memory is illustrated in a Piaget and Inhelder (1956) study in which young children are asked to draw lines representing the level of water in tilted jars. Although all children have seen fluids in tilted glasses or bottles, that they don't actually remember what this looks like is clear from their reproductions (shown in Figure 9.7). Only after children understand that water remains horizontal do they remember correctly.

4. Some Things Are More Easily Remembered

Meaningful material, as we just saw, is remembered far more easily and for longer periods than is material that is less meaningful. Memory for odors also appears to be very persistent. And, as Wynn and Logie (1998) found when they questioned 63 adults about actual events in their lives, personal recollections of real-life, day-to-day events seems to be remarkably accurate and to change relatively little over time.

Particularly striking, important, or emotional events are often remembered more clearly and for longer periods than are more mundane happenings. Such events sometimes give rise to what are called **flashbulb memories.** Flashbulb memories are extremely vivid recollections associated with first becoming aware of some especially emotional information. Such memories, explains Cohen (1996), typically include extraordinarily clear recall of the immediate circumstances in which you first heard the news, of what you were doing, how you

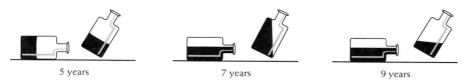

Figure 9.7 Children's drawings of water lines. Note how the children don't draw what they have seen and remember. They draw the water line correctly only when they understand the principle that water tends to remain level.

found out, what you felt, what happened next, and so on. Flashbulb memories are sometimes mass phenomena—as occurred with the assassination of President Kennedy in the United States or the death of Princess Diana in Europe—or they might be more personal, as when you find out you have won an enormous lottery.

Short-Term and Long-Term Memory Compared

Short-term memory is an active memory, says Wickelgren: It includes that which is "currently being thought of" (1981, p. 46). Hence, short-term memory is equivalent to span of attention, and the most important distinction between STM and LTM is not that one lasts for a long time and the other only for seconds, but rather that one is immediately conscious and the other is not.

Other differences between STM and LTM (summarized in Table 9.3) include the fact that as an active, ongoing process, STM is easily disrupted by external or internal events. In contrast, LTM is far more passive and far more resistant to disruption. Also, as we have seen, STM is far more limited in capacity, being essentially synonymous with active attention or immediate consciousness.

Finally, retrieval from STM is immediate and automatic—a fact that is hardly surprising, because what is being retrieved is either immediately conscious or not available. Retrieval from LTM may be far more hesitant, may require a search, and may result in a distortion of what was originally learned.

Table 9.3 *Three Levels of Memory*

	Sensory	**Short-Term**	**Long-Term**
Alternate Labels	Echoic or iconic	Primary or working	Secondary
Duration	Less than 1 second	Temporary, less than 20 seconds	Permanent, indefinite
Stability	Fleeting	Easily disrupted	Not easily disrupted
Capacity	Limited	Limited (7 ± 2 items)	Unlimited
General Characteristics	Momentary, unconscious impression; a passing sensation or association	What we are paying attention to; immediate consciousness; active; maintained by rehearsal	All our knowledge; passive; the result of encoding, storage, and retrieval of information

From *Psychology for Teaching*, 10th edition, by G. R. Lefrançois, p. 175. Copyright © 2000 by Wadsworth, Inc. Reprinted by permission of Wadsworth Publishing Company, Belmont, CA.

Types of Long-Term Memory

One of the most important insights to emerge from memory research is the gradual realization that long-term memory is not just one thing—it consists of different components. Different researchers and theorists have proposed various labels as metaphors for these components. Among the most useful and widely investigated are what are labeled *implicit* and *explicit* memory (Davis, 2001).

Explicit (Declarative) and Implicit (Nondeclarative) Memory

Knowledge, as we saw earlier, can be either explicit or implicit. When the centipede was asked how it managed to walk so elegantly with its many legs, how it always knew which to move next, it was stunned to realize that it had never really thought about the problem. So it tried hard to think about how it walked, and in the end, the poor thing became hopelessly confused and wrapped itself up in a little knot just trying, consciously, to walk as it always had.

Human memories relating to how to walk, how to keep upright on a bicycle, how to hit a home run, or how to do a triple lutz in ice skating are **implicit memories**—also termed **nondeclarative memories** because they cannot readily be recalled and put into words (in other words, they cannot be declared). The sorts of memories that led Watson's subject, Little Albert, to whimper when he saw a rat are also implicit.

In contrast, memories relating to people's names and addresses, their telephone numbers, and the name of their dog are **explicit memories**—also termed **declarative** because they can be put into words (they can be declared). Other examples are memories relating to their last birthday or to what they did last Christmas.

"The main distinction," claim Squire, Knowlton, and Musen, "is between conscious memory for facts and events and various forms of nonconscious memory" (1993, p. 457). One way to remember the difference between explicit and implicit memories, as Rovee-Collier, Hayne, and Colombo (2001) point out, relates to the difference between *knowing* and *remembering*. Explicit memories can be remembered; that is, they can be brought to mind (made explicit). In contrast, implicit memories, although they involve things that one knows (such as riding a bicycle, for example), cannot be *remembered* and verbalized—that is, cannot be made explicit.

Physiological Evidence

The distinction between implicit and explicit memories is especially well illustrated in amnesiacs, some of whom have been extensively studied by psychologists. Many of these amnesiacs have lost huge chunks of declarative (explicit) memory, often forgetting who they are, where they went to school, what they did for a living, who their spouse, children, parents, and friends are, and so on. Yet, they retain many implicit memories relating to motor skills and other items.

Not surprisingly, as Keane and associates (1997) have shown, in simple memory experiments amnesiacs often do quite well on tasks of implicit memory while manifesting impaired recall for explicit learning. Similarly, patients with Alzheimer's disease (which is associated with severe memory loss) also do relatively well on tests of implicit memory despite severe impairment for explicit memory tasks (Monti, Gabrieli, Wilson, Beckett, Grinnell, et al., 1997). Interestingly, amnesiacs can be classically conditioned, Hintzman (1990) reports. This finding is evidence of implicit or nondeclarative memory. In such cases, however, they may retain absolutely no memory of the conditioning itself, thus providing evidence of a declarative memory weakness.

As we see later in this chapter, there is also clear evidence from studies of brain activity in normal subjects, as well as from studies of people with brain injuries, that different parts of the brain are involved in implicit and explicit memory (for example, Broadbent, Clark, Zola, & Squire, 2002).

Two Kinds of Declarative Memory

Studies of amnesiacs also provide evidence of an important distinction between two kinds of declarative memory. There is, for example, the case of K. C., a man who, when he was 30, missed a curve with his motorcycle and suffered severe brain damage, becoming permanently amnesiac (Tulving, Schacter, McLachlan, & Moscovitch, 1988). K. C. is incapable of bringing to conscious memory anything that he has ever done, seen, or felt in the past. He cannot remember himself ever experiencing or doing anything. "K. C.," writes Tulving, "knows that his family owns a summer cottage, knows where it is located, and can point out the location on a map of Ontario, and he knows that he has spent summers and weekends there. But he does not remember a single occasion when he was at the cottage or a single event that happened there" (1989, p. 363). K. C. remembers all sorts of things that are political, geographical, and musical. In fact, he remembers well enough that his measured intelligence is quite normal, and those talking with him might not notice anything wrong. But he remembers nothing of the personal episodes of his life.

Semantic and Episodic Memory

There are at least two distinct types of declarative long-term memory, claims Tulving (1989, 2002). On the one hand, there is stable knowledge about the world, such as abstract knowledge, knowledge that is necessary for understanding and using language, knowledge of principles, laws, and facts, and knowledge of strategies and heuristics. These illustrate **semantic memory**. The evidence shows that K. C. has retained his semantic memory.

On the other hand, there is a body of knowledge consisting of personal memories of events that have happened to the individual. These are not abstract memories (as are rules and principles, for example), but specific memories tied to a time and place. These are autobiographical memories; they always involve the person at a certain time and place. These memories, which K. C.'s amnesia obliterated, are labeled **episodic memory**.

Tulving argues that these two types of memories are sufficiently distinct that it is useful to consider them separately. He suggests that there might be some important differences in the way material is stored in each, as well as in how it is remembered and forgotten. For example, episodic memory seems to be far more susceptible to distortion and forgetting than is semantic memory: Humans have considerably more difficulty remembering what they ate for breakfast 3 days ago than in remembering a poem or a name they learned in elementary school.

Episodic memory, according to Tulving (1989), depends on semantic memory. When Georgina remembers the experience of eating breakfast this morning, she might also remember a variety of abstract things about eating, about breakfasts, or about kitchens or restaurants. In contrast, semantic memory seems to be able to operate independently from, or even in the absence of, episodic memory. Thus, K. C. can know how to play chess—and know that he knows how to play chess—without any memory of ever playing a single game of chess. As Tulving puts it, "It is possible for an individual to know facts without remembering learning them, but not possible to remember without knowing what it is that is being remembered" (1989, p. 365).

Episodic memory, explains Tulving (2002), is closely tied to a subjective sense of time.[2] When people recall specific episodes in their lives, they are also recalling a specific time and place. K. C., whose episodic memory had disappeared with his accident, had also lost all sense of personal time. Although he understood the concept of time and could discuss it as well as any normal person, he had no sense of subjective time. In Tulving's words, "The impairment does not encompass only the past; it also extends to the future. Thus when asked, he [K. C.] cannot tell the questioner what he is going to do later on that day, or the day after, or at any time in the rest of his life. He cannot imagine his future any more than he can remember his past" (2000, p. 14).

Distinctions among the various kinds of long-term memory are shown in Figure 9.8.

Models of Declarative Long-Term Memory

An early metaphor for long-term memory portrays the mind as a sort of motion picture camera (complete with audio, video, smell, touch, taste, and so on; Koffka, 1935). This model views memory as a complete, sequential record of experiences from which people retrieve the isolated bits of information that

---

[2]Your brighter students might want to digress a little here, the Old Woman said, interrupting her reading and motioning that I should shut off the recorder. They might want to take a little time to think about time. Maybe they should read Stephen Hawking's *A Brief History of Time* (1996). Or maybe that would be too difficult. Better, perhaps, that they should reflect on the possibility, suggested by Tulving (2002), that no nonhuman animal is able to ever think about subjective time. Because episodic remembering takes the form of "mental travel through subjective time," it is accompanied by a special kind of self-awareness (labeled *autonoetic*) that animals aren't supposed to have. Harpaz, in reference to this suggestion, writes, "That is dead stupid. Until an animal has enough intelligence to have self-awareness, it cannot have episodic memory by definition. Even if it does, it has to be intelligent enough to discuss it with us for us to know it" (2003).

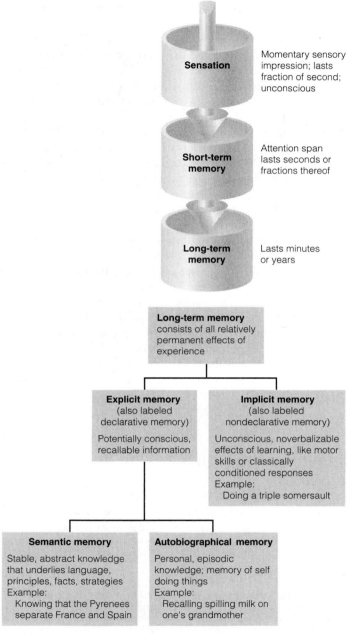

Figure 9.8 A model of memory. Researchers describe different aspects of memory distinguishable by the kind of material involved, how it is learned, and how it is recalled. Studies of memory failure in amnesiacs, as well as imaging studies of the brain, indicate that different parts of the brain are involved in each type of memory.

remain accessible after the passage of time. This is a nonassociationistic model of memory.

Almost without exception, contemporary models of LTM are associationistic. This means they are premised on the fundamental notion that all items of information in memory are associated in various ways. Thus, when you "search" your memory for some item of information, you don't haphazardly produce a long sequence of unrelated responses; instead, you narrow in on the missing item through a network of related information.[3]

Associationistic models of long-term memory are essentially cognitive models. Not surprisingly, they often use a variety of abstract concepts, such as Bruner's *categories* and *coding systems*, Piaget's *schemata*, Hebb's *cell assemblies* or *phase sequences*, or other abstractions such as *nodes* (see, for example, Wickelgren, 1981). But *node, category, schema, cell assembly,* and related terms are simply metaphors, not actual structures. They are metaphors for what can be represented in the "mind." Their single identifying attribute is that they represent.

A node model of mental representation, for example, is simply a model that says people represent knowledge through representations (called nodes, although they could as easily have been called anything else) that are related in countless little-understood ways. Figure 9.9 presents one version of how a small part of a node model might be depicted.

The usefulness of a node model for human memory is that it emphasizes memory's associationistic features. Note, too, that models of LTM are basically information-processing models. As such, they have much to say about the processes involved in memory (such as attending, rehearsing, and organizing). Not surprisingly, most cognitive theorists no longer study learning and memory as separate subjects.

Physiology of Memory

Learning and remembering result in some sort of change in the brain, as we saw in Chapter 5. Understanding the precise nature and location of this change should be very useful for understanding what learning and memory are all about.

---

[3]Abruptly, the Old Woman stopped reading once more. She was still on top of the rock face, but she no longer stood as she had earlier, like a preacher trumpeting out psychology's messages of memory. Instead, she sat on the edge of the cliff, legs dangling into space, apparently unconcerned about the danger of falling. She said did I need a break, but I wasn't doing anything, just half listening as the recorder whirred in the early morning sunshine, so I shook my head no, and the Old Woman said maybe here I should point out, as an aside for all you sharp-minded readers, that the concept of associations is fundamental to most of the earlier, behavioristic theories described in the first chapters of this report. She explained that many of these theories, for example, deal with how associations between stimuli and responses are affected by repetition or reward. She said associations are also very important in the area of cognitive psychology. But cognitive theorists are concerned more with associations between ideas (concepts) and how they are affected by meaning. Then she continued to read from her notes.

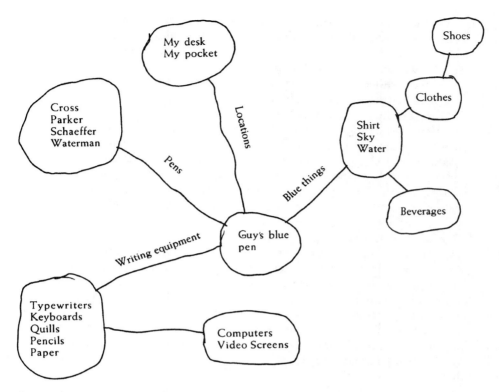

Figure 9.9 A model of a metaphor. Node theory suggests that we remember abstractions (meanings, associations, gists, rather than specifics). Thus, "Guy's blue pen" is depicted as a "node" embedded in a complex web of abstractions (for example, "blue things"), each of which relates to many other nodes that are not shown here.

The Engram

It makes sense, thought the first memory researchers, that a specific and permanent trace should be left in the brain for every experience that is remembered. The trick is to find this trace, sometimes labeled an **engram.** Perhaps, as Wolfgram and Goldstein (1987) argue, the physical basis of memory is less a trace (or an engram) than a code—the secrets of which might reveal the true nature of remembering. The search for this code, or trace, includes some fascinating studies.

Lashley's Rats

Karl Lashley (1924) was convinced that experiences leave specific *engrams* in the brain, and he was determined to find them. As we saw in Chapter 5, Lashley trained rats to run through a maze and, once a rat knew the maze well, he systematically lobbed off tiny chunks of its brain, keeping a careful record of exactly what it was he had removed. Then he would release the rat back into the maze. He knew that he would eventually cut out just exactly the right piece, and the rat would have no idea how to get through the maze.

But it didn't work that way. It seemed that no matter what part of the brain Lashley excised, as long as he didn't kill the rats or incapacitate them physically, they continued to run through the maze (although they did so more and more slowly). He was eventually forced to conclude that memories are scattered throughout the brain rather than located in just one place.

After Lashley died, one of his close associates, R. Thompson, continued to look for the engram. He, too, concluded that memories might have a variety of locations throughout the brain (Thorne, 1995). Later research revealed that these investigators might have been far closer to the truth than many of their contemporaries suspected. For example, Poldrack and Packard (2003) summarize research that indicates that multiple memory systems are often simultaneously active during learning. They suggest that in some cases, there is *competition* among these systems so that injury to one actually improves overall learning.

Penfield's Patients

Wilder Penfield (1969), a brain surgeon, thought he had begun to discover and map human memories when he stimulated the brains of some of his fully conscious patients as they were undergoing brain surgery. Tiny amounts of stimulation applied with minute electrodes seemed to stimulate very vivid and detailed recollections of past experiences. More careful examination, however, later revealed that these memories were not very reliable: One subject who described in detail a visit to a lumberyard had never been there. It's likely, claims Squire (1987), that Penfield's subjects were fantasizing, constructing memories, or perhaps even hallucinating.

Rat Brain and Planaria Studies

A series of studies of rat brains (Krech, Rosenzweig, & Bennett, 1960, 1962, 1966) seemed to show that learning causes specific, measurable chemical changes in the brains of rats. But the changes that were found turned out to be highly global and not very informative. In addition, these studies have seldom been replicated and are generally considered invalid (Johnson, 1992).

Similarly, McConnell (1962, 1976) reports studies that seemed to show that conditioning planaria (flatworms) to curl up in response to a light causes permanent chemical changes that can then be transmitted to other planaria simply by mincing the trained worms and feeding them to untrained worms. However, other researchers were unable to duplicate these results, and McConnell was later accused of "overselling" his planaria research, and of being a "popularizer" (see, for example, McKeachie, 1997; Rilling, 1996).[4]

---

[4]So do you know anything about the Heisenberg uncertainty principle?, the Old Woman shouted down at me as if out of the blue. But before I could even think to answer, she had already begun to explain how the Heisenberg uncertainty principle is drawn from quantum mechanics and how it implies that for no state of any system can all dynamic variables be simultaneously and exactly known. Then, for a long time, she said nothing else, just sat up there watching the golden eagle mounted on a wide-swirling mass of rising air, and I thought I'd missed the point, and then she started talking again, explaining how studies such as the planaria research are good examples of the urgent need for replication in human sciences. She said there are simply too many variables human scientists have still not learned to control in their experiments. She said scientists still haven't learned how to counter

Brain Imaging, ERPs, and ERFs

Although the precise physiology of memory remains undiscovered, early studies of amnesiacs and of those suffering from brain injuries suggested that different brain systems are involved in different types of memory. More recent studies have been greatly aided by the use of new imaging techniques that allow researchers to study neurological functioning in normal patients rather than only in those suffering from brain injuries or amnesia. As we saw in Chapter 5, *EEG (electroencephalogram) recordings* detect neurological activity by monitoring and measuring actual electrical discharges that accompany neural activity in the brain. *Positron emission tomography (PET) scans* detect changes in blood flow associated with neural activity by monitoring the distribution of radioactive particles injected in the bloodstream. And *functional magnetic resonance imaging (fMRI)* is sensitive to extremely subtle changes in magnetic fields that reflect blood oxygen level.

Event-Related Potentials and Fields

When EEG recordings are taken while a person (or an animal) is exposed to a specific stimulus, it's possible to detect electrical activity in the brain that is directly related to that stimulus. That activity is called an **event-related potential (ERP).** Related to ERPs are **event-related fields (ERFs),** which are measures of changes in the magnetic field that result from the flow of electrical currents among nerve cells. These changes can be detected by means of a **magnetoencephalogram (MEG),** which involves a recording of the magnetic field at the scalp, even though that field is less than one billionth as strong as the earth's magnetic field (Roth, Ford, Pfefferbaum, & Elbert, 1995).

ERPs and ERFs are now among the most often studied variables in investigations of memory and learning, as well as in studies of learning disabilities and mental disorders. Many of these studies, for example, use auditory stimuli such as words or tones. These studies typically show that ERPs related to verbal material occur in *both* hemispheres but tend to be stronger and more localized in the left temporal lobe (for example, Gottselig et al., 2004).

Studies of ERPs and ERFs have repeatedly found abnormalities in various mental disorders such as schizophrenia (for example, Guillem et al., 2003). The most common finding is that of *reduced* ERP amplitude among schizophrenics. Reduced ERP amplitude has also been associated with poorer personality development, as well as with learning disabilities (Greenham, Stelmack, & van der Vlugt, 2003).

Research using some of this new technology indicates that injury to certain parts of the brain (specifically parts of the temporal lobe) is associated with losses in declarative LTM (Mayes, 2002). In contrast, nondeclarative memory seems to be associated with other brain structures such as the neocortex, amygdala, and cerebellum. Similarly, following his studies of K. C., Tulving (1989) concludes

---

all the confounding effects of their own investigatory procedures, although they now recognize that these effects do exist. And that, she said, that phenomenon, that's the Heisenberg uncertainty principle, which, in a nutshell, means that investigators almost always have a considerable but not always considered effect on their own investigations. I wanted to protest, tell her it wasn't all that clear, ask her to explain again, but she turned once more to her notes.

that episodic memory depends on intact frontal lobes of the brain, but semantic declarative memory does not. And the emotional aspects of memory seem to be closely related to the amygdala (Rolls, 2000). Note, however, that the bulk of the evidence indicates that human learning—and consequently memory—is seldom associated with a single site in the brain. Even learning as simple as the classical conditioning of the eye-blink reflex involves activity and change in different brain structures (Kress & Daum, 2003).

Many details of the physiology and neuroanatomy of learning remain unknown, say Broadbent and associates (2002). But the new imaging techniques that permit the study of normal brains have already contributed a great deal to the understanding of both normal and abnormal memories. It is likely that as more is learned, metaphors will become more appropriate. In time, psychology might even move from the metaphor to a literal description.

A Connectionist View

The current cognitive metaphor for memory is less concerned with the gross physiology of brain structures than with neuroanatomy and the organization of neurons. This view, as shown in Chapter 8, sees learning and memory as involving changes at the level of the neuron. These changes are reflected in arrangements of associations among neurons (in neural networks, in other words). The view is in many ways highly reminiscent of Donald Hebb's notion of facilitation of conduction among neurons following repeated firing. As we saw, there is now evidence of a biochemical basis for Hebb's theory—evidence that chemical changes in neural receptors occur and facilitate subsequent neural transmission. But psychologists still don't know exactly what happens when people learn and remember. Do they know more about forgetting?

Forgetting

To forget, as the term is ordinarily used, is to be unable to bring into immediate consciousness. Clearly, forgetting does not prove—or even imply—complete loss from memory. There are many things people learn implicitly (like how to skip a stone) whose underlying memories they can't easily translate into symbols or examine consciously. Also, there is a possibility that when someone can't recall something, it has not been lost but simply cannot be retrieved. Perhaps, like a stubborn name lurking on the tip of the tongue, it will be retrievable later—and perhaps not.

Many answers have been proposed for why people are unable to remember.

Brain Injury

Brain injuries impair memory presumably because they affect normal brain functioning. **Amnesia,** a total or partial impairment of memory, is one possible outcome of brain injury, although it can also result from other causes, including disease or emotional disorder or trauma.

Because different parts of the brain are more involved than others in certain kinds of memory, brain injury might result in memory impairments involving only episodic memory—as it did in the case of K. C. In this case, although the patient is unable to remember personal experiences, more general information is retained. In other cases, all past information may be lost, including knowledge of personal identity.

One type of amnesia, reports Brown (2002), involves a complete lack of memory for all experiences before amnesia. Far more common, however, is a form of partial amnesia in which the memory loss is most likely to involve the most recent rather than the most distant recollections. Brown suggests that this is evidence that long-term memories become more resistant to forgetting with the passage of time.

Fading Theory

Brain injury is an uncommon cause of forgetting; there are other far more common causes. For example, one possibility is that people forget some things simply as a function of the passage of time—that whatever traces or changes learning leaves behind become less distinct as time passes. Evidence for this **fading theory** rests on the observation that people often remember recent events more clearly than very distant ones. Clara might at this moment be able to remember most of the items of clothing hanging in her closet, but she would not fare so well at describing what she had in her closet 6 years ago (unless she was in prison then). But if she has periodically reviewed mentally what was in her closet at that time, she will probably do much better. Items that are occasionally remembered are far more resistant to the presumed ravages of time than are items that have never been recalled. Every recollection is a sort of rehearsal and an opportunity for relearning (Altmann & Gray, 2002).

Huang (1997) reports a single-subject investigation of memory loss with the passage of time, involving a 55-year-old professor who attempted to recognize the names of students in classes he had taught as much as $26^1/_2$ years, and as little as 6 months, previously. Not surprisingly, there was a close relationship between time and accuracy of recognition, reflecting rapid early forgetting followed by slower forgetting.

It's worth noting that many psychologists don't consider fading, or decay, theory very useful or accurate. These psychologists point out that time, by itself, does not cause forgetting any more than it causes the erosion of mountains, the melting of glaciers, or the rusting of metal. Other things that occur (during the passage of time, of course) cause these changes. These other things, ERP and ERF research suggest, might well have to do with less effective functioning of the brain. In particular, suggests Friedman (2003), the frontal lobes seem to be involved in age-related changes in the ability to learn and remember.

Distortion Theory

Evidence reviewed earlier shows that much of what is retrieved from long-term memory is distorted. **Distortion theory** recognizes that when people search their memories, what they remember are main ideas and abstractions, the gist of the story but not the details. Later, they generate the details, often distorting the original. Recall that in the Johnson, Bransford, and Solomon (1973) study, subjects were convinced they had seen a never-before presented sentence simply because it made sense.

Eyewitnesses, Loftus (1979) notes, are notably unreliable and easily misled. In one study, she had subjects view a film in which a sports car was involved in an accident. Afterward, subjects were asked the sorts of questions an accident witness might be asked. Some were asked, "How fast was the sports car going when it passed the barn while traveling along the country road?" Others were simply asked, "How fast was the sports car going while traveling on the country road?" There was no barn along the road. Yet, when subjects were later asked if they had seen a barn in the film, about one fifth of the group who had been asked the first question swore they had; fewer than 3% of the second group thought they had seen a barn.

Repression Theory

One theory of forgetting is based on Freud's notion that individuals sometimes repress (that is, unconsciously forget) experiences that are anxiety provoking or traumatic. This might be the case, for example, when an adult experiences difficulty remembering childhood traumas such as sex abuse. However, most highly traumatic (highly negative) experiences are not forgotten. In fact, a study conducted by Porter and Birt (2001) found that 306 adult participants were able to recall traumatic experiences with about the same accuracy and detail as they could highly positive experiences.

Because unconscious repression applies only to rare, highly emotional, and highly negative experiences, **repression theory** is of limited value as a general explanation of forgetting. Still, evidence indicates that when experimental subjects are asked to forget certain information, they are at least partly successful in doing so (Lehman, McKinley-Pace, Wilson, & Slavsky, 1997). However, repression refers to unintentional forgetting. Deliberately forgetting—or, more likely, deliberately not learning—may be quite different from unintentional repression.

Interference Theory

A widely known theory of forgetting holds that new learning can interfere with the recall of old learning (*retroactive interference*) or that old learning can interfere with the recall of new learning (*proactive interference*). These two kinds of interference have been a consistent phenomenon in studies of long-term memory (often employing nonsense syllables). In these studies, learning one list of words and then learning a second related list leads to (a) more difficulty in remembering the first list (retroactive interference) and (b) more difficulty in learning the second list (proactive interference). Interference has also been extensively studied in language learning. For example, Isurin and McDonald (2001) found significant evidence of interference between first and second languages. Not surprisingly, interference appears to be higher for words that are most similar, and interference decreases with increasing exposure to the second language.

What happens in forgetting via interference, suggests Wixted (2004), is that recent experiences are simply not "consolidated"—that is, the neurological changes that underlie memory do not occur. Until a memory is consolidated, it is especially vulnerable to the interfering effects of ongoing mental activity and to the formation of other memories. This, says Wixted, explains why sleep and even certain drugs often improve memory for recent learning. In effect, sleep and drugs such as alcohol have the effect of diminishing competing mental activity.

Fortunately, interference appears to be more descriptive of what happens in the laboratory than of what actually happens in people's daily lives. Although people might occasionally become confused because of competition among items they are trying to remember, indications are that they can continue to learn all sorts of things without running the risk of becoming progressively more subject to the effects of interference.

The fact that laboratory results in memory research are not always reflected in real life has led to a sometimes-heated controversy among some psychologists. Some, such as Neisser (1978), argue that laboratory research has produced no important knowledge and that investigators should study everyday memory in real life. Some, such as Banaji and Crowder (1989), insist that science needs experimental control to produce results that can be generalized. Still others, such as Tulving, claim that the quarrel is uncalled for and that it will not advance science: "There is no reason to believe that there is only one correct way of studying memory" (1991, p. 41).

Retrieval-Cue Failure

Perhaps, as noted at the outset, people don't actually forget but simply cannot remember. That something cannot be remembered is not very good evidence that it is completely gone from memory; this might simply mean that it cannot be accessed. The problem, in Howe and O'Sullivan's (1997) words, might be one of retrieval rather than of storage.

Tulving (1974) recognizes this possibility in his description of two kinds of forgetting. There is a kind of forgetting, he explains, that simply involves an inability to recall—a **retrieval-cue failure**. He assumes that this type of forgetting is related to the unavailability of appropriate cues for recall. In his words, it is cue-dependent forgetting. Many researchers (for example, White, 2002) suggest that this may be one of the most common causes of forgetting. The problem in not remembering, he explains, is related to not being able to discriminate the item from other possibilities *at the time of remembering rather than at the time of learning.*

A second type of forgetting involves actual changes in the memory trace itself and is therefore labeled *trace dependent.* The five possibilities described earlier (brain injury, fading, interference, distortion, and repression) relate primarily to trace-dependent forgetting.

For declarative (conscious, explicit) material, recall seems to be better with certain types of cues. For example, Tulving (1989) reports that the most effective memory cues are those that match the type of recall required. In studies where subjects are required to remember the meanings of words, cues that emphasize meaning are best. But when subjects are asked questions relating to the spellings or sounds of words, retrieval cues that emphasize the sounds (phonemes) or the letters in the words work best. Other retrieval cues and strategies that can significantly improve memory include various well-known aids to remembering.

Educational Implications: Aids to Learning and Remembering

One of the principal aims of education is long-term remembering. And fortunately, the common belief that students begin to forget much of what they have learned very soon after their examinations may not be especially valid. True, a large number of studies support this notion. But, as Semb and Ellis (1994) point out, most of these studies are laboratory studies. In these studies, the material to be learned is usually presented and learned in one session, and learners are tested later at different times. But schools, they suggest, don't usually provide students with just one opportunity to learn. Instead, material is presented at different times and in different ways, often using a variety of presentation modes (such as films, computers, demonstrations, books, and so on). When Semb and Ellis examined 62 studies that had looked at long-term retention of school-taught materials, they found impressive evidence of significant long-term retention. Hence, one of the most important instructional implications of research and theory on memory may well be the rather obvious recognition that repetition over time, using a variety of presentation and learning modes, may be far more effective than the one-time procedures more common in laboratory learning.

It may also be important to systematize and emphasize the various strategies that psychology has shown are effective in moving material from short-term to long-term memory. The most important of these strategies—rehearsal, elaboration, and organization—are also the main cognitive processes of learning.

Rehearsal

To rehearse is to repeat (Her name is Greta; her name is Greta; Greta; Greta; Greta . . .). **Rehearsal,** as noted earlier, is the principal means of maintaining information in short-term memory. It is also one means by which information is transferred to long-term memory.

Elaboration

To elaborate is to extend or add to. **Elaboration** might involve associating what is to be learned with mental images, or relating new material to material that has already been learned. Bradshaw and Anderson (1982) asked subjects to remember the sentence "The fat man read the sign." Those who had elaborated the sentence to "The fat man read the sign warning of thin ice" were far more successful in recalling it than those who had not elaborated.

Organization

To organize is to arrange according to some system. Chunking—placing what is to be learned into related groups—is one example of **organization.** Deliberately organizing textual material with heads and subheads is another example. A fundamental belief of cognitive psychology is that people appear to have a natural tendency to look for relationships—to identify similarities and differences (that is, to categorize and attain concepts).

Systems for Remembering

Various systems developed specifically to improve memory are based on these strategies; accordingly, the strategies emphasize ways of organizing and of elaborating, as well as ways of highlighting retrieval cues. Many of these strategies, notes Bellezza (1996), require considerable skill and practice. Research indicates that they can be highly effective in a variety of situations—for example, with students with learning disabilities (Bulgren, Schumaker, & Deshler, 1994), as well as with normal learners (Richardson, 1995).

Rhymes and Little Sayings

Among these memory aids—or **mnemonic devices**—are acronyms (letter cues) such as NATO, UN, or Roy G. Biv (the colors of the visible spectrum in order). They also include acrostics, which are sentences or expressions in which the first letter of each word stands for something else. For example, the acrostic "Men very easily make jugs serve useful nocturnal purposes" recalls English names for planets in order from this system's sun (Mercury, Venus, Earth, Mars, and so on). These sorts of mnemonic aids provide easily recalled retrieval cues and are a form of elaboration and organization of material.

The Loci System

More complex mnemonics typically use visual imagery, which is far more memorable for humans than are most written or spoken words (Kosslyn, Behrmann, & Jeannerod, 1995). When subjects were exposed to 10,000 pictures very briefly and then shown some of these same pictures again—paired this time with other pictures that had not been included in the first presentation—they were able to recognize more than 90% of the pictures (Standing, 1973). Similarly, when

Bahrick, Bahrick, and Wittlinger (1975) presented subjects with photographs of their former classmates (taken from yearbooks), recognition was approximately 90% accurate after 2 months and had not declined appreciably 15 years later. The human capacity for visual recognition is remarkable.[5]

Mnemonic systems based on visual imagery suggest specific ways in which mental images can be linked visually with other easy-to-remember images. Many of these systems are very old, and very powerful. The **loci system,** for example, is more than 2,000 years old (Hermann, Raybeck, & Gruneberg, 2002). It simply requires learners to form a strong visual image of the item to be remembered and to place it in some familiar location such as a room in a house. The second item is then visualized and placed in another room, the third might be placed in a hallway, and so on. Recalling the items later simply requires that the subject take a mental "walk" through the rooms of the house and attempt to visualize each of the items that have been placed there. Try it with a grocery list. It works.

The Phonetic System

A memory system often used by professional memorizers, guaranteed to impress grandmothers, is the **phonetic system,** described by Higbee (1977). The first step in learning the phonetic system is to form strong visual associations between numbers and consonants. Traditionally, associations make use of the visual appearance of the consonants. Thus, 1 is a *t* (because it has one down stroke); 2 might be *n;* 3, an *m;* 4 a *q,* and so on.

Once you have associated a number with each consonant (vowels don't count), you can then form a word for each number, say, from 1 to 25. For example, number 12 could be "tin"; number 21, a "nut." Now form a strong visual image linking each of these words to its number. Learn these thoroughly, practice them, and then challenge your grandmother to name, or show you, 25 items. As she writes these items on a piece of paper, numbered consecutively, you close your eyes and cleverly link an image of each with its appropriate numbered visual image.

When your grandmother has finished, you are ready: "So do you want me to give them back to you backward or forward?" But she's a devious old lady, and she suspects you have some trick that allowed you to link these 25 items in series. So she throws you a curve: "What was the twenty-first thing I said?" In your newly trained mind's eye, you immediately see your "nut," which you have linked to your grandmother's saying, "And for number 21, let's see, that'd be the stove in the old house," so that now you see the "nut" sitting, red hot, on the stove. You answer, "The twenty-first item? Well now, that'd be that old stove in the other house, the one in which you closed the oven door on the cat." And your grandmother is impressed.

---

[5]The Old Woman said she meant this in a relative sense: The human capacity for remembering images is remarkable compared with the human capacity for remembering poetry, personal experiences, or the faces of dogs, she said. She explained, again, that she did not mean this in an absolute sense.

Summary

1. Various metaphors, that of the computer being highly popular, have been used as comparisons and explanations of human memory. Some extraordinary human memories (like those of Euler and of Luria's subject, S) are capable of astounding long-term recollections, but, unlike computers, most human memories display rapid initial loss of information.

2. Memory is ordinarily defined as the availability of information (recall or retrievability); however, some aspects of memory are not conscious (that is, are implicit rather than explicit). Not all that is stored can be retrieved. Ebbinghaus pioneered the early scientific investigation of memory using nonsense syllables.

3. Forgetting is the inability to bring into consciousness and may involve either storage failure (loss of memory traces, perhaps because of decay or interference), or retrieval failure (failure to recall). Proactive (forward acting) and retroactive (backward acting) interference are often involved in forgetting.

4. The modal model of memory describes a process consisting of short-term and long-term memory. A third stage, sometimes termed the *sensory register*, describes the momentary effect of stimulation (and is sometimes called echoic or iconic memory). This is illustrated in studies of the cocktail party phenomenon, which demonstrate that even material not attended to remains available for a fraction of a second.

5. Short-term memory (STM) lasts only seconds (seldom more than 20), unless there is continued rehearsal (in which case the information may be coded into long-term memory). It refers essentially to the ongoing availability of a small number of items (seven, plus or minus two), and it is termed *active* or *working memory* to emphasize its similarity to immediate attention or consciousness. Its capacity may be increased through chunking—the grouping of related items.

6. Baddeley's model of short-term (working) memory describes two systems: an executive control system concerned with controlling the flow of information in and out of working memory, and two slave systems (the phonological loop and the visual-spatial sketch pad) concerned with maintaining auditory or visual material ready for access by the executive system.

7. Forgetting in STM may be related to decay (loss of memory traces), displacement (replacement of old with new material because of space limitations), interference (where previous learning interferes with new learning), or level of processing (Craik and Lockhart's model).

8. Long-term memory (LTM) is assumed to involve some permanent structural or chemical changes in the brain. Short-term recall, in contrast, may involve no more than temporary electrical/chemical activity. This is essentially Hebb's theory.

9. Long-term memory is highly stable (notably so for images and odors), is generative rather than simply reproductive, is influenced by understanding, and is better for some items (those that are more striking, more meaningful, or more emotional, sometimes leading to *flashbulb* memories) than for others.

10. A comparison of short-term memory and long-term memory reveals that STM is an active, continuing process; that it is easily disrupted by ongoing activities; and that it is highly limited in capacity. In contrast, LTM refers to a more passive process, not easily disrupted by ongoing activities, and essentially unlimited in capacity. Retrieval from STM is either immediate and

automatic or does not occur; retrieval from LTM may be considerably slower and more groping.

11. Long-term memory systems include explicit (declarative) memory, consisting of potentially conscious, recallable information; or implicit (nondeclarative or procedural) memory, consisting of unconscious, nonverbalizable effects of learning (as in, for example, skill learning or classical conditioning). Evidence from studies of amnesiacs and people with brain injuries, as well as studies of normal brains, using imaging techniques such as PET and fMRI scans, suggest that different brain systems underlie these memory systems.

12. Declarative (recallable) memory is composed of semantic memory and episodic memory. Semantic memory includes general, stable, abstract facts and principles (for example, knowledge of language or of the world). Episodic memory refers to private knowledge that is temporal in nature and tied to specific personal events (hence, autobiographical memory).

13. Some early models of memory were non-associationistic (Koffka's notion of a continuous record like a videotape); current models emphasize associations among items in memory and frequently make use of schema or node models—a node or schema being simply whatever it is that represents an idea.

14. Historical episodes in the search for the physiology of memory include Lashley's ablations of rat brains (he didn't find the engram); Penfield's stimulation of his patient's brains (their memories may have been fantasies and hallucinations rather than specific memories); dissections of the brains of enriched rats (changes were global and imprecise); the feeding and injection of trained planaria into untrained planaria (the studies don't easily replicate and, 30 years later, seem to have led no-where); the study of amnesiacs' memories (these support distinctions among different long-term memory systems and indicate that different brain systems may be involved in each); and the development of connectionist models (which argue that memories reside in patterns of neurons rather than in specific changes within single neurons).

15. A great deal of current memory research uses electroencephalograph (EEG) and magnetoencephalograph (MEG) recordings. EEG recordings provide real-time recordings of what are termed *event-related potentials (ERPs)*, changes in the electrical potential of nerve cells as they fire. MEG recordings provide parallel indications of changes in magnetic fields at the scalp during neural activity—termed *event-related fields (ERFs)*. ERPs and ERFs are typically associated with specific external stimulation and allow researchers to identify the exact areas of the brain involved.

16. Some forgetting may result from brain injury; some might result from an ill-explained "fading" process. In addition, some forgetting probably results from distortion, which might occur partly because what is remembered tends to be relatively abstract and because people generate rather than reconstruct when they try to remember. Other explanations for forgetting include repression theory (uncommon, and most appropriate for experiences laden with negative emotion), interference theory (proactive and retroactive interference), and retrieval-cue failure (absence of appropriate cues to retrieve learned material).

17. Learning and remembering can often be improved through rehearsal, elaboration, and organization. Memory strategies include rhymes and related devices, as well as specific mnemonics that use visual imagery extensively (the loci and the phonetic systems).

Motivation

> Persons attempting to find a motive in this narrative will be prosecuted.
> **Mark Twain**

The Old Woman seasoned the doves and wrapped them in what looked like thick pastry. Then she scratched the glowing embers apart and laid the birds directly in the ashes, covering them with more ashes and embers. Later she cracked open and discarded the blackened shells and laid the steaming birds on the platter with the roasted potatoes and we ate them, one each. And when we had done, it was dark and the wolf howled from deep in the forest, and I would have added wood to the fire to warm the night and ease my fears but the Old Woman said not to, that tonight she wanted that nothing should dim the heavens. And for a long time, she lay on her back gazing at the sky, and it seemed that her eyes did not move, almost as though she might be looking at something she had recognized, something familiar. But when I peered hard where I thought she might be looking, I saw nothing, just a jumble of tiny stars lost in the confusion of the Milky Way. Then the wolf howled again, so close this time that between his howls I could hear the rasping in his throat and I would have asked the Old Woman once more, might I build the fire up just a little, but I saw that she had now turned her face to the northern sky where the aurora had just now begun to shimmer and dance in the cold night, brushing the sky with greens and pinks, and for a time the wolf was silent.

Suddenly the Old Woman rose and heaved great lengths of wood on the fire until the flames leaped and flailed about, throwing sparks like diamonds into the suddenly blackened night. And then she motioned that I should turn on the recorder once more.

ⓣhis Chapter

We have done and felt much tonight, said the Old Woman, about which the 10th chapter speaks. She explained that we had eaten and drunk and burned our fears and gazed at splendor—which is to say that we had been moved by thirst and hunger, perhaps by fear and cold, maybe even by love and beauty. She said that these are precisely the things with which this chapter is concerned: What moves human beings? Or, to put it another way, what are the reasons and causes for what people do?

Objectives

Tell your readers, said the Old Woman as she fed still more birch to the fire, that they'll know the difference between causes and reasons once they are completely done with this chapter—that is, after they've read it and carefully translated it into every other language they know. At that point, they'll be in the enviable position of being able to write *tiny but brilliant truths (of the kind that might be baked into fortune cookies) explaining, among other things, the following:*

- *The meaning of motivation*
- *How instincts and reflexes relate to behavior*
- *What needs, drives, and incentives are*
- *The intricacies of attribution theory*

- *The meaning and importance of arousal*
- *The use of motivation in the classroom*

In addition, she said, they will have new insights into the causes and reasons for their own uninspiring, but nevertheless inspired, actions. She sat close to the fire, now, once more taking up her sheaf of notes. Number One Head: Motivation and Emotions, she began.

Motivation and Emotions

Among the most basic questions that can be asked about human behavior are questions like these: Why do people behave? Why do they behave in precisely this manner and not that? Why does behavior stop? Answering these questions is essential for understanding human learning and behavior. These are the questions of **motivation.**

The Latin origin for the word *motivation* means *to move.* Hence, motivation deals with action. A motive is a conscious or unconscious force that incites a person to act or, sometimes, not to act. In this sense, motives are **causes** because, says the dictionary, causes are agents or forces that produce an effect or an action. Thus, the study of human motivation is the study of agents and forces that cause behavior.

But the study of human motivation is also one other thing: It includes a study of **reasons** for behavior. Reasons are rational explanations. They typically involve deliberation, purpose, anticipation of the results of behavior—in other words, reasoning. When Sherlock Holmes inquires about the killer's motives, he is asking for the killer's purposes—her reasons.

To illustrate the distinction between reasons and causes: If Joe naively places his hand on a hot stove, the heat (or, more precisely, Joe's sensation of heat) causes him to withdraw his hand at once. The reason why Joe later avoids going near the stove is his realization that doing so might be painful. The study of human motivation is a study of both reasons and causes.

It's important to note that motives, and motivation, are very closely tied to emotions. Emotions may be centrally involved as causes and reasons for a very large number of human actions. Just as powerful negative emotions accompany painful sensations of heat, so too do powerful positive emotions accompany the attraction one might feel for a love interest.

Emotions, as we see in this chapter, are complex states tied not only to motives but reflected as well in activity of our nervous systems. As Russell (2003) notes, emotions can be very general states experienced as "feeling good," "feeling bad," "feeling energized," and so on. When these states are linked directly to some cause, such as an activity or an object, they can become very powerful sources of motivation.

Reflexes, Instincts, and Imprinting

Motivation theory recognizes that there are biological causes for behaviors such as Joe's sudden withdrawal from heat. These have to do with his nervous system and its wired-in tendency to react to certain situations reflexively. Hence, a **reflex** is one kind of motive, one sort of explanation for behavior.

Reflexes

As we saw in Chapter 2, a reflex is a simple unlearned act that occurs in response to a specific stimulus. Children are born with a limited number of reflexes, such as the blinking reflex in response to air blown on the eye, the knee-jerk reflex, withdrawal from pain, and startle reactions. All these reflexes are normally present in adults as well. In addition, several human reflexes are present at birth but disappear shortly after: the Babinsky reflex (curling of the toes when the sole is tickled), the grasping reflex, the sucking reflex, and the Moro reflex (flinging out the arms and legs when startled or dropped suddenly). (See Table 2.1 for a summary of infant reflexes.)

Most reflexes have clear survival value. As we saw in Chapter 2, some hypothesize that even the Moro reflex might have been useful in some distant past when a tree-dwelling infant accidentally fell from a perch or slipped from its mother's embrace, and the sudden flinging out of its arms helped it find another branch to grasp.

The Orienting Reflex

Another type of reflexive behavior, the **orienting reflex (OR),** is a general tendency to respond to new stimulation by becoming more alert. It is "a mechanism that enhances the processing of information in all sensory systems," explain Berg and Berg (1987, p. 268). In dogs and cats, the orienting response is clear: When they hear a new sound, their heads turn, their ears perk up, and their entire posture says, "What the @#$*! was that?" Not surprisingly, the orienting response is often called the "What is it?" response. MacCulloch and Feldman (1996) point out that the orienting response is an evolutionary development that enables organisms to assess the environment quickly to uncover both potential threats and potential opportunities. Hence, it has important implications for survival.

In humans, the orienting response is not as obvious as in cats or dogs, but it serves the same alerting function. Thus, when exposed to a novel stimulus, heart and respiration rate may decelerate momentarily (this explains the expression "to hold one's breath"), and electrical activity in the brain may change. Interestingly, some of these orienting changes (such as heart rate changes) are present even in the unborn fetus (Groome, Mooney, Holland, & Bentz, 1997).

One very important function of the orienting reflex in humans relates directly to learning and development, notes Alter (1996). Orienting occurs in response to novelty; as the novel becomes familiar (becomes learned, in other words), the orienting response ceases to occur. Thus, in studies with preverbal infants, the disappearance of an orienting response is often used as an indication that learning has occurred.

Reflexes as Explanations

Pavlov and Watson made extensive use of reflexes in their theories, and they were at least partly successful in explaining some simple types of learning, such as emotional responses or taste aversions. Note that both these classes of learning can be important for the organism's survival. Classically conditioned fear of a snarling noise, for example, might lead an animal—even a human one—to avoid a saber-toothed tiger when it hears one clear its throat. And a learned taste aversion might prevent the animal from eating a poisonous toadstool.

Because of their link with survival, reflexes are valid, biologically based explanations for some behaviors. Unfortunately for those who prefer things to be simple, they have limited generality and usefulness as explanations for most human behaviors, the bulk of which are not reflexive.

Instincts

Reflexes are simple unlearned (inherited) behaviors; **instincts** are more complex inherited patterns of behavior that are common to an entire species and are associated with survival. Some early theorists, including James, thought that humans had an enormous number of instincts—more than any other animal. In addition to instincts for jealousy, cleanliness, sucking, pointing at, clasping, and biting (among hundreds of others), James listed a tendency toward kleptomania as a human instinct! (James, 1890/1950). McDougall (1908) and others went so far as to argue that all human behavior results from unlearned tendencies to react in given ways—in other words, from instincts. These theorists thought up long lists of supposed instincts such as gregariousness, pugnacity, flight, self-assertion, self-abasement, and hunger. At one point, Bernard counted more than 6,000 "instincts," including inclinations as unexpected as "the tendency to avoid eating apples that grow in one's own garden" (1924, p. 212).

But perhaps most of these tendencies are not really instincts at all. After all, instincts are complex behaviors (such as migration or hibernation), they are general to all members of a species (the "following" behavior of young ducks or geese, for example), and they are relatively unmodifiable (birds' nesting behaviors, for instance). Given these observations, many psychologists argue that there is no convincing evidence that there are *any* instincts among humans, although instincts are clearly evident in other animal forms and are invariably related to survival and propagation (see, for example, Thorpe, 1963).

Still, not all psychologists believe that instincts play no role in human behavior. Freudian theory, for example, is premised on the notion that powerful, instinctual tendencies, mainly associated with survival and procreation (collectively labeled **id** and often manifested in sexual urges termed **libido**), underlie much of behavior (see, for example, Lear, 1996). These instincts, argues Medici de Steiner (1995), are sometimes apparent in dreams, as well as in actual behavior.

Also, as we saw in Chapter 5, evolutionary psychologists look to biology and genetics as important sources of explanation for human learning and behavior. Sociobiology, for example, argues that human behavior is profoundly influenced by unlearned instinctlike tendencies.

Imprinting

Similarly, theorists such as Bowlby (1982) argue that early attachment between human mother and child has important parallels with **imprinting** among animals. Imprinting describes an instinctual, unlearned behavior that is specific to a species and does not appear until an animal has been exposed to the appropriate stimulus (called a *releaser*), providing that exposure occurs at the right period in the animal's life (the **critical period**). The classical example of imprinting is the "following" behavior of ducks, chickens, or geese, which typically imprint on the first moving object they see. Fortunately, that object is usually their mother, but it need not be. Lorenz (1952) reports the case of a gosling that imprinted on him and followed him around much as it might have followed its mother. As the time for mating approached, much to Lorenz's embarrassment, this goose insisted on foisting its affections on him. The story is that this goose, in a gesture of devotion and love, insisted on depositing beakfuls of minced worms in Lorenz's ear. Its love, as far as science knows, remained unrequited.

Collias (2000) also found that birds such as chickens will imprint not only on the mother hen, but also on their siblings, as well as any other moving object—including a person—providing exposure to the imprinted-upon stimulus occurs shortly after birth. In his investigation, imprinting was strongest if exposure occurred during the first day after hatching, and weakened progressively during the next 10 days (see Figure 10.1).

Imprinting among animals is not limited to acquiring "following" behavior in *precocial* (fast-maturing) birds; it also appears to play an important role in their later sexual behavior. Various studies have shown, for example, that the sexual behavior of adult birds is strongly influenced by their exposure to appropriate stimuli during critical periods early in their development. This is perhaps why adult birds typically seek to mate with members of their own species. When Plenge, Curio, and Witte (2000) raised female birds with parents that had been adorned with a bright red feather on their heads, these female birds later chose to mate with similarly adorned adults. And in a related study, males raised under the same circumstances also showed a significant preference for red-feather adorned adult females (Witte, Hirschler, & Curio, 2000). Interestingly,

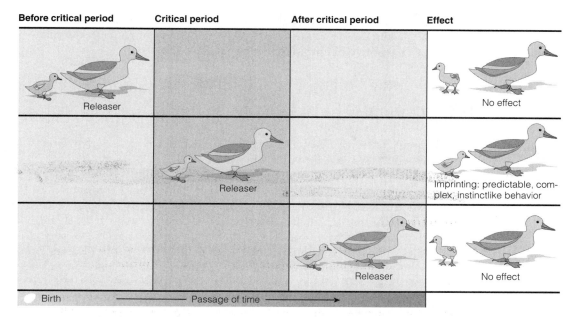

Before critical period	Critical period	After critical period	Effect

Figure 10.1 A representation of imprinting. Under appropriate conditions, exposure to a releaser (a mother duck, for example) during the critical period (within a few hours of hatching) leads to imprinting which is evident in the "following" behavior of the hatchling. Imprinting does not occur in the absence of a releaser, or if the releaser is presented too early or too late.

however, in a third study in which the hatchlings were imprinted on adults with red-dyed bills, the hatchlings did *not* prefer adults with red bills as mating choices (Hoerster, Curio, & Witte, 2000). Not all characteristics can serve as imprinting stimuli.

Although humans do not imprint as do other animals, Bowlby (1982) and others (for example, Klaus & Kennell, 1983) argue that there is a "sensitive period" during which bonds between mother and infant form most easily and that this provides a biological explanation for early attachment. Others suggest that certain behaviors such as sexual abuse—given that those who are abusive have often been abused as children—may reflect a kind of imprinting (Eisenman & Kristsonis, 1995). Similarly, profound fears (*phobias*) may sometimes relate to an imprinting-like phenomenon that results from exposure to an appropriate frightening stimulus. For example, Fredrikson, Annas, and Wik (1997) report that snake and spider phobias can occur either through direct exposure (actually being frightened by a snake or a spider) or through indirect exposure (seeing someone else being frightened, or being warned by a parent about the dangers of snakes and spiders). In their sample of 158 phobic women, they found a close relationship between phobias among parents and grandparents and phobias among children and grandchildren. This, the authors argue, might support the notion that phobias are learned through experience; it might also support the view that genetic factors contribute to the development of phobias, and that these are an example of imprinting among humans.

Psychological Hedonism

Considerable intuitive evidence indicates that human beings seek that which is pleasant and try to avoid the unpleasant (Overskeid, 2002). At first glance, this notion, labeled **psychological hedonism,** would seem to be a good general explanation for most human behavior. Unfortunately, it's not a very useful idea. The main problem with the notion is that it can't be used to predict or even to explain behavior unless pain and pleasure can be defined clearly beforehand, which they often can't. For example, it might appear wise to say that a person braves the Arctic cold in an uninsulated cabin because doing so is pleasant, but it's quite another matter to predict beforehand that this specific person will retire to that frosty cabin. The difficulty is that pain and pleasure are subjective emotional reactions. Although it might be true that people are hedonistic, motivational theory can profit from this bit of knowledge only if pain and pleasure can be described more objectively. For this, suggest Hosen, Hosen, and Stern (2001), we would need to know something about the subjective "hedonic" calculus that people use to evaluate different payoffs.

Drive Reduction and Incentives

One approach to defining pain and pleasure more objectively is implicit in operant conditioning theory's definitions of reinforcement and punishment. At a simple level, positive reinforcers might be considered pleasant, whereas punishment and negative reinforcement generally would not be.

Another approach to clarifying the hedonistic notions of pain and pleasure is to look at basic human needs and drives—assuming that satisfying needs is pleasant and leaving them unsatisfied is unpleasant. Historically, there have been two ways of looking at motivation, says Covington (2000). One view, for a long time the most popular, sees motives as drives that urge the individual to action. Recall that a **drive,** clearly defined by Hull, is a tendency to behave that is brought about by an unsatisfied need. Thus, the need for food, when unsatisfied, gives rise to the hunger drive, which then motivates behavior.

The other view sees motives less as drives that impel the individual to act, but rather as goals toward which the individual strives. The difference between these two views is mainly one of emphasis. Drives, such as the sex drive for example, clearly have goals associated with them. Similarly, a goal—such as the desire to achieve great fame—may lead to powerful drives to behave. As we see later, the emphasis in most current approaches to motivation, which tend to be more cognitive than behavioristic, is toward viewing motives as goals rather than as drives.

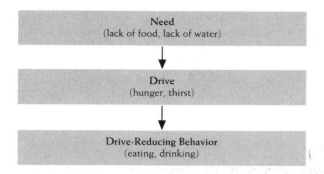

Figure 10.2

The drive-reduction model of motivation. A need (lack) leads to a drive (urge), which in turn leads to a behavior intended to satisfy the need and eliminate the drive. This model is useful for explaining many physiologically based behaviors but is less useful for explaining things like why some people like to read and others don't, or why some like to climb mountains, others like to sing songs, and so on.

Three physiological motives are central to the lives of all humans: hunger, thirst, and sex. These have been studied mainly as drives rather than as goals.

Needs and Drives

Each of the three physiological motives is linked with a **need**—a lack that gives rise to a desire for satisfaction. The tendency to act to satisfy a need is what defines a drive. For example, to be thirsty is to be in a state of need for liquids; this need leads to the thirst drive. Thirst leads to drinking, and the need disappears. Thus, needs bear the seeds of their own destruction (see Figure 10.2).

This explanation of behavior, termed *drive reduction*, is well illustrated in Hull's theory. Hull believed that drive reduction is what accounts for the effects of reinforcers and leads to learning.

Psychological Needs

What the basic **physiological needs** (or physical needs) are seems clear: They consist of the need for food, drink, and sex and the need to maintain body temperature. Some psychologists also believe that people have **psychological needs,** although there is considerably less agreement about what these might be. Likely candidates include the needs for affection, belonging, achievement, independence, social recognition, and self-esteem. Glasser (1998, 2002), for example, describes four groups of needs that are especially important in understanding the behavior of children and adolescents: the need for fun, for freedom, for power and control, and for love and belonging. Harvey and Retter (2002) studied 402 children and adolescents (ages 8 to 16), and found systematic sex and age differences in the importance of these needs. For example, the older children expressed a higher need for freedom than did younger children; boys had a higher need for fun than did girls; and girls had a higher need for love and belonging than did boys. That nonhuman animals also have psychological needs is less clear and somewhat controversial. Some, such as Jensen and Toates (1993) argue that it is difficult, and not especially useful, to try to establish that such needs exist among animals.

One main difference between physical and psychological needs is that physical needs—and their satisfaction—result in tissue changes. Psychological needs, in contrast, are not necessarily manifested in bodily changes but have to do more with the intellectual or emotional aspects of human functioning. In addition, physiological needs can be completely satisfied, whereas psychological needs are relatively insatiable. People can eat until they're not at all hungry, but they seldom receive affection until they desire absolutely no more from anyone.

Maslow's Hierarchy

There are two major systems of needs, says Maslow (1970): basic needs and **metaneeds**. The basic needs are called *deficiency needs* because they lead to behavior if the conditions that satisfy them are lacking. Basic needs include the physiological needs (need for food, drink, and sex, for example), safety needs (such as the need for security), love and belongingness needs, and self-esteem needs.

In contrast with the basic *deficiency* needs, the metaneeds are *growth needs*. They are marked by a human desire to grow, to achieve, to become. They include the need to know and achieve abstract values such as goodness and truth, to acquire knowledge, and to achieve **self-actualization**—which is discussed in more detail next.

Maslow assumes these need systems are hierarchical in that higher level needs will not be attended to until lower level needs have been satisfied. Thus, starving people do not hunger for knowledge. And thus, too, the elderly whose basic needs are met but whose higher level needs are ignored might remain unhappy (Umoren, 1992). (See Figure 10.3.)

Self-Actualization

The most important of Maslow's metaneeds is self-actualization, a difficult-to-define concept. It is best described as the process of becoming oneself, of *actualizing*—that is, making actual—one's potential. But even Maslow admitted, "The exploration of the highest reaches of human nature and its ultimate possibilities and aspirations is a difficult and tortuous task" (1970, p. 67). Even decades later, say Leclerc, Lefrançois, Dube, Hebert, and Gaulin (1998), the concept remains unclear. That's partly because there has been a tendency to view self-actualization as a *state* that the individual reaches when all of that person's potential has finally unfolded. In Maslow's words, self-actualized people "may be loosely described as [making] full use and exploitation of talents, capacities, potentialities, etc.," (1970, p. 150). But when Maslow searched among 3,000 college students, he found only one person that he considered truly self-actualized, using this definition.

The problem, says Rowan (1998), is that self-actualization is not a state but a process, an ongoing search to develop and to grow. As a result, the triangle that has typically been used to represent Maslow's hierarchy of needs is misleading because it's closed at the top. "What is wrong with the triangle," explains Rowan, "is that it suggests that there is an end point to personal growth" (1998, p. 88). But we never reach that end point. (See Figure 10.3.)

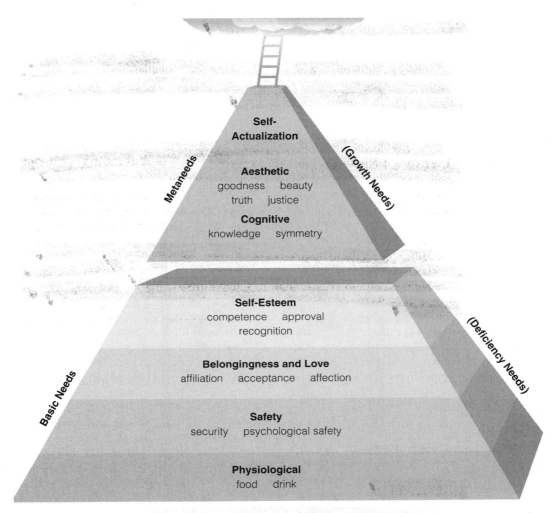

Figure 10.3 Maslow's hierarchy of needs. The open pyramid, suggested by Rowan (1998) indicates that self-actualization is a never-ending process, rather than an ultimate, achievable goal.

Need/Drive Positions: An Appraisal

Need/drive models are important explanations in behavioristic learning theories. Skinner's and Thorndike's conditioning theories are founded largely on the effectiveness of basic drives as human motives. Similarly, Hull relied on drive reduction to explain why habits are acquired and how fractional antedating goal responses become connected. Not surprisingly, common reinforcers in animal research are food and drink—objects that satisfy basic unlearned needs. And among the most common reinforcers in studies of human operant conditioning are those that satisfy learned or psychological needs (praise, money, tokens, high grades, and so on).

Some Problems with Need/Drive Theory

Even though need/drive theory appears to have considerable relevance for explaining human behavior, it has a number of problems. First, need-drive theories typically suggest that behavior results from a need or deficiency in the organism. It would seem logical to assume, then, that the satisfaction of needs should lead to rest. This, however, is often not the case. Even rats that presumably are not in a state of need, having just been fed, given drink, and loved, often do not simply curl up and go to sleep. Instead, they may even show increases in activity.

A second problem with need/drive theory is that there are many instances of behaviors that human beings (and lower animals as well) engage in with no possibility of immediate or delayed satisfaction of a need—as when a rat learns to run a maze in the absence of any reward (Tolman, 1951) or a person gets bored and looks for sensory stimulation (Hebb, 1966). Evidence of exploratory behavior has led some theorists to suggest that a curiosity or exploratory drive motivates many human behaviors (for example, Berlyne, 1960, 1966).

A third major shortcoming of need/drive or drive-reduction theories is that they try to account for behavior through inner states and urges (need for food, for example, is an inner state, and the hunger drive is an urge). As a result, they are hard-pressed to explain why behaviors also seem to be affected by external stimulation. If hunger were solely an internal state, people would always eat only enough to activate the physiological mechanisms that relate to stopping eating. Yet, a great many people eat far more if the foods appear more appetizing; others seem to become far hungrier if they are allowed to anticipate beforehand what they will be eating. Even rats that are given a small taste of food before being placed in the start box of a maze run faster toward the goal box than do rats that have not been "primed" (Zeaman, 1949). If an inner state of hunger is the motive, it follows that the taste of food, however small, should reduce the hunger drive somewhat and that hungrier rats should run faster (see Figure 10.4.)

Incentives

What need/drive positions need to account for is the incentive value of motivation (termed *incentive motivation*). Even for rats, a taste of food seems to serve as an incentive, urging them to run faster. For humans, gifted as they are with the ability to imagine and to anticipate, there is no need for a taste beforehand. All they need know is that the world's most exquisite crêpe Suzette is to be found yonder under the purple sign that reads "Suzie's," and they will walk a little faster.

Basically, the term *incentive* relates to the value of a goal or reward. Thus, a goal is said to have high incentive value when it is particularly powerful in motivating behavior, and to have low incentive value if it is not very motivating. As we saw in Chapter 3, Hull was among the first to use the concept of incentives (for which he used the symbol K) in his theory. He recognized that drive alone could not account for motivation. Among other things, the amount of reward a rat receives affects its behavior, as does its history of past rewards.

The introduction of the concept of incentives into a discussion of need/drive theory makes it possible to account for the fact that monkeys will work

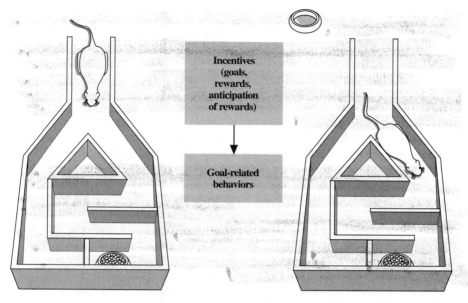

Figure 10.4 Incentives. Drives alone can't explain behavior. In Zeaman's (1949) experiment, rats that had already been given some food (right maze) performed better on a maze that they knew led to food than did hungry rats (left maze).

harder to obtain a banana than a piece of lettuce and that a person might pay more to eat a steak than a hamburger. It also brings what is essentially a behavioristic theory of motivation somewhat closer to the cognitive positions, because anticipating goals and estimating their values involve what are essentially cognitive processes. Later in this chapter, we deal in more detail with goals and rewards, and how they relate to motivation.

Arousal Theory

Three things affect how much effort a person is willing to make (that is, how motivated a person is), according to Brehm and Self (1989): internal states such as needs, potential outcomes, and the individual's estimate of the probability that a certain behavior will lead to a desired outcome. This recognizes both the physiological and the cognitive aspects of behavior, much as Hull's system tried to do (see Chapter 3).

Arousal: Measuring Motivation

Can intensity of motivation be measured? Brehm and Self (1989) say it can be, because intensity of motivation is reflected in changes in the **sympathetic nervous system.** More specifically, such changes are reflected in what is termed

arousal. Hence, **arousal theory** presents both a physiological and a cognitive explanation of behavior.

The term *arousal* has both psychological and physiological meaning. As a psychological concept, it seems to have at least two dimensions, explains Dickman (2002). One dimension relates to *tension* and ranges from high anxiety or even panic at one extreme to great calmness at the other. The other dimension has to do with *energy* and refers to the degree of alertness, wakefulness, or attentiveness of a person or animal. The energy dimension of arousal may also be evident in the organism's vigor, notes Dickman, which appears to be somewhat different from wakefulness.

As a physiological concept, arousal refers to the degree of activation of the organism, which is often measured through changes in heart rate and blood pressure, changes in conductivity of the skin to electricity (called **electrodermal response**), and changes in electrical activity of the brain. Specifically, with increasing arousal, the electrical activity of the cortex (as measured by an electroencephalograph, or EEG) takes the form of increasingly rapid and shallow waves (called **beta waves**). At lower levels of arousal (such as sleep), the waves are slow and deep (called **alpha waves**).

Increasing arousal defines increasing intensity of motivation (and of emotion), claim Brehm and Self (1989). But the relationship between arousal and intensity of motivation is not perfectly linear; that is, a person doesn't continue to become increasingly motivated as arousal increases.

The Yerkes-Dodson Law

At the very lowest levels of arousal, motivation tends to be low and behavior ineffective. This can easily be demonstrated by asking someone at the lowest normal level of arousal (namely, sleep) a simple question like "How many are five?" As arousal increases, behavior becomes more highly motivated, more interested; the person can now tell you with stunning clarity how many five are, and all sorts of other things as well.

But if arousal continues to increase—as might happen, for example, if what woke the person up were an earthquake—performance might deteriorate badly. High arousal, often evident in high anxiety or even fear, explains why students in tense oral examinations are sometimes unable to remember anything and sometimes can't even speak. Anxiety in test situations, Hembree (1988) concludes after reviewing 562 separate studies, clearly lowers test performance. More recent evidence suggests this may be because working memory capacity appears to decrease with increasing arousal (Necka, 2000). Similarly, overly high arousal in sports situations has repeatedly been shown to have a negative effect on athletic performance (Gould, Greenleaf, & Krane, 2002).

In summary, the relationship between performance and arousal, depicted in Figure 10.5, takes the form of an inverted U-shaped function. This observation, first described by Yerkes and Dodson (1908), is known as the **Yerkes-Dodson law:** There is an optimal level of arousal for the most effective behavior; arousal levels above and below this optimal level are associated with less effective behavior.

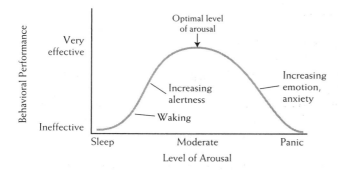

Figure 10.5
The Yerkes-Dodson law describes the relationship between behavioral performance and arousal level. In general, the most effective performance occurs at an intermediate level of arousal.

Hebb's Arousal Theory

Hebb's arousal theory of motivation is based directly on the Yerkes-Dodson law. This law, claims Hebb (1972), gives rise to two important assumptions. First, the optimal level of arousal differs for different tasks. Thus, intense, concentrated activities, such as studying or competing on a television quiz program, demand higher levels of alertness (arousal) than do more habitual behaviors, such as driving a car. For most daily activities, moderate levels of arousal are probably best. Second, the organism behaves in such a way as to maintain the level of arousal that is most appropriate for ongoing behavior. If arousal is too low, the organism will try to increase it; if it's too high, an attempt will be made to lower it.

The value of arousal as a motivational concept is based largely on the validity of this second assumption. If people try to maintain an optimal level of arousal, then it should be possible to predict at least some behaviors. For example, students who are bored (too low an arousal level) in a classroom would be expected to do things to increase their arousal. Actually, this is essentially what happens when students daydream, throw spitballs, read comic books, or talk out loud with other bored students.

Two Functions of Stimuli
Stimuli have two important functions, claimed Hebb (1972): the **cue function** and the **arousal function.** The cue function is the message function; it tells the organism how to feel, think, or react. The arousal function is defined by the general activating, or arousing, effect of stimuli. Interestingly, Hull made exactly the same distinction, referring to the *cue* and the *drive* components of stimuli—a testimony to the appeal of the idea.

In Hebb's terms, the cue function involves the activation of the specific cell assemblies corresponding to the stimulation. In contrast, the arousal function involves the activation—or, more precisely, *preactivation*—of a larger number of cell assemblies. This preactivation is brought about through the *reticular formation*— a structure that forms part of the brain stem and through which most neural pathways branch on their way from sensory systems to the brain. Arousal (preactivation of cell assemblies) is essential for the cue to have its effect, claims Hebb. At extremely low levels of arousal, for example, the individual is asleep and stimulation might have no discernible effect.

The Need for Stimulation

Unless they are tired and in need of sleep, humans, and, indeed, many other organisms, appear to have a clear and strong need to maintain relatively high levels of arousal. When Hebb and his co-researchers lowered students' arousal levels dramatically and kept them at low levels for long periods, they observed some surprising outcomes (Bexton, Heron, & Scott, 1954; Zubek, 1969). In the original—and now-classic—experiments, conducted at McGill University, a group of male college students were asked to volunteer for an experiment. They were told they would be paid $20 a day for doing absolutely nothing (Heron, 1957)—a substantial sum in those days. In fact, not only were they not asked to do anything, but also they were not allowed to do anything. Instead, they lay on cots, getting up only to use the toilet, and sitting up only to eat their meals. Each cot was isolated in a soundproof cubicle, and subjects wore translucent visors that did not allow them to see but permitted diffuse light to enter. Over their ears, they wore U-shaped foam pillows designed to prevent hearing. As a further precaution against the perception of sounds, air-conditioning equipment hummed ceaselessly and monotonously. In addition, participants wore cotton gloves and had cardboard cuffs that extended over their fingertips to discourage tactile sensation. In short, the experimenters tried to make sure that participants would experience a minimum of sensory stimulation as long as they remained in isolation.

Interestingly, none of the subjects lasted more than two days. In some later experiments where conditions of deprivation were more severe (for example, complete darkness, no sound, body immersed in water to simulate weightlessness), subjects often didn't last more than a few hours (see, for example, Barnard, Wolfe, & Graveline, 1962; Lilly, 1972).

Sensory Deprivation

Because the chief source of arousal is sensation, perceptual deprivation should result in a lowering of arousal. This assumption has been confirmed through measures of electrical activity in the brain (EEG recordings) before, during, and after isolation (Heron, 1957; Zubek & Wilgosh, 1963). After prolonged isolation, the brain activity of subjects who are awake is often similar to that normally associated with sleep.

Other effects of sensory deprivation include impairment in perceptual and cognitive functioning that is evident in performance on simple numerical or visual tasks (Heron, 1957). In addition, subjects often become irritable, easily amused or annoyed, and almost childish in their reactions to limited contact with experimenters. For example, they often attempt desperately to engage the experimenter in conversation, acting in much the same way a child does when trying to gain the attention of a preoccupied parent.

Among the most striking findings of sensory-deprivation studies is that subjects sometimes report experiencing illusions of various kinds—in some cases hallucinations—after prolonged isolation. These are relatively infrequent and are markedly affected by the subject's pre-isolation attitudes (Zubek, 1969).

These studies of sensory deprivation tend to add further support to arousal-based explanations of human behavior. There seems to be little question that behavior is more nearly optimal under conditions of moderate arousal. In addition, it seems that people try to maintain arousal at that level. For example, subjects in isolation often talk to themselves, whistle, recite poetry, or (as noted earlier) attempt to draw the experimenters into conversation. Such behavior led Schultz (1965) to hypothesize that the need for arousal is really a need for stimulation.

Sources of Arousal

One important source of high and low arousal is stimulation. But perhaps even more important for theories of motivation, it is the meaningfulness, the novelty, and the surprisingness of stimulation that increases arousal or fails to increase it (Berlyne, 1965, 1966). Much of people's exploratory behavior—that is, behavior designed to discover and learn things—stems from a need for stimulation, says Berlyne.

Arousal is also related to a variety of personal and cognitive factors. Geen (1984) reports evidence that **introverts** are often more highly aroused than **extroverts** by the same stimulation. Also, as Brehm and Self (1989) note, the more difficult and the more important a behavior is, the higher the arousal associated with it will be. Similarly, motivational arousal may be a function of the extent to which the actor assumes personal responsibility for the outcomes of behavior (versus the extent to which these are attributed to luck or other factors over which the person has no control). These are some of the things that cognitive theories of motivation look at.

Cognitive Theories of Motivation

Some early behavioristic theories, both in learning and in motivation, were characterized by what has been described as a mechanistic and passive view of the human organism (Bolles, 1975). In theories such as Hull's, for example, motives for behaving consist largely of the urge to reduce drives related to unsatisfied needs. Behavior is viewed as a question of responding to internal or external prods to which the individual reacts in a relatively helpless way.

In contrast, cognitive positions present a more active view of human behavior. Individuals are seen as actively exploring and manipulating, as predicting and evaluating the consequences of their behavior, and as acting on the environment rather than simply reacting to it.

We should note, however, that although some behavioristic positions do tend to see the individual as more reactive than active, many do not. Skinner, for example, also sees the organism as acting on the environment, as exploring and manipulating—in short, as emitting responses rather than simply responding blindly. Accordingly, a better contrast between behavioristic and cognitive approaches to motivation is that cognitive theories explain the effectiveness of environmental circumstances (such as rewards and punishments) in terms of the individual's understanding and interpretation. Behavioristic theorists see no need to resort to these cognitive events.

A Theory of Cognitive Dissonance

That individuals act on the basis of their information and beliefs seems clear, claims Festinger (1957, 1962), author of an intriguing cognitive theory of motivation known as the theory of **cognitive dissonance.** Simply stated, the theory holds that when a person simultaneously possesses two contradictory items of information (a situation that defines cognitive dissonance), that person will be motivated to reduce the contradiction.

In one study, Festinger (1962) subjected individual college students to an exhausting and boring 1-hour session that the students thought had to do with motor performance. After the session, each participant was told that the experiment was over, but each was then asked to help the experimenter with the next participant. The participants were told that it was important for the research that the incoming person believe the experiment would be interesting and pleasant. Each student agreed to lie to the next participant. As a result, says Festinger, the students would be expected to experience conflict (or dissonance) between their behavior and their beliefs.

Cognitive dissonance theory predicts that subjects will try to reduce the dissonance. One way of doing this would be to retract the lie, an impossibility under the circumstances. The alternative would be for subjects to change their private opinions—to modify their beliefs. As Petty, Wegener, and Fabrigar put it, "Dissonant behavior induces a general discomfort in people and attitude change can eliminate this discomfort" (1997, p. 619).

Festinger used two different treatments in this experiment. Although all subjects were paid to tell the lie, some were given $20 but others only received $1. The effect of this differential treatment was remarkable. The obvious prediction (and the one favored by bubba psychology, as discussed in Chapter 1) is that those paid the larger amount would be more likely to change their beliefs than would those paid the smaller amount. But the opposite was consistently true! Those who received small sums often became convinced that the hour session was really enjoyable; those who were paid the larger sum remained truer to their original beliefs.

Brehm and Cohen (1962) later corroborated these findings in a similar study in which they paid participants $10, $5, $1, or 50 cents for lying. As in the Festinger study, those subjects paid the smallest sum changed their opinions the most, whereas those paid $10 did not change appreciably. The explanation for these unexpected results is that the magnitude of dissonance brought about by a behavior contrary to one's beliefs will be directly proportional to the justification that exists for the act. Students paid $20 to lie have a better reason for doing so and will therefore feel less dissonance. These studies lead to the interesting observation that if criminals (thieves, for example) initially know that their behavior is immoral and if they are highly successful at their chosen vocation, they will be "better" people than if they are unsuccessful. If they make a lot of money by stealing, they are more likely to continue to believe that stealing is an immoral act.

Reducing Dissonance

Dissonance, explains Festinger (1962), can lead to uncomfortably high arousal. Several studies have shown significant increases in physiological measures of arousal accompanying dissonance (Zanna & Cooper, 2000; see also Franken, 2002). Dissonance is an important motivational concept because it provides an explanation for behaviors designed to reduce it. Festinger (1957), Brehm and Cohen (1962), and numerous experimental studies suggest a number of different ways in which this can be done (for example, Beauvois, 2001; Takaku, 2001; and Martinie & Joule, 2000).

1. Attitude Change One way of reducing dissonance, as the experiments just described illustrate, is to change beliefs (or attitudes). Consider the case of Sam Plotkin, who dislikes schoolteachers intensely but who, at a local dance, falls in love with Mary Rosie. When he discovers that Mary is a teacher, he is subjected to a great deal of dissonance, which will disappear when he decides either that he doesn't like Mary or that teachers really aren't that bad.

Cognitive dissonance theory is widely used in social psychology as a way of explaining how and why people change their attitudes. Schauss, Chase, and Hawkins (1997) suggest, for example, that therapists can deliberately manipulate individuals' beliefs and bring about important attitude changes by using cognitive dissonance. Similarly, Morwitz and Pluzinski (1996) show that advance voter polls can cause dissonance among voters when the polls present results

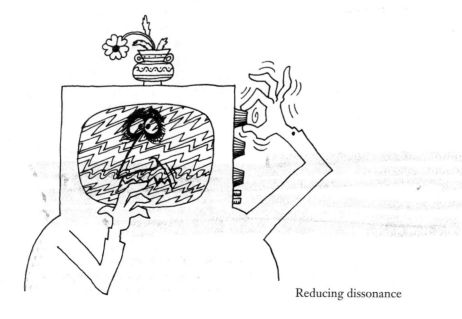

Reducing dissonance

that contradict their expectations, their preferences, or their beliefs. Such polls, these authors argue, can then lead to actual changes in voters' beliefs and, ultimately, in their voting behaviors.

2. Compartmentalization If Sam Plotkin, in love with Mary but negatively predisposed toward teachers, decides that Mary is really not like other teachers—that she is a different type of person, despite the fact that she teaches—what he is doing is placing her in a different "compartment." Compartmentalization, says Festinger (1962), is a fairly common dissonance reducer.

3. Exposure to or Recall of Information Sometimes when two items of information conflict, gaining more information can reduce the dissonance. If a rumor is circulated that wheat flour turns the human liver white, it will probably create some conflict in those who have been in the habit of eating food made with wheat flour. If a person were exposed to the information that white livers are really quite functional, the dissonance might disappear. Similarly, dissonance resulting from doing poorly on a test (a discrepancy between expectations and actual performance) would be greatly reduced if the student learned that all other students had done as poorly.

4. Behavioral Change Situations characterized by dissonance sometimes lead to changes in behavior. Tobacco smokers whose behavior is at odds with the information they have about the effects of smoking can stop smoking, thereby eliminating all dissonance.

5. Perceptual Distortion Quite frequently, however, smokers find it simpler to use other techniques for coping with this problem. For example, they might convince themselves that there is yet no conclusive proof that smoking is harmful, thus using a strategy of selective exposure to information, or perceptual distortion. To avoid dissonance, these smokers might simply insist that all that has been clearly demonstrated by numerous smoking-related studies on experimental animals is that *Rattus norvegicus* would do well to stay away from the weed.

Not surprisingly, when Gibbons, Eggleston, and Benthin (1997) looked at the attitudes of individuals who had stopped smoking but later started again, they found that these relapsers had significantly distorted their perception of the risks associated with smoking.

Summary of Dissonance Theory

Cognitive dissonance is the motivating state that occurs when an individual is in conflict. Ordinary sources of dissonance are incompatibilities between beliefs, between behavior and private opinion, or between two items of information. Dissonance theory holds that these states lead to behavior that is intended to reduce the conflict and reflects the amount of conflict that exists (Figure 10.6).

Collins and Hoyt (1972) argue that people will not feel dissonance unless they also feel personal responsibility for their behavior. In more current psychological jargon, cognitive dissonance is a direct function of the causes to which behavior is attributed.

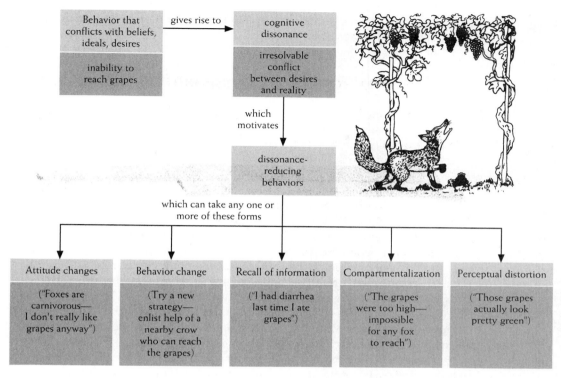

Figure 10.6 A model of cognitive dissonance. Everyone experiences conflicts between beliefs or desires and reality. This conflict can be arousing and disturbing and can serve as a motive for behavior designed to reduce it. There are many ways of trying to ease cognitive dissonance.

Intrinsic and Extrinsic Motives

Cognitive theorists insist that the urge to understand and explain to ourselves why we do things is fundamentally human. We need to be able to attribute our behavior to some recognizable cause.

Some causes of behavior seem clear. For example, we do many things for external goals and rewards, such as a steak or a hamburger or a twenty-dollar bill. These external rewards are closely tied to what are termed **extrinsic motives**. Extrinsic motives are what investigators use when they give rats and pigeons food rewards for their actions—and when they give students high marks and verbal praise for their behaviors. But praise isn't something that can be eaten like a candy to satisfy an urge—and then it's gone. Praise, and perhaps the candy too, might do more than simply satisfy a passing urge. Each might bring about the realization that one has done well, and each might lead to feelings of pride and satisfaction. These feelings, cognitive psychologists insist, can be extremely powerful **intrinsic motives**. In both business and education, where motivating people is tremendously important, appeal to intrinsic motives may be more important than appeal to external motives.

Can External Rewards Decrease Intrinsic Motivation

"When individuals are intrinsically motivated," explain Eccles and Wigfield, "they engage in an activity because they are interested in and enjoy the activity. When extrinsically motivated, individuals engage in activities for instrumental or other reasons, such as receiving a reward" (2002, p. 112). External rewards, such as money, are very powerful motives—witness the lengths to which many people will go to get some. But, caution Deci and Flaste, "While money is motivating people, it is also undermining their *intrinsic* motivation . . ." (1995, p. 27). As counterintuitive as this may seem, some studies seem to indicate just that. For example, Lepper and Greene (1975) gave two groups of children some geometric puzzles to solve. One group was told that they would be rewarded by being allowed to play with some toys; the other group had no reason to expect any reward. Subsequently, both groups were allowed to play with the toys. And both were later observed to see whether they would be sufficiently interested in the puzzles on which they had worked to play with them spontaneously. Surprisingly, as is shown in Figure 10.7, significantly more of those who had *not* expected a reward were motivated to play with the puzzles.

Lepper and Greene (1975) suggest that perhaps the most plausible explanation for this is a cognitive one. It's important for us to make sense of our behaviors, to understand why we do things. Typically, they explain, we resort to two types of explanations for our behaviors: intrinsic or extrinsic. In other words, we recognize that we do things for external rewards—such as money, or being allowed to play with a toy—or for internal rewards—such as because we are interested in them, because we enjoy the activity and derive personal satisfaction from it. Or, we do things for both internal and external motives.

When external motives are large, obvious, and expected, we are most likely to use these motives to explain our behaviors, notes Lepper (1981). That is, we are then most likely to be extrinsically motivated. But when we expect no significant external reward, we have to explain and justify our behavior with more intrinsic motives. Thus, those who expect no external reward subsequently display more intrinsic motivation—more interest—in the activity.

Self-Determination Theory

The finding that extrinsic rewards can undermine intrinsic motivation is not entirely clear. An analysis of 96 studies that examined the relationship between intrinsic and extrinsic motivation concluded that reinforcement doesn't lower intrinsic motivation (Cameron & Pierce, 1994). Perhaps, suggest Deci, Koestner, and Ryan (1999), that's because many behaviors that appear to be directed toward external rewards are a result of the individual's basic *internal needs*. Most important among these are the need to be competent and to be self-determining (autonomous). For example, explain Deci and Ryan (1985), the student who chooses

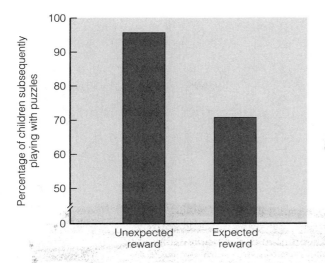

***Figure* 10.7**
Significantly more children who had not expected a reward showed higher intrinsic interest by subsequently playing spontaneously with the geometric puzzles. Based on data from M. R. Lepper and D. Greene (1975), "Turning Play into Work: Effects of Adult Surveillance and Extrinsic Rewards on Children's Intrinsic Motivation," *Journal of Personality and Social Psychology, 31,* 479–486.

a major *because* it will earn him a lot of money may seem to be guided entirely by extrinsic motives but, in fact, may be strongly influenced by the basic needs for self-determination and competence. Self-determined individuals—those who select their own activities freely and autonomously—are those who have *internalized* what might otherwise seem to be external reasons for behaving.

The single most important assumption of Deci and Ryan's (1985) **self-determination theory** of motivation is, as the label implies, that people need to be self-determining, to feel that they are in control of their own actions. By definition, to be intrinsically motivated, we need to be able to *attribute* the causes of our behavior to factors over which we have control (factors that are intrinsic), rather than to external causes.

Attribution Theory

This belief ties in directly with what is termed **attribution theory**—as, also, does cognitive dissonance theory, which is now usually reinterpreted through attribution theory (Westermann, 1989). To attribute in cognitive theory is to assign responsibility or to impute motives. If Rod attributes his stupidity to his parents, he is assigning them responsibility for that condition.

Rotter (1954) was among the first to suggest that people can be differentiated by their tendencies to ascribe their successes and failures to internal or external causes. In his words, there are people whose **locus of control** is external; others are more internally oriented. Those who are externally oriented, says Weiner (1986), tend to attribute their successes and failures to task difficulty, bad luck, good luck, or other factors over which they have no control. In contrast, internally oriented individuals are more likely to explain the outcome of their behavior in terms of their own ability and effort (see Figure 10.8).

	Internal (under personal control)	External (not under personal control)
Stable (do not change)	ability	difficulty
Unstable (change)	effort	luck

Figure 10.8
Attribution theory: explanations of success or failure (after Weiner, 1974).

Attribution and Dissonance

The relationship between attribution theory and dissonance is implicit in the observation that dissonance reflects how responsible the person feels for the outcomes of behavior. By definition, those who attribute outcomes to external causes do not accept personal responsibility for successes and failures. As a result, they are not subject to cognitive dissonance in the same way as are individuals who are more internally oriented. Similarly, those who are internally oriented are far more likely to feel pride when they succeed and shame when they fail. Thus, both dissonance and internal orientation are likely to be associated with emotion, and the motivating power of emotion is considerable. Albonetti and Hepburn (1996) suggest that drug offenders most likely to benefit from a treatment program are those who attribute their behavior to factors over which they have control—in other words, those who accept personal responsibility for their actions.

This cognitive view of motivation is based on the assumption that people continually evaluate their behaviors, look for reasons behind their successes and failures, anticipate the probable future outcomes of intended behaviors, and react emotionally to success and failure. And here is the key concept in attribution theory. It is not the attribution of behavior to one cause or the other that motivates behavior, says Weiner (1992); it is the emotions that occur as responses to specific attributions. The outcomes of attribution, he suggests, might be anger, guilt, gratefulness, or a variety of other emotions (see Figure 10.9). It seems logical that if the emotions are positive, subsequent behaviors will attempt to maintain the conditions that made the attribution possible.

Attribution and Achievement Goals

How people explain their successes and failures appears to be closely related to what psychologists call **need for achievement**—the individual's need to reach some standard of excellence. It seems that those with a high need to achieve are far more likely to attribute the outcomes of their behavior to internal causes. Thus, if they are successful, they are likely to attribute their success to effort (and perhaps to ability as well); if they are not successful, they continue to invoke internal factors, often blaming a lack of effort.

In contrast, individuals characterized by a lower need for achievement may attribute their success to ability, effort, ease of task, or luck, but they are most likely to attribute failure to lack of ability (Graham, 1997; Nathawat, Singh, &

Causal Attributions

	Internal		External	
	Effort	Ability	Others	Luck
Success	Relaxation	Confidence Competence	Gratitude	Surprise
Failure	Guilt (shame)	Incompetence	Anger	Surprise

Figure 10.9
Relations between causal attributions and feelings associated with success and failure.

Singh, 1997). These individuals have low estimates of their own abilities—low evaluations of what Bandura (1991) labels **self-efficacy**.

Self-Efficacy

Self-efficacy deals with the individual's assessments of personal effectiveness (Bandura, 1986, 1993; Evans, 1989). Those with high self-efficacy see themselves as capable, or effective, in dealing with the world and with other people. (See Chapter 11 for a biography of Albert Bandura.)

Importance of Self-Efficacy Judgments

Self-efficacy judgments are significant in determining what people do; hence, they are important as motives. As Schunk (1984) puts it, under most circumstances, people don't do things at which they expect to do very badly. "Efficacy beliefs," says Bandura, "influence how people feel, think, motivate themselves, and behave" (1993, p. 118). Not surprisingly, for example, Slanger and Rudestam (1997) found that level of self-efficacy was one of the variables that most clearly differentiated between high and low risk takers in sports such as kayaking, skiing, rock climbing, and stunt flying. Individuals with the highest judgments of self-efficacy—of personal power—are also those who are most likely to engage in activities that demonstrate the validity of their judgments.

Judgments of personal efficacy influence not only what people will do but also how much effort and time they will devote to a task, especially when they are faced with difficulties. The more Ann believes in herself (the higher her estimates of personal effectiveness), the more likely she will be to persist. In contrast, if she doesn't see herself as being very capable, she is more likely to become discouraged and to give up. This is why, note Zimmerman, Bandura, and Martinez-Pons, self-efficacy judgments are so important in school: "Numerous studies have shown that students with a high sense of academic efficacy display greater persistence, effort, and intrinsic interest in their academic learning and performance" (1992, p. 664). Furthermore, note Phillips and Gully (1997), on average, these are the students who set the highest goals and who achieve at the highest levels. And students characterized by the highest levels of academic self-efficacy also tend to display the highest levels of social self-efficacy (Patrick, Hicks, & Ryan, 1997). These students have the most realistic social goals and tend to be highly successful at forming close social relationships with peers and adults.

Self-efficacy is also a significant factor in the workplace. Harrison, Rainer, Hochwarter, and Thompson (1997) showed that those who have the most positive judgments of their personal competence (in other words, those with the highest notions of self-efficacy) are also those who are most likely to perform well. Notwithstanding the positive role that high self-efficacy plays in relation to goal setting and performance, it nevertheless appears to be true that under some circumstances, high self-efficacy judgments are associated with stubborn commitment to a losing effort. For example, Whyte, Saks, and Hook (1997) demonstrated that many students characterized by a firm conviction that they would succeed (marked by high self-efficacy) escalated their commitment to a failing course of action even beyond the point at which it should have become apparent they would fail. This reveals that although positive evaluations of competence are closely related to setting high goals and investing effort in attaining them, unrealistically high appraisals of one's competence might be associated with unrealistic goals and inappropriate persistence.

Sources of Efficacy Judgments

Why do some people typically have high judgments of personal efficacy, and others much less favorable judgments? The answer, suggests Bandura (1986), lies in the combined effects of four main sources of influence.

First are the effects of the individual's behavior, especially as they are reflected in success or failure. Other things being equal, people who are generally successful are likely to develop more positive evaluations of their personal effectiveness than are people who typically fail. As Weiner (1980) points out, however, people who attribute their successes and failures to factors over which they have no control (such as luck or task difficulty) are less likely to base judgments of personal efficacy on the outcomes of their behaviors. After all, it's not their fault the test was too hard or they studied the wrong sections.

A second influence is *vicarious* (secondhand): It is based on comparisons between the individual's performance and that of others. The most useful comparisons, Bandura (1981) notes, are those that involve potential equals. Thus, children who do better than their age-mates are likely to develop positive judgments of self-efficacy. That these same children might be blown away by somebody older or more experienced would be less relevant for judgments of self-efficacy.

Persuasion is a third type of influence on self-judgments. Those with lower self-confidence can sometimes be persuaded to do things they would not otherwise do. One of the possible effects of persuasion, Bandura (1986) argues, is that people will interpret it as evidence that others think them competent.

High arousal can also affect self-judgments, says Bandura, leading to either high or low estimates of capability depending on the situation and the person's previous experiences in situations of high arousal. For example, some athletes who are anxious before a competition view this emotion as helpful to their performance; for others, arousal may be interpreted as negative. These personal experiences in anxiety-producing situations may subsequently influence the extent and direction of the effects of arousal on self-judgments. Thus, an extreme fear of drowning might lead a person to decide he is incapable of some act like swimming across a river. In contrast, extreme fear might lead another

Table 10.1 *Four Sources of Information Related to Judgments of Self-Efficacy*

Sources of information	Examples of information that might lead Joan to arrive at positive estimates of her personal efficacy
Enactive	She receives an A in mathematics
Vicarious	She learns that Ronald studied hard but only got a B
Persuasory	Her teacher tells her she can probably win a scholarship if she tries
Emotive	She becomes mildly anxious before a test, but feels exhilarated afterward

person to decide that she is capable of swimming across the same river to save her son, who is marooned on the other side.

To summarize, Bandura's four sources of influence on judgments of self-efficacy are *enactive* (reflecting the results of the individual's own actions), *vicarious* (based on comparisons between self and others), *persuasory* (the result of persuasion), and *emotive* (reflecting arousal or emotion). Examples of each of these types of influence are shown in Table 10.1.

Efficacy and Expectancy-Value Theory

Our choices of actions, explain Eccles and Wigfield (2002), as well as our persistence and our performance, are strongly influenced by our expectancies for success (or failure) as well as by the values related to our various options. The interplay of these two variables—expectancy and value—define Eccles's **expectancy-value theory** of motivation.

In this theory, expectancy is defined in much the same way as Bandura defines self-efficacy: "individuals' beliefs about how well they will do on upcoming tasks, either in the immediate or longer-term future" (Eccles & Wigfield, 2002, p. 119). The *value* associated with a choice, on the other hand, reflects four distinct components: *attainment value, intrinsic value, utility value, and cost*.

Attainment value is the personal importance of the task to the individual. Among other things, attainment value reflects such things as how well an activity fits into an individual's plans, and how well it reflects the person's self-image. A person who sees herself as "good" and law-abiding is not likely to ascribe much value to the option of accompanying her cousin while he robs the local convenience store.

Intrinsic value refers to the personal satisfaction and enjoyment that the individual derives from an activity. As Deci notes, people tend to seek out challenging activities for which they have an expectation of success—a feeling of competence or of self-efficacy (Deci & Flaste, 1995). Such activities, he claims, tend to have high intrinsic value. That is, they are highly intrinsically motivating.

Utility value has to do with whether or not an activity fits in with present and future objectives. If Robert, whose goal is to be accepted in a doctoral program, is motivated to take a series of difficult summer courses in physics when he could be lounging about at the lake instead, his choice might well be because of the very high *utility value* of his chosen option.

Table 10.2 *Main Concepts in Eccles' Expectancy-Value Theory of Motivation*

Summary of Theory	Choice, persistence, and achievement are directly linked to the individual's expectancy- and task-related (value-related) beliefs
Expectancy	Personal beliefs about how well the individual is likely to do now and in the future
Value	Task-related beliefs that define the value associated with each option.

Components of Value Judgments

1. Attainment value	Personal importance of doing well; does the option fit in with self-image?
2. Intrinsic value	How enjoyable and personally satisfying is the option?
3. Utility value	How well does each option fit in with immediate and future goals?
4. Cost	How much effort is required? How stressful will each option be? What am I giving up?

Cost of an option, a very critical factor in determining an individual's choices, has to do with the various *negative* possibilities associated with a task. These include such things as the probability of failure, stress and anxiety associated with the task, effort required, other conflicting options, and so on.

In summary, expectancy-value theory is a cognitive approach to motivation that holds that humans make choices based on a sort of mental calculus where the most important factors are expectancy of success and competence on the one hand (feelings of self-efficacy, in other words), and the values associated with the various options (their personal importance; how they fit into plans, goals, and self image; their intrinsic value; and the cost associated with each option in terms of effort, loss of other opportunities, stress, etc.). (See Table 10.2.)

Educational and Other Applications of Motivation Theory

Knowledge about why people behave the way they do can greatly facilitate the psychologist's task of predicting what a person will do in a given situation and of controlling behavior (when it isn't unethical to do so).

Predicting Behavior

Normal social interaction depends largely on being able to predict many of the ordinary activities of others. If these activities were not at least partly predictable, social relations would be chaotic and confusing. When Jack meets his grandmother and says, "Hello," he expects that she will return either the same greeting (or some other appropriate greeting) or that, at worst, she will ignore him. He would be understandably surprised if, instead of responding as expected, she chose to kick him in the shins, run away, faint, or curse in some foreign language.

Controlling and Changing Behavior

Knowledge about motivation has important implications for the control of behavior—a subject that has led to considerable debate among psychologists. Should behavior be controlled? How should it be controlled? Who should control it, and to what end? In short, what are the ethics of behavior control (see Rogers & Skinner, 1956)?

Despite the somewhat appealing humanistic arguments against behavior control, deliberate behavior control is not only a reality but in many cases highly desirable—as a parent whose young child has recently been toilet trained would quickly admit. Toilet training is just one of many behaviors that involve systematic and deliberate attempts to modify behavior.

Motivation plays a key role in changing and controlling behavior. For example, toilet training a child might involve manipulating goals (for example, getting little Sammy to view cleanliness as a desirable condition). In addition, rewards and punishments, which also relate to motivation (and to learning), can be employed. Cognitive dissonance also may be implicated in toilet training: Children who think being clean is desirable may feel considerable dissonance when they have what is euphemistically referred to as "an accident."

Motivation in the Classroom

Motivation theory is highly relevant for teachers, whose function is largely one of changing the motivation and the behavior of students (recall that learning is defined as relatively permanent changes in behavior). It's important that teachers know something about the individual needs and goals of students, about the effects of cognitive dissonance, about the role of arousal in learning and behavior, and about the cognitive factors involved in decision making.

Needs and Psychological Hedonism

Theories based on a recognition of the importance of needs and on the human tendency to seek pleasant outcomes and avoid those less pleasant have obvious instructional implications. It's clear, for example, that basic physiological needs such as the need for food and for drink, need to be reasonably well satisfied if learning is to be optimized. It's less obvious, but no less true that children's psychological needs—for example, the growth needs described by Maslow—also need to be attended to.

As we saw in Chapter 4, the judicious use of rewards (praise, marks, etc.) and perhaps of punishments (loss of privileges, use of noxious stimuli) can also play an important role in the teacher's direction of learning and motivation.

Arousal

The role of arousal in behavior can also be crucial for teaching. Recall that it is the combined novelty, intensity, and meaningfulness of stimuli that most affect level of arousal. Teachers are one of the most important sources of arousal-inducing stimulation for students. The impact of what teachers say and do and how they say and do it is instrumental in determining whether students are either bored or sleeping (low arousal) or attentive (higher arousal). This observation leads directly to an argument for meaningfulness, variety, and intensity in classroom presentations.

Cognitive Dissonance

Cognitive dissonance is one possible source of arousal. Motivation theory suggests that students who are experiencing cognitive dissonance will attempt to reduce the dissonance—and, consequently, to reduce the accompanying arousal. For example, dissonance may occur when students become aware of a discrepancy between their behavior and what a teacher or some other important model (such as a book) describes as being ideal. Such dissonance may well lead students to try to become more like the teacher's description of the ideal. As we saw, dissonance can be reduced in a variety of ways including behavior change, attitude change, or exposure to new information. Teachers can clearly play an important role in setting up dissonant situations to motivate students and in helping them find ways to reduce the dissonance.

Intrinsic and Extrinsic Attributions

The tendency to attribute success and failure to internal or external causes may be a relatively stable personality characteristic, says Dweck (1986). Children who are most likely to make internal attributions—that is, to take personal responsibility for their successes and failures, are also the children who are most likely to strive toward increasing their competence. Externally oriented children are less willing to accept challenges and less likely to strive to improve their competence. One of the objectives of schools, and teachers, is to make children more internally oriented—more *intrinsically* motivated. In this connection, recall that the excessive use of external rewards can sometimes appear to have a detrimental effect on internal motivation. Ames (1992) suggests that teachers need to take pains to make sure that students perceive classrooms as being oriented toward mastery (rather than simply toward performance), and to arrange learning experiences so that all students can develop a sense of personal competence and self-efficacy. Among other things, Ames suggests that teachers present students with a variety of short-term goals that are challenging but that can be accomplished with reasonable effort, that an effort be made to ensure that school work is personally involving, that teachers focus on the processes of learning rather than on its outcomes, that individual progress be emphasized, and that comparisons with other students be minimized.

Self-Determination, Self-Efficacy, and Expectancy-Value Theory

People need to be self-determining, explain Deci and Ryan (1985). They need to feel a sense of autonomy and of personal competence. Defined in other terms, personal competence translates into personal estimates of self-efficacy.

It is worth repeating that judgments of self-efficacy are powerful motivators—they profoundly influence a person's thoughts and emotions. Those who have low judgments of self-efficacy are also likely to feel poorly about themselves, to attempt fewer difficult tasks, and ultimately, to be less successful. Our choices, according to Eccles and associates' expectancy-value theory, are the result of a mental calculation in which we consider our expectancies of success or failure (or judgments of self-efficacy) and weigh these expectancies against our personal judgments of the value of the options we contemplate.

Teachers play a crucial role in providing children with the sorts of experiences that contribute to positive judgments of self-efficacy. Teachers can also play an important role in determining student goals and self-image, important factors in how students judge the value of different outcomes and the potential cost of the efforts required to reach these outcomes.

Summary

1. A motive is a conscious or unconscious force that incites a person to act. Psychological theories of motivation deal with both the reasons and the causes of behavior.

2. Reflexes are simple, unlearned, stimulus-specific responses that explain some elementary human behavior. The orienting reflex (OR) is the general reflexive response an organism makes to novel stimuli; it involves some physiological changes that are related to arousal. Instincts are more complex unlearned patterns of behavior that are more relevant for animal than for human behavior. Imprinting is a complex, instinct-like pattern of behavior manifested following exposure to an appropriate stimulus during a critical period.

3. Psychological hedonism is an expression of the pain/pleasure principle—the notion that people act to avoid pain and to obtain or maintain pleasure. Physiological needs are states of deficiency or lack that give rise to drives, which in turn impel the organism toward activities that will reduce the needs. Psychological needs are sometimes described as learned needs.

4. Maslow, a humanistic psychologist, describes a hierarchy of needs that includes both basic or deficiency needs (physiological, safety, belongingness, and self-esteem) and meta- or growth needs (cognitive, aesthetic, and self-actualizing). Self-actualization is more a process (of developing the highest levels of potential of humanness possible) rather than a state that can be reached.

5. An incentive is basically the value that an activity or goal has for an individual. It is a more cognitive concept than is need or drive.

6. Arousal refers to the degree of alertness of an organism. Its relation to motivation is implicit in the assumption that too-low or too-high arousal is related to less optimal behavior than is a more moderate level of activation (the Yerkes-Dodson law).

7. Hebb's theory of motivation centers on the assumption that there is an optimum level of arousal for maximally effective behavior and that people will behave to maintain that level. Hence, stimuli have both cue (message) and arousal functions. Studies of sensory deprivation support the belief that humans need a variety of sensory stimulation.

8. Cognitive theories present a more active view of the human organism than do

traditional behavioristic theories. One such theory, cognitive dissonance, assumes that conflict among beliefs, behavior, and expectations leads to behavior designed to reduce the conflict (for example, attitude change, compartmentalization, acquisition or recall of information, behavioral change, or perceptual distortion).

9. Extrinsic motives relate to external rewards; intrinsic motives have to do with personal satisfaction and interest in an activity. Some evidence indicates that excessive reliance on external rewards might undermine intrinsic motivation.

10. Self-determination theory is premised on the assumption that individuals have a need for personal autonomy—that is, a need to be responsible for their own actions (to be intrinsically motivated).

11. Attribution theory attempts to explain how individuals assign responsibility for the outcomes of their behaviors. Internally oriented individuals frequently ascribe success or failure to ability or effort; externally oriented individuals are more likely to blame success or failure on luck or on the task being very easy or very difficult. Internally oriented individuals are often characterized by higher need for achievement.

12. Self-efficacy judgments have to do with personal estimates of competence and effectiveness. High evaluations of efficacy are associated with persistence, achievement, and positive self-concepts. They are influenced by the outcomes of behavior, comparisons with others, persuasion, and arousal.

13. Expectancy-value theory is a cognitive motivational theory that describes some of the variables that are considered in the mental calculus that leads to choice among options: specifically, expectations of success or failure (self-efficacy) factored in with the value of each of the options (for attainment value, intrinsic value, utility value, and cost).

14. Knowledge about human motivation is important for predicting behavior, for controlling it, and for changing it. In a practical sense, it is especially important for teachers.

Social Learning: Bandura's Social Cognitive Theory

Children are more in need of models than of critics.
Anonymous

When I arrived at the bush cabin, the Old Woman said to come in and sit down; she wanted to show me something. She acts very much like the cabin is hers and I'm only a guest, although I'm the one who built it and it's really mine. So I went in and pulled a chair up close to the table. I could smell the pot of beans the Old Woman had just taken from the oven, and on the table were two loaves of her freshly baked bread. I was suddenly very hungry. But the Old Woman said no, not to sit at the table, motioning that I should sit on one of the bunks instead. Then she took a plate and heaped it with beans, and cut a thick slab of bread, which she buttered very slowly. I thought she would now offer me the plate, although I found it curious that she had bothered to butter my bread. But no, she offered me nothing. Instead, she sat at the table and began to devour her beans, scooping them into her mouth as fast as she could with both hands, stopping now and again to stuff a chunk of bread into her cheeks until they bulged grotesquely on either side of her wrinkled face. When the plate was half empty, she buried her face directly into it, slurping up great mouthfuls of beans, making all sorts of grunting and snorting noises. When the last of the beans was gone, she licked the plate clean. Then, holding her nose firmly between thumb and forefinger, she blew it forcefully into the plate. Now she motioned that I should turn on the recorder, that she was ready to start the next chapter.

This Chapter

You're shocked and disgusted aren't you, said the Old Woman as she wiped her nose with the back of her hand, bean juices dripping from her chin and eyebrows. But she said I shouldn't be shocked, that the way she had just eaten would seem perfectly normal and exquisitely polite to the people in some Amazonian tribes she knew. She said you would understand this more clearly once she had finished with this, the eleventh chapter.

Objectives

Tell your readers, said the Old Woman, that once they have finished this chapter, they will have a stunningly clear understanding of

- *What social learning is*
- *How imitation works*
- *The three effects of modeling*

- *The various systems that control human behavior*
- *The importance of a sense of personal power and effectiveness*
- *One reason why different cultures continue to be identifiably different*

In addition, she said, tell your students that they will have a keener appreciation for the significance of will and intention in their

lives. Too, they will understand why rich corporations gladly pay "stars" obscene sums of money to endorse their products.

Social Learning

Psychologists often use the phrase **social learning** without defining it, as though everybody already knew what it meant. But, actually, the phrase can be used in at least two distinct senses.

Social learning can mean all learning that occurs as a result of social interaction or that in some way involves social interaction (Salomon & Perkins, 1998). Or it can mean the sort of learning involved in finding out which behaviors are socially expected and acceptable in social situations. Put another way, the phrase *social learning* might refer to the *process* by which we learn (specifically, a process that involves social interaction) or to the *product* of learning (that is, the learning of socially appropriate behaviors).

The Product of Social Learning

The product of social learning is knowledge of what is socially acceptable. Through a process of social learning children learn that it is acceptable to ask a parent or a grandparent to take them to the store and buy them purple gumdrops—and that it is unacceptable to make the same request of a stranger. It is also through a lengthy process of **socialization** that humans learn how to eat a plateful of beans—among a great variety of other social behaviors. They also learn that acceptable behaviors can vary from culture to culture and that they can be very different for different ages and sexes. For example, in some Asian countries, it's quite acceptable—perhaps even expected—for students to bow to their professors and perhaps even to offer them small gifts. In contrast, in North America, few students feel inclined to bow to their professors or to offer them gifts. To do so might indicate lack of social intelligence.

In the same way as socially accepted behaviors can vary among cultures, so too might they vary for different ages and sexes. For example, whereas adults freely call each other by their first names, young children are seldom expected to do the same. For 8-year-old Charles to call his grandmother *Rhonda* might be taken as a sign of lack of respect (or of exceptional precocity—or of an especially advanced sense of humor).

One of the most important tasks of child rearing is to *socialize* youngsters—that is, to teach them socially appropriate behaviors. A society's chief socializing agencies are its major cultural institutions: family, school, church, playground, communication media, and so on. These institutions transmit to children the **mores,** customs, values, habits, beliefs, and other trappings that define human cultures.

Albert Bandura (1925–)

Albert Bandura was born in a small farming community about 50 miles from Edmonton, Alberta. Later he moved to the southern coastal area of British Columbia, where he did his undergraduate work at the University of British Columbia (UBC), graduating in 1949.

"What influenced you to become a psychologist?" Evans asked Bandura. "I have come to the view," he replied, "that some of the most important determinants of career and life paths often occur through the most trivial of circumstances" (Evans, 1989, p. 3). He went on to explain how, because he commuted to the university with a group of premed and engineering students who had to go in very early, he took a psychology course simply to fill a gap in his schedule. The subject fascinated him and, three years after graduating from UBC, Bandura obtained his Ph.D. in clinical psychology from Iowa State University. A year later, he joined the faculty at Stanford University, eventually becoming a professor and department chair.

Bandura's early writings and theorizing stemmed from the predominant theories of the day: Skinnerian and Hullian forms of behaviorism. But even at the dawn of his career, he had already begun to break away from the behaviorists' rejection of the importance of thoughts and intentions. Bandura's approach was more socially oriented; he looked at how people influence each other and at how social behaviors are acquired through imitation. His approach was also more cognitive, assigning an increasingly important role to the human ability to anticipate the consequences of behavior.

In the end, this is a social cognitive theory of human behavior, summarized in his aptly titled *Social Foundations of Thought and Action: A Social Cognitive Theory* (1986).

Bandura has received numerous state and national awards and honors, and has served a term as president of the American Psychological Association.

The Processes of Social Learning

Given the importance and prevalence of social behavior, a fundamentally important learning-theory question is, How do children, and adults, learn socially appropriate behavior?

The answer that has become almost synonymous with the phrase *social learning* is based on Albert Bandura's theory of social learning through **imitation,** also termed **observational learning.** Bandura's theory was partially derived from Miller and Dollard's (1941) theory. The original Miller and Dollard theory was a highly behavioristic approach that closely followed Hull's notions of drive reduction. Basically, the theory argued that behavior occurs as a response to specific drives (such as hunger). These drives are linked to stimuli (such as internal feelings of hunger). Reducing the drive gets rid of the stimulus; this is reinforcing and leads to learning.

The problem with a drive reduction theory, as we saw in Chapter 10, is that both humans and nonhuman organisms engage in many behaviors that don't seem to be directed toward eliminating or reducing stimulation. For example, recall the Hebb sensory deprivation studies in which participants actively seek stimulation when they became bored.

What Bandura did is modify Miller and Dollard's theory of imitation by getting rid of the Hullian drive-reduction component. Bandura's early theorizing was initially based squarely on B. F. Skinner's theory of operant conditioning (Bandura & Walters, 1963) and then later expanded as Bandura came to recognize the importance of cognitive activities such as imagining and anticipating (Bandura, 1977, 1986, 2001). The theory is now commonly referred to as a *social cognitive theory.*

Ⓜain Ideas Behind Bandura's Social Cognitive Theory

We learn a great deal through operant conditioning, explained Bandura early in the development of his theory (Bandura & Walters, 1963). But in many ways, operant learning by itself can be a highly inefficient, even ineffective, way of learning. Imagine if all we could do is wait for a socially desirable behavior to be emitted as an operant, and then hope that subsequent circumstances might prove reinforcing. Take, for example, the simple social behavior of learning how to shake hands. How likely is it that young Peter will spontaneously emit the "hand shaking" operant one day, under the appropriate circumstances, to be sure, and that someone will immediately reinforce him? Or consider the problem of learning how to drive a car. How reasonable is it to expect that if Sheila is given a set of keys and a car, she will quickly learn to drive simply as a result of, by chance, emitting the right sequence of operants—and being reinforced for these operants before running up against the side of the house?

Actually, it would be difficult to learn how and when to shake hands, or how to drive, if the completely inexperienced learner were required to emit spontaneously the appropriate series of responses without any sort of guidance. But the point is that there are very few completely inexperienced would-be hand shakers or car drivers. Almost all youngsters have seen their parents and others shaking hands and driving. Many will even have read instruction booklets describing rules of the road, and they will have listened to peers and siblings talk about how you start and drive cars. In Bandura's terms, they have been exposed to many different **models.**

Much of our learning, says Bandura, involves models. It's called observational learning (or learning through imitation). It results from imitating models. Learning through imitation, says Bandura, is really a form of operant learning.

That's because an imitative behavior is much like an operant; it's not a response to a specific stimulus (as is the case for a *respondent*) but, rather, an emitted response. And imitative behaviors, as we see shortly, are often reinforced, and therefore become learned.

Models

Although there is a tendency to think of models as people whose behavior is copied by others, models are better defined as *any representation of a pattern for behaving.* Thus, although a model may be an actual (perhaps very ordinary) person whose behavior serves as a guide, a blueprint, or an inspiration for somebody else, many models are symbolic. **Symbolic models** include the great variety of models that are represented by things such as oral or written instructions, pictures, book characters, mental images, cartoon or film characters, television actors, and so on. Symbolic models also include computer-based models, many of which are used for various kinds of training programs, such as pilot training with computer-controlled simulators (Shebilske, Jordan, Goettle, & Paulus, 1998).

Often, models aren't examples of highly advanced skills and competencies such as might be displayed by older people or by experts. Even 2- and 3-year-olds imitate and learn from each other, explain Abravanel and Ferguson (1998). In contrast, Lindberg, Kelland, and Nicol (1999) report a fascinating study in which horses *did not* learn to open a feed bin as a result of watching other "model" horses who already knew how to open the bin! If nobody had opened the bin for them, they would have starved.

The Processes of Observational Learning

Observational learning, explains Bandura, is clearly based on the principles of operant conditioning. But perhaps even more important, the theory recognizes the tremendous significance of our ability to anticipate the consequences of our behaviors, to symbolize, to figure out cause-and-effect relationships. The power of models has to do mainly with their *informative* function. Models *inform* us not only about how to do certain things, but also about what the consequences of our behaviors are likely to be. Accordingly, four distinct processes are involved in observational learning.

Attentional Processes
To begin with, we have to pay attention. We learn very little from observing behaviors that have little value for us, and to which we therefore pay little attention. Thus, 30-year-old Robert may have seen his mother making him crepes for breakfast a thousand times. But if he were asked to make his own crepes, he might well be at a complete loss. Despite the inordinately high value he places on eating crepes with wild chokecherry syrup, his mother's crepe-making behavior is of such little value to him that he has learned virtually nothing from observing her these countless times.

Whether or not we attend to a potential model's behavior, Bandura informs us, depends very much on the value of the model's behavior. (Is it important for the observer to be able to roll a cigarette like that? Make such delicate crepes? Throw a horseshoe in that way? Catch a rabbit in a cage?)

Whether or not we pay attention also depends on how distinctive, how complex, how prevalent, and how useful a behavior is. We are less likely to attend to behaviors that are highly common and not very distinctive, or that occur only rarely or that are complex and difficult to perform. Not surprisingly, the most effective models—those that command the greatest attention—are those that are most attractive, most trustworthy, and most powerful (in social power, which can come from knowledge, money, or prestige) (Brewer & Wann, 1998). That's one of the reasons why actors and sports stars can be such effective models.[1]

Retentional Processes

To learn from a model, the observer needs to pay attention and must be able to remember what is observed. This, explains Bandura, might involve one of two different types of representation: visual or verbal. For example, much of what an observer sees can be described in words (verbal representation). Thus, a novice driver learning how to operate a standard shift vehicle might well be able to verbalize the required sequence of actions—depress clutch, place gear shift into first gear, slowly release clutch while applying pressure to the accelerator, and so on. But an aspiring athlete watching an Olympic performer might represent, and retain, the behavior to be imitated as a series of visual images rather than as a series of words.

Motor Reproduction Processes

Imitating requires transforming imagined (visually or verbally represented) actions into actual behaviors. Doing so may well call for certain motor and physical capabilities, or perhaps some verbal and intellectual capacities. In addition, successful imitation implies the ability to monitor and correct performance. For example, a coach might repeatedly demonstrate how to cut in from the wing in ice hockey, or how to lay up for a slam in basketball, but it will all be to no avail if the observer lacks the combination of well-practiced physical skills required for successfully imitating the coach. Similarly, if the athlete remains unaware of how poorly she skates, or of how she cannot jump high enough to reach the basket—in other words, if she cannot monitor and correct her performance— she is unlikely to be able to imitate successfully.

Motivational Processes

Finally, the observer has to be *motivated*. Motives, as we saw in Chapter 10, are the reasons and causes of behavior. When Robert's mother announced that, because

---

[1]That's why corporations gladly pay them such ridiculous sums of money to wear their logos and pretend they eat their potato chips, said the Old Woman somewhat testily, adding that nobody was paying her a dang thing to wear her jacket. Actually, it was my jacket, the one with the Coca Cola™ crest on it. They don't pay me to wear it either.

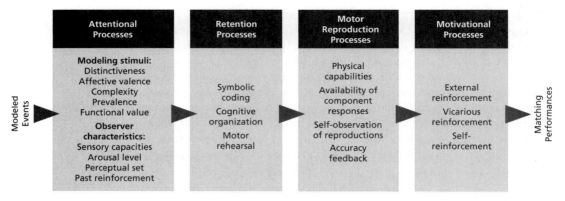

Figure 11.1 The four processes involved in observational learning. From A. Bandura, *Social Learning Theory*, © 1977, p. 23. Reprinted by permission of Pearson Education, Inc., Upper Saddle River, NJ.

he refused to leave the house, *she* would be moving out, he suddenly had an important reason for learning how to make his own crepes. This newfound motivation became apparent when he now learned to make crepes after observing his mother only one or two more mornings. (See Figure 11.1 for a summary of the four processes involved in observational learning.)

Imitation and Operant Conditioning

Simply put, Skinner's model of operant conditioning describes learning as an increase in the probability of occurrence of an operant (emitted response) as a function of reinforcement. Bandura's theory of social learning assumes that imitation is a type of emitted behavior that occurs as a function of observing a model, and that is reinforced. Hence, imitative behaviors are learned in the same way as any operant.

Imitative behaviors, explains Bandura, are extremely common. Similarities in the ways people dress, eat, walk, and talk and differences between cultures are testimony to the prevalence and the power of imitation. Imitation ranks high as an explanation for social learning because it provides a good explanation for complex learning. Skills such as learning to fly a plane can't easily be acquired solely through contiguity or trial and error; they require the presentation of models (usually other pilots, as well as verbal and written instructions). Similarly, children would probably never learn to speak if they had to do so through trial and error, without benefit of the models that are presented by other speaking humans. Also, as we saw earlier, it seems clear that people learn what is acceptable and unacceptable in matters of speech, dress, and behavior largely by observing the models presented by others.

Sources of Reinforcement in Imitation

The relationship between operant conditioning and observational learning can be expressed simply: An imitative behavior is, in effect, an operant; accordingly, when imitative behaviors result in positive contingencies or in the removal or prevention of aversive contingencies, they become more probable (Masia & Chase, 1997).

There are two main potential sources of reinforcement for the observer in observational learning, claim Bandura and Walters (1963). In addition, the model, too, might be reinforced.

First, imitated behaviors are often subject to **direct reinforcement,** when their consequences lead directly to reinforcement. For example, an imitator is often reinforced directly by the model whose behavior is being copied. Proud parents are quick to praise their children for behaviors that resemble those of Daddy or Mommy. Even grandmothers are occasionally heard saying, "Look at little Norbert standing there with his finger in his nose, just like his daddy."

A second source of direct reinforcement has to do with the actual consequences of the imitated behavior. If the activity is socially acceptable or leads to the obtaining of reward, it is often reinforced by its own consequences. A child who learns to say "milk" as a result of hearing her mother say the word 40 times a day for 18 months, may actually get milk as a result of saying the word.

Second, in addition to the possibility of direct reinforcement, the observer in a modeling situation often appears to be influenced by what Bandura (1969) calls **vicarious reinforcement.** This is a type of secondhand reinforcement in which the imitator is not actually reinforced directly. It's as though the observer assumes that if the model does this or that, then this or that must be reinforcing. Therefore, in the imitator's unconscious logic, a similar sort of reinforcement is expected for the imitator.

Another source of reinforcement for imitative behavior, which affects the model rather than the observer, is based on the supposition that simply being imitated may be reinforcing. Thus, entertainers who wear bizarre clothes or hairstyles and are subsequently imitated by their fans may be more likely to persist with their unusual tastes.

Classical Conditioning in Observational Learning

Imitative behavior, as we saw, is typically an operant response whose probability increases or decreases because of the reinforcement contingencies associated with it. Hence, operant conditioning is clearly involved in this kind of learning.

As Powell, Symbaluk, and Macdonald (2002) point out, classical conditioning is also implicated in learning through imitation. Specifically, many of the *emotional responses* associated with models are acquired through classical conditioning. If you see a group of your cohorts laughing uproariously, clearly having a wonderful time, it's likely that their manifestations of fun and happiness will trigger similar emotions in you. Why? Simply because hearing people laugh and seeing them smile has been repeatedly paired with your own emotional reactions of joy, beginning right in infancy. As a result, other people's joyful behavior now serves as a conditioned stimulus (CS) for your own conditioned response (CR) of joy.

Not all **conditioned emotional reactions (CERs)** are positive. Many social behaviors and gestures, such as cries, tears, frowns, raised eyebrows, head shakes, and finger wags, are conditioned stimuli for powerful negative CERs. These behaviors have been linked with negative emotions often enough that, through classical conditioning, they readily elicit negative emotions in observers.

Conditioned emotional reactions may have a profound influence on the likelihood that a model will be imitated. If you witness Edward being punished for climbing on the roof, the CERs that you experience may discourage you from imitating his roof-climbing behavior. But if, instead, Edward clearly has a wonderful time on the roof and, furthermore, Cindy smiles at him and praises him for his courage, you might well find yourself trying to imitate him.[2]

Three Effects of Models

In advanced technological societies, explains Bandura, symbolic models such as those presented by television, books, verbal directions, and the like, are extremely important. In fact, explains Bandura, one problem with older theories of learning is that "most of them were cast long before this tremendous technological revolution in communications. . . . These theories do not encompass the tremendous power of the symbolic environment" (Evans, 1989, p. 6).

Through observational learning, children (and adults) learn three different classes of responses, which Bandura and Walters (1963) describe as the three effects of imitation. These are described here and summarized in Table 11.1.

The Modeling Effect

When observers learn through imitation something that is new for them, they are said to model. Hence, the **modeling effect** involves the acquisition of novel responses. When grandmothers describe how their grandchildren acquire undesirable habits from the neighbor's undisciplined ruffians—habits that are clearly novel, because the grandchildren never did such things previously—they are describing the modeling effect.

The classical experimental illustrations of the modeling effect are Bandura and Walters's (1963) often-replicated experiments on aggression in young children. In these experiments, participants are exposed to filmed, actual, or cartoon models of other children or of adults engaging in novel aggressive behavior with a large, inflated, plastic "Bobo" clown. Occasionally, the model is verbally aggressive; at other times he or she strikes the clown (with fist, foot, or mallet), sits on it, scratches it, or otherwise attacks it. Subjects are later exposed to the

---

[2]"Remember the car," the Old Woman said, interrupting her reading and pulling out the magazine ad she had shown me many weeks ago, the one with the model lounging over a car. I was puzzled that she still had it. "If we measured changes in your blood pressure and your heart rate and perspiration, and all that," she said, "we'd find that you had a CER when you looked at this ad. And that's exactly what the advertisers were shooting for." And then, although I know she doesn't smoke—at least not much—she pulled out a pack of cigarettes, one of those with the Surgeon General's dire warnings printed on the side, along with a picture of a cancerous lung. "Now here," she said, "is a different kind of CER. But it's the same learning principle."

Table 11.1 Three Effects of Imitation, Bandura's Theory

Type of Effect	Description	Illustration
Modeling Effect	Acquiring a new behavior as a result of observing a model.	After watching a martial arts television program, Robert tries out a few novel moves on his young sister, Jenna.
Inhibitory-Disinhibitory Effect	Stopping or starting some deviant behavior after seeing a model punished or rewarded for similar behavior.	After watching Robert, Dick, who already knew all of Robert's moves but hadn't used them in a long time, now tries a few of them on the family cat (*disinhibitory effect*).
		Dick abandons his pummeling of the cat when Jenna's mother responds to her wailing and soundly punishes Robert (*inhibitory effect*).
Eliciting Effect	Engaging in behavior related to that of a model.	Robin starts piano lessons after her cousin receives a standing ovation for singing at the family reunion.

same clown, and their reactions are noted. Frequently these reactions take the form of precisely imitative aggressive responses. When the responses are clearly new for the child, modeling is assumed to have occurred.[3]

Inhibitory and Disinhibitory Effects

Imitation sometimes leads not to the learning of novel responses but, rather, to the suppression or disinhibition of previously learned deviant behavior. Inhibition and disinhibition usually occur as a result of seeing a model punished or rewarded for doing something deviant. For example, a group of thieves may stop stealing after a member of the group is apprehended and punished (the **inhibitory effect**). Conversely, the same group may have begun stealing as a result of seeing a member become wealthy through stealing (the **disinhibitory effect**). The disinhibitory effect involves engaging in a previously inhibited deviant behavior as a result of observing a model. The inhibitory effect involves refraining from a deviant behavior.

A striking illustration of the power of models in disinhibiting deviant behavior is found in some classic punishment studies (Walters & Llewellyn, 1963; Walters, Llewellyn, & Acker, 1962). In these studies, subjects were asked to

---

[3]I have another example of modeling for your keen-brained students, said the Old Woman, indicating that this was not to be recorded. She said it's an example described by Bandura. It involves the film *The Doomsday Flight*, in which an altitude-sensitive bomb is used in an attempt to extort money from an airline. Bandura wrote to the Federal Aviation Administration to find out about extortion attempts before and after airings of this film. As he expected, these attempts went up dramatically, often on the day following an airing. What is perhaps most striking is that many of these attempted extortions involved very precise modeling, including the use of allegedly altitude-sensitive bombs designed to explode at an altitude below 5,000 feet. One would-be extortionist out of Montreal on a London-bound flight was foiled when the airline decided to land in Denver (altitude 5,300 feet) instead. But in Alaska, an extortionist received $25,000; in Australia, another succeeded in getting $560,000 from Qantas Airlines (Evans, 1989).

volunteer for what was described as an experiment in memory. They were then shown one of two short sequences of film: a violent episode from *Rebel Without a Cause* or an excerpt from a film showing adolescents engaged in artwork. Afterward, subjects were asked to help the experimenter with another study designed to investigate the effects of punishment on problem-solving behavior.

Now another male student, who posed as a subject but who was in reality a confederate of the experimenter, sat at a panel working out problems and signaling his answers by pressing a switch. Whenever he answered correctly, a green light would flash on a second panel; when he was incorrect, a red light would go on. This second panel also contained 15 toggle switches labeled 15 volts, 30 volts, 45 volts, and so on. The switches appeared to be connected to the electrodes fastened to the impostor subject's wrists. The actual subject was instructed to administer punishment in the form of an electric shock every time the imposter subject made an error (after he himself had been administered a mild shock to ensure that he realized what he was doing).

Results of this study indicated that exposure to films with violent content significantly increased the intensity of shocks subjects were willing to give (the confederates weren't actually given shocks, because one electrode was always disconnected). This and related studies have often been cited as evidence of the potentially harmful effects of televised violence—about which final conclusions are still tentative, although it now seems likely that television violence does contribute to aggressive behavior. Schneider (1996) notes that a preponderance of the evidence demonstrates a strong connection between violence in the media and actual violence in relation to the treatment of women, pornography, suicide, terrorism, gang delinquency, and "copy-cat" crimes of all sorts.

The Eliciting Effect

A third manifestation of the influence of models on human behavior, the **eliciting effect,** involves eliciting responses that, instead of matching the model's behavior precisely, are simply related to it. In a sense, it's as though the model's behavior encourages similar behavior in the observer. For example, a brother's being praised for winning athletic competitions might encourage another brother to try to excel academically. Similarly, the tastes and the fashions of television and movie heroes might influence the tastes and fashions of their admirers. The eliciting effect, explains Bandura, "is the social facilitation function . . . The whole fashion and taste industry relies on that modeling functioning" (Evans, 1989, p. 5).

Cognitive Influences

Bandura's theory of observational learning (or imitation) is based squarely on a model of operant conditioning. Imitation is a powerful phenomenon by means of which a tremendous variety of social learning occurs. People learn how to dress, eat, speak, drive vehicles, and so on largely through imitation. Imitative behaviors, Bandura explains, are emitted behaviors that can be reinforced either as a direct consequence of the behaviors themselves, or they may be subject to the secondhand (*vicarious*) effects of seeing other people being reinforced or punished.

In Chapter 10, we saw another side of Bandura's theorizing. There, we looked at the role of the individual's personal assessments of competency and effectiveness. What Juan thinks of himself (his sense of self-efficacy) is inextricably linked with decisions he makes about what he will do, as well as with the amount of effort and time he is willing to devote to different activities. If he firmly believed himself to be stupid and incapable of understanding the concepts in this book, he probably would not read it. Thus do cognitions drive actions.

Even in operant learning, claims Bandura, what is most important is the ability to think, to symbolize, to tease out cause-and-effect relationships, and to anticipate the consequences of a person's own behavior (as well as the behavior of others). Moreover, says Bandura, people strive to control events that affect them. "By exerting influence in spheres over which they can command some control," writes Bandura, "they are better able to realize desired futures and to forestall undesired ones" (1995, p. 1). Although punishments and reinforcements affect behavior, they don't exert control as if people were thoughtless puppets. Rather, these effects are largely a function of awareness of relationships and expectations of outcomes—expectations that might span days or even years. Thus, farmers plant wheat in the spring with no possibility of any immediate reinforcement; they know that reinforcement will come in the fall (if it ever rains).[4]

Behavior Control Systems

Bandura (1969) maintains that it is impossible to explain human behavior solely by reference to either internal or external stimulus events; both are inevitably involved in most human behavior. Behaviorism can be defined by its preoccupation with external events, whereas cognitivism deals mainly with internal events; Bandura's view tends to integrate the two approaches.

When Bandura refers to external stimulus events, he means simply that the physical environment is at least partly responsible for human behavior. People respond to the environment. Not to do so would be a mark of a completely nonfunctional being. Even such phylogenetically low forms of life as planaria are responsive to external stimulation.

Internal stimulation refers to more cognitive events (in the form of images, memories, feelings, instructions, verbalizations, and so on) that make up human thought processes. That these events influence behavior is clear: Grandmother would need no convincing whatsoever. Interestingly, though, psychologists sometimes do. To this end, Bandura (1969) cites an experiment performed by Miller (1951) in which a group of subjects were conditioned by means of electric shocks to react negatively to the letter T and positively to the number 4.

---

[4]And students study night and day, the Old Woman grumbled, motioning that this was an aside, not to be recorded. They study and study, she said, even with no likelihood of immediate rewards for their efforts. They know that they will eventually have fascinating and rewarding careers. She paused for a moment, then added, at least the bright ones will.

After conditioning, subjects consistently gave evidence of greater autonomic reaction (arousal) for the stimulus associated with shock (in this case, T). Miller subsequently instructed subjects to think of the stimuli alternately as a sequence of dots was presented to them (T for the first dot, 4 for the second, T for the third, and so on). That there was now greater autonomic reaction to odd-numbered dots demonstrates the effect of internal processes on behavior.

In describing the forces that affect human behavior, Bandura notes three separate control systems that interact with one another in determining behavior.

Stimulus Control

One class of human behaviors consists of activities directly under the control of stimuli. Such behaviors include the host of autonomic (reflexive) acts in which people engage when responding to certain specific stimuli. Sneezing, withdrawing from pain, flinching, the startle reaction, and so on are all examples of behavior controlled by external stimuli.

Behaviors under control of stimuli also include responses learned through reinforcement. When a specific stimulus is always present at the time of the reinforcement, it acquires control over behavior in the sense that it eventually serves as a signal for a response. One illustration of this type of control is found in the contrast between the behaviors of some schoolchildren when their teachers are present and when they are not. By granting rewards for good behavior and punishment for less desirable activity, teachers become stimuli capable of eliciting obedience, fear, caution, respect, love, or a combination of these responses.

Outcome Control

Some behaviors, explains Bandura, are under the control of their consequences rather than their antecedents—that is, they don't appear to be under stimulus control. The outcome control system, which has been extensively investigated by Skinner, relates specifically to activities that become more probable as a function of reinforcement or less probable as a function of either nonreinforcement or punishment. In this behavior control system, control is achieved through operant conditioning (see Chapter 4).

Symbolic Control

The third behavior control system includes the range of human activity that is influenced by "mediation," or internal processes. Thought processes can affect human behavior in several ways. Internal verbalization of rules (self-instructions) can direct behavior, as in the Miller (1951) experiment, in which subjects instructed themselves to think T, then 4, and so on.

A second way in which symbolic processes direct behavior has to do with the way imagining the consequences of behavior affects ongoing activity. Were it not for the ability to represent long-range outcomes symbolically, many tasks that are not associated with either an immediate stimulus or an immediate reward would not be undertaken. Why sow a field of corn if you cannot anticipate a crop in the fall? Why study medicine if you cannot imagine yourself as a doctor?

The importance of symbolization for human behavior appears to be much greater than that of the other two behavior control systems. It also appears that as one goes down the phylogenetic scale, the importance of outcome control and of direct stimulus control increases. Lower animal forms seem to react more to specific external stimulation than to behavioral outcomes. In addition, symbolization does not appear to play an important (if any) role in directing the behavior of many lower animals.

Behavior Control Systems in Action

Although stimulus, outcome, and symbolic control are clearly distinguishable on theoretical grounds, they are not necessarily separate in practice. Much human activity is probably directed by a combination of these three. For example, consider a woman who pursues a bucktoothed, cross-eyed, knock-kneed, pigeon-toed, skinny, redheaded man. Because of stimulus generalization, the pursuer reacts to this man as she would to any other (the stimulus man has been present at the time of many previous reinforcements).

But human behavior is not this simple. The pursuer does not just respond to the stimulus in the blind manner expected of an unsophisticated rat. If her initial approach encounters strong resistance, she may modify it; if it is rewarded, she may intensify it. If the intensification leads to more reward, it may be reintensified; if it leads to a cessation of reinforcement, it may be diminished. Thus, the human female is capable of changing her behavior in accordance with its immediate outcomes.

The direction of activity is even more complex because symbolic processes also guide actions. For example, the woman can represent in her imagination the consequences of succeeding in capturing this unattractive redheaded male. She likely believes that such an ugly man must possess hidden talents to offset his lack of obvious physical qualities. Perhaps she anticipates that he will be an excellent cook.

Bandura's Agentic Perspective

People are *agents* of their own actions, Bandura insists, "They are agents of experiences rather than simply undergoers of experiences. The sensory, motor, and cerebral systems are tools people use to accomplish the tasks and goals that give meaning, direction, and satisfaction to their lives" (2001, p. 4).

There are three main features of human agency, explains Bandura—three human characteristics that define this **agentic perspective.**

Intentionality
People can only be agents of their actions if they perform these actions intentionally. If Graciela gets pushed into her professor, accidentally causing the professor to spill her coffee, she would not be considered the *agent* of that action. But if Consuelo, who pushed Graciela, did so deliberately, Consuelo would be the agent.

Forethought
Intentionality implies planning and anticipation. That is, it implies forethought. As we noted earlier, the ability to symbolize allows people to anticipate the consequences of their actions. Were it not for the ability to predict the likely

consequences of behavior, we could hardly intend to achieve them. Thus, if Consuelo could not foresee the consequences of pushing the hapless Graciela, she could hardly intend to get her into trouble.

Self-Reactiveness and Self-Reflection

As Bandura puts it, "Through the exercise of forethought, people motivate themselves and guide their actions in anticipation of future events" (2001, p. 7). This requires that people be able to examine and react to their own functioning. As an agent of her own actions, Consuelo can not only intend to push Graciela and foresee the consequences of so doing, but she can also reflect on her own actions, as well as on their consequences, and she can react to them. That is, she can reflect upon (think about) the likely long-term consequences of her behavior, both before and after they occur, and she can react to these consequences—again, both before and after they occur. Too, she can change her intentions and her actions as she reflects and reacts.

The fundamentally important point, according to Bandura, is that *we* are in charge: We are the agents. This is not to deny that powerful biological forces shape many of our behaviors. Nor does it deny that much of what we do is under the control of various stimuli and under the control of anticipated outcomes. As well, there are accidental outcomes, unintended behaviors, and unexpected eventualities over which we exercise little control—often precisely because we could not have anticipated them. Clearly, had Graciela expected Consuelo to push her, things might have gone quite differently.

Self-Efficacy

As we saw in Chapter 10, another important aspect of Bandura's theory deals with **self-efficacy.** Self-efficacy has to do with an individual's assessments of personal effectiveness (Bandura, 1986, 1993; Evans, 1989). If Muhamed sees himself as highly capable in dealing with life, he can be said to have high self-efficacy.

Judgments of self-efficacy appear to have a profound influence on what we do or don't do. If Sarah thinks she is especially good at making public speeches— that is, if her judgments of self-efficacy relative to public speaking are highly positive—she may be strongly motivated to seek out and accept opportunities to speak. If, in contrast, she has low estimates of self-efficacy in this area, she will probably be far more likely to avoid public speaking occasions. As Schunk (1984) points out, people tend to avoid doing things that they expect to do very badly.

Of course, judgments of self-efficacy are not always accurate. There are those who continue to see themselves as efficacious, as capable in activities in which they perform appallingly poorly. Others have just the opposite problem—they see themselves as incapable and try to avoid activities where they would perform astonishingly well.

As we saw in Chapter 10, judgments of self-efficacy reflect four distinct influences: enactive (the direct effects of behavior), vicarious (the effects of comparisons with the behavior of others), persuasory (the effects of persuasion), and emotive (the effects of emotions).

The effects of our behaviors on others, or their effects in a more objective sense, often tell us how effective we are. If Samuel fails a lot in school, that would be objective evidence of low effectiveness. And if his parents, his teachers, or his friends make disparaging comments about his performance, the effects of his behavior on others would be an additional, very powerful, social influence that would tend to lower his estimates of self-efficacy.

Similarly, comparisons that Samuel makes between his performance and that of his peers should tell him something about how effective he is. And, significant others, such as parents, teachers, or peers, might succeed in persuading him that he really is a competent and effective individual, that he need only apply himself more diligently.

Educational and Other Applications of Bandura's Social Cognitive Theory

Bandura's theory has several important facets: One, based largely on Skinner's model of operant learning, deals with observational learning—that is, learning through imitation. This aspect of the theory looks at the extremely powerful and pervasive influence on learning and behavior of both actual and symbolic models. It looks at the different processes that are involved in observational learning (attention, retention, reproduction, and motivation), and at the different effects of observational learning (modeling, inhibition-disinhibition, and eliciting).

A second facet of the theory introduces a more cognitive orientation. It recognizes that even in observational learning, the individual's ability to symbolize and to anticipate is fundamentally important. This aspect of the theory looks at the three different control systems that direct human behavior: stimulus control, outcome control, and symbolic control. The first of these, stimulus control, has to do with classically conditioned behaviors; the second, outcome control, deals with operant learning, and the third, symbolic control, refers to the role of cognitive activities such as thinking and imagining.

A third aspect of the theory, even more cognitive, underlines Bandura's belief that we are not simply pawns pushed hither and yon by our reflexes, our drives, or the contingencies of our behaviors. We are in charge, Bandura insists. Despite there being powerful biological forces and behavioral consequences that shape our behaviors, we are the agents of our own actions. We intend them, we anticipate their consequences, and we reflect on our behaviors, our effectiveness, and ourselves as human beings.

Each facet of this theory has clear applications.

Observational Learning

Observational learning has to do with learning by imitating models. As we saw, imitation might be evident in novel behaviors (modeling effect), in the suppression or appearance of deviant behaviors (inhibitory-disinhibitory effect), or in the appearance of behaviors related to those of the model (eliciting effect). Recall, too, that some of the most important models in advanced technological societies are *symbolic* rather than actual. These include books, fictional characters, verbal instructions, and so on.

Teachers use models extensively in the classroom. The instructions and directions they provide are, in effect, models. So too, is the teacher's behavior and that of other students. Research suggests that not all models have the same influence on children. Children are most likely to imitate people who are important to them and with whom they identify—such as parents, siblings, close friends, and respected teachers. Also, as we saw, they are most likely to imitate highly valued behaviors. Each of the three effects of imitation described by Bandura can be used systematically both to promote desirable behavior and to eliminate deviant behaviors.

For example, children might be taught something new by being shown what to do (modeling effect); they might be discouraged from doing something by witnessing someone else being punished for the behavior (inhibitory effect); or they might be encouraged to engage in a certain class of behaviors after being exposed to a relevant model (eliciting effect).

One example of using models to modify behavior comes from a study Martens and Hiralall (1997) conducted in which a teacher was instructed in a three-step procedure for changing inappropriate play behaviors among nursery-school children: (1) identifying sequences of inappropriate behavior, (2) rescripting these behaviors by working out more acceptable interactions, (3) acting out the modified scripts for the children. These investigators found that the teacher was quickly able to learn and implement this procedure, and that the effect was a measurable increase in acceptable play behavior.

Behavior Control Systems

Some classroom behaviors appear to be under relatively direct control of specific stimuli. Thus, early in the school year, most teachers establish clear rules and routines that ensure the smooth and orderly functioning of their classrooms. A verbal signal, a bell, a buzzer, or a gesture might be a specific stimulus that says, "Yes, you may now go to the bathroom," "It's time to put away your books," "You're dismissed for recess," "Take out your math books," and so on. Such routines, says Doyle (1986), are fundamental to effective classroom management. Bringing them under the control of clear stimuli can greatly facilitate teaching.

Many classroom behaviors are affected by outcomes rather than mainly by preceding stimuli. Among important outcomes that are under teacher control are things such as praise and criticism, as well as the enormous range of other reinforcers and punishers that schools can provide for children (see Chapter 4 for a discussion of some of these).

Closely related to stimulus or outcome control, explains Bandura, are the effects of the individual's ability to symbolize and anticipate—that is, to *imagine*—the likely consequences of various behaviors. That Vladimir so carefully follows all the rules and routines in his classroom has to do with his ability to imagine what the consequences of not doing so might be. Similarly, that Ishmael studies so hard may well relate to his ability to anticipate how his parents and teachers will react to his performance on various tests. And his studying may also be linked to his anticipation of a brilliant future as a nuclear physicist.

Personal Agency and Self-Efficacy

Ishmael has strong, highly positive notions of self-efficacy. Self-efficacy judgments are a very important aspect of self-knowledge, says Bandura (1977). Among other things, our judgments of self-efficacy are important determiners of what we do and what we don't do. In addition, positive judgments of self-efficacy are associated with higher physical and mental health. Bandura explains that high self-efficacy provides people with the tools they need to cope with the situations life offers. As a result, anxieties and phobias, important manifestations of human distress, are far less common among those whose judgments of self-efficacy are positive. In contrast, those who have low evaluations of their personal competence are far more likely to judge themselves negatively and to have poorer self-esteem (Bandura, Pastorelli, Barbaranelli, Caprara, & Gian, 1999). Also, a great deal of research underlines the importance of positive self-evaluations for achievement in both school and life (for example, Skaalvik & Rankin, 1995).

Developing positive self-concepts (positive evaluations of self-efficacy) in children, together with an accompanying sense of personal power (of personal *agency*), is an important task for parents and teachers. Bandura describes four main sources of influence that can affect these concepts, each of which is at least partly under the control of parents and teachers. For example, enactive influences are those related to the effects of the child's actions—hence, the importance of presenting children with tasks that allow them to experience success.

Vicarious influences relate to the effect of comparing one's achievements with those of others. In this connection, many educators recommend that teachers avoid highly competitive school situations where learners are placed in a win-lose struggle to see who is best (Johnson & Johnson, 1994). Instead, teachers are encouraged to provide students with their own learning goals so that they can work individually as well as cooperatively at their own pace and in a way that ensures that every student achieves success and feels personally responsible for doing so (Schmuck & Schmuck, 1997).

Teachers are also important agents of what Bandura calls *persuasory* influences—the effects of other people's confidence or doubt. That Sarah's teacher has suggested she not attempt the extra assignment in mathematics because it will be too difficult for her will do very little that is positive for her self-judgments of personal competence.

Physiological states of arousal, evident in high or low excitement or anxiety, also influence judgments of self-efficacy, explains Bandura. As we saw in Chapter 10, arousal, too, is at least partly under a teacher's, or a parent's, control. Teachers are among the most important sources of stimulation in the classroom. What they say and do, as well as the tasks they present their charges, can do a great deal to increase or decrease arousal. Bandura suggests that high arousal can affect self-judgment in different ways. For example, great fear might lead to judgments of low personal competence. If Jessica is deathly afraid of being afraid if she tries to climb the rock wall, she may well judge herself incapable of doing so. If, on the other hand, Jessica is deathly afraid of being attacked by the rampaging bear, she might judge herself capable of outrunning—or outwitting—it.

Bandura's Position: An Appraisal

Bandura's social cognitive theory serves as an important bridge between behavioristic and more cognitive theories. Its behavioristic roots are evident in his use of an operant conditioning model to explain learning through imitation. And its cognitive orientation is apparent in its recognition of the power of our ability to imagine the consequences of our actions, and in Bandura's insistence that we are the *agents* of our own actions.

Bandura's theory also serves as an excellent example of how theories in psychology don't need to be—and probably should *not* be—static and unchanging things. As the spirit of the times change, and as science provides theorists with new information and new possibilities, good theories can also change. After all, our psychological theories are not judged by some absolute criteria of rightness or wrongness. Instead, we judge them by how well they reflect the facts as we know them and, perhaps most important, we look at how useful they are in any of a variety of ways.

Bandura's theorizing does no great violence to the facts as we know them. It tends to reflect research findings well and has successfully incorporated new findings and new ideas over a span of some decades. For example, Bandura's notions about self-efficacy and his assertion that we are agents of our own actions are in close agreement with current notions about *expectancy-value* and *self-determination* in motivation theory (see Chapter 10).

That the theory is useful in a practical sense also seems clear. For example, observational learning theory has been used extensively in an effort to understand the influence of television on aggression and violence among children and adults. The theory also suggests useful explanations for the effectiveness—or lack of effectiveness—of incarceration and other forms of punishment.

Different aspects of Bandura's theorizing have been enormously influential in psychology. His theory of observational learning has become nearly synonymous with the field of social learning theory. And his notions regarding self-efficacy have stimulated an enormous amount of recent research.

Summary

1. Social learning can mean all learning that occurs as a result of social interaction (a process definition), or the sort of learning that is involved in discovering which behaviors are expected and acceptable in different social situations. Socially accepted behaviors vary from one culture to another, as well as for different ages and sometimes for different sexes.

2. The chief agents of socialization are the culture's main institutions: the family, the school, the church, and so on.

3. Bandura's theory of social learning is a theory of imitation (observational learning), stemming from Miller and Dollard's drive-reduction theory of imitation, and based heavily on Skinner's theory of operant conditioning, with a clear recognition of the importance of cognitive variables.

4. Imitative behaviors are operant responses subject to the laws of operant learning. Models can be people or more symbolic patterns for behavior, such as are provided by books, instructions, religions, television, and so on.

5. Observational learning depends on four related processes: attentional (the need to pay attention), retentional (the need to be able to remember and represent what is observed), motor reproduction (the need to be able to produce the observed behavior), and motivational (to need to be motivated, to have a reason to imitate).

6. Imitation can be reinforced directly (by the model or through its own consequences), or vicariously (as a result of seeing someone else rewarded or punished).

7. Conditioned emotional responses (CERs), acquired through classical conditioning, are often involved in determining whether or not a behavior will be imitated.

8. Observational learning may be apparent in the *modeling effect* (novel, precisely imitative responses), the *inhibitory* or *disinhibitory effects* (the suppression or appearance of deviant behavior), and the *eliciting effect* (social facilitation of related responses).

9. Bandura integrates behavioristic and cognitive models by describing three behavior-control systems involving different classes of responses: those that are under direct stimulus control, those that are affected by their consequences, and those that are directed by means of symbolic processes.

10. We are agents of our own actions, says Bandura, as is evident in our intentionality, our forethought, and our self-reactiveness and self-reflection.

11. One of the most important aspects of self-knowledge is reflected in personal judgments of competence, termed *self-efficacy*. Positive evaluations are associated with high achievement and good physical and mental health. Self-efficacy is influenced by the outcomes of our behavior (enactive influences), by comparisons with other people's behavior (vicarious influences), and by the effects of persuasion (persuasory influences) and of arousal (emotive influences).

12. Bandura's theory reflects scientific findings well, is highly compatible with current developments in social-learning and motivation theory, and has important practical implications for parenting, teaching, and therapy.

Analysis, Synthesis, and Integration

> A theorist is an artist, someone with a talent for weeding the essential from the inessential and constructing these marvelous orders.
> **George Johnson**

We spent the morning drifting soundlessly down the Beaver River far beyond the last of the empty cabins, the Old Woman sitting on her lifejacket in the bow, neither of us saying very much, just looking and pointing at the goldeneyes whistling along the banks and at the mergansers in winter colors low in the water under the overhanging willows. Bald eagles patrolled the shoreline from above and the Old Woman said not to start the motor yet, why spoil such a place and such a day.

When the current had taken us beyond the mouth of the creek-with-no-name to the edge of the riffles that mark the beginning of the rapids, the Old Woman said we could stop,

that my enemies would not find me here, and I wondered how did she know, and she took the oar from my hand and pushed hard against the bottom and steered us against the long sandbar at the edge of the island, and I made a fire while the Old Woman cast into the pool and caught a walleye which we cooked and ate, a gray jay appearing as they always do to see would we leave something for it to eat, which we did.

Later, the Old Woman said it was time for the very last chapter and once more I turned on the machine, and on this tape you can hear both the river and the sounds of ducks and songbirds.

This Chapter

This chapter, said the Old Woman, undertakes a very complex task: that of summarizing and evaluating the learning-related theories that make up the earlier chapters of the book. There are two great techniques for taking care of things that are complex, she continued, and I could not tell whether she was being serious or not: oversimplifying and lying. She said she used one of these techniques repeatedly in this ambitious chapter, but she didn't say which. She said the chapter presents a summary of the major learning theories discussed earlier, follows that summary with a rapid evaluation, and ends with two syntheses. In short, the chapter is a summary, an analysis, and an integration of the content of the 11 chapters that have come before.[1]

---

[1]The Old Woman said maybe I should tell you that much of this chapter could, and maybe should, have come at the beginning of the book. She explained that this final chapter is like the skeleton of the book—its frame. She said it was like the emperor, sans clothes; the first 11 chapters are the various imperial garments. She said that if you had glimpsed the emperor first, you might have seen better how the vestments would hang on his frame. But she said she thought there was a danger that the naked emperor would prove not too shocking or too outrageous but simply too bewildering for a naive—and sensitive—student. She said to tell you that here, finally, is the essence of imperial power—the emperor stripped.

Objectives

If I were speaking directly to your readers, the Old Woman said, I would say to them (if they cared to listen), "Much of science is a shared hallucination, a network of self-reinforcing beliefs" (Johnson, 1992, p. 53).

And I think they might shake their heads and say, "Does this mean I've wasted my time studying these theories of learning and behavior, these shared hallucinations?" I would answer no, the Old Woman explained, because there's nothing more useful than a theory, even if it is an invention, a fantasy. A theory doesn't have to be true, although it does have to be other important things: useful, logical, consistent, clear, and so on.

So tell your students to keep studying, said the Old Woman, absently tossing a pebble into the river. Tell them to read this last chapter, reflect on it well. And when they're finished, each student should discuss it with his or her grandmother, because in it are hidden truths and insights that might impress even someone as wise as she. When grandmother and student have talked it over, students will finally understand

- *Why we absolutely need theories*
- *How theories actually work*
- *The essence of each of the major theories that compose this text*
- *Why theories of learning and behavior are really models of human learners*
- *How this entire text might be synthesized*

There is also a small chance that they will have learned to simplify—without lying.

Two Major Approaches to Learning Theory

Theories are invented not just because they might be useful, *the Old Woman read from her notes.* Humans also seem to crave them—or at least seem to crave the order that theories bring. You see, there is much in this planet, and in human behavior, that is chaos; but humans want it to be orderly. "There is an ancient human longing," says Johnson, "to impose rational order on a chaotic world. The detective does it, the magician does it. That's why people love Sherlock Holmes. Science came out of magic. Science is the modern expression of what the ancient magician did. The world is a mess, and people want it to be orderly" (1992, p. 114).

But science doesn't work quite the way it's pictured, Johnson informs us. It isn't simply a question of having a theory, generating hypotheses from it, testing them, and throwing out the theory if the hypotheses don't pan out. Many theorists love their theories so much they're seldom willing to abandon them. Sometimes they stick with them long after everybody else has left.

A theory, Johnson explains, is a form of architecture, maybe a little like a cathedral. When the theory ages and threatens to become useless, theorists don't just build a brand new one. What the smart theorists do, instead, is shore up their old ideas: put in new joists, new rafters, brace the old walls, redo the decaying foundation, patch the roof, paint a little here and there, polish the old gold, and so forth. Those less smart try to make do with what they have (and the rats move in). Later in this chapter, we look briefly at examples of two theorists who have tried to synthesize what they thought was the best they could find in other theories—who have remodeled their cathedrals, hinting at new religions and adding contemporary altars where the new disciples might worship.

Learning, as stated at the beginning, involves actual or potential changes in behavior that result from experience. Hence, the terms *learning theory* and *behavior theory* are often used synonymously.

Among the various ways of looking at human behavior or learning, two broad orientations can be identified; these give rise to the traditional divisions among psychological theory. One orientation assumes that human behavior is, at least in some measure, influenced by activities such as thinking, feeling, intending, wanting, expecting, reasoning, remembering, and evaluating. These processes define what is thought of as "mind." They are cognitive (or intellectual) processes; hence, this orientation is that of the cognitive psychologists.

The other orientation doesn't flatly contradict the first but insists that little scientifically valid knowledge about human behavior can be obtained by investigating the nebulous processes of the mind. Instead, advocates of this orientation concentrate on examining actual behavior and the observable conditions that lead to behavior. Hence, this is the orientation of behavioristic psychologists.

Summaries of Key Theories

Although few positions are entirely and exclusively behavioristic or cognitive, these labels are useful for indicating the general orientation of a theorist and the sorts of topics with which the theory is most likely to be concerned. Thus, behavioristic theories deal largely with investigations of relationships among stimuli, responses, and the consequences of behavior. In contrast, cognitive psychologists are less interested in stimuli and responses than in more intellectual processes: problem solving, decision making, perception, information processing, concept formation, self-awareness, and memory, among others. Table 12.1 (adapted from Table 1.2) distinguishes among the major divisions in learning theory. Each of these positions is summarized in the following sections.[2]

Mostly Behavioristic Positions

Among the major predominantly behavioristic positions are those of Pavlov, Watson, Guthrie, Thorndike, Hull, and Skinner.

Pavlov: Classical Conditioning
The Russian physiologist Ivan P. Pavlov, largely as a result of a single study of a dog being trained to salivate in response to a tone, set the stage for much of the entire world's next 100 years of research and theorizing in human learning and behavior. The model of classical conditioning described by Pavlov, and illustrated by his famous dogs, is part of almost every current course in introductory psychology. More than this, it served as the basis for the development of the first clearly behavioristic positions in psychology. Why? Partly because it provided what seemed like a simple way of explaining both animal and human behavior; perhaps even more, because it pointed toward an approach based on objective, replicable, scientific methods in contrast with the more subjective and introspective approaches that had previously been widely current. Interestingly, many principles of classical conditioning (of generalization and extinction, for example) continue to be applied in clinical psychology, in education, in industry, and elsewhere.

---

[2]The Old Woman pointed at the recorder which meant I should turn it off, that she was going to stop for a while and I wondered, did she need to go to the bathroom? She didn't. She said she thought some students might be interested in another of Blaise Pascal's thoughts, the one in which Pascal wrote that science has two closely related extremes: One is pure, natural ignorance, the state in which all humans are born; the other is a state reached by those lofty souls who have learned all that it is possible for humans to know and who, finally, arrive at the realization that they know nothing, that they are once more in a state of ignorance. But it is a far wiser ignorance than the first state, an ignorance that sees and judges things more clearly. The unfortunate ones, says Pascal, are the ones who have only gone half way between the extremes—those who have learned much of what science knows, but who have failed to learn that they know nothing. These are the souls who most trouble the world, and who see things most obscurely (Pascal, 1820, p. 121). I wanted to protest, explain that we are not ignorant, or even half ignorant, but the Old Woman started to read the manuscript once more and I hurried to turn on the recorder but still, I missed the first few words she said.

Table 12.1 *Major Divisions in Learning Theory*

	Variables of concern	Representative theorists and models
Behaviorism	Stimuli	Pavlov
	Responses	Watson
	Reinforcement	Guthrie
	CS	Thorndike
	US	Hull
		Skinner
A transition: the beginnings of modern cognitivism	Evolutionary psychology	Rescorla-Wagner
	Sociobiology	Wilson
	Stimuli	Hebb
	Responses	Tolman
	Reinforcement	Köhler
	Mediation	Koffka
	Purpose	Wertheimer
	Goals	
	Expectation	
	Representation	
Cognitive theories	Perceiving	Bruner
	Organizing	Piaget
	Decision making	Vygotsky
	Information processing	Information processing
	Problem solving	Computer models
	Self-awareness	Models of memory
	Attention	and motivation
	Memory	

Watson: American Behaviorism

Pavlov's classical conditioning was quickly embraced and championed by John B. Watson, one of the first North American psychologists to define the science of psychology in completely objective terms. He saw psychology as a science that deals with the observable rather than the merely hypothetical—a definition that gave rise to North American behaviorism. Watson assumed that individuals are born with a behavioral repertoire consisting of only a few reflexes and that these early responses become conditioned to other stimuli by being repeatedly paired with them.

Watson was also an important spokesman for environmentalism: the belief that the environment (the nurture side in the historical nature/nurture dispute) determines personality, intelligence, and all other human qualities. One of his better-known claims was that he could make whatever he wanted out of a dozen healthy infants if he were given a free hand in their upbringing.

Guthrie: One-Shot Learning

Like Watson, Edwin R. Guthrie was firmly behavioristic. His theory can be summarized in several major laws, the most important of which states that whenever a response follows a stimulus, there will result a tendency for the same response to occur again the next time the stimulus is presented. Thus, Guthrie maintained that learning is complete with the first pairing of a stimulus with a response and that further practice will not strengthen the response, although it will help ensure that the person (or animal) learns it in many different situations.

Although learning occurs and is complete and relatively permanent after a single trial, said Guthrie, it is possible to remove undesirable habits simply by learning new habits that are incompatible with the old ones. Guthrie suggested three ways in which this can be done: the fatigue technique, the threshold approach, and the method of incompatible stimuli.

Note that for both Watson and Guthrie, the consequences of the behavior are not important in bringing about learning. According to Guthrie, the effect of punishment or reward is simply to change the stimulus situation, thereby preventing the unlearning of a response.

Thorndike: Trial and Error and The Law of Effect

But consequences can be extremely important, argued the behaviorist, Edward L. Thorndike, who is generally credited with introducing the notion of reinforcement in contemporary learning theory through his *law of effect*. This law states that learning is a consequence of the effect of behavior. Specifically, responses that lead to a satisfying state of affairs will tend to be repeated. At first, Thorndike had also believed that unpleasant or annoying states would have an opposite effect, but he rejected this belief after 1930. Similarly, before 1930 he had believed that stimulus-response events that are practiced tend to be more strongly linked, whereas those that fall into disuse tend to be forgotten (the law of exercise). Thorndike later rejected this belief as well. Thus, Thorndike is an example of a theorist whose ideas changed in important ways as a result of new findings and new insights.

For Thorndike, learning consists of the formation of bonds between stimuli and responses largely as a function of the consequences of the responses. He labeled the process of learning a *stamping-in* process; forgetting involves *stamping out*. The system includes a number of subsidiary laws, the most important of which is the law of multiple responses. This law holds that when faced with a problem situation, people tend to respond in a variety of ways until one of the responses emitted is reinforced; in other words, learning occurs through a process of trial and error. Additional laws note that behavior is generalizable, that people respond to the most striking features of the environment, that cultural background affects behavior, and that learning through contiguity does occur.

Hull: A Hypothetico-Deductive System

Clark L. Hull carried to an extreme the scientific approach of behaviorists such as Watson, Guthrie, and Thorndike, developing a resolutely objective and highly complex hypothetico-deductive system. He dedicated himself to one of the most monumental tasks ever undertaken by a psychologist—that of formalizing all knowledge about human behavior to make it possible to predict responses on the basis of knowledge about stimuli. The system was never completed; nevertheless, Hull's work stands as an overwhelmingly ambitious attempt at formal theory building.

Hull's investigations and consequent formulas and equations deal with three aspects of human behavior: input variables (which include physical stimuli as well as such factors as drive condition, previously learned habits, and amount of reward available), intervening variables (which consist mainly of the assumed effects of input variables on the organism), and output variables (which are the characteristics of actual behavior in terms of response latency, frequency of responding, and time to extinction). The system may be partly summarized by the equation, $_sE_R = _sH_R \times D \times V \times K$.

Hull's final system contains 17 postulates, 133 theorems, and hundreds of corollaries from which the nature of his beliefs about learning emerges. One of the central concepts in the theory is habit, which is an S-R connection. A collection of such connections forms a habit-family hierarchy, which is a hypothetical preferential ordering of related alternative behaviors. Habits are related in that they have common goals, represented by Hull's concept of fractional antedating goal responses. An antedating goal reaction is any one of the many reward-related responses that an organism makes as it nears a goal. For example, as it turns the last corner in a maze, a rat may lick its chops. Fractional antedating goal responses are important because they represent Hull's behavioristic definition of expectancy or purpose, and they foreshadow important cognitive concerns.

Hull's use of the concept of intervening variables might seem to be a link between his system and more cognitive interests. Note, however, that these variables are tied directly to input and output variables. Hull didn't intend them to be simply inferences or metaphors.

Skinner: Operant Conditioning

B. F. Skinner stands out as one of the great system builders in 20th-century psychology. He developed a model of operant conditioning—a model based on the notion that learning results from the reinforcement of responses emitted by an organism. Much of Skinner's work has dealt with the effects of different ways of presenting reinforcement (in other words, schedules of reinforcement) on rate of learning, response rate, and extinction rate (extinction refers to the cessation of a response after reinforcement has been discontinued). Among his most important findings is that learning is facilitated in its initial stages by continuous reinforcement, but extinction is slower following intermittent reinforcement. Although Skinner experimented extensively with animals, many of his results are generally applicable to human behavior as well.

One technique developed by Skinner for teaching complex behaviors to animals is shaping, which involves reinforcing successive approximations to the desired behavior. It is widely employed by professional animal trainers.

Skinner discusses the applications of his work to human behavior in several books, including *Walden Two* (1948), *Science and Human Behavior* (1953), and *Beyond Freedom and Dignity* (1971). In addition, many principles of Skinner's theory have been extensively applied in education, medicine, advertising, psychotherapy, and other human activities. One well-known educational application takes the form of programmed instruction—the deliberate arrangement of material to take advantage of the effects of reinforcement. Behavior modification, which includes various systematic programs for changing and controlling behavior and is based primarily on Skinnerian principles, is widely used in education and psychotherapy.

Transitions to Modern Cognitivism

Watson's insistence that behaviorism must be limited to events that can be observed proved a difficult constraint even for those as staunchly behaviorist as Thorndike and Hull. Hull, for example, found himself having to invent unobservable fractional antedating goal responses to explain observable connections. And Thorndike (1931)—who initially had vigorously attacked the gestaltists for resorting to insight as an explanation for learning—found himself speaking of "ideational learning" to explain insight learning.

Evolutionary Psychology

Thorndike's and Skinner's theories were strongly influenced by Darwinian ideas. In a sense, they are theories of the survival-of-the-fittest responses. Evolutionary psychology, too, reflects a profound Darwinian influence. Its primary identifying characteristic is its attention to biology and genetics as sources of explanation for human learning and behavior. Much support for evolutionary psychology derives from studies of phenomena such as autoshaping and instinctive drift, in which animals revert to instinctual patterns of behavior despite reinforcement contingencies that urge different responses. It is as though biological constraints make certain kinds of learning (and behaving) highly probable and make other responses far more improbable.

Sociobiology, an important branch of evolutionary psychology, looks at inherited predispositions as the underlying causes of all social behavior. It draws its evidence heavily from ethology, which is the study of the behavior of nonhuman animals in natural settings.

As Wright (1994) notes, evolutionary psychologists continue to struggle against a belief that has dominated psychology for much of this century; namely, that biology doesn't matter, that what is most important in the study of human behavior is a recognition of the malleability of the mind and the potency of culture in shaping the human character. This doctrine, says Wright, insists there is no such thing as human nature. But there is a human nature, claims Wright. It is apparent in the similarities that one finds among the world's many cultures: for example, the human tendency to worry about social status; a number of basic male-female differences; the tendency of humans everywhere to feel guilt, to seek justice and retribution, to feel pride, remorse, love, empathy.

But today's evolutionary psychologist does not believe that all explanations lie in a genetically determined human nature. Malleability, notes Wright, is built into human nature. Malleability—responsiveness to environmental and cultural realities—is what makes learning and adaptation possible. And underlying this malleability is the wonderfully complex human brain, whose chemical and electrical secrets we are beginning to discover.

Hebb: The Neurophysiology of Learning

Donald O. Hebb's attempt to explain higher mental processes is a much clearer departure from some of the constraints of behaviorism. His is a somewhat speculative, neurophysiological proposal designed to explain thinking and learning by looking at activity in neurons. Thinking, he suggests, involves activity among groups of neurons arranged in closed loops (called *cell assemblies*), or of activity in more complex arrangements of such loops (termed *phase sequences*). Absolutely central to Hebb's theory is the notion that transmission among neurons appears to be facilitated as a function of repeated firing among them. This phenomenon of neural activity ostensibly accounts for learning. A cell assembly corresponds to some simple sensory input (for example, the color of an object or one part of one of its dimensions), whereas activity in a phase sequence corresponds to the whole object. Through learning, cell assemblies and phase sequences eventually achieve some correspondence to the environment: Because different parts of an object are usually sensed in contiguity, cell assemblies related to different aspects of an object will often be simultaneously active and will therefore become related. Interestingly, many of Hebb's notions about neural activity have been supported by more recent research using sophisticated techniques of brain imagery (EEGs and MEGs, for example), to yield measures of change in event-related potential (ERPs) and event related fields (ERFs).

Hebb has been largely responsible for the development of an arousal-based theory of motivation. This theory is premised on the assumption that optimal human functioning is made possible by a moderate level of arousal, and an organism therefore behaves in such a way as to maintain that level. Other theorists (for example, Bruner) have subsequently incorporated these same notions in their systems.

Tolman: Behavior Has a Purpose

Edward C. Tolman was among the first North American psychologists to begin with a behavioristic orientation and eventually develop a system far more cognitive than behavioristic—a theory of purposive behaviorism.

Tolman's system reflects three basic beliefs. First, all behavior is purposive. By this, Tolman meant that behavior is directed, that it is guided toward goals, not by stimuli (as in Hull's system) but, rather, by cognitions—conscious awareness. These cognitions take the form of expectancies that the organism develops with respect to reward.

Second, Tolman emphasized the molar rather than molecular aspects of behavior. In other words, he was not concerned with discrete S-R events as much as with the more global aspects of behaving.

Third, Tolman insisted that what is learned as a function of reinforcement is not a response-stimulus link or a response-reinforcement link but a cognition—an awareness that reward is likely to follow certain behaviors. This awareness or expectancy guides behavior, thus making it reasonable for Tolman to describe his system as one of purposive behaviorism.

The Gestaltists: German Cognitivism

The first cognitive position in American psychology was associated with the Gestalt school. This was the name applied to the system advanced by a group of German psychologists—Wolfgang Köhler, Kurt Koffka, and Max Wertheimer—who emigrated to the United States and did much of their research, lecturing, and writing there.

One sense in which Gestalt psychology represents an important transition in the history of learning theories is that the gestaltists used people for their research about half the time, whereas behavioristic psychologists had conducted most of their research on animals.

The Gestalt position is a cognitive position because of its preoccupation with perception and because of its rejection of trial-and-error explanations of human learning. The Gestalt explanation is that people learn through insight.

The Gestalt approach is one of synthesis: Even physical objects cannot be completely known or understood through an analysis of their parts. "The whole is greater than the sum of its parts" became the familiar Gestalt slogan.

The chief concern of Gestalt psychology was to discover the laws governing perception. The gestaltists were responsible for the elaboration of such "laws" as closure, proximity, symmetry, continuity, and prägnanz.

Modern Cognitivism

This text's chronology (from behaviorism to cognitivism) might make it seem as though more recent formulations are more enlightened, more accurate, and more useful, and that they must therefore have completely replaced older theories by now. This is not entirely so. Many aspects of earlier positions have survived and continue to appear in current theories and applications, though not always in completely recognizable guises. And behaviorism is still a vigorous and growing orientation in psychology, well represented in current professional literature as well as in countless educational and therapeutic programs. But cognitive metaphors are now in the majority.

Bruner: Going Beyond the Information Given

Jerome S. Bruner has developed a loose-knit cognitive theory intended to explain various phenomena in perception, decision making, information processing, conceptualization, and development. His earlier writings deal primarily with concept learning; his more recent interests are largely in the area of development.

Bruner's theory is sometimes referred to as a theory of categorizing. To categorize is to treat objects as though they were in some ways equivalent; accordingly, a category can be thought of as a rule for classifying objects by their properties (attributes). Bruner devoted much of his early work to investigating the strategies people use in learning how to categorize stimulus events.

Bruner's approach to learning and problem solving is premised on the assumption that the value of what is learned can be measured by how well it permits the learner to go beyond the information given. He argues that concepts and perceptions are useful when organized into systems of related categories (coding systems) that have wide generality. One of Bruner's major contributions has to do with his role in the so-called cognitive revolution—his championing of approaches that rejected the constraints of behaviorism.

Piaget: Development and Adaptation

Jean Piaget's theory is a system unto itself, not easily compared with other positions. Although Piaget's major focus is development, much of what he says is relevant to learning and behavior because of the close relationship between learning and development.

Piaget describes development as the evolution of a child's ability to interact with the world in an increasingly appropriate, realistic, and logical fashion. Hence, part of his work is a description of children at different stages of development: the sensorimotor stage (birth to 2 years), the preoperational stage (2 to 7 years, comprising preconceptual and intuitive thinking), the period of concrete operations (7 to 11 or 12 years), and the stage of formal operations (11 or 12 to 14 or 15 years). Each stage is marked by characteristic abilities and errors in problem solving, results from activities and abilities of the preceding period, and is a preparation for the next stage.

Another aspect of Piaget's work discusses the properties of children that enable them to make progress in their development. Thus, he describes intelligence as a biologically oriented process involving a combination of using previously learned capabilities (assimilation) and modifying behavior as required (accommodation). An optimal balance between these processes (equilibrium) constitutes maximally adaptive behavior.

Children construct a view of reality, says Piaget, rather than simply discovering it or learning it passively. Thus do they build notions of time, space, causality, logic, geometry, and so on.

Vygotsky: Culture and Language

Had Lev Vygotsky, the Soviet psychologist, lived beyond his short 34 years, he would surely stand very tall among the giants of psychology. This "Mozart" of psychology had apparently mastered all the leading theories of his day and had already developed a far-reaching theory of human learning and development. This theory grants an especially important role to culture, and especially to its most important invention, language. Cultural interaction, together with the language that culture grants us, insists Vygotsky, is what makes all higher mental processes possible.

Vygotsky was especially interested in the intellectual development of children. He worked in the field of *pedology*, the then-popular Soviet discipline of child development that used tests to determine the developmental level of children. One of Vygotsky's important notions was that children who are capable of X on their own might be capable of X plus, say, Y, with the help of some competent adult or older child. This "Y," specifically, that which the child is capable of achieving with prompting and other kinds of assistance, is the *zone of proximal development*. Good teaching and learning, explains Vygotsky, requires that the educator or parent present the child with tasks that fall within this zone—neither so simple that they can be accomplished easily by the child alone, nor so difficult that even with assistance, the child remains incapable of successful performance.

Scaffolding is a general term for the kind of assistance that skilled educators and parents present children. It can include demonstrating, explaining, providing written or real-life models, systematically developing prerequisite skills, asking leading questions, suggesting, correcting errors, and so on—all within the *zone of proximal growth.*

Neural Networks: Connections

The computer, with its systems and functions, has become increasingly common as a metaphor for human cognitive activity. This metaphor compares human neurology and especially the brain (wetware) to computer hardware (physical components), and computer software (programs) to human cognitive functioning. The two most common forms of computer metaphor are the symbolic (based on the functioning of the digital computer) and the connectionist (based on the functioning of the parallel distributed processing computer). Symbolic models assume that all knowledge can be represented in symbols and manipulated using rules; connectionist models recognize that some learning is implicit (rather than explicit) and cannot easily be verbalized.

Connectionist models consist of interconnected units rather than central processors and are therefore also called neural networks. In neural networks, patterns and strengths of connections represent knowledge. Connectionist models lead to machines whose functioning is in some ways similar to that of humans in that it isn't completely logical or predictable. But these models are descriptions rather than explanations, don't always generate plausible results, and don't always function as a human would.

Still, some argue that humans are on the verge of making machines that can actually think—taking into account all the variables, the contingencies, the qualifications that a human might consider. These machines don't think in a completely predictable, linear, old-fashioned-logic kind of way, but in a fuzzy logic, neural network mode in which the programmer doesn't really know beforehand what the computer will decide because the problem is too complex to program symbolically.[3]

Factors Affecting Learning

Among the important factors that are inextricably implicated in human learning are memory and motivation. In fact, studying memory is just another way of studying learning. And motivation, by definition, deals with the causes and

---

[3]The Old Woman laid the manuscript on the sand and motioned that I should put more wood on the fire. As I laid the driftwood on the embers, I asked the Old Woman what role she thought computers might play in clarifying human thinking, say in 10 years. For a moment, she looked as though she would ignore my question, but then she answered another one, one I hadn't asked. She said that these thinking machines aren't really threats, that they won't replace us. She said that's because they feel nothing. They don't care. They don't have emotion. But she explained that despite their lack of feeling, the day is at hand when computers will act as though they really care, and many people will be fooled, and many will have the living be-gory scared out of them as a result. And then she started to read the manuscript again, and I turned the recorder back on.

the reasons for behavior and for behavior change (which, you will recall, defines learning). Theories in each of these areas include both behavioristic and cognitive orientations, although recent investigations of memory and motivation tend to be based primarily on cognitive models.

Memory

One common memory model is a metaphor that says people process and remember information as though they had two separate memory storage areas or processes—one associated with short-term memory (STM, lasting seconds rather than minutes) and another associated with long-term memory (LTM). STM is an active, ongoing process that is easily disrupted and highly limited in capacity; LTM is more passive, relatively stable, and virtually unlimited in capacity.

Current models of long-term memory tend to be associationistic (that is, they assume all knowledge is related), and they often distinguish between explicit, potentially conscious memory (termed *declarative*) and the implicit, unconscious, nonverbalizable effects of learning (termed *nondeclarative* or *procedural*). Explicit or declarative memory includes semantic memory (stable, abstract knowledge) and episodic memory (personal, autobiographical memory, tied to a specific personal time and place). Studies of amnesiacs and neural imaging studies of brain activity indicate that different parts of the brain might be involved in each of these types of memory.

Motivation

Motivation theory addresses the *why* of behavior—a question with many answers. Some behaviors are reflexive: simple unlearned responses to specific situations. Others might result from instincts, which are more complex inherited tendencies common to all members of a species. Still others might result from urges (termed *drives*) associated with basic biological needs such as those for food or drink, or perhaps with psychological needs such as those for achievement, affection, or self-esteem.

Cognitive theories of motivation present a more active view of human behavior—one quite distinct from that of a reactive organism pushed and prodded by hungers and drives over which it has little, if any, control. Maslow's theory recognizes the importance of both basic (deficiency) needs and metaneeds (growth needs), the highest human need being that of self-actualization. Arousal theory looks at the motivating consequences of too low and too high arousal. Cognitive dissonance theory describes how conflicts among beliefs, behaviors, and expectations give rise to behaviors designed to reduce or eliminate the conflicts. Self-determination theory looks at the human need to be autonomous and self-determining. Attribution theory explores systematic tendencies for people to attribute the outcomes of their behaviors to causes they either can or cannot control. And Albert Bandura's account of the role of self-efficacy judgments shows how personal estimates of competence and effectiveness are associated with persistence, achievement, and positive self-concepts. What these newer cognitive approaches to motivation have in common is that they describe behavior as involving a conscious attempt to make sense out of self and environment.

Social Learning

Social learning refers to the learning of socially appropriate behavior as well as to the processes by which humans learn through social interaction. The phrase *social learning* has become almost synonymous with *learning through imitation* or *observational learning*. Bandura's theory of observational learning describes three possible effects of observing models: (1) we learn new behaviors as a result of seeing others (models) engaging in these behaviors (the *modeling* effect), (2) deviant behaviors can be encouraged or discouraged largely as a function of what we observe to be the consequences of such behaviors (*inhibitory* and *disinhibitory* effect), and (3) seeing models engage in what seem to be highly rewarded behaviors can elicit similar, but not identical, behaviors in observers (the eliciting effect).

Bandura's theory of observational learning was initially based largely on a Skinnerian model of operant conditioning: Imitative behaviors are learned because they are reinforced either *directly* (by the model, for example, or because of the imitated behavior's direct consequences) or *vicariously* (a type of second-hand reinforcement where the consequences of a behavior for the model seem to be reinforcing for the observer).

But, explains Bandura, not all human behaviors are under the direct control of their outcomes—as Skinner might have argued. Some behaviors are controlled more directly by stimuli—as in the case of classical conditioning, for example. Others, perhaps far more important for understanding human behavior, are under *symbolic* control. What is truly important, says Bandura, are perhaps less the direct and immediate consequences of an action or of a stimulus than the peculiarly human ability to imagine the action's consequences, to discover cause-and-effect relationships, to anticipate. As a result of so doing, we enthusiastically engage today in behaviors that have no possibility of being reinforced for weeks, months, and even years.

These three behavior control systems—stimulus control, outcome control, and symbolic control—provide a clear and useful summary of the major learning theories discussed in this text. They illustrate the progression from early emphases on understanding the relationship between stimuli and behavior, evident in theories based on a model of classical conditioning, to an emphasis on the consequences of behavior, apparent in theories such as those of Thorndike and Skinner, finally to a progressively more cognitive orientation. In the final analysis, says Bandura, humans are *agents* of their own actions. As agents, they clearly demonstrate intentionality, forethought, and self-reflectiveness.

Ⓢ ynthesis and Appraisal

The preceding sections summarize most of the learning positions described in this text. Table 12.2 and Figure 12.1 synthesize that information. Table 12.2 lists key terms associated with each theoretical position. Figure 12.1 is more visual; it consists of diagrammatic or symbolic representations of aspects of each theory. Note that neither pretends to be a complete representation of the theories in question.

Table 12.2 *Key Words*

Mainly Behaviorist Positions

Watson	Guthrie	Thorndike	Hull	Skinner
Behaviorism	Contiguity	Effect	Habit strength	Operant
Classical conditioning	One-shot learning	Satisfiers	Hypothetico-deductive	Respondent
Reflexes	Habits	Annoyers	Reaction potential	Schedules
Environmentalism	Threshold	Stamping in	Drive	Extinction
Contiguity	Fatigue	Stamping out	Goal reactions	Rats
	Incompatible stimuli	Trial and error	Habit families	Shaping
		Connectionism	Intervening variables	Superstition
				Programmed instruction
				Behavior modification

	Transition		*Mainly Cognitive Positions*			
Hebb	**Tolman**	**Gestaltists**	**Bruner**	**Piaget**	**Vygotsky**	**Information-processing models**
Cell assembly	Purposive	Perception	Categorizing	Equilibrium	Culture	Neural networks
Phase sequence	Molar	Wholes	Concept formation	Stages	Language	Connectionism
Neurophysiology	Intention	Prägnanz	Attributes	Assimilation	Social speech	Parallel distributed processing
Arousal	Expectancy	Closure	Coding systems	Accommodation	Inner speech	Symbolic models
	Sign-significate	Insight	Strategies	Operations	Egocentric speech	Artificial intelligence
	Place learning			Logic	Zone of proximal growth	Wetware
				Conservation	Scaffolding	Hardware
						Software

Behaviorism

Watson	Thorndike	Guthrie	Hull	Skinner
US → UR	1) $S_1 \rightarrow R_1$ (pleasant)	$S_1 \rightarrow R_1$	$_SE_R = {}_SH_R \times D \times V \times K$	$R + S_1 \rightarrow$ reinforcement
CS → ?	2) $S_1 \rightarrow R_1$	$S_1 \rightarrow R_1$		
CS + US → UR				→
CS + US → UR				
CS → CR	1) $S_2 \rightarrow R_2$ (unpleasant)	$S_1 \rightarrow R_1$		$S_1 \rightarrow R_X$
	2) $S_2 \rightarrow$			

Transition

Hebb	Tolman
	Reward 4 kilometers

Cognitivism

Gestaltists	Bruner	Piaget	Information Processing
		content / structure / function	output / hidden units / neurons / input

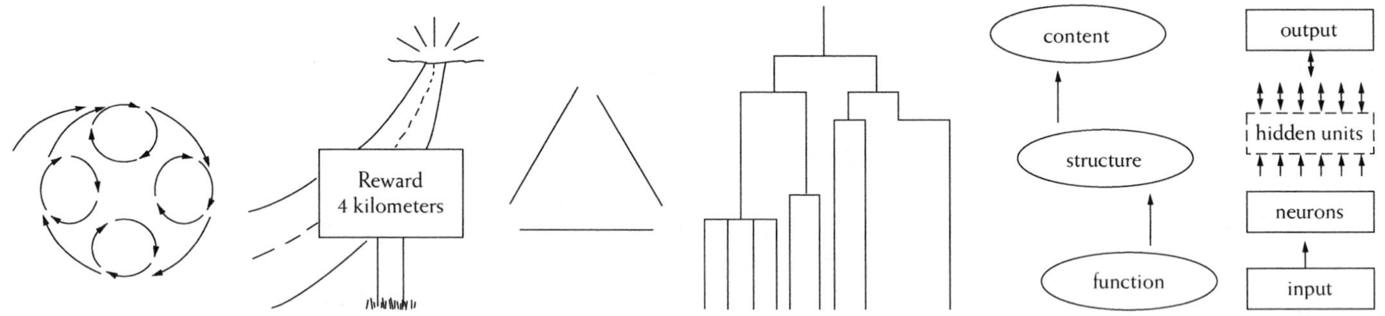

Figure 12.1 Diagrammatic and symbolic representations of the main content of each of the preceding 11 chapters.

Strengths and Weaknesses

An appraisal section follows each of the major learning theories described in this book. This section does not repeat all these evaluations, but simply brings together in one place some of the most important features of earlier evaluations. The following comments are not meant to be an exhaustive catalogue of all the good and bad features of each theory. Besides, criticism and evaluation are quite subjective in the first place—often a matter of taste, or upbringing, or religion. So these evaluations are presented only as suggestions.

Behaviorism

One main criticism of behaviorism is that through its mechanization of humanity it has dehumanized the human animal. Critics point out that humans possess awareness, that feeling is very much a part of behaving, and that surely human interaction with the environment is more than simply a matter of stimuli and responses. These critics contend, further, that conditioning in all of its varieties leaves much human behavior unexplained. Some also react negatively to the use of animals in studies whose results are then generalized to human behavior. Others are appalled and frightened at the thought of applying a science of human behavior to shape and control thought and action.

Behaviorists, in their own defense, maintain that only by dealing with those aspects of human functioning that are clearly measurable and definable can valid and reliable conclusions be reached. Behaviorists point in scorn at the chaotic and confused nature of more "mentalistic" psychologies. They ask what images, feelings, and sensations are, and of what value these might be in developing a science of behavior.

Clearly, behaviorism stresses objectivity and loses some relevance in doing so. Nevertheless, the approach has generated a great deal of applicable research and theory and continues to have a tremendous influence on the development of learning theory. Much of the current emphasis on experimentation and scientific rigor stems from the work of people such as Guthrie, Watson, and especially Hull. Emphasis on the practical applicability of theory owes much to the work of Thorndike. And Skinner's contribution to a practical science of behavior can hardly be overestimated.

A Transition: Evolutionary Psychology and Early Cognitivism

Early behaviorists were certain that their theories, or others based like theirs on objective scientific data, would be widely applicable. If you can condition a rat to press a lever, a dolphin to throw a ball, or a horse to genuflect, then surely you can teach any animal, and—why not?—any person, to do whatever.

Not so. Even among animals, a number of apparently simple behaviors can be conditioned only with great difficulty, or not at all. Certain biological constraints appear to govern much of what animals learn. Thus, pigs reinforced for depositing wooden "nickels" into a piggy bank often appear to prefer rooting around with them, even if doing so means they go hungry. This and related observations, argue a group of psychologists, suggest very strongly that psychology should pay more attention to biology. Sociobiology, an attempt to provide a genetic explanation for social behavior, is one result of this emphasis.

An important contribution of evolutionary psychology and of sociobiology has been to focus increasing attention on the biological roots of human behavior. Related to this, increasing numbers of psychologists are looking at the role of the human brain in learning and behavior. One of the pioneers of this emphasis is Hebb.

The proposal for a theory advanced by Hebb is admittedly based on neurophysiological speculation as well as fact. It has been argued that such an approach is not likely to lead to any new discoveries about learning, or to anything more than an explanation for what is already known or suspected about behavior. Of course, the opposite argument can also be advanced. It can be countered that not all of Hebb's proposal is based on speculation, that there are sources of information about human neurology that are distinct from psychological experimentation, and that a great deal of new information about human neural activity is rapidly leading to a better understanding of learning and behavior. Neural network models of the new connectionism are highly compatible with Hebb's speculation, and owe him an important debt. In addition, some of Hebb's notions concerning arousal have contributed significantly to current theories of motivation.

Hebb, a neobehaviorist, retained a commitment to the need to preserve the objective, scientific nature of psychological investigation. But he also responded to the need to include inferences about profoundly important mental processes such as thinking and imagining, thus serving as a transition from behaviorism to cognitivism.

Tolman, another neobehaviorist, also gave behaviorism a new twist by acknowledging the role of purpose. Many of the first generation of cognitivists were followers of Tolman.

The first psychological theories clearly identified with modern cognitivism were those of the Gestalt psychologists, Köhler, Wertheimer, and Koffka. Unlike behaviorists such as Thorndike who believed that learning and problem solving occur through trial and error, the gestaltists thought people learn through insight. Accordingly, their main concerns were with cognitive topics such as insight, perception, and problem solving. These theories are sometimes criticized for being vague. At the same time, however, they have contributed significantly to counseling practice as well as to the subsequent development of cognitive theories.

Cognitivism

Critics of cognitive approaches to human learning sometimes base their objections on the cognitivists' sometimes less precise and more subjective approach to information gathering and to theorizing. The extensive use of jargon by many contemporary cognitivists and the seeming lack of agreement among different positions have also caused confusion and criticism.

Both Bruner and Piaget have been criticized because their terminology is sometimes confusing and because the metaphors they use are often obscure and impractical. Piaget has also been much criticized for his imprecise experimental methods, his nonrepresentative samples, the extremely small numbers of subjects employed in most of his studies, the lack of statistical analysis in his early work, and for his tendency to overgeneralize and overtheorize from his data. And Vygotsky has been criticized for his lack of precision, and for the global and all-encompassing nature of his theorizing. Cognitive theorists sometimes counter these criticisms by pointing out that they are dealing with topics that are more relevant to human behavior than are questions relating only to stimuli, responses, and response consequences, and investigating these topics sometimes requires making inferences from relatively limited data.

Bruner, Piaget, and Vygotsky continue to have tremendous influence on child-rearing, and especially on practices in schools. Piaget is largely responsible for converting a generation of teachers, parents, and childcare workers into fascinated observers of children and their development. And in recent decades, Vygotsky's theorizing has enjoyed increasing popularity among educators.

Two Eclectic Integrations

Historically, the search in learning theory has been for one best way of explaining human behavior—a search clearly based on the assumption that there is one best explanation. But what if there isn't? What if psychology assumes that because there are many different kinds of human learning, there is a need for many different explanations?

Several theorists have made just that assumption, and the resulting theories are typically an integration of a variety of concepts that have traditionally been associated with separate positions. Among these thinkers are Robert Gagné and Jerome Bruner. Their theories can be viewed as highly useful syntheses of many of the theories discussed earlier in this book.

Robert Gagné: An Instructional Design Theory

People learn in many ways, claims Gagné. They learn through simple Pavlovian conditioning, through Skinnerian conditioning, and through more cognitive processes. These various ways of learning are most evident in the different outcomes of the learning process—of which there are five (see Table 12.3).

Gagné describes the five major outcomes of learning as different kinds of learned capabilities. Thus, there are **intellectual skills,** verbal information, **cognitive strategies,** attitudes, and motor skills (Gagné, Briggs, & Wager, 1992). Intellectual skills are concerned with the *how* of learning and relate well to the learning theories described in preceding chapters. The other four domains are concerned more with the *what* of learning.

One of the most important features of Gagné's theory is that it pays special attention to the conditions that facilitate each of these learning outcomes (Gagné, Briggs, & Wager, 1988). This theory is geared toward resolving very practical issues related to how to design instructional programs and is probably the most influential instructional design theory of the past several decades (Richey, 2000; Zemke, 1999).

Although people learn in different ways, and although the outcomes of learning can be described through different outcomes, Gagné insists that nine instructional events can profitably be used in all types of instruction. We look at these instructional events after a brief look at the outcomes of learning, and at the conditions that assist these outcomes.

Verbal Information

Verbal information is the learning outcome that is perhaps of greatest concern to teachers. Verbal information is defined in terms of what is generally considered **knowledge.** Although it is not always derived only from verbal input (or stored verbally, for that matter), verbal information can be expressed in the form of a sentence—or at least an implied sentence.

Cognitive Strategies

Cognitive strategies are the specific means by which people guide their intellectual functioning. These are the plans (strategies) that govern how people go about learning, remembering, paying attention, synthesizing, abstracting, creating, and so on. They are skills that appear to be largely self-learned even though schools (and teacher education programs) typically pay considerable lip service to them.

Attitudes

Attitudes are affective (emotional) reactions that can generally be described as positive or negative and that have important motivational qualities. Gagné suggests that one important way in which attitudes are learned involves imitation much as Bandura describes it. In Gagné's words, "An attitude is an acquired internal state that influences the choice of personal action" (Gagné & Driscoll, 1988, p. 58).

Motor Skills

Motor skills are the variety of organized, sequential activities that involve the use of muscles. They include all complex behaviors that require an organized pattern of controlled muscular movements. Writing, talking, plucking chickens, and hitting a spittoon from 22 paces are all examples of motor skills.

Intellectual Skills

The domain of behaviors to which Gagné has paid the greatest attention is that of intellectual skills. These include all the skills involved in acquiring information, solving problems, discovering rules, and learning how to talk, to name but a few. In earlier descriptions of his theory, Gagné (1974) distinguished between eight different types of learning. The first four were clear examples of Pavlovian and Skinnerian conditioning (for example, signal learning, stimulus-response learning, and learning of chains); the last four presented more cognitive kinds of learning. In his more recent writing, however, he lumps the first four types under the heading of "simple types of learning" (Gagné & Dick, 1983). To illustrate how Gagné's view integrates the major positions described in this book, the original eight types of learning are summarized briefly here.

Two points need to be noted at the outset. First, the types of learning are not completely independent from one another but are actually hierarchical. The simplest learning is necessary before the learner can go on to more complex types of learning. Second, types of learning are distinguishable largely by the conditions that permit the learning to take place.

Type 1: Signal Learning

Definition: Simple Pavlovian conditioning.

Example: A car horn blasts. A man jumps, startled. The same man sees another car. He jumps again although the horn does not sound.

Important theorists: Pavlov, Watson

Type 2: Stimulus-Response Learning

Definition: The formation of a single connection between a stimulus and a response.

Example: A fat sow is turned clockwise as a psychologist says gently, "Turn." After each complete turn, the sow is given half an apple. The psychologist does this every day for 2 years. After 730 apples and 1,459 turns (the psychologist ate half the apple once), the sow now turns whenever the psychologist says "Turn." That is slow stimulus-response learning.

Important theorists: Skinner, Thorndike, Hull

Type 3: Chaining—Motor Chains

Definition: The connection of a sequence of stimulus-motor behaviors.

Example: A man is seen removing his teeth. He reaches to his mouth with his hand, opens his mouth and inserts his hand, places the thumb and forefinger on the right upper canine, and pulls. He then does the same for his lower teeth. The S-R chain may be simplified as follows:

$$S \rightarrow R \text{ --- } S \rightarrow R \text{ --- } S \rightarrow R \text{ --- } S \rightarrow R$$

| hand at mouth | open mouth | mouth open | insert hand | hand inserted | position fingers | fingers positioned | pull |

Important theorists: Guthrie, Thorndike, Skinner

Type 4: Chaining—Verbal Associations

Definition: The connection of a sequence of verbal stimulus-response behaviors.

Example: One, two, three, four, five . . .

Important theorists: Hull, Hebb, Bruner, Vygotsky

Type 5: Discrimination Learning

Definition: Learning to discriminate between highly similar stimulus input. The learning of discriminations is "essentially a matter of establishing numbers of different chains" (Gagné, 1965, p. 115).

Example: Learning a foreign language involves learning verbal chains in that language. Because these chains are already present in the mother tongue, the learner must discriminate between the two.

Important theorists: Skinner, Bruner, Hebb, Vygotsky

Type 6: Concept Learning

Definition: Concept learning involves responding to a set of objects in terms of their similarities. Gagné distinguishes between concrete concepts, which can be pointed at (dog), and defined concepts (uncle or religion).

Example: A boy learns that an English setter is a dog. He sees a cat and says "doggie." He has developed a "doggie" concept, albeit an incorrect one.

Important theorists: Hebb, Bruner, Skinner, Piaget, Vygotsky

Type 7: Rule Learning

Definition: "A rule is an inferred capability that enables the individual to respond to a class of stimulus situations with a class of performances" (Gagné, 1970, p. 191). Rules enable learners to actually do things, rather than simply being able to state the rule.

Example: A simple rule is exemplified by the statement, "Psychology is fun." Understanding this rule involves understanding the concept *psychology* and the concept *fun.*

Important theorists: Bruner, Piaget, Vygotsky

Type 8: Higher-Order Rules

Definition: Combining simple rules to generate more complex rules that allow the solution of problems.

Example: To find the area of a floor consisting of 24 tiles, each measuring 12 inches by 12 inches, the learner combines the rules: 12 inches equals 1 foot; the area of a tile measuring 1 foot by 1 foot is 1 square foot; the area of surface is equal to the sum of the separate areas of each of its components.

Important theorists: Bruner, Piaget, Vygotsky

Educational Implications of Gagné's Theory: Nine Instructional Events

Gagné's emphasis has gradually shifted toward the more cognitive explanations, and especially toward their usefulness for instruction (Gagné & Medsker, 1996). "Learning," he explains, "is something that takes place inside a person's head—in the brain" (Gagné & Driscoll, 1988, p. 3).[4]

---

[4]You should point out to your readers, said the Old Woman, that this statement implies a false dichotomy: cognitivists on the one hand, who believe that learning takes place inside the head; and behaviorists on the other, who, by implication, must believe that learning takes place elsewhere. In fact, none of the theorists discussed in this entire report would deny that learning takes place inside the head. The point is that Gagné's emphasis, like that of other cognitivists, has been shifting toward events inside the head. In contrast, behaviorists have considered it more fruitful to deal with events outside the head.

Table 12.3 *Gagné's Major Learning Outcomes, Illustrated, with Suggestions Relevant for Instruction*

Outcomes of learning	Examples	Conditions that facilitate outcomes
1. Intellectual skills		
Higher order rules	Learner determines relationships among models of the learner and learning theories	Review of relevant rules; verbal instruction to aid in recall of rules; verbal instructions to direct thinking
Rules	Learner identifies new theory as being cognitive	Learner is made aware of desired learning outcome; relevant concepts are reviewed; concrete examples are provided
Concepts	Learner classifies objects by size and color	Examples presented; learner engaged in finding examples; reinforcement
Discriminations	Learner distinguishes among different printed letters	Simultaneous presentation of stimuli to be discriminated; reinforcement (confirmation); repetition
Simple types of learning (signal learning; stimulus-response learning; chaining)	Learner is conditioned to respond favorably to school	Reinforcement; models; positive experiences in various school contexts
2. Verbal information	Learner writes down Gagné's five major learning domains	Information that organizes content; meaningful context; instructional aids for retention and motivation
3. Cognitive strategies	Learner devises personal strategy for remembering Guthrie's three methods for breaking habits	Frequent presentation of novel and challenging problems
4. Attitudes	Learner chooses to read a learning text rather than a novel	Models; reinforcement; verbal guidance
5. Motor skills	Learner types a summary of this chapter	Models; verbal directions; reinforcement (knowledge of results); practice

Gagné also described nine instructional events that he thought were important for each of the five different learning outcomes that are summarized in Table 12.3. These events set the stage for all learning. In his words, they are the *conditions of learning* (Gagné, Briggs, & Wager, 1992). They should serve all teachers as a basis for organizing instruction, for selecting instructional media, and for evaluating. These instructional events are summarized in Table 12.4.

Jerome Bruner: Models of the Learner

Learning theories, claims Jerome Bruner (1985), are really models of the learner. If we look at the various theories of learning that have been proposed, we get glimpses of the models of the human learner that underlie them.

***Table* 12.4** *Gagné's Nine Instructional Events*

Nine instructional events	Purpose	Possible instructional strategy
Gaining attention	To enable reception of new information	Use highly captivating introduction to establish attention
Informing learners of the objective	To establish expectancy	Inform learners about what they will be able to do following instruction
Stimulating recall of prior learning	To provide anchors to which new learning can be related	Remind/ask students about relevant prior knowledge
Presenting the stimulus	To encourage learners to attend to and learn material	Present new information
Providing learning guidance	To assist students in understanding, organizing, and seeing relevance using semantic encoding (verbalization)	Explain, illustrate, elaborate, show relationships, show applications (perhaps using various instructional media)
Eliciting performance (responding)	To allow the learner to demonstrate learning, or learning problems	Ask for recall, applications, summaries, generalizations
Providing feedback	To provide learner with reinforcement for learning effort	Use verbal or other forms of reinforcement
Assessing performance	To provide learner with opportunity for retrieval	Using formal and informal testing procedures to assess instructional techniques and their effectiveness
Enhancing retention and transfer	To provide learner with an opportunity to apply and generalize learning	Provide practice in different contexts

Tabula Rasa

One of the oldest models of the learner is that of the *tabula rasa* ("blank slate"). This view is premised on the notion that the human is born with no prior knowledge, few inclinations, and no thoughts, although perhaps a few reflexes. All are equal at birth, says the model: Experience subsequently writes its messages on the slate, gradually molding the infant into the child and eventually the adult, accounting for all the eventual differences among people.

The tabula rasa model is sometimes illustrated with the empty-vessel metaphor. The infant's mind, says this metaphor, is like a vessel that is completely empty at birth and that has the same capacity as every other infant's vessel. In time, the waters of experience are poured slowly into the vessel, and in the end some vessels end up fuller than others. Some leak pretty badly.

The tabula rasa model is clearly reflected in the theories of the behaviorists, who undertook to discover and explain the rules by which experience writes its messages or pours its waters—namely, the rules of classical and operant conditioning. When Watson insisted he could make what he wanted of a dozen healthy infants, it was because he firmly believed all infants to be equal at birth and equally susceptible to the influences of experience.[5]

Hypothesis Generator

Some theorists objected to the mechanistic view of the learner presented by the tabula rasa model. Human learners are not so passive, these theorists argued; learners aren't simply pushed this way and that by the stimuli, the rewards, and the punishments that experience holds in store for them. Rather, they are characterized by intentionality. They choose experiences and, perhaps more important, interpret them through their own notions about the world (their own personal hypotheses).

Hull's antedating goal responses provide an early glimpse—albeit a carefully behavioristic one—of the learner as a **hypothesis generator.** Tolman's purposive behaviorism provides an even clearer view of behavior driven by intention rather than simply by external events.

Nativism

The complexity of what the infant and the child have to learn, and the ease and rapidity with which they learn it, suggest yet another model—one that views the human learner not as a blank slate but as possessing a mind characterized by previously built-in constraints and capabilities. **Nativism** holds that the mind is already shaped by important tendencies before any learning occurs. Bruner argues that the infant's mind is not "blooming, buzzing confusion" that James had thought. Rather, it is remarkably sophisticated and well prepared to become the highly complex, culture-using and culture-producing mind of the adult (Bruner, 2000).

Nativistic models are central to the work of **ethologists,** who study and try to understand the behavior of organisms in natural situations. Imprinted behaviors such as the "following" response of young goslings, ethologists explain, are clear evidence of a prewired neurology that constrains and determines behavior. Much the same model underlies psychologists' discovery that some behaviors are more easily conditioned than others, as well as sociobiologists' belief that a wealth of important social behaviors are genetically preprogrammed.

The theories of the gestalt psychologists, too, reflect this nativistic model remarkably closely. Thus, the tendency to perceive wholes rather than parts, to see the best form possible, and to look for patterns and similarities all illustrate wired-in tendencies. Similarly, Chomsky (1972) argues that humans have built-in neurological tendencies relating to language, and these explain how easily and quickly infants acquire language.

---

[5]I want you to tell your super intelligent readers, said the Old Woman somewhat imperiously, that it's a bit of a caricature, a misleading exaggeration, to suggest that most behaviorists adopted this tabula rasa model. Although it's true that aspects of the tabula rasa model are reflected in behaviorists' belief in the conditionability of humans, even the first of the behaviorists, Watson, accepted that infants are born with simple reflexes—hence, not entirely blank. Similarly, Skinner's Darwinian metaphor (the survival of reinforced responses) appeals to the importance of the organism's inherited behavioral repertoire.

Constructivism

The world is not found or discovered, claim psychologists such as Bruner, Piaget, and Vygotsky; rather, it is constructed. The resulting model, **constructivism,** is a model of the learner as a builder of knowledge. It holds that through interactions with the world, children discover how to make meaning out of experience. Thus do children progressively discover rules that govern relationships among events, objects, and phenomena of the real world, as well as rules for abstracting significance and for generating concepts. The constructivist learner is a self-motivated, mastery-oriented learner, driven by a need to know, to organize, to understand, to build meaning. Even adults continue to strive to build meaning and, perhaps far more than the child, to understand the significance of their lives. To this end, they tell themselves stories, personal narratives. And they struggle to understand the beginnings, the middles, and, yes, the ends too of these stories to make sense of them and, by so doing, make sense of their own lives (Bruner, 2002).

As we saw in Chapter 7, Bruner's description of the learner as one who sifts through the data of experience to form concepts and to organize elaborate mental structures corresponding to the world is a constructivist model. The same is true of Piaget's view of the learner as assimilating and accommodating to invent and build progressively more advanced representations and systems of rules for dealing with the world.

Novice-to-Expert

A more recent model of the learner, says Bruner (1985), is one that is less concerned with theory than with the practical business of taking learners who are novices and making experts out of them. One approach suggested by this **novice-to-expert** model is to analyze experts and novices, describe the differences between them, and then devise ways of making the novice more like the expert. The novice-to-expert model is evident in information-processing approaches that use computers to simulate aspects of learning. Connectionism, for example, tries to mimic with neural network models the functioning of the human mind; in other words, it tries to create an expert system. In much the same way, symbolic computer models, such as those illustrated in chess-playing programs, attempt to discover the strategies that account for chess expertise.

In contrast with other models, the novice-to-expert model tends to be domain specific rather than general. That is, different models are developed for different areas (such as playing chess or reading a page).

These five models of the human learner are summarized in Table 12.5.

 **he Last Word**

As this book makes clear, there have historically been a variety of different explanations of learning and, hence, a variety of different models of the learner. Through much of history, the notion has lingered that one model and one group of theories must be more correct, more useful, better than the others. "It was

Table 12.5 *Models of the Learner*

Model	Definition	Theories reflecting the model*
Tabula rasa	The learner is an empty vessel waiting to be filled	Watson, Guthrie, Pavlov, Skinner, Thorndike
Hypothesis generator	The learner is characterized by intentionality and evaluates experience through personal expectations and suppositions	Tolman, Hull
Nativism	The learner is born with some constraints and predispositions that make learning some things (such as language) highly probable	Ethologists, sociobiologists, Gestalt psychologists
Constructivism	The learner invents rules, discovers concepts, and builds representations of the world	Piaget, Bruner, Vygotsky
Novice-to-expert	The learner is a novice in specific domains and becomes more expert as differences between expert and novice functioning are eliminated	Information-processing models; connectionism (neural network models)

*Note that most theories also include elements of other models.

the vanity of a preceding generation," says Bruner, "to think that the battle over learning theories would eventuate in one winning over all the others" (1985, p. 8).

None has clearly won over all, perhaps because there isn't one kind of learning. In the end, the most useful models may well prove to be those that recognize this most clearly and allow for all the various kinds of learning possible in the wealth of circumstances under which learning takes place. Such a model would recognize that the strength of the human learner lies in the enormous range of competencies and adaptations possible.

Ideally, the human learner is flexible rather than rigid, open rather than closed, inventive rather than receptive, changing rather than fixed, and poetic rather than prosaic. Models of the learner and resulting theories should reflect this.

Summary

1. There appears to be a human need to simplify, to bring order out of chaos, to invent theory. One problem in summarizing learning theory is to simplify without lying.

2. The major divisions in learning theory reflect different concerns and different approaches to data gathering and science building. Behaviorists are primarily

concerned with objective, observable events (stimuli, responses, reinforcers); cognitivists are more concerned with mental processes (thinking, problem solving, perception, decision making).

3. Pavlov, Watson, Guthrie, Thorndike, Hull, and Skinner are behaviorists. Evolutionary psychologists, and psychologists such as Hebb, and Tolman, represent the beginning of a transition between behaviorism and cognitivism. Gestalt psychology reflects early attempts to develop cognitively based theories. Bruner, Piaget, Vygotsky, and theorists whose models are computer-based are cognitive psychologists.

4. Studying memory is another way of studying learning. Motivation looks at the causes and reasons for behavior and behavior change. Memory models are primarily cognitive; models of motivation include behavioristic (needs, drives) and cognitive (attributions, self-concepts, need for achievement) approaches. Social learning theory deals mainly with how we learn socially appropriate ways of behaving. Bandura's theory of social learning presents an important and highly integrative account of learning through observation.

5. Major criticisms of behaviorism have to do with its mechanization of humans and its failure to account for such mental events as thinking, feeling, and understanding. Major criticisms of cognitivism relate to its less precise and more subjective approach and to its use of technical terms that are not always clearly defined.

6. Both behavioristic and cognitive models continue to influence psychological theory and practice, as do the more biologically based orientations. Major contributions of behavioristic approaches include an important assortment of approaches for treating behavior problems and emotional disorders, as well as for changing behavior in classrooms.

7. Gagné integrates a range of learning theories in his description of five hierarchical classes of learning underlying intellectual skills (simple types, discriminations, concepts, rules, and higher order rules), as well as four other domains of learning (verbal information, cognitive strategies, attitudes, and motor skills). His description of the conditions that facilitate each of these types of learning, and of the nine instructional events that can be applied for each, have important instructional implications.

8. Bruner describes five models of the learner, which are reflected in different learning theories: tabula rasa (empty vessel, behavioristic), hypothesis generator (intention and prediction; Tolman, Hull), nativism (prewired constraints and predispositions; ethologists, gestaltists), constructivism (invention and building of cognitive representations; Piaget, Bruner, Vygotsky), and novice-to-expert (computer simulation, information-processing models, neural networks).

9. No one has yet won the battle of the learning theories. This battle has largely been abandoned following the recognition that there isn't just one kind of learning, and that there is not likely to be just one kind of explanation.

Lefrançois's Epilogue

The Old Woman is gone, which is sad. "Where are you going?" I shouted at her back as she trudged through the snow toward the beaver dam, the one-eyed orange cat at her heels. "Where are you from?" I yelled when she didn't answer my first question.

"I'll be back," she answered a different question. Right! I've heard that before. Kongor, Kro, and the Old Man said exactly the same thing.

And then she stopped and pulled something from her pocket and hung it on a poplar branch. The cat darted in front of her and dashed into the trees, almost as if he knew where the Old Woman was going. The Old Woman waved once, without turning around, and then she too disappeared. I haven't seen either of them since.

What the Old Woman had hung in the tree was a flag just like the other two I already had folded up in one of the shoeboxes under my bed so that now I have three.

The colors have faded, but you can still see the pig rampant on the right side of the escutcheon, facing the turkey glissant in some unexplained personal interaction. Both are on a field of what could be dandelions. The inscription, fronti nulla fides, is now barely legible, but its meaning is burned forever in my brain. "The forehead is never faithful" is the literal translation, but it actually means "You can't judge a book by its cover." Which is true. Nor can you judge a book by its author, or an author by his or her book.

Kongor—not a real good photo but, what the hey, that was 30 years ago.

Kro and me, both sleeping. Don't be fooled by the wide-open, bulbous eyes and the stupid grin on his face; that's how Korons sleep.

The Old Man. Whenever there was a camera around, he always managed to hide his face.

The Old Woman liked to cook in the bush cabin. But if she saw or heard my camera, she would give me no food.

When the children succeeded in photographing the Old Woman, she was always going, never coming.

She waved once, but didn't turn around. Then she disappeared into the trees. That's the last time I saw her.

Glossary

Absolute threshold The midpoint between a level of stimulus intensity below which the stimulus is never detected and the point above which it is always detected.

Accommodation Modification of an activity or ability in the face of environmental demands. In Piaget's description of development, assimilation and accommodation are the means by which individuals interact with and adapt to their world. (*See* Assimilation.)

Acquisition In conditioning theories, acquisition is sometimes used interchangeably with the term *learning*. It might be used to signify the formation of associations among stimuli or between responses and their consequences.

Action potential A pulselike electrical discharge along a neuron. Sequences of linked action potentials are the basis for the transmission of neural messages.

Adaptation Changes in an organism in response to the environment. Such changes are assumed to facilitate interaction with that environment. Adaptation plays a central role in Piaget's theory. (*See* Assimilation, Accommodation.)

Agentic perspective An orientation, described by Bandura, that emphasizes the extent to which people are authors (agents) of their own actions (rather than simply experiencing that which happens to them) as is evident in their use intentionality, forethought, self-reactiveness, and self-reflectiveness.

Aggregate inhibitory potential ($_s\mathring{I}_R$) In Hull's system, an intervening variable that reduces the likelihood of responding. Reflects conflicting habits as well as the amount of work involved in responding.

Agonist An agent or drug that enhances the activity of some naturally occurring substance. For example, cocaine is a dopamine agonist in that it appears to stimulate the activity of dopamine.

Alpha waves Brain waves associated with restful but waking states of consciousness. Characteristically deep, regular waves. (*See* Beta waves.)

Altruism Selflessness. In an evolutionary sense, a powerful tendency to do things that increase the probability that other related individuals will survive, even when doing these things poses serious risk to the actor.

Amnesia A partial, or total, loss of memory. May often be associated with head injury or disease resulting in brain impairment.

Amygdala A small structure in the limbic system (part of the forebrain) that is involved in emotion and aggression and that plays an important role in the processing and storage of memories that have to do with emotion.

Analog computer A computer that, in contrast with a digital computer, represents variables as changing in a continuous rather than discrete fashion.

Anthropomorphism The tendency to imbue inanimate objects, animals, and gods with human characteristics and feelings.

Arousal As a physiological concept, arousal refers to changes in functions such as heart rate, respiration rate, electrical activity in the cortex, and electrical conductivity of the skin. As a psychological concept, arousal refers to degree of alertness, awareness, vigilance, or wakefulness. Arousal varies from very low (coma or sleep) to very high (panic or high anxiety).

Arousal function In Hebb's and Hull's theories, the motivating function of a stimulus. That aspect of the stimulus that relates to attention or alertness. (*See* Cue function.)

Arousal theory A motivational theory that looks at how intensity of motivation is related to physiological changes. (*See* Arousal.)

Artificial intelligence (AI) Describes models, procedures, devices, or mechanisms intended to simulate or duplicate some of the intelligent functions of human mental activity.

Assimilation The act of incorporating objects or aspects of objects into previously learned activities. To assimilate is, in a sense, to ingest or to use for something that is previously learned. (*See* Accommodation.)

Associative shifting A Thorndikean concept that describes a process whereby a response is gradually shifted to a situation entirely different from that in which it was learned. One way of doing this is to change the initial stimulus very gradually (a process called *fading*).

Assumption A belief important in reasoning, accepted as fact but often unprovable.

Attention A state of the reacting organism that implies a narrowing and focusing of perception—a selection and emphasis of that to which the organism responds. Attention may be equated with short-term memory.

Attitude A prevailing and consistent tendency to react in a certain way. Attitudes can be positive or negative and are important motivational forces.

Attribute A characteristic of an object; a quality or value. (*See* Criterial attribute.)

Attribution theory A theory that looks for regularities in the ways in which people attribute things that happen to certain causes, either internal or external.

Autoshaping Refers to responses that are learned in experimental situations even though they are not necessary to obtain reinforcement. Autoshaped behaviors (like pecking in pigeons) often appear to be part of the organism's repertoire of "natural" behaviors.

Axon An elongated, trunklike extension of a neuron. Neural impulses are ordinarily transmitted from the cell body outward along the axon.

Back propagation A type of neural network model in which the system uses information about the appropriateness of its output to adjust the weightings of the connections among intervening units.

Backward pairing In classical conditioning, the presentation of the US before the CS. (*See* Delayed pairing, Trace pairing, Simultaneous pairing.)

Behavior management The deliberate and systematic application of psychological principles in attempts to change behavior. Behavior management programs are most often based largely on behavioristic principles. (*See* Behavior modification, Behavior therapy.)

Behavior modification The deliberate application of operant conditioning principles in an effort to change behavior. (*See* Behavior therapy; Behavior management.)

Behavior therapy The systematic application of Pavlovian procedures and ideas in an effort to change behavior. (*See* Behavior modification; Behavior management.)

Behavioral field A Gestalt concept defined in terms of the individual's personal perception of reality; also called the *psychological field*.

Behavioral oscillation ($_S O_R$) Concept based on Hull's recognition that the potential of a situation to elicit a response is not fixed but varies (oscillates) around a central point. Hence, behavior is never completely predictable.

Behaviorism A general term for approaches to theories of learning concerned primarily with the observable components of behavior (such as stimuli and responses).

Belief The acceptance of an idea as being accurate or truthful. Beliefs are often highly personal and resistant to change. (*See* Law, Principle, Theory.)

Beta waves Characteristically shallow, rapid brain waves associated with alertness. (*See* Alpha waves.)

Biofeedback The information we obtain about our biological functioning. Also refers to procedures whereby individuals are given information about their physiological functioning so they can achieve control over aspects of this functioning.

Biological constraints Limitations on learning that result from biological factors rather than from experience.

Black box Could be the squarish, blackish box (alluded to in Chapter 8) in which grandfathers keep their family jewels. In psychology, more likely to be a metaphor for the mind, implying its unknown (unknowable?) nature—a metaphor embraced by "radical" behaviorists who refrain from speculating about mental processes.

Blocking A phenomenon in classical conditioning in which conditioning to a specific stimulus becomes difficult or impossible because of prior conditioning to another stimulus.

Brain stem The collection of brain structures that joins the brain to the spinal cord.

Bubba psychology An expression for folk beliefs in psychology, also referred to as *naive* or *implicit* theories. *Bubba* means grandmother.

Categorization A Brunerian concept referring to the process of identifying objects or events on the basis of the attributes they share with other instances. (*See* Category.)

Category A term Bruner used to describe a grouping of related objects or events. In this sense, a category is both a concept and a percept. Bruner also defines it as a rule for classifying things as equivalent. (*See* Coding system.)

Causes Agents or forces that produce an effect or a result. Causes are one aspect of motivation. (*See* Reasons, Motivation.)

Cell assembly A hypothetical structure in Hebb's theory, consisting of a circuit of neurons that reactivate one another. Corresponds to relatively simple sensory input. (*See* Phase sequence.)

Cell body The main part of a cell, containing the nucleus.

Central executive system In Baddeley's model of working memory (short-term memory or STM), that which is concerned with regulating the flow of information from sensory storage, processing it for long-term storage, and retrieving it from long-term storage.

Cerebellum Literally "little brain," this structure is located at the bottom rear of the brain, attached to the brain stem. It controls rapid and habitual movements, and coordinates motor activity.

Cerebral cortex The one-eighth inch thick outer covering of the cerebrum. Its four major divisions (on each side of the brain), the cerebral lobes, are implicated in sensation, hearing, language, speech, and higher thought processes.

Cerebrum The largest, most complex, and most highly developed part of the human brain relative to the brains of non-human animals. Its outer covering, the *cerebral cortex*, is centrally involved in higher mental functioning.

Chaining A Skinnerian explanation for the linking of sequences of responses through the action of discriminative stimuli that act as secondary reinforcers. Most behaviors involve such chains, according to Skinner.

Chunking A memory process whereby related items are grouped together into more easily remembered "chunks" (for example, a prefix and four digits for a phone number, rather than seven unrelated numbers).

Classical conditioning Involves the repeated pairing of two stimuli so that a previously neutral (conditioned) stimulus eventually elicits a response (conditioned response) similar to that originally elicited by a nonneutral (unconditioned) stimulus. Originally described by Pavlov. (*See* Conditioning, Operant conditioning.)

Closure A Gestalt principle referring to our tendency to perceive incomplete patterns as complete. (*See* Continuity, Prägnanz, Proximity, Similarity.)

Coding system A Brunerian concept referring to a hierarchical arrangement of related categories.

Cognitions To cognize is to know. Hence, *cognitions* refers to things that are known. Similarly, *cognition* refers to knowing, understanding, problem solving, and related intellectual processes.

Cognitive architecture A term used in cognitive research to refer to abstract, symbolic descriptions of the human cognitive processing system. Cognitive architecture includes all the systems and processes assumed to be necessary for perception, thinking, problem solving, and other cognitive activity.

Cognitive dissonance A state of conflict involving beliefs, behaviors, or expectations. Festinger argued that cognitive dissonance is an important motive for behavior.

Cognitive map Tolman's term for a mental representation of a physical environment in which goals are located, as well as an internal representation of relationships between behavior and goals.

Cognitive strategies The processes involved in learning and remembering. Cognitive strategies include procedures for identifying problems, selecting approaches to their solution, monitoring progress in solving problems, and using feedback.

Cognitivism A general term for approaches to theories of learning concerned with such intellectual events as problem solving, information processing, thinking, and imagining.

Combined schedule A combination of various types of schedules of reinforcement.

Common sense Widely held beliefs that seem intuitively correct. Sometimes they are correct; sometimes they are not. (*See* Bubba psychology.)

Compensation A logical rule relating to the fact that certain changes can compensate for opposing changes, thereby negating their effect.

Computer literacy The minimal skills required for effective interaction with computers. Does not require knowing how a computer functions, or how to program computers.

Computer simulation Attempts to develop computer systems capable of mimicking the intelligent functioning of humans (including errors and biases). In computer simulation, the emphasis is on process; in contrast, the field of artificial intelligence emphasizes the outcome. (*See* Artificial intelligence.)

Concept An abstraction or representation of the common properties of events, objects, or experiences; an idea or notion.

Concept attainment In Bruner's system, discovering the attributes that identify members of a category. (*See* Concept formation.)

Concept formation In Bruner's system, discovering that different classes exist. (*See* Concept attainment.)

Conceptual change movement A discovery-oriented movement in education, highly compatible with Bruner's theory, where the emphasis is on fostering discovery and mental reorganization rather than simply increasing the number of facts and procedures learned.

Concrete operations The third of Piaget's four major stages, lasting from age 7 or 8 to approximately age 11 or 12 and characterized largely by the child's ability to deal with concrete problems and objects, or objects and problems easily imagined.

Conditioned emotional reactions (CERs) A largely unavoidable emotional reaction associated with a conditioned stimulus, acquired through repeated exposure to specific emotion-related situations.

Conditioned response (CR) A response elicited by a conditioned stimulus. In some obvious ways, a conditioned response resembles, but is not identical to, its corresponding unconditioned response.

Conditioned stimulus (CS) A stimulus that initially does not elicit any response (or that elicits a global, orienting response) but that, as a function of being paired with an unconditioned stimulus and its response, acquires the capability of eliciting that same response. For example, a stimulus that is always present at the time of a fear reaction may become a conditioned stimulus for fear.

Conditioning A type of learning describable in terms of changing relationships between stimuli, between responses, or between both stimuli and responses. (*See* Classical conditioning, Operant conditioning.)

Connectionism E. L. Thorndike's term for his theory of learning, based on the notion that learning is the formation of neural connections between stimuli and responses.

Connectionist model Label for parallel distributed processing (PDP) models of the human cognitive processing system. Such models recognize unconscious, automatic, implicit, nonsymbolic learning. They are based not on the application of previously determined rules but, rather, on the generation (learning) of new rules. The basic metaphor is that of cognitive processing involving complex arrangements and modifications of connections among neural units. (*See* Symbolic models, Neural network.)

Conservation A Piagetian term for the realization that certain quantitative attributes of objects remain unchanged unless something is added to or taken away from them. Such characteristics of objects as mass, number, area, and volume are capable of being conserved.

Constructivism A model (illustrated in the theories of Piaget and Bruner) that views the learner as actively inventing and building representations of reality, rather than as simply discovering what is already out there.

Contiguity The occurrence of things both simultaneously and in the same space. Contiguity is often used to explain classical conditioning.

Contingency A consequence. The outcome of a behavior. What follows behavior. Positive and negative contingencies define the various kinds of reinforcement and punishment. Contingency implies dependency. Events are said to be contingent when the occurrence of one depends on the occurrence of the other. For example, daylight is contingent on sunrise; good grades are contingent on studying (or intelligence, or good luck, or what have you).

Continuity A Gestalt principle evident in our tendency to perceive patterns as continuous. (*See* Closure, Prägnanz, Proximity, Similarity.)

Continuous reinforcement A reinforcement schedule in which every correct response is followed by a reinforcer.

Control group In an experiment, a group comprising individuals as similar to the experimental group as possible except that they are not exposed to an experimental treatment. (*See* Experimental group.)

Counterconditioning A behavior modification technique (similar to Guthrie's threshold technique or his method of incompatible stimuli) in which stimuli associated with an undesirable response are presented below threshold or at times when the undesirable response is unlikely to occur. The object is to condition a desirable response to replace the undesirable one.

Criterial attribute An expression Bruner used to describe the characteristics of objects, events, or experiences that define their membership in a category—in other words, that are essential to their being what they are.

Critical period A period in development during which exposure to appropriate experiences or stimuli will bring about imprinting. (*See* Imprinting.)

Cue function In Hebb's and Hull's theories, the message function of a stimulus—the aspect of the stimulus that tells the organism how it should react. (*See* Arousal function.)

Culture The sum total of the attainments and accumulated customs, beliefs, and mores of a group. Human cultures are typically marked by shared languages, spiritual beliefs, habits, and so forth.

Cumulative recording A graphical representation of number of responses over time (hence, of rate of responding), Skinner used this widely in his investigations of bar pressing and key pecking.

Decay theory An explanation for loss of information in short-term memory based on the notion that the physiological effects of stimulation fade. Similar to *fading* in connection with forgetting in long-term memory. (*See* Fading.)

Declarative memory Explicit, conscious long-term memory, in contrast with implicit memory. Declarative memory may be either semantic or episodic. (*See* Explicit memory.)

Deferred imitation The ability to imitate people or events in their absence. Piaget assumes that deferred imitation is crucial in the development of language abilities.

Delayed pairing In classical conditioning, the presentation of the CS before the US, with both ending simultaneously. (*See* Backward pairing, Simultaneous pairing, Trace pairing.)

Dendrite Hairlike tendrils found on a neuron's cell body. Their function is to receive impulses.

Dependent variable The variable (measurement, outcome, behavior) that reflects the assumed effects of manipulations of the independent variable(s) in an experiment. The "then" part of the if-then equation implicit in an experimental hypothesis. (*See* Independent variable.)

Determinism The belief that all things have causes rooted in antecedent events. In psychology, refers to the belief that all human behaviors are caused by preceding events and conditions, and not by the exercise of free will.

Differential reinforcement of successive approximations The procedure of reinforcing only some responses and not others. Differential reinforcement is used in the shaping of complex behaviors. (*See* Shaping.)

Differential threshold *See* Just noticeable difference.

Digital computer A computer that, in contrast with an analog computer, represents variables through values that change discretely (1 or 0 for example). A digital computer can be programmed to process as though it were an analog computer.

Direct reinforcement Reinforcement that occurs as a direct consequence of a behavior—such as getting paid to work. (*See* Vicarious reinforcement.)

Discovery learning The acquisition of new information or knowledge largely because of the learner's own efforts. Discovery learning is often associated with Bruner and is contrasted with *reception learning*. (*See* Reception learning.)

Discrimination Making different responses in closely related situations, thus providing evidence of discriminating among the stimuli (also referred to as *stimulus discrimination*). The opposite of generalization. (*See* Generalization.)

Discriminative stimulus (S^D) Skinner's term for the features of a situation that an organism can discriminate to distinguish between occasions that might be reinforced or not reinforced.

Disinhibitory effect Involves engaging in a previously inhibited, deviant behavior as a result of observing a model. The inhibitory effect involves refraining from a deviant behavior. (*See* Inhibitory/disinhibitory effect.)

Displacement theory Miller's belief that there are a limited number of "slots" in short-term memory (7, plus or minus 2), and that incoming information displaces older information.

Dispositions Attitudes or inclinations. Changes in disposition are often involved in learning.

Distortion theory A theory of forgetting that recognizes that what is remembered is often changed or reconstructed.

Dopamine A brain chemical involved in neural transmission. *Dopaminergic* cells (those that use dopamine for transmission) are found in at least one of the pleasure centers of the brain, as well as in some areas that control physical movement. Loss of dopamine in areas involved in physical movement results in what is termed *Parkinson's disease*. Excessive dopamine activity in the pleasure centers, such as might result from the intake of cocaine, from electrical stimulation, and from rewards such as food and drink, lead to reactions of pleasure.

Double-blind procedure An investigation where neither subjects nor investigators know who members of experimental and control groups are. (*See* Single-blind procedure.)

Drive (D) The tendency to behave that is brought about by an unsatisfied need; for example, the need for food is associated with a hunger drive. A central concept in Hull's theory.

Dualism Descartes's belief that the mind and the body are separate substances.

Egocentric speech Vygotsky's intermediate stage of language development, common between ages 3 and 7, during which children often talk to themselves in an apparent effort to control their own behavior. (*See* Inner speech, Social speech).

Egocentrism A way of functioning characterized by an inability to assume the point of view of others. A child's early thinking is largely egocentric.

Elaboration A memory strategy involving forming new associations. To elaborate is to link with other ideas or images.

Electrodermal response A measure of skin resistance to an electrical current (also termed *galvanic skin response*). Skin conductivity increases with increasing arousal—and increasing perspiration.

Electroencephalogram (EEG) An instrument used to measure electrical activity in the brain.

Eliciting effect Imitative behavior in which the observer does not copy the model's responses but simply behaves in a related manner. (*See* Inhibitory/ disinhibitory effect, Modeling effect.)

Enactive representation A phrase Bruner used to describe how young children tend to represent their world in terms of sensations and actions (hence *enactive*). (*See* Iconic representation, Symbolic representation.)

Engram A permanent change in the brain presumed to underlie memory.

Episodic memory A type of declarative, autobiographical (conscious, long-term) memory consisting of knowledge about personal experiences, tied to specific times and places.

Epistemology A branch of philosophy concerned with questions relating to the nature of knowledge and of knowing.

Equilibration A Piagetian term for the process by which people maintain a balance between assimilation (using old learning) and accommodation (changing behavior; learning new things). Equilibration is essential for adaptation and cognitive growth.

Ethologist A scientist who studies the behavior and adaptation of organisms in natural situations.

Ethology The study of organisms in their natural habitats. The science of animal behavior.

Eugenics A form of genetic engineering that selects specific individuals for reproduction. Although widely accepted and practiced with animals, the concept raises many serious moral and ethical issues when applied to humans.

Event-related field (ERF) A measure of magnetic fields at the scalp relating to neural activity typically associated with specific stimuli. Highly useful for studying brain functioning.

Event-related potential (ERP) A measure of electrical activity in identifiable areas of the brain, corresponding to specific stimuli. Electroencephalograms (EEG) are typically used in studies of ERPs.

Evolutionary psychology An approach in psychology defined by its attention to biology and genetics as sources of explanation for human learning and behavior. The branches of evolutionary psychology are sometimes considered to include sociobiology and behavior genetics.

Exemplar model A concept learning model that assumes that people learn and remember the best examples of a concept, then compare new instances with these examples. (*See* Prototype model.)

Expectancy-value theory A cognitive approach to motivation that describes decision-making as involving a sort of mental calculus where the most important factors are expectancy of success (feelings of self-efficacy) on the one hand, and the values associated with the various options on the other.

Experiment A deliberately controlled arrangement of circumstances under which a phenomenon is observed.

Experimental analysis of behavior A phrase typically associated with Skinner's system. Reflects radical behaviorism's emphasis on the objective analysis of the variables involved in behavior—specifically, what the organism does, the circumstances under which the action occurs, and the consequences of the action (whether behavior occurs again under similar circumstances). (*See* Radical behaviorism.)

Experimental group In an experiment, the group of participants who are exposed to a treatment. (*See* Control group.)

Explicit memory Also termed *declarative memory*. Explicit, conscious long-term memory, in contrast to implicit memory. Explicit memory may be either semantic or episodic. (*See* Episodic memory, Semantic memory.)

Exteroceptive stimulation Relates to sensations associated with external stimuli and involving the senses of vision, hearing, taste, and smell. (*See* Proprioceptive stimulation.)

Extinction In classical conditioning, the cessation of a response following repeated presentations of the CS without the US. In operant conditioning, the cessation of a response following the withdrawal of reinforcement.

Extrinsic motive A motive associated with external sources of reinforcement—like food, money, high grades, praise, and so on.

Extroverts A term used to describe individuals who are predominantly oriented toward the outside rather than the inside. Principal characteristics of introverts include concern with and involvement in social activities. Those who are outgoing and sociable.

Fading A conditioning technique in which certain characteristics of stimuli are gradually faded out, eventually resulting in discriminations that did not originally exist.

Fading theory The belief that inability to recall in long-term memory increases with the passage of time as memory "traces" fade.

Fatigue technique One of Guthrie's methods for replacing habits, involving the repeated presentation of the stimuli that lead to the undesirable habit so that the organism, eventually fatigued, emits (and learns) a different response. (*See* Method of incompatible stimuli, Threshold technique.)

Fitness A measure of the reproductive success of a variation in a trait. Traits that become more common through generations are said to have a higher degree of fitness. (*See* Inclusive fitness.)

Fixed schedule A type of intermittent schedule of reinforcement in which the reinforcement occurs at fixed intervals of time (an interval schedule) or after a specified number of trials (a ratio schedule). (*See* Continuous reinforcement, Interval schedule, Ratio schedule.)

Flashbulb memories Unusually vivid and permanent recollections of the details surrounding first hearing some emotionally significant news.

Forgetting Loss from memory. May involve inability to retrieve, or might involve actual loss of whatever traces or changes define storage. (*See* Memory.)

Formal operations The last of Piaget's four major stages. It begins around age 11 or 12 and lasts until age 14 or 15. It is characterized by the child's increasing ability to use logical thought processes.

Fractional antedating goal response (r_G) One of a collection of related responses made by an organism before the actual goal response.

Frontal lobe Frontal part of the cerebral cortex, centrally involved in higher thought processes.

Functional magnetic resonance imaging (fMRI) A diagnostic imaging technique that detects extremely subtle changes in magnetic fields in the human body, allowing technicians to view real-time, computer enhanced images of soft tissue. Used extensively to diagnose disease as well as to study the brain.

Fuzzy logic A logic that is relativistic, considers a variety of factors, and has a not entirely predictable probability of being correct. Characteristic of parallel processing-based connectionist models.

Generalization The transference of a response from one stimulus to a similar stimulus (stimulus generalization) or the transference of a similar response for another response in the face of a single stimulus (response generalization). Also called *transfer*. (*See* Discrimination.)

Generalized reinforcer Any of a number of powerful, learned reinforcers that are reinforcing for a large variety of behaviors in many situations (behavioral consequences such as praise, prestige, money, fame . . .).

Genetic epistemology One of Piaget's labels for his system. Literally, genetic epistemology refers to the origins and growth of knowledge.

Gestalt A German word meaning whole or configuration. Describes an approach to psychology concerned with the perception of wholes, with insight, and with awareness. Gestalt psychology is a forerunner of contemporary cognitive psychology.

Habit In Guthrie's system, a combination of stimulus-response bonds that become stereotyped and predictable.

Habit strength ($_sH_R$) A behavioristic Hullian concept; the strength of the bond between a specific stimulus and response, reflecting how often the two have been paired *and* reinforced in the past.

Habit-family hierarchy Hull's expression for a collection of habits (stimulus-response links) that are related because they share common goals.

Habituation A highly common form of learning in which an organism's responses to stimulation gradually diminish or cease altogether. Most often occurs following mild, repetitive stimulation. (*See* Sensitization.)

Hardware The physical components of a computer, including monitors, controllers, keyboards, chips, cards, circuits, drives, printers, and so on. (*See* Software, Wetware.)

Hawthorne effect A label for the observation that subjects who are aware they are members of an experimental group often perform better (or differently) than they would if they did not have this knowledge.

Hebb rule Hebb's supposition that the repeated co-firing of two related neurons would lead to a permanent change in the strength of the synapse (connection) between them.

Heuristic Leading to further discoveries. A theory with high heuristic value suggests new avenues of research, new relationships, and new findings.

Higher mental processes A general phrase to indicate unobservable processes that occur in the "mind" (for want of a more precise term). What we normally think of as "thinking."

Higher-order conditioning A phenomenon in conditioning, where a conditioned stimulus takes on the role of an unconditioned stimulus. Thus, a dog conditioned to salivate to a tone may subsequently learn to salivate to another stimulus, such as a light, that has been paired with the tone, but never with food. (*See* Second-order conditioning.)

Hippocampus A limbic system structure in the forebrain, which is involved in learning and memory.

Holistic education A comprehensive term for educational approaches that attempt to remedy what is seen as the failure of traditional education to educate the whole brain. Advocates of holistic education believe that the right hemisphere—speculatively linked with music, art, and emotion—is neglected by curricula that stress reason, logic, language, science, and mathematics.

Homunculus Literally, a little man or dwarf. Term used for the hypothetical entity assumed by the ancient Greeks to be the cause of human behavior.

Hypothalamus A small structure deep within the brain near the top of the brain stem, involved in a variety of bodily functions including the functioning of the endocrine glands.

Hypothesis An educated guess, often based on theory, which can be tested. A prediction based on partial evidence of some effect, process, or phenomenon, which must then be verified experimentally.

Hypothesis generator A model that has at its core the notion that the learner is characterized by intentionality and by the ability to generate hypotheses (suppositions or predictions) and to interpret experience in the light of these hypotheses.

Hypothetico-deductive system A theoretical system consisting of general laws from which subsidiary principles can be derived and tested. Hull's learning theory is hypothetico-deductive.

Iconic representation A Brunerian stage in the development of the child's representation of the world, characterized by a representation of the world in terms of relatively concrete mental images (icons). (*See* Enactive representation, Symbolic representation.)

Id One of three levels of the human personality, according to Freudian theory. The id includes all the instinctual urges that humans inherit. These are the source of all human motives.

Identity A logical rule that specifies that certain activities leave objects or situations unchanged.

Imitation Copying behavior. To imitate a person's behavior is simply to use that person's behavior as a pattern. Bandura and Walters describe three different effects of imitation. (*See* Eliciting effect, Inhibitory/disinhibitory effect, Modeling effect.)

Implicit learning Unconscious learning, not represented in symbols or analyzable with rules.

Implicit memory Also termed *nondeclarative* or *procedural memory*. Refers to unconscious, inexpressible effects of experience such as might be manifested in acquired motor skills or in classical conditioning.

Imprinting Unlearned, instinctlike behaviors that are not present at birth but that become part of an animal's repertoire after exposure to a suitable stimulus during a *critical period*. The "following" behavior of young ducks, geese, and chickens is an example.

Incentive motivation A motivational concept relating to the attractiveness or subjective value attached to a behavior or goal, and therefore to its effectiveness as a motive.

Inclusive fitness In sociobiology, refers to the fitness of genetically related groups relative to their likelihood of procreation—hence, of survival.

Independent variable The variable that is manipulated in an experiment to see if it causes changes in the dependent variable. The "if" part of the if-then equation implicit in an experiment. (*See* Dependent variable.)

Information processing (IP) Relates to how information is modified (or processed), resulting in knowledge, perception, or behavior. A dominant model of the cognitive approaches, it makes extensive use of computer metaphors.

Inhibitory/disinhibitory effect The type of imitative behavior that results either in the suppression (inhibition) or appearance (disinhibition) of previously acquired deviant behavior. (*See* Eliciting effect, Modeling effect.)

Inner Speech Vygotsky's final stage in the development of speech, attained at around age 7, and characterized by silent "self-talk," the *stream-of-consciousness* flow of verbalizations that give direction and substance to our thinking and behavior. Inner speech is involved in all higher mental functioning. (*See* Egocentric speech, Social speech.)

Input variables Hull's phrase for the complex of stimuli to which an organism responds—the stimulus. Characteristics of input variables include intensity of the stimulus, the motivational state of the organism, the amount of work involved in responding, and the amount of associated reward.

Insight The perception of relationships among elements of a problem situation. A problem-solving method that contrasts strongly with trial and error. The cornerstone of Gestalt psychology.

Instinctive drift Refers to the tendency of organisms to revert to instinctual, unlearned behaviors.

Instincts Complex, species-specific, relatively unmodifiable patterns of behaviors, such as migration or nesting in some birds and animals. Less complex inherited behaviors are usually termed reflexes.

Instrumental learning The learning of voluntary responses as a function of their consequences. Associated with Thorndike's learning theory, and sometimes used interchangeably with operant conditioning. (*See* Operant conditioning.)

Intellectual skills Gagné's term for the outcomes of the learning process. He describes five such skills ranging from discrimination learning to higher-order rules (involved in abstract problem solving).

Interference theory The belief that previous learning might interfere with retention in short-term memory. (*See* Proactive interference, Retroactive interference.)

Intermittent reinforcement A schedule of reinforcement that does not present a reinforcer for all correct responses. (*See* Interval schedule, Ratio schedule.)

Internalization A Piagetian concept referring to the processes by which activities, objects, and events in the real world become represented mentally.

Interoceptive conditioning The conditioning of actions involving glands or involuntary muscles, like vasoconstriction or dilation.

Interval schedule An intermittent schedule of reinforcement that is based on the passage of time. (*See* Fixed schedule, Random schedule.)

Intervening variables Hull's phrase for the complex of assumed variables that intervene between the presentation of a stimulus and the occurrence of a response. Include the organism's habits, expectations of reward, and other factors related to previous responses in similar situations.

Interviews Data-gathering method wherein investigators question participants.

Intrinsic motive A motive associated with internal sources of reinforcement—like satisfaction, and feelings of competence and worth.

Introspection A once popular method of psychological investigation involving careful self-examination followed by an attempt to arrive at laws and principles that explain the introspector's own behavior and can be generalized to others.

Introverts A term used to describe individuals who turn inward rather than outward. Such individuals tend to be more interested in their internal states and less interested in externally oriented, social activities. Those who are sober, reserved, and withdrawn.

Intuitive thinking One of the substages of Piaget's preoperational thought, beginning around age 4 and lasting until age 7 or 8. Marked by the child's ability to solve many problems intuitively and by the inability to respond correctly in the face of misleading perceptual features of problems.

Just noticeable difference (JND) The least amount of change in stimulation intensity that can be detected.

Knowledge A generic term for the information, the ways of dealing with information, the ways of acquiring information, and so on that an individual possesses. Gagné defines knowledge as verbal information.

Latent Not evident; present, but hidden; potential. Latent learning involves changes in capabilities or attitudes that are not immediately apparent in performance.

Latent inhibition A characteristic of taste aversion learning, evident in the observation that aversions typically develop some time after the presentation of the effective stimulus (a poison, for example), but are nevertheless associated with the offending stimulus rather than with some other stimulus. It's as though the connection is potential, or latent, until the occurrence of the unconditioned response (illness). In the event that there is no unconditioned response, no aversion learning occurs.

Lateralization A term that refers to the division of functions and capabilities between the two hemispheres of the brain.

Law A statement whose accuracy is beyond reasonable doubt. (*See* Belief, Principle.)

Law of effect A Thorndikean law of learning stating that the effect of a response leads to its being learned (stamped in) or not learned (stamped out).

Law of exercise One of Thorndike's laws of learning, basic to his pre-1930s system but essentially repudiated later. It maintained that the more frequently, recently, and vigorously a connection was exercised, the stronger it would be.

Law of multiple responses Law based on Thorndike's observation that learning involves the emission of a variety of responses (multiple responses) until one (presumably an appropriate one) is reinforced. Because of this law, Thorndike's theory is often referred to as a theory of trial-and-error learning.

Law of prepotency of elements A Thorndikean law of learning stating that people tend to respond to the most striking of the various elements that make up a stimulus situation.

Law of readiness A Thorndikean law of learning stating that certain types of learning are impossible or difficult unless the learner is ready. In this context, readiness refers to maturational level, previous learning, motivational factors, and other characteristics of the individual that relate to learning.

Law of response by analogy An analogy is typically an explanation, comparison, or illustration based on similarity. In Thorndike's system, response by analogy refers to responses that occur because of similarities between two situations. (*See* Theory of identical elements.)

Law of set or attitude A Thorndikean law of learning that recognizes that we are often predisposed to respond in certain ways as a result of our experiences and previously learned attitudes.

Learning All relatively permanent changes in behavior that result from experience, but that are not caused by fatigue, maturation, drugs, injury, or disease.

Learning curve A graphic representation of the acquisition of a learned response as a function of variables like number of trials, reinforcement, or strength of stimuli.

Learning theory A systematic attempt to explain and understand how behavior changes. The phrase *behavior theory* is used synonymously.

Leveling In Gestalt theory, a tendency to smooth out peculiarities in a perceptual pattern. Also applies to learning and remembering.

Levels of processing Craik and Lockhart's suggestion that remembering is largely a function of the nature and extent of processing of material to be remembered. At the level of the sensory store, little or no processing occurs and forgetting occurs almost immediately. Material in long-term storage has been encoded (processed) for meaning and may be retained indefinitely.

Libido A general Freudian term denoting sexual urges. The libido is assumed to be the source of energy for sexual urges, which are the most important force in human motivation.

Limbic system A grouping of brain structures located beneath the cerebral cortex. These structures are associated mainly with emotion, memory, and reinforcement and punishment.

Loci system A mnemonic system whereby items to be remembered are associated with visual images of specific places.

Locus of control Rotter's expression for an individual's tendency to attribute responsibility for behavior and its outcomes to external sources (for example, the individual blames others for failure) or internal sources (for example, the individual accepts full responsibility for successes and failures).

Logical construct Also termed *hypothetical construct*. A label for assumed or invented entities that cannot be observed and whose existence cannot be proven. In scientific theories, logical constructs follow from observations and are postulated as attempts to explain observations.

Logo Seymour Papert's computer language, designed to allow young children to learn programming skills as easily and painlessly as they might learn an exciting new game. The program uses a "turtle"—a small creature that the learner discovers how to move in different ways while tracing geometric designs on a computer screen.

Long-term depression (LTD) A neurological change defined by a lasting decline in the strength of the connection between two neurons (a decline in synaptic strength).

Long-term memory A type of memory whereby, with continued rehearsal and recoding of sensory input (processing in terms of meaning, for example), material will be available for recall over a long period.

Long-term potentiation (LTP) A lasting neurological change defined by an increase in the responsiveness of neurons, evident in an increase in synaptic strength.

Magnetoencephalogram (MEG) A recording of magnetic fields that correspond to electrical activity of the brain. MEG recordings are obtained at the scalp by means of a *magnetoencephalograph* to yield *event-related fields* (ERFs).

Mechanistic behaviorism Expression sometimes used to describe early behavioristic theories. Denotes a concern with the machinelike, predictable aspects of behavior and a refusal to consider *mentalistic* explanations in addition to directly observable events.

Medial forebrain bundle Group of nerve fibers in the limbic system associated with reinforcement.

Mediational construct A hypothetical entity or process invented by a theorist as an explanation or description of thinking. In theories such as Hebb's and Hull's, mediational constructs served as inferred links between stimuli and responses. (*See* Logical construct.)

Memory The physiological effects of experience, reflected in changes that define learning. Includes both storage and retrieval. Nothing can be retrieved from memory that has not been stored, but not all that is stored can be retrieved. (*See* Forgetting.)

Metaneeds Maslow's term for higher needs—those concerned with psychological and self-related functions rather than with biology. These include "needs" to know truth, beauty, and justice and to self-actualize.

Method of incompatible stimuli One of Guthrie's techniques for breaking habits, involving presenting the stimulus complex associated with an unwanted habit in conjunction with other stimuli that lead to a response incompatible with the habit. (*See* Fatigue technique, Threshold technique.)

Méthode clinique Piaget's experimental method. It involves an interview technique in which questions are determined largely by the subject's responses. Its flexibility distinguishes it from ordinary interview techniques.

Mind A term referring primarily to human consciousness. Often defined as originating from or resulting in the processes of the brain associated with such activities as thinking, imagining, and perceiving.

Mind-body problem A general expression for questions relating to the relationship between the body and the mind.

Mnemonic devices Systematic aids to remembering, like rhymes, acrostics, or visual imagery systems. (*See* Loci system, Phonetic system.)

Mnemonist Professional memorizer.

Model A representation, usually abstract, of some phenomenon or system. Alternatively, a pattern for behavior that can be copied by someone.

Modeling effect The type of imitative behavior that involves learning a novel response. (*See* Eliciting effect, Inhibitory/disinhibitory effect.)

Mores The established social conventions and customs of a group, often considered essential to its identification and preservation as a distinct cultural group.

Moro reflex The generalized startle reaction of a newborn infant. It typically involves throwing out the arms and feet symmetrically following sudden loss of support.

Motivation The causes of behavior. The conscious or unconscious forces that lead to certain acts. (*See* Causes, Reasons.)

Motor skill A behavior that involves muscular coordination and physical skills. Such common activities as walking and driving are motor skills.

Movement produced stimuli (MPS) In Guthrie's system, proprioceptive (internal) stimulation that results from actions of muscles, glands, and tendons.

Nativism A model that reflects the belief that the learner is born with biological and neurological constraints and predispositions that shape reactions to the world and that facilitate certain types of learning and behavior (such as imprinting in geese or learning language in people).

Nature-nurture controversy A very old argument in psychology about whether genetics (nature) or environment (nurture) is more responsible for determining development. Also called the heredity-environment question.

Need Ordinarily refers to a lack or deficit in the human organism. Needs may be either unlearned (termed basic or *physiological*; for example, the need for food or water) or learned (termed *psychological*; for example, the need for prestige or money).

Need for achievement Expression for a personality characteristic evident in an individual's apparent need to achieve success (to accomplish, to succeed, to win, to gain) and to avoid failure.

Negative reinforcement An increase in the probability that a response will recur following the elimination or removal of a condition as a consequence(s) of the behavior. Negative reinforcement ordinarily is the effect of an unpleasant or noxious stimulus that is removed as a result of a specific response.

Negative reinforcer An event that has the effect of increasing the probability of occurrence of the response that immediately precedes it. Negative reinforcement ordinarily takes the form of an unpleasant or noxious stimulus that is removed as a result of a specific response.

Neobehaviorist Label Hull used to emphasize that, unlike the earlier behaviorists, he did not limit his theory to observable stimuli and responses, but also considered what occurs between the presentation of a stimulus and the occurrence of a response.

Nerve Bundle of neurons.

Nervous system The part of the body that is made up of neurons. Its major components are the brain and the spinal cord (the central nervous system), receptor systems associated with major senses, and effector systems associated with functioning of muscles and glands.

Net reaction potential ($_s\mathring{E}_R$) In Hull's system, the result of subtracting the tendency not to respond (called inhibitory potential) from the tendency to respond (reaction potential).

Neural network A connectionist model of brain functioning premised on the functioning of the parallel distributed processing computer. Neural networks are complex arrangements of units that activate each other, modifying patterns of connections. In this model, meaning resides in patterns within the network, and responses are also determined by patterns.

Neurofeedback A form of biofeedback in which participants are given information about their neurological functioning. Typically involves specific information about electrical activity in the brain. (*See* Biofeedback.)

Neuron A single nerve cell, the basic building block of the human nervous system. Neurons consist of four main parts: cell body, nucleus, dendrites, and axon.

Neurotransmitters Naturally produced chemicals that are released by nerve cells and whose function it is to initiate or facilitate transmission of messages among nerve cells. The number of known neurotransmitters approaches 100, the best known of which are serotonin, dopamine, norepinephrine, and acetylcholine.

Nominal fallacy The assumption that naming something explains it.

Nondeclarative memory Also termed implicit or procedural memory. Refers to unconscious, nonverbalizable effects of experience such as might be manifested in acquired motor skills or in classical conditioning.

Normalizing A Gestalt principle describing the tendency for memories to change so that they become closer to other related memories.

Novice-to-expert An information-processing model of the learner reflecting the view that the differences between those who can (experts) and those who can't (novices) can be determined and used to make novices more like experts. Less general and more domain-specific than other models.

Object concept Piaget's expression for the child's understanding that the world is composed of objects that continue to exist apart from his or her perception of them.

Observational learning A term used synonymously with the expression "learning through imitation." (*See* Imitation.)

Occam's razor Also called the *law of parsimony*. A principle, attributed to William of Occam, which holds that unless it's absolutely necessary, things that cannot be proven to exist should not be assumed to exist. Typically interpreted to mean that the simplest of competing explanations is preferable.

Occipital lobe Part of the cerebral cortex located at the rear of the brain, importantly involved in vision.

Operant Skinner's term for a response not elicited by any known or obvious stimulus. Most significant human behaviors appear to be operants (for example, writing a letter or going for a walk).

Operant conditioning The process of changing behavior by manipulating its consequences. Most of Skinner's work investigates the principles of operant conditioning. (*See* Classical conditioning, Conditioning).

Operation A Piagetian term that refers essentially to a thought process. An operation is an action that has been internalized in the sense that it can be "thought" and is reversible in the sense that it can be "unthought."

Operational definition A definition that describes a variable by precise actions (operations) that can be observed and measured.

Organization A memory strategy involving grouping items to be remembered in terms of similarities and differences.

Orienting reflex (OR) The initial response of humans and other organisms to novel stimulation. Components of the orienting response include changes in electrical activity in the brain, in respiration and heart rate, and in conductivity of the skin to electricity. The orienting reflex is an alerting response.

Output variables Hull's phrase for what the organism does (that is, the response). Output variables include response latency, response amplitude, and the number of responses required before extinction.

Parallel distributed processing (PDP) Describes computer processing where several functions are carried out simultaneously and are related to common sets of input and output. PDP systems are the basis for connectionist models of human thinking.

Parietal lobe Cerebral lobes located just above the temporal lobes, between the frontal and occipital lobes. The parietal lobes are involved in sensation.

Parsimonious Avoiding excessive and confusing detail and complexity. Parsimonious theories explain all important relationships in the simplest, briefest manner possible.

Pedology A Soviet discipline of child development, very popular in the Soviet Union in the 1930s, that used Western tests for psychoassessment. Vygotsky and Luria were pedologists. In the mid 1930s, the Soviet government decreed that pedology was a "bourgeois pseudoscience" and ordered that it should no longer be written about, researched, or even discussed, wiping out all pedology centers and putting all pedologists out of work.

Percept A term Bruner used to refer to the effect of sensory experiences. In Bruner's system, percepts are equivalent to concepts. (*See* Concept.)

Performance Actual behavior. Learning is not always manifested in obvious changes in behavior (that is, in actual performance), but instead may be latent.

Periventricular tract Group of nerve fibers in the limbic system associated with punishment.

Phase sequence In Hebb's system, an integrated arrangement of related cell assemblies. Corresponds to a concept or percept. (*See* Cell assembly.)

Phonetic system A particularly powerful mnemonic system that makes use of associations between numbers and letters combined to form words; visual images associated with these words are then linked with items to be remembered. Professional memorizers often use some variation of a phonetic system.

Phonological loop In Baddeley's model of working memory, one of the *slave* systems responsible for maintaining verbal information, such as words or numbers, so that it might be available for short-term (working) memory.

Physiological needs Basic biological needs, such as the need for food and water.

Pineal gland A small, reddish, conical organ found near the base of the brain. Its function remains largely unknown.

Pleasure center Term Olds and Milner used to describe the part of the brain thought to be involved in reinforcement—specifically, a part of the hypothalamus that includes a group of nerve fibers known as the *medial forebrain bundle* located in the *limbic* system (a part of the brain that includes the hypothalamus and the thalamus among other structures).

Population Collections of individuals (or objects or situations) with similar characteristics. For example, the population of all first-grade children in North America. (*See* Sample.)

Positive reinforcement An increase in the probability that a response will recur as a result of a positive consequence(s) resulting from that behavior (that is, as a result of the addition of something). Usually is the effect of a pleasant stimulus (reward) that results from a specific response.

Positive reinforcer An event added to a situation immediately after a response has occurred that increases the probability that the response will recur. Usually takes the form of a pleasant stimulus (reward) that results from a specific response.

Positron emission tomography (PET) An imaging technique used extensively in medicine and in physiological and neurological research. Records changes in blood flow by detecting the distribution of radioactive particles injected in the bloodstream.

Prägnanz A German word meaning "good form." An overriding Gestalt principle that maintains that what we perceive (and think) tends to take the best possible form where *best* usually refers to a principle such as closure, continuity, similarity, or proximity. (*See* Closure, Continuity, Similarity, Proximity.)

Preconceptual thinking The first substage in the period of preoperational thought, beginning around age 2 and lasting until age 4. It is so called because the child has not yet developed the ability to classify.

Premack principle The recognition that behaviors that are chosen frequently by an individual (and that are therefore favored) may be used to reinforce other, less frequently chosen behaviors. (For example, "You can watch television when you have finished your homework.")

Preoperational thinking The second of Piaget's four major stages, lasting from around age 2 to age 7 or 8, characterized by certain weaknesses in the child's logic. It consists of two substages: intuitive thinking and preconceptual thinking. (*See* Intuitive thinking, Preconceptual thinking.)

Primary reinforcer An event that is reinforcing in the absence of any learning. Stimuli such as food and drink are primary reinforcers because, presumably, an organism does not have to learn that they are pleasant.

Principle A statement relating to some uniformity or predictability. Principles are far more open to doubt than are laws but are more reliable than beliefs. (*See* Belief, Law, Theory.)

Principle of belongingness Thorndike's belief that certain responses are easier to learn because, for cultural or logical reasons, they seem to go with (belong with) certain stimuli.

Principle of opposite control Describes the tendency for sensations and movements on either side of the body to be controlled by the opposite cerebral hemisphere.

Proactive interference The interference of earlier learning with the retention of subsequent learning. (*See* Retroactive interference.)

Propositional thinking A Piagetian label for the thinking of the formal-operations child. A proposition is a statement that can be true or false; hence, propositional thinking is the ability to think about abstract, hypothetical states of affairs.

Proprioceptive stimulation Refers to internal sensations (relating to what is termed kinesthetic sensation), such as those associated with movements of muscles. (*See* Exteroceptive stimulation.)

Prototype model An original model that serves as a basis for other models. In concept learning, a prototype is an abstraction of the most average or representative features of a concept, to which new instances can be compared. (*See* Exemplar model.)

Proximity A Gestalt principle manifested in our tendency to perceive elements that are close together as

being related. (*See* Closure, Continuity, Prägnanz, Similarity.)

Psychological hedonism The belief that humans act primarily to avoid pain and to obtain pleasure.

Psychological needs Human needs other than those dealing with such basic physical requirements as food, sex, water, and temperature regulation (physiological needs). Psychological needs described by Maslow include the need to belong, to feel safe, to love and be loved, to maintain a high opinion of oneself, and to self-actualize. (*See* Self-actualization.)

Psychology The science that examines human behavior (and that of other animals as well).

Psychophysics The measurement of physical stimuli and their effects.

Psychotherapy A very general term for the variety of techniques used to alleviate mental disorders and emotional problems. Usually restricted to procedures undertaken by psychiatrists, psychologists, and other specially trained individuals.

Punishment Involves either the presentation of an unpleasant stimulus or the withdrawal of a pleasant stimulus as a consequence of behavior. Punishment should not be confused with negative reinforcement.

Questionnaires Data-gathering devices consisting of lists of predetermined questions to which subjects respond.

Radical behaviorism Label applied to Skinner's behaviorism to distinguish it from other behavioristic positions less insistent on *not* making inferences about mental states. In this sense, radical means *root*. Radical behaviorism maintains that the "root" (or origin) of psychological knowledge is observable behavior.

Random Where the outcome cannot be predicted; attributable solely to chance. In a randomly selected sample, every member has the same probability of being selected.

Random schedule Also called variable schedule; a type of intermittent schedule of reinforcement. It may be of either the interval or the ratio variety and is characterized by the presentation of rewards at random intervals or on random trials. Although both fixed and random schedules may be based on the same intervals or on the same ratios, one can predict when a reward will occur under a fixed schedule, whereas it is impossible to do so under a random schedule.

Rate of learning A measure of the amount of time required to learn a correct response, or of the number of trials required before the emission of the correct response.

Ratio schedule An intermittent schedule of reinforcement that is based on a proportion of correct responses. (*See* Fixed schedule, Random schedule.)

Reaction potential ($_sE_R$) In Hull's system, the probability that stimulus conditions will lead to a response. Reaction potential is a combined function of specific intervening variables that reflect the individual's history as well as present stimulus conditions.

Reaction threshold ($_s\mathring{L}_R$) In Hull's system, the magnitude of net reaction potential required before a response occurs.

Reasons Explanations for or defenses of an action. In psychology, reasons are often treated as motives. (*See* Causes, Motivation.)

Reception learning The type of learning that involves primarily instruction or tuition rather than the learner's own efforts. Often associated with Ausubel, reception learning usually involves expository or didactic methods. That is, the instructor structures the material and presents it to learners in relatively final form rather than asking them to discover that form. (*See* Discovery learning.)

Reductionist Term used to describe theories that try to understand a process or a phenomenon by *reducing* it to its smallest components.

Reflex A simple, unlearned stimulus-response link, such as salivating in response to food in one's mouth or blinking in response to air blowing into one's eye.

Refractory period A brief period after firing during which a neuron is "discharged" and is incapable of firing again.

Rehearsal A memory strategy involving simple repetition. The principal means of maintaining items in short-term memory.

Reinforcement The effect of a reinforcer; specifically, to increase the probability that a response will occur. (*See* Negative reinforcement, Positive reinforcement.)

Reinforcer An event associated with a response that changes the probability of that response occurring again. (*See* Reinforcement.)

Repression theory A theory of forgetting based on the notion that unpleasant, anxiety-provoking experiences might be blocked from consciousness in a self-protective move.

Reprimands A mild form of punishment involving indications of disapproval—usually verbal, but sometimes consisting of gestures (such as shaking one's head to say no).

Rescorla-Wagner model A model based on the notion that contiguity is neither sufficient nor necessary to explain classical conditioning. Instead, it holds that what is learned in classical conditioning are relations among events (expectancies).

Respondent Skinner's term for a response that (unlike an operant) is elicited by a known, specific stimulus.

Unconditioned responses are examples of respondents. (*See* Unconditioned response.)

Response amplitude (A) In Hull's system, the physical strength of a response.

Response cost A mild form of punishment in which tangible reinforcers that have been given for good behavior are taken away for misbehavior. Response-cost systems are often used in systematic behavior management programs.

Response latency ($_st_R$) Time lag between the presentation of a stimulus and the appearance of a response.

Reticular formation The upper portion of the brain stem that appears to be importantly involved in the physiological arousal of the cortex, and in the control of sleeping and waking. Forms part of the midbrain.

Retrieval-cue failure Inability to remember because of the unavailability of appropriate cues (as opposed to changes in memory "traces").

Retroactive interference The interference of subsequently learned material with the retention of previously learned material. (*See* Proactive interference.)

Reversibility A logical property manifested in the ability to reverse or undo activity in either an empirical or a conceptual sense. An idea is said to be reversible when a child realizes the logical consequences of an opposite action.

Sample A subset of a population. A representative selection of individuals with similar characteristics drawn from a larger group. For example, a sample constituting 1% of all first-grade children in North America. (*See* Population.)

Scaffolding A Vygotskian concept to describe the various types of support that teachers and upbringers need to provide for children if they are to learn. Scaffolding often takes the form of directions, suggestions, and other forms of verbal assistance and is most effective if it involves tasks within the child's *zone of proximal growth*. (*See* Zone of proximal growth.)

Schedule of reinforcement The timing and frequency of presentation of reinforcement to organisms. (*See* Continuous reinforcement, Intermittent reinforcement.)

Schema The label Piaget used to describe a unit in cognitive structure. A schema is, in one sense, an activity together with whatever biology or neurology might underlie that activity. In another sense, a schema may be thought of as an idea or a concept.

Science An approach and an attitude toward knowledge that emphasizes objectivity, precision, and replicability. Also, one of several related bodies of knowledge.

Secondary reinforcer An event that becomes reinforcing as a result of being paired with other reinforcers.

Second-order conditioning In classical conditioning, the forming of associations between the CS and other stimuli that take the place of the US (typically other stimuli that have been paired with the US).

Self-actualization The process or act of becoming oneself, developing one's potential, of achieving an awareness of one's identity, or self-fulfillment. The term is central in humanistic psychology.

Self-determination theory Deci and Ryan's cognitive theory of motivation, based on the assumption that people need to be self-determined, to feel autonomous and competent, and to develop close relations with others. The theory is highly compatible with attribution theory.

Self-efficacy Judgments we make about how effective we are in given situations. Judgments of self-efficacy are important in determining an individual's choice of activities and in influencing the amount of interest and effort expended.

Semantic memory A type of declarative (conscious, long-term) memory consisting of stable knowledge about the world, principles, rules and procedures, and other verbalizable aspects of knowledge, including language.

Sensitization A common form of learning in which an organism's response to stimulation increases in intensity. Most often occurs following intense stimulation. (*See* Habituation.)

Sensorimotor intelligence The first stage of development in Piaget's classification. It lasts from birth to approximately age 2 and is so called because children understand their world during that period primarily in terms of their activities in it and sensations of it.

Sensory deprivation Refers to experiments in which subjects are kept in conditions of unvarying sensory stimulation over long periods.

Sensory memory The simple sensory recognition of such stimuli as a sound, a taste, or a sight. Also called short-term sensory storage.

Set A tendency to respond, or perceive, in a predetermined way.

Shaping A technique for training animals and people to perform behaviors not previously in their repertoires. It involves reinforcing responses that are progressively closer approximations to the desired behavior. Also called the *method of successive approximations*, or the *method of differential reinforcement of successive approximations*.

Sharpening In Gestalt psychology, a tendency, evident with the passage of time, to exaggerate the most distinctive features of a memory.

Short-term memory Also called primary or working memory; a type of memory in which material is available for recall for a matter of seconds. Short-term memory primarily involves rehearsal rather than more in-depth processing. It defines our immediate consciousness.

Significant In research, refers to findings that would not be expected to occur by chance alone more than a small percentage (for example, 5% or 1%) of the time.

Similarity A Gestalt principle recognizing our tendency to perceive similar items as though they belonged together. (*See* Closure, Continuity, Prägnanz, Proximity.)

Simultaneous pairing The presentation of CS and US at exactly the same time in classical conditioning. (*See* Backward pairing, Delayed pairing, Trace pairing.)

Single-blind procedure An experimental procedure where either the subjects or the investigator are not aware of who are members of the experimental group and who are members of the control group. (*See* Double-blind procedure.)

Skinner box One of various experimental environments Skinner used in his investigations of operant conditioning. The typical Skinner box is a cagelike structure equipped with a lever and a food tray attached to a food-delivering mechanism. It allows the investigator to study operants (for example, bar pressing) and the relationship between an operant and reinforcement.

SOAR Label for Newell's abstract, 10-component, symbol- and rule-based model of the human cognitive processing system.

Social cognitive theory A label for Bandura's theory, which explains social learning through imitation, using the principles of operant conditioning while recognizing the importance of cognitive activities such as imagining, symbolizing, and anticipating.

Social learning The acquisition of patterns of behavior that conform to social expectations; learning what is acceptable and what is not acceptable in a given culture. Also, learning that involves interaction among individuals.

Social speech In Vygotsky's theorizing, the most primitive stage of language development, evident before age 3, during which the child expresses simple thoughts and emotions out loud. The function of social speech is to control the behavior of others. (See Egocentric speech, Inner speech.)

Socialization The complex process of learning both those behaviors that are appropriate with a given culture and those that are less appropriate. The primary agents of socialization are home, school, and peer groups.

Sociobiology A discipline that applies the findings of biology, anthropology, and ethology to the understanding of human social behavior. Sociobiology looks for biological explanations for behavior.

Software Computer instructions or programs. (*See* Hardware, Wetware.)

Spontaneous recovery The apparently spontaneous reappearance of response that had previously been extinguished. (*See* Extinction.)

Spread of effect Thorndike's observation that rewards sometimes strengthen connections between a stimulus and a specific response and between the stimulus and other closely related responses.

Stimulus discrimination (*See* Discrimination.)

Stimulus generalization (*See* Generalization.)

Stimulus-intensity dynamism (V) Hull's label for the effect of stimulus intensity on the individual. In general, the more intense a stimulus, the higher the probability of a response.

Structure A term Piaget used in reference to cognitive structure—in effect, the individual's mental representations, which include knowledge of things as well as knowledge of how to do things.

Sucking reflex The automatic sucking response of a newborn child when the mouth area is stimulated.

Superstitious schedule A kind of fixed-interval schedule of reinforcement where reinforcement occurs after a fixed time interval no matter what the organism is doing—hence, reinforcement that is *not contingent* on the organism's behavior. Superstitious schedules of reinforcement can sometimes lead to bizarre and unpredictable behaviors.

Surveys A collection of observations based on a sample (often large) representing some population.

Symbolic model A model other than a real-life person. For example, books, television, and written instructions are important symbolic models.

Symbolic representation In Bruner's system, the final stage in the development of a child's representation of the world. Symbolic representation uses arbitrary symbols such as language. (*See* Enactive representation, Iconic representation.)

Sympathetic nervous system Part of the nervous system that instigates the physiological responses associated with emotion.

Synapse A bridge or junction between neurons. In effect, a space between neurons that can be crossed by an electrical impulse.

Synaptic cleft Label for the space between terminal boutons at the ends of axons and the dendrites or cell bodies of adjoining neurons.

Tabula rasa Literally, *blank slate*. A model of the learner based on the assumption that people are born equal, each with no prior learning, inclinations, or thoughts and ready to be shaped by experience—like identical blank slates ready to be written upon.

Taste aversion A powerful disinclination toward eating or drinking certain substances. Taste aversions are easily learned, are highly resistant to extinction, and demonstrate biological constraints.

Temporal lobe Cerebral structure located on either side of the cerebrum, associated primarily with speech, language, and hearing.

Terminal bouton Also called synaptic knobs, these are slight enlargements on the wispy branches at the ends of axons.

Thalamus A tiny structure at the base of the brain that serves as the major relay center for incoming sensory stimulation.

Theory A body of information pertaining to a specific topic, a method of acquiring or dealing with information, or a set of explanations for related phenomena.

Theory of identical elements A Thorndikean theory that holds that similar stimuli are related because two situations possess a number of identical elements, and these identical elements lead to transfer of responses from one situation to another.

Theory of natural selection Darwin's notion that variations that provide individuals of a species with a survival and reproductive edge tend to become more common through succeeding generations.

Threshold technique A method for breaking habits described by Guthrie, in which the stimulus complex associated with an undesirable habit is presented in such mild form that the habit is not elicited. Stimulus intensity is gradually increased. (*See* Fatigue technique, Method of incompatible stimuli.)

Time out A procedure in which students are removed from situations in which they might ordinarily be rewarded. Time-out procedures are widely used in classroom management.

Token Something indicative of something else. In behavior management programs, token reinforcement systems consist of objects like disks or point tallies that are themselves worthless but later can be exchanged for more meaningful reinforcement.

Trace pairing In classical conditioning, the presentation and termination of the CS before the US so that there is a time lag between the two. (*See* Backward pairing, Delayed pairing, Simultaneous pairing.)

Transductive reasoning The type of reasoning that proceeds from particular to particular rather than from particular to general or from general to particular.

One example of transductive reasoning is the following: Cows give milk, and goats give milk; therefore, goats are cows.

Transfer (*See* Generalization.)

Trial and error Thorndikean explanation for learning based on the idea that when placed in a problem situation, an individual will emit a number of responses but will eventually learn the correct one as a result of reinforcement. Trial-and-error explanations for learning are sometimes contrasted with insight explanations.

Turing test The assumption that if thing A duplicates exactly thing B's functions, then thing A must have the same qualities as thing B.

Unconditioned response (UR) A response that is elicited by an unconditioned stimulus.

Unconditioned stimulus (US) A stimulus that elicits a response before learning. All stimuli that are capable of eliciting reflexive behaviors are examples of unconditioned stimuli. For example, food is an unconditioned stimulus for the response of salivation.

Variable A property, measurement, or characteristic that can vary from one situation to another. In psychological investigations, qualities such as intelligence, sex, personality, age, and so on can be important variables.

Vicarious reinforcement Reinforcement that results from observing someone else being reinforced. In imitative behavior, observers often act as though they are being reinforced when in fact they aren't, but they think that the model is.

Virtual reality (VR) A computer-based simulation that typically involves a number of sensory systems (such as bodily sensations, visual images, and auditory signals) in order to produce a sensation of realism.

Visual-spatial sketch pad One of the *slave* systems in Baddeley's model of working memory, concerned with the processing of material that is primarily visual or spatial.

Weber's law Just noticeable differences (JNDs) require proportionally greater increases as stimulus intensity increases.

Wetware The brain's neurons and their interconnections. Corresponds to *hardware* in the computer metaphor. (*See* Hardware, Software.)

Yerkes-Dodson law States that the effectiveness of performance is an inverted U-shaped function of arousal, such that very low and very high levels of arousal are associated with least effective behavior.

Zone of proximal growth (also called the zone of proximal development) Vygotsky's phrase for the individual's current potential for further intellectual development. Conventional measures of intelligence assess current intellectual development rather than potential for future development. Vygotsky believed that the zone of proximal growth (future potential) might be assessed by further questioning and the use of hints and prompts while administering a conventional intelligence test.

References

Abravanel, E., & Ferguson, S. A. (1998). Observational learning and the use of retrieval information during the second and third years. *Journal of Genetic Psychology, 159*, 455–476.

Aguado, L. (2003). Neuroscience of Pavlovian conditioning: A brief review. *Spanish Journal of Psychology, 6*, 155–167.

Ahmad, K., Casey, M., & Bale, T. (2002). Connectionist simulation of quantification skills. *Connection Science: Journal of Neural Computing, Artificial Intelligence, and Cognitive Research, 14*, 165–201.

Ahmad, K. C., & Matthew, B. T. (2002). Connectionist simulation of quantification skills. *Connection Science: Journal of Neural Computing, Artificial Intelligence & Cognitive Research, 14*, 165–201.

Alberto, P. A., & Troutman, A. C. (2003). *Applied behavior analysis for teachers*. Upper Saddle River, NJ: Prentice-Hall.

Albonetti, C. A., & Hepburn, J. R. (1996). Prosecutorial discretion to defer criminalization: The effects of defendant's ascribed and achieved status characteristics. *Journal of Quantitative Criminology, 12*, 63–81.

Alcock, J. (2001). *The triumph of sociobiology*. New York: Oxford University Press.

Alexander, R. D. (1989). Evolution of the human psyche. In P. Mellars & C. Stringer (Eds.), *The human revolution*. Princeton, NJ: Princeton University Press.

Allman, W. F. (1989). *Apprentices of wonder: Inside the neural network revolution*. New York: Bantam.

Alter, I. (1996). On novelty and exploration in the psychoanalytic situation. *Psychoanalysis and Contemporary Thought, 19*, 611–630.

Altmann, E. M., & Gray, W. D. (2002). Forgetting to remember: The functional relationship of decay and interference. *Psychological Science, 13*, 27–33.

APA Guidelines for Ethical Conduct in the Care and Use of Animals. (2002). Washington, DC: American Psychological Association.

Ames, C. (1992). Classrooms: Goals, structures, and student motivation. *Journal of Educational Psychology, 84*, 261–271.

Amit, D. J. (1995). The Hebbian paradigm reintegrated: Local reverberations as internal representations. *Behavioral and Brain Sciences, 18*, 617–657.

Amsel, A. (1989). *Behaviorism, neobehaviorism, and cognitivism in learning theory: Historical and contemporary perspectives*. Hillsdale, NJ: Erlbaum.

Amsel, A. (1992). B. F. Skinner and the cognitive revolution. *Journal of Behavior Therapy and Experimental Psychiatry, 23*, 67–70.

Anastasi, A. (1958). Heredity, environment and the question "how?" *Psychological Review, 65*, 197–208.

Anderson, J. R. (1995). *Learning and memory: An integrated approach*. New York: Wiley.

Annett, J. M. (1996). Olfactory memory: A case study in cognitive psychology. *Journal of Psychology, 130*, 309–319.

Anscombe, E., & Geach, P. T. (Eds). (1954). *Descartes: Philosophical writings*. New York: Thomas Nelson.

Atkins, M. S., Osborne, M. L., Benn, D. S., Hess, L. E., & Halperin, J. M. (2001). Children's competitive peer aggression during reward and punishment. *Aggressive Behavior, 27*, 1–13.

Atkinson, J. W., & Shiffrin, R. M. (1968). Human memory: A proposed system and its control processes. In K. W. Spence & J. T. Spence (Eds.), *The psychology of learning and motivation* (Vol. 2). New York: Academic Press.

Aubrey, C. (1993). An investigation of the mathematical knowledge and competencies which young children bring into school. *British Educational Research Journal, 19*, 27–41.

Ausubel, D. P. (1977). The facilitation of meaningful verbal learning in the classroom. *Educational Psychologist, 12,* 162–178.

Ausubel, D. P., & Robinson, F. G. (1969). *School learning: An introduction to educational psychology.* New York: Holt, Rinehart & Winston.

Baddeley, A. D. (1997). *Human memory: Theory and practice* (Rev. ed.). East Sussex, UK: Psychology Press.

Baddeley, A. D. (2002). Is working memory still working? *European Psychologist, 7,* 85–97.

Baddeley, A. D., & Hitch, G. J. (1974). Working memory. In G. Bower (Ed.), *The psychology of learning and motivation.* New York: Academic Press.

Baeyens, F., Vansteenwegen, D., Hermans, D., & Eelen, P. (2001). Human evaluative flavor-taste conditioning: Conditions of learning and underlying processes. *Psychologica Belgica, 41,* 169–186.

Bahrick, H. P., Bahrick, P. O., & Wittlinger, R. P. (1975). Fifty years of memory for names and faces: A cross-sectional approach. *Journal of Experimental Psychology, 104,* 54–75.

Baillargeon, R. (1987). Object permanence in $3^{1}/_{2}$- and $4^{1}/_{2}$-month-old infants. *Developmental Psychology, 23,* 655–664.

Baillargeon, R. (1993). The object concept revisited. In C. Granrud (Ed.), *Visual perception and cognition in infancy: Carnegie-Mellon Symposia on Cognition* (Vol. 23). Hillsdale, NJ: Erlbaum.

Bakhurst, D., & Shanker, S. G. (2001). Introduction: Bruner's way. In D. Bakhurst & S. G. Shanker (Eds.), *Jerome Bruner: Language, culture, self.* Thousand Oaks, CA: Sage.

Balfour, M. E., Yu, L., & Coolen, L. M. (2004). Sexual behavior and sex-associated environmental cues activate the mesolimbic system in male rats. *Neuropsychopharmacology, 29,* 718–730.

Ballou, M., Matsumoto, A., & Wagner, M. (2002). Toward a feminist ecological theory of human nature: Theory building in response to real-world dynamics. In M. Ballou & L. S. Brown (Eds.). *Rethinking mental health and disorder: Feminist perspectives* (pp. 99–141). New York: Guilford Press.

Banaji, M. R., & Crowder, R. G. (1989). The bankruptcy of everyday memory. *American Psychologist, 44,* 1185–1193.

Bandura, A. (1969). *Principles of behavior modification.* New York: Holt, Rinehart & Winston.

Bandura, A. (1977). *Social learning theory.* Englewood Cliffs, NJ: Prentice-Hall.

Bandura, A. (1981). Self-referent thought: A developmental analysis of self-efficacy. In J. H. Flavell & L. Ross (Eds.), *Social cognitive development: Frontiers and possible futures.* Cambridge, UK: Cambridge University Press.

Bandura, A. (1986). *Social foundations of thought and action: A social cognitive theory.* Englewood Cliffs, NJ: Prentice-Hall.

Bandura, A. (1991). Social cognitive theory of self-regulation. *Organizational Behavior and Human Performance, 50,* 248–287.

Bandura, A. (1993). Perceived self-efficacy in cognitive development and functioning. *Educational Psychologist, 28,* 117–148.

Bandura, A. (1995). Exercise of personal and collective efficacy in changing societies. In A. Bandura (Ed.), *Self-efficacy in changing societies.* New York: Cambridge University Press.

Bandura, A. (2001). Social cognitive theory: An agentic perspective. *Annual Review of Psychology, 52,* 1–26.

Bandura, A. (2002). Growing primacy of human agency in adaptation and change in the electronic era. *European Psychologist, 7,* 2–16.

Bandura, A., Pastorelli, C., Barbaranelli, C., Caprara, G. V., & Gian, V. (1999). Self-efficacy pathways to childhood depression. *Journal of Personality and Social Psychology, 76,* 258–269.

Bandura, A., & Walters, R. (1963). *Social learning and personality development.* New York: Holt, Rinehart & Winston.

Barnard, C. W., Wolfe, H. D., & Graveline, D. E. (1962). Sensory deprivation under null gravity conditions. *American Journal of Psychiatry, 118,* 92–125.

Barrett, L., Dunbar, R., & Lycett, J. (2002). *Human evolutionary psychology.* New York: Palgrave.

Batsell, W. R., Jr., & George, J. W. (1996). Unconditioned stimulus intensity and retention interval effects. *Physiology and Behavior, 60,* 1463–1467.

Beauvois, J. L. (2001). Rationalization and internalization: The role of internal explanations in attitude change and the generalization of an obligation. *Swiss Journal of Psychology, 60,* 215–230.

Beilin, H., & Fireman, G. (2000). The foundation of Piaget's theories: Mental and physical action. In H. W. Reese, (Ed.), *Advances in child development and behavior* (Vol. 27). San Diego: Academic Press.

Bellezza, F. S. (1996). Mnemonic methods to enhance storage and retrieval. In E. L. Bjork & R. A. Bjork (Eds.), *Memory: Handbook of perception and cognition* (2nd ed.). San Diego: Academic Press.

Beltran, C. J. (2000). Donald Olding Hebb: An intellectual biography. *Dissertation Abstracts International: Section B: The Sciences & Engineering, 61,* 2739.

Benjafield, J. G. (1996). *A history of psychology.* Boston: Allyn & Bacon.

Berg, W. K., & Berg, K. M. (1987). Psychophysiological development in infancy: State, startle, and attention. In J. D. Osofsky (Ed.), *Handbook of infant development* (2nd ed.). New York: Wiley.

Berlyne, D. E. (1960). *Conflict, arousal, and curiosity.* New York: McGraw-Hill.

Berlyne, D. E. (1965). *Structure and direction in thinking.* New York: Wiley.

Berlyne, D. E. (1966). Curiosity and exploration. *Science, 153,* 25–33.

Bernard, L. L. (1924). *Instinct: A study in social psychology.* New York: Holt, Rinehart & Winston.

Bernstein, I. L., & Webster, M. M. (1980). Learned taste aversion in humans. *Physiology & Behavior, 25,* 363–366.

Bexton, W. H., Heron, W., & Scott, T. H. (1954). Effects of decreased variation in the sensory environment. *Canadian Journal of Psychology, 8,* 70–76.

Bijou, S. W., & Sturges, P. S. (1959). Positive reinforcers for experimental studies with children: Consumables and manipulatables. *Child Development, 30,* 151–170.

Bitterman, M. E. (1967). Learning in animals. In H. Helson & W. Bevan (Eds.), *Contemporary approaches to psychology.* Princeton, NJ: Van Nostrand.

Bitterman, M. E. (1969). Thorndike and the problem of animal intelligence. *American Psychologist, 24,* 444–453.

Bjorklund, D. F. (1997). In search of a metatheory for cognitive development (or Piaget is dead and I don't feel so good myself). *Child Development, 68,* 144–148.

Blanchard, E. B. (2002). Biofeedback and hypertension: A déjà–vu experience. *Applied Psychophysiology and Biofeedback, 57,* 107–109.

Blanchard, E. B., Andrasik, F., Ahles, T. A., Teders, S. J., & O'Keefe, D. (1980). Migraine and tension headache: A meta-analytic review. *Behavior Therapy, 11,* 613–631.

Bolles, R. C. (1970). Species-specific defense reactions and avoidance learning. *Psychological Review, 77,* 32–48.

Bolles, R. C. (1975). *Theory of motivation* (2nd ed.). New York: Harper & Row.

Bolles, R. C. (1979). *Learning theory* (2nd ed.). New York: Holt, Rinehart, & Winston.

Boring, E. G. (1950). *A history of experimental psychology* (2nd ed.). New York: Appleton-Century-Crofts.

Boujabit, M'B. Bontempi, B., Destrade, C., & Gisquet-Verrier, P. (2003). Exposure to a retrieval cue in rats induces changes in regional brain glucose metabolism in the amygdala and other related brain structures. *Neurobiology of Learning & Memory, 79,* 57–71.

Bouton, M. E., & Peck, C. A. (1992). Spontaneous recovery in cross-motivational transfer (counterconditioning). *Animal Learning and Behavior, 20,* 313–321.

Bowers, T. G. R. (1989). *The rational infant: Learning in infancy.* New York: Freeman.

Bowlby, J. (1982). *Attachment and loss: Vol. 1. Attachment* (2nd ed.). London: Hogarth.

Bradshaw, G. L., & Anderson, J. R. (1982). Elaborative encoding as an explanation of levels of processing. *Journal of Verbal Learning and Verbal Behavior, 21,* 165–174.

Bradshaw, J. L. (1989). *Hemispheric specialization and psychological function.* New York: Wiley.

Branscombe, N. A., Castle, K., Dorsey, A. G., Surbeck, E., & Taylor, J. B. (2003). *Early childhood curriculum: A constructivist perspective.* Boston: Houghton Mifflin.

Bransford, J. D., Brown, A. L., & Cocking, R. R. (Eds.). (2000). *How people learn: Brain, mind, experience, and school.* Washington, DC: National Academy Press.

Brehm, J. W., & Cohen, A. R. (1962). *Explorations in cognitive dissonance.* New York: Wiley.

Brehm, J. W., & Self, E. A. (1989). The intensity of motivation. *Annual Review of Psychology, 40,* 109–131.

Breland, K., & Breland, M. (1951). A field of applied animal psychology. *American Psychologist, 6,* 202–204.

Breland, K., & Breland, M. (1961). The misbehavior of organisms. *American Psychologist, 16,* 681–684.

Breland, K., & Breland, M. (1966). *Animal behavior.* New York: Macmillan.

Brewer, K. R., & Wann, D. L. (1998). Observational learning effectiveness as a function of model characteristics: Investigating the importance of social power. *Social Behavior and Personality, 26,* 1–10.

Broadbent, D. E. (1952). Speaking and listening simultaneously. *Journal of Experimental Psychology, 43,* 267–273.

Broadbent, N. J., Clark, R. E., Zola, S., & Squire, L. R. (2002). The medial temporal lobe and memory. In L. R. Squire & D. L. Schacter (Eds.), *Neuropsychology of memory* (3rd ed.). New York: Guilford Press.

Brody, B. A. (2001) Defending animal research: An international perspective. In E. F. Paul & J. Paul (Eds.), *Why animal experimentation matters: The use of animals in medical research. New studies in social policy.* New Brunswick, NJ: Transaction.

Brooks, R. A. (2002). *Flesh and machines: How robots will change us.* New York: Pantheon Books.

Brown, A. S. (2002). Consolidation theory and retrograde amnesia in humans. *Psychonomic Bulletin & Review, 9,* 403–425.

Brown, H. D., & Kosslyn, S. M. (1993). Cerebral lateralization. *Current Opinion in Neurobiology, 3,* 183–186.

Brown, P. L., & Jenkins, H. M. (1968). Auto-shaping of the pigeon's key peck. *Journal of the Experimental Analysis of Behavior, 11,* 1–8.

Brown, R. E., & Milner, P. M. (2004). The legacy of Donald O. Hebb: More than the Hebb Synapse. *Nature Reviews Neuroscience, 4,* 1013–1019.

Bruer, J. T. (1997). Education and the brain: A bridge too far. *Educational Researcher, 26,* 4–16.

Bruner, J. S. (1957a). On going beyond the information given. In J. S. Bruner and others (Eds.), *Contemporary approaches to cognition.* Cambridge, MA: Harvard University Press.

Bruner, J. S. (1957b). On perceptual readiness. *Psychological Review, 64,* 123–152.

Bruner, J. S. (1964). The course of cognitive growth. *American Psychologist, 19,* 15.

Bruner, J. S. (1966). Toward a theory of instruction. Cambridge, MA: Harvard University Press.

Bruner, J. S. (1983). *In search of mind: Essays in autobiography.* New York: Harper & Row.

Bruner, J. S. (1985). Models of the learner. *Educational Researcher, 14,* 5–8.

Bruner, J. S. (1990a). Metaphors of consciousness and cognition in the history of psycology. In D. E. Leary (Ed.), *Metaphors in the history of psychology.* New York: Cambridge University Press.

Bruner, J. S. (1990b). *The proper study of man.* Cambridge, MA: Harvard University Press.

Bruner, J. S. (1990c). *Acts of meaning.* Cambridge, MA: Harvard University Press.

Bruner, J. S. (1996a). Frames for thinking: Ways of making meaning. In D. R. Olson & N. Torrance (Eds.), *Modes of thought: Explorations in culture and cognition.* New York: Cambridge University Press.

Bruner, J. S. (1996b). *The culture of education.* Cambridge, MA: Harvard University Press.

Bruner, J. S. (1997a). Celebrating divergence: Piaget and Vygotsky. *Human Development, 40,* 63–73.

Bruner, J. S. (1997b). Comment on "Beyond competence." *Cognitive Development, 12,* 341–343.

Bruner, J. S. (1997c). A narrative model of self-construction. In J. G. Snodgrass & R. L. Thompson (Eds.), The self across psychology: Self-recognition, self-awareness, and the self-concept. *Annals of the New York Academy of Sciences, 818,* 145–161.

Bruner, J. S. (1997d). Will the cognitive revolutions ever stop? In D. M. Johnson & C. E. Erneling (Eds.), *The future of the cognitive revolution.* New York: Oxford University Press.

Bruner, J. S. (2000). Human infancy and the beginnings of human competence. In J. A. Bargh, & D. K. Apsley (Eds.), *Unraveling the complexities of social life: A festschrift in honor of Robert B. Zajonc.* Washington, DC: American Psychological Association.

Bruner, J. S. (2002). *Making stories: Law, literature, life.* New York: Farrar, Straus & Giroux.

Bruner, J. S., Goodnow, J. J., & Austin, G. A. (1956). *A study of thinking.* New York: Wiley.

Buckley, K. W. (1994). Misbehaviorism: The case of John B. Watson's dismissal from Johns Hopkins University. In J. T. Todd & E. K. Morris (Eds.), *Modern perspectives on John B. Watson and classical behaviorism.* Westport, CT: Greenwood Press.

Bukacinski, D., Bukacinski, M., & Lubjuhn, T. (2000). Adoption of chicks and the level of relatedness in common gull, Larus canus, colonies: DNA fingerprinting analyses. *Animal Behaviour, 59,* 289–299.

Bulgren, J. A., Schumaker, J. B., & Deshler, D. D. (1994). The effects of a recall enhancement routine on the test performance of secondary students with and without learning disabilities. *Learning Disabilities Research and Practice, 9,* 2–11.

Burnham, J. C. (1994). John B. Watson: Interviewee, professional figure, symbol. In J. T. Todd & E. K. Morris (Eds.), *Modern perspectives on John B. Watson and classical behaviorism.* Westport, CT: Greenwood Press.

Burns, J. D., & Malone, J. C., Jr. (1992). The influence of "preparedness" on autoshaping, schedule performance, and choice. *Journal of the Experimental Analysis of Behavior, 58,* 399–413.

Buxton, C. E. (1940). Latent learning and the goal gradient hypothesis. [Special issue]. *Duke University: Contributions to Psychological Theory, 2.*

Cameron, J., & Pierce, W. D. (1994). Reinforcement, reward, and intrinsic motivation: A meta-analysis. *Review of Educational Research, 64,* 363–423.

Campbell, M., Hoane, A. J. Jr., & Hsu, F-h. (2002). Deep blue. In J. Schaeffer & J. van den Herik (Eds.), *Chips challenging champions: Games, computers and artificial intelligence.* New York: Elsevier.

Carpenter, S. L., & McKee-Higgins, E. (1996). Behavior management in inclusive schools. *Rase: Remedial and Special Education, 17,* 195–203.

Carporeal, L. R. (2001). Evolutionary psychology: Toward a unifying theory and a hybrid science. *Annual Review of Psychology, 52,* 607–628.

Carrillo, M. C., Thompson, L. T., Gabrieli, J. D. E., & Disterhoft, J. F. (1997). Variation of the intertrial interval in human classical conditioning. *Psychobiology, 25,* 152–157.

Casteel, C. A. (1997). Attitudes of African American and Caucasian eighth grade students about praises, rewards, and punishments. *Elementary School Guidance and Counseling, 31,* 262–272.

Cermak, L. (1976). *Improving your memory.* New York: McGraw-Hill.

Cermak, L. S., & Craik, F. I. (Eds.). (1979). *Levels of processing in human memory.* Hillsdale, NJ: Erlbaum.

Chang, F. (2002). Symbolically speaking: A connectionist model of sentence production. *Cognitive Science, 26,* 609–651.

Cherry, E. C. (1953). Some experiments on the recognition of speech, with one and with two ears. *Journal of the Acoustical Society of America, 25,* 975–979.

Chomsky, N. (1972). *Language and mind* (Rev. ed.). New York: Harcourt Brace Jovanovich.

Chotro, M. G., & Alonso, G. (2003). Stimulus preexposure reduces generalization of conditioned taste aversions between alcohol and non-alcohol flavors in infant rats. *Behavioral Neuroscience, 117,* 113–122.

Churchland, P. S., & Sejnowski, T. J. (1992). *The computational brain.* Cambridge, MA: MIT Press.

Cicero, F. R. & Pfadt, A. (2002). Investigation of a reinforcement-based toilet training procedure for children with autism. *Research in Developmental Disabilities, 23,* 319–331.

Cohen, G. (1996). *Memory in the real world* (2nd ed.). East Sussex, UK: Psychology Press.

Cole, S. O. (2002). Evolutionary psychology: Sexual ethics and our embodied nature. *Journal of Psychology & Theology, 30,* 112–116.

Collias, N. E. (2000). Filial imprinting and leadership among chicks in family integration of the domestic fowl. *Behaviour, 137,* 197–211.

Collins, B. E., & Hoyt, M. F. (1972). Personal responsibility for consequences: An integration and extension of the "forced compliance" literature. *Journal of Experimental and Social Psychology, 8,* 558–593.

Cooper, R., & Shallice, T. (1995). *Soar and the case for unified theories of cognition. Cognition, 55,* 115–149.

Covington, M. V. (2000). Goal theory, motivation, and school achievement: An integrative review. *Annual Review of Psychology, 51,* 171–200.

Cowley, G. (1989, March). How the mind was designed. *Newsweek, 113,* 56–58.

Cox, B. D., (1997). The rediscovery of the active learner in adaptive contexts: A developmental historical analysis of transfer of training. *Educational Psychologist, 32,* 41–55.

Craik, F. I. M. (1977). Depth of processing in recall and recognition. In S. Dornic (Ed.), *Attention and performance.* New York: Academic Press.

Craik, F. I. M., & Lockhart, R. S. (1972). Levels of processing: A framework for memory research. *Journal of Verbal Learning and Verbal Behavior, 11,* 671–684.

Crawford, M. L., Harwerth, R. S., Smith, E. L., & von Noorden, G. K. (1993). Keeping an eye on the brain: The role of visual experience in monkeys and children. *Journal of General Psychology, 120,* 7–19.

Crespi, L. (1942). Quantitative variation of incentive and performance in the white rat. *American Journal of Psychology, 55,* 467–517.

D'Esposito, M., & Postle, B. R. (2002). The neural basis of working memory storage, rehearsal, and control processes. In L. R. Squire & D. L. Schacter (Eds.), *Neuropsychology of memory* (3rd ed.). New York: Guilford Press.

Dadds, M. R., Bovbjerg, D. H., Redd, W. H., & Cutmore, T. R. H. (1997). Imagery in human classical conditioning. *Psychological Bulletin, 122,* 89–103.

Darley, J. M. & Latané, B. (1968). Bystander intervention in emergencies: Diffusion of responsibility. *Journal of Personality and Social Psychology, 8,* 377–383.

Darwin, C. (1859/1962). *The origin of species by means of natural selection, or the preservation of favoured races in the struggle for life.* New York: Collier.

Dasen, P. R. (1972). Cross-cultural Piagetian research: A summary. *Journal of Cross-Cultural Psychology, 3,* 23–29.

Dasen, P. R. (Ed.). (1977). *Pigetian psychology: Cross-cultural contributions.* New York: Gardner.

Davis, J. T. (2001). Revising psychoanalytic interpretations of the past: An examination of declarative and non-declarative memory processes. *International Journal of Psychoanalysis, 82,* 449–462.

Davis, P. W. (1996). Threats of corporal punishment as verbal aggression: A naturalistic study. *Child Abuse and Neglect, 20,* 289–304.

Davydov, V. V. (1995). The influence of L. S. Vygotsky on education theory, research, and practice. *Educational Researcher, 24,* 12–21.

Dayan, P., & Abbott, L. F. (2001). *Theoretical neuroscience: Computational and mathematical modeling of neural systems.* Cambridge, MA: MIT Press.

Debigare, J. (1984). The phenomenon of verbal transformation and the Cell-Assembly Theory of D. O. Hebb: An operational model. *Canadian Journal of Psychology, 38,* 17–44.

Deci, E. L., & Flaste, R. (1995). *Why we do what we do: The dynamics of personal autonomy.* New York: G. P. Putnam's Sons.

Deci, E. L., Koestner, R., & Ryan, R. M. (1999). A meta-analytic review of experiments examining the effects of extrinsic rewards on intrinsic motivation. *Psychological Bulletin, 125,* 627–668.

Deci, E. L., & Ryan, R. M. (1985). *Intrinsic motivation and self-determination in human behavior.* New York: Plenum.

DeLancey, C. (2002). *Passionate engines: What emotions reveal about mind and artificial intelligence.* New York: Oxford University Press.

Delius, J. D. (1992). Categorical discrimination of objects and pictures by pigeons. *Animal Learning and Behavior, 20,* 301–311.

deMause, L. (1974). The evolution of childhood. In L. deMause (Ed.), *The history of childhood.* New York: Psychohistory Press.

Demorest, A. P., & Siegel, P. F. (1996). Personal influences on professional work: An empirical case study of B. F. Skinner. *Journal of Personality, 64,* 243–261.

DeVries, R. (1997). Piaget's social theory. *Educational Researcher, 26,* 4–18.

Dewsbury, D. A. (2002). The Chicago Five: A family group of integrative psychobiologists. *History of Psychology, 5,* 16–37.

Dickinson, A. M., & Poling, A. D. (1996). Schedules of monetary reinforcement in organizational behavior management: Latham and Huber (1992) revisited. *Journal of Organizational Behavior Management, 16,* 71–91.

Dickman, S. J. (2002). Dimensions of arousal: Wakefulness and vigor. *Human Factors, 44,* 429–442.

Domjan, M., & Galef, B. G., Jr. (1983). Biological constraints on instrumental and classical conditioning: Retrospect and prospect. *Animal Learning and Behavior, 11,* 151–161.

Domjan, M., Huber-McDonald, M., & Holloway, K. S. (1992). Conditioning copulatory behavior to an artificial object: Efficacy of stimulus fading. *Animal Learning and Behavior, 20,* 350–362.

Doyle, W. (1986). Classroom organization and management. In M. C. Wittrock (Ed.), *Handbook of research on teaching* (3rd ed.), New York: Macmillan.

Draaisma, D. (2000). *Metaphors of memory: A history of ideas about the mind.* (P. Vincent, Trans.). New York: Cambridge University Press.

Dulit, E. (1972). Adolescent thinking à la Piaget: The formal stage. *Journal of Youth and Adolescence, 1,* 281–301.

Dweck, C. S. (1986). Motivational processes affecting learning. *American Psychologist, 41,* 1040–1048.

Dymond, S., & Barnes, D. (1997). Behavior-analytic approaches to self-awareness. *Psychological Record, 47,* 181–200.

Ebbinghaus, H. (1885/1964). *Memory* (H. A. Ruger & C. E. Busenius, Trans.). New York: Dover.

Eccles, J. S., & Wigfield, A. (2002). Motivational beliefs, values, and goals. *Annual Review of Psychology, 53,* 109–132.

Eckland, B. K. (1977). Darwin rides again. *American Journal of Sociology, 82,* 693–697.

Egner, T., & Gruzelier, J. H. (2001). Learned self-regulation of EEG frequency components affects attention and event-related brain potentials in humans. *NeuroReport, 12,* 4155–4159.

Eisenman, R., & Kristsonis, W. (1995). How children learn to become sex offenders. *Psychology: A Quarterly Journal of Human Behavior, 32,* 25–29.

Epstein, W. (1988). Has the time come to rehabilitate Gestalt theory? Meetings of the American Psychological Association (1986, Washington, DC). *Psychological Research, 50,* 2–6.

Estes, W. K. (1991). Cognitive architectures from the standpoint of an experimental psychologist. *Annual Review of Psychology, 42,* 1–28.

Evans, R. I. (1989). *Albert Bandura: The man and his ideas—a dialogue.* New York: Praeger.

Eysenck, H. J. (1982). Neobehavioristic (S-R) theory. In G. T. Wilson & C. M. Franks (Eds.), *Contemporary behavior therapy: Conceptual and empirical foundations.* New York: Guilford.

Falmagne, J. C. (1985). *Elements of psychophysical theory.* New York: Oxford University Press.

Farnham-Diggory, S. (1990). *Schooling.* Cambridge, MA: Harvard University Press.

Fechner, G. (1860/1966). *Elements of psychophysics* (Vol. 1; H. E. Adler, Trans.) New York: Holt Rinehart.

Fernandez, M., Wegerif, R., Mercer, N., & Rojas-Drummond, S. (2002). Re-conceptualizing "scaffolding: and the zone of proximal development in the context of symmetrical collaborative learning. *Journal of Classroom Interaction, 36,* 40–54.

Festinger, L. A. (1957). *A theory of cognitive dissonance.* Stanford, CA: Stanford University Press.

Festinger, L. A. (1962, October). Cognitive dissonance. *Scientific American, 207,* 93–106.

Flavell, J. H. (1985). *Cognitive development* (2nd ed.). Englewood Cliffs, NJ: Prentice-Hall.

Franken, R. E. (2002). *Human motivation.* Belmont, CA: Wadsworth/Thompson Learning.

Fredrikson, M., Annas, P., & Wik, G. (1997). Parental history, aversive exposure and the development of snake and spider phobia in women. *Behaviour Research and Therapy, 35,* 23–28.

Freeman, D. (1983). *Margaret Mead and Samoa: The making and unmaking of an anthropological myth.* Boston: Harvard University Press.

Freeman, W. J. (2003). Neurodynamic models of brain in psychiatry. *Neuropsychopharmacology, 28,* S54–S63.

Friedman, D. (2003). Cognition and aging: A highly selective overview of event-related potential (ERP) data. *Journal of Clinical & Experimental Neuropsychology, 25,* 702–720.

Gabler, I. C., & Schroeder, M. (2003a). *Constructivist methods for the secondary classroom.* Boston: Allyn & Bacon.

Gabler, I., & Schroeder, M. (2003b). *Seven constructivist methods for the secondary classroom: A planning guide for invisible teaching.* Boston: Allyn & Bacon.

Gagné, R. M. (1965). *The conditions of learning* (1st ed.). New York: Holt, Rinehart & Winston.

Gagné R. M. (1970). *The conditions of learning* (2nd ed.). New York: Holt, Rinehart & Winston.

Gagné, R. M. (1974). *Essentials of learning for instruction.* Hinsdale, IL: Dryden.

Gagné, R. M., & Dick, W. (1983). Instructional psychology. *Annual Review of Psychology, 34,* 261–295.

Gagné, R. M., & Driscoll, M. P. (1988). *Essentials of learning for instruction* (2nd ed.). Englewood Cliffs, NJ: Prentice-Hall.

Gagné, R. M., & Medsker, K. L. (1996). *The conditions of learning: Training applications*. Fort Worth, TX: Harcourt Brace.

Gagné, R. M., Briggs, L. J., & Wager, W. W. (1988). *Principles of instructional design* (3rd ed.). New York: Holt, Rinehart & Winston.

Gagné, R. M., Briggs, L. J., & Wager, W. W. (1992). *Principles of instructional design* (4th ed.). New York: Holt Rinehart.

Galef, B. G. (1988). Evolution and learning before Thorndike: A forgotten epoch in the history of behavioral research. In R. C. Bolles & M. D. Beecher (Eds.), *Evolution and learning*. Hillsdale, NJ: Erlbaum.

Gallo, A., Duchatelle, E., Elkhessaimi, A., Le Pape, G., & Desportes, J-P. (1995). Topographic analysis of the rat's bar behaviour in the Skinner box. *Behavioural Processes, 33*, 319–328.

Galton, F. (1870). *Hereditary genesis: An inquiry into its laws and consequences*. New York: Appleton.

Garcia, J., & Koelling, R. A. (1966). Relation of cue to consequence in avoidance learning. *Psychonomic Science, 4*, 123–124.

Garcia, J., Ervin, F. E., & Koelling, R. A. (1965). Learning with prolonged delay of reinforcement. *Psychonomic Science, 5*, 121–122.

Gardner, H. (1987). *The mind's new science: A history of the cognitive revolution*. New York: Basic Books.

Gathercole, S. E., & Baddeley, A. D. (1993). *Working memory and language*. Mahwah, NJ: Erlbaum.

Geen, R. G. (1984). Preferred stimulation levels in introverts and extroverts: Effects on arousal and performance. *Journal of Personality & Social Psychology, 46*, 1303–1312.

Gelman, R. (1978). Cognitive development. *Annual Review of Psychology, 29*, 297–332.

Gelman, R., Meck, E., & Merkin, S. (1986). Young children's numerical competence. *Cognitive Development, 1*, 1–29.

Gibbons, F. X., Eggleston, T. J., & Benthin, A. C. (1997). Cognitive reactions to smoking relapse: The reciprocal relation between dissonance and self-esteem. *Journal of Personality and Social Psychology, 72*, 184–195.

Gilovich, T. (1991). *How we know what isn't so: The fallibility of human reason in everyday life*. New York: Free Press.

Glasser, W. (1998). *Choice theory: A new psychology of personal freedom*. New York: HarperCollins.

Glasser, W. (2002). *Unhappy teenagers: A way for parents and teachers to reach them*. New York: HarperCollins.

Glick, J. (1975). Cognitive development in cross-cultural perspective. In F. D. Horowitz, E. M. Hetherington, S. Scarr-Salapatek, & G. M. Siegel (Eds.), *Review of child development research* (Vol. 4). Chicago: University of Chicago Press.

Goldblum, N. (2001). *The brain-shaped mind: What the brain can tell us about the mind*. New York: Cambridge University Press.

Goldman, W. P., & Seamon, J. G. (1992). Very long-term memory for odors: Retention of odor-name associations. *American Journal of Psychology, 105*, 549–563.

Gottselig, J. M., Brandeis, D., Hofer-Tinguely, G., Borbely, A. A., Achermann, P., & Gottselig, J. M. (2004). Human central auditory plasticity associated with tone sequence learning. *Learning & Memory, 11*, 162–171.

Gould, D., Greenleaf, C., & Krane, V. (2002). Arousal-anxiety and sport behavior. In T. Horn (Ed.), *Advances in sport psychology* (2nd ed.), Champaign, Il.: Human Kinetics.

Gould, J. E. (2002). *Concise handbook of experimental methods for the behavioral and biological sciences*. Boca Raton, FL: CRC Press.

Gould, S. J. (2002a). *I have landed: the end of a beginning in natural history*. New York: Harmony Books.

Gould, S. J. (2002b). *The structure of evolutionary theory*. Cambridge, MA: Belknap Press of Harvard University Press.

Graham, S. (1997). Using attribution theory to understand social and academic motivation in African American youth. *Educational Psychologist, 32*, 21–34.

Grakalic, I., & Riley, A. L. (2002). Asymmetric serial interactions between ethanol and cocaine in taste aversion learning. *Pharmacology, Biochemistry & Behavior, 73*, 787–795.

Greenham, S. L., Stelmack, R. M., & van der Vlugt, H. (2003). Learning disability subtypes and the role of attention during the naming of pictures and words: An event-related potential analysis. *Developmental Neuropsychology, 23*, 339–358.

Greenspoon, J. (1955). The reinforcing effect of two spoken sounds on the frequency of two responses. *American Journal of Psychology, 68*, 409–416.

Gregory, K. M., Kim, A. S., & Whiren, A. (2003). The effect of verbal scaffolding on the complexity of preschool children's block constructions. In D. E. Lytle (Ed.), *Play and educational theory and practice. Play and culture studies* (Vol 5). Westport, CT: Praeger.

Groeger, J. A. (1997). *Memory and remembering: Everyday memory in context*. New York: Addison Wesley.

Groome, L. J., Mooney, D. M., Holland, S. B., & Bentz, L. S. (1997). The heart rate deceleratory response in low-risk human fetuses: Effect of stimulus intensity on response topography. *Developmental Psychobiology, 30*, 103–113.

Guidelines for the treatment of animals in behavioural research and teaching (Jan 2002). *Animal Behaviour, 63*(1), 195–199.

Guillem, F., Bicu, M., Pampoulova, T., Hooper, R., Bloom, D., Wolf, M., et al. (2003). The cognitive and anatomo-functional basis of reality distortion in schizophrenia: A view from memory event-related potentials. *Psychiatry Research, 117,* 137–158.

Gunderson, K. (1964). The imitation game. In A. R. Anderson (Ed.), *Mind and machines.* Englewood Cliffs, NJ: Prentice-Hall.

Guthrie, E. R. (1935). *The psychology of learning.* New York: Harper.

Guthrie, E. R. (1952). *The psychology of learning* (rev. ed.). New York: Harper.

Guthrie, E. R., & Horton, G. P. (1946). *Cats in a puzzle box.* New York: Rinehart.

Guthrie, E. R., & Powers, F. F. (1950). *Educational psychology.* New York: Ronald Press.

Hackenberg, T. D. (1995). Jacques Loeb, B. F. Skinner, and the legacy of prediction and control. *Behavior Analyst, 18,* 225–236.

Halpern, D. F., & Coren, S. (1990). Laterality and longevity: Is left-handedness associated with younger age at death? In S. Coren (Ed.), *Left-handedness: Behavioral implications and anomalies.* Amsterdam: Elsevier.

Hamburger, H., & Richards, D. (2002). *Logic and language models for computer science.* Upper Saddle River, NJ: Prentice-Hall.

Hamilton, W. D. (1970). Selfish and spiteful behaviour in an evolutionary model. *Nature, 228,* 1218–1220.

Hamilton, W. D. (1971). Geometry for the selfish herd. *Journal of Theoretical Biology, 31,* 295–311.

Hamilton, W. D. (1972). Altruism and related phenomena, mainly in social insects. *Annual Review of Ecology and Systematics, 3,* 193–232.

Hanley, G. P., Piazza, C. C., & Fisher, W. W. (1997). Noncontingent presentation of attention and alternative stimuli in the treatment of attention-maintained destructive behavior. *Journal of Applied Behavior Analysis, 30,* 229–237.

Harlan, J. C., & Rowland, S. T. (2002). *Behavior management strategies for teachers.* Springfield, IL: Thomas.

Harnish, R. M. (2002). *Minds, brains, computers: An historical introduction to the foundations of cognitive science.* Malden, MA: Blackwell.

Harpaz, Y. (2003). http://human-brain.org/

Harris, B. (1979). Whatever happened to little Albert? *American Psychologist, 34,* 151–160.

Harrison, A. W., Rainer, R. K., Hochwarter, W. A., & Thompson, K. R. (1997). Testing the self-efficacy-performance linkage of social-cognitive theory. *Journal of Social Psychology, 137,* 79–87.

Harvey, V. S., & Retter, K. (2002). Variations by gender between children and adolescents on the four basic psychological needs. *International Journal of Reality Therapy, 21,* 33–36.

Haslam, S. A., & McGarty, C. (2001). A 100 years of certitude? Social psychology, the experimental method and the management of scientific uncertainty. *British Journal of Social Psychology, 40(1),* 1–21.

Hastie, R. (2001). Problems for judgment and decision making. *Annual Review of Psychology, 52,* 653–683.

Hawking, S. (1996). *A brief history of time* (Updated and expanded tenth anniversary ed.). New York: Bantam Books.

Hays, R. (Ed.) (1962). Psychology of the scientist: IV. Passages from the "idea books" of Clark L. Hull. *Perceptual and Motor Skills, 15,* 807–882.

Hebb, D. O. (1949). *The organization of behavior.* New York: Wiley.

Hebb, D. O. (1958). *A textbook of psychology* (1st ed.). Philadelphia: Saunders.

Hebb, D. O. (1960). The American revolution. *American Psychologist, 15,* 735–745.

Hebb, D. O. (1966). *A textbook of psychology* (2nd ed.). Philadelphia: Saunders.

Hebb, D. O. (1972). *A textbook of psychology* (3rd ed.). Philadelphia: Saunders.

Hebb, D. O. (1980). D. O Hebb. In G. Lindzey (Ed.), *A history of psychology in autobiography* (Vol. 7). San Francisco: Freeman.

Hembree, R. (1988). Correlates, causes, effects and treatment of test anxiety. *Review of Educational Research, 58,* 47–77.

Henson, R. (2001). Neural working memory. In J. Andrade (Ed.), *Working memory in perspective.* Philadelphia: Psychology Press.

Herman, J., & Stimmel, B. (Eds.). (1997). *The neurobiology of cocaine addiction: From bench to bedside.* Binghamton, NY: Haworth Press.

Hermann, D., Raybeck, D., & Gruneberg, M. (2002). *Improving memory and study skills: Advances in theory and practice.* Seattle: Hogrefe & Huber.

Heron, W. (1957, January). The pathology of boredom. *Scientific American, 196,* 52–56.

Herrnstein, R. J. (1977). Doing what comes naturally: A reply to Professor Skinner. *American Psychologist, 32,* 1013–1016.

Herrnstein, R. J., Loveland, D. H., & Cable, C. (1976). Natural concepts in the pigeon. *Journal of Experimental Psychology: Animal Behavior Processes, 2,* 285–302.

Higbee, K. L. (1977). *Your memory: How it works and how to improve it.* Englewood Cliffs, NJ: Prentice-Hall.

Hilgard, E. R., & Bower, G. H. (1966). *Theories of Learning* (3rd ed.). New York: Appleton-Century-Crofts.

Hinde, R. A., & Stevenson-Hinde, R. (Eds.). (1973). *Constraints on learning: Limitations and predispositions.* New York: Academic Press.

Hintzman, D. L. (1990). Human learning and memory: Connections and dissociations. *Annual Review of Psychology, 41*, 109–139.

Hoerster, A., Curio, E., & Witte, K. (2000). No sexual imprinting on a red bill as a novel trait. *Behaviour, 137*, 1223–1239.

Hogan, K., & Pressley, M. (1997). Scaffolding scientific competencies within classroom communities of inquiry. In K. Hogan & M. Pressley (Eds.), *Scaffolding student learning: Instructional approaches and issues*. Albany: State University of New York.

Holcomb, H. R. III (1993). *Sociobiology, sex, and science*. New York: State University of New York Press.

Holyoak, K. J., & Spellman, B. A. (1993). Thinking. *Annual Review of Psychology, 44*, 265–315.

Hosen, R., Hosen, D. S., & Stern, L. (2001). The complexity of motivated human choices that affect psychological well-being. *Psychology & Education: An Interdisciplinary Journal, 38*, 3–27.

Howe, M. L., & O'Sullivan, J. T. (1997). What children's memories tell us about recalling our childhoods: A review of storage and retrieval processes in the development of long-term retention. *Developmental Review, 17*, 148–204.

Hsueh, Y. (2001). Basing much of the reasoning upon the work of Jean Piaget, 1927–1936. *Archives de Psychologie, 69*, 39–62.

Hsueh, Y. (2002). The Hawthorne experiments and the introduction of Jean Piaget in American industrial psychology, 1929–1932. *History of Psychology, 5*(2), 163–189.

Hu, Y. H , & Hwang, J.-N. (2002). Introduction to neural networks for signal processing. In Y. H. Hu & J.-N. Hwang (Eds.), *Handbook of neural network signal processing*, http://www.engnetbase.com/pdf/ENGnetBASE/2359/2359_PDF_toc.pdf, Boca Raton, FL: CRC Press.

Huang, I-N., (1997). Recognition of student names past: A longitudinal study with N = 1. *Journal of General Psychology, 124*, 35–47.

Hull, C. L. (1943). *Principles of behavior*. New York: Appleton-Century-Crofts.

Hull, C. L. (1951). *Essentials of behavior*. New Haven, CT: Yale University Press.

Hull, C. L. (1952). *A behavior system*. New Haven, CT: Yale University Press.

Ilyas, M., & Kumar, H. (1996). Building intelligence into computer-based systems: Some methodological problems of educational computing. *Indian Journal of Psychometry and Education, 27*, 99–106.

Inhelder, B. (1982). Outlook. In S. Modgil & C. Modgil (Eds.), *Jean Piaget: Consensus and controversy*. London: Praeger.

Inhelder, B., & Piaget, J. (1958). *The growth of logical thinking from childhood to adolescence*. New York: Basic Books.

Inoue, Y., & Sadamoto, T. (2002). Effects of single trial of heart-rate biofeedback during ramp bicycling exercise. *Perceptual & Motor Skills, 94*, 127–134.

Irwin, O. C., & Weiss, L. A. (1934). The effect of clothing on the general and vocal activity of the new born infant. *University of Iowa Studies in Child Welfare, 9*, 149–162.

Isurin, L., & McDonald, J. L. (2001). Retroactive interference from translation equivalents: Implications for first language forgetting. *Memory & Cognition, 29*, 312–319.

Jack, S. L., Shores, R. E., Denny, R. K., & Gunter, P. L. (1996). An analysis of the relationship of teachers' reported use of classroom management strategies on types of classroom interactions. *Journal of Behavioral Education, 6*, 67–87.

James, W. (1890/1950). *Principles of psychology* (Vol. 1). New York: Holt.

Jang, J. S. R., Sun, C. T., & Mizutani, E. (1997). *Neurofuzzy and soft computing: A computational approach to learning and machine intelligence*. Upper Saddle River, NJ: Prentice-Hall.

Janssen, J. (2002). Fantasy becomes reality. Treatment of sexual fantasies of sex offenders. *Tijdschrift voor Psychotherapie, 28*, 223–246.

Jenkins, R., Burton, A. M., & Ellis, A. W. (2002). Long-term effects of covert face recognition. *Cognition, 86*, B43–B52.

Jensen, P., & Toates, F. M. (1993). Who needs "behavioural needs"? Motivational aspects of the needs of animals. *Applied Animal Behaviour Science, 37*, 161–181.

Johanson, D. J., & Shreeve, J. (1989). *Lucy's child*. New York: Morrow.

Johnson, D. W., & Johnson, R. T. (1994). *Learning together and alone: Cooperative, competitive, and individualistic learning* (4th ed.). Boston: Allyn & Bacon.

Johnson, G. (1992). *In the palaces of memory: How we build the worlds inside our heads*. New York: Vintage.

Johnson, M. K., Bransford, J. D., & Solomon, S. (1973). Memory for tacit implications of sentences. *Journal of Experimental Psychology, 98*, 203–205.

Joncich, G. (1968). *The sane positivist: A biography of Edward L. Thorndike*. Middleton, CT: Wesleyan University Press.

Jones, M. C. (1974). Albert, Peter, and John B. Watson. *American Psychologist, 29*, 581–583.

Kamil, A. C., & Mauldin, J. E. (1988). A comparative ecological approach to the study of learning. In R. C. Bolles, & M. D. Beecher (Eds.), *Evolution and learning*. Hillsdale, NJ: Erlbaum.

Kamin, L. J. (1968). "Attention-like" processes in classical conditioning. In M. R. Jones (Ed.), *Miami Symposium on the Prediction of Behavior: Aversive stimulation*. Miami, FL: University of Miami Press.

Kamin, L. J. (1969). Predictability, surprise, attention and conditioning. In B. A. Campbell & R. M. Church (Eds.), *Punishment and aversive behavior.* New York: Appleton-Century-Crofts.

Kandel, E. R. (1985). Cellular mechanisms of learning and the biological bases of individuality. In E. R. Kandel & J. R. Schwartz (Eds.), *Principles of neural science* (2nd ed.). New York: Elsevier.

Kandel, E. R., Schwartz, J. H., & Jessell, T. M. (Eds.), (2000). *Principles of neural science* (4th ed.). New York: McGraw-Hill.

Keane, M. M., Gabrieli, J. D., Monti, L., Fleischman, D. A., Cantor, J. M., & Noland, J. S. (1997). Intact and impaired conceptual memory processes in amnesia. *Neuropsychology, 11,* 59–69.

Keith-Lucas, T., & Guttman, N. (1975). Robust single-trial delayed backward conditioning. *Journal of Comparative and Physiological Psychology, 88,* 468–476.

Keller, F. S. (1969). *Learning: Reinforcement theory* (2nd ed.). New York: Random House.

Kelley, H. H. (1992). Common-sense psychology and scientific psychology. *Annual Review of Psychology, 43,* 1–23.

Kellogg, R. T. (2003). *Cognitive psychology* (2nd ed.). Thousand Oaks, CA: Sage.

Kenrick, D. T., Maner, J. K., Butner, J., Li, N. P., & Becker, D. V. (2002). Dynamical evolutionary psychology: Mapping the domains of the new interactionist paradigm. *Personality and Social Psychology Review, 6,* 347–356.

Keri, S. (2003). The cognitive neuroscience of category learning. *Brain Research Reviews, 43,* 85–109.

Kiianmaa, K., Hyytia, P., Samson, H. H., Engel, J. A., Svensson, L., Soderpalm, B., et al. (2003). New neuronal networks involved in ethanol reinforcement. *Alcoholism: Clinical & Experimental Research, 27,* 209–219.

Killeen, P. R. (2003). Complex dynamic processes in sign tracking with an omission contingency (negative automaintenance). *Journal of Experimental Psychology: Animal Behavior Processes, 29,* 49–60.

Kimble, G. A. (1993). A modest proposal for a minor revolution in the language of psychology. *Psychological Science, 4,* 253–255.

Klaus, M., & Kennell, J. (1983). *Bonding: The beginnings of parent-infant attachment* (Rev. ed.). St. Louis: Mosby.

Knowlis, D. T., & Kamiya, J. (1970). The control of electroencephalographic alpha rhythms through auditory feedback in the associated mental activity. *Psychophysiology, 6,* 476–484.

Kobes, B. K. (1991). On a model for psycho-neural coevolution. *Behavior and Philosophy, 19,* 1–17.

Koffka, K. (1922). Perception: An introduction to Gestalt theory. *Psychological Bulletin, 19,* 531–585.

Koffka, K. (1925). *The growth of the mind.* New York: Harcourt, Brace & World.

Koffka, K. (1935). *Principles of Gestalt psychology.* New York: Harcourt, Brace & World.

Köhler, W. (1925). *The mentality of apes* (E. Wister, Trans.). New York: Harcourt, Brace & World.

Köhler, W. (1927). *The mentality of the apes.* New York: Harcourt, Brace & World.

Köhler, W. (1929). *Gestalt psychology.* New York: Liveright.

Köhler, W. (1969). *The task of Gestalt psychology.* Princeton, NJ: Princeton University Press.

Kolb, B. (2003). The impact of the Hebbian learning rule on research in behavioural neuroscience. *Canadian Psychology, 44,* 14–16.

Kolb, B., & Whishaw, I. Q. (1998). Brain plasticity and behavior. *Annual Review of Psychology, 49,* 43–64.

Kollins, S. H., Newland, M. C., & Critchfield, T. S. (1997). Human sensitivity to reinforcement in operant choice: How much do consequences matter? *Psychonomic Bulletin and Review, 4,* 208–220.

Koriat, A., Goldsmith, M., & Pansky, A. (2000). Toward a psychology of memory accuracy. *Annual Review of Psychology, 51,* 481–537.

Kosslyn, S. M., Behrmann, M., & Jeannerod, M. (1995). The cognitive neuroscience of mental imagery. In M. Behrmann, S. M. Kosslyn, & M. Jeannerod (Eds.), *The neuropsychology of mental imagery.* Tarrytown, NY: Elsevier.

Kozulin, A., & Gindis, B., Ageyev, V. S., & Miller, S. M. (Eds.). (2003). *Vygotsky's educational theory in cultural context. Learning in doing.* New York, NY: Cambridge University Press.

Krech, D., Rosenzweig, M., & Bennett, E. L. (1960). Effects of environmental complexity and training on brain chemistry. *Journal of Comparative and Physiological Psychology, 53,* 509–519.

Krech, D., Rosenzweig, M., & Bennett, E. L. (1962). Relations between brain chemistry and problem-solving among rats in enriched and impoverished environments. *Journal of Comparative and Physiological Psychology, 55,* 801–807.

Krech, D., Rosenzweig, M., & Bennett, E. L. (1966). Environmental impoverishment, social isolation, and changes in brain chemistry and anatomy. *Physiology and Behavior, 1,* 99–104.

Kress, T., & Daum, I. (2003). The principle of learning based on multiple brain structures. In R. H. Kluwe, G. Lüer, & F. Rösler, (Eds.), *Principles of learning and memory.* Cambridge, MA: Birkhäuser.

Kuhn, D. (1972). Mechanisms of change in the development of cognitive structures. *Child Development, 43,* 833–844.

Kurcz, I. (1995). Inevitability and changeability of stereotypes: A review of theories. *Polish Psychological Bulletin, 26,* 113–128.

Lambert, E. B., & Clyde, M. (2003). Putting Vygotsky to the test. In D. E. Lytle (Ed.), *Play and educational theory and practice. Play and culture studies* (Vol. 5). Westport, CT: Praeger.

Lana, R. E. (2002). The behavior analytic approach to language and thought. *Journal of Mind & Behavior, 23*, 31–49.

Lantolf, J. P. (2003). Vygotsky's psychology-philosophy. A metaphor for language theory and learning. *Modern Language Journal, 87*, 137–138.

Larsen, D. J. (1999). Eclecticism: Psychological theories as interwoven stories. *International Journal for the Advancement of Counselling, 21*, 69–83.

Lashley, K. S. (1924). Studies of cerebral function in learning. *Archives of Neurological Psychiatry, 12*, 249–276.

Latimer, C., & Stevens, C. (1997). Some remarks on wholes, parts, and their perception. *Psycoloquy, 8*, NP.

Lear, J. (1996). The introduction of Eros: Reflections on the work of Hans Loewald. *Journal of the American Psychoanalytic Association, 44*, 673–698.

Leask, S. J., & Crow, T. J. (1997). How far does the brain lateralize? An unbiased method for determining the optimum degree of hemispheric specialization. *Neuropsychologia, 35*, 1381–1387.

Leclerc, G., Lefrançois, R., Dube, M., Hebert, R., & Gaulin, P. (1998). The self-actualization concept: A content validation. *Journal of Social Behavior and Personality, 13*, 69–84.

Lefrançois, G. R. (1968). A treatment hierarchy for the acceleration of conservation of substance. *Canadian Journal of Psychology, 22*, 277–284.

Lefrançois, G. R. (2000). *Psychology for teaching: A bear is not a choirboy* (10th ed.). Belmont, CA: Wadsworth.

Lehar, S. (2003). *The world in your head: A Gestalt view of the mechanism of conscious experience.* Mahwah, NJ: Erlbaum.

Lehman, E. B., McKinley-Pace, M. J., Wilson, J. A., & Slavsky, M. D. (1997). Direct and indirect measures of intentional forgetting in children and adults: Evidence for retrieval inhibition and reinstatement. *Journal of Experimental Child Psychology, 64*, 295–316.

Lepper, M. R. (1981). Intrinsic and extrinsic motivation in children: Detrimental effects of superfluous social controls. In W. A. Collins (Ed.), *Aspects of the development of competence: The Minnesota Symposium on Child Psychology* (Vol. 14). Hillsdale, NJ: Erlbaum.

Lepper, M. R., & Greene, D. (1975). Turning play into work: Effects of adult surveillance and extrinsic rewards on children's intrinsic motivation. *Journal of Personality and Social Psychology, 31*, 479–486.

Lerman, D. C., Iwata, B. A., Shore, B. A., & DeLeon, I. G. (1997). Effects of intermittent punishment on self-injurious behavior: An evaluation of schedule thinning. *Journal of Applied Behavior Analysis, 30*, 187–201.

Letourneau, E. J., & O'Donohue, W. (1997). Classical conditioning of female sexual arousal. *Archives of Sexual Behavior, 26*, 63–78.

Li, P., & MacWhinney, B.(2002). PatPho: A phonological pattern generator for neural networks. *Behavior Research Methods, Instruments, & Computers, 34*, 408–415.

Li, X. (2002). Connectionist learning: A comparison of neural networks and an optical thin-film multilayer model. *Connection Science: Journal of Neural Computing, Artificial Intelligence & Cognitive Research, 14*, 49–63.

Liben, L. (1975). Perspective-taking skills in young children: Seeing the world through rose-colored glasses. *Paper presented at the meeting of the Society for Research in Child Development*, Denver, CO.

Lilly, J. C. (1972). *The center of the cyclone: An autobiography of inner space.* New York: Julian.

Lindberg, A. C., Kelland, A., & Nicol, C. J. (1999). Effects of observational learning on acquisition of an operant response in horses. *Applied Animal Behaviour Science, 61*, 187–199.

Lindblom, J., & Ziemke, T. (2003) Social situatedness of natural and artificial intelligence: Vygotsky and beyond. *Adaptive Behavior, 11*, 79–96.

Lobb, M. S. (2001). The theory of self in Gestalt therapy: A restatement of some aspects. *Gestalt Review, 5*, 276–288.

Loftus, E. F. (1979). *Eyewitness testimony.* Cambridge, MA: Harvard University Press.

Loftus, E. F., Feldman, J., & Dashiell, R. (1995). The reality of illusory memories. In D. L. Schacter, J. T. Coyle, G. D. Fischbach, M. M. Mesulam, & L. E. Sullivan (Eds.), *Memory distortion: How minds, brains and societies reconstruct the past.* Cambridge, MA: Harvard University Press.

Logue, A. W. (1988). A comparison of taste aversion learning in humans and other vertebrates: Evolutionary pressures in common. In R. C. Bolles & M. D. Beecher (Eds.), *Evolution and learning.* Hillsdale, NJ: Erlbaum.

Lorenz, K. (1952). *King Solomon's ring.* London: Methuen.

Lourenco, O., & Machado, A. (1996). In defense of Piaget's theory: A reply to 10 common criticisms. *Psychological Review, 103*, 143–164.

Lubin, D. A., Cannon, J. B., Black, M. C., Brown, L. E., & Johns, J. M. (2003). Effects of chronic cocaine on monoamine levels in discrete brain structures of lactating rat dams. *Pharmacology, biochemistry, and behavior, 74*, 449–454.

Luria, A. R. (1968). *The mind of a mnemonist*. New York: Avon.

MacCulloch, M. J., & Feldman, P. (1996). Eye movement desensitisation treatment utilises the positive visceral element of the investigatory reflex to inhibit the memories of post-traumatic stress disorder: A theoretical analysis. *British Journal of Psychiatry, 169*, 571–579.

Macfarlane, D. A. (1930). The role of kinesthesis in maze learning. *University of California Publications in Psychology, 4*, 277–305.

Magnussen, S., Greenlee, M. W., Aslaksen, P. M., & Kildebo, O. O. (2003). High-fidelity perceptual long-term memory revisited—and confirmed. *Psychological Science, 14*, 74–76.

Malone, J. C. Jr. & Cruchon, N. M. (2001). Radical behaviorism and the rest of psychology: A review/precis of Skinner's About Behaviorism. *Behavior & Philosophy, 29*, 31–57.

Mandler, G. (1985). *Cognitive psychology: An essay in cognitive science*. Hillsdale, NJ: Erlbaum.

Mandler, G. (1996). The situation of psychology: Landmarks and choicepoints. *American Journal of Psychology, 109*, 1–35.

Markman, A. B., & Gentner, D. (2001). Thinking. *Annual Review of Psychology, 52*, 223–247.

Martens, B. K., & Hiralall, A. S. (1997). Scripted sequences of teacher interaction: A versatile, low-impact procedure for increasing appropriate behavior in a nursery school. *Behavior Modification, 21*, 308–323.

Martinie, M. A., & Joule, R. V. (2000). Trivialization and rationalization acts in a false attribution paradigm: Two alternative modes for reducing dissonance. [French]. Trivialisation et rationalisation en acte dans le paradigme de la fausse attribution: Deux voies alternatives de reduction de la dissonance. *Revue Internationale de Psychologie Sociale, 13*, 93–114.

Masia, C. L., & Chase, P. N. (1997). Vicarious learning revisited: A contemporary behavior analytic interpretation. *Journal of Behavior Therapy and Experimental Psychiatry, 28*, 41–51.

Maslow, A. H. (1970). *Motivation and personality* (2nd ed.). New York: Harper & Row.

Massaro, D. W., & Cowan, N. (1993). Information processing models: Microscopes of the mind. *Annual Review of Psychology, 44*, 383–425.

Mayes, A. R. (2002). Exploring the neural bases of complex memory. In L. R. Squire & D. L. Schacter (Eds.), *Neuropsychology of memory* (3rd ed.). New York: Guilford Press.

Mayo, E. (1930). The work of Jean Piaget. *Ohio State University Bulletin, 35*, 140–146.

McClelland, J. L., & Rumelhart, D. E. (Eds.). (1986). *Parallel distributed processing: Explorations in the microstructure of cognition* (Vol. 2). Cambridge, MA: Bradford/MIT Press.

McCloskey, M., & Cohen, N. J. (1989). Catastrophic interference in connectionist networks: The sequential learning problem. *Psychology of Learning and Motivation: Advanced Research and Theory, 24*, 109–165.

McConnell, J. V. (1962). Memory transfer through cannibalism in planarians. *Journal of Neuropsychiatry, 3* (Suppl. 1).

McConnell, J. V. (1976). Worm-breeding with tongue in cheek and the confessions of a scientist hoist by his own petard. *UNESCO Courier, 32*, 12–15.

McDougall, W. (1908). *An introduction to social psychology*. London: Methuen.

McKeachie, W. J. (1997). McConnell: Mischievous but not malevolent? *American Psychologist, 52*, 269.

Mead, M. (1935). *Sex and temperament in three primitive societies*. New York: Morrow.

Medici de Steiner, C. (1995). Analysing children's dreams. *International Journal of Psychoanalysis, 76*, 45–49.

Medin, D. L., & Florian, J. E. (1992). Abstraction and selective coding in exemplar-based models of categorization. In A. F. Healy, S. M. Kosslyn, & R. M. Shiffrin (Eds.), *From learning processes to cognitive processes: Essays in honor of William K. Estes* (Vol. 2). Hillsdale, NJ: Erlbaum.

Medin, D. L., & Ross, B. H. (1992). *Cognitive psychology*. Fort Worth, TX: Harcourt Brace.

Medin, D. L., Lynch, E. B., & Solomon, K. O. (2000). Are there kinds of concepts? *Annual Review of Psychology, 51*, 121–147.

Mellor, D. H. (1989). How much of the mind is a computer. In P. Sleak & W. R. Albury (Eds.), *Computers, brains and minds*. Boston: Kluwer.

Meltzoff, A. N., & Moore, M. K. (1989). Imitation in newborn infants: Exploring the range of gestures imitated and the underlying mechanisms. *Developmental Psychology, 25*, 954–962.

Mervis, C. B., & Rosch, E. (1981). Categorization of natural objects. *Annual Review of Psychology, 32*, 89–115.

Miller, G. A. (1956). The magical number seven, plus or minus two: Some limits on our capacity for processing information. *Psychological Review, 63*, 81–97.

Miller, N. E. (1951). Learnable drives and rewards. In S. S. Stevens (Ed.), *Handbook of experimental psychology*. New York: Wiley.

Miller, N. E. (1969). Learning of visceral and glandular responses. *Science, 163*, 434–445.

Miller, N. E., & Carmona, A. (1967). Modification of a visceral response, salivation in thirsty dogs, by instrumental training with water reward. *Journal of Comparative and Physiological Psychology, 63*, 1–6.

Miller, N. E., & Dollard, J. C. (1941). *Social learning and imitation.* New Haven, CT: Yale University Press.

Miller, R. (1990). Beyond reductionism: The emerging holistic paradigm in education. *Humanistic Psychologist, 18,* 314–323.

Mills, J. A. (1998). *Control: A history of behavioral psychology.* New York: New York University Press.

Milner, P. M. (1989). A cell assembly theory of hippocampal amnesia. Special Issue: Memory. *Neuropsychologia, 27,* 23–30.

Miskin, M. (1995). Cerebral memory circuits. In J. King & K. H. Pribram (Eds.), *Scale in conscious experience: Is the brain too important to be left to specialists to study?* Mahwah, NJ: Erlbaum.

Mitchell, C. J., & Lovibond, P. F. (2002). Backward and forward blocking in human electrodermal conditioning: Blocking requires an assumption of outcome additivity. *Quarterly Journal of Experimental Psychology, 55B,* 311–329.

Modgil, S., & Modgil, C. (Eds.). (1982). *Jean Piaget: Consensus and controversy.* London: Praeger.

Monti, L. A., Gabrieli, J. D., Wilson, R. S., Beckett, L. A., Grinnell, E., Lange, K. L., Reminger, S.L. (1997). Sources of priming in text rereading: Intact implicit memory for new associations in older adults and in patients with Alzheimer's disease. *Psychology and Aging, 12,* 536–547.

Moore, J. D., Redfield, L. W., & Johnson, L. W. (Eds.) (2001). *Artificial intelligence in education: AI-ED in the Wired and Wireless future.* Amsterdam: IOS Press.

Moray, N. (1959). Attention in dichotic listening: Affective cues and influence of instruction. *Quarterly Journal of Experimental Psychology, 11,* 56–60.

Morgado, L. (2003). The role of representation in Piagetian theory: Changes over time. In T. Brown & L. Smith (Eds.), *Reductionism and the development of knowledge.* Mahwah, NJ: Erlbaum.

Morrison, A. R. (2001). A scientist's perspective on the ethics of using animals in behavioral research. In M. E. Carroll & J. Bruce Overmier (Eds.), *Animal research and human health: Advancing human welfare through behavioral science.* Washington, DC: American Psychological Association.

Morwitz, V. G., & Pluzinski, C. (1996). Do polls reflect opinions or do opinions reflect polls? The impact of political polling on voters' expectations, preferences, and behavior. *Journal of Consumer Research, 23,* 53–67.

Mowrer, O. H., & Mowrer, W. M. (1938). Enuresis: A method for its study and treatment. *American Journal of Orthopsychiatry, 8,* 436–459.

Murawski, D. A. (1993). Passion vine butterflies: A taste for poison. *National Geographic, 184,* 123–137.

Murchison, C. (Ed.). (1936). *A history of psychology in autobiography* (Vol. 3). Worcester, MA: Clark University Press.

Murray, D. J. (1995). *Gestalt psychology and the cognitive revolution.* New York: Harvester Wheatsheaf.

Nairne, J. S. (2002). Remembering over the short-term: The case against the standard model. *Annual Review of Psychology, 53,* 53–81.

Nathawat, S. S., Singh, R., & Singh, B. (1997). The effect of need for achievement on attributional style. *Journal of Social Psychology, 137,* 55–62.

Necka, E. (2000). Intelligence, cognitive strategies, and arousal: Can we control non-cognitive factors that influence our intellect? In U. von Hecker, S. Dutke, & G. Sedek (Eds.), *Generative mental processes and cognitive resources: Integrative research on adaptation and control.* Boston: Kluwer Academic.

Neisser, U. (1976). *Cognition and reality: Principles and implications of cognitive psychology.* San Francisco: Freeman.

Neisser, U. (1978). Memory: What are the important questions? In M. M. Gruneberg, P. E. Morris, & R. N. Sykes (Eds.), *Practical aspects of memory.* San Diego: Academic Press.

Neruda, P. (1972). *The captain's verses.* New York: New Directions.

Newell, A. (1973). Artificial intelligence and the concept of mind. In R. C. Schank & C. M. Colby (Eds.), *Computer models of thought and language.* San Francisco: Freeman.

Newell, A. (1989). Putting it all together. In D. Klahr & K. Kotovsky (Eds.), *Complex information processing: The impact of Herbert A. Simon.* Hillsdale, NJ: Erlbaum.

Newell, A. (1990). *Unified theories of cognition.* Cambridge, MA: Harvard University Press.

Newell, A., Shaw, J. C., & Simon, H. A. (1958). Elements of a theory of human problem-solving. *Psychological Review, 65,* 151–166.

Newell, A., & Simon, H. A. (1972). *Human problem solving.* Englewood Cliffs, NJ: Prentice-Hall.

Norcross, J. C., & Tomcho, T. J. (1994). Great books in psychology: Three studies in search of a consensus. *Teaching of Psychology, 21,* 86–90.

Nucci, L., & Turiel, E. (2001). Message from the Jean Piaget Society. *Cognitive Development, 16,* 657–658.

O'Brien, G., & Opie, J. (2002). Radical connectionism: Thinking with (not in) language. *Language & Communication, 22,* 313–329.

O'Donohue, W., & Ferguson, K. E. (2001). *The psychology of B. F. Skinner.* Thousand Oaks, CA: Sage.

Olds, J. (1956). Pleasure centers in the brain. *Scientific American, 195,* 105–116.

Olds, J., & Milner, P. (1954). Positive reinforcement produced by electrical stimulation of septal area and other regions of rat brain. *Journal of Comparative and Physiological Psychology, 47,* 419–427.

O'Leary, K. D., & Becker, W. C. (1968). The effects of a teacher's reprimands on children's behavior. *Journal of School Psychology, 7,* 8–11.

O'Leary, K. D., Kaufman, K. F., Kass, R. E., & Drabman, R. S. (1974). The effects of loud and soft reprimands on the behavior of disruptive students. In A. R. Brown & C. Avery (Eds.), *Modifying children's behavior: A book of readings.* Springfield, IL: Thomas.

O'Neil, W. M. (1991). In what sense do Tolman's intervening variables intervene? *Australian Journal of Psychology, 43,* 159–162.

Olson, D. R. (1963). *The role of verbal rules in the cognitive processes of children.* Unpublished doctoral dissertation, University of Alberta, Edmonton.

Olton, D. S. (1992). Tolman's cognitive analyses: predecessors of current approaches in psychology. *Journal of Experimental Psychology: General, 121,* 427–428.

Opper, S. (1977). Concept development in Thai urban and rural children. In P. R. Dasen (Ed.), *Piagetian psychology: Cross-cultural contributions.* New York: Gardner.

Orlofsky, D. D. (2001). *Redefining teacher education: The theories of Jerome Bruner and the practice of training teachers.* New York: Peter Lang.

Oswick, C., Keenoy, T., & Grant, D. (2002). Metaphor and analogical reasoning in organization theory: Beyond orthodoxy. *Academy of Management Review, 27,* 294–303.

Overskeid, G. (2002). Psychological hedonism and the nature of motivation: Bertrand Russell's anhedonic desires. *Philosophical Psychology, 15,* 77–93.

Page, R. A. (1992). Clark Hull and his role in the study of hypnosis. *American Journal of Clinical Hypnosis, 34,* 178–184.

Pajares, M. F. (1992). Teachers' beliefs and educational research: Cleaning up a messy construct. *Review of Educational Research, 62,* 307–332.

Papert, S. (1980). *Mindstorms: Children, computers, and powerful ideas.* New York: Basic Books.

Papert, S. (1993). *The children's machine: Rethinking school in the age of the computer.* New York: Basic Books.

Pascal, B. (1820). *Pensées de Blaise Pascal.* Paris: Ledentu, Libraire, quai des Augustins, no. 31.

Pashler, H., & Medin, D. (Eds.). (2002). *Steven's handbook of experimental psychology* (3rd ed.), *Vol. 2: Memory and cognitive processes.* New York: Wiley.

Patrick, H., Hicks, L., & Ryan, A. M. (1997). Relations of perceived social efficacy and social goal pursuit to self-efficacy for academic work. *Journal of Early Adolescence, 17,* 109–128.

Paul, D. B., & Blumenthal, A. L. (1989). On the trail of Little Albert. *Psychological Record, 39,* 547–553.

Pearce, J. M., & Bouton, M. E. (2001). Theories of associative learning in animals. *Annual Review of Psychology, 52,* 111–139.

Penfield, W. (1969). Consciousness, memory and man's conditioned reflexes. In K. H. Pribram (Ed.), *On the biology of learning.* New York: Harcourt Brace Jovanovich.

Penner, D. E. (2000–2001). Cognition, computers, and synthetic science: Building knowledge and meaning through modeling. In W. G. Segada (Ed.), *Review of research in education, 25,* 1–35.

Peterson, L. R., & Peterson, N. J. (1959). Short-term retention of individual verbal items. *Journal of Experimental Psychology, 58,* 193–198.

Petty, R. E., Wegener, D. T., & Fabrigar, L. R. (1997). Attitudes and attitude change. *Annual Review of Psychology, 48,* 609–647.

Phillips, J. M., & Gully, S. M. (1997). Role of goal orientation, ability, need for achievement, and locus of control in the self-efficacy and goal-setting process. *Journal of Applied Psychology, 82,* 792–802.

Piaget, J. (1926). *The language and thought of the child.* New York: Harcourt, Brace & World.

Piaget, J. (1929). *The child's conception of the world.* New York: Harcourt, Brace & World.

Piaget, J. (1930). *The child's conception of physical causality.* London: Kegan Paul.

Piaget, J. (1932). *The moral judgment of the child.* London: Kegan Paul.

Piaget, J. (1946). *Le dévelopement de la notion de temps chez l'enfant* [The development of the notion of time in the child]. Paris: Presses Universitaires de France.

Piaget, J. (1950). *The psychology of intelligence.* New York: Harcourt, Brace & World.

Piaget, J. (1951). *Play, dreams and imitation in childhood.* New York: Norton.

Piaget, J. (1961). *On the development of memory and identity.* Worcester, MA: Clark University Press.

Piaget, J. (1972). Intellectual development from adolescence to adulthood. *Human Development, 15,* 1–12.

Piaget, J. (1976). *The grasp of consciousness.* Cambridge, MA: Harvard University Press.

Piaget, J. (1980). *Les formes élémentaires de la dialectique.* Paris: Gallimard.

Piaget, J. (2001). *Studies in reflecting abstraction.* (R. Campbell, Ed. and Trans.) Sussex, UK: Psychology Press.

Piaget, J., & Inhelder, B. (1941). *Le développement des quantités chez l'enfant.* Neuchatel: Délachaux et Niestlé.

Piaget, J., & Inhelder, B. (1956). *The child's conception of space.* New York: Norton.

Plato. (427–347 BC) *Republic 5.* (1993 translation and introduction by S. Halliwell). Warminster: Aris & Phillips.

Plenge, M., Curio, E., & Witte, K. (2000). Sexual imprinting supports the evolution of novel male traits by transference of a preference for the colour red. *Behaviour, 137,* 741–758.

Poldrack, R. A., & Packard, M. G. (2003). Competition among multiple memory systems: Converging evidence from animal and human brain studies. *Neuropsychologia, 41,* 245–251.

Pope, A. T., & Bogart, E. H. (1996). Extended attention span training system: Video game neurotherapy for attention deficit disorder. *Child Study Journal, 26,* 39–50.

Pope, D. J., & Whiteley, H. E. (2003). Developmental dyslexia, cerebellar/vestibular brain function and possible links to exercise-based interventions: A review. *European Journal of Special Needs Education, 18,* 109–123.

Porter, S., & Birt, A. R. (2001). Is traumatic memory special ? A comparison of traumatic memory characteristics with memory for other emotional life experiences. *Applied Cognitive Psychology, 15,* S101–S117.

Powell, R. A., Symbaluk, D. G., & Macdonald, S. E. (2002). *Introduction to learning and behavior.* Belmont, CA: Thomson Learning.

Premack, D. (1965). Reinforcement theory. In D. Levine (Ed.), *Nebraska Symposium on Motivation.* Lincoln: University of Nebraska Press.

Prytula, R. E., Oster, G. D., & Davis, S. F. (1977). The "rat rabbit" problem: What did John B. Watson really do? *Teaching of Psychology, 4,* 44–46.

Pulvermuller, F. (1996). Hebb's concept of cell assemblies and the psychophysiology of word processing. *Psychophysiology, 33,* 317–333.

Purdy, J. E., Harriman, A., & Molitorisz, J. (1993). Contributions to the history of psychology: XCV. Possible relations between theories of evolution and animal learning. *Psychological Reports, 73,* 211–223.

Quigley, J. (2001). Psychology and grammar: The construction of autobiographical self. *Theory & Psychology, 11,* 147–170.

Raphael, B. (1976). *The thinking computer: Mind inside matter.* San Francisco: Freeman.

Reber, A. S. (1989). Implicit learning and tacit knowledge. *Journal of Experimental Psychology: General, 118,* 219–235.

Reese, E. P. (1966). *The analysis of human operant behavior.* Dubuque, IA: Brown.

Reilly, S., & Grutzmacher, R. P. (2002). Autoshaping in the rat: Conditioned licking response to a stimulus that signals sucrose reinforcement. *Behavioural Processes, 59,* 15–24.

Rescorla, R. A. (1980). *Pavlovian second-order conditioning: Studies in associative learning.* Hillsdale, NJ: Erlbaum.

Rescorla, R. A. (1988). Pavlovian conditioning: It's not what you think it is. *American Psychologist, 43,* 151–160.

Rescorla, R. A., & Holland, P. C. (1976). Some behavioral approaches to the study of learning. In M. R. Rosenzweig & E. L. Bennet (Eds.), *Neuromechanisms of learning and memory.* Boston: MIT Press.

Rice, B. (1982). The Hawthorne defect: Persistence of a flawed theory. *Psychology Today,* February, *16,* 70–74.

Richardson, J. T. E. (1995). The efficacy of imagery mnemonics in memory remediation. In M. Behrmann, S. M. Kosslyn, & M. Jeannerod (Eds.), *The neuropsychology of mental imagery.* Tarrytown, NY: Elsevier.

Richey, R. C. (Ed.). (2000). *The legacy of Robert M. Gagné.* Syracuse, NY: ERIC Clearinghouse on Information & Technology.

Riesen, A. H., Chow, K. L., Semmes, J., & Nissen, H. W. (1951). Chimpanzee vision after four conditions of light deprivation. *American Psychologist, 6,* 282.

Rilling, M. (1996). The mystery of the vanished citations: James McConnell's forgotten 1960's quest for planarian learning, a biochemical engram, and celebrity. *American Psychologist, 51,* 589–598.

Robertson, R., Garcia Y., & Garcia, J. (1988). Darwin was a learning theorist. In R. C. Bolles & M. D. Beecher (Eds.), *Evolution and learning.* Hillsdale, NJ: Erlbaum.

Rockwell, W. T. (1994). Beyond determination and indignity: A reinterpretation of operant conditioning. *Behavior & Philosophy, 22,* 53–66.

Roethlisberger, S. J., & Dickson, W. J. (1939). *Management and the worker.* Cambridge, MA: Harvard University Press.

Rogers, C. R., & Skinner, B. F. (1956). Some issues concerning the control of human behavior: A symposium. *Science, 124,* 1057–1066.

Rolls, E. T. (2000). Memory systems in the brain. *Annual Review of Psychology, 51,* 599–630.

Romanes, G. J. (1883). *Animal intelligence.* New York: D. Appleton. Reissued as Robinson, D. W. (Ed.). (1977). *Animal intelligence: George John Romanes.* Washington, DC: University Publications of America.

Rosch, E. (1973). Natural categories. *Cognitive Psychology, 4,* 328–350.

Rosch, E. (1977). Human categorization. In N. Warren (Ed.), *Advances in cross-cultural psychology* (Vol. 1). London: Academic Press.

Rosenzweig, M. R., Leiman, A. L., & Breedlove, M. S. (1999). *Biological psychology: An introduction to behavioral, cognitive, and clinical neuroscience.* Sunderland, MA: Sinauer Associates.

Rosler, F., Heil, M., & Roder, B. (1997). Slow negative brain potentials as reflections of specific modular resources of cognition. *Biological Psychology, 45,* 109–141.

Roth, W. T., Ford, J. M., Pfefferbaum, A., & Elbert, T. R. (1995). Methodological issues in event-related brain potential and magnetic field studies. In F. E. Bloom & D. J. Kupfer (Eds.), *Psychopharmacology:*

The fourth generation of progress: An official publication of the American College of Neuropsychopharmacology. New York: Raven Press.

Rotter, J. B. (1954). *Social learning and clinical psychology.* Englewood Cliffs, NJ: Prentice-Hall.

Rovee-Collier, C., Hayne, H., & Colombo, M. (2001). *The development of implicit and explicit memory.* Philadelphia: John Benjamins.

Rowan, J. (1998). Maslow amended. *Journal of Humanistic Psychology, 38,* 81–92.

Rozin, P., & Kalat, J. W. (1971). Specific hungers and poison avoidance as adaptive specializations of learning. *Psychological Review, 78,* 459–486.

Rumelhart, D. E. (1992). Towards a microstructural account of human reasoning. In S. Davis (Ed.), *Connectionism: Theory and practice.* New York: Oxford University Press.

Rush, K. S., Crockett, J. L., & Hagopian, L. P. (2001). An analysis of the selective effects of NCR with punishment targeting problem behavior associated with positive affect. *Behavioral Intervention, 16,* 127–135.

Russell, J. (1999). Cognitive development as an executive process—in part: A homeopathic dose of Piaget. *Developmental Science, 2,* 247–295.

Russell, J. A. (2003). Core affect and the psychological construction of emotion. *Psychological Review, 110,* 145–172.

Russo, M., & Jain, L. C. (2001). *Fuzzy learning and applications.* Boca Raton, FL: CRC Press.

Sagan, C. (1977). *The dragons of Eden.* New York: Ballantine Books.

Sahakian, W. S. (1981). *Psychology of learning: Systems, models, and theories* (2nd ed.). Chicago: Markham.

Sakagami, S. F., & Akahira, Y. (1960). Studies on the Japanese honeybee, Apis cerafabricius: 8. Two opposing adaptations in the post-stinging behavior of honeybees. *Evolution, 14,* 29–40.

Sales, B. D., & Folkman, S. (Eds.), (2000). *Ethics in research with human participants.* Washington, DC: American Psychological Association.

Salomon, G., & Perkins, D. N. (1998). Individual and social aspects of learning. In P. D. Pearson & A. Iran-Nejad (Eds.), *Review of Research in Education, 23,* 1–24.

Samelson, F. (1980). J. B. Watson's little Albert, Cyril Burt's twins, and the need for a critical science. *American Psychologist, 35,* 619–625.

Santiago-Delefosse, M. J., & Delefosse, J. M. O. (2002). Spielrein, Piaget and Vygotsky: Three positions on child thought and language. *Theory & Psychology, 12,* 723–747.

Schacter, D. L., Norman, K. A., & Koutstaal, W. (1998). The cognitive neuroscience of constructive memory. *Annual Review of Psychology, 49,* 289–318.

Schauss, S. L., Chase, P. N., & Hawkins, R. P. (1997). Environment-behavior relations, behavior therapy and the process of persuasion and attitude change. *Journal of Behavior Therapy and Experimental Psychiatry, 28,* 31–40.

Scher, S. J., & Rauscher, F. (2003). Nature read in truth or in flaw: Locating alternatives in evolutionary psychology. In S. J. Scher & F. Rauscher (Eds.), *Evolutionary psychology: Alternative approaches.* Boston: Kluwer.

Schmuck, R. A., & Schmuck, P. A. (1997). *Group processes in the classroom* (7th ed.). Madison, WI: Brown & Benchmark.

Schneider, H. J. (1996). Violence in the mass media. *Studies on Crime and Crime Prevention, 5,* 59–71.

Schultz, D. P. (1965). *Sensory restriction: Effects on behavior.* New York: Academic Press.

Schunk, D. H. (1984). Self-efficacy perspective on achievement behavior. *Educational Psychologist, 19,* 48–58.

Scrimsher, S., & Tudge, J. (2003). The teaching/learning relationship in the first years of school: Some revolutionary implications of Vygotsky's theory. *Early Education and Development, 14,* 293–312.

Searle, J. (1980). Minds, brains, and programs. *Behavioral and Brain Sciences, 3,* 417–424.

Sears, I. R., Maccoby, E. P., & Lewin, H. (1957). *Patterns of child rearing.* Evanston, IL: Row, Peterson.

Sejnowski, T. J., & Rosenberg, C. R. (1987). Parallel networks that learn to pronounce English text. *Complex Systems, 1,* 145–168.

Seligman, M. E. P. (1975). *Helplessness: On depression, development, and death.* San Francisco: Freeman.

Seligman, M. E. P., & Hager, J. L. (1972). *Biological boundaries of learning.* New York: Appleton-Century-Crofts.

Semb, G. B., & Ellis, J. A. (1994). Knowledge taught in school: What is remembered? *Review of Educational Research, 64,* 253–286.

Shanks, N. (2002). *Animals and science: A guide to the debates.* Santa Barbara, CA: ABC-Clio.

Shebilske, W. L., Jordan, J. A., Goettle, B. P., & Paulus, L. E. (1998). Observation versus hands-on practice of complex skills in dyadic, triadic, and tetradic training teams. *Human Factors, 40,* 525–540.

Shotter, J. (2001). Towards a third revolution in psychology: From inner mental representations to dialogically-structured social practices. In D. Bakhurst & S. G. Shanker (Eds.), *Jerome Bruner: Language, culture, self.* Thousand Oaks, CA: Sage.

Siegel, P. F. (1996). The meaning of behaviorism for B. F. Skinner. *Psychoanalytic Psychology, 13,* 343–365.

Siegert, R. J., & Ward, T. (2002) Evolutionary psychology: Origins and criticisms. *Australian Psychologist, 37,* 20–29.

Siegler, R. S., & Liebert, R. M. (1972). Effects of presenting relevant rules and complete feedback on the conservation of liquid quantity task. *Developmental Psychology, 7,* 133–138.

Simon, H. A. (1990). Invariants of human behavior. *Annual Review of Psychology, 41,* 1–19.

Skaalvik, E. M., & Rankin, R. J. (1995). A test of the internal/external frame of reference model at different levels of math and verbal self-perception. *American Educational Research Journal, 32,* 161–184.

Skinner, B. F. (1938). *The behavior of organisms: An experimental analysis.* New York: Appleton-Century-Crofts.

Skinner, B. F. (1948). *Walden two.* New York: Macmillan.

Skinner, B. F. (1950). Are theories of learning necessary? *Psychological Review, 57,* 193–216.

Skinner, B. F. (1951, December). How to teach animals. *Scientific American, 185,* 26–29.

Skinner, B. F. (1953). *Science and human behavior.* New York: Macmillan.

Skinner, B. F. (1957). *Verbal behavior.* New York: Appleton-Century-Crofts.

Skinner, B. F. (1961). *Cumulative record* (Rev. ed.). New York: Appleton-Century-Crofts.

Skinner, B. F. (1969). *Contingencies of reinforcement: A theoretical analysis.* New York: Appleton-Century-Crofts.

Skinner, B. F. (1971). *Beyond freedom and dignity.* New York: Knopf.

Skinner, B. F. (1973). Answers for my critics. In H. Wheeler (Ed.), *Beyond the punitive society: Operant conditioning: Social and political aspects.* San Francisco: Freeman.

Skinner, B. F. (1976). *Particulars of my life.* New York: Knopf.

Skinner, B. F. (1979). *The shaping of a behaviorist.* New York: Knopf.

Skinner, B. F. (1983). *A matter of consequences.* New York: Knopf.

Skinner, B. F. (1986). Why I am not a cognitive psychologist. In T. J. Knapp & L. C. Robertson (Eds.), *Approaches to cognition: Contrasts and controversies,* Hillsdale, NJ: Erlbaum.

Skinner, B. F. (1989). *Recent issues in the analysis of behavior.* Columbus, OH: Merrill.

Skinner, B. F. (1996). Some responses to the stimulus "Pavlov." *Integrative Physiological and Behavioral Science, 31,* 254–257.

Slanger, E., & Rudestam, K. E. (1997). Motivation and disinhibition in high risk sports: Sensation seeking and self-efficacy. *Journal of Research in Personality, 31,* 355–374.

Slifer, K. J., Babbitt, R. L., & Cataldo, M. D. (1995). Simulation and counterconditioning as adjuncts to pharmacotherapy for invasive pediatric procedures. *Journal of Developmental and Behavioral Pediatrics, 16,* 133–141.

Smedslund, J. (1961). The acquisition of conservation of substance and weight in children. I. Introduction. *Scandinavian Journal of Psychology, 2,* 110.

Smeijsters, H., & van den Berk, P. (1995). Music therapy with a client suffering from musicogenic epilepsy: A naturalistic qualitative single-case research. Special Issue: European Consortium for Arts Therapy Education (ECARTE). *Arts in Psychotherapy, 22,* 249–263.

Smith, B. (1988). Gestalt theory: An essay in philosophy. In B. Smith (Ed.), *Foundations of Gestalt theory.* Munich, Germany: Philosophia Verlag München Wien.

Smith, B. D., & Vetter, H. J. (1996). A behavioral approach: B. F. Skinner. In G. H. Jennings (Ed.), *Passages beyond the gate: A Jungian approach to understanding the nature of American psychology at the dawn of the new millennium.* Needham Heights, MA: Simon & Schuster.

Smith, G. P. (1995). Pavlov and appetite. *Integrative Physiological and Behavioral Science, 30,* 169–174.

Smith, L. D. (1990). Metaphors of knowledge and behavior in the behaviorist tradition. In D. E. Leary (Ed.), *Metaphors in the history of psychology.* New York: Cambridge University Press.

Smith, L. D. (2002). On prediction and control: B. F. Skinner and the technological ideal of science. In W. E. Pickren & D. A. Dewsbury, Donald A. (Eds.), *Evolving perspectives on the history of psychology.* Washington, DC: American Psychological Association.

Sommer, R., & Sommer, B. (2002). *A practical guide to behavioral research.* New York: Oxford University Press.

Sonderegger, T. B. (1970). Intracranial stimulation and maternal behavior. *APA Convention Proceedings, 78th meeting,* 245–246.

Sonnier, I. L. (1991). Hemisphericity: A key to understanding the individual differences among teachers and learners. *Journal of Instructional Psychology, 18,* 17–22.

Sperling, G. (1963). A model for visual memory tests. *Human Factors, 5,* 19–31.

Sprenger, M. B. (2002). *Becoming a "Wiz" at brain-based teaching: How to make every year your best year.* Thousand Oaks, CA: Corwin Press.

Squire, L. R. (1987). *Memory and brain.* New York: Oxford University Press.

Squire, L. R., Knowlton, B., & Musen, G. (1993). The structure and organization of memory. *Annual Review of Psychology, 44,* 453–495.

St. Julien, J. (1997). Explaining learning: The research trajectory of situated cognition and the implications of connectionism. In D. I. Kirshner & J. A. Whitson (Eds.), *Situated cognition: Social, semiotic, and psychological perspectives*. Mahwah, NJ: Erlbaum.

Stagner, R. (1988). *A history of psychological theories*. New York: Macmillan.

Standing, L. (1973). Learning 10,000 pictures. *Quarterly Journal of Experimental Psychology, 25*, 207–222.

Steier, D., & Mitchell, T. M. (Eds.). (1996). *Mind matters: A tribute to Allen Newell*. Mahwah, NJ: Erlbaum.

Sternberg, R. J., & Ben-Zeev, T. (2001). *Complex cognition: The psychology of human thought*. New York: Oxford University Press.

Takaku, S. (2001). The effects of apology and perspective taking on interpersonal forgiveness: A dissonance-attribution model of interpersonal forgiveness. *Journal of Social Psychology, 141*, 494–508.

Tannenbaum, J. (2001). The paradigm shift toward animal happiness: What it is, why it is happening, and what it portends for medical research. In E. F. Paul & J. Paul (Eds.), *Why animal experimentation matters: The use of animals in medical research. New studies in social policy*. New Brunswick, NJ: Transaction.

Terrace, H. S. (1963). Errorless transfer of a discrimination across two continua. *Journal of the Experimental Analysis of Behavior, 67*, 223–232.

The Jean Piaget Society. (2002). Constructivism (Special Issue). *Cognitive Development, 17*(September–December).

The Scientific American Book of the Brain. (1999). New York: Scientific American.

Thiele, T. E., Kiefer, S. W., & Badia-Elder, N. E. (1996). Delayed generalization testing produces enhanced alcohol aversions in rats. *Alcohol, 13*, 201–207.

Thomas, M., & Karmiloff-Smith, A. (2003). Connectionist models of development, developmental disorders, and individual differences. In R. J. Sternberg & J. Lautrey (Eds.), *Models of intelligence: International perspectives*. Washington, DC: American Psychological Association.

Thomas, R. K. (1997). Correcting some Pavloviana regarding "Pavlov's bell" and Pavlov's "mugging." *American Journal of Psychology, 110*, 115–125.

Thomas, R. M. (2000). *Comparing theories of child development* (5th ed.). Belmont, CA: Wadsworth.

Thorndike, E. L. (1898). Animal intelligence: An experimental study of the associative processes in animals. *Psychological Review Monograph Supplement, 2*(8).

Thorndike, E. L. (1911). *Animal intelligence: Experimental studies*. New York: Hafner (facsimile of 1911 edition; published in 1965).

Thorndike, E. L. (1913–1914) *Educational Psychology* (Vol. 1, 2, 3). New York: Teachers College Press.

Thorndike, E. L. (1913a). *Educational psychology: Vol. 1. The psychology of learning*. New York: Teachers College Press.

Thorndike, E. L. (1913b). *Educational psychology: Vol. 2. The original nature of man*. New York: Teachers College Press.

Thorndike, E. L. (1922). *The psychology of arithmetic*. New York: Macmillan.

Thorndike, E. L. (1923). The influence of first year Latin upon the ability to read English. *School and Society, 17*, 165–168.

Thorndike, E. L. (1931). *Human learning*. Cambridge, MA: MIT Press.

Thorndike, E. L. (1935). *The psychology of wants, interests, and attitudes*. New York: Appleton-Century-Crofts.

Thorndike, E. L. (1936/1949). *Selected writings from a connectionist's psychology*. New York: Appleton-Century-Crofts. (Original work published in 1936).

Thorne, B. M. (1995), Robert Thompson: Karl Lashley's heir? *Journal of the History of the Behavioral Sciences, 31*, 129–136.

Thorpe, W. H. (1963). *Learning and instinct in animals* (2nd ed.). London: Methuen.

Tinklepaugh, O. L. (1928). An experimental study of representative factors in monkeys. *Journal of Comparative Psychology, 8*, 197–236.

Toch, H. H., & Schulte, R. (1961). Readiness to perceive violence as a result of police training. *British Journal of Psychology, 52*, 389–394.

Todd, J. T., & Morris, E. K. (Eds.) (1994). *Modern perspectives on John B. Watson and classical behaviorism*. Westport, CT: Greenwood Press.

Tolman, E. C. (1932). *Purposive behavior in animals and men*. Berkeley: University of California Press.

Tolman, E. C. (1951). *Collected papers in psychology*. Berkeley: University of California Press.

Tolman, E. C. (1952). Autobiography. In E. G. Boring, H. S. Langfeld, H. Werner, & R. M. Yerkes (Eds.), *A history of psychology in autobiography* (Vol. 4). Worcester, UK: Clark University Press.

Tolman, E. C. (1959). Principles of purposive behavior. In S. Koch (Ed.), *Psychology: A study of a science* (Vol. 2). New York: McGraw-Hill.

Tolman, E. C. (1967). *Purposive behavior in animals and men*. New York: Appleton-Century-Crofts.

Tolman, E. C., & Honzik, C. H. (1930). Insight in rats. *University of California Publications in Psychology, 4*, 215–232.

Tolman, E. C., Ritchie, B. F., & Kalish, D. (1946). Studies in spatial learning: II. Place learning versus response learning. *Journal of Experimental Psychology, 36*, 221–229.

Tomasello, M. (1996). Piagetian and Vygotskian approaches to language acquisition. *Human Development, 39*, 269–276.

Tomie, A., Di Poce, J., Derenzo, C. C., & Pohorecky, L. A. (2002). Autoshaping of ethanol drinking: An animal model of binge drinking. *Alcohol & Alcoholism, 37,* 138–146.

Toulmin, S. (1978). The Mozart of psychology. *New York Review of Books, 25,* 51–57.

Trivers, R. (2002). *Natural selection and social theory: Selected papers of Robert Trivers.* New York: Oxford University Press.

Trivers, R. L. (1974). Parent-offspring conflict. *American Zoologist, 14,* 249–264.

Tropea, D., Capsoni, S., Tongiorgi, E., Giannotta, S., Cattaneo, A., & Domenici, L. (2001). Mismatch between BDNF mRNA and protein expression in the developing visual cortex: The role of visual experience. *European Journal of Neuroscience, 13,* 709–721.

Tulving, E. (1974). Cue-dependent forgetting. *American Scientist, 62,* 74–82.

Tulving, E. (1989). Remembering and knowing the past. *American Scientist, 77,* 361–367.

Tulving, E. (1991). Memory research is not a zerosum game. *American Psychologist, 46,* 41–42.

Tulving, E. (2002). Episodic memory: From mind to brain. *Annual Review of Psychology, 53,* 1–25.

Tulving, E., Schacter, D. L., McLachlan, D. R., & Moscovitch, M. (1988). Priming of semantic autobiographical memory: A case study of retrograde amnesia. *Brain and Cognition, 8,* 3–20.

Turing, A. M. (1950) Computing machinery and intelligence. *Mind, 59,* 433–460.

Umoren, J. A. (1992). Maslow hierarchy of needs and OBRA 1987: Toward need satisfaction by nursing home residents. *Educational Gerontology, 18,* 657–670.

Uttal, W. R. (2000). *The war between mentalism and behaviorism: On the accessibility of mental processes.* Mahwah, NJ: Erlbaum.

Uttal, W. R. (2002). *A behaviorist looks at form recognition.* Mahwah, NJ: Erlbaum.

Van der Veer, R. (1996). Vygotsky and Piaget: A collective monologue. *Human Development, 39,* 237–242.

Van Leeuwen, M. S. (2002). Of hoggamus and hogwash: Evolutionary psychology and gender relations. *Journal of Psychology & Theology, 30,* 101–111.

Vargas, J. S. (2001). B. F. Skinner's contribution to therapeutic change: An agency-less contingency analysis. In W. T. O'Donohue, T. William, & D. A. Henderson (Eds.), *A history of the behavioral therapies: Founders' personal histories.* Reno, NV: Context Press.

Vernon, D., Egner, T., Cooper, N., Compton, T., Neilands, C., Sheri, A., & Gruzelier, J. (2003). The effect of training distinct neurofeedback protocols on aspects of cognitive performance. *International Journal of Psychophysiology, 47,* 75–85.

Vogel, J. J., Bowers, C. A., & Vogel, D. S. (2003). Cerebral lateralization of spatial abilities: A meta-analysis. *Brain & Cognition, 52,* 197–204.

von Glasersfeld, E. (1997). Homage to Jean Piaget (1896–1980). *Irish Journal of Psychology, 18,* 293–306.

Vrooman, J. R. (1970). *René Descartes: A biography.* New York: G. P. Putnam's Sons.

Vygotsky, L. (1962). *Thought and language* (E. Hamsman & G. Vankan, Eds. and Trans.). Cambridge, MA: MIT Press.

Vygotsky, L. S. (1978). *Mind in society.* Cambridge, MA: Harvard University Press.

Vygotsky, L (1987). The historical meaning of the crisis in psychology: a methodological investigation. In *The Collected Works of Vygotsky* (R. Van Der Veer, Trans.). New York: Plenum. (Original work published 1927)

Wade, N. (1976). Sociobiology: Troubled birth for a new discipline. *Science, 191,* 1151–1155.

Wagman, M. (2002). *Problem-solving process in humans and computers: Theory and research in psychology and artificial intelligence.* Westport, CT: Praeger.

Waldrop, M. M. (1992). *Complexity: The emerging science at the edge of order and chaos.* New York: Simon & Schuster.

Walker, J. E., & Shea, T. M. (1991). *Behavior management: A practical approach for educators* (5th ed.). New York: Merrill.

Walters, G. C., & Grusec, J. E. (1977). *Punishment.* San Francisco: Freeman.

Walters, R. H., & Llewellyn, T. E. (1963). Enhancement of punitiveness by visual and audiovisual displays. *Canadian Journal of Psychology, 17,* 244–255.

Walters, R. H., Llewellyn, T. E., & Acker, W. (1962). Enhancement of punitive behavior by audiovisual displays. *Science, 136,* 872–873.

Wan, F., & Salili, F. (1996). Perceived effectiveness of reward and punishment strategies by Hong Kong secondary school students. *Psychologia: An International Journal of Psychology in the Orient, 39,* 261–275.

Watson, J. B. (1913). Psychology as the behaviorist views it. *Psychological Review, 20,* 158–177.

Watson, J. B. (1914). *Behavior: An introduction to comparative psychology.* New York: Holt.

Watson, J. B. (1928). *The ways of behaviorism.* New York: Harper.

Watson, J. B. (1930). *Behaviorism* (2nd ed.). Chicago: University of Chicago Press.

Watson, J. B., & Rayner, R. (1920). Conditioned emotional reactions. *Journal of Experimental Psychology, 3,* 1–14.

Watson, R. (1996). Rethinking readiness for learning. In D. R. Olson & N. Torrance (Eds.), *The handbook of education and human development: New models of learning, teaching and schooling.* Oxford, UK: Blackwell.

Watson, R. I. (1971). *The great psychologists* (3rd ed.). Philadelphia: Lippincott.

Webster, S., & Coleman, S. R. (1992). Contributions to the history of psychology: LXXXVI. Hull and his critics: The reception of Clark L. Hull's behavior theory, 1943–1960. *Psychological Reports, 70,* 1063–1071.

Weidman, N. (1994). Mental testing and machine intelligence: The Lashley-Hull debate. *Journal of the History of the Behavioral Sciences, 30,* 162–180.

Weiner, B. (1980). *Human motivation.* New York: Holt Rinehart.

Weiner, B. (Ed.). (1974). *Cognitive views of human motivation.* New York: Academic Press.

Weiner, B. (1986). *An attributional theory of motivation and emotion.* New York: Springer-Verlag.

Weiner, B. (1992). *Human motivation: Metaphors, theories and research.* Newbury Park, CA: Sage.

Wertheimer, M. (1959). *Productive thinking* (Rev. ed.). New York: Harper & Row.

Westby, G. (1966). Psychology today: Problems and directions. *Bulletin of the British Psychological Society, 19*(65).

Westermann, R. (1989). Festinger's theory of cognitive dissonance: A revised structural reconstruction. In H. Westmeyer (Ed.), *Psychological theories from a structuralist point of view.* New York: Springer-Verlag.

White, K. G. (2002). Psychophysics of remembering: The discrimination hypothesis. *Current Directions in Psychological Science, 11,* 141–145.

Whitehead, A. N., & Russell, B. (1925). *Principia mathematica* (Vol. 1, 2nd ed.). Cambridge, UK: Cambridge University Press.

Whyte, G., Saks, A. M., & Hook, S. (1997). When success breeds failure: The role of self-efficacy in escalating commitment to a losing course of action. *Journal of Organizational Behavior, 18,* 415–432.

Wickelgren, W. A., 1981. Human learning and memory. *Annual Review of Psychology, 32,* 21–52.

Wilcoxon, H. C., Dragoin, W. B., & Kral, P. A. (1971). Illness-induced aversions in rat and quail: Relative salience of visual and gustatory cues. *Science, 171,* 826–828.

Wilson, E. O. (1975). *Sociobiology: The new synthesis.* Cambridge, MA: Belknap.

Wilson, E. O. (1976). Academic vigilantism and the political significance of sociobiology. *Bio-Science, 183,* 187–190.

Wilson, K., & Tally, W. (1990). The "Palenque" project: Formative evaluation in the design and development of an optical disc prototype. In B. Flagg (Ed.), *Formative evaluation for educational technologies.* Hillsdale, NJ: Erlbaum.

Windholz, G. (1996a). Hypnosis and inhibition as viewed by Heidenhain and Pavlov. *Integrative Physiological and Behavioral Science, 31,* 155–162.

Windholz, G. (1996b). Pavlov's conceptualization of paranoia within the theory of higher nervous activity. *History of Psychiatry, 7,* 159–166.

Windholz, G. (1997). Ivan P. Pavlov: An overview of his life and psychological work. *American Psychologist, 52,* 941–946.

Wise, R. A. (1996). Addictive drugs and brain stimulation reward. *Annual Review of Neuroscience, 19,* 319–340.

Witte, K., Hirschler, U., & Curio, E. (2000). Sexual imprinting on a novel adornment influences mate preferences in the Javanese mannikin Lonchura leucogastroides. *Ethology, 106,* 349–363.

Wixted, J. T. (2004). The psychology and neuroscience of forgetting. *Annual Review of Psychology, 55,* 235–269.

Wolfgram, C., & Goldstein, M. L. (1987). The search for the physical basis of memory. *Bulletin of the Psychonomic Society, 25,* 65–68.

Wolpe, J. (1958). *Psychotherapy by reciprocal inhibition.* Stanford, CA: Stanford University Press.

Wood, N., & Cowan, N. (1995a). The cocktail party phenomenon revisited: How frequent are attention shifts to one's name in an irrelevant auditory channel? *Journal of Experimental Psychology: Learning, Memory, and Cognition, 21,* 255–260.

Wood, N., & Cowan, N. (1995b). The cocktail party phenomenon revisited: Attention and memory in the classic selective listening procedure of Cherry (1953). *Journal of Experimental Psychology: General, 124,* 243–262.

Woodworth, R. S., & Sheehan, M. R. (1964). *Contemporary schools of psychology* (3rd ed.). New York: Ronald Press.

Wright, R. (1994). *The moral animal: Evolutionary psychology and everyday life.* New York: Pantheon.

Wulf, S. (1938). Tendencies and figural variations. In W. D. Ellis (Ed.), *A source book of Gestalt psychology.* New York: Harcourt, Brace & World. (Original work published 1922.)

Wyatt, W. J. (2001). Some myths about behaviorism that are undone by B. F. Skinner's "The Design of Cultures," *Behavior & Social Issues, 11,* 28–30.

Wynn, V. E., & Logie, R. H. (1998). The veracity of long-term memories—Did Bartlett get it right? *Applied Cognitive Psychology, 12,* 1–20.

Yerkes, R. M., & Dodson, J. D. (1908). The relationship of strength of stimulus to rapidity of habit formation. *Journal of Comparative Neurological Psychology, 18,* 459–482.

Zanna, M. P., & Cooper, J. (2000). Dissonance and the pill: An attribution approach to studying the arousal properties of dissonance. In E. T. Higgins & A. W. Kruglanski (Eds.), *Motivational science:*

Social and personality perspectives: Key reading in social psychology. Philadelphia: Psychology Press.

Zeaman, D. (1949). Response latency as a function of amount of reinforcement. *Journal of Experimental Psychology, 39,* 466–483.

Zemke, R. (1999). Toward a science of training. *Training, 36,* 32–36.

Zimmerman, B. J., Bandura, A., & Martinez-Pons, M. (1992). Self-motivation for academic attainment: The role of self-efficacy beliefs and personal goal setting. *American Educational Research Journal, 29,* 663–676.

Zubek, J. P. (1969). *Sensory deprivation: Fifteen years of research.* New York: Appleton-Century-Crofts.

Zubek, J. P., & Wilgosh, L. (1963). Prolonged immobilization of the body: Changes in performance in the electroencephalogram. *Science, 140,* 306–308.

Name Index

Subject Index

Photo Credits

This page constitutes an extension of the copyright page. We have made every effort to trace the ownership of all copyrighted material and to secure permission from copyright holders. In the event of any question arising as to the use of any material, we will be pleased to make the necessary corrections in future printings. Thanks are due to the following authors, publishers, and agents for permission to use the material indicated.

Chapter 2

Page 32	Archives of the History of American Psychology, The University of Akron
Page 34	Sovfoto-Eastfoto
Page 46	Archives of the History of American Psychology, The University of Akron
Page 55	Courtesy Special Collections, University of Washington Libraries, neg. S-01540-A

Chapter 3

Page 73	Archives of the History of American Psychology, The University of Akron
Page 83	Archives of the History of American Psychology. Courtesy Manuscripts and Archives, Yale University Library

Chapter 4

Page 102	Courtesy of the B. F. Skinner Foundation

Chapter 6

Page 178	Courtesy McGill University Archives, University of California, Berkeley
Page 192	Photo by Dorothy Moore. Courtesy University Archives, University of California, Berkeley
Page 200	(left to right) Photo by Underwood and Underwood. Courtesy Smith College Archives, Smith College; Archives of the History of American Psychology, Mary Henle Papers; Archives of the History of American Psychology, The University of Akron

Chapter 7

Page 220	Courtesy of Harvard University Archives
Page 238	Archives of the History of American Psychology

Chapter 11

Page 362	Photo by Chuck Painter, Stanford News Service. Courtesy Stanford University

Epilogue

Epilogue	Claire Lefrançois, Marie Lefrançois, and Liam Sakowsky

TO THE OWNER OF THIS BOOK:

I hope that you have found *Theories of Human Learning: What the Old Woman Said*, Fifth Edition useful. So that this book can be improved in a future edition, would you take the time to complete this sheet and return it? Thank you.

School and address:_____

Department:_____

Instructor's name:_____

1. What I like most about this book is:_____

_____

_____

2. What I like least about this book is:

_____

_____

3. My general reaction to this book is:

_____

_____

4. The name of the course in which I used this book is:

_____

5. Were all of the chapters of the book assigned for you to read?_____

   If not, which ones weren't?_____

6. In the space below, or on a separate sheet of paper, please write specific suggestions for improving this book and anything else you'd care to share about your experience in using this book.

_____

_____

_____

BUSINESS REPLY MAIL
FIRST-CLASS MAIL   PERMIT NO. 102   MONTEREY CA

POSTAGE WILL BE PAID BY ADDRESSEE

Attn: Psychology/Marianne Taflinger

Wadsworth/Thomson Learning
60 Garden Ct Ste 205
Monterey CA 93940-9967

OPTIONAL:

Your name:_____ Date: _____

May we quote you, either in promotion for *Theories of Human Learning: What the Old Woman Said*, Fifth Edition, or in future publishing ventures?

Yes: _____   No: _____

Sincerely yours,

Guy R. Lefrancois